PENGUIN BOOKS

FEMALE PERVERSIONS

Louise J. Kaplan is the critically acclaimed author of four books, including *Oneness and Separateness: From Infant to Individual*, and numerous articles on child, adolescent and adult development. Dr Kaplan, who has received honorary awards for distinguished service to psychology, is a co-editor of *American Imago*, a psychoanalytic journal. She is engaged in private practice in New York City.

LOUISE J. KAPLAN

FEMALE PERVERSIONS

THE TEMPTATIONS
OF MADAME BOVARY

PENGUIN BOOKS

PENGUIN BOOKS

Published by the Penguin Group
Penguin Books Ltd, 27 Wrights Lane, London W8 5TZ, England
Penguin Books USA Inc., 375 Hudson Street, New York, New York 10014, USA
Penguin Books Australia Ltd, Ringwood, Victoria, Australia
Penguin Books Canada Ltd, 10 Alcorn Avenue, Toronto, Ontario, Canada M4V 3B2
Penguin Books (NZ) Ltd, 182–190 Wairau Road, Auckland 10, New Zealand

Penguin Books Ltd, Registered Offices: Harmondsworth, Middlesex, England

First published in the USA by Doubleday,
a division of Bantam Doubleday Dell Publishing Group, Inc., 1991
First published in Great Britain by Pandora Press,
an imprint of HarperCollins Publishers, 1991
Published in Penguin Books 1993
10 9 8 7 6 5 4 3 2 1

Printed in England by Clays Ltd, St Ives plc

For
Matilda Davidson Miller
and
Ariel Kaplan Iasevoli

Grateful acknowledgment is made to the following for permission to quote from previously published material:

Excerpts from *George Sand* by Curtis Cate. Copyright © 1975 by Curtis Cate. Reprinted by permission of Houghton Mifflin Co.

Excerpts from *Idols of Perversity: Fantasies of Feminine Evil in Fin-de-Siècle Culture* by Bram Dijkstra. Reprinted by permission of Oxford University Press.

Excerpts from "Designers Reveal the Woman Behind the Fashions," by Michael Gross, November 24, 1987. Copyright © 1987 by The New York Times Company. Reprinted by permission.

From *Portrait of a Marriage* by Nigel Nicolson. Copyright © 1973 by Nigel Nicolson. Reprinted with permission of George Weidenfeld and Nicolson Limited.

Reprinted by permission of the publishers from *Memoirs of My Nervous Illness* by Daniel Paul Schreber, Cambridge, Mass.: Harvard University Press, Copyright © 1955, and Introduction to the 1988 edition © 1988 by the President and Fellows of Harvard College. All rights reserved.

Excerpts from *Observing the Erotic Imagination* by Robert J. Stoller, M.D. Reprinted by permission of Yale University Press.

Excerpts from *Adultery in the Novel: Contract and Transgression* by Tony Tanner. Reprinted by permission of The Johns Hopkins University Press.

Excerpts from *The Perpetual Orgy* by Mario Vargas Llosa. Copyright © 1987 by Farrar, Straus and Giroux, Inc. Reprinted by permission of Farrar, Straus and Giroux, Inc.

Reprinted with permission of Charles Scribner's Sons, an imprint of Macmillan Company, from *The Letters of Edith Wharton* edited by R.B. Lewis, Nancy Lewis & William R. Tyler. Copyright © 1988 by R.W.B. Lewis, Nancy Lewis and William R. Tyler.

Excerpts from "Megamall, a New Fix for Future Shopping Addicts," by Isabel Wilkerson, June 9, 1989. Copyright 1989 by The New York Times Company. Reprinted by permission.

Contents

FEMALE
PERVERSIONS

Prologue: The Doctor-Patient Game

The primitive images of femininity and masculinity that find expression in the perversions are reflections of our most exalted ideals of womanhood and manhood. Emma Bovary is a woman enslaved by the feminine stereotypes that were, in her society, ideals of womanhood. But Flaubert's novel, entitled with a female name, like this book, *Female Perversions*, is as much about the men that women endow with the power to dominate them and the corruptions in the surrounding social world that nurture a state of warfare between the sexes.

Thus, the life of Flaubert's Emma and the fates of the women and men I will describe are played out against the background of the perversions in our most revered social institutions—the family, the church, the fashion and cosmetic industries, the pornography industry, the department store, and, not the least perverse among them, the medical profession.

How medical practitioners, psychiatrists, psychoanalysts, and other psy-

chologists, almost all of them male, have been reasoning about male and female sexuality and gender differences will be critical to our understandings of perversions. Doctors are hovering everywhere in the background of *Madame Bovary* and *Female Perversions*.

Gustave Flaubert's father was a doctor. There are four doctors in *Madame Bovary*, all of them male; each of them, if asked, would have given a different response to the question "What is a perversion?" Flaubert clearly demonstrated how the distinctive modes of intellectual approach favored by these four doctors were intimately associated with their differing ideals of masculine virtue. So let us open our explorations by taking a look at Flaubert's doctors, who are not so very different in their ways of thinking about human suffering from many doctors today.

There is Emma's husband, Charles Bovary. His father, once an assistant surgeon in the army (which would make him the fifth doctor), had been forced out of service for corruption. "In opposition to his wife's maternal tenderness, he had a virile ideal of how his son should be raised . . . harshly, in Spartan style." Charles was to have no fire in his bedroom; he was instructed to down large swigs of rum at dinner and to jeer at religious processions. But in the end the mother had her way. Her husband deserted the marital bed to find his comforts with women of easier virtue, so she focused all her emotions and ambitions on her son, pampering him with jam and candied fruit, reading and sentimental songs. She kept him close to her in the "kind nursery" of the farm where he would remain in docile babyhood until he was twelve. Only then did his mother send him to the priest and then to the lycée to learn the ways of the world. Charles, an obedient and submissive boy, worked hard to keep himself near the middle of his class. Later in medical school, he was awed by the mysterious names of the subjects, the parts of the body, and the diseases. He took notes, copied and recopied, memorized, and recited back every word and phrase precisely as he heard it, "like a mill horse who goes about his daily rounds, blindfolded, ignorant of the work he is grinding out." If he had been asked what a perversion was, Charles would have held fast to the definition he had copied into his notebook. He would have thought of a perversion as yet another of those exotic diseases he did not understand. Charles made up for his intellectual submissiveness by remaining in close touch with his patients. As a health officer responsible for healing the simple ailments of simple country families, Charles was used to blood spurting in his face, dirty basins, soiled bed sheets, the death rattle. Though he never would have understood what a perversion is, neither would Charles have placed himself at a distance from those afflicted with it.

There is Monsieur Homais, the smug, up-to-date pharmacist. Homais, who more than once had been summoned before the authorities for practicing medicine without a license, was haunted by a nightmare of being cast into a dungeon for his transgressions. Like all of those who are constantly tempted to violate rules and prohibitions and taboos, Homais was obsessed with normality. To him every deviation was an affront to his compulsion for systematizing and categorizing. He was not satisfied until every manifestation of errant humanity was squeezed into a list or category. He was fond of making inventories and labels, rearranging bottles, and reorganizing shelves. But his greatest pleasure came from boxing abnormalities into normal shapes. Had he been confronted with a question about vagrancy, deviance, or perversion, he would have scurried about his laboratory searching for a prescription that might contain it. But if the deviance did not yield to his formulas, Homais would have written to the newspapers demanding that the aberrant one be incarcerated, put out of sight so that he could no longer display his diseases and sores in public places. Homais, who feared what might emerge from his disorderly soul, was always on the side of the forces that seek "to eradicate, to forcibly conventionalize, or to imprison forever whatever presumes to exist outside those categories and norms."

There is the famous surgeon Monsieur Canivet, who was summoned

to give his opinion on a botched surgical intervention performed by
Charles Bovary. Bovary, inspired by Homais's reformatory zeal and
Emma's lust for fame, had boxed the stableboy's clubfoot into a monstrous wooden and steel contraption. One look at that perverse effort
to correct a deviation, one look at the twisted foot turned gangrenous
by the mechanism that was meant to cure it, was sufficient for Canivet
to decide on amputation. Canivet was coolheaded. He did not flinch at
the sight of blood. Canivet prided himself on his good health and
healthy habits. He never caught cold and every inch of his body was
solid as a rock. The entire world could perish of illness, deformity,
torment, perversion without ruffling his professional self-assurance.
Canivet always beheld the sick from the point of view of the healthy.
And therefore he never hesitated. When the patient's flesh did not
yield to other remedies, he amputated. If asked about perversion, he
would have known at once that this offense of the flesh had nothing to
do with his flesh or his desires. He would think of it as another of
those scourges that must be eliminated, excised, amputated.

Then there is Dr. Larivière, who was different from all the others. A
tear fell on his shirt as he regarded Emma's cadaverous face. He was
conjuring the beautiful flesh that once adorned it, knowing he must
admit that there was nothing he could do to arrest the processes of
death. Larivière belonged to the line of surgeons that sprang from
Marie-François-Xavier Bichat, "to that generation, now vanished, of
philosophical practitioners who cherished their art with fanatical love
and exercised it with enthusiasm and wisdom." When Bichat lectured
that life is only "the sum of the functions that oppose death," he
wanted to impress on his students the narrow border between health
and disease. He would say that the physical properties of flesh and
organs, which tend by their very functioning to lead toward death, are
held back from that inevitable fate by the vital properties that also
inhabit the cells of the body. But, alas, the vital properties too use
themselves up and become exhausted: "Time wears them away." As a

follower of Bichat, Larivière might have wondered if perhaps perversion was less about sexual abnormality than about the failure of the erotic properties to regulate and contain the processes of death—and he would have been right about that. Moreover, Bichat had also wanted to move his students closer to the patient. He advised them to supplement their note taking by opening up a few corpses. "You will dissipate at once the darkness that observation could not dissipate." Unless the clinician penetrated beneath the surface, the symptoms would refuse "to yield up their meaning and offer you a succession of incoherent phenomena." So Larivière, the Bichat disciple, would also have understood that the manifest or topmost layer of perversion could tell almost nothing about its meaning. He would have recognized that before he could understand anything about the meaning of a perversion, his gaze must penetrate the surface. Larivière's glance, "as sharp as his lancet, plunged deep into your soul, through all pretense and reserve, and laid bare any lies hidden there."

Female Perversions is also about our peculiar century of perversion that has disguised its latent sexual and gender corruptions in a manifest devotion to sexual repression and gender conformity. There have always been males and some females who were sadomasochists, fetishists, transvestites, exhibitionists, pedophiles. However, from the mid-nineteenth century on, coincidental with the modern industrial age and the press toward the emancipation of women, the Western world became preoccupied with sexual normality and gender conformity. The bourgeois family, with its work ethic morality and sharply divided gender role conformities, was the emotional centerpiece of the industrial revolution. No sooner did that family system solidify its structures than it began to sicken and crumble into a state of moral and spiritual decadence. Modern sociologists would liken the bright, cheerful, healthy, successful, progressive, gender-orderly bourgeois family to a decaying body: "In the latter day bourgeois society the family suffers a fate that is not really so different from that of the corpse, which in the midst of civilization recalls to mind the conditions of nature, and which is either hygienically cremated or even cosmetically prepared."

The alarms went off. If the bourgeois family should fade away, the monstrosities of gender ambiguity that had been so efficiently held in check by its rigid gender stereotypes might infiltrate the social order, profaning all that had been sacred and overthrowing all that had been essential to maintaining the structures of civilized societies. If the deviant sexualities that threatened civilization could be boxed into categories, the bourgeois family and the social order it represented could be saved. The twentieth-century obsession with perversion and the increasing importance of sexological research were a response to the decaying of the nineteenth-century bourgeois family. As these last few decades of the twentieth century are proof enough, the obsession with sexual normality and gender conformity became a breeding ground for perversion, but now with more devious lies to conceal it. What we are seeing, as a last-ditch effort to contain and regulate the gender ambiguities that are the lot of human beings, is a commercialization and standardization of so-called deviant sexuality. The twentieth century is ending in a conformity of perversion that trivializes the meaning of erotic freedom.

Like Homais, the early-twentieth-century sexologists Krafft-Ebing, Ellis, Tardieu, Molle, and Kaan kept busy naming, compiling, cataloguing, and making extensive inventories of the sexual perversions. Like Charles Bovary, some doctors did not at all understand what they were so diligently copying into their notebooks. Others, like Canivet, thought of themselves as the healthy ones exempt from the "disease" of perversion. They all focused on the manifestly aberrant behaviors without thinking to look beneath the surface to the deceptions hidden there. There were very few Larivières among them.

However, like Dr. Larivière, we are about to scrutinize the world of perversion, penetrate the surface, and lay bare the deceptions that are hidden beneath.

1

What Is a Perversion?

In the mid-nineteenth century, as the bourgeois family was decaying from the illnesses concealed by the gender stereotypes that had been enlisted to preserve it, the subject of sexual perversion became a matter of crucial concern to scientists and the public alike. At the fin de siècle, a new breed of doctor, called a sexologist, came into being. By the mid-twentieth century, perversion had become a new industry of research and profit. The sexologists, who kept their gaze steadily focused on the manifest symptoms of perversion, became adept at amassing instances of unusual or bizarre sexual acts, distinguishing them from normal sexual acts, and providing various labels and categories for them.

Over the course of the century, the diagnostic categories into which the perversions were slotted shifted here and there. But two things about perversion did not change. First, the medical profession is still preoccupied with boxing aberrant sexual behaviors into lists and categories. Second, except for sexual masochism where the ratio of cases is approximately twenty males to one female, less than one percent of the cases cited as sexual perversion have been of females.

On hearing these statistics some people, usually males, are offended at the suggestion that females might somehow have an edge on males. They insist that I have been taken in by statistics, which as we know always lie. Others, usually females, are happy with this evidence of the moral superiority of females. They admonish me for wanting to question whether females really are less perverse than males. No sooner are questions raised about these odd statistics than an array of stock responses is marshaled to explain them away. A favorite tactic is to undermine the statistics by presenting a list of all the exceptions to the rule: women who have the same perversions as men and women who participate vicariously in perversion by "submitting unwillingly" to the deviant sexual demands of men. They say that there are more perverse women than the doctors realize. In fact, women are just as perverse as men. All doctors have to do is look around them and those odd statistics would even out.

Another standard response is to side with the statistics but then to argue that women do not have to resort to perversions since they are given ample opportunity to vent their aberrant sexual desires on their children. A more carefully considered argument, but one that assigns an inordinate weight to biological factors, is that males are androgen-testosterone-driven and are therefore possessed by the urgencies of enabling and maintaining erections. Females, however, because of their estrogen restraints, genital inwardness, and delicacy of human relatedness, are less inclined toward perverse acting-out as a solution to their sexual and moral dilemmas. In this argument, the premise is that the statistics on perversion are correct and yet another proof of all the differences between males and females that we like to attribute to biology and anatomical destiny.

Still another reason offered for the unbalanced sex ratios in perversion is that men must have erections to perform sexually and therefore cannot hide their genital anxieties and inadequacies, whereas women are pretty good at faking sexual arousal and orgasm. Women don't have to employ fetishes and such to prove their sexual adequacy. Indeed, women do not have to employ prostitutes to get beaten and dominated; men will gladly do it for free. Another response, based on the mistaken assumption that the perversions are spontaneous erotic adventures, "kinky sex" undertaken in the spirit of sexual liberation, is that women would be as perverse as men if they were granted greater sexual freedom.

Whatever truth is conceded to each of these standard responses, they all miss the crucial point of *the perverse strategy*. What makes a perversion a perversion is a mental strategy that uses one or another social stereotype of masculinity and femininity in a way that deceives the onlooker about the unconscious meanings of the behaviors she or he is observing. Were we to think about perversion solely in terms of manifest behaviors without going into the motives that give meaning to those behaviors, we could simply conclude that the male perversions are quests for forbidden sexual pleasures and nothing more. However, since deception is so crucial to perversion, unless we lay bare the lies that are hidden there we will be deceived at once. The perverse strategy works on us immediately by using popular and traditional definitions of perversion to distract us from the truth.

What is a perversion? To most people, including most psychiatrists and psychologists, the term *perversion* implies an irresistible attraction toward some abnormal or bizarre sexual behavior. Very likely the first perversion that comes to mind is SM, sadomasochism, "kinky" sex entailing bondage, whips, chains, and black leather boots. Let me state at the outset that the *essential* ingredient in perversion is not the "kinky sex" of bondages and leather boots. Nor is perversion the exotic veilings and unveilings of the genitals in a striptease, the performances of oral or anal sex, sexual intercourse with partners of the same sex, telephone masturbation, or any of these variations of erotic experience that loving or hating sexual partners may engage in at one time or another if they so choose, or may not if that is their choice. What distinguishes perversion is its quality of desperation and fixity. A perversion is performed by a person who has no other choices, a person who would otherwise be overwhelmed by anxieties or depression or psychosis. The male perversions use some manifest form of "kinky sex" to prevail over these otherwise devastating emotional states. Therefore the kinky sex is only a parody of adventurism. It is actually an appeasement of personal demons.

Sexual behaviors per se, kinky or otherwise, are not the key to the female perversions, however, since females use other sorts of behaviors, one could say other sorts of deceptions, to appease their demons. According to most standard definitions, past and present, only the obvious or manifest aims of certain male behaviors—sexual excitement and sexual performance—have been taken as the hallmark of a perversion. The underlying motives, fantasies, wishes, and desires have been thought of as secondary or, more usually, simply ignored. To qualify as a legitimate and official perversion—a paraphilia, as the latest label has it—the aim of the act *must* be sexual excitement and sexual performance. We have missed noticing the female perversions because we have been looking for them in the wrong place. We were led astray by the official definitions. However, the perverse strategy *is* to divert attention away from the underlying or latent motives, fantasies, wishes, and desires. So we should not be surprised if our official definitions, which also keep our focus on manifest, conscious aims, simply mirror the perverse strategy itself.

A perversion is a psychological strategy. It differs from other mental strategies in that it demands a performance. The overall strategy operates in the same way for males and females. What makes all the difference between the male and female perversions is the social gender stereotype that is brought into the foreground of the enactment. The enactment, or performance, is designed to help the person to survive, moreover to survive with a sense of triumph over the traumas of his or her childhood. The perverse strategy is unconscious. The actor, or protagonist, knows only that he feels compelled to perform the perverse act and that when deterred from doing so he feels desperately anxious, panicky, agitated, crazy, even violent. The protagonist does not know that the performance is designed to master "events" that were once too exciting, too frightening, too mortifying to master in childhood. The performer cannot, dare not remember those terrible events. Instead, his life is given up to reliving them, albeit in a disguised, symbolic form. An adult, male or female, who is compelled to perform a perverse ritual expends a great deal of energy and devotes a considerable portion of each day and night attempting to master and control emotions and affects that were overwhelming and uncontrollable in childhood. A perversion, for as long as it lasts—a decade or an entire lifetime—is a central preoccupation of the person's existence.

The preoccupation in a perversion is very different from the preoccupation in a compulsive symptom, such as making and hoarding money or hand washing or constantly tidying up. In a compulsion, the person feels that he is righting a wrong, doing something "good" and morally proper. The activities the person feels compelled to perform entail a heightened awareness of anxiety, and sometimes also shame, but serve to keep guilt unconscious. In a perversion, the person feels that he is doing something "bad" and morally wrong. He is conscious of being compelled to do something secretive and risky, of feeling that he is sinful and wicked and somehow at odds with his moral order. However, he experiences a sense of elation in his brazen defiance of the moral codes. He feels brave and proud rather than frightened and ashamed. Thus, the preoccupation in a perversion allows that issues of sin and moral apprehension should assume prominence and become conscious, but mainly to keep shame and anxiety unconscious. It seems, though, that no matter how many times the person performs the perverse act, he still is haunted by a shivering apprehension of doom and very often consciously wonders why he must suffer so for pleasure. However, as we will see, one facet of the perverse strategy is to keep ideas of sin and guilt in the foreground, not as signals that might deter moral transgression but as vital ingredients in the ritual enactment, which always includes at least a threat of torment, torture, punishment, or suffering. This apprehension of suffering and even actual torment are tolerated, sometimes sought after, because with the spotlight on these unpleasant and painful feelings the pervert manages to keep at bay the terrors and mortifications that were central aspects of his childhood traumas.

The male perversions—fetishism, transvestism, exhibitionism, voyeurism, sexual masochism, sexual sadism, pedophilia, zoophilia, necrophilia—put the spotlight on unusual or bizarre sexual activities, "kinky sex," as a way of triumphing over the traumas of childhood. In a male perversion, the strategy admits into consciousness a defensive, phallic-narcissistic exaggeration of masculinity: most males feel elated, alive, energized, and proud of themselves when they are conforming to this prevalent social stereotype of masculinity. It is the special strategy of male perversion to permit a person to express his forbidden and shameful feminine wishes by disguising them in an ideal of masculinity. Macho genital prowess and the impersonation of fantasized, idealized males are hiding places for the man's humiliating feminine strivings. Moreover, these caricatures of masculinity, based as they are on prowess, aggression, and domination, simultaneously give some semblance of orderly expression to what otherwise would be experienced as a terrifying primitive violence. In a male perversion, intercourse is risk, erection is deception, ejaculation and orgasm more a trial of survival than a quest for pleasure.

Each facet of the perverse strategy works hand in hand with every other one. One element of the strategy is to allow a forbidden impulse of childhood—say exhibitionism—to gain expression, with the purpose of keeping other forbidden impulses—such as aggressive hostility—unconcious. To an exhibitionist, for example, the risky business of exhibiting his penis in public, the brazen rebellion that invites punishment, the potential of getting caught or being shamed are far more preferable to the terrible mortification that might become conscious if the man were forced to acknowledge that he is an ordinary mortal with quite ordinary genitals. Moreover, the exhibitionist, by forcing the sight of his penis on a nonconsenting victim, is giving expression to a primitive, vengeful aggression that, unless disguised and regulated by this "erotic" scenario, would awaken an overwhelming anxiety.

Exhibitionism, like any other perverse performance, entails the kind of sleight of hand that is every magician's stock in trade. The audience is meant to keep their eyes focused on one piece of risky business so that they will not notice that something else is being sneaked in from up the magician's sleeve. While everyone is concentrating on a presumably erotic performance, what is being sneaked in are hatred and vengeance.

Very often, the perverse enactment depends for its success on a *double* sleight of hand, something akin to Poe's purloined letter: a secret desire is out in the open distracting the observer from searching for any further meaning. In sexual masochism what the onlooker sees is a man striving for erection, penetration, and orgasm, behaviors eminently congruent with a prevailing convention of masculine virtue. The risky business—kinky sex—is expressing an acceptable ideal of masculinity—virility—and is being given permission so that other activities more likely to meet with punishment and less enhancing of an ideal image of self can be kept out of awareness. We see the kinky sex, the man being humiliated and demeaned by his dominator, right before our eyes, but we are deceived completely as to his unconscious motives.

What is hidden from the performer himself and from his observing or participating audience, imagined or actual, are the man's secret wishes to be a passive, submissive, denigrated woman humiliated and demeaned by a "phallic" dominator of either sex. The male pervert does, in fact, personally assume the role of a denigrated female or a humiliated infant (characters that, in the mind of a pervert, are basically indistinguishable and represent the same humiliating weaknesses), but all with a tacit understanding between participants and observers that his enactment of these base strivings is in the service of the elevated and manly purposes of erection, penetration, and orgasm. By assuming the mask of a male striving to achieve erection, the pervert is able to pretend that his master or mistress is forcing him to express his forbidden and shameful feminine and infantile strivings. No one can guess his terrible secrets, least of all himself.

While interest in perversions has been restricted to their manifestations in males, perversions among females have gone relatively unnoticed because the manifest activities are different according to the gender stereotype the female is striving to achieve, sometimes but not always including a conscious striving for sexual excitement and performance. A woman who is compelled to a perverse enactment does have a sexual life—sometimes an extensive one, sometimes a limited, "kinky" one, sometimes a totally impoverished one—and this sexual life figures in her perversion. However, the perversion itself is meant to deceive the woman herself and her audience about the forbidden and shameful elements in her sexual life. Even today as we are acknowledging the extent of our clinical and theoretical neglect of perversions in females, the tendency is to cast about for females with the fetishistic perversions that are typical of men—the exceptions to the rule—rather than to plumb the perverse strategy that has managed for so long to keep the female perversions hidden from view.

My thesis is that perversions, insofar as they derive much of their emotional force from social gender stereotypes, are as much pathologies of gender role identity as they are pathologies of sexuality. There is always a subtle collaboration between the individual unconscious with its infantile gender attributions and the structures of the social order with its primitive notions of masculinity and femininity. Socially normalized gender stereotypes are the crucibles of perversion. Therefore, in locating the female perversions, I will direct attention to some socially normalized gender stereotypes of femininity.

A child wants to be loved, protected, and admired by her parents, and she tries therefore to live up to their expectations of "normality," in part by conforming to the social conventions of the world in which she lives. Unfortunately, many social conventions are derived from gender role stereotypes, which are narrowly restricting and ultimately crippling to the sense of self. So while modern societies theoretically allow for more flexible gender roles than traditional societies, they nevertheless, in their political and economic structures, religious rituals, doctor-patient relationships, teacher-student relationships, paintings, novels, films, and advertisements, perpetuate the gender role stereotypes that are the major hiding places for the perversions.

These gender role stereotypes, since they are themselves founded on infantile dichotomies that assign certain narrowly defined characteristics to one sex, and equally narrow but opposite characteristics to the other sex, are eagerly adopted by little children, whose little minds think that way anyhow. Four- and five-year-olds are ready to employ these dichotomized gender assignments as solutions to the ordinary dilemmas of childhood. As one prevalent solution, a little boy seeks to preserve his penis and his masculine identity by giving up his erotic feelings toward his mother, repudiating all remaining vestiges of his feminine or babyish inclinations, and accentuating certain ideals of masculine virtue—bravery, risk, assertiveness, rebellion, domination, virility—ideals that are confirmed and insisted on by the social order as attainments of a normal masculinity. Similarly, a little girl might seek to alleviate her childhood anxieties and narcissistic mortifications by accentuating certain ideals of feminine virtue—passivity, cleanliness, purity, kindness, concern for others, submission. When the social order colludes with these infantile ideals of femininity by insisting on innocence and submission as ways of achieving a normal adult femininity, females learn very early to disguise their intellectual powers as "feminine intuition" and to compromise their active sexual desires into flirtatiousness and a teasing sexual unavailability.

So ingrained are these gender ideals that males and females grow up believing that the intellectual approaches, social roles, and bedroom positions they assume as adults are matters of biological destiny. Both sexes are burdened by the infantile ideals of sexual prowess demanded of men and sexual innocence demanded of women. In a perversion, soul-crippling social gender stereotypes are in a collaboration with infantile gender ideals. I reasoned that if the male perversions manifest as forbidden sexual acts that impersonate and caricature adult genital performance, the analogous female perversions would manifest in behaviors that impersonate and caricature a feminine gender ideal—cleanliness, innocence, spirituality, submission.

Because so little has been studied about the female perversions, I began my search for them by scrutinizing the deceptions in the male perversions. Therefore it was necessary to begin this book with several chapters on male psychology and the male perversions. Later, in the chapters on the female perversions, I bring into stronger focus the elements of the perverse strategy that are latent and disguised in the manifest performances of the male perversions. Some of these elements I have already alluded to: the compulsion toward repetition of childhood traumas, the heightened awareness of wrongdoing to keep in abeyance the demons of anxiety and mortification, the frantic efforts of the erotic energies to bind the energies of sadism and violence, and, especially, the use of the social gender stereotypes to mask cross-gender wishes and desires.

Since the perverse strategy demands a performance, there must also be a script or scenario. Every perverse enactment is based on an unconscious scenario designed to fulfill the central aim of the perverse strategy, which is to keep everyone's attention focused on a deception. The typical perverse performance consists of an elaboration of that scenario in a style, manner, and use of props that will deceive the onlookers, real or imagined, about the underlying meaning of the performance. The perverse scenario or fantasy is insistent and irresistible. It demands that it be enacted, for were there no performance, the person might be assailed by his demons. The entire performance may be so primitive and direct that it consists only of a gesture—a man caressing a pink satin slipper while he masturbates, a man ejaculating as he dismembers a female body, a man putting on an angora sweater. Or the performance may consist of a series of scenes, each with a clear beginning, middle, and end. In specialty houses dedicated to perverse enactments, the stereotyped nature of the stage sets, the props, and the hired performers reassure everyone involved that nothing too dangerous or unpredictable can happen but allow for as simple or complex a scenario as the man desires. Never are the performers in a perverse enactment aware of the unconscious meaning of the scenario they are enacting. Only during an extended course of analysis or therapy will some of the unconscious themes embedded in a perverse scenario gradually come to light. The case studies of male perversion in Chapter 5 illustrate the complexity and richness of the psychological themes that are revealed and yet concealed through the enactment of perverse scenarios.

With each step into this exploration of perversions, male and female, the various elements of the perverse strategy will gradually emerge and become clearer and you will become a more informed reader of perverse scripts. Moreover, each time I confront one of the texts that have shed light on the psychological dynamics of perversion, whether that text is a novel by Gustave Flaubert or a paper on fetishism by Sigmund Freud or a paper on the female castration complex by Karl Abraham, I will approach the text as a new experience in the reading of a perverse script. Unavoidably, every text on perversion bears some features of a perverse scenario because the author's perverse fantasies are stirred up by what she or he is writing about. Anyone who writes about perversion has to be wary of falling prey to the perverse strategy. And so it must be true of my exploration of the female perversions and this text. At this point, for example, I am keeping hidden from readers some very important ideas about the perverse strategy that I have already learned. I will be bringing into the foreground certain aspects of perversion, some of which I will later identify as deceptions. Therefore, I imagine that in reading this book you will occasionally have the experience of being a child who is excluded from the secrets of the grown-ups. By proceeding in this way, with me having some secrets and you not knowing them yet, I am trying as much as possible to bring you with me on the search, to have you follow along in the steps that I took, as I took them myself. I want your gaze to penetrate the surface slowly, layer by layer, so that you will recognize the lies when next you see them.

Let me give some indication of where we are going. At the outset, it will be evident that the male perversions are designed not for making love, but for making hate. Who or what perverse men hate is not at first clear. One of my theses is that many males, perverse or not, have grown up fearing, even despising, the feminine aspects of themselves. In the later chapters on female perversions I will show how certain social stereotypes of femininity serve as screens or disguises for a woman's forbidden and frightening masculine wishes. I will be using the terms "masculine" and "feminine" in their customary stereotyped ways. However, one of my major reasons for exploring the female perversions is to expose the deceptions that are buried in those social gender stereotypes, for whatever else they are about, perversions are certainly about the social constraints placed on human desire.

As the twentieth century progressed and the borders between usual, normal sex and unusual, abnormal sex were increasingly blurred, it became evident that the categories of the sexologists were not too helpful in determining when a merely aberrant act turned the corner to become a perversion or, for that matter, which sexual aberration was merely a variation on the normal. Beyond the obviously bizarre, anti-social acts of intercourse with children, animals, corpses, excrement, who could say? What about oral and anal intercourse? Homosexuality? The diagnostic uncertainty has continued into the end of the twentieth century. In 1952, as part of a monumental effort to regularize and enforce medical concepts of normal and abnormal mental phenomena, the American Psychiatric Association published the *Diagnostic and Statistical Manual of Mental Disorders,* known as *DSM.* In that manual the sexual deviations were grouped with the psychopathic personality disorders, consistent with the fact that most perversions were legal offenses and lending authority to the then prevailing belief that perversions were enacted by persons with antisocial and criminal tendencies. Homosexuality was included under this heading.

In 1958 the original manual was revised, giving birth to *DSM* II, another monumental inventory of mental diseases. Here the sexual deviations were listed under less criminal-sounding categories of personality disorder such as *hysterical, narcissistic,* and *borderline.* While males and females were equally afflicted by these disorders, it was primarily males whose personality peculiarities led them to sexual perversion. Within the next two decades, in harmony with the ongoing revolution in sexual tastes and preferences among the adult population, there gradually evolved a few criteria of mental health that were meant to be less vulnerable to personal interpretation and social bias. In 1980, yet a third manual was published (*DSM* III), and supplanted in 1987 by a revision (*DSM* III-R).* In these latest diagnostic manuals the sexual perversions are boxed into a category of their own and given a more morally neutral and dignified label, *paraphilia* (*para,* "deviant," *philia,* "attraction"). This new sanitized label, which was meant to do away with the stigmata attached to *perversion,* omitted mention of homosexuality and oral and anal intercourse, implying that these practices were no longer to be thought of as perversions. Playful bondage and consenting SM practices were winked at. Nevertheless,

---

* No sooner was this volume published than there was talk of a *DSM* IV, which would correct the flaws of both versions of the third manual. Perhaps, in keeping with the changing moral structure of our society, we will return then to the old-fashioned term *perversion* with its moralistic implications. It is unlikely that a *DSM* IV or *DSM* V will examine the *strategy* of perversion, since manuals such as these are traditionally devoted to easily identifiable behavioral criteria rather than complex psychological issues.

despite the change in official terminology, the words *bizarre, criminal, unnatural, antisocial,* and *immoral* still attach to the behaviors that now fall under the heading *paraphilia.* And the sinister, old-fashioned word *perversion* reflects what people still feel and it is the term everyone still uses, even if sotto voce.

In most of the United States, several of the paraphilias, such as pedophilia and necrophilia, and many of the old-time perversions, such as oral and anal sex, are still criminal offenses. However, the latest psychiatric fashion is to recommend a liberal diagnostic attitude on the part of doctors. The current list of paraphilias still assumes that the essential element in a perversion is that it is an obligatory precondition for sexual excitement and orgasm. It does not explain why the perverse precondition has the power to enable erections. Nor can it account for the female perversions, in which sexual excitement and sexual performance are rarely what first meet the eye and never the crucial or decisive elements.

A man who experiences himself in the grips of his perversion may engage in other forms of sexual activity, but the perverse impulse is the one that is imperative, the activity he finds most sexually arousing and gratifying. In addition to its driven, imperative, repetitive, and stereotyped quality, to qualify as a paraphilia an act must involve at least one of the following behaviors: (1) sexual activities that use a nonhuman sexual object for sexual arousal, (2) sexual activities with humans involving real or simulated suffering and/or humiliation, and (3) sexual activity with nonconsenting partners.

The question of when humiliation, real or simulated, is merely a sexual variation or in fact a full-fledged perversion does require superfine clinical judgment. Technically, the deciding factor should be whether a sadomasochistic transaction is imperative or a matter of voluntary choice by both members of the sexual partnership. When, though, is a sexual appetite a voluntary desire and when is it a desperate need or preoccupation?

If we were to confine our interest to the beginning and end items of the following official inventory of paraphilias—deviant sexual attractions—we would be struck with the thought that there must be a vast difference between a man who uses a fetish to enable erection and penetration and a man who uses the body of a child or an animal or a corpse to bring about those ends. But as we follow along this list of perversions in the order they are presented, we will notice that one perversion blends almost imperceptibly into another. Indeed, as we come to understand the subtexts of a perverse script, we will be impressed with the somewhat arbitrary nature of the official boundaries. Characteristically, one perversion assumes prominence. Nevertheless, the scenario that is built up around the dominant perversion will bring in elements from nearly all the other perversions. A scenario that highlights masochism, for example, uses fetishistic props and transvestite costuming and is frequently enhanced by exhibitionistic and voyeuristic elements. Moreover, I believe that we come much closer to an understanding of the perverse strategy when we do not think of perversions as separate, neatly defined clinical entities but rather as performances that are designed to bring out different elements or facets of the same overall perverse strategy.

I am beginning where I began. In the catalogue of perversions that follows, I append numerous explanatory remarks to the official definitions, thus introducing many of the themes I will examine more closely later. But these asides are only preliminaries. By the time I have completed my survey of the female perversions, I will have modified, or at least amplified, the standard definitions of the male perversions.

Fetishism The basic requirement or obligatory precondition for sexual arousal is that the pervert have in his possession an inanimate object—a leather boot, a lace handkerchief, a black corset—or that he obtain a sexual partner who is willing to wear the inanimate object. However, beyond these fundamentals are numerous possibilities and variations. For example, the fetishist may himself wear the fetish. The fetish may be a part of the sexual partner's body—her breasts, her ankles, her earlobe, a special shine on her nose. The sexual partner herself (or himself) may personify in the fetishist's imagination what the fetish symbolizes. For example, just as a high-heeled leather boot may represent a female with a penis—the so-called phallic woman—so a woman, with or without boots, may be endowed with phallic properties by her fetishistic lover and thus become, for him at least, a fetish. Some fetishists are able to be sexually aroused only by policewomen or nuns or nurses, or women they command to dress up as these personages. The scenario that accompanies the fetishistic perversion may include humiliation of the sexual partner. But more usually her humiliation is the secondary outcome of being forced to degrade and humiliate the fetishist.

Braid cutting, a popular perversion during the nineteenth century, is now an anachronism. Nonetheless, if we think of braid cutting as a general variant of hair and fur fetishism, we will see that it is not such an uncommon perversion. The change in society's fashions from braids to bobs and demi crew cuts has not deterred the use of hair cutting, hair shaving, and hair plucking as obligatory conditions for sexual excitement and erection.

Transvestism Transvestism is a variation on fetishism. The basic requirement for sexual arousal is that the person himself dress in the clothes of the opposite sex, literally cross-dressing. Transvestism was found in many ancient cultures and was labeled a disease by Hippocrates. But until the recent past, around 1930, the medical profession could not decide which variety of cross-dressing was "true" transvestism and which was perhaps an aspect of homosexuality or which perhaps a symptom of sex-gender dissonance, which doctors today label transsexualism. Throughout history women have been cross-dressing as a way of gaining access to educational, social, and political powers that would otherwise be denied them. Thus cross-dressing, loosely speaking, can be readily observed in persons other than transvestites. The latest psychiatric definition, though it is confusing insofar as it goes against popular notions of transvestism, at least succeeds in clarifying just who is and who is not a transvestite. Transvestism is now defined as heterosexual cross-dressing in which clothing is used fetishistically for sexual arousal. For example, unless her cross-dressing is driven and imperative and required for sexual arousal and performance, a woman who dresses in men's clothing would not be considered a transvestite. Nor is the male drag queen, who is popularly thought to epitomize transvestism, a transvestite. The drag queen is a homosexual male, basically a female impersonator, who as a young man appeals to the fantasies and anxieties of other homosexual men by caricaturing the physical and intellectual inadequacies of females. After a while some drag queens grow into their female clothing and begin to feel more at home with their feminine tendencies. At that point their cross-dressing is less a caricature of femininity.

Very few females cross-dress as a means of enabling sexual arousal. The typical transvestite is a heterosexual male who wears female clothing to achieve an erection. Sexual arousal may be followed by sexual intercourse with the man's wife or mistress or a prostitute or by mutual or solo masturbation. Typically the transvestite is not promiscuous and enacts his scenario with only one or two sexual partners. As he gets older the transvestite becomes less dominated by his need to have erections and more directly obsessed with female clothing. Very often, all that remains of his perversion is an interest in looking at and occasionally wearing female clothing. A special pornographic literature has arisen for transvestites. Some of the stories are romantic interludes about a man who is invited to go shopping with a woman to help her select and choose lingerie, frilly dresses, angora sweaters, and silky gowns.

When the impulse to cross-dress is quiescent, the transvestite dresses in hyper-masculine clothing. In contrast to drag queens and transsexuals, transvestites, when they are not cross-dressing, are unmistakably male in appearance and behavior. Many of them are race car drivers, sky divers, military officers, football players, policemen, sanitation men. They enjoy participating in the macho activities that fortify them against the feminine wishes and tendencies that impel them to act out their perverse fantasy. The transvestite's behavior and attitudes are feminine only when he is dressed in female clothing. However, conscious and unconscious feminine fantasies and illusions are present at all times. Some transvestites wear corsets, garter belts, lace panties, or bras under their business suits but continue to behave in an outwardly masculine way. The illusion of being a woman (actually a woman with a penis, since the transvestite is hyper-conscious of being a male) when he is wearing male garments can be enhanced by little symbols of femininity such as paisley handkerchiefs, satin cuffs, silk ascots, combat ribbons, or any kind of dress-up clothing, like a general's uniform for example. Occasionally the transvestite fantasizes his sexual partner as a protective, rescuing, maternal woman who has dressed an innocent boy in feminine clothes to save him from some terrifying fate. However, in the more typical transvestite fantasy the man casts himself in the role of a sexual novice being forced into the humiliating position of wearing women's clothes by a domineering, leather-booted, pointy-breasted woman—a so-called phallic woman. In truth this phallic woman, who has been assigned the role of a powerful and dominating humiliator, is a demeaned woman, a prostitute, a Playboy bunny, a wife or girlfriend who submits, unwillingly or willingly, to the perverse script of the man who directs the performance and pays the bills.

Sexual masochism The masochistic fantasies that accompany sexual intercourse and masturbation are so prevalent as to be considered universal. However, the kind of driven and repetitive acting out of a sexual masochistic scenario that would justify calling an activity a perversion is comparatively rare. On the other hand, as I have already observed, almost every perversion entails a variation on a masochistic script. In contrast to fetishism and transvestism, which are almost exclusively male, sexual masochism is found in both sexes. Contrary to popular opinion, *sexual masochism* is much more prevalent among males in general (the ratio is about 20 males to 1 female) and especially among homosexual males. Some women are driven to act out masochistic scenarios in which they require a man to assume the role of the sadistic humiliator, but more characteristically a woman is a paid and/or willing participant who has been cast in the role of the sadist in a sadomasochistic scenario invented and controlled by her male sexual partner. The male partner requests that he be bound, beaten on the buttocks, straddled, and urinated or defecated on. The woman obeys his commands.

The strange idea that sexual masochism is a male perversion becomes more understandable when we realize that a crucial aspect of the perverse strategy is to give expression to a man's feminine wishes and longings while still keeping him in a position of masculine power. When Sigmund Freud used the term *feminine masochism,* he was referring to the feminine wishes of males. In the novel *Venus in Furs* by Sacher-Masoch, whose name Krafft-Ebing later gave to this deviant sexual attraction, the hero, Severin, draws up a travesty of the marriage contract that will bind him to his grudging mistress, Wanda von Donajew, who despises Severin for his feminine longings and would much prefer a male who would dominate her. She will later bring such a male into Severin's life, and only then can Severin be dominated and humiliated by the ultimate sadist, the super-macho man of his dreams. In the meantime, "Mrs. von Donajew may not only chastise her slave for the slightest negligence or misdemeanor as and when she wishes but she will also have the right to maltreat him according to her humor or even simply to amuse herself; she is also entitled to kill him if she so wishes; in short, he becomes her absolute property."

Transvestism and sexual masochism are perversions that permit the man to identify with the degrading position assigned to women in the social order, but without losing face. As the plot goes, he is behaving as a female, in the standard feminine position, but he is a female with a penis and is behaving as he does only to achieve the manly end of erection and orgasm. And like Severin, the transvestite and sexual masochist long to be in the position of a woman to be dominated and possessed by a powerful male.

Sexual sadism Popular opinion has it that males are by nature inclined toward sadism. In fact, cases of pure sexual sadism, such as mutilation rape and lust murder, are extremely rare. These acts are crimes and the man who commits the act, if he is caught, is treated like a criminal and put behind bars. Nevertheless, it is conceded that in some lust murders the bodies of the victims are never found and the killers never apprehended. Moreover, as we know, there are more cases of modulated sadism—that is, cases of rape and battered women—than are reported. Until recently the males who enacted these perverse scenarios were regarded with a tolerant eye, hardly as perverts and certainly not as criminals. The cops and the rapist traded winks: "boys will be boys." It was customary to blame the raped or battered female for the mischief. It was said that she was a seductress who led the man on and then tried to frustrate him or a recalcitrant wife who had been disobedient or just plain lazy. A woman who accused a man of rape could expect that *she* might be treated as the criminal. She would be accused of perjury or labeled as a hysteric, one of those repressed women whose ungratified sexual longings had stimulated her overactive imagination and caused her to implicate an innocent man in her perverse fantasy.

The truth is that males are not born sadists. However, when their humiliating and frightening feminine strivings rise too close to the surface, some men are driven to rape, mutilation, and mutilation homicide. Others simply come home after a workday or out-of-work day of being put in the humiliating and demeaning position of a female to reaffirm their masculinity by battering their wives and physically abusing their children. These all-too-commonplace enactments, in my opinion, are outcomes of the perverse strategy and belong in the category of sexual sadism, even though they do not entail sexual intercourse.

One motive for perversion among males is the fear of their own feminine wishes. Another is the terror of carrying out the full measure of the destructiveness aroused by the female body or any body that represents to a pervert the weaknesses and femininity he despises and fears in himself. While outright sadism is not commonplace, males with perverse inclinations are trying to regulate destructive impulses that, if not held in check, could escalate to mutilation rape and mutilation homicide. These men are more likely to contain their sadism by using a fetish, dressing up in female clothing, assuming a masochistic role in a sexual scenario, or developing other symptoms such as premature ejaculation and impotence.

Perversions are an instance of the erotic passions frantically trying to restrain impulses toward destruction and death. And fortunately, most of the time, the controlled ritual of a sadomasochistic scenario is successful in achieving this aim.

For the last passion of the Marquis de Sade's *120 Days of Sodom,* the erotic yields to the destructive, as it takes fifteen simultaneous operations on fifteen females to enable the arousal, erection, and ejaculation of the protagonist. For the scenario to work, the victims had to be between the ages of fifteen and seventeen, not a day younger, not a day older. Each girl was branded with a number designating the order she would enter the operating amphitheater and the specific operation she would be subjected to. Her body was placed in a specially designed apparatus and then either sliced, dismembered, melted, boiled, broiled, impaled, poisoned, deentrailed, or some ingenious combination of those basic operations. Whether the girl died after a few minutes, a few hours, or a few days was a matter of relative indifference to the hero, for it was the simultaneous execution of the fifteen different operations that was the precondition for his sexual satisfaction.

This culminating orgy, as with all the rest of Sade's monotonous and repetitive sexual fantasies, is a story only and not an action. Sade's sadism is referred to as "aesthetic sadism"—pornography. The myth about pornography is that it exists to enhance erotic desire. But this too, like everything else about perversion, is a deception. The truth is that pornography manages to contain outright sadism by disguising the murderous impulses in a script that highlights erotic motives.

In this century, the sadism is scarcely veiled by the aesthetics in slasher films and snuff flicks, in which women's bodies are dismembered and hired actresses purportedly murdered—snuffed out—before the camera.

In the sadomasochistic sexual fantasies that make up the bulk of pornographic reading materials and films, women and young children of both sexes are depicted as assuming the masochistic role. These scenarios are usually invented by men and designed for the sexual arousal of men, who unconsciously identify with the person in the submissive (feminine) position. The unconscious aim, as always, is to express yet disguise, even if barely, the man's wishes to be a submissive, denigrated female. As I have previously noted, when it comes to actual behavior between consenting (or paid) partners, more often than not it is the man who demands that a woman enact the role of the sadistic partner. In that way he can identify with the position of the masochist and fulfill his unconscious and shameful feminine longings without anyone's being the wiser.

A person may be preferentially masochistic or sadistic, but most couples who participate in sadomasochistic scenarios are willing, albeit occasionally, to exchange roles. Most often both partners are searching for a good "top," a master who is in complete control of his or her sadism, allowing the slave to be assured that his or her sexual excitement will not go out of bounds either. In many instances, the sadomasochistic transaction in which somebody is dominated and humiliated is more important than who is dominator and who is dominated. The dominated one seeks to have certain uncontrollable inner sensations associated with femininity and weakness localized on the surface of his body by a master knowledgeable about just how far to turn the screws. The master, of course, is free to identify with his slave.

Exhibitionism Exhibitionists are men who are periodically overcome by an irresistible impulse to expose their genitals to unknown women or girls, usually in a public place—where they run the risk of getting caught. The exposure is accompanied by masturbation, which keeps the penis in a state of erection. Typically exhibitionists are heterosexual males, some of whom are married and ordinarily engage in sexual intercourse with women. Frotteurism, or the rubbing against and fondling of an unwilling woman's breasts and buttocks in crowded situations, such as subway cars, is a variant of exhibitionism.

It is thought that the making of obscene phone calls to unknown women is a more socialized version of exhibitionism. The obscene phone caller is besieged by sexual fantasies similar to those of the actual exhibitionist. Instead of forcing the sight of his penis on the eyes of an unwilling woman, the obscene phone caller forces his sexualized patter about the size, movement, and activity of his penis on an unknown woman during or preceding masturbation. Cases have been reported of females who make obscene phone calls or otherwise force their sexual and aggressive fantasies on an unwilling listener, usually a man but sometimes another woman. Some heterosexual and homosexual couples find that telephone masturbation enhances their sexual relationship, but unlike the pervert they are not governed by a preoccupation with this activity.

A few experts insist that the obscene phone call, especially one that emphasizes filthy language with or without references to "dicks" and "cunts," is closer to copraphilia, a perversion in which the obligatory conditions for sexual arousal are excremental activities of some sort. While one can argue about these fine points, obviously the content of an obscene phone call is infantile, since the words reduce sex to a genital exhibition or a fecal activity. Moreover, the content of the phone call is less important than the fact that someone is in the demeaned and humiliated position (the listener) and someone else is in the powerful, dominating position (the speaker).

Voyeurism The voyeur is the proverbial Peeping Tom, the man who achieves sexual arousal while secretly viewing a half-dressed, undressed, or undressing woman. A voyeur does not accost or in other way try to alert the woman to his presence: the typical voyeuristic scenario requires that the woman be unaware she is being watched. Voyeurs prefer to masturbate while watching one or more women undress or masturbate or have sexual intercourse than to themselves engage in sexual intercourse. The stock-in-trade of commercial peep shows is scenes of women or children masturbating—usually nothing more elaborate than that, much to the disappointment of casual voyeurs who are looking for more invigorating secrets. Many females and males are casual voyeurs, and many children and adults occasionally get a kick out of eavesdropping or secretively observing the behaviors of unsuspecting others in restaurants, department stores, and subways. But there is a great difference between these spontaneous voyeuristic adventures and the preoccupation of the Peeping Tom whose life is devoted to his voyeurism. Very few reported cases of compulsive sexual voyeurism are of women. The owners of peep show joints report that each day a woman or two comes for a peep, but very few are steady customers.

Some women are sexually aroused by watching couples engaging in sexual intercourse or mutual masturbation or simply dressing and undressing. However, rarely is their so-called voyeurism a preoccupation or a precondition for sexual arousal. They can take it or leave it. The scenario is fairly flexible and is enacted with other cooperating adults. Sexual arousal is not dependent on an unsuspecting or victimized subject.

Pedophilia Sexual arousal that depends on sexual activity with prepubescent children and adolescents is always a criminal activity and involves an innocent victim. The term *pedophilia* covers a variety of specific crimes, the names of which have less to do with the behavior of the pedophile than with local legal statutes and therefore vary from country to country and in the United States from state to state. Whatever the sexual act or the age of his victim, a pedophile might be arrested and convicted for sodomy, carnally abusing a minor, impairing the morals of a minor, or lewd and lascivious conduct. The pedophile might be a heterosexual married man, a macho single guy, a homosexual, an exhibitionist, a father, an uncle. Whoever he is, the pedophile may simply expose his genitals to an unsuspecting child, masturbate in the presence of a child, induce the child to masturbate him, or masturbate the child. Some pedophiles are more desperate. They can be aroused and gratified only if they penetrate a child sexually. As with any perversion, when the pedophilia does not succeed in controlling the man's sadism, the child might be mutilated or dismembered postcoitally.

Pedophilic acts are considered child sexual abuse even when the man merely masturbates in the presence of the child or when the child is said to have consented to mutual masturbation or penetration.

The typical pedophile prefers young boys, but some prefer girls. He prefers a runaway from another city or a lost or abandoned child with whom he need not have a prolonged relationship. In these respects pedophiles are distinguished from straightforward incest offenders, who prefer daughters, stepdaughters, nieces, or the female children of relatives and neighbors. Incest offenders, if they are males, which they usually are, prefer female children because incest is motivated in part by a fear of cross-gender inclinations. Pedophiles, while they also are desperate to prove their manhood, have another, more dominating motive that rules their lives—a preoccupation with wanting to obscure all differences between the child and adult generations. However, these distinctions between one category of child molester and another are not hard and fast. Some offenders are crossover types such as Nabokov's hero in *Lolita*. Some pedophiles, for example, marry divorced mothers or widows to gain access to their prepubescent children. Others marry women susceptible to their charms, produce children with them, and in that way cross over from pedophilia to incest.

The North American Man-Boy Love Association (NAMBLA), an organization devoted to helping men locate the boys of their choice, is listed in the Manhattan telephone directory. In Great Britain a group of pedophiles banded together to form the Paedophile Information Exchange (PIE). Among the members of PIE were a former British ambassador, members of the household staff at Buckingham Palace, a vicar's son, a scoutmaster, and other upstanding members of the society, most of whom eventually confessed their preference for young boys. When questioned about their sexual preference, pedophiles are uncommonly frank about their distaste for adult females. They have a distaste for all adult bodies, but what fills them with horror is the more obvious way that a woman's body reminds them of the anatomical distinctions between adults and children. They complain that the adult female body is disgusting to them: where women are supposed to have genitals they have a dirty hole filled with menstrual blood. "Boys' bodies are V-shaped, while women's are angular, like a bag of shit tied in the middle," they will say. Or "I like the smooth surface of the young boy's body, I don't like hair on it or any pimples. I don't like to touch that, I can't stand it."

Recent investigations of child sexual abuse in day care centers and nursery schools have raised questions about the pedophilic potential of females. A study of crack addiction among lower-class women has revealed that mothers and grandmothers, under the influence of crack, will sexually abuse their own children or sell them to sexually abusing crack dealers to obtain more crack. If crack should become a widespread middle- and upper-class addiction, we may encounter more instances of female pedophilia and incest. Some researchers have suggested that crack induces a breakdown of the gender stereotypes. I think that the primary effect of crack is to break down the perverse strategy itself. Crack, a substance that provokes violence and paranoia, makes conscious the desperate hatred and vengeance and utter madness that are usually held at bay by the perverse strategy.

Zoophilia Sexual arousal is obtained by stroking or fondling an animal or observing animal intercourse. Some experts distinguish zoophilia from outright bestiality, an activity that involves oral, anal, or genital sex between a human and an animal. Zoophilia and bestiality are extremely rare and are almost never the preferred method of sexual arousal and discharge. The childhood histories of the men and women who have been driven to enact one or another of the more traditional perversions may include sporadic sexual contacts with household pets or other domesticated animals such as horses, cows, and sheep. Pornographic stories, movies, and photographs designed for the sexual arousal of men often depict a woman or child being forced to engage in sexual activities with an animal.

Necrophilia Sexual arousal, erection, and orgasm are possible only with a corpse or dismembered, dying body. Usually a female corpse is preferred, but for some necrophiles the dead or dying body of a male, a child, or an animal suffices. Necrophilia, so far as we know the rarest of all the perversions, nevertheless expresses succinctly a facet of the perverse strategy that is common to all perversions. In its larger meaning perversion is about the deadening and dehumanization of otherwise humanly alive and therefore threateningly dangerous, unpredictable desires.

Therefore, though zoophilia, bestiality, and necrophilia seem a far cry from the comparatively normal-sounding fetishism with which I began this catalogue of perversions, the household pets and dying or dead humans and animals are as much fetishistic objects as are a leather boot, a lace garter belt, or a blue velvet bathrobe. The more dangerous and unpredictable the threat of living desire is felt to be, the more deadened or distanced from human experience the fetish or fetish object has to be.

. . .

Fetishism exemplifies the perverse strategy. In every perversion a part, a detail, always stands for the whole. The perverse strategy employs this detail to symbolize an entire narrative of the traumatic childhood events that led to the perversion. When the detail or part is conscious, moreover hyperconscious because it is the central aspect of a lively performance rather than merely a thought or daydream, the more frightening and dangerous story, in its entirety, can be kept unconscious. A fetish is designed to keep the lies hidden, to divert attention away from the whole story by focusing attention on the detail. In fetishism, the prototypical perversion, an object like a leather boot, a lace garter belt, or a blue velvet bathrobe is employed by a man with the conscious motive of enhancing sexual excitement and erection— and thus his self-esteem as well. However, as I will demonstrate in succeeding chapters, that simple detail—a boot, a bathrobe—is a complex symbol that both expresses and yet conceals all the forbidden and dangerous wishes, all the losses, abandonments, anxieties, and terrors of childhood. While on the surface the sole function of a fetish object is to enable sexual performance, the perverse strategy *is* to focus attention on sexual performance with its manifestly wholesome motive of male virility so that an entire history of desire and punishment can be kept secret and unconscious.

In a male perversion, a fetish of one sort or another is always present, actually or symbolically. In its narrowest meaning, the fetishism in a male perversion entails a displacement of sexual desire away from the whole identity of a woman to some accessory or garment, some object ancillary to her being—a shoe, a corset, a garter belt, a whip, a slipper, a bathrobe. By virtue of its fantasized or actual isolation from the woman's breathing, responding, sensing, pulsating, experiencing body, the fetish object, unlike the woman herself, can be controlled and manipulated. A sexual fetish is significantly more reliable than a living person. It expects neither commitment nor emotional engagement. When the full sexual identity of the woman is alive, threatening, dangerous, unpredictable, the desire she arouses must be invested in the fetish. Unlike a fully alive, human female being with dangerous, unpredictable desires, who must be wooed and courted, fetish objects are relatively safe, easily available, undemanding of reciprocity.

The French analysts say that the term *fetish* originates in the French word *factice*, meaning "ficitious" or "artificial." The sexual fetish, of course, represents artificial or imaginary genitals, and sexual fetishism is about the creation of fictitious and artifical genitals. The mighty penis in eternal erection, the phallus, is as fictionalized as the shortchanged clitoris or mutilated vagina that the phallus is meant to repair and compensate for. Traditionally in most cultures, the female genitals are thought of and represented as damaged organs. In the mind of the fetishist the damaged female genitals must undergo interminable imaginary reparations to be eternally revived as a phallus. The woman whom the fetishist endows with this fictitious genital is transformed into the proverbial "phallic woman." Now that the term "phallic woman" has come into common usage, it is popularly used to refer to any powerful, authoritative, "masculine" woman. However, as I said earlier, the fundamental phallic woman is a woman who embodies a stereotype of denigrated femininity: a Playboy bunny, a centerfold, a call girl, a whore, a go-go dancer, a wife who submits to her husband's demands that she dominate him or urinate on him, the slave who has the power to generate erections in her master because she is imagined as having a phallus hiding under her silky veils. The phallic woman, even when she plays the role of a dominating sadist with pointy breasts and spike heels, is a demeaned and "castrated" woman, a woman who has been temporarily repaired for the purpose of creating erections in the man who is paying the bill.

Whereas the French would like to claim the fetish as an emblem of their tolerance for sexual diversity, it is generally held that the word derives from the Portuguese *feitiço,* meaning "false" or "worship of false values." The word is said to have come into existence to describe "the veneration for, and precious status of, seemingly useless objects that the Portuguese explorers had found in various African religions." Marx spoke of "commodity fetishism" to describe capitalism, with its worship of useless commodities as though they were sacred objects. Freud compared the search for the sacred sexual fetish with the search of "the pious English for the ten lost tribes of Israel."

Among the favored sexual fetishes are articles of leather—shoes, gloves, thongs, belts. Female clothing such as panties, garter belts, and corsets are also standard, as are items that resemble female pubic hair—braids, locks of hair, wigs, fur, velvet. More exotic items are rubber aprons and coats, rubber or leather goods with laces and ties; ropes and whips with or without thorns.* Black is the preferred color of many sexual fetishes, presumably because the contrast between the lighter skin and the darker garment is a reassurance of the phallic potentials hidden beneath the woman's pubic hair, which is always darker than her skin. Depending on the eye of the beholder, black might be an assurance that the woman does have a phallus, while the contrasting skin color would signify that she is in fact damaged and mutilated. However, since fetishes are always strategically ambiguous, it could be the other way around. And white or red or pink often does just as well as black. In addition, the dark-light contrast provides a sense of boundary between one body and another, thus protecting the man from his unconscious wish to identify with and merge his body with the despicable-desirable body of the "castrated" woman.

---

* Robert Stoller, an authority on sexual perversion, has attempted to demonstrate the infinite variability of the fetishistic objects or erotic preferences that might be enlisted to ensure sexual performance. Included in his two-page list of fetishes are such items as cigarette holders; feces; pacifiers; velvet; a single-leg-above-the-knee amputee (those whose sexual preference is for persons lacking a limb or limbs are sufficiently represented, Stoller informs us, to have been given their own designation—amelotatism); other men's wives; other women's husbands; sunsets; Wagnerian sopranos; a woman pulling a toilet chain; handcuffs; copulating flies; hair—braided, flowing, red, blond, cut, shaved; wigs; coral jewelry; cross-eyed women; whipped horses slipping; sucked blood; jodhpurs; men with breasts like women; a smooth-skinned girl covered with lather being shaved.

Simply focusing his eyes on a part of his partner's body that he has fetishized in his imagination—the shine on her nose, the curve of her neck, the pale sliver of ankle showing between her long black skirt and her black shoes—might do the trick for those men who are only slightly terrified of the female body. However, for a full-fledged, genuine fetishist the fetish is an obligatory and actual prop. It must be tangible, visible, inanimate, smellable, and always at the disposal of the fetishist, who cannot perform sexually unless he or his sexual partner wears or manipulates the fetish during foreplay and coitus.

A fetish is often the dominant prop in a more encompassing sado-masochistic scenario entailing restraint, immobilization, binding, hanging—restrictions that lead to pleasurable torments ranging from mild discomfort to excruciating pain. The corsets, gloves, boots, garters, and lacings are like armor that hold together a body that is experienced as a container for leaking, fragmented parts. They hide and reveal. They soothe and lacerate.

If he is going to invent a fetish, a boy usually does so during early pubescence or puberty as an accompaniment to other details that are part of his masturbation ritual. He may model this adolescent fetish on the piece of leather or "borrowed" lace underpants that he used in boyhood to reassure him when he went to sleep at night or while he was masturbating. But the adolescent fetish acquires its perverse meaning in the context of a compulsive and desperate erotic performance meant to allay anxiety and shame—though it does make prominent an uncomfortable sense of guilt.

During early pubescence a boy is frightened by his nocturnal emissions and also by the insistent urgency of his penis, which can be so easily stimulated into erection by an infinite variety of sounds, odors, sights, movements, and tactile sensations from the surface and from inside the body. Grown men, all of whom from time to time experience some problem with their potency, often look back on the ease and frequency of their adolescent erections with forlorn admiration, longing for the golden days of youth. However, they don't remember that when they were adolescents the unpredictability of the erections and all the other strange and unpredictable physical changes were frightening, sometimes terrifying.

While an erect penis and a tight scrotum are symbols of strength, firmness, control, and virility, almost every other change induced by male pubescence signifies weakness, flabbiness, passivity, and femininity. Most of the initial changes of puberty are immensely disquieting to all boys, but especially so to those who have all along been frightened of their feminine wishes. The culture supports the infantile mythology that the penis and the penis alone is the masculine sexual organ. However, the most striking changes of male pubescence, the changes that will transform a boy into a genitally functioning adult, are the awakening and growth of the so-called inner genital organs—the testicles and scrotum, the seminal vesicles, the prostate, Cowper's glands—changes that all too often remind the boy of the femininity, passivity, and weakness that he has succeeded in masking with the phallic-narcissistic bravado of his prepuberty years. To complicate matters, the dramatic rise in androgen production triggers a sudden increase in unstructured, free-floating aggression, which alarms the boy about his capacity to control the sadistic fantasies frequently aroused by images of the female body. Preceding the growth of the penis by a year or more is the enlargement of the testicles and scrotum. Defensively boys will refer to the testicles as "balls," but more often they think of them as feminine organs, like breasts or ovaries, and call them "jewels" or "eggs." The downy quality of the first pubic hairs also threatens to make conscious the boy's unconscious fantasies of being transformed into a woman. The looseness, stickiness, and messiness of the first emissions are associated with babyhood and the pendulousness of the scrotal sac with the female body and femininity. The experiences of passivity in the first emissions and the initial spasmodic ejaculations are overwhelming and terrifying to a boy. Each of these unpredictable involuntary secretions from a mysterious place inside the body is associated with messiness, infection, dirty female secrets. Cowper's glands secrete a preejaculatory mucus that may exude from the penis at any time during sexual arousal. Prostate emissions seem to be coming from nowhere. Wet dreams are associated with urination and babyishness. Boys experience "dry runs" in which they reach orgasm before they are capable of ejaculation. Though nowadays most boys know better, they still often think of ejaculation as a sign of injury produced by masturbation.

The fetish is designed to reassure the boy that he has control over the mysterious substances and sensations emanating from inside his body and over the cycles of erection, ejaculation, orgasm, and detumescence. The fetish also gives him a feeling that he can modulate his hostile aggressive strivings, which he fears might otherwise transform his penis into an instrument of violence.

Usually, as his erotic sensibilities and fantasies come to the fore, they induce more affectionate and tender feelings toward females, and the boy also becomes more secure in his masculine identity. At that time he is able to give up the adolescent masturbatory fetish or fetishistic scenario, albeit with some degree of reluctance but also considerable relief.

A man who remains uncertain about his maleness and masculine identity may never give up his adolescent fetish. Fur pieces, lace panties, leather belts, corsets, patent leather boots may be enlisted in the service of sexual performance throughout adulthood. Very often the fetish continues to be used in exactly the same ritualistic way as when it was invented during adolescence. Fetishes are conservative objects designed to preserve the fictions of the past. Nevertheless, chances are that the adult male will discover a few little ways of elaborating and extending the possibilites of his original fetish. In time, the original fetish may be joined by other fetishes. The scenario becomes more complicated.

A male who managed his boyhood and adolescent sexual anxieties without resorting to a fetish might not invent a fetishistic fantasy until he encounters an emotional crisis that stirs up his long-suppressed feminine yearnings and exacerbates his separation and castration anxieties—marriage, divorce, parenthood, a faltering love affair, the death or illness of a loved one, a loss of power or prestige at work, an assignment to a position of authority, a homosexual temptation.

Unlike other animals, we are creatures whose sexual lives are governed almost entirely by fantasy and very little, if at all, by biological instincts. None of us is ever entirely free of the conflicts or anxieties associated with sexual intercourse. Every person who engages in sexual intercourse invents a fantasy that serves directly or indirectly to alleviate anxiety, enhance self-esteem, and heighten sexual pleasure. Activities that are commonly regarded as perverse—cunnilingus, fellatio, wearing erotic undergarments, enacting bondage scenarios, watching the sexual partner undress or masturbate—could be aspects of any run-of-the-mill sexual relationship. However, the sexual pervert behaves very differently from the countless men and women who evoke erotic fantasies, and sometimes enact them, to heighten their sexual pleasure. The pervert is not making love; he is making hate. The pervert has no choice. His sexual performance is obligatory, compulsive, fixated, and rigid.

Usually, however, the person whose life is dominated by a perversion cannot appreciate the imperative and driven quality of his sexual rituals. He fools himself into believing that he is a free agent and may even proudly advertise the advantages of his unique scenario. He glorifies his sexuality by imagining that it endows him with exceptional powers. As the maestro who has invented a method so exquisitely calculated to both create and repair castration, to inflict and heal, to control the terrors of merger and separation, to rectify all the humiliations and traumas of childhood, the pervert experiences himself as superior to the dull, cautious, and straight citizen. He has contempt for the others, whose goodness, moral rigidity, and banal imagination force them to abide by the roles and positions assigned to them by the social order.

The law-abiding, virtuous citizen sometimes thinks there is some validity to the pervert's view of himself as a rebel. After all, the pervert is able to tolerate, carry out, and elaborate on acts that the average person dares only to imagine or once in a while furtively attempt. Even our playful little bondage games and cross-dressing impersonations are but tame approximations of his fully realized sexual rituals. We are always uncertain about the pervert's position with regard to the social order. Is he the most sorry victim of a social order that preserves itself by assigning to men and women positions of domination and submission? Or is he a transgressor who has found the way to explode the boundaries of a sadistic and tyrannical morality? How often, in high art as in the popular media, the pervert is represented as a heroic being, a moral adventurer who is willing to risk all, while the ordinary mortal is depicted as shrinking in the shadows of normality.

The pervert's clear-cut hostility toward the fundamental structures of civilization puts to shame our cowardly ambivalence. He wishes to obliterate the differences between the sexes and the differences between the child and adult generations. And what's more, he succeeds in translating these wishes into action. When we are not scapegoating and punishing him for his heinous crimes and unnatural acts, we are idealizing him as a culture hero. He is the one with secrets of Great Sex. And we are the naive children who can only imagine what that impressive Great Sex is all about. He is the transgressor we would wish to be. If we could act as he does, then we might also dare to go beyond the narrowing conditions of sex role, family, jobs, and moral obedience. We too could be free of the burdens of relating to other human beings with commitment and responsibility. Like him, we could break down the barriers, storm the barricades, push forward the frontiers of the possible, unsettle reality, defy death.

Perversions are about unsettling reality and defying death. But the rebellion and the bravery are deceptions. For the pervert is rigid and conservative. He lives in terror of his demons. He is eternally searching for the secret of Great Sex and never finding it. Perversions are never what they seem to be.

2

A Memorial
to the Horror
of Castration

Lear: Down from the waist they are Centaurs,
Though women all above:
But to the girdle do the gods inherit,
Beneath is all the fiend's.
There's hell, there's darkness, there is the sulphurous pit,
Burning, scalding, stench, consumption; fie, fie, fie!

King Lear, 4.6

Lear's portrayal of the female as a creature divided at the waist with angelic breasts above and fiendish genitals below is a common enough female gender stereotype. That Lear likens the female to a male warrior with the impressive genitals of a beast reminds us of the phallic woman who plays a significant role in most male perversions. The shifting images of the female in Lear's tirade call to mind the layers of masks in a perversion, where nothing is ever as it first seems to be. A madonna removes her veils to reveal her beastliness. What seems to be love is hate. A monument to life turns out to be a memorial to death.

Lear was not the first nor will he be the last to entertain the fantasy of female as divided between the good nursery breast above and the evil sexual temptress below. Whereas the milky warmth of the breast represents nourishment and divine forgiveness, the sulphurous pit of the vagina represents eternal damnation and death. Sooner or later in every discussion of the male perversions, we come across the idea that many adult males, not only those whose lives are driven by the perverse strategy, are terrified of the female genitals. It is said that men dread any reminder that they were born of the body of women, between one stenching hole and another. It is said that men cannot endure the idea that they are dependent on women for reproduction and childrearing. One basic theme keeps reappearing in different guises: there is something innately horrifying about the vagina, something about that life-giving passage of sexuality and procreation that has perpetually brought to men's minds the stigmata of humiliation, degradation, mutilation, and death.

Gustave Flaubert worshiped madonnalike women, particularly those with baby at the breast, but in his letters to his friends he cursed and defamed and vilified the female, bragging that his greatest wish was to defile and trample every sacred value. Flaubert spent his childhood and early adolescence in the doctors' quarters of his father's hospital, l'Hôtel-Dieu. Clutching the hand of his beloved little sister Caroline, Gustave would peek through cracks in the hospital fence to watch his father performing autopsies. An awesome spectacle, to be sure, for a young boy to witness his father carving up corpses and probing about entrails, but especially so when the boy was well aware that he was peeking at a scene that was forbidden to the eyes of children. Gustave confessed to a friend, "The most beautiful woman is hardly beautiful on the dissecting table of an amphitheater, with guts hanging in her nose, a leg cut open and an unlit cigar resting on her feet."

When he arrived at manhood he realized that "a terrible shyness" would prevent him from touching the body of a "good" woman without trepidation. He preferred his mistress's slippers and handkerchiefs to her actual body. He advised his lusty friend Ernest, "Take care not to ruin your intelligence in commerce with the ladies. You will lose your genius in a womb."

The unconscious fear of being swallowed up into the womb, which Flaubert was capable of expressing openly, is the counterpoint of some men's unconscious wish to be a woman, to merge with her, to be back inside her belly where there are no disturbing facts of life such as the differences between penis and vagina, male and female, child and adult. Merely the thought of a woman's inner sexual and procreative organs —her vagina and her uterus—can be a reminder of these frightening wishes to be eternally united with Mother in some smooth, womblike utopia where the rough and troubling realities of everyday existence can no longer disturb the peace. Such conflicted wishes would be paralyzing without a fetish to rescue the capacities to have an erection and penetrate the female body.

In "Fetishism," a six-page paper published in 1927, Freud described what he believed were the infantile origins of the sexual fetishes that males use to enable sexual performance. In his eagerness to get at the unconscious strategy underlying the symbolic structure of the fetish, Freud hurried over a few very significant details about the fantasy life of little boys. In doing so, he lent support to the gender stereotypes of his age.

Freud's lack of clarity on these crucial details led to some unfortunate misreadings of his paper on fetishism. In trying to understand why Freud would not have been more precise at these critical junctures, I surmised that his haste had as much to do with his long-standing emotional ambivalences toward females as with his intellectual enthusiasms and incomplete knowledge. One of the issues he left clouded and ambiguous, for example, is the meaning of the term *castration* as it refers to the female genitals. Freud states bluntly that "probably no male human being is spared the fright of castration at the sight of a female genital." In this stark proclamation Freud seems to be implying that a little boy's castration anxiety is a more or less natural reaction to the sight of the female genitals. But does a child ever get to see the female genitals? In Freud's day parents imagined that children were too innocent to notice genital differences. So in spite of their Victorian prudishness, they were fairly casual about dressing and undressing in front of the little ones. Nevertheless, surely a little boy would not actually see his mother's genitals and surely Freud does not mean a sight of the vagina. All a little boy might see is his mother's pubic hair. He would notice the absence rather than presence of a penis. It is possible, but unlikely, that he would catch a glimpse of her clitoris and interpret that organ as a shrunken or cut-off penis.

We can follow Freud's reasoning up to a point. What normal little boy, after all, would not react with fright to the sight of an absent part of the body that is very much his and so intrinsic to his sense of self and identity? However, in rushing by his clarifying explanations Freud created the impression that there is something innately and essentially horrifying about the female genitals. This is taking a four-year-old's temporary perception of the female genitals as mutilated for an objective appraisal. In fact, granting the possibility that Freud was referring to an actual moment of horror in which a little boy did catch a glimpse of pubic hair or even the clitoris, one still has to ask if this reaction of horror is the outcome of something seen by the child or something the child imagined as a result of his ongoing fantasy life, anxieties, and emotional conflicts.

To this day, some psychoanalysts speak like King Lear, Gustave Flaubert, and four-year-old boys, as though the inevitable fright of castration has something to do with the inevitably horrifying vision of the sexual organs that lie beneath the female waist. Freud did not help to dissuade his colleagues from these impacted stereotypes of the female body when in his later papers on male castration anxiety and female penis envy he reinforced the tendency to portray the female genitals as castrated or absent organs. Because the anxieties that originally motivated the defensive mental strategies of the four-year-old persist and can all too easily be reawakened in adulthood, even an intelligent and otherwise realistic adult can unconsciously reexperience the fear and discomforts he felt as a little boy. Freud was no exception.

Freud's divided attitudes toward the female would continually undermine and subvert his otherwise revolutionary theories of sexuality. He was one of the few doctors who openly opposed separating off "homosexuals from the rest of mankind as a group of a special character." He had stated emphatically that "all human beings are capable of making a homosexual object choice." Nor did Freud believe that heterosexuality was any proof or sign of normality: "The exclusive sexual interest felt by men for women is also a problem that needs elucidating and is not a self-evident fact." However, whenever Freud wandered from his mission to understand the unconscious mind and the fantasy life of human beings, he was tempted into a sexological, behavioristic view of the differences between the sexes. Then he would think just like the sexologists he was rebelling against and write about male and female differences as though he had the prescriptions for normal femininity and masculinity. Nevertheless, Freud was not a social or sexual utopian, and he rarely faltered from his fundamental premise about the impossibility of a complete gender normality for any human being. "The disposition to perversions is itself of no great rarity," he wrote, "but must form a part of what passes as the normal constitution." Though he wittingly and unwittingly used his psychoanalytic understandings in support of the gender stereotypes of his age, intrinsic to Freud's thinking was his reluctance to view matters of human sexuality in terms of normality or abnormality. Undaunted by his colleagues' outraged reactions, he proclaimed that any adult who had ever been a child had within him all the predispositions and experiences that went into the creation of a perversion. He remained firm in his conviction that the sexual perversions arose out of the unavoidable complexities of being a helpless human child growing up in the care of adults whom he adores, hates, and fears, idealizes, misunderstands, and sometimes understands all too well.

Our most exalted gender ideals and our most demeaning gender role stereotypes still bear the mark of the infantile period of childhood—loosely the ages from birth to about four (depending on the particular family or society it can be a year or two earlier or later). Psychoanalysts refer to that time of human life as *infantile* to distinguish those earlier years from childhood proper, when the child enters the larger social world outside the family and begins to slowly revise his infantile fantasies about the differences between the sexes. In coming to terms with some ubiquitous dilemmas of childhood and adolescence, most girls and boys acquire the emotional and intellectual capacities that will enable them to think in a more generous and less stereotyped way about sexuality and gender. Nevertheless, the infantile versions of feminine and masculine persist unconsciously and therefore continue to influence how the adult woman or man feels and thinks about what it means to be female or male. Infantile fantasies about gender are all that little minds are capable of. The danger comes when these infantile gender attributions are employed by the social order to enforce its conventions of femininity and masculinity. A subtle two-way collaboration takes place between the unconscious mind, with its store of infantile representations of male-female difference, and the social order, with its primitively conceived prescriptions for normal femininity and masculinity. As I have already said repeatedly and will continue to stress, these primitively conceived gender stereotypes are fundamental elements in the female and male perversions.

Freud's ingenious but immensely befuddling paper on the befuddling deceptions of the sexual fetish opens, innocently enough and lucidly enough, with a brief observation about some male patients whose sexual performances relied on the use of fetishes. None of these men had come to consult Freud with any worries or complaints about their fetishes. They were entirely satisfied with them. Indeed, several of the men praised the way in which a fetish had made sexual performance easier and more pleasurable.

Each of these men had revealed to Freud that his fetish was unconsciously experienced as a substitute for a penis, a reassuring symbol of intactness that could mask the woman's absent genital organ. In listening to his patients' fantasies about their fetishes, Freud was struck with the idea that a sexual fetish would have to be something far more crafty than a straightforward phallic symbol. A high-heeled shoe or a whip might and often does suffice as a fetish. However, Freud would insist that a phallic shape is never the *deciding* factor in a choice of a fetish. While shoes and boots and other leather goods are favorites, some other typical fetishes—a fur piece, a corset, a velvet bathrobe, a rubber apron, lace undergarments, a pink satin slipper—could hardly qualify as ordinary phallic substitutes. How could something with feminine qualities come to represent a penis?

Freud was leading up to a new and startling proposition: the fetish represents not a penis but *a substitute for a penis*. The pervert does not model his fetish on the basis of just any chance penis,

> but . . . a particular and quite special penis that had been extremely important in early childhood but had later been lost. That is to say, it should normally have been given up, but the fetish is precisely designed to preserve it from extinction. To put it more plainly, the fetish is a substitute for the woman's (the mother's) penis that the little boy once believed in and—for reasons familiar to us—does not want to give up.

When the little boy was younger, around two or three, he firmly believed that everybody in the universe was made just the way he was. Everybody had a penis, including his mother. However, contrary to the impression given by Freud's paper, the reasons the little boy of four or five does not want to give up this earlier belief about his mother's genitals have more to do with the boy's fantasies, wishes, and anxieties than with the mother's genital insufficiencies.

The model for an adult fetish is not a real penis but a later fictitious substitute for an earlier imaginary penis. The chain of logic from an actual anatomical penis to the imaginary penis that male toddlers assume is universal, to the fictitious penis that an older child constructs to fill in imaginary gaps in his mother's genital anatomy, to the adult male's sexual fetish that allows an ordinary woman with ordinary genitals to be transformed into a phallic woman is confusing enough. Freud's explanation of how the human mind achieves these various levels of deception is at times as confounding as the fetish itself. The fetish is an item constructed out of the tissue of falsehood and artificiality. So we have to remember that what follows is not at all about real genitals, male or female. However, we should not be surprised that male analysts, who had for so long deceived themselves about the true nature of the female genitals, should become confused and confusing about the difference between an actual castration and an imaginary one.

The little boy's wish to cling to a false version of reality is an outcome of the various theories he has adopted in his struggle to figure out the weighty dilemmas of childhood—first questions about the functions of his body parts, including his genitals, and then only later the role the parents' genitals play in making babies. These dilemmas assume a great importance to little children of both sexes. The emotional centers of a child's existence are his own body and his relationship with the two people on whom he has depended absolutely for nourishment, care, safety, protection, and self-esteem. Any new baby that comes along or that might come along is a serious threat to his own position in the family—to his narcissism and his relationship with his parents. The child must figure out where such a pesky intruder into his earthly paradise did come from or might at some future date come from.

Any parent who listens and observes will have little trouble recognizing how involved the child is in solving the problem of where babies come from, how they get inside the mother, and how they get out. What parents find harder to accept is that the child's seemingly innocent questions are intertwined with his theories about genital anatomy and his fantasies about what the mother and father are "doing" together as a consequence of their "being married."

Even when adults do listen, observe, and recognize that most children are brimming with sexual curiosity, some still find it hard to believe that this curiosity is stimulated by the child's own erotic and aggressive fantasies. It is much more appealing to an adult's wished-for image of childhood to view the whole business of childhood curiosity as purely cognitive and intellectual. Nor does everyone so readily embrace the idea that childhood curiosity might lead to the bizarre sexual fantasies that psychoanalysts attribute to children.

Adults are of two minds about children. Not unlike the parents of Freud's day, they assume that children are entirely innocent and never think about sex. Yet at the same time, adults assume that children understand and accept the facts of life when adults inform them about childbirth and sex. Adults are surprised when they learn that the true facts and their opposing fantasies can exist side by side in a child's mind. Adults, even though they also are capable of regressing to similar primitive ways of perceiving and understanding reality, still find it hard to believe how fantastic and unrealistic children's imaginings about sex and gender are. For the most part, a child believes only what he or she wishes to believe. And if it requires some fancy mental maneuvering to make the wished-for obscure the reality, their little minds are quite up to the task.

Perhaps the biggest hurdles to a full appreciation of childhood feelings and thoughts are the adult's wish to sentimentalize the child, the adult's need to see in the child his own lost goodness and innocence, the adult's desire to visualize childhood itself as a pre-satanic Garden of Eden. Under the best circumstances these wished-for ideals of childhood might encourage adults to do everything possible to ensure children's rights to a protected childhood. These ideals might even lend support to social values aimed at a modification of the gender stereotypes and other devastating conditions that prevent little children from growing up into sexually fulfilled, morally responsible adults. However, as I will illustrate in later chapters, the sentimentalization of childhood and the wish that the child mirror for the parent his or her own goodness and innocence have very often led to instances of brutality toward children—not only the more obvious cases of physical abuse, sexual molestation, pedophilic seduction and rape, kiddie porn, pretty girls posed as harlots for lingerie ads, but also those little and big soul murders that are everyday enacted in the name of the best interests of the child.

Parents are right, though, to question what we analysts tell them about the feelings and thoughts of children. We have not always made clear, either in our technical papers or in our public pronouncements, which of the emotions and ideas we attribute to children come from the fantasies and dreams of adult patients and which from our direct observations of children. Over the past few decades, numerous observational studies of infants and children and many analyses conducted with young children have made it eminently clear that it is an error to assume that adults' fantasies about their childhoods reflect directly the actual events of childhood or, for that matter, that the actual events determine the later fantasies. The versions of childhood that adults bring out in their analyses represent fantasies and thoughts filtered through many layers of cumulative life experience that have rearranged, jumbled up, and distorted much of what actually happened in childhood. Furthermore, many of the memories of childhood that arise in the adult mind have turned out to be "screen memories"—memories that date from earlier or later experiences or memories that use a falsification to disguise a truth and partial truths to conceal larger, less acceptable truths. To decipher the actual experiences that are represented in an adult's recollections of childhood requires great ingenuity. Very often the best that can be done is to construct a kind of ideal fiction about how the adult got to be the person he now is. What goes on between analyst and patient in the present reveals a great deal about who the patient now is and how he might have become the person he is, but that doctor-patient interaction is never an exact replication of the patient's infantile past. The older method of arriving at an image of childhood through adult recollections and the newer methods of understanding childhood by observing young children at play or by listening to their fantasies and thoughts as these emerge during a child analysis do not yield the same versions of childhood.

I have had the good fortune to be engaged in all three of these aspects of the psychoanalytic enterprise: a psychoanalyst of adults, a psychoanalyst of children and adolescents, and a researcher in observational studies of little children interacting with their families. Having personally struggled with the formidable task of disentangling and integrating the three methods, I can well appreciate how difficult it would be for the nonprofessional to keep straight which of the psychoanalytic versions of childhood are narratives of normal or average child development and which are consulting room childhoods derived from the fantasies and screen memories of adults.

To illustrate these intricacies of memory and recollection, fantasy and reality, infantile past and adult present, I have likened human development to the creation of a crochet pattern. The crochet needle moves forward, steadily enlarging old patterns and creating new ones. In the process of creating something new, every so often at some crucial juncture the needle reaches back to pull in earlier stitches and patterns, integrating some facet of the old into a new pattern of organization. Whatever was created earlier can always be given new meaning, and some of what is created later will always bear the influence of earlier patterns. A crochet pattern without such backward movements and later interweavings would be dull indeed. Similarly the richness and complexity of a human life consist of the various ways in which fantasies and wishes can always effect new interweavings of past, present, and future. What distinguishes human beings from other higher animals is this capacity to create a life narrative that moves forward and backward in time. The persistence of infantile fantasies in the adult mind always involves regressions backward *and* transformations of those fantasies achieved by the forward-moving development of the mind.

For example, in tracing the infantile origins of the adult fetish we must be cautious. An adult fetish, since it is a concrete representation of a fictitious or artificial genital, may take its inspiration from the fictitious substitute penis of childhood, but the adult version is very different in many significant ways from the childhood version. A little boy's provisional fantasies about the female genitals will influence his erotic fantasies as an adolescent or adult fetishist, but those earlier infantile fantasies will have undergone considerable transformation and reorganization over the course of his mental development.

The little boy whose childhood curiosity, fantasies, anxieties, and wishes lead him to endow his mother with a substitute penis is constructing only a temporary, elusive fantasy of the grotesque genital that the adult fetishist will concretize into a shoe or a fur piece. A little boy's invention of a substitute penis for his mother is a fiction that produces a vague, uncertain image and is merely a provisional solution to some ordinary dilemmas of childhood. The object that a fetishist uses to attain erection and penetration is a tangible object that represents a desperate solution to a lifelong situation of trauma. The adult fetishist cannot introduce his penis into that temple of doom called the vagina without a fetish to ease his way.

As Freud was the first to insist, the extravagant sexual theories of little boys may be outgrown and forgotten but they are never entirely given up. They are repressed and temporarily banished from consciousness but persist as unconscious fantasies that are ready to return to consciousness whenever there is a serious threat, imagined or actual, to a man's hard-earned masculinity. Moreover, when a childhood fantasy about the female genitals returns from the realm of the repressed to haunt the mind of an adult male it has been transformed several times over in the course of development and by then has acquired all sorts of social stereotypes and cultural mythologies. The fictitious genitals of childhood do not return in their vague and provisional childhood form but in concrete images that are bizarre and grotesque. In fetishistic literary images and in the fetishist's imagination, the "castrated" mother endowed with an imaginary penis returns as a disheveled, toothless witch with a broomstick between her legs or a threatening Medusa's face endowed with terrible vacant, staring eyes and a multitude of phallic serpents covering her head. The little boy invents a fictitious penis for his mother in a moment of panic over the safety and importance of his own penis, which he values as a most precious item of his physical being. When adult men panic at a threat to their masculine identity, they may revive in a more elaborated form these infantile images of the female genitals and project them onto the adult woman whom they love, have sexual intercourse with, marry, and create families with. Women, too, as later chapters will show, also bring their infantile fantasies about the anatomical differences between the sexes into their relationships with the men they wish to love in a more generous way.

Freud's paper "Fetishism" is a tangle of his revolutionary insights into the troubled nature of men's sexual relationships with women, his still uncertain formulations on the perverse strategy, omissions in his renditions of child development, gaps in his understandings of gender that he could not fill in because of his stubborn adherence to the gender mythologies of his day, and the mental backslidings that allowed some of Freud's own four-year-old imaginings to infiltrate and subvert his significant discoveries on the nature of the adult fetish. In short, "Fetishism" makes use unconsciously of the perverse strategy and is itself a fetishistic document.

Before we can understand the perverse logic of the adult fetishist we must wonder at the motives that would compel a little boy to invent a substitute penis for his mother. How, in fact, does his little mind accomplish such an extraordinary feat of imagination? If it is not simply the horrible sight of the terrifying female genitals, as Freud bluntly states, what events would lead to this fantasy that his mother is a chimerical creature—a mother still, but a mother with a penis. What sorts of mental strategies would enable a perfectly sane, observant, curious, alert, intelligent boy to adopt such peculiar notions about the female genitals?

Keeping in mind that every child is different and that nothing in human development ever proceeds in an ideal, orderly, expectable way, let us follow an imaginary "normal" boy along the path to his fantastic interpretations of the female genitals. The road to understanding in infancy and early childhood is almost entirely through fantasy. Only gradually does the child learn to subtract his fantasies from more logical and reasonable appreciations of reality, and even then, as I have said, his erotic life will always be a matter of fantasy. At first, in infancy and early childhood, fantasy is the child's *only* method of interpreting the psychological meaning of what he perceives and experiences. Thus, the child's fantasies of castration arise out of his susceptibility to provisional misunderstandings about the nature of reality. By the conclusion of the infantile period of childhood, at age four or five, what a child "knows" about sex and gender is a multilayered concoction of these provisional misunderstandings, with the factual and the fantasy existing side by side without too much conflict.

In the first stage, a child's anatomical fantasies are inextricably intertwined with the developmental concerns that are uppermost in his mind—body image, bodily integrity, and self-definition. Our average little boy starts out his imaginings by being highly invested in his body and in how the various parts of his body work. From a very early time, probably at around five months, he is busily at work studying how his body parts work and comparing his body parts with the body parts of other human beings, dolls, animals, and even inanimate objects like radios and lamps.

In the course of the first year or two of his life the boy has been discovering the functions of all his external body parts. One part—his penis—remains something of an enigma. He has learned that the penis can make pee-pee at various distances and in various patterns. His parents regard it with admiration. However, something tells him that his pee-pee maker must have something even more exciting to do than produce urine. But what else is it for? What else is it meant to do? He has some notion about the something else because he has already had erections while being diapered, while dashing about from here to there, and while fondling, scratching, and pushing on his penis. His highly charged emotional investment in this versatile but mysterious body part raises some other questions in his mind. Does it break off like fingernails and hair and feces? Or is it firmly rooted in place like fingers and toes and arms and legs? For a long time the little boy persists in the comforting belief that all animate and perhaps even some inanimate objects possess a penis. At the same time he entertains the discomforting fantasy that maybe the penis is a removable and detachable part that can be given away as a gift or taken away as a punishment. It is beyond even his very wild imagination to conjecture that any living being would have been born deprived of that most precious and exciting body part. Moreover, since he idealizes his mother and thinks of her as the most powerful person in his life—the one whose warm breast or sweet rubber nipple brought him the gift of a satisfied mouth and a full belly, the one who has eased the raging pains of teething and calmed away the worries of the day, the one who enforces when he eats and what he eats, where he may deposit his urine and feces and where he mustn't, the one who determines when he sleeps and when he doesn't, the one who says no to him and sometimes punishes him for wrongdoings—that beautiful caregiver of enfolding arms, that marvelously omnipotent lawgiver of the nursery must have the most powerful penis of all.

He is noticing that some people have long hair and breasts and wear skirts and dresses and bracelets, just like his mother, and that other people have short hair and beards and wear shirts and pants and big watches and smoke cigars and have no breasts, just like his father. He classifies himself with his father and if his father is a very strong and loving presence in his life, the boy will gradually accept that he is going to grow up to be a daddy person. But he still loves his delicious, sweet-smelling, and powerful mother most of all, and sometimes he wants to grow up to be a mommy person, just like her with breasts and pretty bracelets—and, of course, a penis, he supposes for the moment, for he is not prepared to give up his penis no matter how much he longs to be a mommy. Mother belongs to him. He and mother are the insiders, the sharers of all the intimate delights of the nursery. Everything and everybody that distracts his mother from him—her job, her household chores, her letter writing, her friends, his grandmother, his father—is an unwelcome intruder.

When he is a toddler and proudly walking upright with that exciting penis bouncing along between his big strong legs, the little boy experiments with some intuitions about what else his pee-pee maker might be used for. He pokes his fingers into every hole he can find, as though he had some inkling that his excited penis belongs in a hole of some sort or other. The toddler has one or two vague notions about the additional purposes of the penis, but elaborate fantasies about genital function arise only later in childhood, at the point when he becomes the excluded outsider in the erotic triangle involving him and his mother and father, the so-called Oedipal phase. When he first begins to take note of the difference between his visible penis and his mother's absent penis, his initial observations and theories about anatomical difference do *not* include the notion that these body parts have genital functions—sexual intercourse and procreation.

Leaving aside the more imponderable and threatening question of how a baby might get into the mother, the boy prefers to put his imagination to work on how it gets out. One very satisfying theory is that babies are expelled from the anus just like excrement. This theory allows for the possibility that one day he can make a real baby, just as his mother does. The anal-birth theory has definite advantages. Babies that emerge out of the anus (or from a slit in the chest or belly) are babies that little boys can give birth to as easily as mothers can. Another theory that can be accepted on the basis of his current wishful understandings is that the mother eats something that develops inside like a seed or a plant until one day a baby bursts forth from the anus (or a slit in the chest or belly).

For a time his infantile theories of where babies come from protect his original theory that all beings, including his mother, have a penis. Should he catch a glimpse of his mother's pubic hair or the labia and "tiny penis" of his little sister, he can simply deny what he has seen and replace those unwelcome images with images of what he wishes to see. He has no trouble convincing himself that his mother's penis is hidden away behind the pubic hair, perhaps in her belly, and that his sister's tiny clitoris will soon grow into a real penis.

A year or so later, around age three, when his mind is too grown up to permit these simple denials of the facts of life, the boy does not abandon his first-stage theories on how the body makes and produces babies. He brings them along to the next stage of his investigations, where they continue to influence his fantasy interpretations of what he sees and what he does not see. What are the mother and father doing together on their big bed? He would like to think that they are doing things that he could also do. They are undressing and urinating and showing off their bottoms and making big fecal sticks. Nevertheless, those loud and terrible noises from behind the bedroom door signify that some other events of a far more sinister import are also going on. Sometimes at the dinner table the boy has seen his mother and father transformed into biting, tearing, mean-looking creatures and he has been driven to tears by the terrible screams and yells and curses that they hurl at one another. Repeated experiences of this kind confirm his fantasies that "doing it" entails an act of violence. However, even if a child has very gentle parents who hardly ever fight or scream and yell, he assumes that doing it entails domination and submission. It suits a little boy's wishful view of the universe to assume that Father is forcing Mother to submit.

In his efforts to comprehend the riddles of creation and of human existence, our budding King Lear is developing a split image of the female. If he could accept the full truth, he might have to recognize that his mother has betrayed him. It is intolerable to the boy that his mother should actively desire the father. It would be an insupportable mortification to accept that his adorable mother, his nursery breast, his personal possession, should have desires other than eating and feeding or cleaning the bottoms of little children. Therefore, it follows that when his parents are "doing it," the father must be forcing the mother to do terrible things she does not want to do. Considering the state of marital relations in the early part of this century, reality may very well have confirmed the boy's comforting fantasies that his mother hates "being married" and only "does it" when forced to. To think that *his* mother prefers the father to him or that she really likes to "do it" is a mortification too terrible to reckon with. The boy prefers to believe that being married and making babies is about fighting and making up and all the terrible but exciting things that fathers inflict on mothers in bed.

When little children fantasize about what their parents are doing in bed, they play imaginatively with being one parent or the other in that imaginary, misperceived, and fantastic scene of sexual intercourse. Any infantile fantasy of the parents' sexual intercourse is referred to nowadays as a primal scene fantasy: "primal" because the fantasy is one of the primal or ubiquitous human sexual fantasies; "scene" because the fantasy entails a dramatic action and a dramatis personae of two main characters and a third party who is excluded from the action. The primal scene is a fantasy that represents a child's (or adult's) distorted impression and personal mythology concerning human sexual relations. The primal scene is unfamiliar. The fantasy is an everyday matter. Most of us are conscious of having a fantasy when we have sexual intercourse. Most of us take these sexual fantasies for granted and welcome them as enhancers of our sexual pleasure. Every human adult has at least one central primal scene fantasy and several others that are unconscious, which he or she imposes on the erotic situation. The conscious and unconscious erotic fantasies we all use to enable and enhance sexual pleasure allow us to identify with both the submitter and the dominator, both powerful adults (mother and father disguised as harem girl and sheik, patient and doctor, secretary and boss), while some shadowy third party, implicitly or explicitly, is assigned the role of a helpless, frustrated, humiliated, excited, curious onlooker.

To be excluded from what the parents enjoy together—all those submissions and dominations, those terrible but exciting forcings—is for a child a narcissistic mortification. However, most children, those with ordinary devoted parents, those whose lives have not been absorbed by painful bodily illnesses, deprivation, and other kinds of abuse, recover from this ordinary trauma of childhood with its inevitable wound to a child's self-esteem. Moreover, by virtue of accommodating to these ordinary facts of life, the average child also learns his first lesson in managing feelings of envy and jealousy and affects of shame, anxiety, and guilt in ordinary, expectable ways.

My research and clinical work have convinced me that the primal scene mortification is the crucial traumatic element in the Oedipus complex even for the average child with ordinary devoted parents, who has had the opportunity to master the painful emotions generated by this ubiquitous childhood event. In its very naming, the Oedipus complex is obviously based on the male child's fantasies and gives only a limited appreciation of how a little girl might experience this inevitable tableau of childhood. Moreover, even what is commonly understood about the male Oedipus complex is an exceedingly narrow version of how the male child responds to the knowledge of the differences between the sexes and generations.

The term *Oedipus complex* has achieved a widespread notoriety, regularly appearing in the childrearing columns of magazines and newspapers and influencing, for better or worse, how we understand paintings, plays, novels, and the lives of their creators as well as the unconscious motives of all human beings. But the term *primal scene,* which by now also appears in contemporary studies of literature and art, has yet to filter into the popular imagination. Most people, including most nonanalytic psychologists and psychiatrists, still think of the

Oedipus complex in the simpler way that Freud originally described it: the boy experiences erotic feelings and wishes toward his mother and wants his father out of the way; the boy is guilty about his murderous wishes toward his father and fearful of the father's retaliatory rage; the boy's castration anxiety, his fear that his father will castrate him, leads him to relinquish his erotic longings for his mother and to identify with the power and authority of his father and thereby acquire a conscience or superego. This schematically accurate but limited version of the child's earliest experience of the sexual triangle, with its focus on guilt and castration anxiety, underplays the full emotional resonance of the primal scene. The familiar narrower version has the advantage of putting the spotlight on the child's desire and the child's anxiety and guilt. We can easily appreciate why a small and powerless boy would like to think that his big and powerful father takes him for a serious rival, even if it means he must suffer now and then a terrible anxiety and guilt. In the primal scene, however, it is the parents' mutual desires that are dominant while the child, as an outsider, must endure his exclusion passively and helplessly.

Every child constructs a set of fantasies about those mysterious scenes from which he is excluded. These fantasies, which reflect at first the child's infantile versions of sexuality and then increasingly what he encounters of his culture's versions of adult sexuality, constitute the primal scene. In that scene the child, or the adult who is feeling like a child, is the humiliated and enraged outsider. The parents are the insiders who know the secrets of desire and withhold them from the child.

Since a child's narcissism depends on not entirely recognizing the anatomical differences between the sexes anyway, he or she capriciously identifies with both parents in the primal scene. The little boy "knows" by eighteen months or so that he is a male. But even at four years when he has begun to appreciate the sexual and procreative implications of the genital differences, the fact of being male does not prevent him from wishing to have the father do to him what he imagines the father is doing to the mother. This all makes complete sense to a little boy since he looks up to his father and is still very much identified with his powerful and adored mother. The boy child, since he so much values his exciting penis, suffers intensely the narcissistic mortification of recognizing that his genitals are too insignificant and puny to satisfy his mother's desires. Moreover, his mother is also a rival for the love of his father. And this father, whom he also worships and adores, does not think him worthy of the terrible punishments and forcings that he bestows on the mother. A little boy cannot for long sustain these mortifications. If he can convince himself that there are no real differences between the sexes or between the child and parent generations, his narcissism will be salvaged and he will not feel so intensely his rage at being excluded from the primal scene.

Our first question concerned the motives that would impel a little boy to invent a substitute penis for his mother. It is this humiliating knowledge of his own anatomical insufficiency that the boy sees in his mother's absent genitals. It is not *her* castration but the terrible knowledge of *his* genital limitations that compels the boy to endow his mother with a new substitute penis. Another compelling motive is his wish to be a mommy just like his adorable mommy so that the father will do to him all the terrible and exciting things he does to the mother. To be sure, however, the boy must be a mommy with a penis.

At this stage in his tireless but not always satisfying investigations of the facts of life, usually around age four or five, the boy must bring to bear on his observations and fantasies a mental strategy more advanced than simple denial. Freud identified this special unconscious mental strategy as disavowal. The newly avowed facts of life—that the sexual intercourse between his mother and father, the primal scene, entails somehow the anatomical differences between his mother and father—must be disavowed as quickly as possible. With the advantage of this more advanced but still primitive mental strategy, disavowal, the little boy does away with all his frightening and humiliating observations. His solution is to endow his mother with a substitute penis, for with that magical gesture all parties in the primal scene have essentially the same genital equipment. The mother's absent genital—that otherwise mortifying reminder of the mother's erotic desire for the father and the father's desire for her—has been successfully disavowed. Now that Mother has her substitute penis there is no difference between himself and Mother or between Mother and Father or between Father and himself. All differences have been abolished.

It is this fictitious, artificial, substitute genital, which the average child reluctantly gives up believing in during the gradual course of arriving at manhood, that serves as a model for the adult sexual fetish.

The fact that the adult fetish is modeled not on any chance penis but specifically on the substitute penis invented for the mother does not entirely explain why many sexual fetishes are items of female apparel or various parts of the female body. Surely, a more plausible representation of a penis should be a straightforward phallic symbol—a pen, an umbrella, a whip, a high-heeled boot. However, the substitute must be able to represent simultaneously the two contradictory fantasies in disavowal. Avowal confirms reality: mother has no penis. Disavowal negates that reality: mother has a penis.

Freud wrote the telling line "The horror of castration sets up a memorial to itself in the creation of the substitute." In other words, the substitute penis of childhood has two missions to accomplish, two equally fantastic fantasies it must express. It must triumph over the mother's "castration." It must also retain the moment of horror when the sight of her absent genital forced the little boy to recognize that there were real and consequential differences between the sexes. It is these differences between his mother's genital and father's genital that the boy holds responsible for his exclusion from adult delights. To accomplish the disavowal of that unwelcome news, the little boy incorporates into his vision of the mother's absent genital another image of the mother, an image of the moment before she was "castrated," the last moment when the little boy could still sustain his fantasy that he was the center of his mother's universe.

In Freud's day a child might make this unwelcome discovery at any time as he watched his mother undressing or bathing, but usually the discovery came while he was naughtily peeking up at the mother's body from under her skirts. Many of the substitute penises Freud heard about from his male patients were "memorials" to those sorts of occasions. The substitute penis, on which the adult fetish is modeled, could be the mother's feet, the smell or sight of her leather shoes or boots, her pink slippers, her stockings, her garter belt, any article of clothing she was wearing, her pubic hair, some odor from her body, or some fantasy the boy had been entertaining about her just at the moment when he recognized the unwelcome news. Therefore, a sexual fetish may be a foot with special odors, or white shoes, or gray stockings, or a black garter belt, or lace panties, or a hank of hair or piece of fur or velvet, or a blue velvet bathrobe, or a handkerchief, or a toilet odor, or any sense impression that captures the moment before the moment of horror.

In the late 1960s prostitutes who were interviewed about the types of garments their more prosperous clients wanted them to wear inadvertently confirmed Freud's thesis. They reported that many men are not at all satisfied with the latest lingerie fashions. The men requested that the prostitutes wear the kind of "kinky" underwear worn by women a generation earlier, from the time when the men were little boys. "It's like they want us to dress up like their mothers," the prostitutes said. In London, prostitutes reported a sudden demand for gas masks and bathrobes, the very garments that mothers would have been wearing in the air raid shelters when the middle-aged adult fetishists were little boys of four or five.

Ingenious as it is, Freud's idea that the fetish is a memorial to a moment of horror is misleading. In fact, the precise moment that the fetish allegedly memorializes is as much a mythology as the mother's castration. As with all such vivid and impressive "moments," this recollected moment of horror represents a series of events and impressions that occurred over a period of time. The very notion of a mother's castrated genitals is an infantile fantasy, one that will acquire new meanings as the little boy passes from childhood to adolescence to manhood.

The adult fetishist is a man who has revived (who probably has never given up) the infantile fantasy of the castrated/not castrated female genital, now along with all the distortions it has acquired in the course of his growth into manhood. He revives the fantasy to verify a masculine gender identity that is uncertain and wavering. The adult fetishist can assert his masculinity only with a fantasy that there are no differences between the sexes. He is not a totally psychotic man whose version of genital anatomy is delusional. He is like a creature split in two. Part of him acknowledges that the woman does not have a penis, while the other part disavows that unwelcome and frightening piece of knowledge.

The average child's temporary fantasy, meant to assuage his narcissistic mortification at being excluded from his parents' sexual life, becomes for the adult pervert a preoccupation that dominates his life. He has never accepted that he has been cast out of the Garden of Eden. He has taken a bite of the apple but never really digested the knowledge that the genitals of males and females are essentially and irrevocably different. His perversion erases the distinctions between the sexes and allows him to live on in the never-never land where boys and girls can still be either sex, children are just as grown up as grown-ups, and grown-ups are really merely children in disguise.

If "no male human being is spared the fright of castration at the sight of a female genital," why is it that the great majority of men tame that anxiety sufficiently to have heterosexual relationships relatively free of dread, while some men become homosexuals and avoid the female body altogether and still others must perpetually fend off castration anxiety by using a fetish to enable erection and sexual performance? Freud admitted he had no answer to that question.

A general answer is customarily found within the complementary and interacting factors that contribute to the determination of any man's sexual identity. These factors are the degree of innate bisexual-ity, a biological factor that will influence gender identity only insofar as it evokes responses in the environment; early constitutional factors such as the boy's physical appearance and temperament; and the fantasies, conscious and unconscious, that these characteristics and tendencies elicit in the parents and the traumas the boy suffered before he had to recognize the differences between the sexes and generations. However, even if we had access to all that information, which we never do, there would be no way to predict with any degree of certainty which boy will become a homosexual, which a fetishist, transvestite, pedophile, and so on, or which a run-of-the-mill perverse heterosexual, or which a little bit of each.

We can appreciate how a boy who has been threatened with having his penis removed or damaged when he is discovered fondling it or masturbating will be particularly predisposed to regarding the female genitals as an emblem of the horrible castration that might befall him. But even the little boy who never hears such a threat will project his infantile theories of castration onto the female genital. As I have been insisting, the fantasy of the castrated female genitals derives its power not so much from the actual sight and innately horrifying vision of the "absent" female genitals, as Freud's paper is traditionally interpreted, but rather from the humiliating news it imparts to the child. How that news is greeted by the child is greatly overdetermined by other things going on in his mind at the time. It is determined partly on the basis of his infantile theories of intercourse, pregnancy, and birth, partly on his innocent wishes to be a woman like his mother, but largely on the basis of his past and current relationships with his mother and father.

Furthermore, none of these fantasies and wishes and parent-child relationships is generated in a social vacuum. Any social gender stereotype that perpetuates these infantile theories will make it more difficult for the boy to come to terms with the humiliating news that he is only a child who cannot satisfy his mother's every desire.

Though the outlines of the story about our average little boy's genital fantasies are fairly universal, each specific story and its eventual outcomes is infinitely variable. Much will depend on the numerous ordinary and fortuitously fortunate and unfortunate events that may come into play during the entire course of the child's development from birth onward. Is he an only child? Is he the youngest sibling or the eldest? How many other children compete for the attentions of his parents? Is he the only male in a family of many female siblings? Does he grow up in a household with an extended family of grandparents, uncles, aunts, and cousins? Is he raised by nannies and tutors or by his own mother and father? Has he witnessed childbirth or sexual intercourse? Did those scenes confirm his sadistic fantasies? Does his parents' "being married" present to him images of tender sexual love or images of abuse and frightening sadism? Were there miscarriages, abortions, deaths of younger or older siblings? Did one of his parents die or disappear during his childhood? Does his father respect his mother's intelligence or does he treat her like a household slave? Does his father have a mistress? Does his mother have a lover? Do his parents get divorced? Is he an adopted child? Is the boy raised by a stepmother or stepfather? Is his mother frightened of sexual intercourse? Does his mother denigrate his father? Does his mother convey the impression that she has sexual desires that are fulfilled by his father? Does the boy grow up in an environment of poverty? Is his father unemployed? Does his mother have interests outside the family, a job, a career, a calling? Does his mother support the family?

And then there are those factors that are regularly found in the childhood histories of male perverts. Is his father an absentee father? Is his father terrified of his own feminine wishes? Is the little boy growing up in a subculture or social environment that sustains itself through the denigration of women? Are the images of sexual intercourse in his society confirming of his childhood fantasies of sadism and castration? Has his mother turned to him for the fulfillment of her unfulfilled social ambitions and sexual desires? Has his infancy been characterized by prolonged physical illnesses, traumatic separations, physical and sexual abuse, or other threats to his physical and mental integrity? And, most important, have these devastating abuses and deprivations aroused in him a hatred and primitive hostile aggression that he feels he cannot control or regulate? Will his life be dominated by an unconscious vengeful hatred toward his abusers and deprivers that he later feels compelled to express toward the female or her substitutes—children, animals, corpses.

Recent studies of perversion have compellingly demonstrated how very early abuses and deprivations predispose the intensity and content of the four- or five-year-old boy's castration anxiety. These earlier traumas play a much larger role than Freud recognized in determining which little boy is destined for a perverse sexuality and which little boy will grow up with a capacity for integrating tender, erotic, and aggressive feelings in his relationships with women, which little boy will become an adult male capable of making love and not hate. Before the time when the knowledge of the parents' sexual and procreative life became a fact of life inducing the painful affects of anxiety, mortification, and rage associated with the primal scene, the boy who is predisposed to perversion has suffered extensively from other traumas, among them painful physical injuries and illnesses, physical abuse, sexual abuse, mental torment, deprivations of mothering or fathering, the loss of one or both parents through death or desertion, the expectation, even as an infant, that he must be a good parent to parents who have themselves suffered extensively from childhood traumas. Not only do these infantile traumas predispose the adolescent or adult to enlist the perverse strategy as a solution to sexual and gender conflicts, but they shape the content of his primal scene fantasies.

In fact, the more extensive and severe the earlier traumas, the less able the person is to enlist the perverse strategy, which itself depends on a capacity for fantasy and symbolization. Some children are so overwhelmed by the traumas they suffer that their immature minds can work only at shutting out the pain and the events themselves: "What is happening is too terrible. It is not happening." It is then that in adolescence or adulthood the boy or man fantasizes a primal scene of lust murder and barely controlled body mutilation or suffers severe depression and utter madness. When the traumas were at least somewhat manageable through fantasy and symbolization, the perverse primal scene that the boy creates allows him a re-creation and simultaneous rectification of those traumas.

The more familiar primal scene scenario entails two adults and an ambiguous outsider who represents the once excluded child. But in a perversion, where there is always a confusion between hurting and loving, between abandonment and reunion, overlaying the three-person primal scene is another scene with only two characters—a helpless child and a "caring" parent. Here, a once abused or abandoned child may take the role of either hurting parent or child being hurt, but this time the hurting is done with the care and control of a ritualized perverse scenario. The hope is that "this time it won't hurt so much." In the two-person scenario, a child is reunited with a lost parent, re-creating in a controlled way an abandonment that he once suffered helplessly and passively. The hope is that "this time she will come back."

In Chapter 5 "Perverse Scenarios," we will see how these unconscious scripts, when they can be brought into consciousness, always contain bits and pieces of the traumatic infantile history that preceded the so-called moment of horror. But what happened *after* that "moment" in the child's life will have reorganized those bits and pieces of the *before* life into a new pattern. The later three-person primal scene fantasy functions as a new pattern that transforms the earlier infantile traumas, carrying them forward with new interpretations relating to the anatomical differences between the sexes and to the differences between the generations.

A perverse scenario is also an attempt to regulate and control aggression. In an infant or young child, every painful experience arouses some degree of aggression, for aggression is a helpless child's way of responding to physical or emotional hurt. For example, when a little child is frightened, unless someone is there to hold him, to console him, to relieve his hurt or reassure him that relief is coming, the child experiences in addition to his fear an awesome rage, which then exacerbates the fear. Whenever, therefore, he suffers an anxiety that he cannot surmount or master in an ordinary way, either through fantasy or through the comforting presence of a parent or other caregiver, he has a corresponding reaction of crude aggression that always exacerbates the anxiety.

The anxieties of childhood that are surmounted and mastered in average development are unmasterable by a person predisposed for perversion or worse mental suffering. These anxieties of childhood, which in severely traumatized children become insurmountable, are *annihilation anxiety*—in earliest weeks of infancy, a fear of not being held, of falling forever and fragmenting into nothingness; *abandonment anxiety*—around eight months or so, a fear of being deprived of an emotional dialogue with the person on whom the child depends for survival; *separation anxiety*—in the middle of the second year of life, a fear of emotional separation from that person; and *castration anxiety*—finally, at around four or five, a fear of being deprived of genital and procreative power. In a perversion, the earliest anxieties of annihilation, abandonment, and separation combine forces to create a terror of loss of bodily integrity and self-identity. In these circumstances, the more focused castration anxiety engendered by the primal scene mortification is transformed into a diffuse fear of a destruction of the entire body and the self—*mutilation anxiety*. The point is that the aggression with which the severely traumatized child reacts to his physical and emotional sufferings is also traumatizing. The child cannot, of course, direct this aggression toward the actual parents on whom his survival depends or even consciously recognize that they are the agents responsible for his suffering. Unconsciously, however, the rage *is* directed toward the parents, toward their bodies and their genitals. The mutilation anxiety in a perversion is the result of an unconscious fear of retaliation for the mutilations the child has wished on the traumatizing and depriving parents. Therefore, the severely traumatized child suffers from the fear of his own violent aggression, which he is sure will one day return to mutilate his body and his genitals.

Many of Freud's colleagues and followers assumed that Freud's single-minded focus on castration anxiety meant that he was excluding or diminishing the importance of the earlier infantile anxieties. In reaction, they protested the limitations of Freud's vision by vigorously exaggerating the significance of the earlier anxieties and minimizing the importance of castration anxiety. This either-or way of thinking about human sexuality stands in the way of a full and rounded appreciation of the interweavings of earlier and later experiences in the determination of a person's sexual preferences and gender identity. The desire to avoid any knowledge of the distinctions between the sexes and the differences between child and parent generations is at the heart of every perversion. Perverse scenarios are attempts at rectification of the early infantile abuses and deprivations, but they are also dedicated to creating primal scenes in which a once betrayed and humiliated child defeats and humiliates the betraying parents. Any attempt to understand perversion that reduces a perverse scenario to *merely* issues of bodily integrity, loss, and separation will effectively cloud over the immense significance of the pervert's preoccupation with rectifying the mortifications of the primal scene and forestalling mutilation anxiety. Therefore, to my mind, theories of perversion that diminish the role of genital and generational difference can succeed only in reflecting the perverse strategy. They are in themselves fetishistic fictions.

For example, those who wish to diminish the importance of the roles of genital difference, genital sexuality, the castration complex, and the primal scene in the creation of a perversion frequently take refuge in the idea that sexual fetishes are descendants of those innocent asexual security blankets, the so-called transitional objects of infancy. There is some truth to this idea, but it is a limited and partial truth.

It is true that the capacity to imagine something that is absent and then symbolize it in a representable form appears early in human life. The young child caresses his treasured shred of odorous cloth against his cheek, thereby creating an illusion of safety and well-being when he is separated from the sweet-smelling mothering presence that usually makes him feel held together, secure, and valuable. It is not surprising, therefore, that an adolescent or adult would choose to allay his sexual anxieties through a method analogous to the one he used during infancy when the threat of separation from the mother was equivalent to an annihilation, a fragmentation of self and identity. Even though his mother is not there, a baby feels restored to her presence when he holds and smells his security blanket. The adult fetishist who requires that his sexual partner wear an object that he can smell, touch, and see is also desperate to believe that something that is *not there, not true,* really is there, is true.

Apparently—and, as I see it, this is the crucial point—the fetishist brings to his misperception of anatomical differences the themes of *absence* and *presence* that belong to early infancy. A little boy who has not been able to make emotional sense of the mysterious absences and presences of his mother will bring his anxieties about abandonment and separation to the later time when he begins to reckon with the differences between the sexes. As an adult, he will reduce a genital difference to a dichotomy—an absence of something or a presence of something.

The baby's illusion is that the mother's absent breast—and all the essential and delectable sensations that her breast evokes—has been restored by the security blanket. The fetishist's illusion is that a woman's absent genital can be restored to a phallic presence by his fetish. Nevertheless, the analogy between a baby's security blanket and a grown man's sexual fetish has its limitations. While it is true that we can trace a line of descent between the former and the latter, there are some very important distinctions between a soft, milky-smelling blanket and a black leather boot or lace garter belt or fur piece or blue velvet bathrobe.

Though both transitional object and fetish involve magic and illusion, the magic of the transitional object is flexible and can be applied to many situations. The security blanket serves as a bridge from the very immediate and familiar "me" world to the unfamiliar "not-me" world. It is pliable in its shape and versatile in its uses. One little fellow who was on the verge of consigning his treasured security blanket to oblivion still insisted on taking it with him when he went visiting. When the door opened to an unfamiliar household, he threw his blanket across the threshold, waited a few seconds, and then followed it in. A few months later, the little adventurer was eagerly looking forward to exploring new places. He left his blanket at home. His blanket had helped him realize that some strange, exciting places could also be warm and welcoming and safe.

A man who is driven by a perverse fantasy is terrified of open, ambiguous spaces that remind him of his wish to be swallowed up in the womb, and he is frightened also of soft, friendly things that invite him to cling and remind him of his shameful feminine wishes. He prizes strong, upright, sturdy structures that inspire in him feats of daring and prowess. He would have very little use for his fetish unless it was capable of alleviating the anxiety that some awful fate would befall his penis if he should insert that most prized organ into the cavernous emptiness of a vagina. Yet so desperate is he to prove his masculinity that he *must* have erections and he *must* enter the vagina as many times as possible. Alas, though, no matter how many times the lace garter belt or blue velvet bathrobe enables him to penetrate this forbidden and dangerous territory, the vagina will never become a safe haven. Sometimes he so dreads that terrible hell below the waist that he can only masturbate and make love (or is it hate?) to his fetish or a child, an animal, or a corpse.

The perverse scenario has many subtexts related to flaws in a man's body image, dislocations in his earliest human attachments, basic faults in his sense of self and identity. However, the energy that drives the male perversion is genital excitement. Whatever else he fantasizes about, a perverse male always uses the perverse enactment to preserve the idea that he is a *real* man even as he grants his unconscious wishes to be a woman or an infant who is the center of his mother's desires, which are to nurse and wipe the bottom of her adorable baby.

Another difference between a security blanket and a sexual fetish is the type of bodily excitement invested in it. There is an immense difference, for example, between the *sensual* delights of sucking and touching and smelling, which serve to enliven the entire skin surface and inner organs of the child's body, and the concentrated, focused *eroticism* of genital excitement and arousal.

Yet a further distinction is that each experience of reassurance regulates a different degree and level of aggression. A security blanket is sucked, chewed, pinched, cast aside, stepped on, crumpled up, thrown in the corner. It is often neglected, and it usually falls apart from years of tender abuse. But the blanket is invested primarily with tender, loving feelings and is rarely, if ever, destroyed in violence or hatred. The blanket is created to serve the aggression of growth, the expansion of self, the enabling of a little child's mastery of his expanding world. The sexual fetish, because it is essentially an object evoking a "moment" of horror, of confusion, anxiety, humiliation, and even immutable hatred, arrests growth and stands in the way of further explorations of reality. By transmuting this terror and hatred, which might otherwise lead to impotence, premature ejaculation, or murderous rape, into a simulation of tender abuse, a sexual fetish enables erection and penetration. A crucial element in every sadomasochistic scenario is that a fetish-like object be present to allay the man's anxiety about mutilating his own body or the body of his sexual partner. For the fetishist, every coitus is a risk and a trial of survival. The fetishist uses the fetish to tame his sadistic impulses and also to alleviate the anxieties about merger and separation and loss of identity that are evoked during the act of entering the body of another and afterward at the moment of detumescence—*le petit mort*.

So while it is impossible to understand the meaning of perversion without a full recognition of the significance of annihilation and abandonment and separation anxieties, it is equally crucial to keep in mind that no man would be compelled to fetishism or other perversions unless he was also suffering from an extreme form of castration anxiety tantamount to a mutilation anxiety.

If a severe castration anxiety is a central motive of fetishism and the male perversions, what about the female perversions? Do females also experience castration anxiety? Or is that anxiety reserved for males, who are the possessors of a more obviously vulnerable genital organ? What we have learned in recent decades about the child's relationship to the mother and about female sexuality and feminine gender identity has extended and enriched our comprehension of the conscious and unconscious sexual fantasies of males. Indeed, in the early psychoanalytic explorations of the differences between the sexes, these very same male fantasies about the female genitals and femininity were influencing the way that analysts tried to comprehend the riddles of female sexuality. After we explore a few of the fetishistic fantasies that went into the early psychoanalytic theories of female sexuality, we will return to Freud's fetishistic fetishism paper and some further ramifications of the male castration complex. These more complete understandings will advance our account of the special motivations of the male perversions and suggest a good point of departure for the female perversions. In switching from male psychology to female psychology, I want to encourage some greater mutual understanding between the sexes. The perverse strategy operates in the same overall way for males and females, but there *are* differences between the sexes that are significant, and these differences are in some measure responsible for the differences between the male and female perversions. These same differences are what might engender love *or* hatred between the sexes, appreciation and delight *or* suspicion and animosity. The problem is not with the anatomical differences between the sexes but with the social gender stereotypes that are attributed to those differences and the way in which the perverse strategy makes use of those stereotypes.

Freud initiated the enterprise of discovering the castration complex in the little girl with a premise that was bound to distort how females feel about their bodies, their desires, and what they want from life. Freud's followers assumed that since so much of a male's adult psychology was determined by his childhood castration complex, a corresponding process must play an equally significant role in the psychology of the female. That assumption, itself based on incomplete appreciations of the male castration complex, immediately presented another dilemma. How could the little girl, who is already lacking a visible genital, experience anxiety about its potential castration? It followed that female castration anxiety must be about an absent genital, a genital not there. And thereby came the "scientific" rationalization for the just-so story of female penis envy.

3

The Female Castration Complex: The Inner Genital World and Separation Anxiety

Her fate is one of "lack," "atrophy" (of her genitals), and "penis envy," since the penis is the only recognized sex organ of any worth. Therefore she tries to appropriate it for herself, by all the means at her disposal: by her somewhat servile love of the father-husband capable of giving it to her; by her desire of a penis-child, preferably male; by gaining access to those cultural values which are still "by right" reserved for males alone and therefore are always masculine, etc. Woman lives her desire only as an attempt to possess at long last the equivalent of the male sexual organ.

All of that seems rather foreign to her pleasure, however.

Luce Irigaray, New French Feminisms

The early psychoanalysts prided themselves on their appreciation of the unconscious fantasy life. However, when it came to genitals they were often more impressed with the concrete biological facts, where the differences between a penis and clitoris *are* sizable, than with the unconscious fantasies attributed to those facts. The female was portrayed as the sex without a genital. Or, as the feminist psychoanalyst Luce Irigaray summed up these matters, "Ce sexe qui n'en est pas un"—"This genital which is not one," the linguistic and psychological equivalent of the "sex which is not one." All that a female can experience as a reaction to anatomical differences between the sexes is the envy, rage, and depression that follow from being a have-not. Analysts also had the habit of taking the terms *phallic* and *castrated* literally, forgetting that these refer only to infantile fantasies about the distinctions between the sexes. A penis is an anatomical part. A phallus is a fictitious genital, a symbol of power, and it is a fact that traditionally, in most societies, those with penises have the power, a power associated with an erect penis and its sexual performance. Males, however, are not inherently phallic and females are not castrated beings—except in the eye of a beholder who is reacting to a genital difference the way a child does. By equating one anatomical part, the penis, with a phallic power and other anatomical parts, the vagina and clitoris, with a castrated vulnerability, psychoanalysts were reflecting the power structures and gender stereotypes of their social order.

The first full-scale depiction of the castration complex in females was written by one of Freud's closest disciples, Karl Abraham, and published in his 1920 paper "Manifestations of the Female Castration Complex." Believing the manifestations of the castration complex in women to be "so numerous and multiform," Abraham worried that his brief paper would not do justice to the subject. He was, however, thorough. He left to the world an all-encompassing catalogue of men's typical complaints and nagging worries about the Female.

Abraham's catalogue of disappointed and envious women, masculine and vengeful women, phobic and frigid women is probably a fair accounting of the psychological solutions available to many women in the early twentieth century. But Abraham's persistent focus on what he took to be the shortcomings of female anatomy I regard as a fetishistic literary device that serves, like a piece of fur, a leather apron, or a lace garter belt, to obscure the intricacies of female sexual desire. What men have always feared in women and Abraham would conceal-reveal in his explorations of the ever inscrutable female were the soft, the vulnerable, the passive, the receptive, the enigmatic—all those cryptic uncertainties that males find it necessary to repudiate in themselves in order to confirm their basic sense of self and masculine gender identity.

Abraham starts off his explorations of the female castration complex with a tale about a little girl who tried to work out her genital disappointments with a drama of three cigars. His portrayal of the little girl's response to her lack of a penis is as narrowly conceived as the hypothetical "moment" of castration horror that is said to epitomize the male castration complex. It leaves out all the emotions and fantasies that the girl brings to her discovery. It leaves out the ongoing conflicts and dilemmas that were influencing the girl to interpret a difference as a lack. It leaves out what her parents were like and how they felt about having a little girl and the ideals of femininity they had communicated to her. I will consider those missing aspects of Abraham's narrative. In the meantime I will embellish Abraham's stark, one-paragraph portrayal of this quite marvelous little girl with some details from everyday reality.

A two-year-old girl is deeply engrossed in acting out a little drama she has invented on the spur of the moment. Her new baby brother is napping. Her big brother is doing his schoolwork. Now she has her parents to herself. They are relaxing with their afternoon coffee and are free at last to concentrate on her and participate in her show. She begins by removing three cigars from a cabinet. The cigars are her only props. Her parents are both audience and actors. First she hands a cigar to her father. She gives the second cigar to her mother. Now father and mother have the same. Then she places the third cigar decisively in front of the lower-middle part of her body right between her thighs. Her mother puts the cigars back in the cabinet. After waiting a few minutes the little girl plays out her drama once again, in exactly the same way—and then again. The repetition of the game makes it clear that the little girl's actions are not arbitrary or accidental. She has observed that only men smoke cigars. By handing the cigar to her mother, the little girl is giving to her mother what the father has. Now the mother and father are equals. With the third cigar she announces that she is an equal and, moreover, is equal to the grown-ups too. As Abraham interprets the drama, the little girl wishes that any adult of either sex can have a penis. Although she is feeling her lack, she is comforting herself with the fantasy that when she grows up to be a mommy she will acquire her penis.

About a year or so later, the girl begins to become impatient with dramatizing her wishes and waiting patiently for them to be fulfilled. Most of the time she is cheerful, playful, and emotionally engaged with friends and family. But every once in a while she returns to her dilemma. She clumps about the house, brooding, cranky, nagging, glum. It is hard to think straight when you are confused by so many mixed and contradictory feelings—disappointment, envy, jealousy, rage, revenge, helplessness, humiliation, frustration—and love. She decides, in any event, to forgive her parents, whom she loves too much to really chew up into little pieces.

Her child mind reckons that the giving of gifts is proof that one person loves another person. The mother has shown her love by giving the child milk from the breast. The child has returned that love by giving the mother feces from the inside of her body. Why then should not a loving parent give her a penis and maybe a baby too? Of course these dreams of glory are also doomed to disappointment. The little girl's self-esteem, sense of power, and love of her own body—every facet of her precious narcissism—undergoes a severe test of endurance.

As she comes to realize that her father, whom she regards as the giver of penises, has no intention of granting her wishes, she resigns herself to waiting for a handsome prince of her own generation who will give her all the wonderful things she has wished for from her father—a baby surely, but maybe a penis too. These new hopes spur her on to become a worthy princess. She becomes a miniature version of her mother, each day learning some new way to be a mommy: adopting an even-stepped, springing walk, dressing up in hats with fluttering veils, baking tortes and stuffing chickens, rubbing tired backs and feeding hot soup to the sick. In this way Abraham's envious and disappointed little girl reconciles herself to growing up into Abraham's normal womanhood.

There is much to question in Abraham's version of normal womanhood and I will return to these questions in a later chapter. But first I will amplify and amend his account of how little girls react to the anatomical differences between the sexes. Like all just-so stories— "How the Leopard Got His Spots," "How the Camel Got His Hump" —Abraham's "How the Girl Overcomes Her Penis Envy and Gets to Be a Normal Woman" lacks every subtlety of character motivation or subplot intrigue. It is a straightforward morality tale on how bad girls who continue to want a penis grow up to be vengeful and disappointed women and how good girls who reconcile themselves to their lack get to be well-adjusted, feminine women.

Shortly after Abraham published his 1920 essay on the female castration complex, a number of female analysts hastened to call attention to the fact that females are not, in fact, the sex without a sex organ. They asserted that female children, from a very early age, not only explore their external genitals—the clitoris, labia, and vulva—but also evidence an intuitive awareness of their vagina. By 1924 Abraham was writing to Freud, expressing his doubts about his earlier version of the female child's genital awareness. "I have recently wondered whether early in infancy there may be an early vaginal awakening of the female libido," he wrote. What female analysts had observed and insisted on —an early and primary vaginal awareness—Abraham was proposing to Freud as a reevaluation of the psychoanalytic theory of the erotogenic zones and of female development. However, neither he nor Freud pursued these matters any further.

Not until forty years later, when the child analyst Judith Kestenberg presented the findings from her observational studies of infants and toddlers, were these earlier proposals about young girls' vaginal awareness given any direct confirmation. On the basis of her observations, Kestenberg claimed that around the age of two and one-half, toddlers of *both sexes,* by way of various body movements and play activities, communicate an awareness of their inner genitals. So strong was her conviction about the vital significance of the behaviors she was observing that she flew in the face of psychoanalytic convention by proposing a new erotogenic zone and naming a phase of child development the *inner-genital phase.* Lamentably, Kestenberg's theories have not yet achieved widespread acknowledgment within the psychoanalytic community.

I have been impressed with the validity and importance of her observations. Not only have I seen similar behaviors in my research nurseries, but her interpretations of those behaviors are confirmed by the fantasies that children, adolescents, and adult men and women bring to their understandings of the differences between the sexes.

It is expectable that children will focus their attention on those bodily parts and bodily experiences that assume importance to the parents. Preceding the inner-genital phase, parent and child are concerned with the *products* of the inside of the body, primarily the food that goes into the mouth and the feces that come out of the anus. In contrast to these definable and locatable body sensations that can be controlled and regulated by the sphincter muscles of mouth and anus, inner genital sensations share with other inner organ sensations a diffuseness and experience of uncontrollability. These arousals have no definable relationship to body products or sphincter muscle controls.

As the mother and father pay less attention to the child's bodily needs, they stimulate and control her bodily functions less, allowing the child to become more aware of stimulations originating from inside her body. Unlike eating and toileting, activities that seem to an infant and young toddler to be what parents care most about, nobody in the environment is concerned about where, how, or when the inner genital arousals are experienced. These body sensations receive no reciprocating gestures from the parents and thus remain for the child to figure out their significance. The genital arousals that emanate from inside the body are a source of mystery to children of both sexes. As Kestenberg said:

> Inner-genital sensations, though resonant with outer-genital excitations, are neither localized nor productive. Vaginal sensations of a nagging quality are elicited by excitation of external genitals in ordinary, bodily care, by pressures from neighboring organs. . . . The boy too has to contend with some unclear inner-genital feelings that may result from resonant excitation from proximal parts of the penis (bulb, crura), movements of testicles, contractions of spermatic cords and pressures on the prostate and seminal vesicles.

Kestenberg observed that young children of both sexes try to solve the problems posed by the diffuse uncontrollability of these inner sensations by externalizing them, projecting them onto outside objects that *are* visible and tangible and *can* be controlled and manipulated. Since children cannot express in words their fantastic theories about the insides of their bodies, they can only hint at these vague, intuitive fantasies through the verbalizations and behaviors that accompany their playful investigations of animate and inanimate objects—baby dolls, trucks, balls, blocks, mechanical toys, erector sets, sand, and water. During the inner-genital phase, children can be observed using "everything that moves, appears to move or can be made to move, seems alive and can be used to represent inside stirrings." Of course, these playful investigations, enjoyable as they are, do not solve the problem of locating or comprehending the emotional significance of the cryptic inner genital sensations.

From birth onward the female child, no more or less than the male, is trying to make sense of her bodily experiences. In the early months of life, what a body part can do and how it feels as it acts or is acted on is one aspect of self experience. The parents' responses to the child's body—whether they caress the surface of her body with looks of mirroring admiration, or rebuff what the body does or does not do with frowns of disappointment, or behave as though certain bodily experiences do not exist—lend emotional resonance to these body-self experiences. The other major aspect of the self experience concerns the fantasies and wishes that are being developed in connection with the child's vigorous but confusing emotional attachments to her mother and father. By the middle of the second year of life the little girl is capable of interpreting and representing her body and her world through symbolic means, but still largely only through fantasy and fantasy play rather than with symbolic reasoning or word logic. This limitation leads to some fascinating and very often distressing *mis*interpretations. What were at first mere sensualities in the child and mirrorings of love or disappointment or disinterest in the parent are now brought into the realm of fantasy where the experiences of self and other become invested with various more complicated emotional meanings, some of them tenderly sensual, others hostile and destructive, most of them various combinations of affectionate and hostile emotions.

In the late fifties and sixties, when Kestenberg was studying the body movements and play activities of infants and toddlers and discovering that two-and-one-half-year-olds have an intuitive, sensorimotor awareness of their inner genital world, Margaret Mahler was conducting observational studies of infants and toddlers as they were experiencing the emotionally charged process of separation-individuation. Like Kestenberg, Mahler was a pioneer in two respects: she believed in the vital significance of the preverbal parent-child interaction *and* in the value of direct child observation for enhancing the psychoanalytic understanding of the human condition.

By demonstrating the primary significance of the first caregiver, customarily the mother, and clarifying the differing reactions to separation of female and male children, Mahler also illuminated the process that initiates the emotional life of a human being. When this process goes wrong, a human being will have difficulty taming his or her own aggression, ascertaining the boundaries of self and other and of time and space, loving others, nurturing the young, mourning the dead.

The human dialogue begins in the infant's first partnership outside the womb. The infant experiences the bliss of oneness with mother, the unconditional love that is the basic dialogue of human existence. The next series of mother-infant dialogues, from around four months to three years, concern the way the infant separates from the state of oneness with the mother. As the infant separates, she learns the conditions of actual love and acquires the sense that she is herself and nobody else. All later human dialogues have in them, among other strivings and longings, a striving to reconcile her longings to restore the lost harmonies of oneness with her equally intense need for separateness and individual selfhood. How a child learns to reconcile the contradictions between these two fundamental human strivings is the story of separation-individuation, the second, or psychological, birth.

Though Mahler and Kestenberg worked independently, they later shared their findings and each of them recognized the psychological interactions between the different developmental phenomena they had discovered. The critical phase of separation-individuation, rapprochement, which begins at fifteen to eighteen months, is resolved at around two and one-half to three years. Thus the resolution of the separation-individuation process and the occurence of the inner-genital phase discovered by Kestenberg correspond chronologically and interact psychologically.

The rapprochement phase is the crisis of the separation-individuation process. In the complicated resolution of that emotional crisis the child is acquiring the rudimentary forms of the varied emotions, thoughts, fantasies, and values that are involved when one human being relates to another down-to-earth, actual person. Oneness is the essence of human love. The vitality of love comes from the partnership of two in-the-flesh human beings who comprehend and respect each other's separateness. At the beginning of the rapprochement phase, as much as the child wants to return to the bliss of oneness, she also refuses to relinquish her sense of separateness, her urgent desire to claim her body and mind as her own. By three years, an average child comes to a first tentative resolution of these conflicting strivings and thereby also achieves her initial sense of separateness and identity. A three-year-old's sense of well-being and self-worth comes from her having built up inside her enough good-mother and good-self experience to permit her to function as a separate person even when she might have envious-hateful thoughts about her parents. She doesn't begin to suppose that she has to be a perfect all-good child or a clinging, helpless nonentity to protect herself and her parents from her awful wickedness.

Certainly, how she interprets the value of her genital organs and how she learns to regulate the envy, jealousy, mortification, and rage aroused by the primal scene will be strongly influenced by how well she resolves the dilemmas of separation-individuation. On the other hand, the primal scene, with its emphasis on the sexual and procreative functions of the genitals, will serve as a new organizational framework for all earlier infantile experiences of the body and self. Like a crochet needle, the mind reaches back into the infantile past and draws the earlier experiences and fantasies about body, self, and other into a new mental and emotional organization. Then and only then, in the context of the primal scene fantasies evoked by the child's exclusion from the parents' sexual life, will these earlier merely cognitive and sensual experiences acquire *erotic* meanings.

Abraham's inventive little girl constructed her drama of the three cigars in the context of her working out the crises of separation-individuation and trying to comprehend the source and meaning of excitations emanating from her inner genital world. From Abraham's narrowly conceived account we cannot tell anything at all about how these experiences might be influencing her clever enactment. However, in any discussion of how a little girl responds to her observations of the external genital differences, it is imperative to appreciate whether she is simply making note of bodily differences or investing the differences with fantasies having to do with self and other or making interpretations with erotic connotation.

As with the little boy and his "moment" of discovering the absent female genital, a little girl's discovery of the penis is not a one-time occurrence. It is a discovery that will acquire new meanings in the context of each new understanding of how her body functions, each new experience of the emerging self, each recognition of the different social roles assigned to females and males. The female castration complex, like the male castration complex, is a not a once and for all response arising at a particular moment in childhood—the so-called oedipal phase. It is based on fantasies and misinterpretations that begin in infancy and go on to acquire new meanings and new interpretations throughout life.

Therefore, as I did earlier in my discussion of the male castration complex, I will follow a hypothetical "normal" little girl as she brings to her discoveries of the anatomical differences between the sexes all manner of provisional theories, fantasies, and misinterpretations. The female child proceeds with her investigations in a pattern fundamentally similar to that of the male child, but she endows her discoveries with fantasies that pertain mainly to female development. Nevertheless, by understanding more about female development we will be learning something very important about the underground fantasy life of males. To put it briefly for the moment: there is a female castration complex, but it is *not* about a genital not-there. The female castration complex concerns, among other things, anxieties that pertain to the damage or mutilation of *female* genitals. The major interest of the little girl is in her own genitals, which, except for the clitoris, labia, and vulva, are completely *internal*.

The earliest concerns of any child are with bodily integrity and completeness and all those experiences of her body that contribute to a coherent sense of self and self-esteem. Thus when a one- or two-year-old first notices a penis, her observations challenge her about being different from others. As the little boy wonders with some consternation, "Where is hers?" she is puzzled and worried too: "Where is mine? Where is it?" She might wonder why she doesn't have one and come to the conclusion that she is being punished for being bad. She might wish to be like another person who has one, or she might want to have one of her own, or want to grab one away from someone who has one, or want to stand up to urinate as though she has one like her brother does. None of these penis *wishes* have in them the experience of *envy* that they will acquire later in childhood when the anatomical differences between females and males, adults and children, acquire larger social meanings. Nor does the average two-year-old interpret her anatomical difference as a difference related to gender and genital functioning. She does not understand that the penis is a genital.

By the middle of the second year of life, if not earlier, children arrive at a core gender identity having to do with a recognition that they are either female or male. Feminine and masculine gender identity, on the other hand, have to do with the erotic meanings that are attributed to the sexual and procreative functions of genital organs and sex role differences, which are social differences based on social gender ideals. The penis the two-year-old girl observes and notes and sometimes wishes to have is not yet invested with sexual and procreative attributes with gender ideals concerning the respective social roles of females and males. Only after the girl has resolved the considerable emotional conflicts entailed in becoming a self separate from the mother will she have acquired the cognitive capacity to attribute erotic gender meanings to a bodily difference or the emotional capacity for envy of those with *phallic* power. Until then, the penis is something that her father and brother and other males have and she doesn't and that perhaps her mother does or doesn't have. Nevertheless, even such a young child will already be noticing some reactions of emotional and social significance that will influence her later interpretations.

Her parents are responding to her discoveries of her own genital parts with an emotional tone that is very different from the mirroring admiration that greeted her discoveries of her hands, feet, eyes, mouth, nose, and belly button. They know, even if she doesn't, that genitals play a role in gender differentiation and they are responding to their little girl's genitals and her genital puzzlements with the value judgments that they have come to attribute to having or not having a penis. As the little girl is gradually bringing her observations, wonderments, puzzlements, and wishes about penises into a connection with some of the other mysteries of life, how her parents have been communicating their feelings and fantasies about the differences between females and males will play a considerable part in her fantasies and wishes. Moreover, no matter how reasonable or unconventional her parents are, the child, because of the infantile nature of her own mind, will interpret her parents' spoken and unspoken communications about gender in one or another stereotype. She idealizes the mother and father as all-good, omnipotent beings and she exaggerates in black or white, good or bad, either-or images the standards and values they communicate.

Gradually, as various gender erotic, social role fantasies get attached to the little girl's observations of bodily differences, her psychological development will proceed more and more along lines that can justifiably be called feminine rather than simply biologically female. But none of these early "feminine" fantasies are permanent or irrevocable, except as they remain as unconscious fantasies that can be evoked by later experiences. The dichotomous stereotypical gender ideals of infancy, especially when these resemble so much the primitive gender stereotypes enforced by the social order, are always ready to spring to life in later childhood, adolescence, or adulthood in response to personal and social crises.

Like the boy, the girl arrives at some preliminary notions that a baby grows inside the mother's tummy and then emerges from the anus or bursts forth from the navel. She is not yet thinking of the penis or the vagina as connected with procreative functions. How the baby gets into the mother's tummy is a mystery and so it will remain for many years to come. However, other things about having babies do impress themselves on the little girl in a spontaneous, barely conscious connection with some immediate bodily sensations. Some mothers and fathers still talk about storks and fairies, and others tell "the truth" about where babies come from. But a little girl gets the idea all on her own that she can grow a baby inside her tummy as a mommy does, and her happy fantasy is confirmed by the special kinds of arousals she senses coming from inside her pelvis and abdomen. Just as a little boy her age will intuit that his penis is for poking and intruding, the girl intuits that the vague, excited flutterings that come from inside her body have to do with where babies sleep while waiting to get out.

If her parents don't prohibit it, the little girl will derive a special kind of excitement from fondling her clitoris, rubbing and squeezing her labia and vulva and the rim of her vagina, and sometimes venturing a little rub inside her vagina. She intuits that all of these excitations are very different from the way her toes, eyes, nose, arms, and chest feel. But she is not at all sure about the differences between one kind of excitement and another. Nor is she able to distinguish between the inner place where feces come from and the inner place where babies come from. As she becomes adept at anal sphincter control she begins to have a clue that some inner bodily fullness can be controlled and some cannot. She learns that the pressure of feces can be relieved by her own efforts at retention and discharge. However, the pleasurable excitations of her external organs, as they spread via the expanding and contracting middle organ of the vagina to the innermost uterus, give rise to worrisome interior sensations that cannot be controlled. Unlike the products of digestion, these experiences are of elusive substances that cannot be held on to or expelled with a sphincter. The little girl bends her head down all the way to her knees hoping to get a glimpse of what is going on in there. The unfathomable depth and uncontrollable excitability of her inner genital world convey a sense of the uncanny, of awesome cavernous spaces. These exciting and sometimes frightening inexplicabilities also stimulate her curiosity, enrich her fantasy life, and expand her emotional range.

As part of the female child's tireless investigative spirit, she begins to look with new eyes at her brother's penis, which he does not hesitate to exhibit to all interested parties. The body part she once merely noted with a worried "Where is mine?" and occasionally wished to have for herself is now invested with some disquieting misinterpretations.

Now at two and a half or so, she compares herself with her brother, her father, and her little male friends and finds herself wanting. Now she associates other deficiencies in her self-experience with not having a body part. Now she is also frightened because she fantasizes her condition as a retribution for some wicked fantasies and thoughts she has been entertaining. The various meanings she is now attributing to her observations of the anatomical sex differences derive in part from her own physical sensations of inner genital vulnerability and also from some events of central psychological import that are occurring simultaneously at this time. The girl has begun to reckon with the conflicting emotions that have arisen in connection with her efforts to separate from her mother and become an independent self. The fantasies evoked by this inevitable emotional upheaval will profoundly influence her interpretations of not having a penis.

The girl and her mother are going through some rough times. It has become imperative to the little girl that she assert her separateness from her mother. She is refusing to do anything her mother wants her to do. She and everyone else around her are unsettled by her piercing protests: "No," "Mine," "Won't." There are moments, sometimes days on end, when these monosyllabic assertions are more important to her than the power of naming things or pronouncing bigger words, such as *refrigerator* and *pelican*. Some days the fury the girl feels toward her mother is like a dark cloud that envelops them both. As the cloud settles around them, the little girl loses track of whom the fury is coming from. The little girl perceives the mother as a frightful creature who feeds on the bodies of little girls. A terrible fright enlarges her fury into a terrible rage that carries the girl back to the time when all she could do about rage was bite and tear.

If you have ever seen a two-and-a-half-year-old in the throes of a temper tantrum, you might appreciate that, to her infantile mind, the frustration and fury she is venting are tantamount to devouring up and demolishing the world and everybody in it. This wild, destructive rage, for the moment unameliorated by any tenderness or concern, is indiscriminate and lacking in focus. The fury is not yet clearly associated with feelings of envy or with the erotic meanings it will acquire in the context of the triangular primal scene. During rapprochement, the crisis of separation-individuation, a biting, consuming rage is one side of the intense emotional ambivalence that characterizes the little girl's feelings toward her mother.

On the other side are other, very different, but in their own way equally frightening emotions. These emotional experiences are derivatives of fantasies and wishes associated with the warm, sweet, swallowing sensations of the mouth and belly. The little girl would wish to give up all this awesome fury and lonely independence and cuddle in her mother's lap, even deeper than her lap, back into her belly maybe, to join all the other babies. Or better yet, she would wish to be swallowed up into a smooth, empty belly where there are no disturbing facts of life like penises and potential rivals to deal with. The girl sometimes longs to be inside that warm, sweet belly and be born all over again—this time as a good little girl with the power to bring happiness and pleasure to her beloved and protecting mother. But these wishes have in them another terror. What if her wishes did come true? What if her mother did swallow her up and never let her out again? All these confusing longings of being swallowed up, with their counterpoint of terror, make it very hard for the little girl to let the soft evening darkness swallow her up for a gentle sleep. After a fitful night of vague, scary dream thoughts about being inside dark caves and drowning and being flushed down the toilet, the next day she wakes up in a grumpy mood, determined to shout as many *No's*, *Mine's*, and *Won't*s as possible. Not only that: when she sits on the toilet she refuses to give a feces baby to the mean mother who never gave her a penis. The girl's resentment about being deprived of a penis gets all mixed up with her conflicts about separating from her mother. Every once in a while her anger and resentment about not-having join in with her assertive *No's* and *Mine's* to transform a lively, alert, and curious little girl into an immensely confused and confusing, cranky, impossible to please, inconsolable, hard to like monster.

From the little girl's point of view, a fantasy of acquiring a penis may now provide a temporary relief from the intense love-hate relationship with her mother. To have a penis would be a concrete assurance that she is different from her mother and would alleviate the anxiety of her wishes to remerge with her. To have a penis would be to have a larger external clitoris with which to locate and discharge the nagging excitements and tensions coming from inside her body. Sometimes the wishful fantasy of having a penis is consoling and reassuring. At other times it makes the little girl more difficult and unreasonable than before. At these times she is sure the mother has a penis underneath her pubic hair, and if she can't get her hands on her pubic hairs when they take a bath together, she will pull and tear at her mother's blouse, her skirt, her necklace, trying to coerce the mother to give to her what she has already given to everyone else. Although she is coercive and resentfully demanding that her mother give back what she has withheld or taken away, the little girl continues to long for the safety of her mother's comforting arms. But the mother can do nothing right: she says hello or good-bye in the worst possible way, selects exactly the wrong little polo shirt, serves the wrong dessert, buys the wrong cereal, places the puzzle piece too correctly, dresses the girl too abruptly, too slowly, holds her too close, too far away.

As the girl becomes more secure in being a self separate from her mother and as her physical and emotional individuation has proceeded to the point where she has internalized her parents' caregiving capacities and simple nursery moralities, she is more confident that she no longer needs their actual presences to be fed or toileted or played with or to feel admired and loved. By three years of age, the average girl has proved that she is able to do for herself whatever the parents previously had done to her or for her. She has emerged from her previous condition of humiliating physical and emotional dependency. During this initial phase of coming to power the girl, no less than the little boy, has a temporary experience of enormous self-confidence. She has begun to focus her attention on her clitoris, and her control over this organ of discharge is immensely reassuring to her, still mystified as she is by those nagging, inexplicable inner genital sensations.

The little girl, who at this moment in her life is feeling all-powerful and all-mighty, does not want to know about her limitations. With her immense, but altogether imaginary, phallic power, she sometimes imagines herself in a competition with the father for her mother's affections. As I emphasized in Chapter 2, girls and boys even after they "know" that they are either female or male do not entirely accept the idea that they can be only one sex. When they first begin to have erotic fantasies about what is going on in the parents' bedroom, a boy is sometimes wishing that he can be loved by the father in the way the mother is loved by him. A girl is sometimes wishing she can make love to the mother the way the father does. And these wishes are quite understandable when we appreciate how passionately children adore both their parents and how closely identified girls and boys are with their mothers during the early months and years of life. Why shouldn't a little girl want to keep her mother tied to her by becoming her lover? Why shouldn't a little boy want to be just like his mother and be loved by the father?

The little girl of three or four is quite comfortable identifying with either parent in the primal scene. Whereas before she could imagine only feces-babies, her mind is now entertaining the possibility that what the parents do together has something to do with making babies, and she may occasionally entertain the fleeting fantasy that she is just as capable of putting babies inside the mother as her father is. This *phallic* (what Kestenberg would term outer-genital) competition, in which the little girl is doomed to defeat, is connected with the child's fantasies of who is doing what to whom in the parents' bedroom and it has a decidedly erotic flavor. The dimming of the little girl's phallic ambitions toward her mother initiates the next emotionally charged drama of childhood.

Whereas some months earlier a girl or boy could confidently play at being both sexes and entertain erotic wishes toward the parent of the same sex—the boy to be penetrated by the father, the girl to penetrate the mother—in the more decisive later primal scene triangle, the mother is recognized by the child as an insurmountable rival for the father's erotic desires and the father is recognized as an insurmountable rival for the mother's erotic desires.

The primal scene now becomes a traumatic event that establishes, more certainly, the differences between the child and the adult. The caregiving, child-adoring, saintly, asexual mother is transformed into an adult sexual being. The girl gives up her doomed competition with the father and transfers to him the erotic fantasies she had attached to her mother. Here too she will be defeated. A four- or five-year-old girl can't win a sexual competition with her mother, and the father won't give to the girl what she imagines he gives to the mother. From the parents' point of view they are obeying the incest taboo and protecting the child from precocious exposure to adult sexuality. From the child's point of view her exclusion from the primal scene is the result not of her immaturity but of her physical inferiority. It is now that an envy of the parental genital power arises. And the child is in helpless fury about the loss of her grandeur and omnipotence. Now as the little girl takes in more fully that she is excluded from the sexual excitements of the parents, the *sensualities* of infancy will acquire a wide range of *erotic* meanings. Sensuality is a bodily experience. Eroticism is a bodily experience associated with fantasies that assign the life-giving functions of sexuality and procreation to the genital organs.

All along the girl has been noticing the secondary sex characteristics of adults—pubic hair, breasts, scrotal sacs—with a certain degree of awe and wonderment. Now she understands these observations as discrepancies between the child's genital anatomy and the parents'. Since a child has little appreciation of the parents' limitations or any confidence that she can overcome her own limitations in the future, she experiences these anatomical discrepancies as a narcissistic mortification. The idealized power and attributes of the parents are counterparts to the child's fantasized inferiority. She is not really inferior. She is merely smaller and less genitally adequate than her grown-up parents, who are capable of having sexual intercourse and making babies. But to her childlike mind, her exclusion from the primal scene means that she is inferior and her parents are superior. In the context of experiencing herself as genitally inferior, the girl idealizes and envies the parents' genitals. She interprets her exclusion from what goes on between the mother and father as a contest between those who have the supplies and those who are deprived. Her envy and rage at being excluded is divided: the envy goes to the parent of the same sex, the one who is getting the babies and the penis; the rage is directed to the parent of the opposite sex, the one who is giving out these "trophies" and withholding them from her. Sometimes the envy and rage are divided the other way. The girl has not entirely given up wishing to advance her loving relationship with her mother, and in that scenario she envies the father for possessing the impressive genital that makes him attractive to her mother and rages toward the mother for desiring what the father has to give and treating her like a nobody who has nothing to offer.

The mother's genitals announce her sexual and procreative powers and the unwelcome news of the difference between the child and adult generations. The father's genitals are idealized as the symbols of the power and authority that exclude the child. Moreover, his penis is imagined as a removable part that can be transferred from one person to another as a trophy of desire and admiration. The penis the little girl envies in her father is a fictitious genital—a phallus. It is this imaginary and idealized penis that she wishes to steal from him so that her mother will once again love her and only her. It is this idealized penis that she imagines the mother getting from the father and that she wishes to steal from the mother.

In her mortification at being the outsider in this adult exchange of genital-erotic pleasure and erotic power, the little girl focuses the indiscriminate, unfocused rage that she had experienced toward the mother during separation-individuation on the hated and envied genitals of the mother and father. She also fears her parents for their moral superiority. She is the bad, wicked one who deserves punishment and they are the judges who will mete out the suitable punishments. In a child's mind, justice is harsh and punitive. The *lex talionis*—eye for an eye, tooth for a tooth—reigns supreme. Thus, the retaliation for her genitally directed envy and rage will be a castration of her own genitals.

The average child goes on to more socialized, tamer interpretations of hostility and aggression, and with them more humane interpretations of justice and morality. But at this time of life, around four or five, what is awakened in both male and female children is a fear of retaliation from the parents whom they envy and hate, idealize and venerate. The boy's mind has grown up sufficiently for him to realize that his penis cannot fall off by itself like a fecal stick. The boy has replaced this misinterpretation with the fantasy that the vengeful, powerful father can damage, mutilate, or remove the boy's genital as punishment for the boy's wishes to take his place with the mother.

When we look at the sexual triangle from the point of view of the girl child, the mother-daughter relationship and the mother's retaliation assume prominence. Thus, the female castration complex can be distinguished from the male complex in several respects—and as we will see in later chapters these are crucial to the female erotic life and to the form and content of the female perversions. As I have indicated, except for the clitoris, labia, and vaginal introitus, which do not participate except indirectly in procreation, a female's sexual and procreative organs are internal. Therefore, for a female, the imagined castration entails a destruction of internal organs. The boy feels vulnerable to castration because his penis is observable, whereas the girl feels that the entire inside of her body is vulnerable. Moreover, for the girl the retaliating castrator is the mother, the same mother toward whom the girl experienced such profound ambivalence during the crisis of separation-individuation.

As I emphasized in the last chapter, this traditional version of the oedipal drama, with its traditional emphasis on retaliation and castration, while it is accurate, underplays the full range and extent of a child's painful and troubling emotions. As with the boy, the little girl's fears of retaliation are *in part* a defensive fantasy meant to screen out other terrible feelings. The primal scene in which the girl is the excluded third party is the critical trauma of her childhood. The castrations and body mutilations that all children imagine as a retribution for their sinful erotic wishes and their envy and rage are *in part* screens for the mortifications of the primal scene. Some children are threatened with terrifying physical punishments that are the equivalent of a castration. Some children do have violent and abusive parents and have every reason to evoke fantasies of castration. But even children with empathic and nonpunitive parents experience some castration anxiety. A child will often exaggerate his or her own guilt and the parents' punitive rage to assuage the narcissistic humiliation of being a creature with small and inadequate genitals. Anxiety and guilt are painful affects that, even in adulthood, screen out shame and shelter the person from feeling small, inadequate, and helpless. For a small, inadequate, and helpless child particularly, it is sometimes better to suffer anxiety and guilt than to suffer shame and a lessening of self-esteem. Scary as these childhood retaliation fantasies are, it is more satisfying, more enhancing of narcissism, to imagine oneself as a rival worth defeating than as a puny, genitally defective outsider.

The recognition of the genital capacities and prerogatives of the mother and father brings with it a collapse of the little girl's narcissistic grandeur. The mother has first claims on the father, and to compound the insult the mother has the sexual and procreative wherewithal that makes her exciting and desirable to the father. The girl has little to compensate her for this crumbling of her childhood omnipotence except the promise that when she grows up she will have big breasts and be able to produce babies just like her mother. There is not much to console her for her present narcissistic humiliation. And the higher valuation of the male sex in her social order, which by now she is painfully aware of, is not conducive to a healing of these narcissistic injuries. Furthermore, the dubious promise of babies to come is also a promise of some mysterious and possibly painful physical changes that will take place within her body. With all her anxieties about a castration of her inner genital organs, these promises about her eventual inner genital capacities for sexuality and procreation are not entirely reassuring.

The early psychoanalysts were correct in their assumption of a female castration complex, but they were mistaken in interpreting that complex as a female child's responses to not having a penis. Females do have genitals of their own: a vagina *and* a clitoris and a vast inner genital world. Even as young children, females are aware of these genital organs and, moreover, they do have considerable emotional investment in them. Just as the little boy's "moment" of horror is a simplified version of his castration complex, so the little girl's penis envy is a simplified and incomplete version of her castration complex. The female castration complex is much richer and far more intricate than simply a response to not having a penis, which turns out to be merely one of a host of things to worry about in light of all that could befall the little girl's own sexual and procreative organs. The female castration complex concerns a guilt for having entertained prohibited wishes toward both parents, the narcissistic mortification of being unable to fulfill these wishes, and the humiliation of being excluded from the adult prerogatives. And if she has suffered earlier from unmanageable traumas and abuses, this later anxiety and narcissistic wound will coalesce into a composite of anxieties—annihilation, abandonment, separation, and castration—the mutilation that the almighty gods might perform on her body in retaliation for *all* the provisional wishes and fantasies of childhood.

In a defensive response to her castration complex, a little girl will repress and deny the initial awareness she had of her mysterious, uncontrollable, and *vulnerable* inner genital world, focusing all her genital arousals and fantasies on her more controllable and visibly intact clitoris, labia, and vulva. She may sometimes imagine the introitus as the entrance to "a secret garden" where babies and lost penises are hiding. But until the physical changes of puberty, especially menstruation, reawaken the inner genital world, she defensively represses it.

The standard psychoanalytic explanation that girls turn to the father out of an anger with the mother and a disappointment in their mutual genital inferiority is unnecessary and, except in instances of developmental trauma where this sort of emotional transfer may fit the case, it explains very little. In average circumstances, a little girl's erotic strivings toward her father evolve out of her identifications with her mother. Her manifold positive identifications with her mother's childbearing capacities and sexuality contribute to a strengthening of her wishes to be a wife and mommy in relation to her father. The difficulties the girl has during separation-individuation concern her pronounced ambivalence toward her mother. In a response to her castration complex the girl defensively represses her inner genital world to quell the anxiety-arousing fantasies of maternal retaliation. One motive of her turn toward her father is to gain his reassurance and protection from the retaliatory mother. But despite these more or less typical outcomes of her childhood dilemmas, the little girl's capacity for intimacy, albeit a conflicted and sometimes frightening intimacy, with the same-sex parent leaves her better off in many respects than the average little boy.

In noting the intensity of mother-daughter ambivalence, some contemporary psychologists have recommended that the female child's development would be less troubled if the mother played a less dominant role in childrearing. Certainly it would be better for all concerned, mothers and fathers, female and male children alike, if fathers were more attuned to what it feels like to be a child and more comfortable in assuming a caregiving role and if mothers did not derive their sole satisfactions and self-esteem from caregiving. If fathers were more involved in child care and domestic life and mothers more involved with the larger social order, there would be less of this primitive collaboration between infantile gender ideals and the gender stereotypes of the social order. However, if mothers were to surrender completely their caregiving functions to fathers, this would obviate the positive outcomes of what is, after all, only a temporary and developmentally appropriate ambivalence. When the girl is given the opportunity to engage her mother in the resolution of these emotional struggles, she enlarges the range and flexibility of her emotional responses. It is tender battle, and if fought with compassionate understanding on the mother's part it brings mother and daughter into a closer harmony, advances and cements their relationship, and contributes to the girl's internalization of reliable and protective mothering—a superego presence that is loving and beloved. With that protecting mother inside and an actual caring mother still reliably present outside for comfort and support, the girl is less guilty and anxious about her erotic wishes and fantasies with regard to her father and more able to achieve a *gradual* independence from both parents.

We know that a little boy suffers from having to so quickly separate from his mother and from not having enough opportunity to work out his ambivalence toward her. We tend to forget that an essential aspect of the boy's castration complex concerns a fear of retaliation from the mother whose "absent" genital provokes in him an envy of her sexual and procreative powers and a helpless fury for reminding him of his genital insufficiencies. In the next chapter I will show how male bonding generally and the boy's identification with his father's imaginary phallic powers in particular are very often based on their mutual envy and fear of the female. All too often, therefore, a little boy's independence and assertiveness are founded on an infantile ideal of what a real man should be. He has very little opportunity to integrate the feminine and masculine aspects of his identity.

The way things now stand in our society, typically the little girl is given permission to linger longer in the land of make-believe. And this permission is something a little boy, burdened so quickly with having to be a real man, envies in little girls. A girl need not be as decisive as a little boy in relinquishing her childhood fantasies and wishes. Her conscience evolves more gradually and therefore she has a greater chance to moderate its infantile, either-or, harsh, and absolute qualities. The potential tenderness, compassion, and enduring affection in the mother-daughter relationship that contribute so much to the mercy and compassion of a little girl's conscience should not be taken away from females. These tendernesses should, however, be given more to males, from their mothers and their fathers. It is vital to expose the deceptions of the "law of the phallus." The solution, however, is not to do away with motherhood but to heal the soul-crippling ruptures between the caregiving and lawgiving functions in the child, in the family, and in the social order.

I am aware that I am talking here only about an ideal of a generally positively toned mother-daughter relationship, a relationship that in the best of circumstances allows for a more gradual and gentle accommodation to the ways of the world. However, as we know, much can go awry in the early mother-daughter relationship. Any situation that might signify a loss of protective mothering—a mother's self-hatred, depression, neglect, emotional unavailability, her physical abuse of the girl, or physical illnesses and other insults to the integrity of the little girl's bodily and emotional self—will exacerbate and prolong the expectable ambivalence a girl experiences toward her mother and thereby will exacerbate her castration anxiety.

If the mother had been wishing for a boy to fulfill her own thwarted ambitions and instead got a disappointing little girl who lacked the penis and phallic powers the mother was longing for; if the girl was led to feel that she was a mean, ugly, stupid little girl every time she expressed her willfulness and disappointment; if the girl was forced, with enemas or nasty-tasting medicines, to give up her feces-babies when she wanted to have control over the giving or withholding of those gifts; if the contents of her body were treated as objects that could be pulled out and taken from her against her will; if her mother was unable to tolerate the confusing feelings stirred up in her by her daughter's conflicts and responded with a reciprocal rage; if, when the little girl was longing for fondling and cuddling and skin contact, her mother was unavailable and preoccupied; if the little girl's curiosity about her genitals was interpreted to her as an evil and dirty sexuality; if she was punished and threatened for masturbating; if her hands were tied down or her fingers covered with gloves so that she could not touch her "dirty" genitals; if her father cared only for cute little baby girls and had no interest whatsoever in assertive, independent older little girls; if her father reacted to the girl's seductive appeals by sexually abusing her; if her father was the sort of tyrannical patriarch who demanded that little girls be clean and virginal and yet looked the other way when his sons or stepsons or brothers intruded their hands and penises into his daughter's insides; if the little girl grew up in a world that every day confirmed that females are the unwanted, degraded sex—then the primitive rage that accompanied her earlier discoveries of the genital differences will now attach itself to the envies and mortifications, jealousies and depressions, of the primal scene drama, a drama that is centered on a young child's first, still provisional attempts to reconcile and integrate her feminine and masculine identifications. As I have been saying, the typical little girl has had the benefit of a long period of identification with the parent of the same sex. Whatever problems and dilemmas that kind of close identification might lead to, typically the female child feels more assured than the male child of her gender identity.

Nevertheless, despite any initial advantages for a girl in her identifications with her mother, chances are that the little girl's infantile fantasies about the differences between the sexes will be validated by the gender stereotypes that are imposed on her in the course of growing into womanhood. The female child's castration complex is perpetuated by the incompatibilities of female desires and female ambitions with the social roles traditionally assigned to women. In other words, throughout their lives females have experiences of their bodies and minds that they are told are allowed only to males. Males, of course, have analogous experiences of their bodies and minds that they must repudiate in the interests of fitting themselves into some stereotype of masculinity.

4

Other Memorials: The Male Castration Complex

Males also have inner genitals. How a boy experiences his inner genital world profoundly influences his fantasies about the differences between the sexes, his responses to the separation-individuation process, his later responses to the humiliations of the primal scene, and his attitude in adolescence and manhood toward the female and femininity.

The assertive freedom and triumphant exhilaration with which the boy darts away from the mother during separation-individuation serve to mute his conflicts over wishing to remain an extension of his powerful mother. The boy's characterization of himself as belonging to a category with his father and not belonging to a category with his mother is also immensely reassuring. More often than he wants to recognize or admit, the two-year-old boy is still yearning for the loving support of his mother and he still longs to be carried about and enfolded in his mother's sweet-smelling arms. As much as he wants to assert his independence and autonomy, he also wishes to be so close to her as to feel he is inside her. As part of this longing to merge with the mother, he entertains the fantasy of having a body like hers, a body with an inner cavity that can make and hold a baby. So powerful sometimes are these yearnings to be mother/be a mother/be inside mother that they momentarily override his fear of losing his penis. But not for long. This is the other powerful motive that compels the little boy to invent a substitute penis for his mother. He counters the anxiety of his feminine wishes by imagining that his mother has a penis too. Now there is no difference between them. He can be a mother, make a baby, be back inside mother, and still have a penis.

What boys seem to need most from the mother and continue to need and, as lovers and husbands, go on to get from other women is an all-present but unobtrusive Mother who is willing to stand by in the wings ready to rescue the mighty acrobat as he recklessly hurls his body through the open spaces. The best mother of all is an acrobat's assistant, one with sweet-smelling, strong, protective arms. After his long day of surmounting the heights and running about, she will lure him back to her arms with sugar cookies, rub his back, and tuck him into bed with stories and lullabies. However, she must never enfold him, cling to him, possess his body or reengulf him into her dangerous insides. The boy who grows up exaggerating his phallic prowess to protect himself from his quite ordinary wishes to be a passive, enfolded baby or a submissive mommy who can be penetrated by the father or a powerful mommy who can produce babies out of her belly is always on the run, escaping from the entrapments of the female. In the female he dreads not only the loss of his separate self but the loss of his masculine identity *and his penis.* When he is clearly and definitively outside the Female, he and his penis are safe.

As we have seen, one important reason why adult men so fear what they interpret as the "castrated-castrating" vagina is that a woman's enigmatic genitals remind a man of his wishes to be loved as a woman is, to have organs that make babies like a woman has—and of his incapacity to achieve those wishes. A little boy envies his mother's baby-making capacities and sometimes wishes to "castrate" her. It is this set of frightening fantasies and wishes that also encourages a little boy to endow his beloved and saintly mother with a substitute penis. With this gift he is making reparations for his sadistic wishes toward her.

A boy also needs to believe in a *phallic* mother so that he can continue to entertain his feminine wishes without having to give up his own penis. For a boy, the wish is to be a mommy, but a mommy with a penis. For an adult, this fundamental fetishistic fantasy, which comes most vividly to life in transvestism, is to be a woman, but a woman with a penis. In the male's repudiation and defensive disavowal of the female genitals we detect another set of fears. The male finds his own inner genital world cryptic and elusive. The fantasies and wishes associated with that world are a huge threat to his masculine identity.

That mysterious world is analogous to the mysterious inner genital world of the female. In the embryo, the testes evolve from the same tissue as the ovaries, and the scrotal sac from the tissues that in females become the labia majora. Like the upper vagina and uterus and ovaries, the male inner genitals, the testicles and innermost genitals—the prostate, the seminal vesicles, and spermatic cords—are immature and nonfunctional until puberty. Nevertheless, even in their immature form these organs are physically connected, via a vast neural network, to the penis, and they make their presence known in ways that are subtly different from the workings of the other inner body structures.

The boy's inner arousals can be immensely disquieting, not only because they give rise to uncontrollable sensations of fullness and loss but also because they resonate with wishes of being a mommy and having babies just like a mommy does. Kestenberg's studies of male toddlers are not conclusive about the intensity of inner genital arousals or about the extent to which the young boy's fantasy life is influenced by them. However, there is no question at all about the boy child's awareness of his scrotal sac and testicles or the fact that these observable, semi-external inner genital body organs are sometimes associated with femininity and other shameful, frightening fantasies that must be banished from consciousness. So frightening are these fantasies that many grown men continue to think and act as though the penis is their only genital organ.

As early as 1923 Freud had noted:

> It is remarkable, by the way, what a small degree of interest the other part of the male genitals, the little sac with its contents, arouses in the child. From all one hears in analysis one could not guess that the male genitals consist of anything more than the penis.

The very denial and neglect of such a visually prominent body part as the scrotal sac should have alerted psychoanalysts to wonder about the defensive undervaluation of them. However, until the late 1950s, when the psychoanalyst Anita Bell undertook a thorough investigation of that peculiar oversight, it was more or less implicitly accepted that the penis was the only genital organ that figured significantly in the mental life and imagination of the male. Bell reviewed numerous pediatric films of male children and interviewed nearly two dozen of her colleagues who had treated male children and adolescents. What she learned confirmed her hunch that the scrotal sac and testicles play a prominent role in male psychology, "in the areas of pleasure-unpleasure, the development of the castration complex, body image and feminine identifications." Moreover, her investigations dovetailed with and indirectly corroborated what Kestenberg, during those same years, was discovering about the inner-genital phase of little boys.

Usually by the first or second year of life, and normally at least by the age of six the testicles have descended into the scrotal sac. But since 90 percent of all male children also have an inguinal ring that remains open until approximately age six, the testicles can temporarily retract into the inguinal canal and seemingly disappear. Retraction of the testicles due to feelings of apprehension or cold persists until age six and in some males throughout adolescence and adulthood. The testicles visible to little boys as "ballees" or "nuts" that lie within their sacs can and do completely disappear from time to time. Moreover, they cannot be made to reappear voluntarily. Testes, even when they no longer retract, still continue to move involuntarily in response to fear, cold, anger, and defecation.

From the physical-anatomical point of view alone, it should be evident that the scrotal sac–testicle unit would play a significant role in the male castration complex. The testicles can disappear. The scrotal sacs are anatomically close to the anus and sometimes look to a child like his feces, which do break off and disappear. Males of all ages sometimes imagine their scrotal sacs as analogous to female breasts. In their physical appearance and in their function of producing seeds, the scrotal sacs and testicles are susceptible to various connotations of femininity. Whereas the penis is associated primarily with erotic pleasure, little boys and adult males report sensations of tender comforting from fondling their scrotal sacs. One adult happily reported to his therapist, "It's as though the scrotum is the feminine part of me. When I hold the soft balls it feels pleasant and comfortable. They hang like a soft, mushy bottom." Little boys whose parents give recognition to the testicles and scrotum will speak their minds. "Look, I have a nut," said a two-year-old to his father. After he discovered his second nut, his father explained that this is where the seeds were for making babies. "Oh good, then I can make babies too," the boy said. Though their immature minds will still misinterpret the scrotal sacs as cavitylike structures that can actually hold babies, some boys are able at least to recognize them as a significant part of their genital anatomy. A bright boy of five enlightened his three-year-old sister about the facts of life by proudly showing off his scrotal sacs. "See, there are two, one to make boys and one to make girls."

In various legends of creation a female is born out of parts of a male. Eve is taken from one of Adam's two sides. Some revered and influential goddesses are born from the skull-cavities of the gods. Zeus swallows his pregnant wife, Maia, and several months later Pallas-Athene springs forth from his head—in some legends fully armed with a shield bearing an image of the threatening, gaping-mouthed, stony-eyed, serpent-haired Medusa. A few goddesses have come into the world directly from the testes. Aphrodite, for example, was born of Uranus, whose youngest son, Cronus, had cut off his father's testicles and thrown them into the sea where they were nourished by sea substances to provide the essence of Aphrodite's being. In many cultures a manly pride is associated with the procreative capacities of the testicles. The testicles thus are given masculine connotations, but only in special circumstances and under special conditions.

For example, in cultures where the man's capacity to impregnate a woman is considered the confirmation of manhood, the testes may be more revered than the penis. "Balling" is the slightly more tender term used for "fucking," with the provision, however, that the balls be appreciated as a part of a penetrating organ. When the testicles can be visually identified as part of the penis, as when dancers and actors and bullfighters pad them together within a codpiece or when the penis and testicles appear as a firmly held together unit within the confines of a pair of tight-fitting jeans, then the testicles are considered "ballsy" and "macho." Bell noted that "when the Pope is enthroned, as part of the ceremony he is told: '*Habit testicularis et bene pendentis*' [Have testicles and let them hang well]." Nevertheless, the tendency to associate the scrotal sac, the testicles, and the unseen innermost genital organs with the inscrutable female and her inscrutable inner cavities is more typical.

It is no wonder that males would overvalue the penis, which never disappears, is nonambiguously masculine, and is associated with feats of urinary exhibitionism and with the erotically pleasurable and culturally valued performance of erection. From an early age most boys are countering the inscrutabilities of their inner genital world by focusing their emotions and fantasy life on their more certain and reliably present external genital, the penis. Moreover, because the passions and anxieties and humiliations associated with the primal scene enforce their fear of their feminine tendencies, all these vague "inner space" sensations are now associated with a disgraceful and forbidden femininity.

The tendency for little boys to exaggerate the powers of the penis and silence their inner genital world is often exacerbated by the ordinary developmental dilemmas that every boy must solve on the way to arriving at a masculine gender identity. The male child's separation-individuation is problematic in that he has to declare his independence from a mother with whom he has been physically attached but from whom he soon recognizes he is physically different. To affirm his identity as a male he feels that he has to effect his separation from her quickly and decisively. Generally, therefore, a boy is given less opportunity than a girl to work out his ambivalences toward his mother. The intensity and quality of the little boy's castration anxiety are reflections of the extent to which he regards as forbidden and shameful his wishes to be a mommy and to linger awhile in babyhood. In a family where those expectable and fleeting wishes are regarded with suspicion, even horror, a little boy will feel especially compelled to flee from his mother rather than to gradually separate.

Indeed, when he is four or five, he will turn away from his mother in a nearly complete renunciation of femininity and embrace and identify with his father's attitudes, values, power, and authority to protect his penis from the imagined wrath of the father and to preserve his self-esteem from his disgraceful feminine wishes. These identifications with the power of the father serve the wholesome purpose of bringing son and father together in a bond that is reassuring to both generations. Unfortunately for himself and for the women he will go on to love, the boy's comforting sense of belonging to a strong and powerful, phallic, masculine world is all too often sustained by an emotional participation in the father's fear and distrust of females. In this over-idealization of the father and his powers the boy engages in an implicit hatred and denigration of the mother.

Traditionally, male bonding perpetuates the gender stereotypes of childhood. Nevertheless, the boy who has been able to effect a positive alliance with his father has a far greater chance of eventually arriving at a more wholesome view of the female sex than a boy who has been deprived of *benevolent* fathering. The absence of a paternal presence in a boy's life can wreak as much havoc on his masculine gender identity as can a tyrannical and abusing father or a father who is terrified of his own feminine longings. It stands to reason that without an emotionally available father, a boy would have difficulty working through and mastering the knowledge that he is not the center of his mother's life. If his mother should collaborate with the boy's wish to maintain the fantasy that she is merely an extension of him or with his wish to believe that the father counts for nothing at all in her affections and desires, that all the mother needs to make her happy is her adorable, brilliant son, she encourages her son to avoid any knowledge of the primal scene. He remains tied to his mother's apron strings forever. He lingers in a Garden of Eden where there are no real or significant differences between the adult and child generations. Later in childhood or adolescence, when the significance of the fact of his father's presence in his mother's life becomes inevitably known to him, he must suddenly acknowledge that he was born of a desire between his mother and father and is enraged about the deception that has been perpetrated. The boy suffers the humiliating betrayal of his mother more intensely than he would have earlier, and the hostile aggression he experiences toward both parents for their deception is the equivalent of a force that would destroy the world.

Thus, in either circumstances—when a boy flees from his attachment to mother to the safety of his identification with his powerful phallic father or when he remains forever attached to his mother in an infantile way—he will grow up with a fragile sense of self and an uncertain masculine gender identity.

The key to a male's acceptance of the full range of his sexuality is his identification with the benevolent aspects of his father, the benevolent and loving internal father that is merciful, caregiving, nurturing, supportive, and accepting of immaturity, vulnerability, softness, and sensitivity. A boy who has internalized a wrathful, tyrannical father as the model for his own authority and power or a boy whose father was not present to help him separate from an engulfing and possessive mother will be more terrified of his feminine strivings and thus more in dread of the vagina and all things female. He will perceive the female as a dangerous catcher of men whose entire being is bent on swooping up, swallowing, possessing, and engulfing—stealing his manhood and appropriating his genitals. At the climactic moment of erotic surrender, as the active, pulsating, masculine erection subsides in conjunction with the more passive (feminine) ejaculatory spasms and inner pelvic expansions and contractions, the male yearns to give himself up to his passive, receptive, feminine-baby wishes. However, a man who dreads these sensations and wishes will quickly extricate himself rather than linger in the entrapping, engulfing vagina. To such a man, erection is life; ejaculation and detumescence, death.

As Kestenberg once remarked, nothing is better calculated to evoke violence in a male adolescent than remarks that liken him to a woman or a baby or remind him of the inner spaces of his origins. When the boy becomes more assured of his masculinity he is less prone to react with macho violence to such taunts and less inclined to refer to females and feminine longings as "pussy," "wimpy," "baby," or "retard." Nevertheless women, by their very existence, remind men of their frightening feminine desires.

Kestenberg said that "extreme denial of the 'inside' makes the man unable to identify with women; it motivates him to seek out phallic women and makes him more prone to perversions *based on externalization*" (emphasis mine). Kestenberg implies that males early in life acquire a tendency to externalize onto the environment whatever is inscrutable and ambiguous in themselves. Female children during the inner-genital phase are also externalizing their inner genital sensations. But even then, at that early time of life, little girls typically are also giving expression to their cryptic inner sensations by eliciting from their caregivers cuddling, fondling, and other immediate tactile experiences—and little boys typically are not. For by two years, children of both sexes have already learned a few fundamentals about the social stereotypes of feminine and masculine. And these rudimentary adult gender ideals correspond to nothing more or less than the way two-year-old girls and boys solve the dilemmas evoked by their mysterious inner genital world. The boys are out in the world, exploring; the girls, even the more adventurous ones, are at home making elaborate nests for their dolls and cuddling with their stuffed animals. How convenient it is to attribute these early differences to genes and hormones and then to rationalize them as nature's prescriptions for normal masculinity and femininity: males are born to adventure and females are born to decorate the nest and cuddle little babies.

Whatever other arbitrary misfortunes females may suffer as a result of the social gender stereotyping that cripples them emotionally and narrows their life choices, females as a rule are less prone to gender confusion than males. They are also less prone to externalize their gender conflicts and are more likely to express them through tactile experiences and the medium of the body. The female suffers from being denigrated and demeaned and in that connection may wish to have the advantages of males. But it is more the male who suffers from his forbidden and shameful wishes to be female. Furthermore, it is these wishes that may incite in him a murderous envy and thus a fear of retaliation from females.

The perennial interest of male philosophers in deciphering what females are about and what it is they want can be interpreted as diversions of attention from men's curiosity about their own mysterious insides. Males tend to externalize the emotions and the feminine parts of themselves they cannot comprehend or tolerate. Men who cannot accept the finality of the differences between the sexes and the generations will externalize their gender conflicts through enactments entailing actual characters, actual stage settings, and special props—fetishes.

Sometimes all a man needs is his fetish, for embedded in the fetish is the drama, the characters, the stage set, and an entire history of the lost desires and confused imaginings of childhood.

Near the conclusion of "Fetishism," Freud relates a little tale. He describes one man's fetish—an athletic supporter—a sort of elaborately designed jock strap that in Freud's day was also worn as a swimming garment. This piece of clothing covered up the genitals entirely and concealed the distinction between the sexes. Freud's apparently simple story of the athletic supporter fetish has in it a few befuddlements. Only one thing seems certain: the garment in question is masculine. But who is wearing the athletic supporter? Is it the man or his sexual partner? Usually the woman wears the fetish object—the black leather boots, the blue velvet bathrobe, the pink satin slippers—or the male simply fondles, smells, or gazes at his fetish. Freud's remarks are not much help. He explains that the transformation of this quite ordinary athletic supporter into a revered fetish had been inspired by a fig leaf on a statue the man had seen in childhood. This explanatory comment only deepens the ambiguity. Though we might presume that the fig leaf in question was meant as a cover for the genitalia of a male statue, occasionally fig leaves are used to mask the reality of the female genitals. At this point in Freud's tale, the sex of the wearer of the athletic supporter *and* the sex of the statue are both in doubt. Not arrested by Freud's lack of clarity about these matters, readers usually go along with the assumption that a woman was wearing the fetish object, that female genitalia were being covered and disguised, and that the fig leaf was on a female statue. However, a closer reading reveals that it was the man himself who wore the fetish garment and that it was *his* genitals that were being disguised. The statue remains clouded in gender ambiguity.

As the next chapter will demonstrate, most fetish objects are created to allow the man to express his forbidden and shameful feminine wishes and yet remain male. But Freud's athletic supporter story reveals some other motives in the male perversions. In the fetishistic fantasies I have been stressing thus far, the man unconsciously imagines he is a woman, but a woman with a penis. However, what are the fantasies of a man who is wearing an athletic supporter as his fetish, a man who is impersonating a male? By masking his genitals with a garment that allows for genital ambiguity but is still reassuringly male, the protagonist of Freud's little story identifies with a powerful, idealized phallic male. The general drift of Freud's athletic supporter tale is toward the fetishist's identifications with his father, his father's position in the world, his father's position in sexual intercourse, and his father's attitudes toward the female sex.

By using a male garment as his fetish, a man is participating in the power of his father's genitality. Freud's fetishist has created a different sort of "memorial" than the fetishist who employs a female garment to attain erection and penetration. It is not a memorial to his mother's absent genital and that last moment before he was banished from the Garden of Eden. It is a memorial to his father and his father's powerful and *superior* genital. Many fetishists hold to the infantile belief that it was the father's violence that created the mother's mutilated genital. In his unconscious fantasy the fetishist who wears a male garment is participating in a violent and sadistic sexuality. These men are extremely envious of and competitive with women and therefore fear the woman's retaliation for their mutilation wishes toward her. To them the mutilated vagina is also a retaliating mutilating vagina, the infamous *vagina dentata*. By participating in the father's imagined sadism, these males are reassured of their maleness, but this identification only serves to increase their mutilation anxiety. For they live in perpetual dread of some terrible retaliation from women.

Whether he uses a female garment or a male garment, the fetishist is expressing a hostility toward the female, whom he would like to castrate and whom he also reveres and idealizes. The fetish protects the woman from the full extent of his hostility. The fetish protects him from his feminine wishes *and* from carrying out his hostile, castrating wishes *and* from the retaliation of the female.

Every fetishist reveres his fetish and also treats it with contempt and hostility. This very sort of divided attitude, Freud pointed out, is exemplified by the *coupeur de nattes,* the pervert who can have an erection and perform sexually only by cutting off a lock of a woman's hair or snipping out a scrap of silk from one of her dresses or, in a more civilized manner, merely stealing her handkerchief. Yet another variant of this divided attitude, suggests Freud, is the Chinese custom of mutilating the female foot and then revering it like a sacred fetish.

The Chinese custom brings Freud to the last sentence of his fetishism paper. That concluding sentence alone, a kind of literary *coupeur* or Chinese mutilation, is quite enough to reveal Freud's ambivalent attitudes toward the female and her mysterious genitals. "In conclusion," announces Freud, "we may say that the normal prototype of fetishes is a man's penis, just as the normal prototype of inferior organs is a woman's real small penis, the clitoris." Is Freud alluding to a child's fantasy, an adult fetishist's fantasy, or his own unrepressible infantile version of the female genitalia? Freud's intimacy with the workings of the unconscious mind did not exempt him from a typical, albeit unconscious, attitude toward the female genitals, an attitude that expresses simultaneously an idealizing reverence and a hostility based on all the unwelcome news that is called to mind by the female genitals.

The memorial to the horror of castration that Freud describes is a memorial to another typical fantasy about the anatomical differences between male and female genitals. In braid cutting most obviously, but somewhere in all perversions, the fantasy of restoration is as powerful as the fantasy of mutilation. A cut-off or absent penis, when symbolized by cut-off hair, can grow back. A sexual fetish always represents the two equally fantastic fantasies of phallic and castrated. The *coupeur de nattes* literally cuts off a woman's hair but symbolically castrates her. Hair, unlike the genitals that might otherwise be removed, can grow back. The *coupeur*'s fetish, the woman's cut-off hair, enables erection and sexual performance, and in the act of penetration the *coupeur* can imagine his penis as fixing her castration. On the basis of these fantastic reasonings, the physical anatomical penis is imagined as a phallus—*an idealized fictitious penis with magical powers*—a kind of fetish rather than an actual anatomical part of an alive person with ordinary strengths and ordinary weaknesses.

In many perverse patients, male and female, I have encountered the fantasy that an erect penis is a magical fetish endowed with the power to "fix" a woman's castration. The man wants to make reparations to the woman for his hostile wishes. He is always fixing women with his phallus (or other imaginary phallic powers) and is always regretting the burden. The woman is looking to find the perfect phallic man whose erect penis can fix her and then lamenting after a while that once again another of these magical penises has not done the job. The magical phallus, of course, is as much a mythological genital organ as is the castrated vagina.

Every perversion is an attempt to unsettle the boundaries between the real and the not-real. Even those, like Freud, who devote their lives to unveiling the not-real, are standing with one foot in that magical territory. Freud's concluding sentence on the inferiority of the female's *real* small *penis* is tantamount to a disavowal of the significance of the actual female genitals. The female genitals are the emblem of that unwelcome news that Mother and Father share a desire that excludes the child. The mother does have some genitals of significance and the father does desire her for having them. The little boy, of course, is competitive with his mother for his father's love. He envies her the power she has over his beloved and mighty father and would just as soon imagine her genitals as insignificant and puny, castrated if necessary.

In the first part of his paper, Freud explains why and how a part of the female body or a female garment could become the model for the typical sexual fetish. At the conclusion of his paper, Freud selects a male garment as the memorial to the horror of castration. Where at first he says that the adult fetish is modeled on the substitute penis the little boy invents for his mother, he concludes by saying that the prototype for the fetish is the superior male genital. These are not contradictory assertions, for the fetish is in fact modeled on the fictitious, artificial genitals of both parents. Nevertheless, Freud's way of contrasting the male and female genital organs and the gender ambiguities inherent in the tale of the athletic supporter suggest a missing train of thought, some conscious or unconscious connections that Freud does not reveal to the reader. Something other than a simple misogyny helped to shape the conclusion of Freud's paper on fetishism.

Immediately preceding his ruminations about the paternal identifications expressed in the athletic supporter fetish, Freud compares a son's disavowal of his father's death with a fetishist's disavowal of the female genitals. "The patient oscillated in every situation in life between two assumptions: the one, that his father was still alive and was hindering his activities; the other, opposite one, that he was entitled to regard himself as his father's successor." Very likely, these thoughts were connected with Freud's feelings about his own father's death, which he had long ago referred to as "the most important event, the most poignant loss, of a man's life." The connections between a son's reactions to his father's death and a theory about sexual fetishes should not be passed by without comment. The man who probed his own dreams and unconscious fantasies and in the process discovered *his* Oedipus complex could not have been unperturbed by such associations. For a little boy to triumph over his father for his mother's affections and desires is only a delicious, dangerous guilt-provoking, and narcissistically satisfying childhood fantasy, real enough to a child. But for an adult to continually challenge and undermine the prevailing sexual conventions with his insistence on the inevitable and intrinsic perversities of human sexuality could constitute a real, immediate danger. Freud's unwelcome news was always putting throne and altar in danger, and he was well aware that he was stirring up some panicky and hostile reactions among his medical colleagues. His father, Jakob, had been unorthodox in his religious and political beliefs and had given courage to his son's intellectual originality by always challenging his half-formed ideas.

But surely even the daring and provocative Freud was occasionally anxious about challenging the medical authorities of his day. As the intrepid explorer of the unconscious fantasy life of human beings, Freud would insist that issues of human sexuality should never be reduced to prescriptive normalities. As an ordinary man responding to the promptings of those fantastic and grotesque images of childhood that are banished from consciousness but never entirely given up, Freud would sometimes react by giving his assent to the power structures and female gender stereotypes of his age. Thus, a paper that begins with a courageous avowal of the fantastic imaginings that make up a male's infantile fantasies and wishes about the female genitals concludes with a disavowal, an affirmation of those fantastic distortions: "the normal prototype of inferior organs is a woman's real small penis, the clitoris."

Freud, of course, also had a mother, Amalie Nathansohn Freud. And more than once he had declared that no love could ever hold a candle to a mother's love for her son, which was "altogether the most perfect, the most free from ambivalence of all human relationships." Amalie was about to celebrate her ninety-second birthday when Freud had the "sudden" inspiration for "Fetishism," which he sent off to his publisher two weeks later. It was Amalie who had personally nurtured and tended the creativity of her golden Sigi, by making his intellectual ambitions the emotional center of her life and a physical center of the household, where his study was a holy space.

Freud was of two minds about the importance of a mother in a son's life, or for that matter about the son's identifications with his mother's caregiving and procreative functions. In the first half of Freud's fetishism paper the mother-son relationship assumes center stage, but by the conclusion, after recalling a son's conflicted feelings about his dead father, Freud was asserting the law of the phallus. Male bonding is immensely reassuring to males, for among other advantages it subdues an anxiety about a male's feminine identifications and an envy and fear of the power of the female.

And yet with all its mystification and off-putting ambivalence, Freud's analogy of a death to a castration, though it succeeded in obfuscating one fact of life, captured another, something else of great significance that is also disguised in a fetishistic fiction. A perverse scenario always leaves room for an enactment of a child's reaction to the death or disappearance or absence of a beloved parent. Freud had not given sufficient recognition in his theories to the child's first relationship—the primordial relationship with the caregiving mother. That idealized, unconditional, perfect love is always lost in the discovery of the reality of the mother's sexual and procreative capacities. Behind the absent-restored penis is the shadow of a lost-resurrected breast, the uncontrollable and confusing comings and goings of the mother, which are made to seem controllable by the person who possesses the fetish. The sexual fetish, like all fetishes, is constructed to represent absences and losses of every kind—castrations, deprivations, separations, illnesses, abandonments, annihilations, deaths—as well as to represent the powers that can diagnose, protect, ameliorate, heal, remedy, fix, and ressurrect. The sexual fetish is indeed a versatile memorial.

5
Perverse Scenarios

Men sometimes feel that their penis controls them, leads them astray, causes them to beg favors at night from women whose names they prefer to forget in the morning. Whether insatiable or insecure, it demands constant proof of its potency, introducing into a man's life unwanted complications and frequent rejection. Sensitive but resilient, equally available during the day or night with a minimum of coaxing, it has performed purposefully if not always skillfully for an eternity of centuries, endlessly searching, sensing, expanding, probing, penetrating, throbbing, wilting, and wanting more. Never concealing its prurient interest, it is man's most honest organ.

Gay Talese, Thy Neighbor's Wife

Fetishism exemplifies the perverse strategy. The fetish is designed to divert attention from a whole story by focusing attention on a detail. By focusing our attention on the penis and protesting that the penis is man's most honest organ, Talese is, all unwittingly, demonstrating the perverse strategy. The fixation of a male's attention to his penis is a measure of his defensive avoidance of something else: perhaps some other, less illustrious body part, perhaps some bodily experience less easily focused and more softly diffuse than a hard, manly erection, perhaps the less than manly wish to be the submissive one who is penetrated by a penis. Very likely the manifest "prurient" interests of a penis that is "endlessly searching, sensing, expanding, probing, penetrating, throbbing, wilting, and wanting more" are there to disguise the man's unconscious desires to submit, to be vulnerable, to open his body to being passively penetrated and probed—just like a woman or a baby. But then Talese must have realized all this. Does he not wonder whether the penis is "insatiable or insecure"? Why does it *demand proof* of its potency? We assume that the more a man insists on the deception of the eternally erect penis, the more frightened he is of his passive, feminine longings. In perversions, the sexual enactments that grip the attention of the actors and the anonymous spectator (the imagined or actual audience) are there to permit a secret fulfillment of wishes and fantasies that are experienced as shameful and frightening.

The Victorian gentleman of the previous chapter, whose erection depended on his wearing an athletic supporter, had grown attached to his fetish and was not at all disturbed about the central role it played in his sexual life. He would have been puzzled, and no doubt mildly amused, had someone asked him about its symbolic structure. The symbolic meaning of a fetish can be deciphered only through an interpretive reading of the perverse scenario in which it appears. Like the owner of the athletic supporter, most men do not regard their fetish or their fetishistic perversion as anything to worry about. They will resist attempts to inquire into its meaning. After all, a man's fetish is his ally. He creates it because it protects him from becoming conscious of some wishes and fantasies that would otherwise frighten and humiliate him. The perversion holds at bay the anxieties, depression, and madness that might otherwise afflict him. How then might we decipher the code of the perverse strategy if the very value of its secrecy is in managing to keep everybody happily entranced by a comforting deception?

Many of the men who use specialty houses, massage parlors, and alleyways as the settings for enacting their perverse scenarios do so in an effort to keep their domestic life uncontaminated by their perverse wishes and desires. Moreover, by making use of commercialized settings, standardized props, and professional humiliators and dominators, they allow the personal elements of the perversion to be *im*personalized and thereby accomplish a more extensive disguise than if they were to leave these dangerous matters to chance. However, it is also true that many perverse scenarios are enacted in domestic surroundings. The sexual partner of the fetishist, the dehumanized, fetishized love object, is often a wife or girlfriend or neighbor. And if we leave out the helpless children and family pets and barn animals and corpses who are sometimes enlisted as fetish objects, the customary partner is a consenting or at least a cooperating adult. Though the domestic perverse enactments are as precisely ritualized as those performed on standardized stages with standard props and experienced hired actors, they bring out the personal themes of a perverse scenario in much finer detail and with much greater clarity.

In a perverse enactment one perversion, say exhibitionism, appears to be more dominant than all the others. However, embedded in each script are always elements from some of the other perversions, if not as crystal-clear enactments, then as whispered hints, fleeting shadows, secondary props, and background tonalities. Each man creates a personal script in which the various nuances of fetishism, transvestism, exhibitionism, voyeurism, masochism, and sadism might be muted in the first act and then perhaps highlighted in the second or third. In every script something or someone is treated as a fetish object, which is why fetishism is considered the prototype of all sexual perversions.

And always there is at least a thread of sadomasochism. The more adept we become at reading perverse scripts, the more we come to realize that every perversion is an effort to give some expression to, while yet controlling, the full strength of potentially murderous impulses to chew up, tear apart, explode, hack to pieces, burn to ashes, rip through to create one hole out of mouth, belly, anus, and vagina. By violating every boundary between one body part and another, the pervert totally eliminates the distinction between the sexes and with it all distinctions between child and adult generations. With its sadomasochistic nuances, the perversion makes apparent its paradoxical essence.

Perversion is a social transgression that regulates aggression and thereby protects the structures of the social order—most of the time.

Only when the perversion can no longer sufficiently disguise or regulate the underlying shameful, frightening, forbidden, and dangerously unpredictable impulses, fantasies, and wishes do outright madness, rampage, violence, rape, mutilation, incest, and murder result. Furthermore, the sadomasochistic motifs that are an integral part of every perverse scenario are also disguises for still deeper layers of meaning. What looks like a seeking for pleasure in pain or humiliation will turn out to be a ritualized reenactment of an infantile trauma. The underlying aim of the vast majority of sadomasochistic enactments is not pleasure in pain but a repetitive cycle of losing love and finding love, of castration and restitution, of abandonment and reunion, of death and resurrection.

To illustrate a few of these unconscious motifs and multilayered levels of meaning that are embedded in a perverse scenario, I have selected four case studies that were reported in the psychoanalytic literature between the 1920s and the 1980s. I will shortly present a narrative version of these technical case reports in a language and a chronology that make the data more accessible to nonprofessional readers. In the interest of presenting a coherent narrative, I have embellished the case material with the textures of ordinary life and omitted certain edifying details that would distract from the themes I wish to highlight. Here and there, to emphasize a point implicit in the analyst's report or to present a somewhat different perspective on the data, I have supplemented the case material with a few brief comments of my own, these in italics.

Each of the four analysts considered seriously the effects of early infantile traumas on the extent and level of the patient's castration anxiety. The analysts were also keenly aware of how a man's feminine wishes and fantasies influenced his perceptions of the female genitals.

The analysts were less clear about how the later primal scene trauma reached backward in time to bring the traumas of early infancy forward and into its sway. Since our usual orientation in time makes us aware only of a forward-moving process, it is always much easier to imagine how an event that occurs earlier in life might influence what comes later. Moreover, our usual conceptions of causality insist that what comes earlier causes what comes later and not the other way around. It takes a bit more imagination and an appreciation of the ingenuity of human memory to discern how later events might influence the way a person comes to interpret his past. Recall my analogy of the crochet pattern to describe the forward and backward movements of human recollection and fantasy. All the analysts remarked at this possibility of *retroactive* trauma even if they did not make explicit how it functioned in their patient's perversion.

In a general way, most contemporary analysts appreciate that the trauma of the primal scene puts the earlier infantile traumas into a new perspective by transposing them into a situation where they are given erotic and genital interpretation. What was once a trauma of oral deprivation, for example, becomes a trauma of genital insufficiency. The primal scene trauma consists not only of the sadomasochistic, submission-dominance fantasies the child attributes to the parents' sexual behavior, but of his exclusion from this exciting imagined scene and his having to acknowledge his own anatomical inferiority compared with his mighty parents. Most children survive this inevitable childhood mortification by advancing their moral and intellectual life. The child's wounded narcissism will be healed as he identifies with both parents' authority and power and recognizes that he must postpone to the future any fulfillment of adult sexual desire. However, the child who is predisposed to perversion in adulthood is the child who is already too traumatized to be able to endure the knowledge that his mother experiences an *active* desire for the father. In most cases of perversion we find that the parents have colluded with the child's wish to obliterate knowledge of the father's role in the mother's life by conveying the impression that the father does not count. In other cases we discover a tyrannical hypermasculine father who was terrified of his unconscious feminine wishes.

The fundamental wish in a perversion is to obliterate all knowledge of the differences between the child and adult generations. The perverse adolescent or adult will arrange his perverse scenario so that he may live forever in the never-never land where there are no real or significant differences between the sexes and no difference between infantile sexuality and adult sexuality.

To be successful a perverse script must enable several triumphs at once. First, the script must arrange to skip over the primal scene mortification, which it accomplishes in two basic ways: by erasing parent-child differences and by reducing genital sex to mother-baby gratifications. Therefore, the usual perverse scenario consists of the protagonist taking on one or both parental roles in the primal scene while someone else is the excluded child. The pervert is conscious of transgressing the sexual codes of his society, but the excluded other is some unconscious representative of society itself—usually a father or mother, the analyst, or the straight person who doesn't have the recipe for Great Sex.

Second, the perverse strategy must arrange for a rectification of the earlier traumas. In this subplot the actors are a child and a parent, with a reversal of roles so that a once abused and traumatized child now assumes the role of the abusing parent. The sexual partner, the "loved one," is treated to the humiliation of being excluded, cast away, abandoned. The sexual partner is also a child subjected to physical or mental abuse but now with the protagonist disguised as a parental caregiver and lovegiver.

Third, whenever possible the perverse strategy must arrange for a reunion between a child and the beloved almighty one who has gone away, abused, tormented, defiled, and demeaned him.

The Great Sex in a male perversion uses the penis and the vagina but reduces sex to infantile acts of peeping and exhibiting, diapering and spanking, urinating and defecating, submitting and dominating and an infinite variety of personal variations on those infantile themes, thus enabling a rectification of both levels of trauma, the early infantile trauma and the oedipal primal scene trauma.

In the following perverse scenarios, the enactments use penises and vaginas, but the Great Sex is about alcoholic humiliation, hair cutting, wearing jodhpurs, and being tied to the mother's apron strings.

Each of the four analysts was impressed by the degree of sadism toward the female sexual partner. The sadism in these cases was carefully regulated by the symbolic nature of the patient's perverse scripts. Therefore, as a contrast to these four strategically symbolic perverse scenarios, I have included the much briefer case reports of two men who were eventually imprisoned because of their inability to sufficiently regulate their sadistic aims. With these cases, which follow after the case of Mr. G, my commentaries are speculative and based primarily on my knowledge of other, similar cases entailing outright mutilation of a female body.

THE CASE OF MR. G:
"Now go to Hell! I've finished."

Several months after a marriage consisting of some tender affection and a long series of failed penetrations, Mr. G created a sexual script that gave him, if not what most men would consider complete sexual satisfaction, at least an opportunity to express his manly powers while secretly gratifying a number of disguised infantile wishes. Since his wife after a while refused to participate in his sexual script, Mr. G had to seek fulfillment with other women. Mr. G's repetitive and ritualized script was a controlled acting out of the traumas he had suffered passively as a vulnerable and helpless child. What had been a trauma for little George was transformed into a triumph by Mr. G's adult perverse scenario.

Mr. G's script required an adaptable woman. To qualify for the starring female role, a woman had to look as though she were capable of changing from one type of woman into another. As the several scenes in Mr. G's scenario unfold, we realize that his erection, ejaculation, and orgasm depended entirely on his ingenuity in arranging a situation in which a woman of refinement, elegance, and cleanliness could be degraded to the rank of prostitute. For the plot to work, the woman had to be unaware of Mr. G's intentions. He could not ask her questions about her interests. He could not instruct her about how to behave. The required behavior had to come to her quite naturally. Mr. G had to judge from appearances alone which woman would be capable of fulfilling the role of his fetishized object.

It was imperative that the woman wear moderately high-heeled shoes. Black shoes, Mr. G felt, were disgusting. Brown shoes, which had something attractive but forbidden about them, would do nicely. But white shoes were the ideal, because then the transformation from purity to soiled degradation would be clearly observable. So far Mr. G's demands might seem fairly commonplace, not too difficult for him to arrange and rather simple for the average woman to fulfill.

His next requirement was more idiosyncratic but one that at least half the refined women in post–World War I London might fulfill—a rosy complexion, especially a slight rosy flush on the nose. This sign would indicate to Mr. G the extent of his potential sexual companion's desire for alcoholic beverages. Though all the other fetishistic elements were necessary, the woman's *slightly* flushed nose was crucial to Mr. G's script. The woman must not be a puritanical abstainer. Yet she must not be one of those vulgar women who was in the habit of drinking to excess. One might presume that Mr. G's perceptions about a woman's alcohol tolerance would have had to be extremely sharp. But he found that his sensitivities to this criterion rarely failed him. Moreover, the uncertainty concerning the degree of alcohol consumption that could be tolerated by the woman endowed Mr. G's script with just the right touches of intrigue, suspense, anxiety, and excitement. Would the slightly flushed nose become swollen and red?

Having ascertained that her social class, shoes, and the flush on her nose met with his standards, Mr. G would approach a woman he had met at a museum, a library, a concert hall, or some other respectable and culturally refined place and invite her to dinner. To a casual observer there would be nothing at all unusual about Mr. G's behavior toward his dinner companion. As the dinner progressed, Mr. G would make verbal sexual advances, being careful to express himself subtly, gently, and unobtrusively so as not to offend the woman or alert her to his designs.

Sometime toward the middle of the dinner, and not before then, Mr. G would invite the woman to join him in a glass of wine. If the lady accepted, Mr. G would begin to get sexually excited. The outcome was still uncertain: the woman now must get drunk in a particular way. Nevertheless, her accepting a glass of wine was sufficient to indicate that the script could move ahead to act two—the drunk scene. If the woman did not perform the drunk scene properly, there was always tomorrow night's refined woman with white or brown shoes, a rosy complexion, and a slightly flushed nose.

Next the woman's mouth came under Mr. G's scrutiny. Mr. G would keep filling the woman's glass with wine, all the while studying the shape of her mouth with growing anxiety. He would master his anxiety about the appearance of the woman's mouth by having a glass or two of wine himself. When at last the woman began to give him evidence of her own intoxication, which Mr. G always interpreted as a sexual euphoria resembling his own, Mr. G felt more certain of the successful completion of his script. This evidence consisted of "a slackness of the mouth," a "derangement of hair or dress," an increased redness and swelling of the nose. The refined lady was beginning to look spoiled.

At this point, Mr. G needed only a few further proofs of the woman's readiness to comply with the denouement of his sexual script. It was essential that he charm the now intoxicated woman into taking a stroll in the fresh air. Mr. G was by now sexually aroused and alert to every nuance of the woman's behavior. Her staggering gait and her need to urinate were the signals he was looking for. When those signs were given, Mr. G knew that he could keep the woman walking until she was on the verge "of falling and collapsing." It was then a simple matter to coax her into a visit to Mr. G's hotel room. Then, at last, the moderately high-heeled shoes could play their part.

In his room, as Mr. G readied himself for full erection and ejaculation, he stared longingly at the woman's shoes, which, owing to the long walk and the woman's staggering gait, had been nicely dirtied and spoiled. After removing the woman's shoes and waiting some minutes for them to cool down (Mr. G could not bear to handle shoes too soon after they were removed from a woman's body, "while they were hot and smelling"), Mr. G arranged them at the foot of the bed so that he could see the toe of one and the heel of the other. With his eyes fixed on the woman's shoes, he began to masturbate. He rarely touched the woman or even spoke to her. In his mind, Mr. G ran through each exquisite detail of the erotic dinner scene and the suspenseful walk to the hotel. When he came to the part about the shoes positioned at the foot of the bed, with desperate haste he proceeded to ejaculation. At the moment after the ejaculatory triumph, Mr. G threw the woman's shoes away with anger and contemptuously dismissed her: "Now go to Hell! I've finished."

The scenes leading up to this moment of triumph were highly charged and erotically exciting, but Mr. G obtained only a modicum of sexual pleasure from his orgasm. Nevertheless, he was immensely gratified by the successful staging of his scenes of seduction. As he told his analyst, the masturbation was merely a way of "ringing down the curtain." He prolonged this experience of power and narcissistic gratification when, the morning after, he fantasized that the woman felt physically ill and moreover mortified by her evening of dissipation and humiliation. Mr. G admitted to a pleasurable sense of conscious spite. He also congratulated himself on his skillful relationships with women.

Mr. G's mother had been an alcoholic. She had died of alcohol excess when George was seven years old. Until that time her behavior with George consisted of short periods of excessive and maudlin physical closeness that alternated with long periods of hostility and neglect. The cycle of closeness-rejection began when George was an infant. After she had nursed her son as frequently as possible for nearly four months, Mrs. G's alcoholism became so severe that little George had to be transferred to a wet nurse. When George was a toddler, his mother was extremely careless about exposing her body to him. While under the influence of alcohol, she would make a point of urinating and defecating in full view of her little boy and then she would retire to her bedroom for the remainder of the day. During her prolonged periods of neglect, George consoled himself for his mother's absence by playing with her shoes. Sometimes he would put on her shoes and toddle about the house. Very often he could make himself feel better only when he put one of his mother's shoes in his mouth.

George's father, unfortunately, did very little to discourage his son's interest in the mother's shoes. Indeed, with the conscious intention of easing his son's sadness, the father contributed a few embellishments that served to heighten George's associations between women's shoes and a comforting mothering presence. The father instructed little George to *not* wear his mother's shoes but instead to play the game of "fetching Mother's slippers." To add to the suspense of this marvelous game, the father would hide the mother's slippers in a box. The activity of searching out the hidden slippers and then giving them to his mother when she reappeared for the evening meal gave little George enormous pleasure. Now that he was older, the slipper game began to offer George more complete satisfaction than merely wearing his mother's shoes. On those rare occasions when his mother was in a playful, motherly mood, she invited him to ride-a-cock-horse on her pretty, slippered foot.

When George was five years old, his father, again with the conscious intention of cheering up his little boy, encouraged him to have a little wine with his meals, even managing to override the mother's worried protests. The practice was finally stopped after George, who rightfully felt that alcohol was the strongest rival for his mother's love, several times bit the edge of the wineglass so hard that it broke off in his mouth. When at the age of five he was excluded from the parental bedroom at night, George conjured up images of his parents naughtily sipping wine together. After his mother died, George assumed her place in the father's bed. He experienced shameful pleasure and hostile resentment as he submitted to his father's affectionate caresses, which the father intended as consolation to his son for the loss of his mother.

George's involvement with shoes and alcohol were prominent during his childhood and adolescence. While his mother was still alive, she gave him a pair of her shoes to wear to keep him company on his first days at school. It was not long before George's classmates made him keenly aware that real boys did not wear ladies' shoes to school. He grew ashamed of the pretty shoes. Since he did not want to hurt his mother's feelings, he solved his dilemma by kicking and soiling the shoes until they were too spoiled to be worn. From then on, he preferred to wear boys' shoes, but only those with a slightly feminine shape. Every time a new pair was needed, he grew excited. The moment he got a new pair of shoes, he proceeded to dirty them. When he was sixteen years old, he decided to experiment with drinking alcohol, thinking of it as an introduction to the sexual excitement that goes on between grown-ups. The feeling of intoxication made him euphoric. But he reserved his special intoxications for the days when he acquired a new pair of shoes.

One day, when the still-virgin George was nineteen years old, he saw the housekeeper taking a drink of wine. The sight made him sexually excited. So he decided to play a trick on her. He mixed a potion of gin, which he disguised with the color of wine and induced the servant to drink until she fell unconscious. After carrying her to her bed, he went to his own room and masturbated for the first time. Around the same time, he discovered, much to his delight, that his new stepmother liked a drink or two at night. And, miracle of miracles, she appreciated nothing so much as receiving presents of shoes. He devoted himself to arranging situations in which he induced his stepmother to drink. Then he would borrow her newest pair of shoes, go to his room, arrange them prettily at the foot of his bed, and masturbate as quickly as he could.

George's adolescent sexual euphorias came to an end when he became worried about the effects of masturbation on his physical and mental health. He determined to get married and have a normal sexual life. However, no sooner was he married (to a very proper, alcohol-abstaining, pale-complexioned young lady) than he developed ejaculatio praecox. He was never able to penetrate his wife. After several months of repeated failed coitus, he had the idea to take his wife to dinner, insisting that she wear her white satin wedding shoes for the occasion. He then, for the first time, staged the program that eventually became his sole means of achieving erections and ejaculations. That night, he managed to penetrate his wife and to remain erect for nearly two minutes. The next morning his wife woke up feeling ill and very ashamed of herself for having had so much to drink. She lamented to her newly potent husband, "I have lost my womanhood." Thereafter, Mr. G's marital jealousy took the form of imagining his wife getting drunk with other men.

Mr. G's repeated attempts to carry out the scenario with his wife led to increasing alcoholic excess in himself and considerable alarm in his wife. Soon she no longer complied with his demands and instead made every effort to curb his alcoholism. He resisted her reformatory efforts and finally found himself beginning and ending his day with a bottle of gin or whiskey. After a time, he let himself be persuaded to seek psychological treatment for his alcoholism. His sexual perversion, which he now acted out with strange women, did not come up in treatment for quite some time.

The haste of the final scene of Mr. G's scenario was a reflection of his overall character structure. In everyday life he was impatient to get the pleasurable part of any experience over as soon as possible. Every potentially pleasurable experience was accompanied by a nearly conscious thought: "Get it over!" "Get it finished!" "Put it down!"

Mr. G ate hurriedly, gulping down his food without much pleasure. When he became intoxicated, he liked to consume vast amounts of alcohol as quickly as possible. He always masturbated hastily and with anger and resentment. He was known to make biting remarks and would grind his teeth at those who angered him. The biting sadism associated with all acts of pleasure could be fairly easily traced to his childhood rage. Even during her moments of motherly indulgence, George's mother was impatient to get to her own gratifications; little George was expected to perform all bodily functions as quickly as possible—eating, urinating, defecating. "There, I've done my job," implied the mother. "Now get out of my sight."

When Mr. G's perversion came to light, his analyst was able to begin to interpret a few of the childhood traumas that were embedded in his scenario. As Mr. G scrutinized his dinner companion for signs of her sexual excitement—a rosy nose becoming swollen and red—he was suspensefully anticipating the appearance of her hidden penis—the white shoe turned soiled and degraded shoe. The scene was interpreted as a grown-up elaboration of the "fetch mother's slipper" game of his childhood. However, Mr. G's analyst was not so completely absorbed in the "phallic woman," "castration anxiety" themes to be blind to the other subtle meanings of his patient's shoe fetishism. For example, from his patient's associations to the special arrangement of the woman's shoes the analyst was able to discern that one of the shoes (with the toe showing) represented the nipple and the other (with the heel showing) represented the penis. The pair of shoes displayed together represented the offered and withdrawn nipple and the seen and not seen penis. This analyst was able, through his sensitivities to the complexities of Mr. G's perverse script, to convincingly demonstrate the reciprocal interactions between the early traumas of abandonment and separation and the influence of castration anxiety in Mr. G's primal scene enactment. Furthermore, I doubt that analysts who are still arguing over the relative importance of pre-oedipal and oedipal issues in the creation of a perversion could render the total picture much better than Mr. G's analyst did in 1924. According to the analyst, the "nipple"—that is, the infant's satisfying or frustrating relationship with the first caregiver —becomes the organizing focus of the child's relationships with the outside world and with other human beings. The "penis," on the other hand, forms the nucleus of the male child's self-esteem, the central focus of his narcissism, self-image, and identity. By using his penis and genital performance to heighten his narcissism, the adult pervert compensates for early deprivations of mothering. "There is a tendency to compensate for withdrawl of the object fetish (nipple) by pleasurable interest in the subject fetish (genital)."

Like Mr. G's analyst, I am convinced that the male perversions generally and some female perversions as well use the fetishistic scenarios of penises and vaginas to compensate for all the deprivations and traumas of childhood. The scenario uses genital performance, but the motive is less to achieve sexual pleasure than to triumph over infantile trauma. The primal scene fantasy lends a genital interpretation to the earlier traumas, while the traumas of nurturance and caregiving become prominent in the content and form of the primal scene enactment.

The key emotional components of Mr. G's perverse scenario were the humiliation and sadistic vengeance toward a mother who had tantalized him with expectations of gratification and then had withdrawn from him: "Now go to Hell! I've finished." He sought to compensate for these deprivations with a perverse enactment that gave him, if not oral or genital gratification, at least the triumph of revenge. Mr. G created a narcissistic triumph out of traumas of abandonment and separation, by treating a woman as he was once treated as a helpless child.

The clinical case of Mr. G was one of the first to illustrate the role of early infantile trauma in the creation of a perverse scenario. Mr. G's analyst demonstrated the ways in which Mr. G's infantile sexual life and adult character structure were intimately interwoven with his desperate compulsion to repeat a ritualized version of infantile traumas relating to abandonment and separation. And although the analyst did not explicitly call attention to the primal scene structure of his patient's enactments, that structure was implicit in the humiliation of Mr. G's sexual partners, who were seduced and then sent away, thrown away, excluded from the sexual pleasures he himself enjoyed. The analyst stressed that Mr. G got his revenge on his mother "for her hypocrisy in deceiving him with the father, by unmasking her sexuality and exposing her as a prostitute." Mr. G reduced the primal scene to a staging of an erotic dinner scene (making the nipple appear) and then got his revenge by throwing away the shoe and getting rid of the woman (punishing the nipple).

Little George was never helped by his father to comprehend the meaning of his mother's death. The father in fact used his little boy to comfort himself and tried by every means possible to deny the loss both for himself and for his little boy. Mr. G never recovered from the loss of his mother so early in childhood. But now she would always be with him every time he enacted one of his triumphant alcoholic seductions. The underlying aim of Mr. G's sadomasochistic enactment was not pleasure in pain but a repetitive cycle of losing love and finding love, of castration and restitution, of abandonment and reunion, of death and resurrection.

Some scripts are less scrupulously executed than Mr. G's. They neither succeed as gracefully as his to both express and control the sadistic attack on the woman's body nor achieve such a highly complex and rich symbolization of the primal scene. Some men have been so severely traumatized in childhood that they are barely capable of premeditating a perverse scenario. They go right to madness, rampage, rape, and mutilation.

Krafft-Ebing's catalogue of lust murder, "lust potentiated as cruelty," begins with the German citizen Andreas Bichel, who killed and dissected with butcherlike precision the young girls he first ravished. "I may say that while opening the body I was so greedy that I trembled, and could have cut out a piece and eaten," Bichel recounts. In London during the years 1887–1889, numerous bodies of women were found ripped open and mutilated by an unknown man. Jack the Ripper, he was called. He first cut the throats of his victims and then ripped open their abdomens and groped about their intestines. With some of his victims, the Ripper also cut off their genitals and either hid them away or tore them to pieces and left them behind with the rest of the corpse. The infamous Vacher, also a ripper, strangled, cut the throats of his victims, ripped open their abdomens, mutilated the corpses, especially the genitals, and eventually gratified his sexual lust on the corpses. The Italian Vincenz Verzeni, who had been unable to keep track of all his victims or all the various mutilations he had inflicted on them, confessed, after he was sentenced to life imprisonment, to his greatest pleasures:

> I had an unspeakable delight in strangling women, experiencing during the act erections and real sexual pleasure. It was even a pleasure only to smell female clothing. The feeling of pleasure while strangling them was much greater than that which I experienced while masturbating. I took great delight in drinking Motta's blood. It also gave me greatest pleasure to pull the hairpins out of the hair of my victim. I took the clothing and intestines, because of the pleasure it gave me to smell and touch them.

Leger, another lust murderer, had only one victim, for he was caught immediately and imprisoned for life. His victim was a girl of twelve. First he violated her, then mutilated her genitals, tore out her heart, ate of it, drank the blood, and buried the remains.

Such occurrences of outright sexual sadism are thought to be extremely rare. However, since we have reports of only the cases of men who get caught, instances of partial or total destruction of the sexual partner's body as the means to erection and orgasm are probably more prevalent than the official statistics indicate.

THE CASE OF MR. N:
Drenching Blood, Stiffening Blood

In the late 1940s Mr. N was sent to a French psychiatric prison hospital following his murder and dismemberment of a young woman. Several years earlier he had been released from prison after serving time for murdering another girlfriend. The first judge had given Mr. N a light sentence for what he regarded as an ordinary *crime passionnel,* provoked by the young lady's sexually seductive behavior. Between the two murders of his sexual partners, Mr. N had led a peaceful and uneventful life as a minor civil servant.

Only moments after the second woman was dead, Mr. N embarked on a sexual scenario that entailed a deliberate, albeit frenzied, cutting up, evisceration, and cannibalistic demolishing of assorted parts of the young woman's body. Only when her body was nearly totally destroyed did Mr. N manage at last to achieve orgasm.

Mr. N was relieved to be back in prison and wanted to cooperate with the psychiatrist who had been assigned to his case. Try though he might, Mr. N could recollect nothing at all about his childhood or his parents. He was able, however, to trace his bloody mutilations to his experiences in World War I. He reported to the attending psychiatrist that during the 1914–1918 war he had been a stretcher bearer. He recalled that he derived a special pleasure from feeling the blood of the wounded drenching his uniform. Soon after that erotic revelation, he recognized that his pleasure was considerably heightened as the blood soaked through to his underwear and slowly stiffened against his body. Like many outright sexual sadists and also many other, more restrained perverts, Mr. N was afflicted by hypochondriasis. He was always imagining that his insides were damaged or diseased. After discovering the extraordinary erotic pleasure of wearing blood-soaked, stiffening underwear, Mr. N took to visiting slaughterhouses where he, like other hypochondriacs of his day, sought a cure for his imaginary illnesses by drinking potions of warm blood. Though Mr. N was not quite a vampire, the very thought of drinking blood was calming and immensely erotic.

Fortunately, this time Mr. N was not released for good behavior. As in his previous life outside the prison hospital, Mr. N was an exemplary prisoner-patient and remained so until his death.

The three analysts who reported the case of Mr. N called attention only to the oral aggression and infantile cannibalistic fantasies underlying his fascination with blood and dismemberment. They presumed that Mr. N's blunt sadism indicated a personality and ego structure too primitive to construct any kind of elaborate symbolic scenario. When, as is typical of cases of outright sexual sadism, there is so little mental activity intervening between the murderous impulse and its enactment, there is also good reason to assume a paucity of symbolic capacity in the sadist.

Mr. N could reveal very little about his inner emotional experience, but he told his doctors just enough to give us an inkling of a few premeditations. And wherever there is prethought, some symbolic functioning is still intact. I do not think we should be deceived by the bluntness of Mr. N's script to assume that there was no script at all beyond the manifest bloodthirsty cannibalism. Therefore, I repeat what I said in the first chapter: the typical perverse script consists of an elaboration of a fantasy in a manner and with props that will deceive the onlookers, real or imagined, about the underlying meaning of that fantasy. Some scenarios consist of a series of scenes, each with a clear-cut beginning, middle, and end. However, to repeat some earlier remarks, the entire enactment may be so primitive and direct that it consists only of a gesture—a man caressing a pink satin slipper while he masturbates, a man ejaculating in the act of dismembering a female body, a man putting on an angora sweater.

Crude as Mr. N's symbolic handiwork was, I will venture a few speculations. Picture, for a moment, Mr. N's increasing erotic excitement as the blood drenching his uniform gradually seeped through to stiffen on his underwear. Think of the transformations of the state of the blood as constituting a "plot" and the blood itself as characters and prop. Perhaps this simple little plot might represent Mr. N's own psychological transformation from a "castrated" female into a stiff and potent phallic male. Perhaps in his initial realization that he could gain erotic pleasure from the sensation of his uniform being transformed into "bloody rags," Mr. N was unconsciously expressing a crude symbolization of his shameful feminine wishes.

Furthermore, in Mr. N's preoccupations with bloody uniforms and dismembered women's bodies we might detect the source of his pathological worries about his bodily illnesses. From what I know about the mental life of sexual sadists, I do not regard as farfetched the theory that Mr. N's hypochondriasis was a reflection of his anxieties concerning the inscrutable, mysterious, soft, diffuse, and—owing to the strength of his feminine wishes— potentially penetrable insides of his own body. Mr. N chose not to be a warrior but rather a caregiver. In the costume of gentle, caring stretcher bearer, Mr. N could enjoy with impunity the blood of the wounded soldiers stiffening onto his body. After his discharge, in his pose as a manly lover, he could dismember his female sexual partners and poke about the insides of their bodies without any consciousness of shame or anxiety. The very fact that Mr. N's erotic excitements were associated with wearing bloody uniforms, dismembering the body of another human being, and drinking blood suggests that the terrors motivating Mr. N's perversion were themselves more primitive than the ordinary ubiquitous anxieties of childhood. While we know nothing at all about Mr. N's childhood, I would conjecture from his adult behavior that by the time he arrived at the discovery of the genital differences, he was bringing to those observations primitive terrors of annihilation and abandonment.

My general thesis is that sadomasochistic scenarios involving any actual mutilation of the self or other are the mental creations of persons who were severely traumatized in infancy by profound insults to their bodily integrity. In some cases that I am familiar with, there was an almost complete absence of the ordinary pleasurable skin contact that brings the surface of an infant's body to life. And often this early absence of life-giving stimulation was supplemented later by sexual or violently aggressive attacks on the child's body. In some instances, parental neglect led to accidents and injuries requir-

ing painful and prolonged surgical interventions. Persons so abused never feel securely held together within the boundaries of their own skin. They never feel confident that the containers they call their bodies are strong enough to protect them from "invading" forces—from inside or outside. As adults they will create a perverse enactment to control and regulate what they experience in themselves as leaking-out body substances. In males, these leaky substances —mucus, urine, feces, even ejaculate—are unconsciously equated with a helpless dependency and a vulnerable femininity. The performance of body mutilations, primitive and horrifying as it is to an observer, is reassuring to the protagonist, who can then feel more secure about his body boundaries, his self-identity, and his masculine narcissism.

As with all fetish objects and substances, the blood that figured so prominently in Mr. N's blunt and barely disguised perverse scenarios represented both abandonment and reunion, castration and reparation, death and ressurection.

By definition, a sadistic act always has a touch of the erotic. Mr. N was a two-time sadistic murderer, sadistic because he confessed to the erotic components that distinguish simple murder and an act of sadism. (Perhaps all premeditated or scripted murders are always something other than "simple murder.") But unlike that of most sexual sadists, Mr. N's life, so far as we know, was not built around the need to repeatedly reenact his scenario. His perversion was not a full-time occupation. The Jack-the-Ripper characters who *repeatedly* murder female victims with the manifest aim of achieving erection moderate their sadistic impulses toward women even less well than the pathetic Mr. N, who had been civilized enough to twice arrange to land himself in protective custody. A sexual pervert with irresistible sadistic impulses needn't be a violent Jack the Ripper or a relatively mild-mannered Mr. N. Other men, with equally malignant feelings toward females and their bodies, find rather ingenious ways to achieve erection in the course of inflicting damage on a woman's body.

THE CASE OF MR. O:
"Maybe this time it will/won't happen"

Mr. O was another man whose erotic desires were not sufficiently strong to adequately modulate the murderous elements of his perverse scenario. His enactments, however, had slightly more symbolic restraint than those of Mr. N. Mr. O tried, whenever possible, to masturbate on rooftops. With one hand regulating the stimulation of his penis, the other hand would hurl bricks at women in the street below. With merely the comforting thought that one of his bricks *might* be landing on a woman, Mr. O could achieve erection and orgasm. Whether or not the brick actually hit the woman was a matter of relative indifference to Mr. O. The moment of throwing the brick and wondering if it would or would not land on a woman was the moment that counted. The erotic excitement depended on not knowing the outcome. The risk of perhaps being caught in his criminal act heightened the thrill of Mr. O's sexual adventures. When a brick did hit the target, Mr. O always waited for evidence of shock on the part of passersby or the victim before attempting to escape. It was the look of shock on someone's face that brought down the curtain on that afternoon's sexual performance. Mr. O was eventually imprisoned. However, he never revealed to himself or anyone else the fantasies and wishes he was enacting through his masturbation ritual.

Once again on the basis of slender data and my familiarity with other, similar cases, I will speculate about Mr. O's perverse script. I surmise that the look of shock on his victim's or an observer's face had something to do with situations of infantile trauma in which Mr. O was the passive victim of an adult's brutalizing surprise attacks on his body. Mr. O's identification with some "potentially" mutilated woman reflected the trauma of having his body brutally penetrated by a child molester, possibly a family member. The uncertainty that gave to his enactment its special drama and increment of excite-

ment—*"Maybe this time it will/won't happen"*—is an essential element in Mr. O's dubious triumph over a childhood trauma.

Men like Mr. N and Mr. O are strongly identified with the mutilated women they attack. They are predisposed by earlier severe traumas to regard the female genitals as a horrible wound and to interpret the primal scene as a surprise attack. In their limited sexual escapades, they can affirm their masculine identity, feel for a moment like intact, coherent, whole males, without ever having to actually engage the potentially dangerous body of a living, breathing, experiencing, actively desiring female.

THE CASE OF MR. R:
The Triumphant Hair Cutter

Mr. R, a professional man in his late twenties, a husband and the father of a little boy, suffered intensely from his hair fetish. More accurately, it was not the fetish that troubled him but the fact that his wife would no longer participate in the fetishistic scenario that he had invented. Because of his professional duties, which brought him into contact with prominent members of his community, Mr. R was most troubled by his slovenly dress, poor hygiene, and some "disgusting" habits such as picking his nose and eating the secreta or rubbing it into his clothing and the upholstery of his car. In the course of exploring the sources of those symptoms, Mr. R's analyst discovered his perversion.

In her introduction to Mr. R's case, his analyst mentions in passing that though the fetish is usually equated with the phallus, "it may also signify the uterus or the vagina." She encouraged her patient to explore his feminine identifications and the relationship between those identifications and his bloodthirsty, sadistic fantasies. It was this analyst's attunement to the various nuances of her patient's feminine wishes and feminine identifications that made special contributions to our knowledge of perversion. I could not help wondering whether Mr. R's analyst was more aggressive about these explorations because she was a woman or whether the frightened and shy Mr. R was

able to express such reactions more readily with a female analyst. The case of
Mr. R is one of the few reported cases of perversion that explicitly calls
attention to the man's envy of female genital functions and the relationship of
that envy to so-called masculine sadism.

The only way that Mr. R could get a satisfactory orgasm was to cut off a lock of his wife's hair during foreplay or occasionally after he had already penetrated her. He also indulged in daily masturbation while fantasizing that he was cutting a woman's hair. Once in a while he would have a masturbatory fantasy of cutting a man's hair. As he walked through the city, he would peer into every barbershop he passed with the hope that he might see a woman having her hair cut. When his sexual anxieties mounted or his professional life became particularly stressful, Mr. R would have to travel to one or another of the few barbershops that employed a female barber. At those times he had to have his hair cut by a woman or his anxiety would become unbearable.

Mr. R had certain specifications for the way his wife was to comb her hair. She had to wear bangs covering her forehead (the equivalent of masculinity and therefore not castrated), while her back hair had to fall into soft waves down to her shoulders (the equivalent of femininity and therefore castrated). He collected pictures from magazines of all women who had their hair cut in this manner. At work he suggested to his female employees that they might also like to wear their hair this way. Accustomed as they were to their boss's peculiar ways, the women simply ignored him and continued filing and typing. Though he was a pompous martinet, the women recognized that he was a shy and frightened man who would never press them to do the weird things he sometimes hinted at.

Before he had met his wife, a softly pretty, compliant woman, Mr. R was able to have satisfactory sexual relations with several girlfriends. He had been drawn to aggressive girls with long blond hair. Several of these women admitted to him that they were bisexual. Mr. R did not react at all adversely to that news. The knowledge of their relative disinterest in men relieved him of the necessity of gratifying them sexually.

Except for his perversion and his slovenly habits, Mr. R gave his wife very little trouble. He was faithful to her and was kind and considerate to her and to their son. She, in turn, was more than willing to do what she could to make her husband happy. Sometimes, though, while Mr. R was cutting his wife's hair, he had the disturbing fantasy that he was gouging out pieces of her scalp.

Over the years, as these sadistic fantasies acquired more and more prominence, Mr. R's fetishistic demands on his wife became increasingly bolder until finally it was impossible for her to comply. One day, after his analyst would not give in to his request that she approve of his perversion, he reacted to this expression of his analyst's authority by displacing his fury toward his analyst onto his wife. When he came home that night, he requested that his wife allow him to shave all the hair off her head. When he noted his wife's hesitancy, he reminded her that she could simply wear an attractive wig for the time her hair was growing in. Her refusal made him so tense that he began to cry. He accused his wife of trying to emasculate him. He was amazed that this scene between them aroused a fantasy in him that went quite against his image of himself as a considerate husband, a passive and gentle man who was fearful of most people he met. He had an image of seizing his wife, pinning her down on the bed, and hacking away at her hair. Even in this fantasy, the kind Mr. R managed to save his wife from the full extent of his fury. He imagined her as wriggling free, grabbing his testicles, and trying mightily to pull them off.

After the disturbing rejection by his wife (and his analyst) and the even more disturbing fantasy that followed, Mr. R waited some days before bringing up any more requests about hair cutting. He then ventured a modified proposal. Perhaps he could shave her head *and* his. With this modification Mr. R had hoped to accomplish two things. First, he thought it would convince his wife to give her permission.

Second, he had figured out that his hair would grow in faster than hers. In that way he could prove himself to be stronger and better than his wife (and his analyst). Once again, his wife thwarted his plans. She found his mutual shaving plan no more to her liking than his first request.

Mr. R had no choice but to curb his shaving impulses. He had to be content with mere hair cutting. Nevertheless, he could not resist cutting his wife's hair closer and closer to her scalp. Finally, Mr. R grew ashamed of his wife's peculiar appearance. Nearly the last straw for Mrs. R was when her husband started complaining about her lack of ingenuity in finding suitable hats or bandanas to cover up his crude handiwork. Then and only then did she voice any overt rebellion. If he insisted on mutilating her, she protested, then he would have to suffer the embarrassment of her appearance.

One night Mrs. R could bear it no longer. She declined absolutely to let Mr. R continue to cut her hair so close to the scalp. Her adamant stance brought Mr. R to a state of unbearable tension. This time he did not cry. Nor did he conjure up a sadistic mutilation fantasy to control his aggression toward his wife. Instead he spent the entire evening in the bathroom, shaving off all the hair from his head and his body. His frightening and ridiculous appearance did not in any way distress him. But for weeks after his hair shaving episode, Mr. R had difficulty in obtaining an emission during masturbation. Until his hair grew back, he was impotent during intercourse.

After a while Mr. R began to recover some memories from childhood. Every single one of these first recollections was about hair and hair cutting. Hair, obviously, was the screen that would conceal, yet symbolically reveal, the traumas of childhood, until Mr. R's mind was ready to allow these traumas greater consciousness. The most vivid and emotionally resonant memories from Mr. R's childhood were of his mother drying her long golden hair in the sun. To dry the underneath hairs, she would throw her hair over her face. As a toddler, Robert was horrified yet intrigued by the disappearance of her face. What a great relief it was when his mother's face finally reappeared. Robert was extremely jealous of a male cousin who was always described as having "beautiful locks." Robert himself felt very unloved and unwanted. His parents were always lamenting that poor little Robert was the only one in the whole family that did not have "beautiful locks." It was true. Robert had very straight, unruly, drab-colored hair. His father had wavy hair and also wonderful curly pubic hair that fascinated Robert.

One afternoon when Robert was four years old, he and a playmate had great fun cutting each other's hair. He was found out and scolded for being a naughty boy. He was told that for his punishment he would have to stay "funny-looking" until his hair grew in. Around this time, Robert invented a new hair game. He induced the little girl next door to let him rub mud into her hair. They both enjoyed themselves immensely until the little girl's mother recognized the culprit and reported Robert to his parents. Throughout his childhood, Robert's mother cut his hair in a girlish Dutch bob with bangs over his forehead, and his father did not intervene on his behalf. At age twelve he began to resent the feminine appearance of his haircut and demand that he be sent to a proper barber. Until his analysis, memories of hair and hair cutting adventures had effectively screened out every other item of Robert's childhood history, including the fact that he had several times witnessed his parents' sexual intercourse.

After recalling all he could about hair and hair cutting, Mr. R began at last to remember some other details from his childhood, which had till then been a total blank. When he was ten years old a little sister had been born. Robert, who had managed to remain totally innocent about all matters having to do with sexuality, was deeply puzzled by his little sister's peculiar anatomy. He also wondered where exactly she had come from. After working over these dilemmas for nearly a year, Robert ventured to ask his parents to explain the differences between boys and girls. His very proper mother and father were both far too embarrassed to answer him. A brother, four years his senior, informed him that girls looked the same way in front as boys looked from behind. That more or less clinched Robert's association between female genitals and dirty, smelly anal functions. He soon afterward acquired a case of pruritus ani (severe anal itching) that would continue to afflict him throughout adolescence and adulthood. Nothing more was said about sex or genitals until Robert was thirteen, when his father decided it was time to let him in on the facts of life. The father took Robert aside for a "man-to-man." He warned him about two things. He must never masturbate. He must never get a girl into trouble. And that was that for Robert's sexual enlightenment.

Robert continued his sexual researches on his own. A year after his father's lecture, he went for a walk with a neighborhood girl and tried to convince her to let him cut her hair. He insisted on clipping just one lock, explaining that he wished only to demonstrate how the barber should cut her hair. Between that quixotic erotic enactment and Mr. R's first sexual experience, five barren years elapsed. He also recalled that at the age of eighteen and for a year or so afterward he had been a daredevil, more or less the hero of his adolescent friends. He could not understand how or why he had become such a shy and frightened man. Mr. R did not masturbate until he was nineteen. At age twenty-one he attempted intercourse with a prostitute. He was impotent. That year Mr. R realized that his erections and orgasms depended on the cooperation of a female partner whose body and emotional attitudes could represent a combination of masculine and feminine qualities. For a time the aggressive girls with long blond hair would do the trick. But after his marriage to his compliant, extremely submissive wife, Mr. R became obsessed with hair and hair cutting. Since gender ambiguity in his sexual partner had made sexual intercourse possible in the past, this ambiguity found some representation in Mr. R's hair cutting scenario.

All Mr. R knew was that he *had* to cut his wife's hair or he would become unbearably anxious and tense and intercourse would be impossible for him. According to his analyst, the cutting of his wife's hair was an enactment of two unconscious wishes, each with its own built-in reassurance. First, Mr. R could reassure himself about his own fears of castration: "I will cut my wife's hair. But hair (in contrast to genitals) can always grow back again, proving that castration is reversible." Second, he could reassure himself that his wife was strong, powerful, and phallic and yet not quite as powerful as he. "I will cut her hair and find the penis. But I can always cut it again and prove myself more powerful than she." Sometimes keeping track of the balances of power at home and in his analyst's office was much too confusing. There would be days, sometimes weeks, when Mr. R withdrew from all relations with his wife and contented himself with masturbation. He found that he could alleviate his tension with the fantasy that he could be both sexes at once and did not need any sexual partner at all. Or for that matter, perhaps he could perform his own analysis without his analyst.

Mr. R began to complain again that his analyst was interfering with his perversion. Her powerful and penetrating interpretations were beginning to make him feel defeated and worthless. He wanted to be able to free himself of his dependency on this authority figure and to cure himself. He carried similar attitudes of absolute independence over to his work situation. Once his father had been a partner in his business, but he fired his father for interfering. Though Mr. R was always overworked and fatigued, he could never abide a partner in his business. He had to control every situation himself. After he decided he could do without either wife or analyst, Mr. R became acutely aware of his wish to be both sexes at the same time. He would imagine that he was able to take his penis into his mouth and thereby become a complete circle unto himself. He recognized that he longed to be a fusion of masculine and feminine. He sometimes dreamed that he had breasts like a woman and a penis like a man. He envied women their capacity to bear and produce children.

After exploring these bisexual fantasies with his analyst, Mr. R went into a period of considerable improvement and regained his trust in her capacity to help him. Then a bit later, as his sadistic fantasies once again came to the fore, his hair fetishism intensified. He could have sex only when he had absolute control over his wife, and he lost all desire when she indicated any signs of her own active sexual desire. Because he was able to acknowledge that he still thought of himself as a "funny-looking boy," he was also able to admit that he was extremely competitive with his pretty wife. With this awareness of his competition with his wife came the conscious realization that he thought of his penis as a destructive weapon that could injure a woman during intercourse.

Now some further memories of childhood came to mind. Mr. R remembered wishing he could be a Christ Child, for if he were the Christ Child and his mother the Madonna, this would be proof that his father had never had intercourse with his mother. Mr. R recognized at long last that his parents, even his adored, emotionally distant, angelic mother with the long blond hair, had carnal knowledge. He then recalled that when he was six years old, he had walked in on his parents while they were having sexual intercourse. He had no idea what was going on. He knew that he was excluded from whatever it was and that he shouldn't have been in the room in the first place. As he always would, the six-year-old Robert figured things out for himself. Since his father just the other day had held him down and forced medicine down his throat, he was certain that "doing it" had something to do with his father forcing something into his mother. A picture of a Greek priest with long flowing hair hung on a wall near his parents' bed. That priest represented to him the perfect neuter, celibate and bisexual. Gentle little Robert certainly didn't want to do the violent terrible things his father did. He wished instead that he could be a priest when he grew up. As a child and now as an adult he wanted so much to be a good, kind person. As a child, soon after his sister was born, he was immensely distressed to find himself irresistibly drawn to killing rabbits and cats. As an adult, he was shy and kind and considerate. However, his dreams were filled with images of people being run over and mutilated, and his sexual fantasies were violent and sadistic.

As he recalled bits and pieces of his buried childhood, Mr. R figured out on his own, presumably without interference or suggestion from his therapist, a few theories about the meaning of his perversion. He had sometimes wondered why he wasn't a shoe fetishist like the other perverts he had heard about. He realized after a while that hair did seem like the right fetish for him. By serving as a symbolic equivalent of the genitals, hair could allow him to express his castration wishes and fears while simultaneously directing his attention upward to "higher matters" and away from the genitals, which were so close to the "lowly, dirty matters." With this strategy the dirty matters could be expressed by smearing mucus and wearing smelly clothes, and the higher matters could be expressed by cutting his wife's hair. He thought that perhaps he cut his own hair because he really wished to be a tower of strength but feared that he would use his strength as a dangerous weapon. He began to see that his wife resembled his mother and wondered whether, when he cut his wife's hair, he was "attempting to take his mother out of his wife." On another occasion he mused that perhaps he was trying to cut his pretty wife down into the humiliating childhood image of himself as a "funny-looking" boy. He recalled that his father used to take him into his bed for Sunday naps and wondered whether his involvement with hair was a cover-up for his dread of homosexuality. Mr. R was able to recognize that the dangerous and unpredictable longings that he had previously projected onto his wife represented his own feminine wishes and desires. He felt that his analyst had helped him bring out his masculinity, which until then he had associated with sadism and violence. He allowed himself to be competitive with his professional colleagues and got along much better with them as a result. He was more congenial and emotionally available to his friends and less patronizing of his female employees. He continued to indulge in hair cutting fantasies when he was under stress, but he never had the impulse to enact them. Still, however, he maintained an inordinate fascination with his wife's hair styles, which she now combed and cut any way she pleased.

Mr. R's hair-cutting scenario allowed him to attack the part of his wife's body that symbolized the genitals, but because the attacks took place in the context of a ritualized performance Mr. R was able to protect his wife from outright genital mutilation. At the same time, his perverse scenario successfully regulated the delicate balance between Mr. R's masculine and feminine strivings. Finally, Mr. R created a primal scene fantasy in which he could identify with both sexes—a mother being castrated by the father and a father whose angry penis is castrating the mother. The once excluded child became the triumphant "hair cutter" who at last had discovered the secret recipe for Great Sex.

THE CASE OF MR. B:
Jodhpurs

Since early adolescence, Mr. B had daydreamed about becoming an army officer who would distinguish himself on the field of battle. He was sure that when he was old enough to fulfill this ambition his intelligent and forceful father, who had contempt for his son's comparatively unimpressive intellectual ability and had always held him in disdain as a physical weakling and a momma's boy, would realize that he was worthy of love and admiration. He imagined himself discharging his rifle to the right and to the left, mowing down every German soldier in his path and then becoming the favorite of his idol, General Patton. When at last he was old enough, he enlisted for training at officer's candidate school. However, Mr. B was shy and could not relate to the boisterous and outspoken young men in his troop. He consistently did poorly at his studies. And the moment he set foot on the training field, Mr. B was frozen on the spot. He could not move in any direction—forward or back, to the right or to the left. He could not fire a single shot, not then and not ever. He admitted to the army psychiatrist that he was terrified that his testicles would be shot off. He was soon discharged from OCS for intellectual and emotional ineptitude and cowardice.

The profound humiliation that Mr. B suffered, first from having to acknowledge to himself how frightened he had been and then from realizing that he might never have another opportunity to win his father's love and admiration, led to the severe depression that prompted him to seek analysis.

At the start of his analysis the twenty-three-year-old Mr. B had never had sexual relations with a woman or a man, although he had seriously entertained thoughts of both possibilities. His sexual life consisted of dressing up in leather garments and masturbating. Mr. B was not concerned about the emotional barrenness of his sexuality or his fetishism, which he did not think important enough to mention to his analyst for nearly a year.

After his depression subsided and he no longer felt so keenly the humiliation of his discharge from OCS, Mr. B reported that he had for quite some time been preoccupied with riding clothes, not only the various leather garments he wore when he masturbated but the riding jodhpurs worn by women. Merely the sight of a woman wearing jodhpurs would arouse him. His sexual excitement was heightened *if* the woman's calf muscles were firm and large enough to produce a bulging impression under the jodhpurs, *if* the woman also wore tight-fitting boots, *if* there was a suede patch at the inner part of the knee, *and especially if* the jodhpurs had been constructed to produce a pronounced bulge at each side. Moreover, continued Mr. B, when it came to leather riding pants he was a compulsive shopper. Indeed, he was always thinking about jodhpurs, cruising the department stores searching for the right kind of jodhpurs, sometimes ending up with a half dozen pairs of leather pants.

He worried about what his parents might think of him should they discover the stacks of riding clothes hidden in his closet. Therefore, when he was not preoccupied with purchasing leather pants, he found himself sneaking about in out-of-the-way neighborhoods with his latest collection of riding pants looking for garbage pails and alleyways where he might dispose of them. Thinking about jodhpurs, planning purchases, collecting, wearing, and disposing of leather riding pants constituted for Mr. B a full-time preoccupation. And every once in a while, he would don a pair of his favorite leather pants, stroll seductively about certain side streets, and fantasize about picking up a strong, handsome man who might make love to him.

Tough leather riding pants were the central focus of Mr. B's preoccupation, but he was also fascinated by leather jackets, gloves, and hats and guns and fast cars.

Mr. B had another preoccupation, one that seemed to him rather feminine and antithetical to his preoccupation with leather goods. On some days he would be overcome by a longing to stroke hair, and he frequently fantasized that he was stroking the hair of his ideal woman, a "Park Avenue Girl" with long blond hair, a Gentile who was aloof and unreachable. In exploring this fantasy with his analyst, Mr. B began to recognize that the blond, aloof girls represented the feminine side of his own self, the femininity that he was so desperately trying to repress with his jodhpur, leather goods, and gun preoccupations. By thinking of himself as the adoring one of the adorable long-haired beauties, Mr. B fantasized himself in the masculine position while simultaneously identifying with the woman whose long silky hair he was stroking. One day, as he spoke about this longing to stroke hair, he recalled that at the age of four much fuss had been made over his own long, blond, silky hair. Other memories of Mr. B's early childhood then began to emerge.

Mr. B remembered that around the age of five or six he had gone with his mother and his aunt, both blond women of Scandinavian descent, on a vacation to Scandinavia. Little Billy was one day watching his mother and his aunt as they changed from their riding clothes into their bathing suits. The moment they removed the boots and jodhpurs, the two women seemed to Billy to be two entirely different women. He hardly recognized them. Here was one of those magical "moments of horror" that analysts long to recover in the memories of their patients. The image of women in jodhpurs was interpreted by Mr. B's analyst as that notorious last moment when a little boy can still continue to maintain the fantasy that his mother has a penis. According to Mr. B's analyst, who was a foremost authority on the ubiquitous phallic woman, the bulges on the sides of the jodhpurs had encouraged Billy's fantasy that his mother and aunt, those adorable, unreachable creatures with long blond hair, were phallic women—women yes, but women with a penis.

One of the things that strikes me as inexplicably odd is that Mr. B's analyst did not relate his patient's jodhpur fetish or his castration anxiety to his fear of having his testicles shot off. Surely the bulges on each side of the jodhpurs resembled two testicles, perhaps also two breasts. Of course, any article of clothing may come to represent symbolically a woman with a penis. However, the testicle and breast interpretations deserve at least a mention and perhaps some serious consideration even in a very brief rendition of this case. Until very recently, psychoanalytic writings on the subject of male castration anxiety left out any discussion of the testicles and focused all attention on "man's most honest organ, the penis." As we now know, in the fantasy life of males the testicles and scrotal sac are often associated with femininity. Furthermore, the more reliable and observable and controllable penis is defensively imagined as an "antidote" against a man's shameful feminine longings. Mr. B's analyst was not unaware of the strength of his patient's feminine wishes. Therefore, the analyst's case report and his patient's analysis could only have been enhanced had the analyst explored the possible role of testicles and scrotal sac in his patient's fantasy life.

In any event, Mr. B's analyst tells us that little Billy became very curious about the bulges in his mother's jodhpurs. Something told the little boy that his curiosity about jodhpurs was naughty. He dared not ask his mother. But he questioned his aunt many times about those mysterious bulges, and each time she patiently explained how they were sewn and constructed. Billy was not at all reassured by his aunt's explanations and soon after the "moment of horror" he would no longer venture into the water, fearing that the fish would gobble him up. His mother and aunt tried to assuage his fears by pointing out that the fish in the lake were much smaller than he. But that logic was as little reassuring as his aunt's narratives about the way jodhpurs were sewn together. His penis, after all (and his testicles), was much smaller than the fish. From then on Billy was haunted by dreams of sharks with big open mouths swimming toward him in the water. He was terrified when he went to use the outhouse that something might come out of the dark hole to injure him. Mr. B described that period of his childhood as feeling like "a worm among Giants."

Mr. B then recalled some other dramatic events that had preceded the "moment of horror." Between the ages of two and three he had great difficulty being separated from his mother or sleeping alone in his own bed. Up to the age of four his mother often slept with him. Furthermore, she dressed him like a girl and never bothered to cut his beautiful long, blond, silky hair. When he was four years old, after having been unusually close to his mother, with very little indication of his father's presence either in her life or his, Billy's parents went on an extended vacation, leaving him alone with a maid. Mr. B remembered suffering greatly from this abrupt abandonment by his mother. Shortly after his parents returned, his mother presented him with the gift of a new little baby brother. No doubt Billy had noticed the bulge in his mother's stomach long before that.

It is clear from what he did mention in his case report that Mr. B's analyst appreciated the contributions of abandonment and separation anxieties and feminine identification to his patient's reaction of horror when his mother and aunt were transformed into "castrated" women. "Historically, the pregenital identification with the phallic mother cannot be given up in the phallic phase in spite of the new reality ([the mother's] penislessness) because separation from the mother is experienced as an equal, if not greater danger than the loss of the penis. Both phases of danger, i.e. separation and castration are defended by the fetishistic compromise." The jodhpur fetish succeeded in alleviating the abandonment, separation, and castration anxieties because it affirmed Mr. B's identification with his phallic mother and his identification with his super-masculine father. In the primal scene fantasy that accompanied his masturbation, Mr. B was identifying with both parents in the primal scene. Though Mr. B's analyst does not mention it, certainly it is significant that Billy went on this trip with his aunt and mother the year after he was greeted by a rival baby in the family. No doubt Billy's inquiries about the jodhpurs were related to his curiosity about where babies come from. How was this new baby's presence in his life related to his father's presence in his mother's life? Do babies emerge from bulging body parts? Do little boys have babies growing inside their scrotal sacs? Would the fish in the lake try to eat up his scrotal babies as he had wished to do to the rival baby inside his mother's bulge?

Shortly after Mr. B recalled the traumatic abandonment surrounding the arrival of his baby brother, another memory emerged into consciousness, this one from early puberty. At that later time, Billy had a recurrent fantasy of "dancing naked with his long blond hair in front of his father and the lower part of his body was indistinct." In connection with the memory of this fantasy, Mr. B thought of how much he had always been in awe of his father's big red penis, how much he had hated that penis, and how intimidated he had been by his super-masculine father. As he thought about his conflicted feelings toward his father, that awesome creature appeared to him in a dream that took place in a pagan, Germanic banquet hall. His father was one of many barbaric, gigantic, shaggy, furry, wild bears of "truly epic proportions." "How much I envied them. I was like a crumb on the floor," Mr. B recalled.

When he was approaching adolescence Billy had wanted to follow his mother's ambitions for him by becoming an artist. But at puberty he began to evaluate artistic ambitions as entirely too feminine. He wanted so much to please his father and to win his love and admiration by acting like a man. However, since Billy had been deprived of a close relationship with his father, all he could do was emulate his father's walk, big mustache, pipe, rough manners, and clothing. In his efforts to understand what a real man was, he became fascinated with guns and fast cars. But the long-haired blond beauty with ambiguous genitals who resembled himself as a long-haired blond boy united with his long-haired blond mother still longed to be sexually desired by the father. She-he could not be silenced. In desperation, Billy joined OCS, fiercely determined to live up to his exaggerated ideals of manhood.

Eventually, Mr. B found a substitute for his jodhpurs in a psychological compromise that also managed to reconcile his wishes to be a blond "castrated" feminine beauty with his caricature of masculinity. Though his unconscious feminine longings and his unconscious preoccupation with castration had made Mr. B particularly terrified of any person with a physical deformity, he married a woman who in childhood had been a victim of polio and as a result had a permanently crippled leg. She was a commercial artist and so fulfilled Mr. B's mother's ambitions. But like his father, she was extremely domineering and much superior to Mr. B intellectually. With her crippled leg and her masterful, masculine ways, she embodied the disavowal that he had attempted in his fascination with jodhpurs. She was both castrated and phallic/not castrated. In his relationship with his wife, Mr. B could be the submissive, feminine, silky-haired child and, because sexual intercourse with his fetish-wife was possible, still be a real man like his father.

THE CASE OF MR. K:
Apron Strings

Mr. K had been happily married for twelve years. However, he explained to his analyst that despite their otherwise good, normal, healthy, productive life, he and his wife could not conceive a child. Actually, their sexual troubles had begun many years earlier when on the night of the wedding Mr. K could not get an erection. After a year or two of marital celibacy, Mr. and Mrs. K decided to seek help at a clinic that specialized in marital counseling. The bits and pieces of sexual knowledge that Mr. K picked up during these sessions led him to an interesting but mysterious revelation. Much to his amazement, he discovered that he could get an erection if he wore an apron and performed a special ritual that went with the wearing of the apron. The idea of the apron ritual seemed to come from a far distant past— he could not remember exactly where or when.

Mrs. K was not too pleased with her husband's revelation. However, the marital counselor helped her understand that if she loved her husband and was eager to have a child, she should agree play her part and do as her husband instructed her.

Following the script dictated by her husband, Mrs. K would begin the foreplay ritual by reprimanding him for not wearing his apron. He would resist. Then Mrs. K would get angrier and angrier. Finally she would hold him down on the bed and force him to wear the apron. At that point Mr. K would have an erection. Then, in order for Mr. K to be able to penetrate his wife, she would have to tie the apron as tightly as possible. The only variation on this very limited script was that once in a while the ritual began with Mrs. K wearing the apron and then forcing Mr. K to wear *her* apron. Mr. K would then imagine that he was being forced to wear an apron that belonged to a woman. Unconsciously, this meant that Mr. K was a woman, but a woman with a penis—the typical transvestite fantasy.

As in most cases that start out looking like a pure fetishistic perversion, for Mr. K the border between fetishism and transvestism was barely distinguishable. Furthermore, as Mr. K's analyst would realize in thinking over the sad fate of Mr. K, embedded in the rather obvious scenario of fetishistic cross-dressing was yet another perversion, perhaps the essential one, exhibitionism. It turned out that the apron script was only partially successful in improving Mr. K's sexual performance, making it necessary for Mr. K to go from one sex specialist to another exhibiting his impotent penis and announcing that he wasn't a man to be taken seriously after all.

The ritual of the apron had improved the couple's sexual relationship in a mechanical way by enabling Mr. K to have an erection and penetrate his wife. However, Mr. K still could not ejaculate or have an orgasm. The signs that would reveal a desire for his wife were not there. He could not bring her sexual satisfaction. He could not impregnate her. Mrs. K made it clear that she only suffered her husband's apron ritual. She just lay there while he pumped away, on and on, and she kept hoping and praying that perhaps tonight the erection would lead to ejaculation and impregnation. As things went, the only way Mrs. K could satisfy herself was by masturbating while watching romantic plays and movies on TV. Mr. K was amused and tolerant of Mrs. K's method of achieving orgasm, which he found "very odd."

A therapist at one of the fertility clinics had advised Mr. K to take advantage of the fact that he was able to ejaculate at the climax of two recurrent dreams. One of these ejaculation dreams was that he was in a hurry to get somewhere but could not get his leg into his trousers. As his excited anxiety mounted, he achieved orgasm and woke up. The other dream entailed running to catch a train. Mr. K's anxiety at being unable to run fast enough also led to orgasm and awakening. The sex therapist suggested that Mr. K attach a receptacle to the end of his penis and capture the semen from his wet dreams. On three occasions the plan worked, but like the apron ritual, the dream ritual was only partially successful. Alas, although Mr. K dutifully collected his semen, he always managed to be too late in getting the specimen to the clinic. He seemed determined to avoid the one outcome of sexual intercourse that might have brought home to him the differences between the sexes and the generations. The capacity of the father to impregnate the mother and the mother's capacity to carry and bear a child were the pieces of knowledge in the castration complex that Mr. K would have no part of.

While I concur with the overall wisdom in this analyst's interpretations of his patient's fetishism-transvestism, I would want to make more explicit the relationship between the strength of Mr. K's feminine wishes and his fear of ejaculation. Undoubtedly, the less controllable, spontaneous "leaking out" of the ejaculate and the inevitable detumescence would unconsciously signify, especially to a conventional, rigid man like Mr. K, a realization of his unconscious feminine wishes and therefore terrify him. On the other hand, ejaculation would have been a confirmation of his manhood. For, as Mr. K's analyst eventually understood, the ejaculation would have been the proof that he was capable of fatherhood. Either way, therefore, ejaculation would be a confirmation of something Mr. K was determined to disavow—the differences between the sexes and generations.

There was a great deal more at stake in Mr. K's full scenario than the obvious fetishistic cross-dressing could express. The fetishism could succeed partially, only insofar as it fulfilled Mr. K's wish to remain tied to his mother's apron strings. Yet it also had to fail at the moment of ejaculation to fulfill Mr. K's wish to continue to exhibit his penis as merely a harmless infantile penis. I am, therefore, in complete agreement with the analyst's larger premise, that Mr. K's "refusal" to acknowledge fatherhood was the fundamental psychological motive of his patient's perverse strategy. I want only to supplement this premise with the suggestion that the psychological refusal gained support from a primitive body anxiety about physical ejaculation. Mr. K had learned, early in childhood, that he could remain in control of the feminine and masculine aspects of his personality only by remaining a little boy frozen in time without any adult desire.

The intimate connections between the psychological and the physical is implicit in the history of Mr. K's childhood, which amply demonstrates the way five-year-old Karl's loss of control over his urinary and anal functions was an unconscious attempt to disavow the genital function of the penis. Karl's childhood "impotence" was in the service of his wishes to disavow the differences between the sexes and to remain at one with his mother, emotionally but also physically.

Karl was the last child of his aging parents and the only boy. His three sisters, who still lived at home, were all much older than he. His father's mother also lived in the house until her death when Karl was five years old. As Mr. K thought over the significant events of his childhood, he recalled that his mother, but sometimes also his father, had forced him to wear an apron the moment he returned from school. The idea was that he should not dirty himself while having tea or playing. Being forced to wear a woman's apron was humiliating, and Karl was not encouraged to rebel when he observed that his father did not protest when the mother insisted that he wear an apron to the table. At this point in her life the mother no longer felt any sexual desire for her husband. She dominated and controlled Karl's father as though he too were nothing other than a dirty little boy—and the father allowed her to do so.

Mr. K wondered if perhaps his own behavior may have contributed to his mother's overconcern with his cleanliness. Though little Karl did not like being forced to wear a feminine garment, he also did not want to acknowledge that he was about to become a big boy with a big boy's penis. During the months preceding his entrance to school, he refused to wear underpants. He was constantly soiling his trousers with urine and feces. Mr. K recalled how much he had enjoyed rubbing his penis against his trousers. The drops of urine and feces reassured him that his penis was still there. But each day he exhibited his penis to his mother as merely a toilet penis. And each day, even as she expressed her resentment and anger, she dutifully inspected his trousers for the dirty "traces" and then dutifully laundered them, confirming that Karl was still her little momma's boy. Mr. K.'s analyst summed up this perverse scenario, "The voyeurism of the mother was satisfied by the exhibitionistic behavior of the child."

Moreover, the apron that Karl was forced to wear to the table and at playtime was not just any apron. It was an apron that had been designed especially for him by his mother in the same month that he started school. The material for the apron came from workman's overalls that had always been worn around the house by Karl's grand-mother, who had died the summer before he started school. His mother had cut out the material from her mother-in-law's overalls and had sewn the apron for her son. So just at the age when his theory of the universal penis might have met with disillusionment (living in a house with a mother, grandmother, and three older sisters should have made that disillusionment inevitable), his mother handed him his fetish, an apron made from the very cloth of the workman's overalls that had contributed to the ambiguity of his grandmother's appearance. It was "a gift cut from the 'body' of another woman dressed up as a man." Mr. K could not remember what eventually happened to his childhood apron. It just disappeared.

As Mr. K reminisced about his childhood, he was impressed and amazed at the way the apron had reappeared, as though by magic, in his adult sexual rituals. His new apron, which hung on a peg over the marital bed, like a lucky charm, did not succeed in making him a father or his wife a mother. The fetish apron, though it helped Mr. K to have manly erections, still had embedded in it the idea of a dirty little boy with merely a toilet penis, a little boy whose penis would never be required to give sexual satisfaction or produce a child. Thus the apron allowed Mr. K to act as if he were a real man while it continued to protect him from having to fully acknowledge the differ-ences between the sexes. Like all fetishes, it had become a substitute for the "something" that was both there and not there. His phallic delusion could be maintained: "Under the female garment there is a penis." At the same time, the apron never worked as a proper fetish would; indeed, Mr. K was only impersonating a proper fetishist. The apron's function was to keep Mr. K safe from the frightening life-giving responsibilities of paternity. The erect penis was there, but since it could never ejaculate it had no adult powers. After making some progress in understanding the childhood origins of his adult plight, Mr. K abruptly decided he would do better to go to a clinic that specialized in test tube babies. Mr. K left his analyst as he had left the previous marital counselors and sex therapists, effectively declaring the impotence of this latest in a long string of father figures.

The analyst concluded that Mr. K's halfhearted attempts to bring pleasure to his wife and to make a baby had made a mockery of the function of fatherhood. Mr. K could masquerade as a grown-up-man-with-wife without ever acknowledging that there was any real difference between himself and his mother or between the child and adult generations. Karl's mother had colluded with his infantile fantasy that she had no active sexual desires for his father. The father, by not "exercising his authority to separate mother and child," had played his role in maintaining the pathological mother-son alliance and left little Karl "attached, engaged, anchored to his mother." Mr. K did not devise the fetishistic cross-dressing scenario until he decided that he should at least make a good show of wanting to impregnate his wife. However, as his analyst later understood, Mr. K's true perversion dated from the time he began to exhibit his impotent penis at the various sex therapy clinics, unconsciously announcing to the world, through his own incapacity for grown-up sexuality and paternity, his father's betrayal of him.

In the primal scene enactment of the apron ritual, Mr. K was identifying with the father who was forced to wear a woman's apron and yet by constantly defeating his capacity for paternity, he was expressing his unconscious rage toward his father who had negated his paternal role. Mr. K had created a triumph out of the traumas of childhood. Of course, except in a perversion, it is no triumph at all for a little boy to defeat his father or for a man to defeat his wife's desires for sexual intimacy and motherhood. And though he grew to physical manhood, the sad and tragic conclusion was that Mr. K could only impersonate a man and even that only while safely tied to his mother's apron strings, which is where he would remain eternally.

6

Feminine Stereotypes and the Female Perversions

At the beginning of the twentieth century, women were changing in ways that were making men wary and uncomfortable. By 1920, when Karl Abraham wrote his paper on the female castration complex, many women had already declared their personal independence and were publicly protesting the confining domesticities that had been assigned to them in the bourgeois family. By then a new phenomenon as insidiously dangerous in its way as the mythology of the castrated-castrating vagina was giving men another method for keeping women in their place: intimidation with a myth of normal femininity.

One of the most powerful instruments of the social order is its doctrine of normality, especially its conventions of gender normality. If need be, society, which cares only to preserve its own structures, will make use of an infantile fantasy about gender difference to keep the social roles of men and women firmly in place. Abraham was particularly susceptible to the twentieth-century preoccupation with normality, the mania for defining normal femininity and normal masculinity, the fetishistic urge to box the ambiguities of human sexuality into easily recognizable, contained categories, the gender stereotypes that are always on hand to help perpetuate infantile mythologies about the distinctions between the sexes.

As Karl Abraham looked about him, he regarded with woeful eyes the parade of female types that surrounded him. There were envious young ladies with probing parasols and restless garden hoses, Medusas with fixed stares that could turn a man and his defenseless penis to stone, housewives who avenged their childhood disappointments by repeatedly inciting their husbands' appetites and then burning dinner (or by arriving late to appointments or by failing to have vaginal orgasms), frigid women who made their husbands impotent, masculine women who never gave up the childhood ploy of trying to adopt the male position and who as adults had the gall to stand up and march through the streets chanting for their feminist causes. There seemed no end to the assortment of dissatisfied, nagging, petulant women who refused to reconcile themselves to the normal feminine attitude of passive-submissive expectancy. What had happened to the normal woman, the sweet, passive wife, the mother who blessed her children and husband with sugar cookies, back rubs, hot porridges, and lullabies?

From all accounts of his life, Abraham was a genial, good-hearted man whose sincere wish it was to help women get over their childhood complexes and be able to arrive at what he believed to be a more satisfying, *normal* femininity. He was convinced that a little girl might become a fairly normal woman despite all her childhood humiliations and disappointments. A female's life could go on in an orderly way if as a woman she would reconcile herself to her normal sexual role. She could surmount her childhood mortifications if she would adopt an expectant attitude toward her husband, opening herself to passive sexual gratification and receiving from him the gift of a child—if not the actual penis itself. "Her castration complex will thus give rise to no disturbing effects," Abraham writes. The gifts the little girl had waited so long to receive will be given to the woman if she abandons her wish to be a male and if she is expectant, receptive, and passive.

Abraham complains that women are rarely able to assume the normal position that has been assigned to them. The wish to be a male prevents them from attaining a normal femininity. For some women, those closest to the normal end of the spectrum, the wish to become a male will express itself only in an occasional dream. At the other extreme, some women exhibit severe and pathological manifestations of their castration complex—penis envy. Abraham introduces his catalogue of adult women pathologically afflicted by penis envy with a mortified bride who nearly strangled her husband. The bride is one of Abraham's little cigar girls who grew up into a romantic princess and expected that all the injustices of childhood would be righted in a relationship with a husband. How this bride had been anticipating her first night of "being married"! But her first intercourse was too horrible for words, even worse than her mother had warned. That penetrating penis was a terrible confirmation of her worst childhood nightmares that there were real and significant differences between the sexes. She tried to restrain her bitter tears, her rage at being once again so mortified. She managed finally to fall asleep, only to be startled into wakefulness by an irresistible impulse to place her fingers around her husband's neck and strangle him and chew off pieces of his skin and attack his body violently in every way imaginable. Fortunately, this bride loved her husband sufficiently and was sufficiently neurotic, inhibited, and guilty to recover her senses before her murderous impulses could be translated into action.

According to Abraham, the poor bride's homicidal impulses were a response to her being confronted with the disparities and inequalities between the two sexes. The very act of being penetrated was a painful reminder of all the injustices she had suffered at the hands of her deceitful father, who never did bestow her with a baby—or a penis either. In this interpretation, Abraham was once again reducing everything to the anatomical difference. It is apparent also that Abraham considered the bride's reactions from the point of view of a disappointed husband who had expected that his penetrating penis would fix his bride and make her happy and fulfilled. Abraham did not at all recognize how the groom's desire to prove his masculinity with his penis might be misconnecting with the bride's wish to fulfill her femininity in a relationship of tender mutuality, where all her organs of erotic desire—her skin, her clitoris, her nipples, her hair, her eyes—are enlivened and brought into play. The burden for the groom was to prove himself with his virility. The burden for the bride was to prove herself with her kindness, patience, and willingness to passively wait for him to teach her the facts of life. She might, had she been brought up in a different age, have thought it permissible to participate actively in bringing about her erotic fulfillment. For both partners in this old-fashioned honeymoon scenario, the humiliations and disappointments of childhood were repeated. His penis could not fulfill the woman. Her long-standing anticipation that one day a handsome prince would bring her everything she had been deprived of and excluded from in childhood brought her to yet another painful disappointment.

Abraham is quick to reassure his readers that the bride's *archaic revenge* is not a widespread solution to the penis envy conflict. Most women have been able to construct more refined remedies for their disappointments than the vengeances that would, if fantasy were transformed into action, result in strangulation, flesh tearing, dismemberment, and homicide. Some women—the masculine types—solve the problem quite simply and directly. They never even attempt to reconcile themselves to their normal feminine condition. They do not accept the inevitability of the differences between the sexes. They never make the slightest concession to the normal female position. Instead, says Abraham, they become homosexual and then adopt the male position in erotic relations with other women. Or they express the wish to be male in a "sublimated" form by pursuing masculine professions and engaging in masculine occupations. Speaking of the latter group, Abraham does not hesitate to expose his feelings about emancipated women: "Such women do not, however, consciously deny their femininity, but usually proclaim that these interests are just as feminine as masculine ones. They consider that the sex of a person has nothing to do with his or her capacities, especially in the mental field. This type of woman is well represented in the women's movement of today."

Now, if truth be told, all little cigar girls are engaging in a fetishistic fantasy. If everyone in the family has the same cigar, then there is an equality—no differences between the sexes or the generations. However, one of the many difficulties with Abraham's narrow version of the female castration complex is that it cannot account for which little cigar girl turns out to be a vengeful bride whose only recourse to disappointment is rage and which little girl becomes a woman who continues to find imaginative ways to fight for social equality between the sexes.

Once again, though, Abraham is reassuring. The vast majority of women will not resort to outright primitive violence, homosexuality, or the pursuit of feminist causes and unfeminine male occupations as a solution to their castration complex. Instead, the average woman constructs what Abraham and the analysts of his day thought of as neurotic solutions.

It is evident from Abraham's account that he, like most analysts and other doctors, had not thought very much about perversions in women. The gender mythology that Abraham subscribed to is familiar even today. Men, normal and perverse, cared about sex, whereas normal women cared more about love and relationships. Only the virile woman with active sexual desires and unrepressed masculine wishes would be drawn to perversion. Along the way Abraham called attention to women who prefer, even enjoy, oral and anal sex. He stated flatly that these sexual responses represent a perversion based on penis envy. According to his reasoning, oral and anal sex are not sexual variations but means of avoiding the genital contact that would remind women of their genital inferiority. And other than his condemnation of these perverse practices and homosexuality as well as of perverse brides who actually murder their husbands, Abraham did not recognize that several of the neurotic solutions he was describing could very well be reflections of the perverse strategy. Just as Abraham was far more comfortable if he could believe in the firm separations between normality and abnormality, masculinity and femininity, he also liked to think of perversion and neurosis as clearly distinct clinical entities.

Abraham was satisfied that most women would adopt relatively harmless unconscious neurotic strategies to resolve their castration complex. These strategies would inflict some degree of suffering on the woman and perhaps the members of her immediate family who must watch her sufferings. However, they had the advantage of dampening any sort of violent acting out, sex role reversal or disruptions of the gender status quo.

At one end of the vast range of Abraham's neurotic solutions, the woman would continue to entertain unconscious fantasies of being a male or possessing a male genital—Abraham's *neurotic wish fulfillment type*. At the other end, the female castration complex would be expressed in an unconscious refusal of the feminine role and a repressed, and therefore disguised rather than directly acted out, impulse to obtain revenge on the privileged male—*the neurotic revenge type*. As a rule these two types of solution to the female castration complex are not mutually exclusive but rather supplement one another in various proportions and differing degrees of intensity within the same woman.

The predominant unconscious fantasy that underlies the wish fulfillment solution, a euphemism for the so-called masculinity complex in women, is "I am the fortunate possessor of the penis and can exercise any male function just as well as any man" or "I must and shall receive the gift of a penis one day; I absolutely insist upon that!" According to Abraham, any woman who assumes she is equal to a man or demands the right to be equal to him is acting out her masculine wishes. As he saw it, the symptoms she might acquire as a way of restraining and disguising such forbidden masculine wishes would be neurotic compromises. They would express simultaneously the wish to be a man and the taboo against such a wish. Her symptoms would mask her masculine wishes behind an affliction that is typically feminine. The affliction would demonstrate her obedience to the inner authority that forbids these masculine wishes—but would also sneak in the wish in a disguised form. As an example of this sort of neurotic compromise, Abraham cited the case of a woman who, when sexually aroused, was afflicted with attacks of redness and swelling of the nose, which he interpreted as the equivalent of an erection displaced from the genital area to the face. Everyone would see that this woman was afflicted with a feminine weakness but would not be able to recognize it as a disguised manifestation of her masculinity. Then there are the women who proudly bemoan their uncontrollable fixed stare, which unconsciously they equate with an erection. Abraham reported, "Just as male exhibitionists seek among other things to terrify women by the sight of their phallus, so these women unconsciously endeavour to attain the same effect [on men] by means of their fixed stare." In a category with these Medusa types, he also placed the gentle woman who is forever poking her frilly parasol into the grass and others like her who demonstrate feminine nurturance by watering their pretty gardens but perform these acts with masculine garden hoses. While all this seems a little quaint and silly, Abraham's portrayals of these female neurotic types contain certain fascinating perversities worth paying attention to.

Abraham was writing about some commonplace symptoms in females and was not realizing that he was actually demonstrating a key strategy of the female perversions. It is my contention that in the female perversions a display of a stereotypical femininity acts as the disguise for what a woman experiences as a forbidden masculine striving. And though Abraham wanted to show that neurosis and perversions were different, he came up with an analogy between the male perversion exhibitionism and the "neurotic" Medusa with her castrating, staring eyes.

Abraham was right that women learn to disguise their intellectual and sexual strivings behind afflictions or conventions that reflect a gender stereotype of femininity. But, as we will see in later chapters, the motives for those all-too-commonplace feminine masquerades and the disguises themselves are more complex and subtle than Abraham could have realized. Just as men learn to disguise their forbidden feminine wishes behind a stereotype of male virility, so women learn to disguise their forbidden masculine wishes behind a stereotype of female innocence, weakness, and self-sacrifice. Women also employ social gender stereotypes to express the desires and ambitions that are forbidden to them, and in those stereotypes of normal femininity we will discover the female perversions.

The same methods of disguise are at work in Abraham's female revenge solutions. Here, Abraham gives us a clue about how females regulate and distill their sadistic impulses toward males. The more conforming woman cannot tolerate the aggression and sadism expressed in her unconscious wishes to emasculate those who possess the penis she desires. Yes, a few brides and daughters and sisters do actually mutilate and murder the men they envy. But most do not. The more typical gentle and caring woman has to acquire a disguise for her unconscious wish to emasculate and mutilate her husband or father or brother. She becomes fearful of situations that might tempt her to inflict harm on those she loves. She develops a phobia, a fearful avoidance of situations and places that symbolize situations and places where her vengeful feelings might be acted out. A phobia will limit a woman's own life but succeed in protecting the bodies and mental health of her family. In that way the woman's desire for revenge can be satisfied by her conscious imaginings of a father, a brother, a husband, a son being run over and losing a limb or two. She is perpetually thinking of all the terrible things that could happen to her loved ones. But then to appease her conscience for these vengeful thoughts, she protects her loved ones from such terrible fates by never riding a horse, never driving a car, never going to school or taking a job or competing with them, successfully at least, in any activity. A woman who adopts such a solution to her castration complex is behaving in an appropriate and normal feminine way but all along is unconsciously "enjoying" the conscious revenge fantasies in which her loved ones are being crippled and maimed.

Abraham goes on to note that the fear—that is, the disguised wish —of mutilating a man's body might turn about and express itself as an attraction toward physically mutilated or emotionally crippled men. In this so-called neurotic sexual attraction, I believe, the perverse strategy accomplishes one of its characteristic deceptions. An avoidance motivated by unconscious guilt has been replaced by a preoccupation with mutilation that regulates a female's sadism toward males and assuages her anxiety and guilt. The woman allows herself to become erotically aroused, but only with a man who limps or wears a patch over one eye or who has lost an arm or leg by amputation or accident. Whereas an intact male might suffer the full brunt of her hatred and vengeful attitudes, a mutilated man is protected. From our knowledge of the male perversions, we can see that this "neurotic" solution has in it a fetishistic device. Mr. B, whose life was dominated by wearing, collecting, and disposing of leather jodhpurs finally solved his castration complex by marrying a domineering woman with a leg crippled by polio. Was this resolution of Mr. B's gender conflicts a neurotic compromise or was it merely a more socially normalized perversion? I would say the latter. Furthermore, all perversions are motivated, in part, by a desire to protect the loved one from the lover's mutilating sadism. Surely a choice of lover or husband based on these unconscious motives is not very different from the fetishistic love object choices of males.

After going through a variety of other neurotic wish fulfillments and revenges, near the end of his paper Abraham arrives at the least overtly violent but, to his eyes, the most unconsciously vengeful of all women—the frigid woman, whom he likens to a prostitute. "Frigidity," Abraham declares, "is practically a *sine qua non* of prostitution."

In contrast to prostitution, an activity that, with rare exceptions, is limited to the unfortunate underclasses, frigidity is widespread among normal middle- and upper-class females, who stay off the streets and find more domesticated, everyday ways to emasculate their husbands and lovers. As a rule, the frigid woman is consciously ready to assume her proper female role. She is not overtly phobic about intercourse or marriage and, with her suggestively lowered gaze, she seems to promise every variety of sexual delight. To be sure, at the moment just before his penetration or perhaps a few minutes later, at the moment of his climax, she disappoints the man: "I did not get what was promised to me. Now I will not give you what I promised." According to Abraham, frigidity is an ingenious strategy for diminishing the worthiness and significance of the penis.

With his discussion of the vengeful and emasculating frigidity of women Abraham recalls an analogous act of sexual vengeance by men. He refers his readers to an earlier paper of his in which he compares the common disturbance of male potency—ejaculatio praecox—to frigidity in women. In that 1917 paper he describes premature ejaculation as an "ejaculation with regard to the substance of the emission, and a micturition with regard to the manner of it." In the childhood histories of male patients afflicted with premature ejaculation, Abraham found infant boys who were difficult to train in matters of toilet cleanliness, boys who were bed wetters up to a late age, men who continued to react to any kind of excitement with a desire to urinate. Unable to attain pleasure through masculine genital sexuality, they turned "to what is for them the most intense pleasure—to the passive one of allowing bodily products to flow out."

As with the frigid female's passively inflicted, sadistic vengeance on males, this passive sexual attitude on the part of a man is the outcome of his sadistic-vengeful attitudes toward females. Many of these men seem to be characterologically lethargic, lacking in energy and masculine get-up-and-go. They strike the observer as decidedly unmanly. On the other hand, some premature ejaculators are hyperenergetic. They throw themselves into a state of energetic haste in everything they do —whether it is eating, drinking, playing, exercising, working, having sexual intercourse. Some of these more irritable-excitable hasty ejaculators also tend to be quarrelsome, to have fits of rage, to commit violent acts, to beat and harangue their wives and lovers. In the more lethargic, passive types, the underlying violence has been counteracted by the opposite character trait—cowardice. In their dreams, these same cowardly men very often express the fantasy of killing the woman by copulating with her. The cowardly premature ejaculator does not murder his sexual partner. Nor does the irritable premature ejaculator. They only murder her sexual pleasure.

Ejaculatio praecox, since it blunts rather than enhances the woman's sexual pleasure, effectively protects the male genital from castration by a vengeful father. "My father needn't worry, I'm still a little boy and not a real man after all. He can keep the wife. I keep the mother." Not surprisingly, men who suffer from this symptom also suffer from peculiar notions about the female genitals. They are fearful that they could lose their penis in the vagina during the sexual act. They exhibit a marked clumsiness in the performance of the sexual act and prefer experienced women who can help them guide the penis into the vagina —much as a little boy would enjoy his mother's manual guidance during urination. Thus, the man expresses a kind of childish love for the woman, but by soiling her *ante portas* with a substance he equates with messy urine, he expresses his hostility. In a more easily identified male perversion, the man takes all this infantile hanky-panky one step further. He takes on the "feminine" role and hires a female prostitute to urinate or defecate on him.

As much as premature ejaculators live in dread of the awesome vagina, they also look upon it as an inferior organ. They have an inordinately high estimation of the value of the penis. Abraham admits, but remains blissfully oblivious to, the personal import of his revelation: "Quite a number of those who suffer from ejaculatio praecox have a disdain for women in general; they cannot cease scoffing at their imperfections. In many cases this attitude is expressed in a violently affective antagonism to the present-day feminist movement."

Obviously Abraham understands something very important about why certain men would have a disdain for women. In the next few paragraphs he unwittingly reveals some other motives underlying the male denigration of women. Again with no hesitation, he continues his discussion of premature ejaculation by equating certain parts of male genital anatomy with femaleness and certain parts of female genital anatomy with maleness. The paragraphs in which Abraham compares premature ejaculation with frigidity reveal, unequivocally, the misinterpretations of female anatomy that will inform his later 1920 paper on the female castration complex. In frigidity the clitoris, "a male-like organ," has taken over all the excitement from the vagina. In ejaculatio praecox, the excitability of the penis is lost, so that the man's sexuality "has lost its specific male character."

> Ejaculatio praecox and female frigidity have still further corresponding characteristics. Besides a deficiency of genital sensitiveness there frequently exists in the male patients a particular erotogenic state of the perineum and posterior part of the scrotum. These parts correspond developmentally to the introitus vaginae and its surrounding parts. The relation between ejaculatio praecox and female frigidity might now be stated as follows: The leading zone in each sex has surrendered its natural importance to those parts of the body which are the equivalent of the leading zone in the opposite sex.

In his efforts to comprehend the riddles of the feminine mystique, Abraham brings to the surface the typical male fantasy that the male *inner* genital organs are intrinsically female. Abraham's method of differentiating male and female genital anatomy confirms my thesis that men who place an inordinately high value on the penis do so in the interest of repudiating their own passive, feminine, and infantile wishes. The three years intervening between his two papers did very little to modify Abraham's perspectives on the male and female genitals. Using the anatomy textbooks of the day for his rationale, he declared that since the perineum of males is a passive organ, it is the equivalent of a female genital; the clitoris, since it is an active organ, is the equivalent of a male genital. In 1920, as he discusses the relation between the female castration complex and frigidity, Abraham restates his original premise: "In cases of frigidity the pleasurable sensation is as a rule situated in the clitoris and the vaginal zone has none. The clitoris, however, corresponds developmentally with the penis."*

Abraham proceeds on the basis of this premise. He says that in some cases the vagina has lost all its sensitivity, thereby effectively erasing its existence. In other instances, vaginal sensitivity is retained but is experienced without pleasure. The contractions of the female organ that would ordinarily signify an orgasm are completely absent. "It is these contractions that signify the complete and positive reaction of the woman to the male activity, *the absolute affirmation of the normal relation between the sexes*" (emphasis mine).

Now, while I am not prepared to state that premature ejaculation and frigidity are perversions per se, I do maintain that these widespread sexual dysfunctions commonly labeled as neurotic do have *elements* of the perverse strategy. Certainly, for example, they are unconscious

---

* In 1966 Mary Jane Sherfey countered the still prevailing view that the clitoris was a male organ. She brought out evidence from anatomy textbooks on the human embryo that purportedly demonstrated that males and females were originally endowed with female genitals. "Female development pursues a straight course," while "male development can be considered as a deviation from the basic female pattern. . . . Embryologically speaking, it is correct to say that the penis is an exaggerated clitoris, the scrotum is derived from the labia majora, the original libido is feminine." Two years later Sherfey's evidence was called into question and largely discredited on the basis of her quoting the anatomy textbooks out of context. Sherfey was right to argue that the clitoris is not a male organ and that clitoral excitations are as central to the female sexual response as vaginal sensations. But arguments about the primacy of femaleness are what Simone de Beauvoir would have called counter-penis arguments. Theories that claim that male organs are female organs are simply shadow images of arguments that female organs are male organs. Female genital organs are female and male genital organs are male. On the other hand, feminine wishes in men and masculine wishes in women are acquired in the course of every child's growing up into manhood and womanhood. The problem for both sexes is the fear of those wishes and how such fears interfere with the mutual understanding between the sexes.

strategies that both conceal and reveal sadistic wishes toward the opposite sex. They murder pleasure and disguise an act of hate as an act of love. They are attempts to avoid knowledge of the primal scene mortifications by rendering genital sex as acts of infantile virtue: for the premature ejaculator, sex is a urination that keeps him tied to his mother's apron strings, but as a good little boy who won't be any challenge to his father; for the frigid female, sex is a virtuous submissiveness that assures everyone she is just a passive, clean little girl without any nasty, active, clitoral excitements that might invite parental retaliations. In the male sexual dysfunction, the man is unconsciously expressing his passive, submissive wishes but under the cover of trying to behave like a real man. In the female sexual dysfunction, the woman is unconsciously being active and dominating but under the cover of trying to be a virtuous female who doesn't care much about sex. Abraham was on to something about the kinship between frigidity and prostitution. By taking the active, dominating role and appearing to care about sex as much as or even more than a man, the prostitute, who typically is frigid despite her outward appearance of active sexual interest, is making conscious what is unconscious in her proper, middle-class sisters—the wish to be *more* than a man and more sexually potent than any man. The castration complex in the female disorder, frigidity, concerns a frustration of masculine wishes, and penis envy to be sure. But frigidity is also about the anxiety of exhibiting active sexual desire in a social order that forbids these desires to "nice" women and an envy of those who are entitled by convention to be active and penetrating and conquering in bed and elsewhere in the world.

In his version of the female castration complex and its effects on the female sexual life, Abraham focuses entirely on the external genital disparities in what I have interpreted as a typically male defensive maneuver designed to sharpen the frighteningly uncertain boundaries between biological maleness and biological femaleness, between masculinity and femininity. He declares, "The girl has primarily no feeling of inferiority in regard to her own body, and does not recognize that it exhibits a defect in comparison with the boy's. Incapable of recognizing a *primary* defect in her body, she later forms the following idea: 'I had a penis once as boys have, but it has been taken away from me.' " It is always ambiguous in these accounts of penis envy—and Abraham was certainly not the only analyst guilty of the ambiguity—whether the writer is speaking about a little girl's temporary feeling that she is defective or whether he is speaking of an actual defect. I find it impossible to accept that the ambiguity is merely an accidental slip of phraseology, especially coming from an analyst, who should know better.

If we take him at his word, Abraham is saying that females transform their biological anatomical *defect* into a less humiliating psychological loss. "I was born with a penis but someone stole it from me" is a fantasy more enhancing of self-esteem than the belief "I have been born without a penis." According to Abraham, a female's fantasy of getting back a penis that was stolen from her allows her to go on believing that she was born just like a male with all the bodily equipment that males are endowed with. In Abraham's simplified and biologically concrete version of female psychology, the girl takes comfort in the idea that she became "defective" only through treachery.

Little girls, frequently and consciously, and adult women, at least occasionally and unconsciously, do entertain the fantasy "I had a penis once, but it has been taken away from me." However, when Abraham declares that this female fantasy is a response to "a primary defect," he is confusing actual genital differences with an infantile fantasy of being phallic or castrated. His theory of the female castration complex represents a denial, or at best a disavowal, of the existence of the female genitalia—and all the unwanted knowledge that an acknowledgment of the clitoris, vaginal introitus, and female inner genitals would imply for female *and* male development. Essentially Abraham is going along with the childhood fantasy that caring women and devoted mothers do not have active sexual desires, that the sexual desires of normal feminine women can come to life only through a man whose penis will bestow her with erotic feelings and a true knowledge about the facts of life. His version of the female castration complex is another example of how infantile fantasies about the distinctions between penises and clitorises and vaginas persist in the adult and are often used as justification for social conventions and cultural mythologies about the biological superiority of the male sexual organs and the corresponding innate inferiority of the female sexual organs.

However, since we now realize that a little girl's temporary fantasy of the absent or stolen penis is only one facet of an intricate childhood mythology composed of numerous provisional misinterpretations about the differences between the sexes, what is it that a *woman* really wants, what is it that a *woman* imagines has been stolen from her?

A female's *forbidden* masculine wishes have the same disastrous impact on her life as the analogous forbidden feminine wishes have on the life of a male. What adult women and men want is to regain access to the parts of themselves that they have learned to distrust and fear in the course of growing up from childhood to adulthood. Yes, they do suffer from the sense that they had something once—powers, ambitions, longings that they had regarded as intrinsic to the little person they were—and that these precious treasures were stolen away. In a society where there are real and considerable disparities between the powers granted to men and the powers granted to women, the distinctions between male genitals and female genitals are a convenient way to symbolize all sorts of dissatisfactions, injustices, and disappointments. When the fantasy of a stolen phallus (a fictitious genital that is represented in fantasies and dreams by social trophies such as cars, pocketbooks, emeralds, babies, statues, paintings, mink coats) does come up in an adult woman's analysis, it is serving as a symbolic equivalent of a power that might compensate for many devastating disappointments and losses commonly suffered by females.

Paramount among these painful losses would be the loss of the soothing, protecting mother of infancy and the loss of the mother's positive value in a social order that denigrates females. Analysts have good reason to wonder why so many girls and women whose actual mothers were and are powerful, intelligent, protecting, generous, and tender create in fantasy maternal representations of demeaned servants, hysterical scatterbrains, and vindictive crazy witches. It is not unusual that in the transition from family life to the larger social order the girl begins to question her comfortable and easygoing identifications with the loving, protective, and admired aspects of her mother. If the girl discovers that this same powerful and beloved mother is a denigrated household slave or worthless female or is regarded by the father as a nagging witch, she starts to repudiate the feminine aspects of her own self. How much more self-enhancing it is to identify with the father, to idealize him as a knight in shining armor who will rescue her from the retaliatory witch-mother who is intent on mutilating her daughter's sexual and procreative organs. However, in the long run, this familiar solution of turning to the "good" father as a haven from the "bad" mother can only intensify a woman's anxiety that her sexual and procreative organs will be mutilated for daring to compete with her mother. Therefore, in this repudiation of her mother and affirmation of her father's superiority, she will also be losing the internalized sources of love, protection, and admiration that came originally from her mother. The loss of a protective inner mothering experience is among the more devastating losses that most females experience in the course of growing up into womanhood.

Some women defensively exaggerate their masculine identifications in a wholesale repudiation of femininity. In a compensation for this painful loss of a good internalized mother, they hunger for the power that men have and despise everything and everyone that reminds them of femininity. In this way, some women *do* become the crazed witch-mothers of the next generation of little girls and little boys. Yet others will retreat from the more integrated and wholesome identifications they have established with their mother to those exaggerated infantile ideals of feminine virtue—cleanliness, modesty, submissiveness, passivity—infantile ideals that are everyday confirmed by a social order with stereotyped versions of femininity.

The longing that is symbolized in an envy of an idealized phallus I would interpret as a longing for aspects of the self that have been lost in the course of trying to become a normal woman. Yes, there is envy of those who do not have to surrender these powers. What was once loved in the self and then lost or abandoned will be envied in those who are given the entitlement to own and keep those powers. The female child who grows up in a society with rigid role definitions of femininity and masculinity is each day discovering that the path to womanhood will be strewn with lost aspects of herself. As I have said, these social stereotypes of gender will sometimes encourage her to repudiate her femininity. She will try in every way, straightforwardly or deviously, to belittle women in order to gain the power that men have. However, more common is the opposite and equally unfortunate female solution. If the girl has solved her infantile castration complex by going along with the gender stereotypes of her society, she will be learning to repudiate her masculine wishes and masculine identifications—an outcome that is disastrous to female development. Each day she is discovering that an array of intellectual ambitions and sexual strivings that she had valued as part of who she is and who she could be are considered masculine. She is learning that such ambitions and strivings are unfitting for virtuous, clean little girls who, if they want to catch a man, had better be finding their identities by developing relationships with others and by learning to cook, clean, and care for others. When she arrives at puberty, if she has not already abandoned, buried, and forgotten her active sexual strivings and intellectual ambitions, she must relinquish them before she becomes an adult woman, or she must disguise them sufficiently so that no one will be the wiser. Indeed, as I will demonstrate, a not uncommon female perverse scenario entails a masquerade of denigrated, submissive femininity that hides a woman's forbidden and dangerous "masculine" ambitions.

A little girl on her way to becoming a "normal feminine" woman can fall easily into the pattern of thinking of herself as a member of the weaker sex, of her mind as a vague and nonthreatening spiritual mist, of her sexual position as dependent and submissive. She becomes fearful of acknowledging in herself those vivid childhood experiences of emotional independence and intellectual power. The active erotic strivings that had been so much a part of her experience of who and what she was, are phallic strivings appropriate only to males. She gives up her active sexual desires and her active intellectual ambitions in the anticipation that one day she will fulfill her desires and ambitions through a relationship with a man.

Those women who could attain a sense of self only by forcing themselves into a stereotype of normal femininity do feel that they have been cheated, that they had something once, a very precious and marvelous sense of wholeness and narcissistic completion, but that somewhere along the way their treasures were stolen from them. Some women go crazy from having lost their treasures and having to be someone much less than who they once could have been. Other women decide to take vengeance on the world and their own bodies and minds by repudiating everything about themselves that is soft, tender, nurturing, and merciful and instead fit themselves into a caricature of masculinity, becoming harsh, cruel, rapacious, tyrannical—even if it means being cruel to their own body. Still others, those who managed, very often against enormous odds, to keep the intelligent, logical, wise, curious, venturesome, commanding, courageous parts of themselves alive, would learn that they had better keep these characteristics and ambitions and strivings hidden behind a stereotyped femininity of intellectual vagueness and exaggerated submissiveness—or somebody *would* steal their treasures away.

Nevertheless, we've come a long way since Abraham's catalogue of frustrated and vengeful women. Women have thrown away the parasols and garden hoses that Abraham saw as symbols of their repressed masculine wishes; they have pursued careers, callings, and professions that their mothers and grandmothers would have considered unfeminine; they have discovered within and on the surfaces of their bodies a vast erotic enterprise.

Sadly though, the phallic-castrated fictions and feminine-masculine gender stereotypes that held sway at the beginning of our century have not changed that much. Even though contemporary end-of-the-century women are outwardly very different from their beginning-of-the-century counterparts, they are still struggling to make sense of the losses they experience in growing up into womanhood. And now that the heyday of sexual liberation is over, very few women fool themselves that erotic freedom and enlarged erotic sensibilities will improve their relationships with men. There is more sex, plenty of it and in a multitude of variations that are celebrated in porno magazines and porno TV shows and in ordinary R-rated films. But commercialized, consumer sex is not at all the same as liberated sex. It is simply another, more devious way of keeping the gender fictions of masculinity and femininity firmly in place. If anything, now that women have greater options in work and sex, men seem to dread them even more than they ever did. The mythologies about the anatomical differences between the sexes persist and continue to create a state of mutual distrust and sexual antagonism between men and women. Fortunately, largely through the efforts of female analysts and the critiques of feminist writers, the sources of these mythologies and the reasons for their proliferation and persistence have been reassessed and reinterpreted. Unfortunately, some of these reassessments have helped to reinstate the old gender tyrannies, but in a new guise.

In 1922, one of Abraham's analysands, Karen Horney, attempted the first critique of his theory, in the essay "On the Genesis of the Castration Complex in Women." Horney did not solve all the problems raised by her analyst's provocative thesis, nor did she confront some of the fundamental issues I have been raising. However, she had the courage to challenge the premises of her analyst's views on female psychology. Since Horney was herself training to be an analyst, she wanted to be respectful of Abraham and Freud. Her rather fierce arguments were, as she delicately put it, "wrapped in a little cotton-wool."

Horney argued that what had seemed too self-evident to need explanation—the female disadvantage because of her genital "disadvantage"—was not acceptable. "The conclusion so far drawn from the investigations—amounting as it does to an assertion that one half of the human race is discontented with the sex assigned to it and can overcome this discontent only in favorable circumstances—is decidedly unsatisfying, not only to feminine narcissism but also to biological science."

Horney was not about to contend that females do not experience castration reactions and penis envy. What she was looking for was a more satisfying explanation for penis envy. In thinking over her personal analysis with Karl Abraham and her own work with several female patients, she came to believe that a little girl's development is feminine from the beginning. A little girl is *not* born as a little man who must be transformed into a normal little motherly woman via the magic wand of penis envy. Penis envy is the outcome of the little girl's disappointment in her sexual love for her father, *not* the other way around as Abraham had proposed. The little girl does *not* turn to her father to acquire a penis. Her desire for a baby from him does *not* originate in a wish to obtain a substitute for her lost penis. She does *not* become a little woman because her desires to be a little man have met with frustration. The crucial emotional event in a little girl's life, Horney asserted, is the frustration of her feminine longings for her father. It is this oedipal frustration and disappointment that motivates the girl to abandon aspects of her inborn feminine nature, reject her identifications with her mother, and identify thereafter with the more advantageous and idealized characteristics she attributes to her father. As Horney saw it, the most harmful outcome of the female castration complex was that many women were led to repudiate their "innate" femininity and to defensively acquire masculine traits.

Horney was on the right track when she would not accept that penis envy was derived from a little girl's reactions to her biological inferiority. She was right, more right than she may have realized at the time, to insist that the significant questions have to do with the psychological context and eventual outcomes of that envy, which we now realize reside in the defeats and mortifications of the "oedipal" primal scene. It makes a great deal of difference whether a girl's envy of the penis is based on a sense of innate anatomical inferiority or whether it is a secondary reaction based on the disappointment of her infantile wishes and desires.

But Horney did not go far enough. She was trying to prove that little girls turn to their fathers in a "natural" way and not out of a disappointment with their mothers. While it is true that girls turn to their father for motives other than disappointment in the mother for their shared genital inferiority, Horney's implication that female babies come into the world equipped with an innate femininity that endows them with an innate attraction to the opposite sex was misleading, wrong, and, I think, surreptitiously misogynist. In human beings, where fantasy plays such a large part in erotic desire, female attraction to the opposite sex is no more a biological given than any other femininity.

A human being is born female or male, and during puberty a person undergoes profound hormonal changes that induce femininization and masculinization of the body according to his or her biological sex. Femininity and masculinity, however, are social concepts relating to sex role stereotypes, gender ideals, and gender conventions. A female acquires her femininity in the course of growing up in a family and social order with all kinds of stereotypes, fantasies, and ideals about gender. The femininization of her body during adolescence will decisively influence her femininity. But even during puberty when biology plays such an impressive role in shaping gender identity, the body and mind of the adolescent girl are not a blank slate on which anything can be written. In hunter-gatherer societies the adolescent's body is scarified, mutilated, literally carved into a standardized femininity or masculinity, literally written upon to bring her or his errant sexual desires and ambiguous gender identifications under control. Nevertheless, even in these societies that require for their subsistence a nearly absolute gender conformity, the scarifications and mutilations represent an effort to reconcile opposing tendencies—circles and lines, sun and moon, hard and soft, ancestors and descendants, masculine and feminine, past and future.

In modern societies, what is "written" at puberty is psychological rather than literal and therefore theoretically open to reinterpretation and revision in the future. A female child's femininity arises gradually over an entire infancy, childhood, and adolescence in a context of coming to terms with the gender conventions of her social order. In saying that femininity is not a biological essence, I am not diminishing its importance. A coming to terms with social gender conventions is not a resignation or a surrender or a forced matching of oneself to a gender stereotype. It is the gender stereotypes of femininity implied in theories of essentialism that I am objecting to. Indeed, gender stereotypes of femininity are always employed by philosophies and social doctrines that would assign women some biologically determined, innate femininity. Whenever a myth of primary femininity crops up— and it has appeared at least once in every century and two or three times in our own age—it is associated with reactionary social trends and with gender stereotypes of femininity. Some of the characters are the virgin mother, the household guardian, the perfect mother, the child bride; some of the characteristics are maternal sexlessness, intellectual vagueness, eternal caregiving, submission.

Psychological femininity always includes some degree of identification with the femininity of the father (and the father's mother *and* father) and some degree of identification with the masculinity of the mother (and the mother's father *and* mother). For that reason alone, a female's femininity would include masculine characteristics, identifications, desires, and ideals. A female who strives for pure femininity can achieve only a caricature of femininity—a female impersonation that is, as I will show in later chapters, a perversion of feminine gender identity. Women who conform to gender stereotypes are women who have been arrested at a prestage of gender identity. On the other hand, a female whose femininity is arrived at through a series of solving and resolving the inevitable conflicts of being human is an interesting, dynamic, and complicated woman who is capable of evoking in herself the masculinity *and* femininity of her father or the femininity *and* masculinity of her mother and arranging and rearranging who she is and what she wants out of life until the day she dies.

The psychologically relevant questions are how a female gets to be a woman and what kind of woman she has gotten to be at any stage of her life. Biology ensures nothing except a basic core of gender certainty that one is definitely either male or female. And even that so-called core gender identity, which is not achieved until about eighteen months or so, is already contaminated by gender stereotypes. As I described earlier, two-year-old boys tend to externalize their gender dilemmas onto the environment and little girls of the same age tend to solve theirs through cuddling, fondling, and other immediate tactile experiences. Boys and girls are ready, at age two, to fall quite "naturally" into their gender stereotypical roles; males care more about adventure and exploiting the environment, and females care more about love and caregiving. However, this readiness for each sex to fall into some normalized gender role does not mean that human beings are destined for these roles by virtue of their anatomical differences. It is one thing to assert a primary vaginal awareness in little girls and quite another to insist that this bodily experience is tantamount to a natural, God-given femininity.

About these always difficult matters of nature and nurture, Horney vacillated. For example, in her early papers she portrayed the little girl as "naturally" flirtatious, coy, and seductive. Her later papers condemned these so-called natural femininities as social gender stereotypes. As Horney's career progressed, she more and more turned from her initial biological emphasis to a sociological approach. However, the unconscious fantasy life that brought out the relationship between these two perspectives on human development always eluded her.

Horney's revisions of the psychoanalytic theory of female psychology were immensely supportive of women's attempts to find alternatives to the patriarchal ideals and ideologies that are unfriendly, sometimes outrightly hostile, to female development. Whether or not a woman ever heard of Karen Horney, something new was in the air that was changing the way women were thinking about being women. Women who had been ashamed of their bodies and their menstruations, women who had repudiated their mothers and their femininity in order to fit into a male-dominated society were at last speaking to one another in their own voices about the ways they experience their bodies and the manifold ways that their own minds go about interpreting the world. The capacity of women to speak as women to other women about the concerns of women was a crucial first step in women's liberation. But it was only a first step and, like every other time in history when women were ready to take the second or third steps, women hesitated there and then slowly but surely retreated back into some myth or other about primary femininity.

To my mind, there are several ironies in this latest outcropping of primary femininity. The first of these ironies is that the myth is achieving prominence now, as it often has in the past, at a time when women are asserting their power, initiative, and authority and beginning to undermine the law of the phallus in family life and making a considerable and forceful impact on educational systems, legal institutions, and political structures. The myth is once again being manipulated by those hostile to feminist causes in support of political movements and social philosophies that would deprive women of the ownership of their bodies and minds. For example, the antiabortion, pro-life movement is founded on a myth of primary femininity that would have it that females are destined for motherhood and that sex, even procreation itself, is man's business. My questions, though, are not about these obvious hostilities toward women. But why have certain women chosen this moment in history to repudiate their masculine ambitions and strivings in favor of a mythical feminine destiny? What are they frightened of? It must be that some women are once again wanting to believe that there are such things as woman's good, virtuous business and man's bad, sadistic business. It must be that they are frightened of assuming power, frightened of their intellectual ambitions and active sexual strivings.

In their efforts to confirm and express what they assume to be their innate femininity, many women have turned to denigrating males and masculinity. They proclaim that only those bewitched females who deceive themselves into emulations of the idealized phallic male are guilty of wanting to achieve power in a phallocentric world. These "masculinized" women are said to be abettors of the male conspiracy to dominate and penetrate and violate and conquer and destroy the earth as males have done to women throughout the ages. Masculinity is equated with rapaciousness. Femininity is equated with nurturance and caring. Feminine ways of thinking and imagining are innately diffuse, vague, rambling, inchoate, volatile, dispersible, a veritable sea of milk and honey. Females are the spirit of the fluid, while males represent all that is solid, the firm, the tangible, the rigid and unchangeable, the measurable, the categorizable, the logical, the knowable.

These newest myths of primary femininity turn out to be a reflection of Abraham's prescriptions for normal femininity. Abraham claimed that women who cannot suppress the masculine side of their personalities are defective females. Some feminists hold to the view that when a woman becomes too logical, too assertively intellectual, she betrays her femininity and impoverishes her soul. In a final irony, in 1944 the psychoanalyst Helene Deutsch, whom feminists generally regard with good reason as a traitor, concurred with the myth of primary femininity:

Woman's intellectuality is to a large extent paid for by the loss of valuable feminine qualities: it feeds on the sap of the affective life and results in impoverishment of this life either as a whole or in specific emotional qualities . . . for intuition is God's gift to the feminine woman; everything relating to exploration and cognition, all the forms and kinds of human cultural aspiration that require a strictly objective approach, are with few exceptions the domain of the masculine intellect, of man's spiritual power, against which the woman can rarely compete. All observations point to the fact that the intellectual woman is masculinized; in her, warm intuitive knowledge has yielded to cold unproductive thinking.

Whatever form it takes, a myth of primary femininity always lends credence to the social conventions that define the positions—whether sexual or social—of domination and submission as respectively masculine and feminine. Unconsciously such positions are interpreted as phallic and castrated, respectively. Horney and Deutsch would have aligned themselves along opposite ends of the psychoanalytic spectrum and were diametrically opposed in their approaches to understanding female development. However, they were very much alike in that neither Horney with her later sociological emphasis nor Deutsch with her fundamentally biological perspective appreciated the intimate collaboration between the language of social indoctrination and the language of the unconscious. They did not distinguish between biological facts and unconscious fantasies about those facts. They did not reckon sufficiently with the unconscious fantasies that went into the creation of the phallic and castrated chimeras that are perpetuated in social sex role stereotypes.

Anatomically, the penis and the clitoris and the undifferentiated embryonic tissue out of which they both emerge are referred to in textbooks as phallic. That, of course, is where Freud and Abraham got the scientific rationale for their interpretations of the clitoris as an obviously pathetic penis and a less than glorious phallus. Biological technicalities can always be enlisted to enforce already existing social conventions. And a social convention or ideal can always be reduced to a biological imperative. To confuse matters further, sometimes a fantasy comes decked out as a scientific technicality and finds itself ensconced in an anatomy textbook or manual of mental disorders. Traditionally and in many religious rituals the male reproductive organ in erection has been designated as the icon of fertility—the symbol of all desire, the phallus. It is, or should be, evident that in its very exaggeration the phallus must be a caricature of masculinity. The phallus, the eternally erect male genital, has always been a strategy for denying the sexual vitality of females and, as I have been suggesting, for denying the inner genital vitalities of males. The phallus is a statement that the penis is the only organ that actively participates in the making of babies, while the rest of the male sexual-reproductive organs and the female sexual-reproductive organs (except for the "masculine" clitoris) are passive. In the olden days married women were instructed that if they wished to become pregnant they could accomplish that aim by sitting for an hour or so, or a day or so if necessary, on a long bench shaped like an erect penis.

The phallus is still generally understood as a symbol of fecundity, potency, and authority. And the exaggerated erect male organ is still widely employed as a figurative representation of phallic power. Objects that are shaped like erect penises, such as swollen nostrils, parasols, and garden hoses, are understood as "phallic symbols." When the ordinary person uses the terms *penis* and *phallus* interchangeably, that is one thing. But only out of confusion between ordinary language and technical language would a psychoanalyst speak of the anatomical penis as a literal equivalent of a phallus—and yet many of them still do.

When Freud termed the phase of development following the oral and anal phases the phallic phase, the confusions multiplied. Was Freud referring to the literal possession or nonpossession of an anatomical part or a child's interpretations of having and not having or an adult's regressive version of human genital anatomy? On this score Freud's texts are as contradictory and ambiguous as the scrambled double-negative texts of the unconscious, where the distinction between the real anatomical penis, the fictitious phallus, and the fetish are also never entirely certain.

Phallic, however, does seem just the right word for the fanciful and exaggerated powers that little boys and girls attribute to their minds and bodies when they are about three or four years old. The phallic fantasy allows them to disavow and put away everything about their bodies that is passive, inscrutable, uncontrollable, vulnerable. They imagine that they know everything and can do everything. By assuming this phallic position, they compensate for all the humiliations of childhood by imagining themselves as fecund, potent, authoritative, dominating, penetrating conquerors of the world. Both little girls and little boys exaggerate those qualities in themselves to make absolutely certain that their wishes to be sucked back into the mother's belly will not be granted. At that time in their lives, both little girls and little boys idealize the penis as a phallus—an awesome, eternally erect body part that is detachable, a trophy that can circulate from one family member to another.

The trouble is not with the unconscious meanings of *phallic* or *phallus* or the fact that little children misinterpret and exaggerate the powers of this fictionalized genital. The serious trouble, the suspicions and warfare between the sexes, starts when the social order designates those powers as capacities allowable only to those that possess the anatomical penis. The dilemmas the little girl will encounter in becoming a woman have to do not with the anatomical differences between her own genitals and the male genitals but with the interpretations and social meanings that accrue to those differences. When the presence or absence of the penis becomes the yardstick for categorizing human beings as sexually active or sexually passive, phallic or castrated, powerful or vulnerable, valued or degraded, dominating or submissive, then we are dealing with psychologically troubling issues for both sexes. These categorizations and dichotomized interpretations of the anatomical differences are made first by little children struggling to understand how their bodies function and where babies come from, but then later are perpetuated as the social order enlists these infantile dichotomies in support of its gender role assignments.

Central to my thesis about the sexual perversions, in males and females, is the idea that they are pathologies of gender stereotyping. When the infantile fantasies of phallic-castrated are carried over into the social conventions of femininity and masculinity, they will come to life in those grotesque caricatures of gender that in males have been given the label *perversion*.

Whereas Freud had warned that heterosexuality was not to be taken for granted as a sign of normality, Abraham assumed that heterosexuality was a self-evident fact of gender normality. Abraham was, as I have said, a generous and genial man and about most clinical and theoretical matters a rather venturesome analyst. Though I have used Abraham as my example of the misguided and unconsciously misogynist analyst, I am convinced that consciously he wanted only to help women to fulfill their natural biological destiny. Because he was so much himself a victim of the gender stereotypes of his age, Abraham was unable to appreciate that the feminine normalities he was assigning to females— passivity, submissiveness, expectancy, and the normal social roles of marriage and motherhood—could also find expression as perversion. My contention is that these social gender ideals of normal femininity are enlisted by the perverse strategy and become the hiding places for some of the female perversions.

Perversions are designed to accentuate regressive outcomes of the castration complex over the more advanced and less stereotyped, more mutable, and less rigidly fixed gender identifications and social ideals that girls and boys acquire in the course of arriving at womanhood and manhood. As I have been arguing, the present definition of perversion is derived from the psychology of males, and the definition itself is based on the infantile ideal of masculine virtue, virility. In the preceding chapter I showed how the manifest perverse scenarios of males put the focus on erection to lend expression to a number of other latent themes, primarily those concerned with shameful feminine strivings and a sadism toward the female body. The male pervert is aware only of a compulsion to repeat a rigid sexual scenario but unaware of his feminine strivings or the hostility and sadism that underlie his acts of love—this despite the fact that his perverse scenarios entail his assumption of feminine and infantile roles within the context of a sadomasochistic scenario.

Some perverse women are obviously "bad girls," with "kinky" sexual appetites. Because they enact their desires in settings that are easily identified as sexual, it is easy to locate these fallen women and to label their behavior as perverse. For example, in her manner of attiring herself in garters, black stockings, and leather boots, a call girl, a prostitute, or a go-go dancer transforms her body into the fetish object that turns a man on. She becomes the most valuable part of him. Without her, he is nothing. She becomes the phallic woman that is capable of generating his erections and orgasms. She complies in a denigration of her female body for which she gains revenge by demeaning a powerless and impotent man. But any woman is capable of transforming herself into an object of value that can circulate, be given away, and received.

In certain socially sanctioned sexual relations—in dating, courtship, marriage bartering, or marital power struggles—a woman is encouraged to think of her body as a commodity, an item of detachable parts that can be traded, given, and received, a container for phallic trophies like youth, beauty, and luxury. However, if she equates her intellectual and sexual powers with phallic trophies that can be detached, taken away, stolen from her, she will do everything in her power to deceive the world that she is only a helpless, passive, suffering, absolute feminine type. Some women might disguise themselves as normal feminine types—the obedient wife, the nurturing mother, the passive, surrendering mistress, the expectant receiver of the phallic goods—so that no one will ever suspect the extent of their wishes to possess, to be instrumental, to dominate, to penetrate, to take over, to will, to succeed, to win. Since the social order designates the feminine virtues that make a woman desirable and valuable, any allegedly normal outcome can be a subterfuge for perversion. The good wife who passively awaits the penis into her vagina and the good mother who devotes her life to child care are as likely to be involved in a perverse scenario as the kinky porno star.

A fetish is the concrete representation of an imaginary phallic trophy and is therefore any desirable or valued object that is detachable, replaceable, and capable of circulating from one person to another. Insofar as the anatomical penis is imagined as an object that can be given or taken away, loaned or stolen, insofar as it is imagined as being detachable, displaceable, and replaceable, it is no different from feces, children, gifts, amulets, money—all of which can be fetishized. Some women can feel confirmed in their feminine identity only when they are sexually excited and in a relationship with a type of man they have identified as a phallic man. They think of themselves as damaged and imagine the men they have intercourse with as possessors of the magical phallus that can fix them. By thinking of a penis as a phallus, the woman is transforming a penis into a fetishistic object. She is dehumanizing the man and making sure that her lover is only a penis and nothing more. In contrast to the anatomical penis with its ordinary weaknesses and strengths, the phallus is an idealized fetishistic object that has been designed to fix castrations, rectify mortifications, bring back the dead. All exchanges of desire that use human beings or parts of human beings as though they were phallic trophies that can be given or taken away are perverse transactions.

If her husband does not give her the sexual pleasure she has been anticipating, a woman can get her revenge by using her children for sexual fulfillment. "You did not give me pleasure, I will steal the child from you." If she is not given the phallic trophy of a baby from her husband, she can borrow a baby for a little while or steal one and try to keep it. The so-called maternal erotomania of child kidnapping is a perversion because it uses and abuses a living human being as though "it" were a phallic trophy meant to fix a castration or bring back the dead.

Men, because they have learned to externalize what they fear in themselves, tend to perform their perverse scenarios using actual stage settings, actual persons as characters and tangible fetishes as props. The manifest focus of a male perverse scenario is the erect penis and the sexual performance of the penis. This is not because a male is incapable of a larger range of erotic expression but largely because the typical male is frightened of the other, more inscrutable, uncontrollable, and therefore "feminine" aspects of his genitality. The sources of erotic pleasure in adult women are not as palpable and locatable as in adult men. In childhood, a female may keep her attention focused on the clitoris to escape knowledge of her less controllable and less tangible inner genital world. However, a woman's erotic life includes a vast network of outer and inner skin surfaces that are intimately connected, emotionally as well as physically, to her cryptic inner genital organs, and this buried and forgotten erotic potential is brought back to her, as welcome or unwelcome news, when she begins to menstruate. If this news is interpreted by her as yet another evidence of her "castration," the outer skin surface of her body remains as a locatable "place" where she can interpret and play out some of the more inscrutable sexual arousals that are emanating from inside her body. In "delicate self-cutting," anorexia nervosa, and other body mutilations such as hair plucking, polysurgical addiction, and some forms of cosmetic surgery, the skin surface of the body or the whole body becomes the arena of enactment. Through fantasy and symbolization, the skin or the hair or the body itself becomes the characters, the stage setting, and the fetish prop, the "place" where the abandonments of infancy can be rectified, the "place" where a woman can play out being both sexes in the primal scene.

Though sexual excitement and genital arousal will not always or usually be at the forefront of a female perversion, we should not be surprised to find fantasies, motives, and disguises analogous to those employed by male perverts. In another female perversion, "womanliness" itself is used as a masquerade that disguises the woman's forbidden masculine wishes. A variety of female impersonations and feminine gender stereotypes may be used to hide the sexualities and intellectual ambitions that women have learned to fear in themselves. I have already alluded to the perverse elements in the conventional female sexual dysfunction of frigidity, particularly the sadistic vengeance disguised as an act of conventional feminine virtue. Similarly, nearly every female perversion disguises vengeful sadistic aims beneath a cloak of feminine masochism.

The way I see it, the myth of primary femininity is itself a disguise for the forbidden and frightening masculine ambitions and strivings that "nice" women are not supposed to entertain. The conventional femininities of intellectual vagueness and exaggerated submissiveness are ingenious hiding places for what a woman imagines as a stolen phallic trophy. If a likely hiding place for a forbidden femininity in males is beneath the uniform of a transvestite businessman, policeman, and general, a logical place to begin looking for a forbidden masculinity in females is beneath the rustling petticoats of a conventional female type.

7

The Temptations of Emma Bovary

It is better not to touch our idols; the gilt comes off on our hands.

Madame Bovary

When he was an adolescent, Flaubert announced to his friend Ernest: "I dissect ceaselessly; I enjoy this especially when I come upon an element of corruption in something I generally considered pure and when I discover gangrene in 'nice' places, I raise my head and laugh." Years later he confessed to his lover, the poet Louise Colet, an innocuous quirk: "Beneath beautiful appearances I search out ugly depths; and beneath ignoble surfaces I probe for the hidden mines of devotion and virtue. It's a relatively benign mania, which enables you to see something new in a place where you would not have expected to find it." Louise had grown accustomed to Gustave's little penchant for paradox, his celebrations of what he seemed to be subverting, his way of undermining what he seemed to be glorifying. An incurable closet Romantic, Flaubert would be officially acclaimed as the head of the realist school. How right it was, then, that he should have created, as the centerpiece of his first realist novel, a heroine whose romantic illusions impelled her to transgress the social realities that defined her as a provincial wife. In deciding on a conventional female type for his protagonist, Flaubert was allowing his "benign mania" a vast arena in which to romp. Whereas a man was free to explore his sexuality, a woman had always to contend with desires that would lead her on and social decorums that would hold her back. Madame Emma Bovary was bound by the contractual obligations of the term *Madame*. However, Emma's adulterous passions and neglect of her motherly duties mark her as a threat, a subversive force, an underminer of the structures of the bourgeois family. Admire her or not, we sympathize with Emma's desire to give voice to her illusions. At the same time, the triteness and ineffectuality of her transgressions show her to be a casualty of the mediocrities that surrounded her.

Bovary was supposed to have been Flaubert's curative immersion in banality, an attempt to expunge from his writings the theological mysticism that just barely disguised the sadomasochistic fantasies in *Temptations of Saint Anthony*. "I am in an entirely different world now, that of a minute attention to the most banal details. I have my gaze focused on moldy mosses of the soul." The erotic extravagances of the saint were to be boxed in by the stoical impersonalities of the madame. But at every point of his novel, Flaubert, like his errant heroine, subverts and undermines his stated intentions. In a novel based on the life of a banal feminine type, Flaubert managed all unwittingly to allow his mania for perversity free rein.

I am not about to embark on one of those "wild analyses" of Emma's character or the character of her creator. However, I will be using *Madame Bovary* as the template for developing some of my ideas about the nature of the female perversions. Not by chance, as I was beginning to think about writing this book, I chose to reread *Madame*

Bovary and discovered there in one form or another, directly or indirectly, in every character and every turn of the plot the personal and social factors that facilitate the perverse strategy and also some prototypes of the female perversions that I had already discovered through my clinical practice and research. Since I would not use my patients to illustrate what I was discovering about the female perversions, I was happy to discover Flaubert's penchant for creating perverse scenarios. Moreover, Flaubert's condemnation of the gender stereotypes of his day was consonant with my thesis that these stereotypes are central aspects of the perverse strategy.

On nearly every page of *Madame Bovary* there is a fetish of one sort or another: not only the false beliefs and deceptive ideologies of social progress that were infiltrating the modern world, but a whole assortment of fetishistic icons from everyday life, the banalities that are always fetched up into something other than what they actually are—napkins in the shape of bishops' hats, country stews with Parisian names, green silk cigar cases, cradles in the form of boats, clocks inlaid with tortoiseshell, damascened rifles. *Madame Bovary* exposes the social conventions and social fetishes that inform and perpetuate the perverse strategies of men and women. Flaubert was appalled by the mindlessness of the Bovary world, the slightness of the intellectuality Emma strives for, the kitsch with which she envelops her vain desires, her lusting after social fetishes. But Flaubert did not place himself beyond the frailties of Emma. Like Emma, whose illusions of perfection always deceived and eluded her, Flaubert, who tormented over every word and phrase, dreaming that his music might move the stars, knew that the perfection he sought would elude him.

Flaubert warned his friend Ernest Feydeau, "Save your eternally erect penis for style, fuck your inkwell." Five years earlier in a letter to Colet, Flaubert had acknowledged that his pen would be expressing all that he had relinquished in actual life. "I no longer have a penis, thank God. I'll find it again when I need it, and that is just the way it should be." While at work on *Bovary,* Flaubert was always wanting to expose his obsessions and penchants and manias and weaknesses to Colet, whose body he caressed less than a half dozen times a year but whose adorable slippers he treasured away in a desk drawer and would occasionally interrupt his writing to stroke. One evening while writing one of these confessional letters, he paused in mid-correspondence to drink a glass of not very good rum. Intoxicated by the concoction of bad rum and the caresses of Louise's sweet-smelling slippers, he returned to his letter with a seven-page indulgence, comparing the merits of different writing styles to styles of shoes. The fetishistic atmosphere of his new novel permeates the concluding pages of Flaubert's letter to Colet.

I could give a course on the question of boots compared to literature. "Yes the boot is a world," I would say. What beautiful comparisons one could make on the buskin or the sandal. What a beautiful word is *sandale* and how impressive it sounds. Isn't that so? Those that have the tips which turn up in the form of a point, like moon crescents, and which are covered with gold sparkling spangles which are all burdened with magnificent ornamentation resembling Indian homes. They come from the Ganges River. With them one can walk in pagodas on floors made of aloe blackened by the smoke of perfume pans and smelling of musk. They drag one in the harems on rugs disordered with arabesque-like drawings. It makes one think of endless hymns of love satisfied. The *Marcoub* of the Arab peasant which is round like the camel's foot, yellow like gold, with coarse sutures tightening the ankles, a shoe made for a patriarch and for a shepherd, dust is becoming to it. All of China can be found in the Chinese shoe which is garnered with pink damask and which carries embroidered cats on its upper leather portion. . . .
This other literature is affected, light, twisted, of no consequence. The heel is so high that the equilibrium is defective. There is no more solid base and on the other hand one adds

padding around the calf, useless philosophical chatter. The academic chases and destroys the poetic; this is the rule of the buckles. And now we are in the hands of the anarchy of the cobblers. We've had the leggings, the moccasins, and the shoes of the mayor . . . the dulling noise of the Celtic galoshes . . . the tired, overused boots of the gay working girl and the awful worn-down boots of the knifers. One smells of rotten straw and the other of sewers. There are drops of tallow on the sentences of one and traces of shit all along the style of the other. . . . All these garbage products have to be thrown away. And one has to come back to the strong boots or the bare feet and especially stop at this point my digression of a cobbler. . . . Good night.

Emma's transgressions, her refusal to submit to the prescriptive normalities of a provincial wife, are expressed by her determination to find herself in another feminine stereotype. She would become a slave of love. Keeping in mind Flaubert's little penchant for paradox, we will not be taken in by Emma's feminine masquerades. As with any perverse script, beneath the surface of Emma's history we will find the unexpected in places where we least expect them to exist. We begin, though, as we must, with the surface, as Emma searches for the meaning of her own life by surrendering herself entirely to Rodolphe Boulanger. Her love for him is everything she has ever dreamed of, so immense that she imagines it could bring the stars to tears.

How little deserving Rodolphe is of poor Emma's slavish adoration. He is hard-hearted. And because he has spent a lot of time in the company of women, he is coldly calculating in his evaluations of Emma. He is devoid of any capacity to appreciate a yearning soul reaching for the stars. All he can hear are her trite words of love. For Rodolphe Boulanger, Emma Bovary is just another bored housewife, "yearning to live in town, to polka every night. Poor little woman. Gasping for love, like a carp on a kitchen table gasping for life. With three gallant words she'd adore me. I am sure of that. She would be affectionate and charming. Yes. But how would I get rid of her afterward?"

How unlike Emma he is: Emma, who would dare to sneak away from her marriage bed and snoring husband, knowing that she was protected from the villagers' eyes only by the misty dawn; Emma, who would dash breathlessly through the muddy countryside, setting up wooden planks along the way to protect her pretty boots—and all for just one hour of Rodolphe's caresses; Emma, who is willing to risk all to breathe life into her illusions. Rodolphe, on the other hand, is frightened of intimacy and cannot tolerate the untidiness of love. When the actual woman beneath the rustling petticoats begins to show, a man like Rodolphe cannot sustain his interest. The novelty of Emma's innocence falls away "little by little like articles of clothing." Exposed in all its nakedness, her innocence reveals "the eternal monotony of passion which has always the same form and speaks always with the same tongue." When Emma declares her passion—"I am your servant and your mistress. You are my king, my idol. You are so good. You are so handsome. You are intelligent. You are strong"—her phrases are to him no different from those of his past mistresses. Rodolphe can only assume that Emma's surrender is the same dreary feminine fakery. The bored housewife is a garden-variety siren. These women are all the same underneath. If you've seen one, you've seen them all. His narrow mentality cannot appreciate that a full soul very often must "overflow into the emptiest of metaphors."

A half century after *Bovary* was published, Edith Wharton, whose bold command of language allowed her now and again to touch the stars that Emma spent her life reaching for in vain, lamented the triviality of her metaphors in a letter to her erratic and careless lover William Morton Fullerton, a prodigy of her friend and mentor Henry James and a sophisticated journalist of vast erotic know-how. After a night of passion in which Edith had exposed more of herself than she had dreamed possible, Morton would not be satisfied until she also revealed her innermost thoughts. She began her letter of compliant revelation by explaining the differences between them—how he had spent his emotional life while she had been carefully hoarding hers.

And I'm so afraid that the treasures I long to unpack for you, that have come to me in magic ships from enchanted islands, are only, to you, the old familiar red calico and beads of the clever trader, who has had dealings in every latitude, and knows just what to carry in the hold to please the simple native—I'm so afraid of this, that often and often I stuff my shining treasures back into their box, lest I should see you smiling at them!

She revealed that when he held her she could not speak "because all the words in me seem to have become throbbing pulses, and all my thoughts are a great golden blur." Sometime later, recalling Fullerton's careless remark that she had the unfortunate habit of serving up "the stalest of platitudes with an air of triumphant discovery," she vowed never again to permit a romantic excess to slip uncensored from heart to pen. In her mid-forties, Wharton could be as effectively silenced by Morton's critiques as she had been at age twelve by her mother's haughty dismissal of the first line of her first attempt at making up a story. The twelve-year-old Edith Jones had started off her story with a social nicety about an untidy drawing room and her mother's only observation was, "Drawing rooms are always tidy." After that chilling commentary, Edith would not risk making up stories until three years later when she produced a racy novella, *Fast and Loose,* which she wisely kept secret from her mother and everyone else except her dearest friend, a girl very much like herself who dared to have intellectual and literary ambitions. But then Edith composed a mock review that was far more devastating than anything her mother might have proffered. "Every character is a failure, the plot a vacuum, the style spiritless, the dialogue vague, the sentiment weak and the whole thing a fiasco." The next year, Lucretia Jones, who kept a notebook of her daughter's poetry, saw to it that a volume of her verse did get published. Unlike fiction, which had to be founded on real events and hard facts, verse, after all, represented the vague stirrings of imagination and therefore was a suitable ambition for a girl. Edith would not publish anything else until 1890, after a decade of devoting herself to dressing up as a proper New York–Newport debutante, being courted, getting engaged, surviving the humiliation of a broken engagement and the illness and death of her beloved father, getting married, and suffering the wedding night and the three weeks of nonconsummation, the consummation, a henceforth sexless marriage, a "nervous breakdown," and the first of her husband's long series of mental collapses.

By 1908, the year she fell in love with Fullerton, she had become an immensely wealthy real estate heiress, a best-selling and highly respected writer of fiction, an intimate of Teddy Roosevelt and Henry James. She was fulfilling her childhood literary ambitions. Moreover, the content of her early short stories and novels made it clear that she had struggled against the entrapments of a stereotyped femininity. She had refused to be only an ornamental object; she had refused to appear as a fragile, innocent, lovely thing. She had won the first stage of her battle to be true to her powers. Something still held her back from assuming the reins.

How powerless she felt in the presence of Fullerton. She was unable to write. Even reading became impossible, as every page would be covered with his name. Edith determined to get hold of herself. But in the blaze of her passion, there was no longer any self to hold on to. "This pinch of ashes that slips through my fingers? Oh, my free, proud, secure soul, where are you?"

If a worldly navigator like Wharton could so lose her bearings with Fullerton, it is not surprising that Madame Bovary's provincial brain would have been totally befogged by Boulanger. How confused she was by the mélange of femininities he assigned to her—Madonna, friend, sister, lover. The day she surrendered to Rodolphe, Emma, who had never been fully sure of who or what she was, found her calling. She belonged in "that lyrical region of adulteresses." Emma found her self by losing herself in a stereotype. She moved from the oppressions of housewife into the tyrannies of adultery. She gave up one standard model only to acquire another. The sisterly voices of adulteresses sang to her and enchanted her. She will at last possess the joys of love and be granted

> that fever of happiness, of which she had so long despaired. She will experience passion, ecstasy, delirium. She was enveloped in a vast expanse of blue, where the sparkling heights of emotion lit up her every thought. Ordinary existence appeared to be far away, down below, in the shadowy valleys between the peaks.

Rodolphe Boulanger's words were so sweet they could make Emma cry and his caresses were "so ardent they drove her mad." Emma's protestations of love, her ecstasies, her deliriums, her platitudes were tiresome to Rodolphe. After a few months, he was so bored that he no longer even bothered to summon up sweet talk or ardent caresses. Rodolphe's glossy infatuation could not survive the impact of the real woman. As the reality of Rodolphe's dimming ecstasy dawned on Emma, it acted as a spur to her mad artistry.

> And so their great love affair, in which she had immersed herself, seemed to be subsiding under her like the waters of a great river being absorbed by its own sandy bed, and she was noticing the mud at the bottom. She wished to disbelieve what she was seeing; she redoubled her tenderness.

Emma's conviction that her life was meaningless without Rodolphe, her willingness to become an extension of him, her desire to comply totally with his wishes and desires, her disavowal of the muddy bottom that was belied by Rodolphe's majestic phallus, is common enough in certain women's attitudes toward the men who survive on their slavish adoration. Provincial housewives succumb willingly to their thralldom. Great novelists swallow their marvelous words and turn to ashes in the presence of the men who inflame their souls. But there is no precise word, either in English or in French, for such idealizations and subservient attitudes. The German word *Horigkeit,* which in English loosely means "extreme submissiveness" or "sexual enthrallment" or, more precisely, "sexual bondage," does capture the spirit of Emma's attitude toward Boulanger and Edith's toward Fullerton. When this subservience and submissive dependency on an idealized authority, an attitude typical of a young child toward the parents, becomes a pronounced feature of an adult relationship, it is tantamount to a perversion.

It was Krafft-Ebing who first made the distinction between the sexual masochism that is more typical of males and the sexual bondage that is more typical of women. However, he insisted that sexual bondage is not a perversion. When Krafft-Ebing discovered that next to fetishism, sexual masochism was the most prevalent perversion in males, he wondered why there were but two "scientifically established" cases of sexual masochism in women. He offered an explanation that confirmed the gender stereotypes of his day and obscured completely the nature of female desire. About women, Krafft-Ebing declared that "the instinct of feminine servitude is everywhere discernible."

> In women voluntary subjection to the opposite sex is a physiological phenomenon. Owing to her passive role in procreation and long-existent social conditions, ideas of subjection are, in women, normally connected with the idea of sexual relations. They form, so to speak, the harmonies which determine the tone-quality of feminine feeling.

Thus, an inclination toward subordination to men (which Krafft-Ebing conceded might be, in part at least, an adaptation to long-standing social conditions) is a normal manifestation of female sexuality. Masochism in females represents merely a pathological increase, an abnormal twist of the female's normal instinct of subjection. Sexual masochism, however, is another matter altogether. Sexual masochism is a perversion and females are not much given to that sort of expression of their instinct for subjugation.

These reflections on the differences between females and males brought Krafft-Ebing to the phenomena of *Horigkeit,* sexual bondage or extreme sexual submissiveness, which, "numerous as the examples of male *Horigkeit* are, every observer of life who is at all unprejudiced must allow that they are far from equalling in number and importance the cases of female *Horigkeit."* The reasons for this sex distinction were eminently clear to Krafft-Ebing. For men, love is only an episode, whereas for women, who after all have no other important interests, love for a man is the principal and central focus of their lives until they have children. To retain a man's love, a woman will make all concessions necessary to a male and willingly plunge herself into deeper and deeper bondage to him. All of this comes quite naturally to women.

Unlike sexual masochism, "sexual bondage is not a perversion and not pathological: the elements from which it arises—love and weakness of will—are not perverse." The sexual bondage of women, in that it is simply an aberration of a normal female trait, is *abnormal,* but not perverse. However, Krafft-Ebing agreed that certain oversexed females may become perverse. The transition from merely abnormal sexual bondage to perverse sexual masochism may take place in masculine females who by virtue of their "hyperaesthetic" natures are given to sexualizing love. Krafft-Ebing's ideas on these matters, quaint as they seem, are still prevalent. Males (and masculine women) are by birth predisposed to sexualizing love, whereas normal feminine females are predisposed to pure love and the weakness of will that lead them into sexual bondage.

The first of Krafft-Ebing's two cases of sexual bondage is of a Mr. N, an otherwise "mentally sound" man, with no traces of "constitutional taints" or "perverse sexual instincts," who nevertheless had been held for several years in "fetich thralldom" by an "avaricious and vindictive" woman who had captivated and controlled him until finally "this monster of a woman had brought the weak and infatuated N. to become the murderer of his wife and children." Krafft-Ebing portrayed this man as a victim of a nefarious woman.

His second case was Mrs. X, thirty-six years old and the mother of four children. In contrast to his male case, who was the helpless victim of a female, Mrs. X is depicted as the victim of her own degenerate femaleness. Mrs. X had never been entirely sound; when she was five she masturbated and throughout her childhood and adolescence was nervous, excitable, and neurasthenic. For the first nine years of her marriage to a man many years her senior, Mrs. X had suffered the tortures of unsatisfied sexual desire and therefore "yielded more and more to onanism." At last she succumbed to a man "in whose arms she found that gratification for which she had so long languished." But now she was tormented with guilt for her sexual transgressions and lived constantly with the fear that she would become insane or commit suicide. She made repeated efforts to give up this liaison without any success. Her greatest terror was that she might lose her lover.

She got deeper and deeper into the bondage of this man, who recognizing and abusing his power had merely to dissemble as if he would leave her in order to possess her without restraint. He abused this bondage of the miserable woman only to gratify his sexual appetite, gradually even in a perverse [sic] manner. She was unable to refuse him any demand.

In the early 1940s the psychoanalyst Annie Reich treated several women whose submissive dependency on men who held them in sexual thralldom was sufficiently extreme to qualify as *Horigkeit*, which she translated as "extreme submissiveness." In each case, the woman's daily life was pervaded by the fantasies that bound her to her enchanter. Her sexual thralldom was the center of her existence and she considered nothing else in her life meaningful or worthwhile. Reich speculated that there must be men who display similar attitudes toward the haughty women who hold them in sexual bondage—the familiar Blue Angel scenario. Reich, however, had found these pervasive and exaggerated attitudes of submissiveness only in her female cases. As we will see at the conclusion of this chapter, this female perversion illuminates some of the latent fantasies in the Blue Angel perverse scenario said to be typical of males.

By now the extremely submissive woman is legendary. During the late decades of the twentieth century, women who are slaves of love have been seeking therapy with increasing frequency. And books that describe the plight of women who love too much or women who persist in falling in love with the wrong kind of man are runaway best-sellers.

In Krafft-Ebing's time, the average woman would have had little opportunity to breathe life into her romantic dreams of submitting to some dominating and powerful male. Her wayward desires *and* her wanton torments would have been held in check and nicely disguised by the costumes and attitudes of the normal, ordinary, submissive housewife, the perfectly feminine woman, the ideal of womanhood. The normal woman was resigned to achieving her childhood ambitions by adopting a passive-expectant, submissive-adoring attitude toward the man who loved or married her. However, this "willing" subjection to a male was not by any means instinctive, as Krafft-Ebing contended. It was a matter of survival for a woman who wanted to have a husband and children. As Abraham prescribed, to achieve normality the woman must become "reconciled to her own sexual role and to that of the man, and in particular to the facts of male and female genitality; she desires passive gratification and longs for a child. Her castration complex thus gives rise to no disturbing effects." If her submissiveness were not *extreme*—with its implication of caricature—Abraham's normal woman who survives by adapting to the passive, submissive roles society expects of her does not sound very different from Emma Bovary, Edith Wharton, Mrs. X, Reich's patients, and the countless women of our modern world who persist in loving the wrong kind of man.

Now the *extremely* submissive woman has been liberated to explore the depths and range of her spiritual and sexual dependencies with any man she chooses. Whereas sexual intercourse with some dreary husband might have been a chore at best, now sex with the right man can be an experience of extraordinary intensity. And now convention no longer requires that she be burdened with a sexually bumbling husband or be tormented with guilt if she betrays her wifely duties. However, as we are finding out, torment and mental anguish are as much a part of the liberated woman's sexual scenario as they were for poor Mrs. X.

The *Horigkeit* script begins with a deception, a dominant theme that diverts us from the whole story—a fetishistic device. When the extremely submissive woman first tells her story to her therapist, she reports that her soul has been burned to ashes by her passion for a man, who because he grants her extraordinary sexual pleasure has been elected as the only right kind of man to penetrate her vagina. In these early moments of therapy, the question to the therapist seems to be, "Is that pleasure permitted or forbidden?" The focus is put on issues of sin and guilt. One woman is married to a decent and considerate but sexually and socially unexciting man and is hoping that therapy will relieve her of guilt and thereby give her permission to elope with her lover; another is unmarried but wants to marry her fiery but elusive enchanter; still another woman is wishing to free herself from the man who holds her in bondage and forevermore to entrust her body and mind only to a caring and considerate man, but she cannot give up the sexual ecstasy. However differently she presents her plight, each woman is highlighting her quest for sexual pleasure. For the moment, she is hyperconscious of her feelings of guilt, but the torment, the abuse, and the humiliation she suffers are experienced as incidental or secondary features, the unfortunate side effects of seeking sexual pleasure. If these torments could be eliminated, they would no longer interfere with the woman's capacity to obtain full sexual pleasure: "If only I didn't have to suffer so for love."

The woman is not aware that her torment is an essential ingredient of her sexual pleasure, that she actively creates situations that will torment her. She tortures herself by imagining her lover with other women. She lives in dread because she leaves evidence of her love affair for her husband to discover. She lets slip the words and phrases that are guaranteed to invoke her lover's contempt or rage. She evaluates the goodness in her life as worthless and pitiful so that she can come to her magnificent lover in a state of worthlessness and deprivation. It takes time for her to recognize that she seeks her torment with dedication, that she must abase herself, remain in a state of humiliating subjection, so that her lover can remain in his position of domination.

Horigkeit, like all perversions, is a full-time occupation. The woman afflicted with *Horigkeit* lives only for her moments of ecstatic *unio mystico,* the sexual union in which the man's mighty phallus confirms the outlines of her feminine self. Without this she is relentlessly self-critical; she sees herself, for instance, as fat and sloppy, her legs too short, her nose long; she never knows how to dress right, her haircut is shabby and dull, her work is nothing much, and she is socially inept and intellectually dishonest. She is quick to acknowledge that she is nothing without her lover. She speaks of her lover's erect penis the way the fetishist speaks about his lover's pink satin slippers or blue velvet scarf. With it inside her or potentially inside her, she feels complete and whole and good and electrifyingly alive. Convinced that she, as herself, worthless and defective as she believes herself to be, could not possibly be loved, that only a phallic being is deserving of love, she comes to her therapy armed with her lover's penis as the trophy of her power over her therapist. As much as she is longing for compassion and understanding, she is convinced that only power and domination make a person valuable. Better to display with pride her defiance of the moral order. Better to torment and dominate her therapist with her terrible plight than to admit how frightened she is of being abandoned. As the slave of love knows all too well, love can always be taken away, but power is eternal.

She is bound to her lover because only an eternally erect penis, a phallus, can confirm her femininity. With him inside her she is a woman, yes, but not like those other, ordinary women—her mother, her sisters, her friends, her therapist. When things are just right, the look in his eyes confirms her very existence but especially her extraordinary femininity: "No other woman can do for me what you do. I am nothing without you. You are Everywoman, madonna, sister, friend, lover, angel." The only events that count in her life are those magical moments when she is encircled in her lover's phallic aura.

What she is waiting for all day is the reunion with her Great Man, who might, just might, see her for one hour later that evening. When separated from her lover, the slave of love feels as though she does not exist, as though she resides in an empty world. Without him the terrible anxieties, the depression, the madness that she is always keeping at bay threaten to become conscious. At the beginning of such an attachment, the woman will experience only a mild apprehension of doom and attribute this unpleasant feeling to her sinfulness, her need for secrecy, and her guilt at having a clandestine affair. Later an experience of torment and a sense of impending disaster begin to take on serious and devastating proportions. Separations from her loved one bring on feelings of panic. When she is separated for too long from the man that resurrects her being, the slave of love succumbs to a nameless and terrible dread. She trudges through the day like a zombie. At other times, as a distraction from these feelings of deadness and emptiness, she is on the go, moving from here to there, aimlessly. Through it all, she is waiting for him, thinking of him, preparing her body for him, bragging to her friends of his beauty and charm, complaining to them how bad he is for her. Then, sooner or later, there is the magical reunion, the restitution of a feeling of worth and well-being, of aliveness.

Not infrequently, after the first days or months of ecstasy, the man pretends disinterest or in fact becomes actually impotent, bored with sexual intercourse; he becomes aloof and distant. In situations of sexual bondage, it is not unusual for sexual intercourse to become less and less central to the relationship. After a while, sex is practically nonexistent except as a facilitator of the woman's humiliation. A heightened eroticism plays a considerable part in the initial stages of her bondage, but finally it is not her lover's capacity to provide erotic pleasure that binds the woman to him but his ingenuity in creating a situation of submission and dominance.

> With the narcissistic entitlement of those who hold themselves aloof from any intimate relationship, Rodolphe soon detected other delicious pleasures to exploit in this love affair. He decided that all modesty was now inconvenient. He treated her coarsely. He made her into something compliant and corrupt. On her side, she was hypnotized by a kind of idiotic infatuation: adoration of him and voluptuousness for herself, a numbing euphoria; and her soul, sinking into that drunkenness, shriveled and drowned.

The longer the man refuses or is unwilling or disinterested, the greater his emotional distance, and the longer his disappearances, the more valuable he becomes to the slave of love. The more he neglects her or threatens to leave her, the more the woman submits to his power. The more profound her feelings of loss and despair, the more ecstatic the reunion. The woman allows herself to be lowered to a state of abject humiliation, despair, and panic so that she can be resurrected to a state of sexual ecstasy. By granting or withholding his penis, the man enables and facilitates these cycles of castration and restitution, abandonment and mystical reunion, death and resurrection.

Why would any woman put up with such conditions? Why does she stay in a relationship with a man who repeatedly humiliates and abuses her? It is hard to believe that a woman entrapped in a scenario of sexual bondage would not accept kindness or tenderness or satisfaction or pleasure without torment, if it was offered to her.

However, what we are observing in these scenarios entails a force more powerful than a quest for pleasure. Nor is the woman seeking pain either. The manifest erotic pleasure and the psychological pain of bondage lead the observer astray. The latent elements in a perverse scenario cannot be deciphered exclusively through a language of pleasure and pain, a language of desire and fulfillment. Perverse performances are about desperate need. The actresses and actors are using penises and vaginas as instruments for playing out the repetitive cycles of castration and restitution, abandonment and reunion, death and resurrection.

In perversions, the compulsion to repeat a trauma is decisively more powerful than the seeking of pleasure and the avoidance of pain. Those who offer comfort or concern or understanding watch helplessly as an entire life gets used up, bit by bit, in an effort to maintain these cycles of castration and restitution, abandonment and reunion, death and resurrection, until sometimes the dread punishments are meted out. It is as though the slave of love is seeking castration, abandonment, and death through the medium of love and pleasure. The only one who can save her from the terrible fate that awaits her is a tyrant who knows how to calculate the delicate balances, a hard-hearted person who knows just how to keep the cycles going.

Ultimately, the *Horigkeit* script is about unbearable losses, profound depression, and death. What is going on is a desperate attempt to master a situation of trauma, a series of childhood traumas so indelible that the pleasures and satisfactions life might offer are given up to mastering the traumas.

The game that is being played out with penises and vaginas is an adult version of the "there it goes, now it has come back" game of infancy. There comes a point in every childhood, usually around the age of eighteen months, that the little child becomes aware of the independent comings and goings of her mother. While the child sometimes feels that she cannot go on existing without the mother, the mother comes and goes as she pleases. The little girl wants to be able to tolerate her mother's disappearances without having to cry and protest like a baby. So she invents a game that enables her to feel that she has some control over the cycle of loss of love and the return of love. At first she still needs her parents to participate in the game. She takes all her toys and throws them one by one into corners, under beds, behind doors, so that the whole family has to get involved with hunting for them, picking them up, and returning them to her.

As she played this game one little girl would give out with an "o-o-o-o," voicing the pleasure and satisfaction she got from hiding her toys and having people find them. The mother realized that the inarticulate "o-o-o-o" was her little girl's way of saying "gone." A few months later, as the little girl learned how to play the game on her own, her mother watched and understood more. Each morning before her mother and father went to work, the little girl would play with a wooden toy wagon on a string. The girl did not pull the wagon along behind her as it was meant to be used. She threw it over the edge of a couch and watched it disappear with a mournful but excited "o-o-o-o" and then slowly pulled it back toward her and watched it reappear with a joyous "b-a-a-a." For a while, the "gone and back" game was more important to the little girl than food or cuddling or fun and games with her parents. Then, as the little girl got used to the idea that loved ones would go away but would always come back, she stopped playing the game and pulled the wagon along behind her in a light-hearted, playful way. The ordinary life of pleasure and pain was restored and went on.

The difference between the childhood game of "gone and back" and the adult game of extreme submissiveness is that the latter is deadly serious and unending, a full time preoccupation. Moreover, the cycles that are repeated in the adult game, by virtue of their being played out with genitals and not little wagons on a string, are highly eroticized and heavy with moral implication. The adult "gone-back" is about a love that was once given and a love that was taken away, but in circumstances that were so overwhelming that the child could not make sense of the loss or master it. Perverse scenarios are about the ordinary pitched at the level of the extraordinary. They are not outside the range of human experience.

Ordinarily, growing up consists of a series of emotional losses that are compensated for by a series of gains. First, in the land of milk and honey the average baby is given the kind of nearly unconditional love that infants typically evoke from their caregivers. The mother mirrors everything the baby does in such a way as to enable the baby to feel as though she has created the world around herself. But before too long the baby is expected to begin to fit her desires and powers into daily routines of her family and to accommodate herself to the desires and powers of her parents. In the average family, there is an unspoken understanding between parent and child that the loss of the mirroring love will be compensated for by the acquisition of a new kind of love and the pride and sense of power that come from being able to learn new things and master new skills. Slowly but surely, the average child gives up some parts of herself that once made her feel grand and powerful and exchanges them for other qualities that are more in keeping with the social order in which she lives. But little girls and little boys are not so submissive as all that. All children are little perverts. They keep the relinquished part hidden behind the screen of the normal part and are always busily sneaking in pleasure, snatching pleasure from defeat. Every adult human being has a perversion lurking in his or her neurotic compromises and so-called normal attitudes.

The legends of finding love and losing love, of mourning the losses, of refinding the lost loves, of immortalizing our past loves in our present loves are embedded in the narrative of every human life. For all of us there will be those irreconcilable injuries and humiliations that persist and infiltrate adult existence. They may become the seeds for despair, for those monotonous repetitions of losing love and regaining love, of humiliating others and getting humiliated ourselves. Or, as so often happens, the leftover traumas can be incentives for change, challenges that keep us striving to refind the lost perfections of childhood.

For some children, however, the ones who got just enough mirroring love to survive and to become human but seldom as much as they were yearning for and seldom at the right time or in the right place, the loss of a love that once existed is senseless. They cannot comprehend why once, or once in a while, or every so often, they had experienced some moments of mirroring admiration and tender care but now the parents no longer applaud the things they had once in a while loved the child for. As she tries to figure out why she has been dropped like this, why she has been cast away, why this terrible thing has happened to her, a little girl cannot imagine that it is due to some weakness or failure or cruelty or ugliness in her mother or father. It must be because she has been bad, because she is worthless, because she has committed some terrible crime. From then on the child is always asking herself, "What is this terrible crime? What awful thing did I do or wish to do that makes me deserving of banishment? Why were my powers taken away from me? What were they? Where are they?" She does not feel compensated in any way for her terrible losses. She is convinced that her parents no longer love her because she is stupid, mean, ugly, a creature of no value at all. When such a little girl grows up into womanhood, she feels she is nothing at all. And if she does have any powers, she makes sure she keeps them hidden, or they will once again be stolen from her.

She gets her revenge, though. She learns how to snatch pleasure from her defeat. She is neat and tidy, but her closet and her dresser drawers and her bedroom are always in a state of chaos. She sucks her thumb until she's fifteen and drives her mother crazy. She plucks the hairs from her scalp until she is nearly bald. She starves herself nearly to death. By committing such terrible crimes she makes some sense of why love was taken away. She extracts justice from these defiant pleasures. And her little perversion, which is at first committed in secrecy but then made known to the world by the messy room, the wrinkled thumb, the bald spots, the emaciated body, is her triumph. And with all its display of self-hatred and suffering it is a show of power, an act of vengeance on those who took love away.

When she grows up she sneaks a dirty, clandestine pleasure in a scenario that repeats the cycles of losing love and refinding love. Each time she has sex it is a crime and another attempt to understand the crimes she committed as a child. Each time the sex is an act of vengeance on the ones who gave love and then took love away. Each time she awaits the terrible punishment that will surely come—the castration, the abandonment, the void. She seeks over and over again to make sense of the senseless losses she experienced as a child.

A woman who starts out with a conviction of her own worthlessness can find sexual pleasure only in a fantasy of being part of a more powerful personality and of overcoming her inadequacy in this way. But such idealization can only breed envy. For if a woman feels she cannot survive unless she is attached to some idealized phallic being, sooner or later she will resent and envy his power.

There are moments of violent rage when the extremely submissive woman becomes conscious of her extraordinary resentment and envy toward the man who has the power to give or deny her his magnificence. How much in this extraordinary power he resembles the almighty parents who also gave but then denied her their love, who went away but then did not return until she was frantic. But her Great Man, whom she has endowed with absolute power, the power of an almighty parent, an omnipotent god, is typically exploitative and narcissistic and very often an experienced con artist who thrives on his power over such women. And she will cooperate with him by disbelieving any perception of hers that might belie his magnificence. Despite an unconscious envy that would destroy him, her god must be kept in his position of power. For he confirms who and what she is and he knows just how to maintain the cycles of love lost and love regained. One way of keeping a tyrant in power is to imagine that he might choose another slave. And this fantasy of the rival slave—what she looks like, where she lives, what she does, and how she does it—becomes another torment but keeps the image of the almighty one glowing.

Sometimes, though, the "tyrant" is an ordinary man, a man who must go to work every morning and return late every night; a man whose interest in philosophy makes him seem like a powerful god but also abstracts him and makes him seem distant; an unexceptional man whose departures and returns are more important to the woman than his actual presence. He becomes invested with tyranthood by virtue of his physical and emotional comings and goings, which are interpreted as a giving of love and a taking away of love. In extreme submissiveness the erotic desire is not directed toward an actual person but rather toward a situation of tyranny. The sexual partner qualifies not on the basis of who he or she is but for his capacity, willing or otherwise, to assume the role of the tyrannical controller of the "gone-back" game.

That is why Rodolphe is irresistible to Emma. Because he is so cold, rational, calculating, and instrumental, Rodolphe can excite the submission of Emma. When Rodolphe decides that Emma is longing for his sexual domination, it is as though he arranges for her seduction in the woods of Yonville less for his sexual pleasure than for her enlightenment and education. He will save her from her dreary existence. Nevertheless, his calculations include the idea of abandoning her. The moment he decides to capture Emma, he is wondering, "But how would I get rid of her afterward?" The threat of abandonment is an essential ingredient of a perverse script. The master could never dominate the slave unless that threat was paramount.

The perversion must be able to protect the respective separate roles of slave and master and contain the cruelty of the master within a carefully regulated script. The perverse enactment arranges for possibilities of bodily violation and mutilation, threats of separation from the master, threats of abandonment, threats of annihilation and death.

The slave acquiesces to her bondage because she trusts the master's capacity to control and manipulate the threats. A tyrant must always be potent or the slave feels castrated and abandoned. A Rodolphe can retain his position of domination only through an Emma's strivings to submit. When the slave of love begins "to see the muddy bottom," she redoubles her efforts to keep her tyrant's image pristine. Reality is a feeble adversary of the fantasy of union with the perfect man who mirrors everything the woman ever wished to be. The muddy bottom can always be camouflaged by a fantasy of the eternally erect phallus that, in her mystical union with him, she imagines as belonging to both of them.

When at the age of eighteen Sofia Andreyevna Bers married the thirty-five-year-old Count Tolstoy, a wealthy landowner and prominent writer, and she confessed that she would ask nothing more of life than to "make myself a serious feminine world" and "love nothing and no one except Lyova," we can believe that social convention prevented her from making an independent life for herself. Marrying an important man like Tolstoy would have been considered achievement enough in a young girl's life. However, even the compliant little Sofia was soon complaining to her diary:

> I can't find any occupation for myself. He is lucky to be so clever and talented. But I'm neither the one nor the other. One can't live on love alone; and I am so stupid that I can do nothing but think of him. . . . I have given my life to him. I live through him.

As she grew older, Countess Tolstoy longed for engaging work. She was always imagining new schemes, wishing for some activity she might devote herself to other than her adoring love for her magnificent Lyova. "What was reverie and fancy ought now to become serious work—a *real* life, not merely a life of the imagination." By the time she wrote those words, Sofia Tolstoy was already immersed in a very real life: thirteen pregnancies, the raising of the nine children who survived, sewing shirts for the entire family, managing her husband's estates, staying up late into the nights peering through a magnifying glass trying to decipher her husband's manuscript corrections, copying and recopying his writings, including seven rewrites of *War and Peace* alone. Each day she would try to leave a bit of time to play the piano and develop her photographs. But the countess never managed to have a *real* life that was *her* life.

Every day analysts are hearing, in one form or another, of the extreme perfectionism of the brave woman who has come to confront her internal demons and make sense of the repetitive scenario that is consuming her life. She has no trouble at all confessing to us how worthless she is. She will reveal quite openly that she is never satisfied with her appearance or the value of the work she does. One of Reich's patients declared that she could never find a composition book of the "right" size in which to copy the most complicated matters of science in the "right" order. Another patient would spend days on end until she found the right dress, the right pair of shoes, the right words for a letter. In the end nothing was ever right. She continued to feel like a crippled bird, a castrated nothing, a clumsy oaf with two left feet, a dumb bunny, an intellectual fake. Still another, after looking for years for the right notebook and working at her thesis on the nature of reality, managed to solve her personal and philosophical dilemmas by marrying the philosopher she worshiped, feeling certain that through her extraordinary passion for him she would discover the nature of reality.

Extreme submissiveness is an expression of a prevailing and enduring social mythology about the respective powers of females and males. The special kind of perfection these women strive for is a perfection that can be achieved only through having intercourse with a superstar, a man with a huge brain, a huge amount of money, a huge reputation, a huge penis.

Nor does it matter if reality confirms these attributions of hugeness and infallibility. If the man does not actually possess these qualities, the social order has fetishistic images enough for any man to become the perfect phallus for any woman. Any man in uniform might do— general, fireman, policeman, judge. Depending on the unconscious appeal that a social stereotype holds for the woman, the continually erect penis could be attributed to a black man, an Italian man, an Irishman, a rabbi, a priest, a crippled man, a man covered with tatoos, a man with a patch over one eye.

The phallus of the great man has been imagined, created, fabricated by the woman with as much dedication and passion as it requires to compose a symphony, paint a painting, direct a play, invent a machine —any talent that the woman may possess but is afraid to expose to the world. Count Tolstoy was a great writer, a man of wealth and power. His actual greatness did not depend on Sofia's submission to him. Nevertheless, he found it convenient and emotionally gratifying that Sofia should have time to devote herself to her own ambitions only after first giving virtually all her energies and devotion to supporting his. On her side of the bargain, Sofia invested her already great and tyrannical husband with sexual and moral tyrannies that kept her enthralled and him ensconced in his position of domination.

Edith Wharton could recover from her enthrallment to the man she had endowed with a magical phallus. Though her mother's disparagement of her ambitions was experienced as a loss of love and a humiliation, it also acted as a challenge. Edith Jones was able to sneak her mischievous tale *Fast and Loose* and then turn her perverse victory into a clever defeat by criticizing the writing more harshly than her mother ever could. Her mother looked askance at her "long words" and accused her of having "less heart" than her brothers. Following the mother's example, most of the household called her Puss or Pussy, but her brother Harry, who suspected the tough intelligence under the frilly dresses, amused himself and teased the Puss by calling her John.

Edith detected how her mother's chilling matter-of-factness had shriveled the literary imagination in her father. "I have wondered what stifled cravings had once germinated in him, and what manner of man he was really meant to be." Edith's father had communicated his yearnings for the loose and the fanciful, endowing his daughter with an unassailable conviction that she was destined to one day fulfill his unexpressed longings and unfulfilled ambitions. Very likely this unconscious bond between Edith and her father took the sting out of her mother's critiques. Her words did not squelch her daughter's literary ambitions. Instead they acted as an incentive. Edith's sexual strivings were another matter. She would keep her sexuality hidden and unexpressed until she was forty-five.

Even then, Mrs. Wharton could allow herself sexual fulfillment only in a clandestine relationship with a man who came and went in ways that were agonizing to her. Nevertheless, after two years of Fullerton's "inconsistencies and incoherences," Wharton declared that her "own sense of worth" would not allow her to accept his cruel and capricious treatment of her. "My life was better before I knew you," she wrote to him. "That is, for me, the sad conclusion of this sad year. And it is a bitter thing to say to the one being one has ever loved [*sic*] d'amour." She tells him how lacking he is in that capacity for complete surrender, that *aimer d'amour,* which is to love with all self-giving love. And then two and a half years after this angry and bewildered, half-hearted attempt to free herself from her enthrallment to Fullerton, Wharton was able to repossess her self-esteem and her trust in the felicitous metaphors of her own frank and straightforward language. What she then wrote to Fullerton exposed the intimate ties between Fullerton's superficial character, his literary dandyism, and the falsity of his "aimer d'amour." After reading his stilted and affected manuscript on international politics, Wharton advised Fullerton to "adopt a franker idiom." Where she had once written to him extolling his literary virtues, the marvelous way in which he could instantly discriminate "between the essential and the superfluous in people and things," and his "radiant reasonableness," she now tells him that his work has been hung "with all the heavy tin draperies of the *Times* jargon—that most prolix and pedantic of all the dead languages. . . . You've read too much French and too much *Times*. I can't too strongly urge you to drop both tongues for a few weeks, and go back to English."

Wharton had been only slightly touched by *Horigkeit*. At the age of forty-five she had allowed herself to surrender to the sexual ecstasies of her *aimer d'amour* just long enough for Fullerton to awaken her "from a long lethargy, a dull acquiescence in conventional restrictions, a needless self-effacement." Wharton's capacity for romantic surrender had enabled her to bring to life, in Fullerton's arms, an extensive sexual repertoire that managed to dazzle her experienced lover, who regarded her at least the equal of any of his previous or concurrent lovers, a veritable George Sand in the disguise of a proper American lady who kept a tidy drawing room. However, most women who surrender themselves to a situation of sexual bondage are more like Sofia Tolstoy than Edith Wharton. Most slaves of love are captivated by that perverse romanticism that leaves them with no wings to soar.

Extreme submissiveness resembles the more familiar romantic love, which is also an ecstasy of *unio mystico,* a sexual passion so intense that it dissolves the boundaries between the lover and the beloved. The difference is that in a romance, a true *aimer d'amour,* the surrender, the mystical union is mutual. Neither actor in the glorious sexual partnership is required to enact the role of slave or master, except playfully or occasionally. In romantic love the slave-master fantasies and enactments are meant to enhance sexual pleasure. It is quite the other way with *Horigkeit,* in which the eroticism is elaborated in the service of psychological or physical torment. The extraordinary romantic surrender of ordinary falling in love becomes a perversion when "the only possible sexual excitement consists in the feeling of one's own insignificance as compared with the magnificence of the loved one." Then we are dealing with the moral tyranny that is a crucial aspect of the perverse strategy.

The feature, for example, that defines Wharton's affair with Fullerton as perverse rather than a simple grand passion, a marvelous self-enhancing romantic love, was her insistence on her worthlessness and her willingness to accept his tyranny over her. Moreover, we know from her diaries and letters and fiction that Wharton was preoccupied with issues of sin and guilt. Before and after Fullerton, she would not make up or imagine a love affair that did not entail some person's profound mental and physical torment. When it came to the conflict between desire and authority, Edith Wharton was always appeasing the authorities. Her eroticism could flourish only in a forbidden relationship where sin and guilt were conscious. But what then was unconscious?

Why did Edith Wharton insist so that her treasures were nothing at all? Why did she swallow her lovely words in deference to a man who she realized had so little capacity to appreciate the poetry of love? We ask, "Why do so many modern women insist that they have no wings to soar, that they are crippled and castrated, that they are nothing?"

The slave's bondage to her master is a cover story that conceals a multitude of meanings. The perversion of sexual bondage brings into the foreground the social stereotype of feminine submissiveness with its heightened consciousness of sin and guilt and its exaggerated abject humiliation, but it does so to assuage anxiety and keep hidden other shameful and forbidden crimes.

Flaubert warned us that a glorious surface may conceal a vulgar depth, that the moldy mosses of banality may be the camouflage for a flourishing jungle of romantic excess. The banality of extreme submissiveness is a cover story. Embedded in the manifest scenario of extreme submissiveness are some latent themes that are more pronounced and manifest in the other female perversions we will encounter.

As part of the scheme of extreme submissiveness, there is a hyper-consciousness of guilt about a sinful sexuality, but nevertheless an aspect of guilt that remains unconscious. Even the abasement and humiliation in extreme submissiveness are a cover story for a shame that associates power with greed and rapacious, sexual virility—a caricature of masculinity. One of the reasons the extremely submissive woman is so frightened of her powers is that she associates power with trickery and betrayal, with rebellion and defiance, with sadism and domination. In these glorifications of suffering and worthlessness we suspect that someone is paying for stolen treasures. Someone is keeping hidden the delicious powers that everyone assumes she has given up.

For example, as a patient's life is being consumed by her bondage to the great men who always abuse her, we sometimes discover that the slave of love has been building another life, a stronger life, where she has been becoming a master. All the time she has been suffering from her erotic enthrallments she has been making lots of money in her business, or becoming a successful doctor, or preparing hundreds of paintings for an exhibition, or delivering lectures on microbiology. These powerful, masterful activities would arouse massive conscious anxiety if she did not do something to appease the gods. And there is also the unconscious guilt at having surpassed the gods who have the power take love away. If a woman had a mother who drudged her life away, slaving in the kitchen or in the family candy store, this woman is not supposed to make a fortune as the owner of a gourmet food shop. For surely she would be castrated and abandoned unless she paid for this terrible crime by becoming the suffering mistress of a womanizer who made her into something compliant and corrupt. A truly feminine woman is allowed to passively submit to her faithless lover, but she is not entitled to become a neurosurgeon while her father is a pharmacist and her two brothers are simple country doctors. A woman whose parents are concentration camp survivors is not supposed to win a Guggenheim grant unless she pays heavily for having survived her ambitions and won. She must not marry a generous, considerate man but only a hard-hearted narcissist who will abuse her and reduce her soul to ashes. And sometimes her triumphs of ambition and intellect must also be surrendered before the woman feels allowed to survive. And, therefore, if she feels she has not paid enough for her triumphs, she may allow her lover to abuse and destroy her emerging talents along with abusing and destroying her soul.

Under the cover of the suffering life that the "authorities" are watching, another secret life is being sneaked in. Sofia, after all, did steal time away from her endless copying of *War and Peace* to peek through lenses at the world around her, take photographs, and develop them, activities that very few women or men of her day knew anything about. Edith Wharton, who had been temporarily silenced by the "radiant reasonableness" and sparkling wit of Fullerton, was appeasing the gods but all along preparing herself to write about the "untidy drawing rooms" of her childhood and the adulterous and incestuous love affairs that would have appalled her mother and to win the Pulitzer Prize for *The Age of Innocence*. Under the cover of suffering, crimes flourish. The torment of sexual bondage is a sort of pay-as-you-go plan. If the slave pays by surrendering her soul to her master, then she can continue with her forbidden occupations until the next bill comes. One forbidden occupation is her sexuality; the other is her intellectual ambition.

There is more. Under the mosses of bondage, something lush is going on. If real power is a crime that will bring castration and abandonment, there is still another way to be more powerful than the almighty others who have the power to take love away. The slave of love turns her defeat into victory and the master's victory into defeat. She has more pride in her self-inflicted suffering than he can ever have in abusing her *aimer d'amour*. "I ask for my pain. I frustrate myself because I choose to do so." "It is not you who robs me of love, I rob myself." There is the pride of conquering a sense of helplessness by manipulating others—her friends, her husband, her therapist—into sadistic, guilty, or helpless responses. Her pride in her enslavement to her lover makes everyone else impotent. Even with her lover, whom she allows to dominate and tyrannize her, she somewhere comprehends that her abject surrender has more power over him than if she were to rebel. The obedience of the slave kills the commands of her master.

Because she does not resist her enslavement, she proves that she can endure anything. There is pride in being an exception, a special victim of fate. "I ask for my pain. I have more pain than anyone." The scarred wrist, the whip marks, the cigarette burns, the bald scalp, her exhibition of her masochistic submissions to her master are her badges of triumph.

Thus the suffering and self-denigration of extreme submissiveness and other female perversions are methods of avoiding retaliation. The idea is to buy love with suffering, to appease in order to maintain a life-giving, vital relationship with the almighty other. Suffering is a seduction of some critical, rejecting Other. And this is a theme in every perversion, male or female, for the worthless one must always retain the hope that one day love will come back. If she is to survive separation and castration anxiety, depression and madness, she must be able to go on believing that the almighty gods who abandoned her in childhood have not disappeared forever.

Emma's affair with Rodolphe culminates in a decisive abandonment. Rodolphe deserts Emma on the eve of their planned elopement, throwing her into a profound melancholy. Months later, after Emma has nearly recovered from her black despair, she runs into her former platonic lover Léon Dupuis. She completes her recovery by unconsciously arranging a situation that enables Léon to seduce her. The slave has been watching her master, and when he abandons her and releases her from bondage she keeps him with her forever by identifying with his powers and emulating his masterful ways. Emma has learned a few lessons about submission and domination, and she does not hesitate to use them in her next love affair. With Léon, she assumes the initiative from the start. Léon finds his soul in Emma. Léon goes along with everything Emma believes, all her tastes, all her desires: "He was becoming her mistress, more than she was his. His soul was carried away by her sweet words. Where, where had she learned this corruption, so pervasive and yet so artfully concealed that it was nearly intangible."

Now Emma knows the ropes. She turns the tables. She manipulates the distances between herself and Léon like a professional tyrant. Emma sets the scenes and controls the interludes of romance, arousal, and consummation. Like a sexually starved housewife who has acquired her first lover, Léon sighs, "At last I have a real mistress." It is clear from the beginning that Emma will be dominating Léon. Now Léon is the slave of Emma.

In Emma, Léon has found the perfect woman. His mother had warned him that Emma was the transgressor of family life, one of those perverse masculine women, a Medusa, a temptress, a monster. Léon had no patience with his mother's foolish lectures. For him, Emma was a lady of style. She was the woman of love in the novels he had read. She was the *Odalisque Bathing,* the feudal chatelaine, the *Pale Woman of Barcelona*—and "above all Angels."

After a few months the serf becomes frightened and wary of the power of his feudal tyrant. Léon tries to resist his enthrallment, his increasing submersion into Emma's personality. "He rebelled against Emma for her power. He resented her because of this constant victory over him, even tried to steel himself against desiring her; and then at the creaking of her boots he felt himself go limp like a drunkard at the sight of whiskey."

And one day when Léon fails to show up to their hotel room, Emma has only contempt for him. In her rage she thinks of him as "incapable of heroism, weak, banal, softer than a woman—greedy and cowardly too."

As with the occasional woman who is afflicted with a male perversion—fetishism, transvestism, exhibitionism, sexual masochism—a man afflicted with *Horigkeit* might be said to be afflicted with a female perversion. Charles Bovary, who dies clutching a lock of Emma's hair, and Emma's second lover, Léon Dupuis, have found the feminine parts of themselves in a Blue Angel scenario of sexual bondage to Emma.

Charles was ruled by a mother who had been emotionally abandoned by the father. She had turned to her son for fulfillment.

Bovary's mother kept him tied to her apron strings; she would cut out cardboard dolls for him, tell him stories; keep up an interminable monologue of melancholic gaiety and cajoling baby talk. In the emptiness of her life she transferred all her shattered little vanities and thwarted ambitions to her son's head. She day-dreamed of important stations, envisioned him grown up, tall, handsome, and witty, making his career as a civil engineer or a magistrate.

So Emma had thought she would find the fulfillment of her thwarted ambitions in marriage to a doctor. But from the day they were married it was evident that Emma would be the dominating spirit and Charles the obedient, adoring one. "It was he who could have been taken for the virgin of the night before, while the bride exposed nothing that could reveal anything." Charles was enthralled by Emma's feminine graces and could hardly stop himself from constantly touching her rings, her shawl, her hats with fluttering veils. What joy, what fulfillments as he gazed at her combing out her long tresses or arranging her skirts and fichus. For Charles, "the universe did not extend farther than the circumference of Emma's petticoat." And when Emma's body became full and ripe with child, Charles's happiness was complete.

Baudelaire was the first to call attention to the uneasy mixture of feminine and masculine traits in Emma's character. He recognized at once that Flaubert had "infused into the veins" of this most feminine of creatures a great quantity of "virile blood." "Like Pallas, sprung forth fully armed from the brain of Zeus, this strange androgyne harbored all the seductive charms of a man's soul in a most attractive woman's body."

In the midst of his commentary on the fetishistic interchangeability of substances in *Madame Bovary*—things turned into humans, humans beings turned into things, men becoming women, women becoming men, Vargas Llosa refers to the ambiguities in Emma's moral character, where corruption is mistaken for virtue, where selfishness is mistaken for charity. He entitles this section "Madame Bovary, a Man." He demonstrates how the lack of precision in Emma's morals is reflected in the fluidity and uncertainty of her sexual identity. "Beneath the exquisite femininity of this young woman a strong-willed, determined male lies hidden."

Emma's entire manner began to alter as a result of her compliance with the erotic demands of Rodolphe. "Her gaze became bolder, her talk freer. She even had the impertinence to parade with Monsieur Rodolphe, a cigarette in her mouth *as though to purposely defy the whole world.* At last those who were still in doubt doubted no more when she appeared one day, stepping down from the Hirondelle, her waist squeezed into a mannish-styled, tight-fitting vest."

By submitting to Emma's masculine powers Charles could express his forbidden feminine strivings and still be reassured of his masculinity. At the same time he could adore with impunity the femininities that were forbidden to him. In his enthrallment with her gestures, clothing, hair styles, he could enwrap his soul in femininity and no one would be any the wiser.

Strictly speaking, a *Horigkeit* scenario is neither particularly female nor male. The attitude of extreme submissiveness, which Emma Bovary assumed in her affair with Rodolphe Boulanger, was a hiding place for her masculine ambitions. Charles Bovary, who craved to lose himself in sexual bondage to a woman who would dominate him with her haughty unavailability, was looking to fulfill his feminine wishes. Since it is a central aim of the perverse strategy to disavow the differences between the sexes or generations, in a perverse scenario, who is humiliated child and who almighty parent, who is on top and who on bottom, whether penis or vagina is the magical phallus, who is masculine and who feminine are arbitrary assignments. The roles are interchangeable. The submissive one is identifying with the powers of the dominating one. The dominating one is fulfilling in the submitting one the parts of himself or herself that are forbidden and shameful.

While these sorts of cross-gender, cross-generational fantasies are present, consciously or unconsciously, in every sexual relationship, what we witness in a perversion is a tyranny of gender roles, an imperative, repetitive, stereotyped scenario in which masculine wishes must masquerade in the caricature of submissive femininity and feminine wishes must disguise themselves in the caricature of masculine virility.

In his Emma, Flaubert is always putting something new in a place where one doesn't expect to find it. The outward appearance of the fainting and expiring virgin, the silk petticoats, the straw hats with fluttering veils, the delicate lace fichus, the pink satin slippers, the Algerian scarves, the religious melancholies, the romantic clichés are Emma's frailties and also her strongest weapons. With these feminine frivolities she masks her dominating spirit, her desire to penetrate the veil of illusion. Says Flaubert, "A man, at least, is free; he is able to explore all passions and to range the world, surmount obstacles, savor the most exotic pleasures. But a woman is constantly thwarted . . . at once excited by the susceptibilities of the flesh yet held in her place by social convention." Emma masqueraded as a sexually submissive *femme évaporée* to conceal from the world, and from herself, her active sexual strivings and intellectual ambitions, which in her world were the prerogatives of males.

8
Masquerades

> "More clumsy I couldn't be." And—and—(here she hesitated
> for a word and if we suggest "Love" we may be wrong, but
> certainly she laughed and blushed and then cried out) "a toad
> set in emeralds."
>
> Orlando, wondering who she/he is

When, in the early years of this century, Vita Sackville-West strolled along Piccadilly and sat at the cafés of the Palais
Royale masquerading as a young man named Julian, no one recognized
her as the well-bred wife of the diplomat Harold Nicolson. In her pose
as Julian, the lover of her adorable Violet Keppel, soon to be married
to the impotent Denys Trefusis, Vita enjoyed fantasizing what people
would think if they knew that the handsome boy with the *"voyou"*
appearance was "the silent and rather scornful woman they had perhaps
met at a dinner-party or a dance." No doubt about it, a large part of
Vita's satisfaction was her ability to put one over. "I never appreciated
anything so much as living like that with my tongue perpetually in my

cheek, and in defiance of every policeman I passed." When at Monte Carlo, a mother and father eyed Julian as a prospect for their daughter and a French officer exchanged war reminiscences with *him*, Vita's triumph was complete.

Granddaughter of a Spanish dancer and a milord, daughter of their illegitimate daughter, who married her father's immensely wealthy and noble nephew, Vita was brought up at Knole, a palatial country mansion allegedly containing as many staircases as there are weeks in the year and 365 rooms to match. A slave-master mentality was integral to her aristocratic breeding. She grew up with a conviction that, in human relationships, there were only two possible positions, one of rapacious domination and the other of docile submission. She cared more for palaces than for people, and she admitted that she loved her dogs more than she loved any of her friends. She had contempt for the blacks, the Jews, and the proletariat and despised the middle class. Democracy was a plague, *la populace* a menace. In her gardening column for *The Observer,* she spoke to her humble suburban readers about gardens with moats around them. The garden that she and Harold would create after they became Lady and Lord Nicolson had a moat, a moat walk, a lime walk between the nuttery and the rose garden, two hundred cyclamens, and an aviary. Her gardens were considered works of art. She nurtured her flowers and trees and birds with all the tenderness and concern that a fairy godmother might bestow upon a beautiful princess.

Her female lovers were quick to intuit the moral and sexual ambiguities that made Vita so entrancing. At the height of their affair, Violet scribbled a note on a scrap of paper: "The upper half of your face is so pure and grave—almost childlike. And the lower half is so domineering, sensual, almost brutal—it is the most absurd contrast, and extraordinarily symbolical of your Dr. Jekyll and Mr. Hyde personality." Vita knew that her lover was referring to her potentials for good or evil, but she also appreciated the double intent of Violet's words and knew that Jekyll and Hyde referred to the feminine and masculine sides of her personality. She claimed that she was too weak to struggle against this duality in her personality. However, there was no real contest. The good Dr. Jekyll got very short shrift in Vita's scheme of gender. Aside from her enduring affection for her husband and her sporadic flashes of tender concern for the welfare of the many lovers who were quite ready to abandon husbands, children, mansions, and occupations all for a night, a week, a year, an eternity of love with Vita, Vita rarely exhibited her feminine side. Dr. Jekyll's outlets were the gardens, the gardening columns, the birds, and the dogs. Vita embraced the harsh, domineering Mr. Hyde persona while trying her best to prevent anyone, including herself or her two sons, from recognizing the caring, nurturing, conventional Dr. Jekyll.

Virginia Woolf was another lover whose appreciation of the complicated desires of the fabulous Vita survives in written form. In a letter she tells Vita that there is "something reserved, muted" a "central transparency" that fails her in her writing. Upon reading this Vita writes to her husband, "Damn the woman, she has put her finger on it. There *is* something muted. What is it, Hadju? Something that doesn't come alive. I brood and brood, feel that I am groping in a dark tunnel." In *Orlando,* the novel that Vita's son Nigel would call "the longest and most charming love letter in literature," Virginia grants to Vita one boyhood and manhood after another, tosses her gaily about from one sex to the other, costumed as a sexually avid Elizabethan youth, a sexually experienced duke in the service of King James, and later transformed into a ravishing woman whose form combined "the strength of a man and a woman's grace," a Turkish ambassador who could dress in those Oriental coats and trousers "which can be worn indifferently by either sex" and decorated by strings of emeralds and pearls. After Turkey Orlando is returned to England and admitted to the literary circle of Alexander Pope. His/her early mornings are devoted to lounging about the library in a "China robe of ambiguous gender," late mornings to gardening in heavy knee breeches, middays to attending luncheons in flowered taffeta, afternoons to visiting court sessions in a lawyer's gown and wig, evenings to junketing about the streets and alleyways of London dressed as a dashing nobleman in search of the usual macho excitements.

Nigel appreciated the versatility of this public love letter and all that it meant to his mother. "Virginia by her genius had provided Vita with a unique consolation for having been born a girl, for her exclusion from her inheritance, for her father's death earlier that year. The book, for her, was not simply a brilliant masque or pageant. It was a memorial mass."

In her autobiographical confessions, Vita makes evident her conflicted feelings about her own mother who, perhaps mercifully, was frequently off on the Continent visiting her lover. "Mother used to hurt my feelings and say she couldn't bear to look at me because I was so ugly." "Although the most incomprehensible, she is certainly the most charming person on earth, whom I adore." Little Vita was determined to be hardy and brave, "as like a boy as possible." Not just any boy, but a boy who enjoyed dominating the playmates who were willing to obey his commands and tormenting the unlucky ones who would not, "stuffing their nostrils with putty and beating a little boy with stinging nettles." The will she drew up at age nine confirmed the general impression of Vita's vigorous tomboyishness. To her mother and governess she leaves some conventional V-shaped brooches. To her father she leaves her pony and cart, a cricket set, and a football. Other males are the recipients of her whip and her ships. A neighborhood boy is to get the bounty of Vita's playroom: "My armour. My swords and guns. My fort. My soldiers. My tools. My bow and arrow. My pocket money. My target."

After her tumultuous affair with Violet, Vita never again dressed as a Julian. She retired to the countryside and, except for the occasional flowered taffetas when she showed up in London in the role of her husband's dutiful hostess, adopted permanently the traditional garb of the Kentish countryside—man-tailored rough shirt, big-pocketed leather jacket, sturdy whipcord jodhpurs tucked into knee-high heavy workman's boots.

I agree with Robert Stoller that a female transvestite, like any other *overtly* masculine woman, has "a lifelong daydream with the theme that if she were a man rather than a woman, she could undo the past and find a loving mother inside some female erotic partner." Perhaps a few of these mothers and daughters were present in Vita Sackville-West's sexual relationships with women. Was Vita yearning to find a loving mother in her female sexual partners? Was she always wishing that if she were a man, then her mother might love her? From the time she was a little girl, Vita knew that because she was a female she would never inherit the palace with 365 rooms. Even though she was an only child, Knole would have to go to the nearest male heir. Was she always wishing to one day get the trophy of power that would have been the sign of a mother's true love? Neither her own autobiographical confessions nor Virginia Woolf's love letter, which concludes by restoring Vita to Knole, gives us decisive answers to those questions. It is not even entirely certain that Vita was a genuine transvestite. We do know that Vita Sackville-West learned very early to conceal her femininity, which she equated with a loathsome vulnerability, in the costumes and attitudes of a brutish, masculine type. There is certainly something perverse in Vita's desperation to find her feminine identity in a caricature of male virility, her equating of nurturance and surrender with a susceptibility to debasement, her division of the world into phallic and castrated beings.

As we near the end of this century, we have become accustomed to seeing women in jeans, pantsuits, trousers, and man-tailored outfits complete with button-down oxford shirt and tie. We scarcely turn around for a second look. Very often the woman is dressed in the height of fashion, making it eminently clear that the lady in pants is a very womanly woman. In a more or less conscious "let's-pretend," a woman might entertain a fantasy that she is a high-stepping cowboy or a debonair Fred Astaire. The whole business has become an ordinary convention.

However, even now as a degree of androgynous dress has been allowed also to men—earrings, gold chains, scarves, frilly shirts, purses—a man who wears a complete female outfit in public will still attract attention. Chances are he is a drag queen, a female impersonator who gets a kick out of displaying himself as a caricature of femininity. With him there is still an element of fun and pretense.

A transvestite, on the other hand, is not a playful fellow. He is serious, secretive, and typically not at all eager to exhibit himself or his feminine wardrobe in public. He is, nevertheless, preoccupied with female clothing. He wears a bra and lace panties under his business suit daily. He wanders around department stores luxuriating in the sight, smell, and feel of bras, panties, negligees, blouses, evening gowns. He can't get enough of touching women's clothing, buying it, stealing it, looking at photographs of it, reading descriptions of it. He is obsessed with planning his next masturbatory ritual, deciding which clothes he will wear, and where, when, and if he should or should not steal them. He reads all the fashion magazines. He photographs himself dressed up in women's clothing.

He does not comprehend the motives underlying his preoccupation and behavior. He is aware only that he is fascinated with women's fashions and that when a certain vague urge seizes him, he is compelled to dress up in women's clothes. When he resists the urge, he is overcome with anxiety or depression and even feels a little crazy.

A transvestite is a heterosexual male who is in dread of his feminine longings. He is proud of his masculine identity. Moreover, he is one of those males who, because of the strength of his feminine wishes, has been particularly impressed with a horror of the female genitals and the superiority of the male genitals. His essential dilemma is how he can gratify his longings to be dependent, vulnerable, and submissive while reassuring himself that he is still a powerful and dominating male. The transvestite accomplishes this ingenious sleight of hand by dressing up as a phallic woman, a caricatured female who has a penis under her skirts. His blue wool skirt, beige silk blouse, angora sweater, cobalt earrings, and beige alligator purse make a rather pathetic fashion statement but a strategic psychological one: "I am a woman, but a woman who has not been castrated. Under these marvelous female clothes is a penis."

When a little girl dresses up in boy's clothing, nobody thinks about it twice. But let a little boy so much as put a lace scarf around his waist and he is already suspect. Should he add a few more dainty touches to his costume or begin to dress up like a female every day, the neighbors will be whispering how the poor little fellow must be all mixed up about whether or not he is a real boy. Most child psychologists would concur with the neighbors' assessments. Should we be more precise about the issues, we would have to add that the boy wants very much to be a real boy.

I am distinguishing this lad from one who has a choice in these matters, one who occasionally tries on his sister's or mother's clothes. What I am referring to is a little boy who feels *compelled* to wear female clothing and sometimes even consciously thinks he might like to be a girl. Such a boy must be plagued by an insurmountable anxiety —a terrifying mix of abandonment, separation, and castration anxiety. The scarf, skirt, piece of lace, silky dress reassure him about a number of things that are very important to little boys: his body parts are all there and in one piece; he has refound his disappearing mother and has been reunited with her; like that magnificent, all-powerful female creature, he has a penis under his skirt; like his adorable mother, he is desired by his father; like his phallic mother, he can now submit to his father without feeling like a castrated woman; his terrifying father shouldn't be concerned with having to castrate his little rival, for the boy is only a charming, ineffectual little girl; there are no humiliating differences between the boy and his father or the boy and his mother; everybody is equal. When he puts on his mother's dress or scarf the little boy feels reassured about all those things. Then and only then can he go on with being a real boy.*

A boy who is too feminine gets the reputation of being a sissy. And if he insists on dressing up in skirts, that diagnosis will be confirmed. After a while the boy will learn to keep his little masquerade a secret. And he will stop confessing his wish to be a girl. Then the secrecy, the anxious feeling that he is committing a crime adds to the excitement of dressing up. Later, during adolescence, dressing up in female clothing will become part of his masturbation ritual.

A little girl, on the other hand, is allowed to play at boyish roles and dress up in boy's clothes. Everybody assumes she is just pretending. Nobody seems to worry very much about her boyish pretenses until she reaches adolescence. Then she is expected to forget all about her cigars and cowboy hats and conform to a socially accepted feminine role, which to everybody's relief she usually does.

What distinguishes a female transvestite from other women who cross-dress are her unconscious motives and the fantasy life that reveals these motives. There have always been women who cross-dressed. In certain periods of history, many women did so. One story has it that in the sixteenth century a girl dressed up as a male, moved to another village, took up the masculine trade of weaver, fell in love with a woman, and married her. The couple lived together for five months and the wife was satisfied, "so they say." The cross-dresser was brought to justice and hanged, "for using illicit devices to supply her defect in sex." In the seventeenth century, a woman named Marie changed her name to Marin, donned men's clothes, and announced "his" intention to marry a thirty-two-year-old widowed mother, who was his "satis-

---

* Follow-up studies of boys who began dressing in female clothing during early childhood suggest that not all of these boys become adult transvestites. Many of them become homosexuals. However, the males who participated in these studies may not be representative of all the gender-conflicted boys who dress in female clothing and express wishes to be a girl. It is my impression that, without therapy, the majority of boys who are compelled to dress in female clothing *will* become transvestites, some will become homosexuals, and others will arrive at a heterosexual adjustment but remain devoted to the enactment of a perverse scenario that includes cross-dressing elements.

fied" lover. The lovers were put on trial and Marin was condemned to be burned alive for the crime of sodomy. Marin appealed, insisting that he was truly a man. The doctor who examined him probed and probed until he found Marin's penis and even caused it to ejaculate with semen that was not watery like a woman's but "like a man's thick and white." This doctor, Jacques Duval, who had written a book *On Hermaphrodites,* defended his patient on the basis of his own unconventional notions of gender, which had it that all bodies contain both male and female elements. "There are not two radically different structures but only one—outward and visible in the man, inverted and hidden in the woman."

In Holland, during the seventeenth and eighteenth centuries, 119 cases were recorded of women who tried to pass themselves off as men. These were not temporary cross-dressers from brothels or the stage or carnivals, but women who had consciously decided to impersonate men for several days to upward of a dozen years. The motives of these women were not unlike motives of other women who had impersonated men in earlier centuries. Many cross-dressed to join the army or navy, for patriotic reasons, for excitement and adventure, for wanting to remain close to their soldier and sailor husbands, for desiring to earn a better salary than they could if employed in female occupations. Others were lesbians, or, as they were called in those centuries, tribades. Since tribadism was a sin and a capital crime, a woman who loved another woman was wise to cross-dress and impersonate a man. Those who have studied the unusually high rate of cross-dressing among women that began around 1600 and continued until around 1800 speculate that the phenomena coincided with certain anxieties among men about changing female behavior. "Male fears of 'women on top' have erupted intermittently throughout Western history, and one of the periods of greatest insecurity seems to have included the decades on either side of 1600." During that period the public seemed inordinately preoccupied with the dangers of witches, assertive women, and effeminate dressing by men. There was a growing alarm of a satanic, chaotic world turned upside down "if the proper boundaries between inferior and superior, man and woman, ruler and ruled were not obeyed." However, with this rash of cross-dressing among women in Holland and other Western nations, there is no evidence of motives or fantasies that would make these women deserving of the label "transvestite."

In our age, the garments that women wear are even less of an indication of whether they are transvestites, occasional cross-dressers, or very stylish, very womanly women. Sally, one of Stoller's patients, however, had an extensive fantasy life that gave her good reason to speculate that she might be a transvestite.

From the time she was pubescent, Sally was turned on sexually by dressing up in male clothing. Moreover, she had invented a dressing-up masturbation ritual that would give her a fantastic orgasm. At age eleven, Sally had already realized that the sexual excitements she was beginning to experience could be heightened when she put on Levi's jeans. A year or so later she was elated to discover that wearing boots could further intensify her sexual arousal and her climax.

Sally would loll about the house planning for the delicious moment when she could begin dressing up in her jeans. The idea was to try to put off the ritual as long as possible. The luxuriating anticipations that preceded the jeans ritual could bring tears to her eyes. It was like eating the cake but saving the frosting until the last possible moment.

At age forty, Sally can still recall the thrill of slowly pulling her Levi's up her legs, hips, thighs, and the exquisite erotic sensations that built and culminated in a super-orgasm, "at that fabulous moment when the in-seam in the crotch collided with my pubic area." Sally also remembers distinctly the fantasies she had as she was slowly drawing her jeans up to her crotch. She imagined that she was making love to a vulnerable young girl. She imagined she was holding the sweet girl in her arms, rocking her, reassuring her that she was safe. Then, right after the super-orgasm, Sally would hurriedly put on the rest of her clothes and strut out of the house wearing the jeans and a pair of men's engineering boots. The soft, vulnerable, sad girl now felt strong, assertive, powerful, sexual, more attractive than any boy or man she knew.

"The neat part is that those same feelings are still available to me now, many years later," Sally says. The thrice-divorced Sally, who has since learned to enjoy seducing actual sweet young girls, to love them and leave them, is still faithful to her Levi's and her Levi ritual. Just as she did when she was twelve years old, Sally waits to begin pulling on her jeans until she aches with desire, until she feels the need in her breasts, her gut, and her genitals.

I wear boots almost exclusively now, and in the acceptable fashion of today, and they continue to fit my moods, and to make me feel secure within myself, but don't cause any sexual excitement. My Levi's are the single exception. Women's Levi's are available now, and I own several pair. I have never become sexually aroused while wearing women's pants, even when the pants have a 'fly' and appear to be men's pants. No other men's pants excite me. Only the blue denim Levi's.

When Sally wore Levi's, she never failed to seduce the girl of her choice, who was always young and pretty, with long, silky black hair, a girl who looked not yet used by men, a girl who had never "yet mothered a child." Sally can also explain something about why these relationships are so important to her: "It gives me a feeling of power to own them. I'm not sure what I mean by 'power' but that's the only way I know to describe the sensation. I think if I were in fact a man I would be powerful."

Though Sally feels strong, powerful, and masculine in her Levi's, the fantasy that accompanied the ritual of putting on the jeans depicts her as two different *females:* a maternal phallic woman making love to a girl *and* a sad, vulnerable, lonely girl being held securely and warmly in the arms of a tender, protective mother. If we look further, we will

discover a few other women in those marvelous blue denim jeans. Like
Vita Sackville-West, whose mother turned her over to nannies and
governesses, Sally also had a mother who rejected her, a mother who
granted tenderness once in a while and then took her love away.
Apparently, both mothers had little tolerance for nursery mothering
but did give license to independence and rebellion in their daughters.
Sally was pregnant by the age of twelve and had to have an abortion.
Almost always, in an unwanted teenage pregnancy there is an unconscious wish to be reunited with mother and a rebellious vengeance
toward the mother who took her love away.

Vita's son Nigel said that his mother seemed shy of children and
probably didn't much like them. He and his brother Harold lived
separately from their mother and father, in a cottage with their nanny.
"The high point of each day," he wrote, "was our descent to the house
at 6 p.m., when we would find our mother bent over her current book,
patient of our intrusion, uncertain how to amuse us." Nigel shrugged
this routine off as an aristocratic tradition. It was the way most boys
and girls would be treated if they were of high birth. It was the way
Vita Sackville-West's mother had treated her, and Vita said of her
mother, "Mother didn't soften, any more than she would soften towards me when I cried; yet she can soften marvellously if you touch
the right chord—I have noticed this in other hard people." In Virginia
Woolf, whom Vita described as an angel, she would find reflected the
fragile, vulnerable part of her own self, the buried part, the "central
transparency" that was so reserved, so muted. "Virginia is very sweet,
and I feel extraordinarily protective towards her. The combination of
that brilliant brain and fragile body is very lovable. She has a sweet
and childlike nature."

If it is frightening and demeaning to be found needy, or to ask to be
taken care of, or to admit that one has longings to surrender one's soul
to the arms of a loving mother, then dressing in blue denim jeans or
jodhpurs and workman's boots is a good subterfuge. To enact the role
of a dashing hero who can rob some bumbling, impotent giant of his

most valuable treasure, as Vita Sackville-West did, is another ingenious and satisfying solution, especially for a woman who never recovered from the mortification of knowing that her mother much preferred her male lovers to the little girl, who so much adored her.

Though transvestism assumes different forms in males and females, the fundamental transvestite fantasy makes manifest an aspect of the perverse strategy that is latent in every perversion. The transvestite fantasy employs an infantile ideal of masculinity to disguise what is felt to be a shameful and frightening femininity. In a more general way, the caricatures of masculinity and femininity expressed in the transvestite fantasy are a metaphor for any perverse strategy that makes evident and manifest one gender stereotype as a way of keeping hidden other gender stereotypes that are felt to be shameful and frightening. For, in fact, every male perversion entails a masquerade or impersonation of masculinity and every female perversion entails a masquerade or impersonation of femininity.

Not too long ago the Canadian psychoanalyst, George Zavitzianos, was struck by an offbeat feature of the perverse scenarios of two of his patients, one male, the other female. While this peculiar feature was present in many other case histories, nobody previously had thought to look more closely at it or question it. After grappling for some years with the psychological meaning of what he was observing, Zavitzianos realized that he might be dealing with a previously unrecognized form of perversion. He hazarded that one might call this rather perverse perversion *homeovestism,* or dressing up in the clothes of the same-sex person.

In Zavitzianos's male patient, twenty-year-old Larry, the homeovestism had been preceded by a childhood history of transvestism. From the age of three, Larry had episodes of dressing up in his mother's clothes and decorating and draping his body in his older sister's colorful ribbons and dainty pinafores. But at seven, when his mother was hospitalized for a severe illness, the episodic transvestism became a nearly daily occurrence. Some years later, when Larry noticed on his body signs of puberty, he tried to overcome the shameful feminine longings of his childhood by asserting his masculinity. However, he was dismayed to discover that he was unable to achieve erections unless he wore a jock strap. As the approach of manhood became more imminent and his body took on a manly shape, Larry began to compare his own penis with those of the other males he knew—his older brother, the boys in the locker room, his father. All those penises were awesome. He judged his own to be small and puny. Convinced that he could only borrow manhood, Larry would masturbate with a jock strap covering his penis and testicles and spend long hours looking at himself in a mirror, fantasizing that he had a large, powerful penis just like those of the phallic men he so envied and admired. Larry's adolescent homeovestism prefigured the homosexual relationships that would eventually become his predominant sexual outlet. As an adult Larry could be sexually aroused only with partners who could mirror the magnificent phallic man he so desperately wished to be. Occasionally he found a suitable woman partner. But on the whole, the scenario of phallic mirroring worked out much more simply and directly with a male partner.

On the basis of his understanding of Larry's sexual scenarios, Zavitzianos suggested that *some* of the traditionally cited cases of male fetishism, including the man with the athletic supporter who appears at the conclusion of Freud's classic paper "Fetishism," may in fact be homeovestites. The borders among fetishism, transvestism, and homeovestism are vague. When a man progresses from observing or caressing a female garment to actually wearing the fetishistic garment, he probably has crossed the border from fetishism to transvestism. Or, if the article of clothing the man uses to enhance his sexual performance is a male garment—an army uniform, a fisherman's mackintosh, a jock strap—the apt term might be *homeovestism*. Thus, any person dressing in clothes of his or her own sex could be a homeovestite.

The quirky notion of a sexual perversion called homeovestism provides an important clue to the fundamental principle underlying the female perversions. Just as not everyone who cross-dresses is a transvestite, not everyone who dresses in the clothes of his or her own sex is, of course, a homeovestite. But we can guarantee missing the point of the perverse strategy if we take a conventional, sex-appropriate way of dressing as a sign that the person is free of gender conflict. The basic rule is that perversions should never be taken for what they seem to be. The typical transvestite wears the lace panties and garter belt under his macho uniform or business suit; he hides his feminine longings and only in private dresses up as a woman. A woman who dresses up like a man may be showing off her manliness to hide her feminine longings. A woman like Emma Bovary, who acts or dresses exactly like some stereotyped notion of a woman, may be a female homeovestite, a woman who is unsure of her femininity, a woman who is afraid to openly acknowledge her masculine strivings.

Zavitzianos's female patient, Lillian, did not begin her analysis to cure her homeovestism. Dressing up in women's clothes was a comparatively benign manifestation of a more profound emotional plight. When she was twenty years old, Lillian had been referred to Zavitzianos by her college dean for stealing. Her analysis, which lasted six years, went on to reveal a long string of other crimes and misdemeanors. Her favorite activity was shopping and spending money wildly. And though her mother showered her with gifts and money, Lillian would steal money and forge checks. Lillian was a kleptomaniac who also stole books, underwear, stockings, jewelry, dresses, "and anything that could enhance her appearance as a woman." She had been sexually promiscuous since the age of thirteen, imagined having children of her own, and enjoyed taking care of other people's children. However, Lillian mistreated the infants and toddlers she babysat, hurting them physically, masturbating the boys, and hugging the little girls so hard that they cried. Her homeovestism was expressed in occasional driven-impulsive acts of "dressing up" as the valued and valuable phallic woman she wished to be. "Lillian had a tendency to imitate the manners of women she envied and admired, and also tended to dress like them. Most of these women were married or pregnant. She found it particularly exciting to steal from them."

Originally Lillian felt no shame or guilt about her activities, only a vaguely anxious excitement and sense of power. She consented to treatment because she had been certain she could fool her therapist with a false case, one that would manipulate him into getting her reinstated in college without having to delve into her feelings and thoughts. But Zavitzianos persisted, and Lillian gradually uncovered the childhood history and unconscious motives of her juvenile delinquency.

Each of the details in Zavitzianos's accounts of Lillian's adolescent and adult personality make some sense in the context of her early family relationships. Lillian's mother made no secret of her disappointment at not having given birth to a boy. She was depressed and perhaps emotionally depleted at the time Lillian was born. Consequently, Lillian was rarely touched, caressed, or cuddled. Although the mother eventually grew attached to her very pretty and lively baby, she still could not bear to handle her more than was absolutely necessary. To make matters worse, one of the mother's compensatory gestures was to masturbate her little daughter. It was the one source of mutual pleasure in this highly ambivalent mother-infant relationship.

When Lillian was three years old she was displaced from the parental bedroom by a little brother. During her pregnancy the mother had been more hopeful and consequently more patient and loving with her daughter. Lillian's participation in her mother's pregnancy was the high point of her childhood. The birth of her brother brought home some unwelcome news. Lillian reacted to the sight of her brother's penis and the glimpses of her mother's resumed menstrual flow with intense anxiety. As soon as her infant son was born, Lillian's mother became totally preoccupied with his care. It was obvious to little Lillian that her mother enjoyed cuddling and caressing him. Now

Lillian had no mother at all. Even the traumatically arousing sensations of her mother's fingers fondling her clitoris and labia were gone. Lillian's severe castration reactions were compounded by unmanageable abandonment and separation anxieties. Lillian was bereft. She would try to console herself by wearing her mother's dresses and stuffing the fronts with pillows. In that way Lillian recaptured the days when she felt united with her marvelously exciting, pregnant mother.

The prospect of a new child on the way had cheered Lillian's mother. She enjoyed having her little daughter with her when she went shopping for maternity clothes. Toward the end of her pregnancy, the mother had also begun to enjoy reading stories to Lillian, who had by then become a very talkative, less babyish, less physically demanding child. Lillian had been valued for her interest in words and books. But when her brother was born, story time came to an abrupt end along with everything else that Lillian shared with her mother. Much as another child might have used a soft, cuddly security blanket to substitute for the mother's presence, Lillian started to take books to bed with her. She would surround herself with books, hold a few in her arms, pretend that a mother was reading to her, and then slowly drift into sleep.

Nearly a full year went by before anyone thought to read a book to Lillian. Then one day, when Lillian showed some interest in learning how to read the words in her books, her father took over the story time function. Although he had not given much attention to her until then, he enjoyed teaching his little daughter how to read. However, as she sat on her father's lap listening to the stories he read to her and looking at the magical letters he pointed out to her, Lillian reacted like most children who have been sexually abused during infancy. The sexual fantasies that other little girls are barely conscious of overwhelmed Lillian, preventing her from feeling comfortable about the cuddling, warmth, and protectiveness that her father was now offering to her along with his reading instructions. Lillian tried hard to suppress her impulses to touch, to hold, or swallow her father's penis. Only by concentrating intensely on the words in the book and sometimes by pretending that she was reading the words just like her father could Lillian dispel these disquieting sensations and thoughts.

Lillian's early childhood was very troubled. Her distress and grief and loneliness and humiliation worsened as she approached adolescence. Lillian could not avoid noticing that her body was growing unambiguously into the body of an "ordinary" woman. As an adolescent the only way Lillian could overcome sensations of bodily disintegration and terrifying feelings of loss and abandonment was to steal women's clothing and to wear the garments wherever and whenever possible. Her attacks of kleptomania and homeovestism coincided with the onset of menstruation. Lillian was able to explain to her analyst that when she wore beautiful and expensive dresses she would feel like a valued child from a different family—important and rich. She would imagine she had been born to a mother and father who adored her and caressed her little body with looks of admiration. On a less conscious level, the sensations of having her body inside these glorious clothes gratified Lillian's lifelong wish to be absorbed through her mother's skin and transported back inside her smooth belly. In that way Lillian could be reborn with the magnificent body part that she imagined had made her brother so valuable to her mother. Now she would find eternal love and be reunited with her mother.

In Lillian's mind there were two Lillians, who would split apart on occasions, especially when she was shoplifting. One was a nice, sweet, normal girl who never masturbated and never stole, a polite, rich, high-class girl who wore gorgeous clothes and had a glorious mother who adored her. The other image was of an unhappy, deprived girl, a bad, dirty girl who masturbated and stole the goods that she felt had been stolen from her. The good Lillian would look on while the bad Lillian stole; the good Lillian was an accomplice in crime by covering up so effectively for the bad Lillian. When Lillian stole women's clothing and jewelry, she was stealing the two childhood gifts she had been deprived of: the nipple that had not been freely given to her and also the exciting, desirable genitals that had been stolen away from her when her brother stole her mother.

Inside her stolen dresses and jewelry Lillian experienced herself as though she were a rare and costly jewel, an emerald of incomparable size and shape. In a very direct way, the velvety and silken garments provided the skin eroticism she had been deprived of as an infant. Furthermore, the contact of the expensive clothing on her skin put edges on Lillian's blurred and indistinct body image, lending a focus to the diffuse inner genital sensations that had been reawakened by her menstrual cycles.

Lillian was promiscuously heterosexual. It was she who made the advances, very often on the first date and usually with a boy somewhat younger than she. She found it impossible to achieve any sort of tenderness in her sexual encounters and barely contained the vengeful sadism that was stirred up when she had intercourse. Nevertheless, during her heterosexual escapades, Lillian did not use a fetish or feel compelled to wear stolen female clothing and jewelry as a means of achieving sexual arousal. The presence of her current lover's actual erect penis was enough to reassure Lillian that she was an adored and valued little girl with a penis. The once terrifying and forbidden fantasies of the little girl on her father's lap could now be gratified with relative impunity. By grabbing and pulling at her lover's penis, performing fellatio, making it erect and bringing it to orgasm, or by simply looking at the penis in a state of erection, Lillian could convince herself that she was taking the penis inside her and thereby repairing her own damaged genitals. Lillian was anhedonic—without any sexual feelings, neither arousal nor orgasm. She was frigid but experienced immense power and narcissistic gratification from her ability to cause erections and orgasms in her male companions, imagining that she had "absorbed the boy's experience" and that "his power and his feelings of pleasure were actually hers." In her extensive, rigidly ritualized heterosexuality, Lillian was one those women who believe that the anatomical penis is a magical phallus that can repair a castration and undo separation. In her homeovestism, Lillian impersonated the phallic mother in order to overcome abandonment, separation, and castration anxieties of a severity that was tantamount to the mutilation anxiety that characterizes the perversions.

If we did not have access to Lillian's inner life and her perverse fantasies, her lively heterosexuality might be taken for granted as, if not absolutely "normal," perhaps a sign of her sexual liberation. The good Lillian was the "normal" girl, who proved her femininity by seeking and finding immense narcissistic gratification in sexual relationships with men and dressing up in gorgeous, expensive women's clothing.

Is poor motherless Emma Bovary an average bored, dissatisfied wife dressing up for an afternoon of delicious adultery or a homeovestite in the disguise of a banal female type?

> While performing the role of virtuous housewife, inwardly she was burning with passion at the thought of that head of black hair curling down over a tanned forehead, of a body so muscular and yet elegant, and, finally, of this man so coolly rational and self-possessed and yet so hot-blooded when sexually aroused. It was for him she filed her fingernails with the meticulous care of a sculptor, that there was never enough cold cream on her skin nor enough patchouli in her handkerchiefs. She loaded herself with bracelets, rings, and necklaces. When he was on his way to her, she would fill two big blue glass vases with roses and arrange her room and her person like a courtesan awaiting a prince. The maid was kept busy washing and ironing her lingerie . . . dimity petticoats, fichus, lace collars, and pantaloons with drawstrings, full around the hips and narrowing toward the bottom.

In this scene, Emma's thoughts and actions could be taken as expressions of a typical homeovestite fantasy. For any conventionally feminine woman adorned with bracelets, rings, and necklaces, with undergarments of satin and frilly lace, may be entertaining an unconscious fantasy of acquiring the phallic powers of the man she worships or imagining that she is transforming her worthless, inadequate body into the body of a phallic woman.

Furthermore, the concept of homeovestism, with its implication of gender impersonation, may also be more faithful to what is going on when a woman dresses up to exhibit herself as a valuable sexual commodity than the term *exhibitionism,* which technically is appropriate only when applied to those rare women who express revenge for their childhood deprivations and humiliations by exhibiting their genitals to nonconsenting male victims. In an offhand way, the psychiatric profession and the public alike often speak of stripteasers and women who act in porn movies or who pose for pornographic magazines as exhibitionists. While the basic gratifications of exhibitionism—genital reassurance and revenge on persons of the opposite sex, as well as "easy" money and even theatrical ambition—play some part in attracting women to these callings, ultimately the countless women who dress up in women's underwear, veils, or other semi-exposing female garments to pose in sexually explicit or sexually suggestive postures do so to reassure themselves that they will not be abandoned or annihilated. Their very existence is at stake. The fetishized body of the porno actress is all that is left of a little girl who could never make any sense at all of why love had been taken away from her.

A woman who participates, willingly or unwillingly, in male fetishistic scripts and in male pornography is thought of as a victim, as a passive, unwilling subject. It is true that she is a victim of a social order that permits and encourages men to exploit women. However, it is also true that she is involved in a retribution scenario, a vengeance on those who have been assigned the power to abandon and mutilate. These contradictory attitudes of submissive dependency and vengeance are characteristic of the prostitute, the call girl, the porno star who puts herself in willing bondage to her pimp, her client, her director, or any man who is willing to bully or enslave her. With her cold calculations, high-strutting boots, and scornful sweet talk she triumphs over her positions of abasement by humiliating and exploiting the hundreds of other men who are dependent on her sexual favors. Now she can be the one who gives love and takes it away. But other motives are more relevant to the plight of these women, who are desperately needy and longing to find a loving mother somewhere. By transforming herself into a fetish, a dehumanized object that enables men to have erections and ejaculations, a powerless, helpless, and socially victimized woman can experience enormous power. And then as we go more deeply into these scenarios we learn of still further motives. The men's excited responses to her body reassure the woman that she actually exists. So a crucial motive of a woman who cooperates in the fetishization of her body is her anxiety about bodily fragmentation and nothingness—her dread of annihilation.

Olympia, the *Raunch* centerfold, striptease artist, and go-go dancer interviewed by Stoller, stresses that she and other women like her are not aptly described by the label *exhibitionist*. And I think she is right in insisting on this diagnostic refinement and also right to think of herself as a female impersonator. Olympia volunteered to narrate the story of her life and the circumstances surrounding her calling, and in doing so she rendered a touching portrait of a woman who earned her right to exist in the world by transforming herself into a fetish. Stoller proposed an erotic equation to represent the relationship between the female who acts as a fetish and the fetishistic male—"masochisma matches machismo." Olympia epitomizes the "dumb blonde, bubble-headed, bubble-busted, bubble-butted" starlets, the exotic dancers, the go-go girls, the centerfolds, the phallic women who drive men wild by posing in the nude or seminude, withholding till the last possible moment whether or not they are phallic or castrated, whether or not they will give love or take it away.

Because she was convinced that she lacked natural femininity, Olympia learned long ago that the best she could do was dress up as a woman. Before she discovered her calling, Olympia was always uncomfortable in her body. She explains to Stoller that she is able to appear to be more feminine than the average woman only because she has been extremely devoted to her craft, which depends on a conscientious study of feminine movements and styles of dress. In expressing these ideas about her femininity, Olympia seems aware of the split images of herself. "I always thought I had the grace of a truck driver but I discovered that it's not a matter of gracefulness, it's a matter of knowing how to do things by studying. For example, I could show you two ways of sitting on the floor, one graceful like an accomplished dancer and one like a clod."

Olympia describes her body as a container or at best a tool for accomplishing her craft—turning men on. "Without the container, I could totally disperse and be in a billion places all over the universe at the same time." In the way she dresses, styles her hair, carries herself, Olympia imagines that she is decorating femininity onto the outside of her body, which she thinks of as a container-tool.

Likely, Olympia's account of her relationship with her mother is a retrospective fiction, the kind of narrative of childhood that an adolescent girl or adult female might construct to try to make sense of her current predicament. Nevertheless, what Olympia tells us is a felicitous version of her adult fantasies about her mother. Her account can be taken as a partial truth that hides other, more frightening details. Olympia is sure that very early in life she was sexually turned on by looking at her mother's naked body. She slept with her mother and her mother liked to walk around the house nude. Olympia claims that as a child she suffered from eye strain just from trying to look through her mother's pubic hair to see what was underneath. Olympia's mother was also something of a practical joker. She would dress up in gloves, a hat, a belt, and nothing more and pretend to be going to the supermarket.

Olympia recollects that she was interested in go-go dancing from the time she was five. She would turn her dresser drawers upside down, stand up on them and dance in the nude.

Among Olympia's other recollections of childhood are a few toileting scenes: she would imitate a dog going "potty" in the backyard, she accompanied her father to the men's room so that her "peepie" would not be mutilated by one of the razor-wielding fiends that her parents were sure hide out in ladies' rooms. In their well-intended conscious efforts to shield Olympia from adult sex criminals, her mother and father unconsciously placed her in precisely the kind of situation that would traumatize a little girl. Though she had been frustrated in her attempts to see beneath her mother's pubic hair, Olympia could freely peek at the row of tinkling penises, an activity that she describes as one of her "favorite forms of [childhood] entertainment." Olympia concludes her toilet *mémoires* with a poignant commentary: "I had quite a bit of difficulty as a child. I was suicidal for a time, because I never felt attached to my body. I just felt completely detached from my body; I felt like a completely separate entity from it."

Being a living, breathing fetish allows Olympia to be in contact with her body. She regards her dancing and posing as creative enterprises that are direct deflections of her sexual energies. She also aspires to be a science fiction writer, another form of creativity that would allow her to express her sexual fantasies. For example, Olympia thinks of the female sex organs as something not there, a space, a void. In this speculation on the differences between the sexes, she sees women as having a definite advantage over men, who always are worried about their genital inadequacies. Olympia reasons like Karl Abraham: with nothing there, women have nothing to worry about. Olympia's fantasy of the vaginal-ovarian void inspires in her a science fiction plot:

Wouldn't it be interesting . . . if there were a linkup, that people are linked up to everything in nature. Like a black hole in space so that on the day that a black hole in space became activated and began to suck up the whole universe, all the vaginas in the world also became activated to sucking to a lesser extent: pulling up the carpets, the little knickknacks and all of them turn themselves inside out and disappear.

Surely as male pornography is a revenge on women, Olympia's creative fantasy of world destruction is a *vagina dentata* come to life, a nightmare of archaic revenge gone haywire. Olympia's vaginal vengeance fantasy meshes with the male fantasy of losing his penis inside the dread vagina. However, her fictional genital apparatus accomplishes much more than simply holding the penis captive and swallowing it up. If the phallus stands for the most priceless treasures, those trophies of power that are most valued in the social order, Olympia's suctioning vaginal orifice proves itself a worthy adversary. The suctioning powers of the vaginal void turn all items of social value, especially the decor that constitutes the cozy patriarchal household, inside out and make them vanish forever.

Women like Olympia, including culture heroine Marilyn Monroe, are prisoners in bodies that cannot come to life except through impersonations of femininity. These female female impersonators are as dominated by their rigid sexual scenarios as are the men they capture, captivate, and serve. They know they are lost. Says Stoller, "So they are vulnerable to those who promise them a connection. They are not just willing to serve as fetishes; they have no other options." Because few of us can escape from that nagging sense that most humans lead, at best, only partially realized sexual lives, it comforts us to believe that the Olympias, Marilyn Monroes, Emma Bovarys are revolutionary types, that they represent the ways and means to push forward the frontiers of what is possible and to unsettle reality. But in a social order that preserves its structures through the trivialization of the sexual life, our fetishized culture heroines are the most mundane commodities of all. As the fetish props of presidents and kings and famous men and aristocratic Boulangers and literary Fullertons and investment bankers and firemen and judges, the fetishized Olympias and Marilyns are the most obvious victims of a commodity fetishism that infiltrates every corner of the social order.

In the fashion industry, a cornerstone of modern industrial economy, the female perversion of dressing up as a woman and the male perversion of transvestism are, like Poe's purloined letter, nicely disguised by being right out in the open. Obviously, not every dress designer is a latent transvestite and not every fashion model or every woman who wears designer clothes is a homeovestite. However, in the overall scheme of the perverse strategy, the fashion industry, which thrives on its obvious social stereotypes of femininity (and masculinity), represents the many other social institutions that exist on the basis of a power structure in which someone is put in a dependent, passive feminine position and someone else is assigned to the powerful, dominating masculine position. The fashion industry makes explicit and visually concrete the various ways in which infantile fantasies of femininity and masculinity can be enlisted by the social order to preserve its own structures.

Men with transvestite tendencies, many of whom had episodes of dressing up in female clothing as children, may never as adults actually cross-dress as a way of assuring masculinity and genital prowess. Instead they solve their gender and sexual dilemmas by becoming involved with a fantasy of dressing up women in female clothing and fixing *their* imperfections. These men are so preoccupied with the grandiose fantasy of fixing women that we might justifiably think of them as afflicted with a Pygmalion complex. Because many of these men, like Pygmalion, also have special talents, their preoccupation enables them to know exactly how to take the raw medium of a woman's body and transform it into a beguiling image of femininity.

Pygmalions are not confined to the fashion industry or to males. A Pygmalion might be a college professor, a film director, a psychiatrist, a cosmetic surgeon, a Casanova, a father or mother, any man or woman who survives mutilation anxiety with the fantasy that his or her phallic powers can fix a wounded, castrated being.

Pygmalions are proficient at spotting some slightly bedraggled, carelessly dressed, intellectually underachieving, unfashionably plump creature and realizing at once that she is the woman who can be counted on to fall right in with their Pygmalion fantasy—a woman who believes she needs fixing, a woman who imagines that a man or his magical phallus can fix her. On her side, the flesh-and-blood Galatea surrenders her body, soul, and mind, allowing her imperfect self to be remolded into Pygmalion's image of the perfect woman. While not entirely impotent, some Pygmalions have difficulties maintaining erections and frequently are unable to ejaculate within the vagina. These genital handicaps do not, however, prevent them from fancying themselves as ideal lovers capable of rousing women to unparalleled heights of passion. Armed with the fantasy that they are fixing a damaged woman, Pygmalions are at least sometimes able to give sexual pleasure to a woman and even to achieve orgasm themselves. However, for the average Pygmalion, the best of all possible scenarios is one that allows him to act out the fixing fantasy without having to engage in any potentially dangerous and unpredictable sexual intercourse.

Our modern-day Pygmalion enjoys nothing so much as taking an unformed girl and transforming her into a highly valued, sexually exciting woman—the ideal phallic woman he wishes he could be. He becomes consumed with the passion of decorating her body, choosing her shoes, gloves, hats, changing her hairstyle, controlling her eating habits, monitoring her table manners, improving her speech, directing her thoughts, analyzing her conflicts so that she may someday become a normal submissive woman—until that moment when the woman at last matches his image of an ideal woman. Then he loses interest. Like Shaw's misogynist, Professor Henry Higgins, he abandons his puppet-woman as soon as he has finished fixing her. Without a pang of guilt, feeling quite honorable and justified—after all, he has made the grubby girl into something much better than she had been—he turns his attention to his next fixing project. So long as there is some pathetic Eliza–urchin girl ready and willing to be fixed up into a princess, the man afflicted with a Pygmalion complex is not likely to suffer consciously from his sexual difficulties or gender conflicts.

Unconsciously, men who thrive on the fantasy of fixing damaged women are haunted by images and fantasies of mutilated bodies, "castrated" males and females. These fantasies are expressions of their unconscious hostility toward the women they consciously want to help. In the fashion industry, the terrifying unconscious fantasies and images which also haunt the minds of every Pygmalion film director or college professor are given expression in the fashions designed for women. Because of the extensive visibility in our society of fashion, in magazines and newspapers and in department store advertisements, Pygmalion fashion designers are in a position to bring out into the open what is going on unconsciously in many social institutions, industries, and professions that are devoted to fixing women. As we will see in later chapters, even parenthood, one of our most sacred social institutions, is sometimes converted into a perverse endeavor aimed at fixing a child so that the child will mirror for the parent the ideal self the parent wishes to be. There are plenty of parents who think of themselves as Pygmalions who can mold a perfect child. In this perverse employment of the parenting function, a fixing of the child includes an indoctrination into a gender stereotype and is also a reparation for the unconscious hostility toward the child that the parent might otherwise express more directly.

Consciously, like the good parents and talented sculptors they wish to be, the fashion industry Pygmalions are preoccupied with happy visions of satin dresses, elegant pantsuits, and bouffant hair styles. However, one doesn't have to go too deeply into their fantasies to grasp that these Pygmalions unconsciously regard women as degraded, filthy, bleeding creatures "always with the rag on." The punitive fashions that fashion industry Pygmalions invent for women, such as the hobble skirt, shoes modeled on the Chinese bound foot, the corset, the whalebone collar, are disguised expressions of a "moment of horror" transformed into hatred. The fear-hatred is only somewhat better camouflaged by the transparent blouses, the feather and fluff that make women look like playthings, ornaments, creatures that are not meant to be taken seriously.

Most Pygmalions, whether they are in the business of teaching or cosmetic surgery or fashion design, expend a great deal of energy on making amends for their unconscious sadism toward the "weaker sex." Pygmalions are forever making reparations to women, silencing their retaliation, and keeping them under control by convincing them that "without me you are nothing."

Olympia is always surrounded by her retinue: her hairdresser, dance instructor, voice teacher, costumer, stage manager, publicity agent, and her choreographer, who issues the command "Cut out your sex life completely so we can rechannel your energy." Olympia agrees with her Pygmalions that she would not exist unless they created her. "All I am is the physical likeness in the act. Without them I would be nothing."

Beneath their impeccable satiny skins and sinuously perfect bodies, a great many fashion models are Olympias and Elizas who survive anxiety and depression with the fantasy that they can be fixed. Beneath their hypermasculine or pseudofeminine cloaks, some of the photographers, hairdressers, and dress designers who mold fashion models into this year's image of the perfect woman are true Pygmalions.

With the advent of the women's movement, dress designers have become ingenuously circumspect. They no longer force their images on women or appear to be dictating to women. "Nowadays it is quite impossible to order women: 'You will wear that,'" Christian Lacroix admitted to Michael Gross, a reporter for the *New York Times*. Gross tells us that the women's movement has transformed the former dictators into "alchemists turning desire into dress."

He lets the alchemists speak for themselves. Emanuel Ungaro proclaims his fascination for the women he serves: "I could talk for hours about women. Why are they so incomprehensible?" Even Yves St. Laurent makes his token bow to women's desires: "The women choose. We have to feel and sense what women want." Taking his cue from Ungaro and St. Laurent, the amused reporter indulges in a bit of reportorial irony by invoking the name of Freud: "As Freud once asked, what do women want?" Azzedine Alaïa knows. Women "want to be both free and feminine." Kenzo agrees. Women today are "more free. . . . They know what they want, what they can do. So fashion changed, too. The message is liberty."

Given his turn to speak out for freedom, Issey Miyake announces that his dresses and suits are the result of an intimate, unspoken collaboration between his liberated designs and the liberated woman: "I try to be free. The women must also be free." Moreover, Miyake would like to help women in their struggle for freedom. He says if only he could, he would put a tag on his designs that reads, "Take these clothes as you like."

As the spokesperson for the female minority in the women's fashion industry, Sonia Rykiel addresses the contradictions within a woman's soul. Whether they are short, tall, fat, or thin, most women are just like Sonia. Sonia's ideal woman "is fragile, but strong." She is a working woman who must also take care of men, children, houses. "I try to explain that in my clothes. They are clothes for everyday life. That is the real life of woman."

St. Laurent, the pioneer of the pantsuit, finds this domesticated image of femininity unpalatable. He is not impressed with the fragile virtues. Above all, he does not want his women to be look-alikes. "I like a woman to be arrogant and daring. The woman who is arrogant doesn't look like anyone else." Ungaro is also attracted to female arrogance, perhaps more so than St. Laurent. Ungaro's woman must be a walking sexual provocation. "There is something very mean in her way of seduction." The truly liberated women are "female Don Giovannis . . . [who] conquer people around them." Ungaro realizes he is a sculptor of women, a Pygmalion of sorts. He compares himself to Michelangelo, who, after his statue of David was completed, demanded, "Why don't you speak?" Detecting the misogynism beneath Ungaro's love of women, Gross comments, "Particularly with male designers the line between worship and warfare can blur."

Jean-Paul Gaultier hits on precisely the right motto to appeal to his Galateas: "Women can do everything men can do, and they can do it sometimes better." He describes his ideal woman, "the daughter of the one who made women's lib," and his ideal of the liberated woman: "She knows her power, but she uses it in a determined way, with a jerk and a twist. I hate the image of servility." When it comes to his thoughts on female power, this latter-day champion of the liberated daughters of "lib" is strategically ambiguous. "A lot of young girls dress like prostitutes, but inside they may be pure, puritan, strict and reserved. Codes are changing."

Scarcely had Vita Sackville-West decided that it wasn't such a bad idea for a woman to dress up as a man than the predicament of women had begun to ease, at least for the intellectually gifted or artistically talented. From the dashing Vita-Julian and Levi's-clad Sally, to the homeovestite-kleptomaniac Lillian to Emma in her dimity petticoats and tapering pantaloons, to the female-impersonating Olympia to the Galatea-Elizas who submit to the men who fix damaged women, to the Don Giovannian daughters of women's lib who submit only to their dress designers, we come, finally, to women who have been liberated to express their intellectual and artistic talents but who nevertheless feel that some awful fate will befall them unless they masquerade as self-demeaning feminine types. In 1929, the psychoanalyst Joan Rivière informed her colleagues that some powerful and liberated women had taken to disguising themselves as women.

At the beginning of the twentieth century, most of the women who followed intellectual pursuits and professional callings were overtly "masculine" women. Abraham detected them at once. In those innocently straightforward days it was only the rare and unusually courageous woman who would dare to imagine that she might become philosopher, doctor, sculptor, poet, composer, musician, banker, head of a corporation. Because these women were different from the average woman, they did not hesitate to make themselves or their talents visible to the world. But before too long, this very visibility of female power was perceived as a threat to the social order and some women went scurrying for cover in their various unconscious masquerades.

In her paper "Womanliness as a Masquerade," Rivière describes a unique type of gender identity solution that became available to women some years after females were finally given permission to pursue "masculine" intellectual ambitions. Instead of outright suppression of these women, who might one day threaten the law of the land by rejecting the feminine virtues that had traditionally been assigned to them, society achieved a sort of compromise. Women could be as masculine as they wished, provided they still upheld the feminine side of things. The social order was providing new roles for women, but now the women were going to have to find a way to express their masculine ambitions and still be considered feminine women. "Of all the women engaged in professional work to-day, it would be hard to say whether the greater number are more feminine than masculine in their mode of life and character. In University life, in scientific professions and in business, one constantly meets women who seem to fulfil every criterion of complete feminine development."

Who are these marvels of "complete feminine development"? They are the legion of professional-intellectual women who are also wives and mothers and excellent housekeepers, who maintain an active social life, who are involved in the cultural life of their community, women whose dress and hair styles—whether or not they wear pants and bob their hair—are impeccably and unmistakably feminine. Moreover, they have excellent sexual relationships with their husbands, including frequent sex and orgasm.

Rivière, a translator of Freud's writings into English and one of his most talented and original intellectual "daughters," a disciple of the daring Melanie Klein, a contemporary of Karen Horney, did not accept that every woman with this flawless femininity is as unconflicted about her femininity as she would have others and herself believe.

Once we begin to look beneath the surface, the woman who masquerades in her womanliness is immediately recognizable. Rivière describes a patient who had every outward sign of "complete feminine development." One symptom gave away the masquerade. Though the patient was a highly respected, well-paid, much admired, immensely successful lecturer, who traveled about Europe lobbying for the intellectual and cultural causes she was emotionally committed to, each of her grand performances would be followed by a severe anxiety attack. Sometimes the patient would be apprehensive all night, unable to sleep, imagining all the inappropriate things she might have said or done and all the terrible consequences that might ensue. In this unreasonable fear of punishment, Rivière's patient was conscious of feeling like a criminal but could not figure out what her crime could be. Because of the increasing severity of her post-lecture anxiety, she became obsessed by a need for reassurance. She finally developed another symptom that replaced this awesome anxiety and guilt but left her wondering about her driven and repetitive solution.

This was the patient's appeasement to the gods for her crimes: Immediately after completing her speech or lecture, she would have an urge to seek the attention and compliments of some man who had witnessed her performance. Rarely was the man qualified to judge her performance. It was enough that he was an older man—a father figure of a sort. The first order of business was to make sure that some fatherly type pay homage to her intellectual superiority. She needed to hear this man's tribute to her intellectual powers, but more important she also needed his implicit approval of a public display of her considerable and impressive talent. With those reassurances out of the way, she went quickly on to the more imperative matter. Scarcely skipping a beat, she would transform herself into a hip-wriggling, eyelash-batting seductress. What she needed now was some sign from the man that she was sexually attractive. In contrast to the magisterial style with which she had commanded and captivated her audience, there suddenly appeared at the back of the auditorium a flirtatious girl, a silly chatter-box, a pure and simple coquette.

The patient intuitively chose the men who were most suitable to participate in her stereotyped script. They were kindly father figures but also the sort of men who feared any woman who might make real sexual demands on them. It was clear that she was impersonating a seduction, that she was one of those harmless flirts to whom a man could safely offer his sexual attentions. And since the men were also reassured by her "masculine" intelligence, they could be confident that no actual sexual performances would be expected by this temptress.

Were it not for the severe anxiety attacks, sleepless nights, and, later on, the degrading female impersonations that she was compelled to perform following her public speaking engagements, the patient might have gone through life rather oblivious to her gender conflicts, some-what aware, to be sure, of her rivalries with men but not at all moti-vated to peel away the mask of womanliness. After all, until she began to wonder at the incongruity between her intellectual power and her ridiculous post-lecture flirtations, the compromised womanliness that was so much a part of her character had effectively masked the gender conflicts that were generating her anxiety reactions.

Why would an intelligent woman like Rivière's patient reassure herself by compulsively behaving like a flighty, dim-witted girl? Why would a woman who had the genuine goods feel that they were stolen goods? As I indicated at the outset, one motive for the masquerade came from her social order, which had begun to feel threatened by the increasing visibility of powerful women like her. But as always in these masquerades, there is a collaboration between a woman's infantile ideals of femininity and masculinity and her social order with its prim-itive stereotypes of gender.

It was Rivière's thesis that her patient used her womanliness as a mask, both to hide the possession of masculinity that her patient had unconsciously interpreted as a theft of her father's phallic powers *and* to avert reprisals if she was found to possess them—"much as a thief will turn out his pockets and ask to be searched to prove he has not the stolen goods." Rivière was careful to insist that there was no sharp distinction between "genuine womanliness" and a masquerade. She implied that whenever womanliness is used as a device to avoid anxiety and retribution it is a masquerade.

The crimes that so troubled Rivière's patient were infantile crimes based on unconscious infantile fantasies. Using Rivière's classic paper as the template for my own analytic cases of women who have found it necessary to hide their intellectual powers behind a masquerade of a self-demeaning femininity, I have constructed a narrative about the infantile fantasies of a woman, whom I shall call Janet. As with all narratives derived from the analysis of an adult woman, this one is not an exact replica of what a person felt or thought, consciously and unconsciously, as a little child. Moreover, *composite* narratives, such as the one I am about to present, are even less faithful to any actual infantile history than the usual reconstructed version. An approximately true-to-life portrait can be constructed only out of the innumerable little details that are unique to each individual, and I am leaving those out and giving merely a type, an outline. Therefore, I must acknowledge that there is something fetishistic about this device of a composite portrait, which reveals but keeps hidden all the various Janets that it represents.

Nevertheless, let us say that "Janet" was born to a mother who had already given birth to two daughters. The mother this time had been especially longing for a son. When Janet was born, she took one look at her baby girl and decided that she would do nicely for the son she never had. From birth, Janet was alert, lively, curious, eager, persistent, and determined to get what she wanted when she wanted it. The world had changed since the mother was a little girl. Now a little girl could aspire to be much more than merely a wife and mother, a nurse or a kindergarten teacher. Therefore, it was altogether in keeping with the times that Janet's mother would elect a female child to fulfill her own frustrated masculine ambitions. And Janet, being the kind of baby she was, had no trouble at all falling right in with her mother's fantasies. As a result of this unconscious bargain between Janet and her mother, Janet sailed through her separation-individuation with relative ease. Even during the ordinarily trying and difficult rapprochement phase, Janet's *No*'s and *Mine*'s and her petulant willfulness were welcomed by her mother as confirmations that Janet would grow up to be a special kind of girl. Consequently Janet's *no*-saying was rarely challenged or opposed with an appropriate *no*-saying limitation from her mother, and Janet barely suffered at all the usual disappointments, frustrations, and humiliations of infancy and toddlerhood. Janet was the queen bee of the nursery and she knew it and so did her two sisters and her father. While this amiable intimacy between mother and daughter made for a peaceful nursery, the rest of the household, especially the father, had mixed feelings about this fantastic baby girl, and Janet sensed that too.

Janet was not a traumatized child. But the exceptional status her mother had conferred on her was a deception for which Janet, later in childhood and adulthood, would pay heavily. Janet was being deprived of an opportunity to work through and master the ordinary childhood anxieties of abandonment and separation and to gradually tame the aggression that these painful affects might have aroused. Fortunately, the strength of her aggressive strivings encouraged Janet to assert her individuality and separate selfhood despite her unusual closeness to her mother. The problem was that Janet continued to cling to the fantasy that she could satisfy her mother's every desire, that her mother was an extension of her own self, a possession that belonged to her and to no one else. So when the time came for Janet to reckon with her father's presence in her mother's life and to recognize that she was prohibited from and furthermore incapable of possessing her mother the way the father did, she could not accept that inevitable defeat of her childhood ambitions with any grace or equanimity. Janet was determined to keep her mother for herself and could not accept that her father had powers that she did not. She also now desired her father and wanted him and his powers to be given to her and not to the mother. However, unlike other little girls who also entertain such wishes, the queen bee of the nursery was totally unprepared for any fact of life that would belie her exceptional status, much less the unwelcome news that she was only a very little princess bee who had a long way to go before she had the sexual and procreative powers of a queen.

Janet tried to remedy all this in fantasy. Her first fantasy solution didn't work for long, but for a while and at moments it calmed her jealous rage—a little bit. Since she envied her father for his powers, she thought she might seduce him into handing them over to her if she behaved like a perfect little princess. Since she was in a rage with her mother for having so cruelly deceived her, she began to think of her as a wicked stepmother who didn't deserve the father's love anyway. Janet's unique little mind was able to conjure away the nasty facts of life with her unique version of a very commonplace childhood fantasy, one that shows up in various disguises in the Snow White and Cinderella and Red Rose fairy tales that little girls for centuries have loved to have read to them—over and over again. The fantasy of being given the phallus, or magical powers, that the king-father had mistakenly given to the wicked, undeserving queen-stepmother was immensely satsifying to Janet. The king would assure her that she was fairest in the land and the one most deserving of his approval and love. Moreover, the king would protect her from the queen's jealous retribution. He would say, "I give my magical powers to you. They belong to you and not to the wicked queen and certainly not to your two mean and ugly sisters."

However, things do not always work out for Snow Whites and Cinderellas as nicely as they do in fairy tales. In fact, they never do, and little girls feel guilty about entertaining these naughty fantasies. In real life, the king does not come back as a handsome prince to marry the princess, and little Janet would be frightened that her father would punish her for still wishing to take his place with the mother. The wicked queen does not fall off a cliff and disappear, and Janet would be terrified that her mother would one day get her revenge and steal back the powers that rightfully belonged to her. Nor is this easygoing version of things commensurate with the violence of the retaliations and vengeances that Janet conjured up as the just punishments for her wishes to triumph over both parents.

The ordinary fairy tale solution could not do the trick. Janet was too observant and smart to be able to deny that her mother and father had a sexual life together that excluded her. Moreover, her jealous rage was too enormous to be managed in any peaceful way. The unconscious bargain struck between Janet and her mother of Janet fulfilling what was unfulfilled in the mother played a considerable role in the intensity and violent content of the unconscious fantasies provoked by Janet's exclusion from the primal scene. With the mortification of the primal scene, the anxieties of abandonment and separation that had been held in abeyance by the fantasy of being mother's "everything" now sprang to life with an unmanageable intensity and with them an unleashing of a violent and terrifying aggression.

On the outside, the four-year-old Janet was acting like a very angry, grumpy, dissatisfied, impossible to please little girl. She devised all kinds of ways to be mean to her mother. She treated her like a lowly servant who was beneath contempt. She tormented her mother by clinging to her and having a tantrum every time her mother paid attention to anyone else but her. She teased her sisters unmercifully, provoking them to hate her and join forces against her. As for her father, Janet forgave him a little more readily. Proud and independent as she was, she allowed him to hold her on his lap and read to her when she was feeling particularly sad. But he could rarely do anything right, and Janet would lose or break every one of the gifts he gave her. Janet's parents knew something was troubling her. They interpreted her tantrums and nasty behavior as signs of Janet's difficulty in growing up—which they were. No one could have understood from Janet's outward behavior, including little Janet herself, how desperate she felt or what was going on unconsciously.

To appreciate the full fury of Janet's reaction to her fall from grace, we have to make the interpretive leap of understanding what all this meant to her unconsciously. Unconsciously, Janet's reaction of jealous rage was the equivalent of a ruthless destruction of everything that stood in the way of her childhood wishes. Moreover, since little girls do have an awareness of their inner genital world, even little girls like Janet who are very early assuming a defensive exaggeration of phallic power, they also surmise that mothers have inner genitals. What better vengeance against the betraying mother than to penetrate and devour her mother's insides, to chew up all the leftover babies and the penis—the glorious phallus given to the mother by the father. Then, for good measure, little Janet lopped off her father's penis so that he would lose his power over her mother. In short, she destroyed every part of her parents that they had and she didn't have, especially those genital parts that made the mother desire the father or the father desire the mother. In Janet's four-year-old mind, where the distinction between sadistic fantasies and actual crimes is always ambiguous, she had vengefully destroyed the envied and hated parents' genitals and she, in a triumph of wish fulfillment, had appropriated the father's phallus for herself. Since a phallus is not a penis but an imaginary and detachable part, it can also be destroyed several times, in several ways, and still be appropriated. However, if the phallus had been given to the mother and now little Janet had stolen it for herself, then the mother is the one who will devise a punishment suitable to the crime. One day the mother, by now transformed into a crazed witch-mother in a reflection of Janet's own crazed envy and rage, will destroy her daughter's body, devour her insides, mutilate her beautiful face, carve up her sexual organs so that she cannot bear children, torture her, and eat up her children—should she dare to have any. This is not the sort of fantasy life that can be tolerated for very long, even unconsciously. Sooner or later a more reasonable solution must be found to the rage and to the disappointment that provoked the rage in the first place.

Some little girls with similar unconscious fantasies might solve the whole business of their terrible jealous rage and the parents' terrible retaliatory rage by retreating to some stereotyped image of the good, clean, well-behaved, submissive, obedient little girl. However, Janet was not about to hide her ambitions and talents to assuage the gods.

How might a little girl atone for her crimes against her parents without relinquishing the powers she supposes she has stolen from them? Little Janet recovered from her jealous rage by devising a clever strategy that would appease both parents and yet still allow her to triumph over them. Janet's first order of business was to devise a way to placate her mother, a quite ordinary, kind, and generous mother who in Janet's dreams and unconscious fantasies was the equal in vengeful fury to Snow White's cruel stepmother. It was Janet's unconscious strategy for appeasing her mother that gave form and direction to her masquerade, her character perversion if you will.

The coup de grace was little Janet's strategy of keeping her stolen "masculinity" but fooling the gods by putting her determination, persistence, intellect, and ambition to work for her mother. In fact, from now on, instead of tormenting her mother she would act just like a powerful, protecting father to her mother. By placating her mother's rage in that way, she would be giving back to her mother what she had stolen from her and yet would still triumph over her father by becoming a bigger and better daddy than he was. Janet would be a proper, self-sacrificing daughter-momma and also the majestic, powerful son-daddy her mother had been wishing for.

After she started school, Janet took pride in reading aloud to her mother. It was not long before she was able to solve many mental and physical problems that were beyond her intellectually inhibited mother. As an adolescent, she helped her incompetent mother repair broken toasters, stereos, and TV sets. She alone could find her scatterbrained mother's missing eyeglasses and misplaced keys. The proud mother, whose own narcissism was gratified by having such a marvelous daughter who was as competent and masterful as a son might have been, was delighted to acknowledge Janet's superiority over her. She bragged to all her friends about her brilliant and beautiful daughter— the valedictorian, the summa cum laude, the college professor, the world-famous lecturer, the potential Nobel Prize winner.

By the time she was an adolescent, Janet's infantile fantasy of being masculine but also virtuously feminine, a son but also a daughter, a Big Daddy but also a Big Momma, had become an entrenched aspect of her character structure, and all she had to do was look around to the conventions in her society to see if she could make that infantile fantasy work in the grown-up world.

To review what I said earlier, in the 1920s it was evident that the ideal of the passive, submissive woman who simply carried out the law of the father and stayed at home and cared for children and polished furniture was not appealing to every woman. Quite a few women were rebelling against that bourgeois ideal of femininity and very soon there would be more and more of these troublesome types. It was imperative that the social order devise an accommodation, a way of placating the feminists who were marching through the steets proclaiming that they were the equals of men and could do anything men could do. It was decided that women would be allowed to express their "masculine" ambitions, but only *if* they could also prove that they were still virtuous, self-sacrificing feminine types. Now at the close of the century, the social order is still reconciling itself to the emancipated woman, the woman who is demanding that she be treated on an equal footing with men. Thus, even today the accommodation of the social order still gives a plausibility and permission to the infantile strategy of masquerading as a feminine type.

When Janet arrived at womanhood, she continued to use what she unconsciously imagined she had stolen and to put it in the service of women less fortunate than herself. She was extremely self-sacrificing and completely devoted to the women who needed her assistance—her two older sisters, her students, her less talented female colleagues. All she required in return was gratitude and a recognition that she was superior to them. In one way or another, the women she assisted had to make tribute to her superior know-how. So long as they recognized that she and she alone was the powerful, dominating one, she would protect them and give to them unstintingly. When Janet's supremacy was not acknowledged, all her buried childhood passions would rise to the surface. At home, in the privacy of her study, she would fall into paroxysms of rage, realizing only that she felt slightly anxious and very hostile toward some woman who was prettier or smarter than she —a colleague, a friend, a passing acquaintance. Usually, though, Janet got all the gratitude and acknowledgment she required. There were plenty of women around whom she could care for, help, and rescue. So most of the time, Janet's fierce rivalry with women could be kept neatly under wraps.

Janet paid a heavy price for living out this scheme she had concocted. There seemed to be no limits to her need to placate and make reparation to the helpless, "feminine" women in her life. She could never do enough for her mother. She would give up a precious evening with her husband and children to try to help out a friend in crisis. She would neglect her own writing to rewrite a student's mediocre thesis. After a strenuous day of rescuing vulnerable female students, she sometimes would drive fifty miles to help her sick sister care for her children and then drive home to make dinner for her own family. The strain of this continual placation and reparation was exhausting. Janet suffered occasionally from excruciating back pains, which she cheerily minimized. No pathetic weakling she. As Rivière pointed out about her patient, the device of placation and reparation "was worked to death, and sometimes it almost worked her to death."

Janet was a respected and admired member of a lively, intellectual community. Moreover, as part of her intellectual calling, she was a feminist who lobbied successfully for the social and cultural causes that would make the world a better place for all women. The securely established, tenured male professors at the university where Janet taught were impressed with the way she tempered her intellectual brilliance with a proper submission to their authority, and they referred to her as a saint. Her younger male colleagues, who were unconsciously threatened by the number of papers and books she wrote, would joke about the Big Momma, who didn't have to be taken seriously anyway. But a few of her equally brilliant and self-sufficient female colleagues saw through the masquerade and knew that with all her pretentious saintly ways and just feminist causes, Janet was merely another Big Daddy in disguise.

At the end of a long day of placation and reparation, the undaunted Janet was ready and willing for sex. As much as she needed to play Big Daddy to all the helpless women in her life, the truth was that she also needed to assure herself of her femininity by having sexual intercourse as frequently as possible. It was imperative that she get more sexual pleasure than those inferior feminine women like her mother. She was determined also not to be beaten out by her husband. She always wanted more sex than he did. It was crucial that he not have an orgasm before she did. She was as afraid of impotence as any man. In bed, as in her post-lecture masquerade, she played the role of a subservient woman. However, under the screen of that impeccable femininity she orchestrated the sexual scenario, essentially robbing her husband of his active masculinity. Her performance was efficient. As when baking cookies, polishing the silver, waxing the grand piano, shopping for gourmet groceries, purchasing the right books, arranging for dinner parties and theater excursions, keeping the household accounts and paying the bills, she obligingly tended-to her husband's sexual needs. She brought to the marital chamber all her practical know-how and managerial skills, making absolutely certain that everything came off without a hitch. She performed fellatio with alacrity and was an inventive bed partner, more than willing to dress in whatever clothes and assume whatever position her undemanding, overwhelmed, and rather passive husband might require. Though he never asked for very much and might have been relieved with less, Janet would do everything necessary to make sure her husband had an erect penis to give her. She used her womanly arts, almost as a man would use a fetish, more as a device to avoid anxiety than as a means of obtaining sexual pleasure. In Janet's bedchamber, there was a great deal of adroit sexual performance, but very little feminine *jouissance*. Sex was an exercise in domination and penetration. Every movement, every gesture was focused, determined, phallic. There was no time or space in Janet's erotic script for suspenseful absences, the scattered, the undetermined, the enigmatic.

Reading this account of Janet's life, no one would doubt that Janet's strategy was far less tormenting and troubling than the strategies of an Olympia or a Sally or all the many women whose solution to gender conflict is extreme submissiveness and a life of sexual bondage. Except for her humiliating fits of rage after she recognized some other woman's superior beauty or power, her occasional backaches, and the bouts of fatigue that resulted from the do-or-die intensity of her day-to-day reparations, Janet's masquerade of womanliness protected her from becoming aware of thoughts and emotions that might otherwise have been immensely troubling to her. Her masquerade, her character perversion, was eminently successful in that it covered over her infantile "crimes," her guilt and fears of retaliation, and all the disappointments and mortifications of childhood. Janet's masquerade of womanliness was a screen for an entire childhood history. It was the trace left of a complicated narrative of deprivations, losses, defeats, clever tactics, unsuccessful self-deceptions, the fantasized triumphant usurpation of the phallic powers of the adult generation. But every psychological strategy works in this way—phobias, paranoid suspicions, jealous rages, obsessional ideas, compulsive rituals, hysterical paralyses. Why then am I likening Janet's masquerade to a perversion?

First of all, I am emphasizing that there is never a clear distinction between a so-called normal womanliness and a perverse masquerade of womanliness. Every adult person has a perversion that has grown up alongside his or her neurotic or normal solutions to gender conflict. Janet's perverse strategy represents a stage in the formation of a typical neurosis rather than a full-fledged perversion. Nevertheless, in certain crucial respects, the strategies that express and conceal Janet's infantile fantasy of the stolen phallus do have the characteristics of what I would label as a perversion. For Janet, the common childhood fantasy of usurping the genital powers that belong to the parents became a furtive enactment of everyday life; her masquerade of womanliness was a full-time preoccupation; her driven character was based on an attempt to reconcile a rigidly dichotomized view of masculinity and femininity. Janet's preoccupation with placation and reparation indicated that this most womanly of women, who managed to present herself to the world as the epitome of a successful adult woman, still confused masculinity with a phallic power and femininity with a castrated vulnerability. Moreover, her castration anxiety, her unconscious fantasy that her own genitals would be destroyed in retaliation for her childhood fantasies, was sufficiently severe to indicate that it gathered *some* of its force from the more primitive anxieties of abandonment and separation, tantamount to the mutilation anxiety that characterizes all perversions.

Janet's psychic bargain was exhausting but it worked efficiently in that it left exposed only a remnant of what it was all about. Janet's character perversion succeeded until she become powerful and famous enough to display her powers to the world. After that, Janet's post-lecture apprehension, her vague sense of impending retaliation for her crimes of intellectual power, threatened to expose everything. So she quickly devised a strategy that would replace her anxiety and guilt and take care of all this foreboding sense of crime and punishment. Janet's post-lecture performance, her perverse enactment—"reassure me that I am deserving of my powers but don't take it all too seriously for I am really only a castrated woman"—expressed succinctly the fuller masquerade of womanliness that constituted an entire way of life devoted to a socially normalized but unsuccessful resolution of Janet's feminine and masculine identifications. The humiliation of pretending to be a demeaned woman was a small price to pay for assuaging the other, more frightening feelings that kept her awake and trembling after every successful and brilliant lecture. Janet's visible display of a self-denigrating femininity—"See, I have nothing at all"—appeased her guilty conscience, which then gave her permission to keep her powers.

In Riviere's day, women like Janet were still unusual. Now I see them everywhere, in my clinical practice, among my friends and colleagues. Many a brilliant and successful woman unconsciously interprets her genuine powers as stolen phallic trophies. She exhibits her talents and achieves her ambitions but is always devising some appeasement for having won. She is always edgy that something terrible will happen unless she goes through a placation to the gods. She survives the winning and the keeping of her hard-earned power by presenting herself to her male colleagues as a saint, a self-demeaning, self-sacrificing, masochistic woman. She is always making reparations to other women by acting like a Big Daddy who has the power to rescue them. She thinks of sex as an exercise in power and domination and is as terrified of inner genital excitement as any macho male.

Now at the close of the twentieth century, with all the token permission given to women to express their intellectual ambitions and erotic strivings, there is still created an atmosphere of retaliation that makes many women hold back from a full-hearted, open display of intellectual mastery and active sexual desire. A woman fears, very often justifiably, that if she challenges authority or succeeds in roles and professions that have traditionally been defined as masculine, she will be punished. For a woman like Janet, who unconsciously interprets her intellectual gifts and talents as stolen powers anyway, these fears of retaliation are exacerbated. So while it is good sense for any woman to think twice about the potential envy and fear she is likely to arouse in men and other women when she shows her power, not every woman will seek refuge in a masquerade of womanliness or advertise her mind as a nonthreatening spiritual mist or display herself as a submissive or masochistic feminine type. Only a Janet, who unconsciously confuses power with a rapacious theft of phallic trophies, will find it necessary to propitiate the gods by devising a strategy that employs a caricature of femininity to disguise her forbidden "masculine" strivings. And nowadays, a Janet can easily find a willing collaboration with her perverse strategy in the primitive social gender stereotypes that are still upheld as ideals of womanhood and manhood. As Janet puts on her mask of self-demeaning femininity, no one will be any the wiser, least of all herself.

9
Stolen Goods

Money is the universal means and power, exterior to man, not issuing from man as man or from human society as society, to turn imagination into reality and reality into mere imagination. Similarly it turns real human and natural faculties into mere abstract representations and thus imperfections and painful imaginings, while on the other hand it turns the real imperfections and imaginings, the really powerless faculties that exist only in the imagination of the individual into real faculties and powers.

Karl Marx, "On the Power of Money
in Bourgeois Society," 1844

What distinguishes kleptomania, the impulsive stealing of material goods, from plain old theft is the erotic excitement that accompanies the filching of the goods. Psychoanalysis has revealed a whole unconscious fantasy life that underlies and accompanies *kleptomania*. Yet there is a mythology in the psychoanalytic understanding of kleptomania that also warrants attention. The mythology is an amalgam of partial truths based on the usual misinterpretations of the genital differences between males and females. For example, kleptomania is frequently said to be the prototype of the female perversion and therefore analogous to fetishism, the prototype of the male perversion. This analogy between kleptomania and fetishism is derived from the idea that females are the genital "have-nots" who suffer from penis envy and males are the genital "haves" who suffer from castration anxiety. Thus, the fetish in fetishism is an item of genital reassurance, a substitute for the woman's absent penis; and the stolen commodity in kleptomania is an item of vengeance, a compensation for a stolen penis. The male fetishist is interested in achieving erection and penetration. The female kleptomaniac is interested in vengeful emasculation of her deprivers, those who she imagines have what she does not have. "What they once took from me, I am entitled to steal from them."

Even after psychoanalysts recognized that there were male kleptomaniacs, men who stole for excitement and security, the thefts were said to be attempts to acquire the superior genital equipment of the father. The psychoanalytic mythology that the stolen goods in kleptomania are stolen penises persists in the face of considerable evidence that the item filched by a kleptomaniac has a symbolic structure very much like the structure of any other fetish. In fetishism, the blue velvet bathrobe, the green earrings, the fur wrap are memorials to absences and losses from every level and dimension of experience. In kleptomania, the stolen goods are also versatile memorials to a variety of absences and losses. Absence—yes, of love, of a sense of wholeness, belonging and well-being, but surely not of an actual penis. Loss—yes, of a power that all infants imagine they have, certain adults actually have, and many others seem to have in great quantities, but not a loss of the anatomical penis.

The neatly drawn border between fetishism and kleptomania is artificial. Male fetishists sometimes steal the items that will enable them to perform sexually. Kleptomaniacs of both sexes sometimes use their stolen trophies as fetishes that enable sexual excitement. As we will see, the penis envy interpretation of kleptomania arose out of the same socioeconomic conditions as the commodity fetishism, which encourages human beings to use things as a substitute for feelings and persons. Fetishism involves the use of deadened and dehumanized objects as a substitute for living, excited persons. Fetishism allows material goods to substitute for feelings. In that sense, kleptomania is an aspect of fetishism, just like every other perversion, and not a distinct disorder with a motive based on penis envy rather than castration anxiety.

Kleptomaniacs of both sexes are more involved with escaping from threats to their psychological survival than with erotic pleasure. For the average kleptomaniac, excitement and fundamental security are indistinguishable. Kleptomaniacs sometimes steal when they are about to be anxious or depressed. The excitement of stealing and the goods that they steal reassure them that they will not be abandoned or annihilated. For instance, they steal when they would otherwise be worried about work, selecting furniture, changing a hair style, writing a term paper, having to wait on line. The excitement and sense of risk they experience when they are stealing makes them feel elated and powerful. The comfort they feel when they are in possession of a stolen trophy forestalls anxiety, the humiliation of having to wait, the letdown of having failed at some enterprise. If her needs for emotional security are frustrated, the kleptomaniac will sometimes react with violence. The theft forestalls worse mayhem by muting any awareness of hostility and sadism. The violence has to do with the depriving ones, the almighty parental gods from her infantile past, whose images the kleptomaniac wishes to protect. Thus, the theft is an act of vengeance that protects these deprivers from the full extent of her violent destructiveness. Her deprivers seem to her to be in the present and she is aware of a contempt for the department store, the museum, the office, the library from which she steals: "I have been deprived, therefore I have a right to steal."

What the kleptomaniac has been deprived of and what she is stealing, the emotions and fantasies that enliven her theft, how the theft relates to her childhood deprivations and humiliations can be understood only by a reading of her unique unconscious script.

There are, however, some prototypical kleptomania scripts. All of them make clear that the thefts have to do with accusations, the filching of withheld gratifications, and risk, deceit, triumph, revenge, and violence. In kleptomania, the penis envy lament that sometimes appears in a dream or a fantasy is, in fact, a disguise for an accusation against the parents that they have withheld the gratifications that enable a child to feel loved, admired, safe, and protected. For the deprived and neglected child, every withholding of gratification is interpreted as justification for filching the trophies of power and love that were withheld. And all of these personal fantasies of power and love, which in kleptomania become attached to phallic symbols, might otherwise be invested in other symbols of power. However, in a social order where a commodity fetishism is the rule and most of the actual social and economic power resides in the hands of a few powerful superior males, the kleptomaniac feels a vengeful envy and experiences the stolen goods as phallic trophies.

In kleptomania, the perverse act moves into the public domain, where the theft is an accusation against the social environment and a vengeful attack on its traditions, edifices, and monuments, akin to acts of vandalism and pyromania. The locale in which the theft occurs—department store, hotel, museum, nightclub, cemetery—is the emotional equivalent of a depriving and frustrating breast. In kleptomania a desire that once attached itself to a human relationship is transferred to a thing, a social commodity.

Every perversion entails a displacement of emotions and desires away from living, mutually participating human partners to dehumanized fetishized objects. Kleptomania highlights this displacement of aggression, lust, envy, vengeance, anxiety, depression, and agitated madness from personal relationships to material goods. The economy of personal psychology, with its unconscious balance accounts of love and power, and the socioeconomic structure, with its arbitrary balances of submission and domination, converge in kleptomania.

In modern societies where virtually every dimension of human life and feeling has been gradually permeated by the commodity fetishism that Marx described in 1847, it is inevitable that a material good—a steak, a cowboy hat, an umbrella, a ruby ring, a black silk dress—

might be a substitute for the mutualities of a freely given care, love, admiration, acceptance, erotic fulfillment. In the commodity form of society, which is rapidly colonizing every nook and cranny of the globe, it becomes an everyday matter that we should lavish our loving attention on things rather than persons. These days, sex itself is merely another commodity and, like any other commodity, it is used as a substitute for every other feeling and desire.

Commodity fetishism is an artifact of a recent stage in the evolution of authority in human societies. We have progressed from the absolute law of the tribal elders to the tyrannies of the law of consumerism. In this gradual social evolution, the family has always played a significant role in communicating to children the political and socioeconomic values of society. Each social system generates the family structure that will preserve its own status quo. Depending on the degree of power held by the rulers of the state, the family is assigned less or more power to exert its influences on the child. If absolute and final authority is invested in the tribal elders, the city-state, the church, the feudal lord, the tsar, the commissar, then the parents assume less responsibility and have less authority over their offspring. But whatever form the family has taken throughout history and however weak or strong it was in relation to other social institutions, its function has been to bring the unformed, untamed desires of the younger generation into some harmony with the law of the land.

What we have now is the law of consumerism, with its worship of things. From an early age, our children are learning that material goods are a substitute for security, self-esteem, and love and that sex is merely another of the commodities that can be purchased in the marketplace. Some say, and I suspect they are right, that the law of consumerism is the age-old patriarchal tyranny in its newest guise. In any event, the effects of consumer mentality on family life and on the relationships between children and parents have yet to be calculated. We do know that the interactions between family structures and social structures are subtle and that what happens to the child in the family can also turn about to affect society. Will the families of the future resist the law of consumerism and undermine it? Or is the whole business of buying (or stealing) security and admiration and love and power and sex so much easier than dealing with the complexities of relating to dangerously alive and unpredictable human beings?

In all times and in all places, even before a child is born, the material social world is penetrating the womb indirectly with its sounds and movements, directly with the substances that enter the baby-to-be through the expectant mother's body. The sounds, movements, and substances may be translated to the baby-to-be as expressions of love and protection or substances of hatred and destruction. To a newborn, the world he or she enters is a good world, the self a good self, when the love and protection of the mother's holding environment brings the world to the baby in a way that makes the baby feel that he or she and the world are in harmony. However, when an infant feels unheld or dropped too much of the time, she or he gets to be a greedy and vengeful child. The hungerlust of infant panic-desperation will later transpose to the larger social environment, where the deprived and neglected child eventually becomes an adult who feels that the only way to be held is to chew up, tear apart, tear out, disembowel, rip off, grab, and snatch, swindle, poach—all with an inner sense of entitlement: "What was not given, I have the right to take."

These impulses to steal what was not freely given play a part in all perversions. Whether a patient's dominant perversion is fetishism, transvestism, homeovestism, extreme submissiveness, or female impersonation, there is always an element of kleptomania, the wish to steal what was not freely given, the wish for vengeance on those who gave love and then took it away. Sooner or later, in every therapy of a perversion, there will be a theft or series of thefts, either in fantasy or in enactment. I have already shown cases of female perversion where a subtext of kleptomania was part of some more encompassing perverse strategy.

Lillian (discussed in Chapter 8), whose dominant perversion was homeovestism—dressing up in the clothes of a powerful, phallic woman—began her homeovestic career at the age of three when she consoled herself for the disappearance and loss of her exciting pregnant mother by donning her mother's dresses and stuffing them with a pillow. She was not given these dresses—she had to filch them and perform her little impersonation secretly. Later, when Lillian menstruated, she would be overtaken by an irresistible impulse to filch the velvet gowns and emerald necklaces that would enable her to feel like a powerful, valuable, and desirable woman. I did not mention earlier that Lillian was for a short while also an exhibitionist who would appropriate her father's flashy open-top sports car and speed along busy highways to exhibit her menstrual pads and bleeding genitals to horrified truck drivers.

In the perversion, the once excluded child is the triumphant one— the one who steals the power of the depriving parents, the one who uses this power to do to others what was once done to her, to humiliate and frighten them as she was once humiliated and frightened. From Lillian's case we learned how a little girl might equate all of her earlier infantile deprivations with genital deprivations. During her mother's pregnancy she had her mother all to herself. With her brother's birth, she lost her mother completely. Moreover, this pregnancy was an announcement of the role that the father played in the mother's life. How much poor little Lillian envied the power of her father! And then, seeing her little brother's penis where she had nothing at all led to the collapse of Lillian's fantasy that she was the center of her mother's universe. It was clear that the mother had given to the brother everything she had withheld from Lillian—cuddling, lullabies, attention, and a penis. Stealing for the adult Lillian was a reassurance of her existence and a vengeful triumph over her depriving mother. We saw how the eroticized excitement that accompanied her kleptomanic attacks arose out of a prolonged situation of infant neglect, which was then exacerbated by the premature and therefore traumatic eroticization of Lillian's genitals. The combination of maternal neglect and maternal sexual molestation brought Lillian's genitals to life while the rest of her body—her skin surface, her musculature, her mouth and eyes—were deprived of freely given security, love, and encouragement.

For a deprived and sexually molested child like Lillian, one body part is interchangeable with another, and any body part is interchangeable with any commodity or other material good. Even the penis was for Lillian merely another item of reassurance. She cared nothing at all for the many men she had intercourse with. The man's erect penis was proof enough to Lillian that she was a safe, valued, and loved person. Though she did not, of course, steal these penises, in devoting herself so assiduously to making them erect, without any regard for her partner, it was clear that she regarded the erect penis as just another phallic trophy, designed to fix her and make her feel less depressed and anxious. It was not erotic fulfillment that assuaged Lillian's desperate fears of abandonment, separation, and castration, but the psychological fantasy that she had attained the security and love and power she had been deprived of as a child. Her vengeance was directed toward these men whom she treated as though they were nothing at all. Lillian performed her various thefts in a social world where the fungibility of material goods with security and love and power encourages the fantasy that things and fragments of things can compensate for the absence of significant human relationships.

Olympia (also discussed in Chapter 8) was not a kleptomaniac, but she got the anatomy-commodity interchangeabilities just right with her science fiction tale of the suctioning vagina. She believed that she belonged to the sex with an absent genital organ. And, as she portrayed these matters, a penis was a burden. All that genital did was create problems of performance. Her void, on the other hand, could make a mockery of phallic power. Olympia knew that the goods of the material world, the household trophies of the patriarchal order, were her enemies. The centerfold, Olympia, displayed her body to multitudes with a cheery smile and a big heart. But her science fiction fantasies made clear Olympia's bitter envy and contempt for those who were given what she was deprived of. Everything she had not been given— holding, protection, nurturance, a sense of value—was interpreted as a deprivation of phallic power. Her own body was merely a container, on which she inscribed her fetishized body parts. The contrast between her void and the powers that were given to others was painfully apparent. Olympia intuitively grasped Marx's thesis that household commodities are fetish objects. Since they are no longer real physical objects, commodity fetishes are not regulated by the laws that govern the relations between real physical things. Commodities are governed only by the artificial value relations of the marketplace, and as such they are destined to be obtained through artifice, deception, robbery, and trickery. Olympia felt that she had every right to suck up and demolish every commodity that symbolized the patriarchal order that had deprived her of her very being.

In his treatise on *Madame Bovary*, Tony Tanner remarks, "At a certain indefinite point the fetish need not be in any way related to a woman or women in general . . . but attaches itself directly to objects." As he explains this displacement of feeling, commodity fetishism "may take over increasingly large areas of the person's approach to life in general, and thus it can permeate an entire society's modes of feeling and dealing." Vargas Llosa, the confessed *Bovary* addict, then echoes Tanner:

> In *Madame Bovary* we see the first signs of the alienation that a century later will take hold of men and women in industrial societies (*the women above all, owing to the life they are obliged to live*): consumption as an outlet for anxiety, the attempt to people with objects the emptiness that modern life has made a permanent feature of the existence of the individual . . . things, once the servants and instruments of mankind, become its masters and destroyers.

Unlike Olympia, who received her inspiration directly from her painful experiences in the material world, the two *Bovary* theoreticians Tanner and Vargas Llosa took their interpretations from Marx:

As this perverting power, money then appears as the enemy of man and social bonds that pretend to self-subsistence. It changes fidelity into infidelity, love into hate, hate into love, virtue into vice, vice into virtue, slave into master, master into slave, stupidity into intelligence, intelligence into stupidity.

The case of Janet (discussed in Chapter 8), who used a mask of self-demeaning, self-sacrificing womanliness to disguise her professional ambitions and intellectual powers, has a subtext on the way the gender conformities of the social order collaborate with unconscious fantasies about phallic and castrated beings. In Janet's case, where the deprivations of infancy and childhood were of the ordinary, expectable kind, the theft of a phallic trophy was an imaginary event that had meaning only in her unconscious fantasy life. But even in these least insidious of circumstances, the infantile fantasy of stealing a phallic trophy went on to acquire a larger social meaning that gave a plausibility to Janet's infantile solutions to her gender conflicts. No person grows up with a clearly demarcated sense of femininity or masculinity. A person's gender identity is always conflicted to some extent; it is an interplay of infantile fantasies, unconscious conflicts, family values and attitudes, and the manner in which the gender conventions of the social order first infiltrate the family structure and then, later, all too often collaborate with infantile gender attributions. Janet grew up in a social environment that gave permission to women to pursue intellectual and professional careers on an equal basis with men. Nevertheless, Janet feared retribution from the men she competed with and retribution from the females whom she triumphed over. On a purely personal level, all this fear of retribution stemmed from Janet's ferocious envy of her father's power to do and have with the mother everything she could not and her rage at the mother who was given what was withheld from the daughter. It was the fury and humiliation of being excluded from the primal scene that drove little Janet wild and motivated her infantile strategy of playing the role of daddy to her mother. As an adult she could still be this Big Daddy, but only in the mask of a self-demeaning, self-sacrificing woman. In the course of her analysis, as Janet was coming to some greater understanding that she was *only* a woman just like her mother and sisters, this mortification led to a phase of kleptomania. With these kleptomanic enactments she was able to bring out into the open the terrible childhood fantasies that were too painful and frightening to remember. Instead of stealing imaginary trophies from her mother's belly, she would steal books from her university library. It was these thefts and her fantasies and dreams about stealing from me and my library that were a key to the unconscious meaning of her symptoms and her childhood fantasies of the stolen phallus. Janet stole not just any books but obscure and difficult books written by men who were famous in her field of endeavor and, as she informed me, "impossible for you or any of my colleagues to understand." These thefts gave Janet a feeling of enormous triumph, especially since the librarian was a very passive and unambitious woman who looked up to Professor Janet as a potential Nobel Prize winner. She was so easy to hoodwink. Every minute of risk heightened Janet's excitement. She would stop by the librarian's desk with her trophy of the day, pausing to chat, brazenly flipping through the pages. On some days her triumph was complete as she would watch gleefully as some other less clever thief was stopped at library door by the guard. With just a twinge of anxiety, Janet marched bravely by this guardian of the treasures, with a mischievous wink and coquettish smile. He waved her out, with a mock bow and a flirtatious grin, which Janet interpreted as his permission to steal what belonged to the pathetic librarian. Janet, now an eminently successful woman, who had every advantage of her social class and position in the world, was still involved in fooling the grown-ups and finding ways to get their permission to keep what she had stolen. In Janet's case these criminal enactments were in the service of recollecting her childhood traumas; they were thefts in the service of advancing her analysis. Nevertheless, they were actual thefts and expressed the essential spirit of the kleptomanic mission and its relationship to the institutions of the social order. Janet's infantile solution fits into our social order that still, as we near the end of the twentieth century, defines intellectual ambition as masculine and still sees professional women like Janet as viragos bent on appropriating male goods and territories.

In certain crucial respects Janet's emotional situation is not too different from that of Joan of Arc, who also dared to compete with men on their own ground. As long as Joan's ambitions went no further than a misty holiness and spiritual communication, the fact that she cut her hair short and dressed in men's clothing did not trouble anyone very much. But from the moment she let her masculine ambitions show, she was endangered. Her holy voices were then interpreted by her enemies as voices of the devil. And when she triumphed on the field of battle, she was properly punished for her unholy presumptions. Janet, because she harbored an unconscious wish to steal what the father could give to the mother, had some personal reasons to fear retribution from men and from women. These childhood fears were then confirmed in a social situation where men were immensely fearful of women anyway, especially of those with "masculine" aspirations. Janet would have had very little to worry about if she had confined herself to her self-sacrificing behavior with her mother, sisters, and other less fortunate students and colleagues. For this she would only get backaches and exhaustion. However, Janet's anxiety and sleepless nights arose when she dared to give lectures that were brilliant and authoritative, when she dared to compete openly with her male and female colleagues. Her symptoms began when she displayed her phallic trophies.

Men are far less likely to wish women harm when they behave like proper feminine types—tenders of the domestic hearth, nurturers of children, whores, mistresses, saints, potters, weavers, quilt makers, and painters of desert flowers. Let a woman openly declare her ambitions in territories that have been defined as masculine or to show her powers in those arenas! That's when the mayhem starts. And that's usually when women run for cover in their masquerades of womanliness. That's when some adult women will reawaken the infantile fantasy that the intelligence they hide under the skirts, or pants, is a stolen trophy that can be stolen back from the stealer.

Psychoanalysts understood the stolen goods in kleptomania to be the deprived woman's triumph over her penis envy. The stolen phallic trophy was seen as a triumph over nature and anatomical destiny: "What nature withheld from me, I have stolen." But it was this emphasis on the laws of nature and anatomical destiny that arrested psychoanalytic knowledge about gender identity and its relationship to perversion for several decades. Freud himself would often warn his readers that the terms *feminine* and *masculine* were elusive and unfortunately all too often misunderstood in terms of conventions of active and passive. Yet at other times he would revert to equating the social conventions of active and passive with the anatomical destiny of sperm and ova, penis and vagina, male and female. Like most ordinary people, psychoanalysts went along with the assumption that the gender stereotypes of femininity and masculinity faithfully represented the laws of human nature. Males were destined to dominate and penetrate and females to submit and receive.

That kleptomania, familiarly called shoplifting, is an impulsive act seen more frequently in females than in males is true. The female-male statistics on shoplifting are valid and reliable across many modern societies. However, the reasons why females are more likely to be shoplifters or kleptomaniacs and males are more likely to be guilty of burglary, robbery, and fraud have very little to do with the differing destinies of the genital have-nots and the genital haves and a great deal to do with the way scientists (mostly men) have reasoned about the relationship between female anatomy and female power. Kleptomaniacs are not penis stealers. They are the many women (and men) who have learned to use commodity fetishes as substitutes for human relationships, to use things as a way of forestalling anxiety, depression, madness, and violence.

As I said at the outset of this chapter, the kleptomaniac/penis envy interpretation arose out of the same socioeconomic conditions that encourage human beings to use things as substitutes for persons. Human history is dotted with decades and eras and ages when women have been allowed to assume the reins of power and to express themselves as equals in politics, business, art and literature, science, and family life. However, males have never stopped, for very long, equating the female desire for political, social, intellectual, and economic power with a desire to rob males of their masculinity. Males are driven and possessed by these infantile fantasies about the virago female. They are convinced that the castrated ones are out to castrate the phallic ones. And with their infantile fantasies that the father's penis is a mutilating organ that created the mother's mutilation, it is no wonder that males would fear retaliation from women. The males stick together in their bonds of maleness so that the females they envy and fear will never have a chance to steal the goods and powers that "rightfully" belong only to males. The penis-stealing female is a creation of males who find refuge from anxiety, guilt, shame, and madness in the exaggerated and imaginary power of the phallus and therefore live in dread of losing this power. Whenever it came to trying to understand why males and females had a greater or lesser proportion of economic power, artistic ability, scientific acumen, criminal tendencies, and sexual deviation, the phallic-castrated fantasies arrested scientists, the vast majority of whom were males, at various prestages of knowledge about the relationship between gender and power.

Until the late nineteenth and early twentieth century, when criminology would achieve the status of a social science, everybody had casually observed but rarely thought to investigate the fact that females made up a very low proportion of the criminal population. When at last that fact became a question worthy of investigation, the issues and dilemmas were dealt with and reasoned through in much the same manner as present-day scientists have been coping with the low rate of sexual perversion among females. As I trace the history of this reasoning, the reader might easily substitute for criminality the word *perversion*.

Criminality, like perversion, was considered a male activity. The theories offered in explanation for a low crime rate among females sought to account both for the large number of women who did not engage in criminal activity and for the small number of women who did. In both instances, the answers were found in the deficiencies of female physical development and rarely, if ever, in any superiority of female moral development. Occasionally, a brave soul would suggest that the low criminality rate among women was a sign of female moral integrity, just as some people today interpret the low perversion rate among women as the female's greater virtue and moral nobility. Nevertheless, in dealing with criminal women, it was usual to argue that specific *weaknesses* in female nature were responsible for the low crime rates in the female population.

Caesar Lombroso and William Ferrero, in their 1899 *The Female Offender,* attributed the lower incidence of crime among women to a less active cerebral cortex, which "leads more easily to motor and hysterical epilepsy, or to sexual anomalies [*sic*], than to crime." As for the female criminals, they, like their brothers in crime, were atavistic throwbacks to an earlier stage in human evolution. When Lombroso and Ferrero discovered that imprisoned women did not have the stigmata that were traditionally used to identify born criminals—moles, prehensile feet, hairiness, misshapen skulls, peculiar facial proportions —they were perplexed. But not for long. On the basis of the few physical similarities between born male criminals and female prisoners, such as large stature and muscular strength, Lombroso and Ferrero resolved that female criminals were pseudo males, genetic relics of a time when females had not fully differentiated themselves from males. The reason women offenders revealed fewer of the stigmata signaling inborn degeneration was attributed to another, even more pathological deficiency: the female of the species had evolved less far from her origins, and women were therefore too primitive to have acquired signs of degeneracy. On the other hand, women could appear to be more law-abiding than men, but only because of their essential conservatism—"a conservatism of which the primary cause is to be sought in the immobility of the ovule compared with the zoosperm."

While later sociologists and psychologists found the Lombroso-Ferrero formulations to be atavistic, unscientific, and perhaps even laughable, in fact they kept to the overall drift of the Lombroso-Ferrero arguments and preserved it in a new guise. Whether they held to a biological determination or a social determination, social scientists were in agreement that feminine women were incapable of criminality because of their feminine weaknesses—passivity, lower intelligence, and lack of ambition—whereas masculine women were criminal because of their driven hunger for masculine power. Here and there, tucked in among the statistics and the theories, was a likely alternative: females may be just as much endowed with criminal mentality as males.

But if females were to turn out to be as innately criminal as males, how were the scientists to explain that women commit fewer criminal acts than men? Here they were back to the beginning of the dilemma about female criminality and again there was a ready answer, not very different in spirit from the old Lombroso-Ferrero arguments. In contrast to males, who are simply and straightforwardly criminal, females are endowed with a greater deceitfulness and a greater capacity to mask or disguise their criminal activity. On this score, female penologists were in complete agreement with their male mentors. By and large female penologists made every effort to gather the facts that would support the secrecy-deceitfulness assessments of the criminal woman. Some, speaking from the authority of their "personal" experience with feminine nature, would supplement these assessments with a few theories of their own. Female penologists would argue that females in general were fundamentally less honest and more devious than men. Female offenders were more deceitful than male offenders and more adept at suppressing the facts, denying their deeds, falsifying details, and misleading the staff members of the prisons and hospitals to which they were committed. To bear witness that these thoughts about female deceitfulness were not the result of male bias, Margaret Sanger would be cited as testifying that concealment was one of the most legitimate of a woman's arts.

It would have been ungenerous and furthermore unscientific to offer these facts and interpretations about female nature without attempting to link nature with the appropriate psychological motives. All the motives necessary were found, and, as usual, in the most obvious place —female anatomy. It was simple enough to conclude that the weaknesses of the female—her smaller body frame, her diminished muscular strength, her menstrual moodiness—required that she resort to indirection in all matters, including her criminal inclinations. It had been agreed by all concerned, and the statistics bore it out, that manslaughter, aggravated assault, robbery, burglary, and auto theft were male crimes. However, by bringing in the element of female deceitfulness, even these long agreed upon verities now had to be questioned.

It had to be conceded that perhaps the facts were merely statistical artifacts. Law enforcement agents were known to be chivalrous and lenient toward women offenders. Women themselves were secretive about their crimes. Putting these two facts together, it could be argued that female criminals were protected from incarceration by a low degree of detectability, which would account for the built-in distortion of crime statistics. On the basis of this reasoning, it would be hard indeed to continue to have confidence in female crime statistics. No one could be sure, after all, which were female crimes. For a time, the whole question of female versus male crime was in a complete muddle. But throughout it all, scientists remained relatively secure in their basic assumption that certain criminal activities could be definitely assigned to the female of the species—prostitution, adultery and abortion, infanticide, and *shoplifting.* Shoplifting was always cited among the crimes that were tied to the biological essence of femaleness.

In 1950 an American sociologist, Otto Pollak, took the bull by the horns. Because he set out to perfect the sociological method and to right the wrongs done to women in previous comparative studies of criminality, his book *The Criminality of Women* was hailed as a classic, a gem of scholarly objectivity, an example of the very best that sociology had to offer. Pollak was not going to accept at face value the prevailing half truths—half mythologies about the female criminal. Furthermore, he was not going to fall for some unproven biological interpretation. Surely, Pollak protested, the specificity of female criminality was intimately linked to the narrowness of a woman's life in modern society.

Nevertheless, one half truth that Pollak accepted from the start was women's innately greater deceitfulness, secretiveness, trickery, and pretense. Pollak, though he was a master sociologist, did not hesitate to assert that not enough attention had been paid to the role of physiological differences in explaining women's greater susceptibility to concealment. Interestingly, like many of those who try to account for the male-female perversion statistics, he related feminine fakery to women's sexual performance, suggesting that a woman's genital arrangements, her secretive inwardness, not only encouraged her to practice deceit but also made it fairly easy for her to do so. The way Pollak described the situation, the step from orgasm fakery to criminal fakery was virtually inevitable. He explained how pretense of sexual response is impossible for a man. A man must achieve an erection to perform sexually; he cannot disguise his absence of desire.

Woman's body, however, permits such pretense to a certain degree and lack of orgasm does not prevent her ability to participate in the sex act. It cannot be denied that this basic physiological difference may well have a great influence on the degree of confidence which the two sexes have in the possible success of concealment and thus on their character pattern in this respect.

Pollak did not mention or, for that matter, seem aware that a long personal history of character development in a social order that denies active sexuality to women precedes orgasm trickery. Pollak goes on, trying to square the fact of female deceitfulness with the perspectives of a scientific sociology. At every turn his good sociology is defeated by his ambivalent attitudes toward the female. He recognizes that the society is always commanding and commending a female for her secrecy. For men secrecy is always experienced as a deviation. For women it is a "technical necessity and a social command." Pollak rejected the findings of other sociologists that some women criminals are known to have "fits of veracity." According to Pollak, "these cases of so-called veracity are cases of treachery committed by women informers acting from spite or fear, and treachery is in itself an act of insincerity and deceit."

The male thief is a specialist who sticks to his method and line of work. The female thief, who knows no rules and has no theft specialties except those associated with her line of work as a prostitute, is always posing "new riddles for pestered detectives." False accusation of sexual harassment and rape is a form of perjury and a criminal offense that women, particularly unmarried women, are more prone to commit than men. Pollak alerts law enforcement officers to the special psychological motivations of these female criminals. "How often the accusation of an unmarried woman against a man [for sexual harassment or rape] may indicate an experience which she consciously fears and abhors but unconsciously desires."

During menopause, when women are at last relieved of their proneness to crimes stemming from sexual secrecy, sexual repression, and sexual revenge, they lose their physical attractiveness and become guilty of crimes of irritability and restlessness such as arson and breach of the peace and the infamous shoplifting.

In general, because of the limitations placed on women's roles in society, female criminals have preferred certain types of victims—children, husbands and lovers, neighbors and other persons they are in close contact with. While it may be true that women steal mostly from people they know, the high rate of shoplifting and pickpocketing among female criminals shows that some women, at least, are able to branch out into the public realm despite the limitations placed on women in general. Pollak contends that this insidious spreading out of kleptomania into the larger social order had grown to dangerous proportions during the Second World War as women began to take over the jobs previously held by men. The emancipation of women and the new social roles they were permitted were major factors in the decreasing incidence in crimes against husbands, lovers, and children and the rising tendency of female crimes against property, such as—once again—shoplifting.

Though he strives throughout for an objective sociological stance that will demonstrate the weaknesses underlying the biological theories of female criminality, Pollak is always drawn back to a near Lombroso-Ferrero reductionism. Here again, the objective male scientist is led into mischievous subjectivism by the usual stereotypes of female nature. Pollak was obsessed with women's cryptic insides, their concealed genitals, their secretive menses. Pollak overcame his biases sufficiently to be able to perceive how the social roles assigned to women provide the temptations and the opportunities to commit the kinds of secretive and undetectable crimes that are typical of female criminals. Unfortunately, Pollak's more reliable sociology is permeated by his suspiciousness of the female. As he ponders the infinite ways in which the society induces and supports the "secret" crimes of women, Pollak is mysteriously drawn to a conclusion that implicitly contradicts his better arguments. Females, he concludes, are as inclined toward criminality as are males: "One can but marvel at the masked character of female crime, which can so conceal the results as to give the impression that women are less criminal than men."

Pollak is at his sociological best when he clarifies the special social arrangements and forces that are designed to induce special desires in women and then provide special opportunities for criminal activities associated with these desires. About one thing Pollak was correct: the criminal activity called shoplifting, which the more psychologically minded would think of as an impulse perversion called kleptomania, is a direct outgrowth of the social roles assigned to women as the primary shoppers and consumers of material goods.

Very rich women just shop and then shop some more and even steal a trophy or two, now and then, whenever they might otherwise get depressed or anxious. Not-so-rich women are kleptomaniacs who replace an experience of deprivation or anxiety with an impulse to steal what they feel deprived of. And poor women merely shoplift, steal what their families need in the way of food and clothing with an occasional extra—a trinket, a record, a bottle of perfume, some little trophy to assuage the violence of deprivation. Modern sales techniques, with their exploitation of the female role of shopper, create desires that lure women into their various commodity crimes. With an uncanny precision about this match between an artificial desire and an unnecessary commodity, merchandise is displayed and advertised so that visual temptations are put in a woman's way before she ever gets to the objects she originally thought she wanted to purchase. She comes to the store for a chair and leaves with a hat, lipstick, perfume, another new kitchen gadget that she will never use—and no chair. Which means she will have to go back another day and succumb to a few more temptations for useless commodities.

How like the modern-day ad man and dress designer was Monsieur L'heureux, the happiness peddler, who worked up Emma Bovary's appetites for luxuries she could not afford by, as Tanner put it, "trying to transform the vagueness and indistinctness of erotic-emotional desire into a specific greed for an infinity of unnecessary commodities." In modern societies, it is logical that the factory and the corporation should be the domains of male crime while the home and the commodity marketplace—department store and grocery store—should be the domains of female crime. The commodity fetishism of modern industrial societies thrives on the domestic imprisonment of women, who are trained from childhood to find the satisfactions of all their desires in material goods. Women are assigned to the role of decorating their households with soft armchairs and pretty curtains. They are meant to inscribe on their bodies the decorations and ornaments that appeal to the eyes of men. They are meant to costume their bodies with the garments that make them exciting and alluring. Every dangerous emotion that might encourage women to rebel against their domestic imprisonment can be assuaged by a commodity. If women are to stay in their assigned place it is essential that they should not think too much or feel deeply. Fear, sadness, anger, terror, grief, rage, social ambition, moral dilemma can be banished by material objects, commodity fetishes.

Emma Bovary never had much tolerance for the heavy sentiments of loss and sadness. If she felt troubled, she groped about for diversions and amusements—novels, songs, flowers, combs for her hair, a vase, bracelets, subscriptions to fashion magazines, a French petticoat, a new love affair. When these could not forestall or ease her anxiety or depression, which at best they might do for only short periods of time, Emma had no other resource but to wallow in the deprivations and terrible injustices of her life until a new distraction came along. Because she felt that she had no real power to do anything substantial to ameliorate or alter the conditions of her existence, in the end she relied on the interchangeable and borrowable power of gold to keep herself in the state of erotomanic excitement that would distract her from loss and disappointment.

Gold, however, was Emma's last resort. At the convent Emma was already practicing the art of distracting herself from difficult thoughts and emotions. When she learned of her mother's death, for example,

Emma went through various tentative stages of mourning this terrible loss, but very quickly arrived at the wish that sealed her own fate. The first few days after her mother's death she cried a great deal. Like any child who cannot tolerate for too long sentiments or affects that are painful, Emma soon found some nice ways to feel better. She asked for a memorial picture that should be decorated with strands of her mother's hair. As she mused, ever so lightly, on the meaning of life and death, Emma's youthful mind meandered in Lamartinian dells, listened to harps, the songs of dying swans, the falling leaves, the pure virgins, even the voice of the Eternal One. Then she made her wish. She requested that when she died, she be buried in the tomb with her mother. With that wish, she awoke from her pastoral ramblings surprised "to find herself tranquil and with no more sadness in her heart than wrinkles on her brow."

Soon afterward, as these spiritual musings grew tiresome, Emma began to require more palpable substitutes for feeling and desire. Though the sisters had tried to impress their little charge with the spirituality of Christ, his tangible and visibly suffering body was what impressed Emma. Emma adored the church for the fragrances of the altar, the glow of the candles, the flowers. The music she loved for its romantic lyrics, the literature for its erotic stimulation, the sermons for their references to fiancé, husband, and eternal marriage, the body of Christ for its wounds, the face of the Virgin for her sweet smile.

It was a simple matter, then, for the fifteen-year-old Emma to transfer her religious passions to the romantic novels smuggled in by the convent laundress. Within those dusty, crumbling pages she encountered Mary Stuart, Héloïse, Agnes Sorel, Joan of Arc, and other suffering and celebrated women who "stood out for her like comets that lit up the black immensity of history." Her wealthy friends let her rummage through their secret keepsake books. Her eyes would be dazzled by the names of the unknown authors who signed their pieces as "count" or "viscount." Her fingers would smooth the satin bindings.

Her hands would tremble as she lifted the diaphanous tissues that veiled the illustrations of refined Englishwomen relaxing in carriages and of sultans in the arms of dancing girls.

Emma's wedding cake was a triumph over the monotonies of the natural world, the epitome of a commodity fetish. It substituted tinseled and sugar-coated objets d'art for the sentiments of marriage. It was a three-tiered affair that started off with a square of blue cardboard on which stood a clay temple with porticoes, colonnades, and niches holding plaster statuettes studded with gilt-paper stars. On the second layer was a meringue castle surrounded by fortifications made of candied angelica, almonds, raisins, and slivers of orange. The uppermost tier was a marzipan green meadow with sugar rocks surrounding blueberry jam lakes with tiny nutshell boats. And on a grassy knoll above the lake sat a little cupid in a chocolate swing with two *real* rosebuds at the top.

And then she and Charles were invited to Vaubyessard, the château of the marquis d'Andervilliers. What Vaubyessard offered in the way of the material world put to shame the little cupid wedding cake. From the moment she entered Vaubyessard, Emma was enveloped by the aroma of flowers, linens, and well-seasoned meat and truffles. Her eyes took in silver platter covers, crystal pieces, napkins folded in the shape of bishop's miters, red claws of lobsters, quails still covered with plumage. Then she saw the dozen or so men of the Andervilliers family. Their clothes were made of finer cloth than any of the other guests'. Their hair gleamed with a more refined pomade and curled more subtly toward the temples.

Their indifferent gaze had the appeased look of constantly satisfied appetites and evident beneath their genteel manners was that peculiar brutality that derives from careless domination of all things, of muscles flexed and vanity flattered from race horses and commerce with fallen women.

After the ball at Vaubyessard Emma would forevermore confuse the sensualities of luxury with the elations of the heart. Paris was Emma's Golden Kingdom. Into that captious sieve Paris, Emma poured every mirage her thirsty imagination could conjure. Opening nights, the races, the soirées, the latest fashions, the opera, the world of ambassadors, salons paneled with mirrors, dresses with bustles, velvet tableclothes fringed with gold. Since Paris was out of the question, Emma picked up a few trinkets from Rouen to enliven the tedium of her existence in Tostes. She bought charms for her watch, an ivory workbox with a vermeil thimble, two large vases of blue glass for the fireplace. These meager tokens of refinement didn't work. How could she escape the prison walls of Tostes? Emma would sit for days without moving a muscle. Her moods were unpredictable. A burst of exultation would be followed by a sullen mood in which she remained totally silent. Some mornings she cried. For several days running, she would alarm Charles with blasphemies. She suffered heart palpitations. She lost weight.

To cure his adored Emma of her nervous disorder, Charles gives up his successful practice as a country doctor and moves his little household to the lively market town of Yonville. There Emma meets the Satan of her desires, Monsieur L'heureux, the dry goods merchant. L'heureux takes one look at Emma Bovary and knows that it is only a matter of time before she is his.

> He was clever, the shopkeeper. . . . No one knew what he had been before. Some said a peddler, others a banker. One thing was certain: he could do complicated calculations in his head that would have frightened Binet, the tax collector. Polite to the point of obsequiousness, he always held himself tilted, at half rein in an ambiguous posture of either bowing or inviting.

On the morning he meets Emma, L'heureux spreads out before her eyes half a dozen embroidered handkerchiefs, three Algerian shawls, straw sandals, embroidered collars, English needles, four egg cups carved out of coconut shells by convicts. He is not discouraged when Emma says she feels no need for any of his goods. Her rejection only serves to inspire the highest refinement of his marketing technique, which is to stimulate need where none has existed. Sensing Emma's special attraction to the Algerian shawls, he flicks his fingernail along the silk. "How much are they?" asks Emma. "Nothing, a mere trifle. . . . We are not Jews! . . . I always work things out with the ladies. It is not the money I care about. I could even give you some if you needed it."

L'heureux does not make a sale and Emma compliments herself for resisting his temptations. But L'heureux has secured his prey. He has calculated on Emma's predilection for consuming goods as compensation for the emptiness of her life. Again Tanner sees precisely the relation between Emma's longings and the commodity fetishism of her world. "Emma will soon be unable to distinguish between kinds of needs, appetites, desires and longings and will try increasingly to compensate for a dissatisfaction of the emotions with a satiation of *marchandises.*" When Léon deserts her for Paris, Emma buys the most luxurious of the Algerian shawls, a blue cashmere dress imported from Rouen, fourteen francs' worth of lemons for her nails, an Italian dictionary and grammar, and some serious books on history and philosophy. A few months later, soon after she recovers from her depression over Léon by succumbing to Rodolphe, she orders from L'heureux a new wardrobe of hats, boots, and petticoats. True to his word, L'heureux never asks for money. He chats about the new goods from Paris and all the trifles of fashion news that women love to hear about. He makes himself always obliging. Emma yields to this lenient way of satisfying all her whims. She buys gifts for Rodolphe, a hunting crop with a silver-gilt handle, a seal with the motto *Amor nel cor,* a scarf to be used like a muffler, a green silk cigar case resembling the one that had belonged to the viscount at Vaubyessard. When at last L'heureux turns up with a bill for 270 francs for these gifts, Emma has no funds.

The shrewd L'heureux suggests that he will wait for payment on the smaller gifts but he must ask the good doctor Bovary to return the hunting crop. Emma gasps, "No, you mustn't." L'heureux, having so cleverly duped Emma into revealing her sins, thinks, "Aha! I've got you."

Without so much as a thought to the consequences, Emma steals her husband's patients' fees, hands L'heureux enough money to silence him, keeps the two five-franc pieces he gives her for change, and vows to be, from then on, a good, thrifty, honest wife. Emma's petty theft of her husband's fees is her initiation into her financial enslavement to L'heureux. The elopement with Rodolphe will cost her a cloak, two trunks, a traveling bag, and a number of items that she has never ordered but that L'heureux nevertheless charges to the Bovary account. When the elopement fails, L'heureux adds to his list of unpaid goods curtains, a rug, fabric for the armchairs, several dresses, and an assortment of toilet articles.

Toward the end of the dark winter in which Emma has tried vainly to distract herself from the loss of Rodolphe, she turns for a brief time to the convent imagery of her innocent childhood. She insists that Charles buy her amulets and rosaries. She looks to Christ to save her soul. "She nearly swooned with celestial ecstasy as she offered her lips to accept the body of the Savior." Now that she is no longer in a state of sinful adultery, Emma immerses herself in the nobler joys of humility and sacrifice. Bolstered by her newfound purity, she rises high above the earth, her soul blending in with the heavens. The curé approves of Emma's conversion. Nevertheless, the driven intensity of Emma's passions worries him. Emma's religious leanings might end in heresy, perhaps even spiritual extravagance. So the curé orders for Emma's edification some cautionary pamphlets. But Emma, who yearns so for tangible physical goodness, never had much patience with the polemics of purity. At the convent she had soon rebelled against the disciplines, the prayers, retreats, novenas, sermons, the lectures on bodily modesty and salvation of the soul. As she had eluded the influences of the sisters, she now distills the good curé's pamphlets and manuals—*Think It Over, The Man of the World at Mary's Feet, Some Errors of Voltaire*—into her own concoction of forgetfulness and remorse. She plunges into these books until she is permeated with erotic melancholy. When she kneels before her gilt-encrusted prie-dieu (which she purchased the year before to console herself for the loss of Léon), she whispers to the Lord "the same delicious words she had once murmured to her lover in the throes of adultery." Emma sees nothing wrong with trying to charm faith as she had charmed Charles, Léon, and Rodolphe. Is she not like one of those grand ladies of yesteryear who poured out at the feet of Christ all the tears of a heart wounded by life? Emma becomes charitable. All winter long, she sews clothes for the poor and sends wood for the fires of women in labor and invites the homeless to sit at her kitchen table and drink soup. By spring, she is back to craving the luxuries of the material world.

L'heureux has been waiting. Armed with the certain knowledge that infidelity sooner or later transforms a dutiful wife into a woman determined to ruin herself, L'heureux plays on Emma's irresistible hunger for luxury. He contrives a scheme of "power of attorney." Patiently he tutors his avid pupil with some fundamental financial principles, a few impressive legal terms, and some well-worked ploys for inducing an overworked husband to place all his financial assets in a wife's more capable hands. "Then you and I could arrange our little affairs together."

Emma has very little trouble convincing Charles to sign over to her his money and property. She uses the Bovary farm at Barneville and the house in Yonville as collateral for her loans. The promissory notes and the interest rates spiral geometrically. Before Emma realizes what is happening to her, the financial duplicities that L'heureux has arranged to keep her in luxury bring her debts to two thousand francs. Emma could pay up, then and there, and escape her fate. But L'heureux knows his customer better than she knows herself. As she offers the bank notes, L'heureux restrains her: "It pains me, word of

honor, to see you give up all at once a sum so *consequential* as that."
Emma regards the bank notes in a new light. Endless nights of love
could be purchased by a miserable little shack in Barneville that nobody cares about. With a mind dizzied by L'heureux's lightening of
calculations, Emma guiltlessly signs four promissory notes for one
thousand francs each in exchange for the tangible cash of two thousand
francs. "Her ears rang as though gold pieces were bursting out of their
sacks and were tinkling about her on the floor." What circumstance
has denied to her, gold will now give her. The luxury of Vaubyessard
and an unfettered existence like Rodolphe's are now hers. With the
power and courage of gold she is the equal of any man.

What a scene there was the following Thursday at the hotel, in
the room with Léon! She laughed, cried, sang, danced, sent for
sherbets, wanted to smoke cigarettes—she seemed to him wildly
extravagant but adorable, superb.

He could not comprehend what inner forces drove her into
this reckless pursuit after the sensual pleasures of life. She was
becoming irritable, greedy, and voluptuous. She would walk
with him in the streets, her head high, unafraid, she said, of being
compromised.

Flaubert's depiction of Emma's final downfall through her enslavement to material goods presaged Frank Norris's best-selling end-of-
the-century novel *McTeague,* in which the sexually driven, gold-lust-
ing Trina finally destroys the hero, McTeague. However, Flaubert had
a profound sympathy for Emma's plight and did not think himself
exempt from the passions and social conditions that led to her pitiful
end. Consciously at least, Flaubert's condemnation was not of Emma
or her passions, but of the social conditions that bound her in the role
of a demeaned woman. By the end of the nineteenth century, writers
who were drawn to the degeneracies of female desire were more consciously and determinedly intent on their repudiation of the dangerous

female. Moreover, by then, Norris's image of the virago-female had the backing of science. All women who gave up motherhood and wifely duties to indulge themselves in sexual fulfillment were lusting after male potency, the material symbol of which is gold. Whereas maleness can never be obtained, the gold that stands for maleness and male power can be stolen, poached, snatched, suctioned up. Like Flaubert's Emma, for whom physical need, emotional appetite, sexual desire, and longing for material objects are interchangeable sensations with interchangeable satisfactions, Norris's Trina cannot distinguish between the masculine energy she hungers for and the sensual qualities of gold.

> Not a day passed that Trina did not have it out where she could see and touch it. One evening she had even spread all the gold pieces between the sheets, and had then gone to bed, stripping herself, and had slept all night upon the money, taking a strange and ecstatic pleasure in the touch of the smooth flat pieces the length of her entire body.

When Norris created the emasculating, gold-hungry Trina he anticipated Abraham's 1920 catalogue of penis-envying women. In 1986 Trina would become merely one in a long list of viraginous women in Bram Dijkstra's catalogue of the nineteenth-century "virgin whores of Babylon." However, Dijkstra, in *Idols of Perversity,* holds these images of the female up to the light to reveal the minds and souls of the terrified males who created them. He begins by reciting some prevalent male images of the female at the turn of the twentieth century. Eve, as every man knows, had started the whole confusing battle of the sexes. When she plucked the fig leaf to cover herself, it was the beginning of her passion for buying expensive clothing. She had merely disguised her essential exhibitionism in a false modesty. Pandora continued the tradition of female deceptiveness by pretending to a good-hearted earthy simplicity while concealing the greedy curiosity that would drive her to open the box containing all the ills of the world. These were the common, longstanding complaints about the female that were simply given their special nineteenth-century twists. In 1895, there was the Venus-Pandemos who triumphed over all of man's "idealistic aspirations; she ridiculed chastity, the family, the fatherland, the future life, drama and the world of dreams." There was Wedekind's Lulu, "created for every abuse, to allure and to poison and seduce, to murder without leaving any trace." Then there were the legion of women who refused motherhood, the vengefully infertile women whose gaping wombs were described in 1896 as "a fountain of life from which flows, every month, death itself, in a flood of debris, a wreckage which repeats itself continuously—a tide of blood which gushes forth in memory of shame and cruelty." There were the Danae who lasciviously opened their limbs to make sure that Zeus's shower of golden coins would hit the mark. According to the twisted mythology of the day, it was not Zeus who was deceitful in his scheme of disguising his semen as gold but the Danae who tricked the mighty god by pretending a desire for motherhood and wanting only gold. In another mythological transformation, Judith, the noble, self-sacrificing heroine of the Bible, was portrayed in 1900 as a head-huntress with sharp, hungry teeth and malicious eyes, a lustful predator eager for the fruit of men's brains, a wild creature who clawed at the severed head of Holofernes. There were Delilah pawing the tresses of her soon to be emasculated Samson, the bestial maenads who protested Orpheus's diatribes against sexually active women by making mincemeat of his entire body, and Salome drooling over the decapitated head of John the Baptist.

Trina, Salome, Judith, Lulu, and their virgin-whore sisters were the culminating images of the nineteenth-century primal woman—a composite of the goods-consuming middle-class housewife who declined housework and motherhood and instead spent her husband's slave wages on trinkets and the syphilis-bearing prostitute who grabbed all the rest and then with the "sword blades gaping in the blood-red hollows" of the "savage Nidularium blossom under her meagre thighs" devoured the insides of the man's body and scraped out his brain. What Flaubert, with his madonna-whore ambivalence, could only partly grasp about the relationship between Emma's personal plight and the changing economic structures of the modern world, Dijkstra expresses decisively.

> The masochism, then, of the late nineteenth-century male, and his manipulation of the image of woman as an all-destroying, rampaging animal was an expression of his attempt to come to terms with the implications of his own marginalization, his removal from the true seats of power in his society. . . . Woman, who at mid-century had of necessity been the first to explore the realm of masochism, now found herself pushed into the role of the surrogate sadist, so that the male could vent his pent-up frustrations in an orgy of masochistic self-indulgence. With her apparent hunger for gold, her outward purity and inward lust, her seeming self-sufficiency and blood thirsty virginity, she was the perfect foil to the pervasive masochism of the artists and intellectuals—the cultural middlemen—of the turn of the century. Spending the male's money, woman symbolically wasted his seed, and in wasting his seed she caused him to lose the most precious source of nourishment of his transcendent intellect.

Of course, women did not invent a money-trade economy, nor are they the only ones who might choose to worship the commodity fetishes it produces. Commodity fetishes are everywhere in the social order. They are reminders of our alienation from nature and from our personal selfhood. And yet they represent a way of escape from our anxieties, our plights, the terrible depression and madness that might overtake our souls. Without illusions of some sort we would all succumb to despair. The problem with illusion is not that it deceives us. That is its gentle purpose. For who among us could bear the severe realities of civilized existence without some sense of the soft, the comforting, the soothing, the healing, the ameliorating, the milk and honey of the lost Eden of infancy? There are distinctions, though, between illusions and fetishes.

To grasp these distinctions, we need only to recall for a moment the differences between an infant's security blanket, the so-called transitional object, and an adult's sexual fetish. Both are tangible, inanimate objects that have been endowed with magical properties that ease the strain of relating to the world of reality. In contrast to the transitional object that serves as a bridge between the comfortably familiar and the unfamiliar, the sexual fetish arrests growth and prevents any further exploration of reality. By serving as a cushion and a haven, the transitional object enables the little human adventurer to test the new realities of his expanding world. The security blanket can be given up when its developmental purpose has been served. The sexual fetish is hard, unyielding, ritualized, unbending. It is a prop that can never be given up because the territory of female sexuality is an eternally unknowable and dangerous environment. The transitional object is invested with tender feelings and the aggression of expansion and growth. It says to the child that no matter how far he wanders, or how much his inquiring body attacks or penetrates the outer world, that world will never disappear and he will never be alone. The sexual fetish is an object of congealed hatred, born of a horror that can never be assuaged. The fetish says to the pervert, "Without me you will never be safe." Without the fetish, every penetration into the unknown would entail murder and death. In a perversion, every tumescence is a bringing to life, every detumescence a killing.

Social fetishes—icons, amulets—lie somewhere between the realm of shared illusion and the realm of secretive perversion. The Zuni, for example, who believe "the sun, moon, stars, the sky, earth, and sea, in all their phenomena and elements, and all inanimate objects, as well as plants, animals and men, to belong to one great system of all-conscious and interrelated life," are renowned for their skill at creating fetishes out of natural material and carving fetishes out of semiprecious stones.

In addition to the carved amulets that represent game animals, water animals, and prey animals, they have created the *mili,* a representation of the breath of life, which is a perfect ear of corn filled with the seeds of sacred plants and covered with the feathers of birds. The rain priests are possessors of *Ettone,* a representation of mother earth, which consists of painted reeds filled with seeds and water, wrapped into a bundle to which is attached an arrowhead and several beads. Among the Zuni, it is understood that the purpose of these fetishes is "to assist man, that most vulnerable of all living creatures, in meeting the problems that face him during his life." The fetishes are regarded as living things that must be carefully tended. They are used for warfare, hunting, diagnosing and curing diseases, initiations, gambling, witchcraft, and protection against witchcraft. The Zuni fetish is an icon of shared belief and therefore more like a transitional object than a fetish. The commodity fetish is an object that substitutes for belief, but in it there is an absence of belief, a fending off only of despair and violence.

Nowadays, along Fifth Avenue and Rodeo Drive, well-booted women and men wear the Zuni necklaces and collect their carved figurines of animals, which to the modern Zuni and to us are only commodities. What are our icons of belief? We have been so alienated from nature and our common humanity that it is very hard these days to tell whether our amulets and crosses and flags and uniforms and art treasures are icons of belief or false icons that, like fetishes, only substitute for belief. A genuine icon is meant to enable groups and communities to convene, and because the group shares ideals and illusions there is a tacit agreement not to put to test the truth or reality of these fictions. They are illusions that comfort us and bring us together into shared realms of experiencing. But these days our social icons and uniforms and flags and crosses and art collections are functioning like fetishes. Instead of bringing us together, they insidiously undermine our possibilities for communion or human relatedness. The fetishized icon separates one person from another and functions instead as though it were a law unto itself. It becomes a dogma that demands submission and obedience. Rather than offer comfort or provide a haven from the harsh realities or protection from the unknown forces that surround us, the fetishized icon involves a constant trial of survival. It is a prop that must be constantly replenished. Fetishized icons are interchangeable and as long as they can be replenished we are deceived into believing that we are safe, that we are having fun, that we are engaged in the interchange of human emotion.

This terrible moment of fetishistic deception is happening now. But it has been a while in preparation. As early as 1880, after initiating the process of building railroads and factories and housing complexes and exploiting the forests and the fields and the air, the master builders of the industrial age were already putting their acquisitive energies to a new project, *the department store.* The sober work ethic that had inspired the first wave of industrialization would slowly yield to the pleasure values and interests of a consumer society. The department store would be the trademark and symbol of all the palaces of consumption of the future. The premise was that eventually, sooner or later, every human interest and desire could be and would be commercialized. What Marx predicted in the mid-nineteenth century is coming to fruition at the end of the twentieth. "All our inventions and progress seem to result in endowing material forces with intellectual life and stultifying human life with a material force."

On June 9, 1989, the same week that the half million Chinese students and workers were peacefully assembled in Beijing's Tiananmen Square to demand the democratization of their society, eventually to be defeated by guns and tanks, The *New York Times* headlined the beginning of the age of the megamall, the newest symbol of American democracy and "a new fix for future shopping addicts."

The producers of the first megamall acclaimed the democratic ethos that gave birth to the megamall concept. "The coming of the megamall followed three decades in which malls transformed the way people shop and entertain themselves. At least once a month, 94 percent of all adults in the United States visit a mall to make a purchase, see a movie and even date." The official name of the first of the new breed of shopping center will be Mall of America. It is now rising up on seventy-eight acres in Bloomington, Minnesota, and, "when completed in the late 1990's, is expected to offer shopping addicts 9.5 million square feet of Utopia." As part of the ground-breaking ceremony that took place on June 14, 1989, a squadron of F-14 fighter planes soared overhead while a band played the *1812 Overture.* By 1992 the mall will be as big as seventy-eight football fields. Shoppers will be able to browse for an entire day without covering the four central "anchor" department stores and eight hundred specialty shops lining four indoor streets on three levels. "Coming here will be a two or three day event," said Rick Geshwiler, Bloomington's director of planning. Stores are only the half of it. "A roller coaster will roar through the middle of the mall and a creek will babble past flume rides and merry-go-rounds in the mall's own 300,000 square foot, indoor amusement park." And there will be nightclubs and restaurants and theaters and health clubs and a miniature golf course.

At first some Bloomington citizens feared the advent of the megamall and, preceding the turning of the first mounds of Bloomington soil, they organized a peaceful protest march, dubbed "Maul the Megamall." The protest died of apathy. After all, how could a handful of people convince their commodity-hungry neighbors to resist the wave of the future? As Geshwiler never tires of explaining, "This is the next level of retailing. It's like the difference between a space station and bus station." Kurt Laughinghouse, the mayor of Bloomington, did not need to use guns or tanks or threats of torture to break up the protest march. He simply prevailed on his citizens to rejoice with him, "It's a different world when you have a megamall."

From academia, we hear Samuel Kaplan, a sociologist from Bryn Mawr College, commenting, "Malls are a new form of entertainment. . . . They're magnetic. They're like collecting pools for middle-class people on shopping binges. It's getting to the point where people say,

'Let's spend the weekend at the mall.' It fills a kind of anthropological need to be around other people."

Because of our increasing alienation, we no longer care to pursue the issues of our religious, social, political, and sexual plights. In his effort to describe the fetishistic nature of the social dogmas that substitute for knowledge and true belief, Gustave Flaubert claimed that dogmas like Reformation or Enlightenment or romanticism or realism or industrialization had always changed and would continue to do so, but what he hoped would never change was a belief in "amulets, sacred fountains, votive offerings . . . priests, monks, hermits, in short, the belief in a force superior to life and the need to place oneself under the protection of this force." It seems, however, that Flaubert's faith in the durability of belief was misplaced. He might have done better to stick to his usual cynical wish to trample on every sacred value. Now the citizens of the world will be comforted by placing their bodies and souls under the protection of the megamall. Not unlike the sexual fetishist, we have arrested our inquiries into the nature of reality. We blindly and frantically worship our false icons, the commodity fetishes that substitute for belief and sense of community—plaster madonnas, schools that look like warehouses, gold-anodized aluminum TV aerials, mini-series, mini-skirts, and midi-skirts, liposuctioned thighs, postfeminist Don Giovanna chic, LY 163502 aphrodisiac pills, pregaphones that allow expectant mothers to speak to their unborn children, bonding bibs that hold bottles of milk so that fathers can feed like mothers, zygote intra-Fallopian transfers, surrogate mothers, kiddies in black garter belts, dial-a-porn sexual release. Fetishized icons substitute for any further process of coping with or addressing the painful and harsh realities of existence. Depression and anxiety will be vanquished. Pleasure is in, and in every variety and shape, and anyone can buy it, or steal it, at a megamall.

10

For Female
Eyes Only

Man in his lust has regulated long enough this whole question of sexual intercourse. Now let the mother of mankind, whose prerogative it is to set bounds to his indulgence, rouse up and give this whole matter a thorough, fearless investigation.

Elizabeth Cady Stanton, letter to
Susan B. Anthony, 1853

For the average man, the sight of unadorned, unposed, unscripted female flesh is a real turn-off. He often likes to look at dimpled buttocks and full, firm bosoms with erect nipples, but he averts his gaze from the female genitals in the flesh. Affected in this manner by stark-naked femaleness, a fin de siècle philosopher, Otto Weininger, proclaimed, "The genitalia are the chief difficulty in the way of regarding woman as theoretically beautiful." For the especially timid fellow, the furry folds of the vestibule leading to the exalted but dreaded vagina are much easier to take when merely suggested by lace panties and black garters. Another man insists that a direct look at the split beaver, the opened muff, the swollen lips are the very best. However, even that hardy adventurer will confess his need for some protection. When the menacing mouthpiece of female desire is veiled by lighting, costumes, poses, and settings, when the adventurer's eyes are shielded by the aesthetics of "for male eyes only" pornographic photographs, magazines, VCRs, peep shows, and films, then and only then is he turned on.

Many of the creators of male pornography claim that they are advertising the beauty of a woman's body and thereby freeing women from the chains of a false modesty and virtue. However, this fantasy of liberating sexually repressed women is analogous to the Pygmalion fantasy of repairing damaged women, but in pornography the unconscious hostility is even less well disguised. Like the fashions that Pygmalion designers create to fix women, pornography images are like Chinese mutilated feet. The aesthetics of male pornography are developed around a denigration of women and a fear and hatred of the female body.

Pornography is a male invention, a literature of harlotry designed to detoxify and repair the actual female body. Thus, with the avowed aims of arousing erotic desire in men and freeing women from the bonds of sexual repression, female bodies are stripped, bent over, spread apart, twisted. Labia are pierced. Breasts are lassoed till they swell to an abnormal size. Nipples are pinched with clothespins. Breasts of pregnant women are shown expressing streams of milk. Buttocks are branded. The genitals of prepubescent girls are licked by dogs. Nymphomaniacs are sated unto death. Lesbians suck one another off. Virgins are subjected to exotic practices that turn them into groveling nymphomaniacs.

Could there be a pornography "for female eyes only"? Could women be sexually aroused by the sight of male bodies in positions of humiliation and torment? Or is the entire notion of a female or "feminine" pornography a contradiction in terms? In these speculations about the possibility of a pornography designed for women, there are two opposing camps. In the one camp are those who argue that women might achieve a female pornography if they could learn to fashion erotic images that are faithful to their own more fluid, diffuse, softer, romantic sexuality. The other camp asserts that this would be exactly the wrong approach, for any glorification of those stereotypes of feminine desire would be misunderstood as a capitulation to the patriarchal values that have, throughout the ages, given license to the subjugation and denigration of women. Instead, there should be a counter-pornography, a pornography in which the woman demeans the man. If men are permitted to jerk off by peering at contorted and tormented women's bodies in *Cavalier, Club International, Chic, Swank, High Society, Playboy, Penthouse, Hustler, Screw,* and *Fuck,* why shouldn't women have women's magazines with photos of tormented men to excite their masturbatory lusts?

"Liberated women publicize their staring at men's pants and penises; they demand not only equal rights but equal drives," says Robert Stoller, the interviewer of Olympia the porno centerfold, the therapist of Sally the transvestite, an authority on the variations, deflections, deviations, and aberrations of the erotic life. Suppose, he wonders, that women, in their search for sexual equality, began to suffer from the same sexual anxieties as men. Wouldn't it be awful if women were to fall into the trap of imitating their enemies, those pathetic perverts who are slaves to the urgencies of the stiff penis and the stringencies of ritualized erotic performance? Stoller is happy to report that women needn't resort to the kind of sorry images that turn men on. "There *is* a pornography just for women!"

Stoller is alluding to modern-day romance novels, referred to in the trade as "bodice rippers," so named for the tearing hands of the lusting hero, or "bodice busters," named for the mirroring, by a sympathetically aroused female reader, of the heaving breasts, erect nipples, and arching spinal columns of the heroine. These sagas of seduction feature a strong-willed, independent, "but nevertheless" completely feminine heroine who dares to act out the sexual adventures that the ordinary housewife, secretary, lawyer, internist, waitress, salesgirl, nurse, school-teacher, psychiatrist only daydream about.

The male pornography of twisted bodies with properly posed breasts and softly lit labia is clearly marked as a product designed for sexual arousal. There is honesty in advertising here. The consumer knows exactly what he's getting for his money. However, the female erotic life tenders itself in sweet disguises. The millions of women who read these romantic pages are in fact indulging in erotica, whether or not they are aware of it or willing to acknowledge it. "Bodice rippers" have been produced in many forms; science fiction, detective stories, historical fiction, family sagas, fotonovellas, true confessions.

The most popular is the romance novel. One imprint alone, Harle-quin, generally credited with being the originator of the mass market romance series concept, sends out more than fifty titles a year to approximately two hundred million readers. The average reader is between twenty-five and forty-nine and spends thirty dollars of her monthly salary on romance novels. Forty percent of the readers are college graduates. The Harlequin romances are published in more than one hundred countries in twenty-one languages. *The Harlequin Story* informs: "If all the words of all the Harlequin books sold last year were laid end to end, they would stretch 1,000 times around the earth or 93 times to the moon. That's a distance of one quarter of the way to the sun." In Japan, where neither *Reader's Digest* nor *TV Guide* could crack the market, "Harlequin" quickly became a household word. In a Japanese dictionary of modern language, *harlequin* is defined as "a word describing romantic sentiments." The English word *harlequin* is itself a translation originally derived from the Italian character *arlecchino* of the commedia dell'arte. *Arlecchino*, "always in the air," is the precisely right logo for the romance novel.

The original Harlequin formula was "clean, easy to read love stories about contemporary people, set in exciting foreign places." Over the past two decades, as the Harlequin enterprise expanded its marketplace, it enlarged its visions of romantic turn-on. Now Harlequin caters to every nuance of feminine erotic taste, providing loyal readers with an inviting assortment of romantic delights. The basic Romance series stresses a clean, fresh approach to sex, where heroines are virtually innocent to start with and metaphorically so after the seduction; sexual tensions are subdued and passionate language kept to a minimum. Moving a tiny notch up the scale of erotic tension, another Harlequin series prides itself on its realism, "in which the sensual scenes evolve naturally and reflect shared feelings and desires central to the characters' sexual involvement." With Superromance we begin to encounter mature heroes and heroines who appeal to the more "passionate reader." Another series depicts current values and thus high levels of sensuality and very aggressive heroines; yet another "delivers suspense and romance in perfect harmony." A highly sensuous group of romances written for "today's women" dispenses "the promise of love— the guarantee of satisfaction." The Special Editions series recognizes the seamier side of erotic life and bravely "tackles sensitive issues" while simultaneously embracing the traditional "romantic ideal that love can, indeed, conquer all." And not to neglect women who still need to have their romance ribboned by traditional values, there is a series that brings "the reader all the wonder and magic of the heroine's discovery of a love that lasts a lifetime."

Although today's reader of romance novels has a wide range of romantic turn-ons to choose from, the basic Harlequin formula is pretty much as it always was. Many of the more contemporary heroines do not enter the scene as literal virgins, and some enjoy assuming the top position. Their souls, however, are essentially feminine and eternally virginal. As the novel begins, the heroine is on the alert to the hard muscularity of the man into whose arms she will soon be surrendering her body. As we meet this venturesome young lady, she is on the verge of knowing the unknown. The reader attends as the virgin patiently peels away each of the many shells of phallic hardness until at last she arrives at the soft custard of domestic desire at the center of the man's being—the caring, protective, loving, *husband*.

Romance novels are not without moral standards. A women who got her *husband* should no longer be burdened by sexual adventures. Incest, adultery, abortion, and husband stealing are taboo. If she had not been a married woman, an adultress to boot, Emma Bovary, an archetypal arlecchina, would have been the ideal heroine for one of these trite seduction scenarios. Emma would, in any case, have been an avid Harlequin reader. She would not have hesitated to betray her higher literary ambitions for the meatier sensualities of the romance novel. Most congenial to Emma's erotic tastes would be the Intimate Moments series, which promises "to sweep the reader away into a world where life is exciting and dreams do come true."

Those engaged in the writing and publishing of these reading materials seem to be dimly aware of what they are up to. They acknowledge that they are delivering a form of sexual release in the guise of offering merely an innocent escape from a humdrum existence. One publisher described romance novels as "the publishing industry's answer to the Big Mac." "They are juicy, cheap, predictable and devoured in stupefying quantities by legions of loyal fans." A well-known writer of romance novels revealed the secrets of her craft. The hero and heroine are obsessed with one another, and the plots simply chronicle their meetings and partings "in a dizzying succession of exotic locales." Many of the heroines "move about so much they practically live out of suitcases. Their love affairs are almost always consummated on ships or in hotels."

Although the locales of Yonville-l'Abbaye and Rouen are not exotic and Emma does not live out of a suitcase, she travels the distance, sometimes under enormous hardship, so that her body will be clasped in the arms of her lover. Indeed, because she is so madly intent on actualizing her romantic illusions, Emma, in a half dozen years, clocks more mileage from the hearth than most women of her social class and station in life would do in a lifetime. The loyal maid Félicité is kept busy ironing dimity petticoats, fichus, muslin collars, and pantaloons while Emma's adoring houseboy Justin keeps himself in a state of erotic delirium polishing Emma's worn-out, mud-encrusted boots. The Bovary household is in a frenzy of preparation for Emma's assignations.

When Rodolphe meets Emma at the country fair, he grasps her hand, a hand that trembles like a "captive dove trying to resume its flight." But this gentle capture is only the first scene in Rodolphe's well-practiced seduction scenario. The dove is released, but only temporarily. Experienced as he is, Rodolphe calculates the extent and tolerance of Emma's impatience for his touch and decides that six weeks will be the exactly right emotional distance. When he returns, Emma is ready and willing to yield her full body to his full embrace. Rodolphe and Emma will be traveling only a short distance, on horseback, riding side by side through the nearby woods of Yonville, as he slowly and masterfully executes the final details. A glance, a few verbal innuendos. For the consummation, which is by now inevitable, he invites Emma to dismount. He feasts his eyes "on the slice of white stocking that, between the black of her skirt and her black boot, aroused in him an image of her naked flesh." He grasps her by the wrist; he moves toward her, smiling strangely; he has a fixed look in his eyes; his teeth are clenched. To overcome Emma's last resistances, Rodolphe softens up his approach with tender words: "In my soul you are like a madonna on a pedestal, revered, pure, and immaculate. I can't live without you. I need your eyes, your voice, your thoughts. Be my friend, my sister, my angel." Now he stretches his arm around her waist. Emma tries feebly to get free. She protests, " 'I am mad to listen to you.' . . . She tilts back her white neck that swells with a sigh; her resistance overcome, weeping, trembling all over, hiding her face, she surrenders."

Horses will continue to play a significant role in Emma's love affairs, much the way limousines and yachts do for today's brave arlecchinas. Emma's passion for Léon, initiated in the cathedral of

Rouen and finalized in a horse-drawn carriage that carouseled through the avenues of Rouen, the way sexual assignations were customarily "done in Paris," has become one of the most famous consummation scenes in modern literature. After much simpering protestation, the panting, now sexually knowledgeable, socially ambitious Emma finds Léon's invitation to do it Parisian style irresistible. And off they go.

The only flash of female flesh is Emma's bare hand reaching through the yellow curtains as she casts away the torn-up fragments of her now superfluous virtuous farewell letter to Léon. "Scraps of paper fluttered in the wind to alight farther along like white butterflies on a field of red poppies all in bloom." The streets, squares, and boulevards that the cab traverses on its twelve-hour voyage are listed in order of appearance and reappearance. That bare hand, those fluttering white butterflies, those meandering streets and alleyways convey more erotic intensity than any juicy Big Mac romance novel. Rouen, however, is not Paris, and "the bourgeois stared in wonderment at an event so extraordinary in a provincial town—a carriage with drawn blinds that kept appearing and reappearing sealed more tightly than a tomb and tossing about like a ship at sea."

When the English got wind of the goings-on of Emma Bovary, they too were stunned into wide-eyed astonishment. The reviewer for the July 11, 1857, *Saturday Review* needed an aesthetic rationale that would preserve his literary dignity.

> It was not without considerable hesitation that we determined to review *Madame Bovary.* . . . Though it is not a work which we can recommend to any man, far less any woman, to read, its success appears to us to be a fact worthy of the attention of all who take an interest in the condition of French society. . . . Indeed, the volume contains not a few passages which would of themselves justify very strong language if there were any danger that M. Flaubert's example would be followed in this country, or that his book would become popular amongst English readers.

We do not, however, feel ourselves called upon to make use of any very indignant expressions. There is no fear that our novelists will outrage public decency. Their weaknesses forbid such dangerous eccentricity quite as much as their virtues.

French society was not quite as decadent as the English reviewer imagined. And even Paris of the late nineteenth century was still eons from our own free-for-all world where anything and everything goes and only the most blatant forms of erotic violence and female denigration can be recognized as pornography. The year that this review appeared, 1857, the Public Ministry of Paris, in bringing Flaubert to trial, declared that *Madame Bovary: Provincial Morals* was (1) an offense against public morals and (2) an offense against religious morals. In his opening remarks, the prosecutor slyly suggested that the deceptively innocent subtitle be replaced by the more accurate *The Story of the Adulteries of a Provincial Housewife.* The editor of *Revue de Paris,* the magazine in which *Madame Bovary* had been serialized, had already suppressed the passage about Emma's downfall in the carriage, but the ministry was not satisfied. Yes, the carriage ride and the fluttering scraps of paper had been eliminated, but the editor had allowed the reader to go from Léon's irresistible argument "It's done in Paris!" to the honeymoon tryst, the three fabulous days, in the hotel room.

The lawyer for the defense had a ready answer. He contended that the suppression of the carriage ride scene had been the most ridiculous gesture possible. The absence of the carriage ride could only arouse the reader to more fantastic flights of erotic imagination than what might had been left on the page. He advised that since the censors had been so foolish as to cut the carriage ride, they were even more foolishly "two words too late," since they had made it all too clear that Emma had stepped into the carriage with Léon.

In his summing up, the prosecutor cautioned the court that lascivious details cannot be canceled out by a moral ending, "otherwise one could recount all the orgies imaginable, one could describe all the depravities of a harlot, so long as she were made to die on a pallet in the poor house." And who were the innocents that would be contaminated by Monsieur Flaubert's pornographic tale? Would it be a man like those in the courtroom, strong of moral purpose, a man who gets "his instincts from below and his thoughts from on high?" The prosecutor responded to his own query:

> The light pages of *Madame Bovary* fall into hands that are even lighter, into the hands of young girls, sometimes of married women. Well then! When the imagination will have been seduced, when this seduction will have reached into the heart and the heart will have spoken to the senses, do you think that a very dispassionate argument will be very effective against this seduction of the senses and the feelings?

The prosecutor and the defense lawyer each used the nefarious influence of romantic novels to bolster their opposing arguments. They were of one mind about the damaging effects of the literature of seduction on a sensitive, innocent female mind. However, the defense lawyer took the courtroom by surprise by showing the connection between convent literature and romance literature. To convince the ministry of the depth of Flaubert's religious sentiments, he called attention the author's remarkable depiction of the dangers of the typical convent education, which, with its emphasis on trinkets and icons and sentimentality, could have as seductive an influence on a young girl's mind as romance novels. The lawyer pointed out that French girls are sent to convents to learn the duties of religion but instead are inspired by the materialistic atmosphere to a religious sensuality that leads them directly to the romance novel. A convent could never provide a proper sanctuary for a country girl like Emma who was drawn to the excitements of storms at sea, a girl whose temperament was more sentimental than religious or artistic, a girl who sought wild emotions and had no patience with calm landscapes. Emma was precisely the sort of girl who would linger at the confessional, prolonging the ecstasies inspired by the priest's whispered references to heavenly lovers and eternal marriages. Her eyes feasted on the images of the sick lamb, the Sacred Heart pierced with arrows, and poor Jesus suffering as He stumbled under His cross.

The defense lawyer then quoted passages from the novel that traced Emma's path from the traditional paraphernalia of convent life to the erotic novels that were sneaked in by the "old maid" laundress who once a month came to the convent, her aprons loaded down with reading materials. For a trinket or a kind word, she would happily loan her romance novels to the susceptible girls.

There was always love, lovers, mistresses, tormented ladies swooning in lonely gazebos, coach-boys dying at every relay, horses ridden to death on every page, somber forests, heartaches, vows, sobs, tears, and kisses, gondolas in the moonlight, nightingales in the thickets, and gentlemen brave as lions, soft as lambs, virtuous beyond belief, always stylishly dressed, and weeping like mourners.

After "soiling her hands" with the old maid's novels, Emma paved her own way to Walter Scott and the historical novels, which were to be the ultimate undoing of her innocence. If the purveyors of our contemporary romance novels were to lay their hands on the reading materials that circulated secretly in Emma's convent, would they appreciate the subtle eroticisms of the illustrations that adorned them? Young men clasping white-robed girls in their arms. English ladies relaxing in carriages as their team of horses is led by two small postilions in white breeches. Girls dreaming away on sofas, gazing at the moon, feeding turtle doves or "plucking daisy petals with their tapered fingers that curved upwards like pointed slippers." The exotic landscapes, the Tartar minarets, "sultans with long pipes, reclining under bowers in the arms of dancing girls," would be too tame for the book jackets that lure the two hundred million contemporary Emmas to purchase the delectable romances that surreptitiously kindle their secret erotic desires.

Though he has always been something of a pioneer in the study of male and female eroticism, Stoller was not the first to expose the erotic allures of the mass market paperback. Feminist writers had been exploring the territory for nearly three decades, collecting, sorting, and arranging, deciphering what they discovered about the pornography of feminine and masculine desire. In her 1979 essay "Mass Market Romance," Ann Barr Snitow reported:

> In a less sexist society, there might be a pornography that is exciting, expressive, interesting, even perhaps, significant as a form of social rebellion, all traits that in a sexist society are obscured by pornography's present role as escape valve for hostility toward women, or as metaphor for fiercely guarded power hierarchies. Instead in a sexist society, we have two pornographies, one for men, one for women. . . . How different is the pornography for women, in which sex is bathed in romance, diffused, always implied rather than enacted at all.

In their contents and in the degree of overt hostility toward females, the two forms of erotic turn-on are immensely different. One is graphic, visual, specific; the other imaginative, vague, and nongraphic. However, in the positions assigned to heroine and hero there are certain unsettling similarities. A long and highly respected tradition of "for male eyes only" pornography is that a woman or a child be depicted in a submissive, degraded position. To add a little spice, the child or woman is shown performing sex on or having sex with an animal, preferably one with a gigantic penis. When he is staring, peeping, or gazing at the porno photo or flick, the man is unconsciously identifying with the person in the passive, feminine, submissive position while simultaneously feeling safely ensconced in the macho position of the looking and violating one.

Until the late 1970s, when female porno stars were being encouraged to keep up with the times and assume the top position, the correspondence of female-child-bottom/male-adult-top was followed religiously in magazine and film pornography. However, for centuries, in porno parlors, houses of prostitution, hotel rooms, and bedchambers, it was the tradition for the male who did the paying to assume the bottom position. Every hired sadist, prostitute, call girl, and male hustler knows that the most popular scenarios require that the one who pays is the one who is bound, strangled, whipped, stomped on, urinated on, defecated on by his dominator of the evening. As one prostitute explained to the 1986 attorney general's Commission on Pornography:

> Having me urinate on them, commonly referred to as golden showers, was a popular request.
>
> Again my customers, who were mostly professional types, would bring many examples in magazines or books of the types of bondage they wanted or of other acts they thought would satisfy their sexual desires, like me acting like their mother, enemas, spanking or cross dressing, men dressing in women's undergarments or clothing.

The schoolteacher ties her pupil to his chair until his errors are corrected. The nurse spanks her recalcitrant patient until he begs for an enema. The nun flagellates her cringing penitent until he confesses to the sins that will grant him a golden shower. The mother stomps across her bad boy's chest until her spiked heels penetrate his skin. Actually, who is on bottom and who is on top matters little in these infantile interpretations of grown-up sexuality and grown-up authority. The essential element in a perverse script is that one body must assume the bottom, passive-feminine position and some other body must assume the top, active-masculine position. Whether enacted in a whorehouse by a bad boy-bottom with a hired sadistic momma or on a yacht with a panting virgin being overcome at last by her phallic man, sadomasochistic scenarios are triumphant celebrations of the familiar patriarchal logos: every slave longs for a master; every bottom needs a top and a good top is hard to find.

If women are to have their own pornography, should they act the submissive roles as in the more traditional mass market paperbacks? Or should they step into the dominant position, as slavishly, submissive Emma finally does with her sexual serf Léon, as do the sophisticated, demi-virgins of the latest Harlequin Desire series, with their hard-shelled but oh so narcissistically vulnerable lovers? Could a feminine pornography designed to express female erotic preferences succeed in undermining the social categories of bottom-top and submission-domination, or would it simply end up reflecting the same time-worn gender stereotypes?

The feminine, soft-focus erotic scenarios that are proposed as antidotes to male pornography succeed no better in altering the submission-dominance structures. The innocent fuzziness only serves to obscure the degree to which women have been brainwashed into a compliance with their sexual and emotional bondages. In fact, most attempts to create a specifically female pornography demonstrate the profound investment most women have in perpetuating the social categories of masculine and feminine that keep women (and men) in a state of subjugation.

In her diaries for the years 1940 and 1941, Anaïs Nin explained the difficulties she encountered in trying to create a truly feminine pornography that would nevertheless satisfy her anonymous male patron, the Collector, who was paying her a dollar a page to turn out high-toned erotic turn-ons. Since at first she did not want to give the Collector "anything genuine," she whipped up a concoction of stories she had heard and pretended they were from the diary of a woman. After he received these initial half-hearted attempts, the Collector telephoned Nin with his critique: "Leave out the poetry and descriptions of anything but sex. Concentrate on sex."

So I began to write tongue-in-cheek, to become outlandish, inventive, and so exaggerated that I thought he would realize I was caricaturing sexuality. But there was no protest. . . . I spent days in the library studying *Kama Sutra,* listening to friends' most extreme adventures.

But the Collector wanted more explicit sex and please, "Less poetry."

Finally, in order to satisfy her patron, Nin became the madame of what she termed her "snobbish literary house of prostitution." She gathered around her some poet friends who also needed some extra cash: for rent, to pay the dentist, to buy paper, to fix a typewriter. "As we have to suppress poetry, lyrical flights, and are condemned to focus only on sensuality, we have violent explosions of poetry. Writing erotica becomes a road to sainthood rather than debauchery." The timid poets composed orgies. The frigid wrote of frenzied fulfillment. Those with the deepest poetic sentiments found their revenge in bestiality. After a while the literary prostitutes in Nin's "house" began to hate the Collector.

In her 1976 preface to *Delta of Venus,* a volume containing some of Nin's efforts for the Collector, she describes the conflict she had experienced as she tried to satisfy his obsession with sex and still not compromise her feminine self.

For centuries we had had only one model for this literary genre —the writing of men. I was already conscious of a difference between the masculine and feminine treatment of sexual experience. I knew that there was a great disparity between Henry Miller's explicitness and my ambiguities—between his humorous,

Rabelaisian view of sex and my poetic descriptions of sexual relations. . . . I had a feeling that Pandora's box contained the mysteries of woman's sensuality, so different from man's and for which man's language was inadequate.

After rereading the tales she selected for inclusion in *Delta of Venus*, Nin was relieved that she had not entirely suppressed her own voice, that she had managed, after all, to express what sexuality was like from a woman's point of view.

The *Delta* tales stick to the sexuality the Collector ordered, with the obligatory female-submissive-bottoms and male-dominant-tops, but they are adorned at various moments by the relationships and emotions that give to sex its "color, flavor, rhythms, intensities." Nin had sneaked in what she understood as mysteries of female sexuality, the Pandora's box of female desire. Nevertheless, she gave to the Collector the requisite prostitutes, lesbians, women whose vulvas and mouths are swollen from being forced to do what their clients demand of them and who love nothing better than to be licked by dogs and end up groveling with desire for the masculine touch that hurts and humiliates. To keep the cash box filled and the Collector's penis erect, her heroines had to be depicted as an assortment of bad, kinky girls turned on by bestiality, domination, humiliation, or innocent girls turned kinky by male lust. In her role as a madame of pornography Nin adhered to the submission-dominance, innocence-lechery motifs.

Perhaps the most famous attempt to create a "feminine" pornography is *The Story of O*, published in France in 1954 and purportedly written by an unknown woman, who called herself Pauline Réage. However, so offensively misogynist do many women (and men) find Réage's novel that rumors continue to circulate that the pseudo-anonymous Pauline must have been a man. In his preface to *O*, Jean Paulhan, a writer and literary critic who was elected to be one of the forty immortals of l'Académie Française shortly after his laudatory preface, "Happiness in Slavery," was published, goes into some detail about the delicate feminine touches that reassure him of the author's female identity. He admits to some initial confusion about the heroine O who, in her devotion to sexuality, aroused his suspicions that she was aspiring to a virile or masculine ideal. However, Paulhan decided that Madame Réage's narrative of a woman's voluntary sexual bondage, the piece-by-piece enslavement and deeper and deeper humiliation to which she consents, represents the lost childhood that men long for in themselves and envy in women. "Women at least are fated to resemble, throughout their lives, the children we once were." Réage, therefore, was not only a female but a genuinely feminine female.

In his Introduction, André Pieyre de Mandriargues states that although Réage had used all the standard formulas of centuries-old pornography—the binding corsets, the brandings with hot irons, the chains, the riding crops—she was actually describing "the tragic flowering of a woman in the abdication of her freedom, in willful slavery, in humiliation." Admirers of O continue to find ways to ennoble Réage's pornography. Most literary critics have tried to find an elevating social message in O and therefore have focused on Réage's method of bringing the reader into an intimate connection with the dynamics of slave-master relationships. In contrast to the more distant, intellectual male writers, like Genet, who have also tried to plumb such relationships, Réage was able to slip into the skin of her slavelike heroine.

Since it *is* true, at any rate, that slave and master are inseparable, Réage's readers are afforded the possibility of identifying with O's submissions *and* her master's dominations. *The Story of O* demonstrates how the master's stern resistance to being absorbed into the slave he secretly wishes to be matches up with the slave's willingness to give up her separate existence in order to remain connected to her all powerful master. O is a high-toned morality fable that exemplifies Stoller's earthy motto "masochisma matches machismo." In O's progressive dehumanization, as there is progressively less of O's self, she transforms her master, creating in him the omnipotent, omniscient, coherent other in whose arms she can take refuge.

The master is turned on by the slave's submission to him. The slave is turned on by the master's domination over her. The reader is turned on by being in the positions of both slave and master. Paulhan makes a valid point when he says that females at least have the right to remain childlike and submissive and that males envy them for that privilege. I have shown how the male—Charles Bovary, Léon, Rodolphe, Fullerton, Mr. R, and Mr. B—expresses, in his identification with his female "victim," the feminine and infantile desires that have been forbidden to him. Analogously, women identify with the men they have assigned to the top position as a way of expressing the masculine desires that are forbidden to them. Emma's masculine strivings and ambitions had to be hidden away beneath her pose of extreme submissiveness. Perhaps Réage, in her subjective, intimate, "feminine" way, has done nothing more nor less than Flaubert did in his cold, dissecting, objective "masculine" realism. Flaubert, who had been determined to rid his writing of romantic extravagances, found some expression for them in his identification with Emma's romantic excesses and thereby illuminated the eternal fate of the female, who is always being led on by the obscure desires of the flesh and held in bondage by the social constraints that forbid to her any expression of sexuality, except as that inscrutable and dangerous sexuality is controlled and directed by a master or as she impersonates the role of dominating master. O, who strips away her bourgeois soul to find her true self in the house of perversion, is nothing more nor less than our modern-day Emma.

And what about Réage? With all her feminine delicacies, she sometimes seems more identified with O's enslavers than with O. The fact that a "porn" novel was written by a female (possibly) does not guarantee at all that the pornography is feminine, or even female. If some females and many males are "turned on" by the flowering of O's sexual life under conditions of bondage, humiliation, and progressive dehumanization, then the pornography of Réage, for all its avowed intimate moral intensity, is essentially not so different from the standard male pornography. Réage may have produced a literary product worthy of the attention of *l'Académie Français,* and she may have given to the world a morality tale on the depths of human degradation and humiliation, but insofar as her novel *is* an erotic turn-on Réage, with all her mischievous irony, is, like her heroine, expressing a slavelike identification with her masters. The masters, the male readers, of course are turned on through their identification with O. Very few male readers want to have the burdens and responsibilities of Sir Stephen, O's perpetually virile master.

The effects of male pornography depend on the wearing down of resistance and the gradual dehumanization of human flesh. Whoever the body and whichever the way, pornography entails a deadening of otherwise living, breathing, and therefore dangerous and unpredictable flesh. The dehumanization of the female body that Réage so "hauntingly" portrayed in her mid-twentieth-century novel has progressed to the point where, now in the last decade of this century, the erotic undercurrents that her admirers claim gave a certain moral tone to O's slavery are no longer powerful enough to contain or disguise the primitive destructive aggression that lies at the heart of the pornography enterprise. Whether she was a woman or a man in the mask of a woman, Réage was deceived if she believed that pornography was about erotic love. Pornography has always been about making hate in the guise of an erotic scenario that could contain the hatred. The difference these days is that the guise is gone. The grinning mask of death is right out in the open. Perhaps Réage was saying just that. O's first master, her lover René, sends her to the Castle of Roissy for her elementary lessons in opening her bodily orifices to the mysteries of sexuality. This accomplished, he hands her over to the cold and calculating Stephen, whose beatings, brandings, and chainings lacerate her body into a further openness. Réage's novel ends with O placed on her back in the middle of a *public* courtyard to be possessed one after the other by her master, Stephen, and the physically grotesque Commander who wants only to open the thing that O has become and poke with his penis and tongue and fingers and toes into all her openings, natural and manufactured, all the way, all at once. The chain around her neck and the one connected to the rings in her labia have been unfastened. The owl's mask with plumage that covered her shoulders and back has been removed. Now that Stephen has put her body on *public* display and given her body to another man to be opened all the way, the O that was once a flowering sexual being will be free to be nothing at all—a Zero.

Three decades after O's sexual flowering, the 1986 United States Attorney General's Commission on Pornography attempted to bring some order to the unruly world of porn. That commission was a forthright but underfinanced and feeble reaction to the inadequate and short-sighted legislative response of the 1970 commission to the comparatively tame, but hardly innocent, pornography of the 1950s, '60s and early '70s. For one thing, the 1970 commission had failed to appreciate the historical momentum underlying the dehumanization they were observing. In their historical overview of the progress of pornography in the United States, the 1986 commission concluded:

The pornography industry has grown considerably over the last thirty years. . . . the industry has gone from a low yield, covert business to a highly visible multi-billion dollar industry. Over five hundred fifty million dollars of this may be attributed to retail sales in the Los Angeles area alone. The remaining billions of dollars worth of materials are distributed throughout the United States and abroad. In the 1950's, "adults only" pornographic establishments were dark and dingy stores and theatres located in the less desirable parts of urban areas. The sex-related materials of this period generally depicted women in seductive poses and were not readily available to the public. . . . The females depicted in the films were often partially exposed in the breast area and the males, for the most part, were fully dressed.

The first of these films to be a major economic success was produced in 1959 for $24,000 and was about a man who was unable to see clothing on women.

By the early 1970s it was evident that the pornography industry was expanding rapidly. The 1970 commission had already noted that the latest crop of "exploitation films" were dealing with "perversion, abortion, drug addiction, wayward girls, orgies, wife-swapping, vice dens, prostitution, frigidity, nymphomania, lesbianism." Not long afterward films and pulp paperbacks designed to appeal to paraphilias became increasingly prevalent. Sadomasochism, and bondage and discipline were the major themes; children, animals, amputees were major characters; visual displays of ejaculation, urination, defecation, and milk-squirting breasts were the staples of the industry. Child pornography was featured in magazines such as *Moppets* and *Where the Young Ones Are,* and one-third of the nearly three-billion-dollar porn industry was derived from kiddy porn operations.

Only fifteen years later, the 1986 attorney general's historical overview concluded:

> The 1980's have seen the complete transformation of the industry into a big business with large scale distributors, theatre chains and technological advances such as home videos, subscription television, Dial-A-Porn and computer sex subscription services. Distribution locations have become large complexes operating out of modern industrial centers. The major distributors own their own buildings and have incorporated all aspects of production into their businesses.

Pornography has become the industry that epitomizes every other social force and institution that exploits the poor, the helpless, women, children, *and* men. However, under the banner of free speech, even social revolution, the porno industry has found some of its strongest defenders among the victims. Some radical feminists, for example, are continuing to deceive themselves about the revolutionary potential of pornography. In her article on the mass market romance novel, which was intended as an antidote to the moralistic stringencies of Women Against Pornography, Ann Snitow argued that feminine romance erotica preserves gender stereotypes whereas hard-core pornography is a *potential* force for dynamiting the presently conceived categories of masculine and feminine that keep women subjugated and oppressed. She contended that soft-core, soft-focus feminine "erotica" left out "too much of what is infantile in sex—the reenactment of early feelings, the boundlessness and omnipotence of infant desire and its furious gusto." Snitow was saying that a polite good-girl erotica that eliminates the exaltations of masochistic surrender and the explosions of the boundaries of the self will lead to a further narrowing of the possibilities of female sexual experience. She claimed that diffuse feminine erotica is no more valid a representation of human desire than the driven, power-hungry, selfish, woman-hating sexuality of hard porn. As nurses ass-fuck their patients, as guardians masturbate their wards, as old men fuck young girls, as servants screw their mistresses, "all social constraints are overwhelmed by a flood of sexual energy. . . . Class, age, custom—all are deliciously sacrificed, dissolved by sex."

Snitow was writing under the lingering influence of the utopian sexual politics of the 1960s, when it was thought that sexual liberation would be the handmaiden of social liberation. At that time there *was* a revolution in sexual values and attitudes and in that revolution women *were* freed to explore a fuller range of erotic responsiveness. And there is no question in my mind that the greatest danger to women, and men, would be if we were to revert to the puritanical sexual slaveries that made women ashamed of their bodies and essentially denied and disavowed the active sexuality of females. Nor do I believe that a ban on pornography could solve the problem of the gender stereotyping underlying the pornography enterprise. Pornography depends for its vitality on the gender stereotypes that support the fundamental structures of our social order. And until we question those structures and institutions, erotic literature, pornography, the erotic life itself will be what it always has been—a reflection of those structures but never a potential underminer of them.

Ellen Willis is another feminist writer who was inspired to take arms against the goody-goody, sanitized version of female sexuality that was implied by the political platform of Women Against Pornography. In the same year (1979) that Snitow published her paper, Willis published "Feminism, Moralism, and Pornography." According to Willis, even the term *erotica,* the nice girl's euphemism for pornography, suggests that lovemaking should be devoid of vulgarity or power or aggression. She conceded that porn is the product of male imagination and therefore sexist, but she nevertheless affirmed its legitimacy on the basis that each woman is entitled to do what she wants with her own body. And if some women are turned on by the images and words that have been designed for the sexual arousal of men, they should not be deprived of this expansion of their sexual life.

Both Snitow and Willis were bravely asserting a point of view about female sexuality that was not popular with some of their more conservative feminist colleagues. However, when they affirmed the radical impulses underlying the pornography enterprise, they were allowing themselves to be deceived by the perverse strategy. Nothing could be more repressive and reactionary than the images of women (and men) as they are portrayed in porno films and literature. By defending the right to produce a feminine pornography modeled on the masculine kind, radical women unwittingly lend support to the power structures that oppress women, children, and men. What has not been sufficiently appreciated is that, like perversion itself, the literature of perversion—pornography—is about death, murder, primitive sadistic aggression, and dehumanization. This has always been the case. However, as I have been stressing, until the recent past, the erotic elements had been sufficiently strong to contain the aggression and the business of sexuality had been largely a private and personal matter. It is the *public* display of O's body and the reducing of her flesh to a Zero that reveals the death mask grinning behind the mask of love. Our mass media, computerized, consumer sex is a democratized version of the old Roman orgies, which were also celebrations of mutilation and death in the guise of erotic love. Whenever sex goes public, buyer beware.

Because gender stereotyping is fundamental to the hierarchical structures of most civilized societies, whether one is pro-pornography or anti-pornography one ends up supporting one form or another of a repressive sexual psychology. In the United States, the various commissions assigned to investigate the pornography industry have been showcases designed to exhibit the government's interest in protecting women and children from male exploitation. The lawyers, doctors, ministers, rabbis, psychologists, educators, social reformers, and feminists who devoted considerable time and spirit to these investigations wanted nothing more than to put their special talents and callings to work for a good and noble cause. But the pornography debates bring out the ironies of a gender politics that is itself based on gender stereotypes. As anyone who scrutinizes the commission reports soon realizes, the women against pornography movement can and will be used by any conservative government in support of repressive legislation—the rescinding of rights to abortion, free speech, and free press. On the other hand, those who defend pornography under the banner of its potentially radical impulses are actually defending the latest brand of repressive sexuality, one of those old tyrannies of gender in a new guise.

Pornography has become the handmaiden of the new law of the land, the law of consumerism. From the nineteenth-century tyranny of the taboos on female sexuality we are now poised to succumb in the twenty-first century to the servitude of consumer sex. One day soon we will all be free to visit the nearest megamall, purchase next year's wardrobes for the whole family, go to the hairdresser, down a juicy burger and some fries, and linger for a while at a porno peep show before going on to buy our paper flags, plastic Madonnas, and Zuni fetishes. Returning home calmed and reassured by our purchases and erotic titillations, we will turn on the video screen and watch the bottoms and the tops assume their usual positions.

While the theoreticians of female desire debate the present virtues and potential values of pornography, the technicians and purveyors of porn are thriving. And they have the cooperation and protection of organized crime syndicates who use their laundered porno profits to fund an international drug trade. There are also the landlords who rent the pornographers space, the realtors who handle the land and space transactions, the bankers who process their currency transactions and help them launder their profits, the transportation companies and interstate carriers who ship obscene materials, the academics who act as their expert witnesses, the prosecutors, judges, zoning board members, health department officials, all of whom ignore the organized crime participation in the production of porn. The treatment of those who testify against the pornography syndicate resembles the worst scenarios of a grade B porno flick. According to several witnesses for the 1986 commission, even minor infractions of the pornography code of honor such as disobeying rules regarding pricing, territory, or failure to pay "the street tax" are severely "disciplined." An inside informer testified that one disobedient was held by his arms up against the wall in an alley while a car ran into him "with the front bumper up against the wall and shattered his knees. That's a pretty good discipline."

As we might expect, the telephone company found a way to cash in on the porno enterprise. The company turned adversity into triumph. The recorded messages referred to as "dial-a-porn" began in 1982 as a result of the federal government's deregulation of the traditional dial-it services that included weather reports, prayers, jokes, and sports scores. In response to being forbidden to produce such services, telephone companies throughout the United States held lotteries to select the future providers, who would thenceforth be responsible for production expenses and the content of messages, while the phone companies stayed on as the official transmitters and, in the long run, greatest financial beneficiaries.

In New York, one Dial-A-Porn provider earns two cents per call and the telephone company earns 9.4 cents. In California, Dial-A-Porn providers earn $1.26 per call while the telephone company earns seventy-four cents. . . . The telephone company for the state of New York has earned as much as thirty-five thousand dollars a day from Dial-A-Porn calls. Pacific Bell estimates that their company earned twelve million from Dial-A-Porn calls between October 1984 and October 1985.

There are two types of dial-a-porn calls. The simpler, more intimate type has the customer carrying on a live conversation with a paid performer who will be as sexually explicit as his or her customer desires, if need be verbally assisting him or her to perform sexual acts during the conversation. In the second type the customer receives a prerecorded message when he or she dials a 976 number, such as 976-SLUT or 976-LUST. These prerecorded messages describe acts entailing lesbianism, sodomy, rape, incest, excretory functions, bestiality, sadomasochistic abuse, and sex acts with children. One dial-a-porn number in California offers the caller a choice of five "pleasures," among them sadomasochistic abuse, urination, and anal intercourse.*

Commercial pornography broadcasts loud and clear the dehumanizations that are usually screened out and disguised by the less overtly commercialized, more personalized perverse scripts. The hucksters who write the porno scripts, run the show, hire the models, orchestrate the

---

* On June 23, 1989, the United States Supreme Court declared that a federal ban on commercial phone messages that are "indecent" but not "obscene" violated the right to free speech. At the same time the Court upheld the ban on "obscene" messages. A 1988 law had made it illegal to offer either indecent or obscene messages. The June 23 ruling was considered a half victory for the two-billion-dollar-a-year dial-a-porn industry. Now messages with "prurient interest" containing "offensive depictions" of sexual conduct and with no serious artistic or political merit will be fined $500,000 with a maximum two-year jail term. But there is still a lot of arguing room about the difference between "indecent" and "obscene."

bondages and submissions, and package and market and merchandise the paperbacks, videos, films, flicks, and photos are keen to their customers' tastes and fantasies, which often resemble their own and which, with all their manifest variety, are as monotonously and eternally the same as a provincial landscape.

In the 1986 report, among the fifty or so pulp paperbacks under *A* alone were all the ingredients of O's sexual flowering and then some: *Abbie's Lesbian Love; Abused, Defiled, and Degraded; Abused Vietnamese Virgins; A Girl and Her Dog; Alice: Sex-Crazed Runaway; Anal Compulsives Needing Rear Service;* and *Arab Captives.* Among the films were *A Taste of Cherry; A Woman's Torment; Always Ready for Four; An Unnatural Act; Anal Annie Just Can't Say No; Angel in Bondage;* and *Audra's Ordeal.* Magazines included *A Cock Between Friends; A Date with Pussy; Amateur Bondage #3; Animal Action; Anal Virgins; Asian Suck Mistress;* and *Ass Fucking Bi-Sexual 3-Way.*

In every industry, the executives are grateful for staples with a long shelf life, classical models and traditional styles that are reliable, dependable money-makers. Even more than in most businesses, monotony and sameness, rigidity and stereotyping are the hallmarks of the porno enterprise. Still, as with any commodity, changing porno styles are welcomed and recognized as necessary to the continuing vitality of the trade. It took a while for the porno hucksters to realize the extent to which their not so classy versions of femininity might influence clothing styles and makeup, department store ads, and window design. They used to be humble before their elegant Madison Avenue mentors. They used to keep one ear to the ground. They used to emulate the changing images of the female by keeping tabs on the changing displays in Bloomingdale catalogues, by studying the covers of *Harper's Bazaar, Vogue,* and *Cosmopolitan.* Nobody knew quite how it happened, but there came a day when nobody could tell who was emulating whom. There were seasons when you couldn't tell the difference between a *Penthouse* girl clad in spike-heeled black leather boots with strands of rope around her breasts and a *New York Times Magazine* lingerie model. One year it was skinny models; the next year lesbians and androgynous bodies were the rage. During the Brooke Shields and Jodie Foster years, prepubescent models were proudly advertising their buttocks in skin-tight designer jeans and their breast-buds in kinky nightwear. Child molesters would collect and trade Shields and Foster type ads, showing them to their victims as a way of assuring the children that it was okay to pose for porno photographs.

Child pornography is any part of a process whereby children, "from as young as one week up to the age of majority, are induced to engage in sexual activity of one sort or another, and the process by which children are photographed while engaging in that activity." Until feminist groups convinced the 1970 commission that there was a real and present danger, child pornography had been a mainstay of the post-Vietnam porno industry. Magazine publishers and film producers, who were offering $200 a day and more for a child model, had no difficulty recruiting. Some parents, among them the film producers and technicians, would pose and act with their children. Others would consent only to hire out their children to perform oral sex on hired adult models or to submit to anal and genital sex with adult males—supposedly always simulated, but very often not. The work was routine. The pay was good. The formulas for inducing sexual excitement were easy for the producers to follow, and the titles of the films and books were fairly straightforward: *Infant Love, Children and Sex, Lust for Little Girls, Little Girls, Lollitots, Uncle Jake and Cousin Paula, The Child Psychiatrist.* In 1982 after the use of prepubescent children for porno flicks and photos became technically illegal, the child pornography industry went clandestine. By 1986 the manufacture of kiddy porn had become a cottage industry, pretty much run by child molesters, who take photographs of children engaging in sexual activities and then simply keep the photos as personal mementos, trade the photographs with other child molesters, or sell them to the clandestine pedophile market. As they always have, child molesters continue to collect and trade photographs of prepubescent children posed suggestively for legitimate lingerie and clothing ads. Sexually oriented computer communications are now used between pedophiles. Child molesters can easily trade information about potential child victims. Commercially produced child pornography in magazine form, motion picture films, and videotapes are still available and are sold under the counter in many stores that feature sexually explicit adult material. The formulas are still as simple and easy to follow as they ever were: Use boys from six to thirteen and girls from six to fifteen. Emphasize the lechery of the adults and the innocence of the children. Emphasize the child's hairlessness, tiny privates, and slightly budding breasts.

The kiddy porn variant highlights the innocence-lechery motif latent in most, if not all, sexual fantasies, perverse scripts, and soft-core erotica. The seduction of an innocent by a lusting, insatiable male has been a staple of the sexual fantasies that enliven the sexual encounters between men and women. The fundamental fantasy, rooted in what little boys and girls prefer to imagine about adult sexuality, is that decent women are virginal and lacking in desire until they are awakened, seduced, bludgeoned, or raped into it. The father is supposed to lust after the mother. But the mother, who desires only her adorable child, does not ever think about or experience sexual desire. She is the gatekeeper who makes sure that pleasure does not run riot.

This fixated infantile primal scene fantasy, devised by the humiliated child to salvage his self-esteem, has always been exploited by the social order in support of its conventions of normal femininity and masculinity. The social order needs its tops and bottoms, its hierarchical structures, and the infantile mind in all of us is always ready to be exploited by those structures. Nevertheless, in its infinite self-serving wisdom, society overlooks a certain degree of variation from the norm that women are innocents and men are lechers. To keep the bottoms happy, most societies find ways to normalize gender variations that seem to be gaining in popularity anyway. As in domestic bedchambers and legitimate PG films, it is now acceptable porno practice to allow females to be the aggressive, dominant ones—at least now and again. Currently, with mass media cooperation, kinky sex between loving couples, androgyny, homosexuality, and video and telephone masturbation are available to men and women of all ages. However, when some feminists take this sort of overt permissiveness as a sign of society's increasing tolerance for women's sexual liberation, they are mistaken. Throughout history, whenever women begin to look as if they might be wandering too far from the hearth or getting too far out from under, the archaic time-honored prescriptive normalities of feminine-submissive, masculine-dominant, female-innocent, male-lecher will be brought back into style. And as always they will be reinforced by whatever rationale is at hand at the time. The first step, very often, has been to reinforce the ever-ready innocence-lechery theme. And thus child pornography has been *one* aesthetic medium for keeping women in their place.

During the late nineteenth and early twentieth century, as it became evident that women were becoming less and less willing to squeeze their bodies and minds and souls into the domestic and sexual conventions that their husbands and fathers and mothers were recommending for them, the sanity of men whose erections were dependent on the fetishistic fiction of female innocence was threatened. As Bram Dijkstra emphasizes in *Idols of Perversity,* "Afraid to deal with women who were strong and independent and who dared to make demands, the late nineteenth century male molded the child into the image of a woman he could handle. The helplessness, weakness and passive pliability of ignorance he could no longer find in woman he began to attribute to the child."

The sexual revolution of the late twentieth century did not eradicate woman-hating. Indeed, the growth of the pornography industry and its expansion into kiddy porn were all too logical responses to the threat that women might begin to express the full range and depth of their sexuality. But when kiddy porn was outlawed, what could take its place? How would men allay the horrors and hold at bay the awesome brutalities that are evoked by images of an in-the-flesh, actively desiring female body? If women attempt to break out of their fetishized molds, there are all sorts of ways to push them back in. Kiddy porn is not the only alternative. In recent history the sexual liberation of women was paralleled by a gradual transition from the "woman-loving," innocent porn of World War II to the overt woman-hating post-Vietnam porn.

Soon after *Life* published its World War II photojournalistic pinups of Rita Hayworth in a bosom-clinging satin slip and Betty Grable in a buttock-hugging playsuit and Chili Williams in a crotch-creased polka dot swimsuit, there suddenly were a lot of other fetishized female bodies around for men to stroke to. There were the girlie magazines— *Flirt, Titter, Wink, Eyeful, Giggles, Sir, Gala, Focus,* and *Cuties*—and the popular sub rosa *New York Times Magazine,* with its advertisements of scantily clad women in bathing suits, negligees, and undergarments. If a man required outright nudity, he could have it—"minus pubic hairs," the courts insisted—in the down-to-earth aesthetic reality of the nudist magazines *Modern Sunbathing and Hygiene, Sunshine and Health,* or the more exclusive *Art Photography.*

Then in December 1953 Hugh Hefner brought out the first issue of *Playboy.* Marilyn Monroe, who found the boundaries of her existence through the fetishization of the container called her body, was the first nude centerfold. And each month thereafter a color photograph of a nude woman faithfully appeared at the center of Hefner's magazine for men, which also featured lovemaking tips, cartoons, satires, and articles of manly interest. Within two years the circulation rose from 60,000 copies per month to 400,000. Millions of ordinary middle-class men and college students seemed to be satisfied by the down-to-earth assortment of clean-cut all-American nudes and bikini-clad girlies in *Playboy.* Then, before anyone knew what was happening or just why it was happening, these tame, some would complain conventional, respectfully dull masturbation inspirations shifted to brutality, violence, exploitation, and blatant misogyny.

Even hardened porno models—the ones who had already traveled the route from pretty porn to masochistic porn to Emperor Crown lesbian porn to animal porn and child porn—were alarmed by this growing trend in the porno industry. "The hating way in which women are portrayed has escalated so fast. They used to be afraid to portray it at all, but now you see everything—women being skewered, women being killed."

The pinnacle achievement of this shift from clean-cut porn to blatant woman-hating porn was the snuff genre, so named for films in which porno actresses were purportedly murdered, snuffed out, as the cameras were rolling. Originally, around 1975, these were underground films smuggled in from South America. They were meant to cater to a select audience of well-to-do men whose jaded sexual palates could be revived only by watching the dismemberment and mutilation of a female body. A year later, a film called *Snuff* showed at X-rated and neighborhood theaters to throngs of aphrodisiac-deprived men. For the denouement, a man dismembers a woman's body piece by piece. The screen is bathed with images of chopped-up fingers, sawed-off arms and legs, blood oozing from every natural and newly created orifice—a *Story of O* with the blood and guts showing. When the producers and distributors of *Snuff* were brought to trial, they defended their artistic right to produce sexual entertainment by claiming that they were being accused of crimes they did not commit. The rapes, tortures, dismemberments, and murders had only been simulated.

Snuffing keeps the failing penis erect. It is also an unconscious strategy for scaring the sexually emancipated woman back to the safeties of hearth and home, *Küche und Kinder*. From pretty porn to snuff, the chief commodity incentive is woman-hating. When women take up the sword to challenge the premises of the pornography industry, a few of them may do it in a delicate "feminine" way. We should not be surprised, though, that others may choose to challenge in a less than friendly emulation of their enemies.

In a good-natured, wholesome literary frolic, *Ladies' Own Erotica,* that very nearly proves the impossibility of a pornography "for female eyes only," the members of the Kensington Ladies Erotica Society of Los Angeles in 1984 presented a series of vignettes, short-short stories, and poems on the nature of feminine sensuality, mixing these samples of genital erotica with a selection of colorful recipes for various erotic meats, vegetables, and desserts. Compared with the hard stuff of male porn, the Kensington erotica is a sweet-and-sour confection, so genteelly feminine that a reader might find herself longing for a taste of the less classy Harlequin Temptations. The Ladies of Kensington had in mind a different sort of erotic turn-on. They wished to illustrate the essential differences between pornographic and erotic fantasies and to enoble the latter as the only legitimate foundation for sexual intimacy between men and women. They wished to transform the mundane encounters of suburban housewives into magical assignations of the soul.

Sabina, the leader and editor-to-be, set the direction and tone of their mission: "Do we really know what turns us on or do we just go along accepting and acting out what male writers proclaim as erotic?" The Kensington group soon realized how much they had been indoctrinated about the helplessness and victimization of women. They dutifully researched the works of Anaïs Nin, Henry Miller, and Nancy Friday and even "glanced" at *Penthouse, Chic,* and *Playgirl.* They were "not amused" by what they read or saw and they were determined not to produce another *Story of O.* Out of those initial realizations came their first rule: the Kensington erotica would have no victims and no victimizers. No submitters and no dominators. They would prove to the world that sexual arousal does not have to depend on the brutalizing victim-oppressor scenarios designed by males. And here the Kensington group arrived at the heart of the matter. Implicitly they were posing the essential questions about pornography: Are brutality and humiliation intrinsic to a good sexual turn-on? Or can men be taught through feminine pornography about the erotic tendernesses that are the turn-ons for women?

Ladies' Own Erotica is not an antimale or antimisogynist pamphlet.

More like a schoolmarmish manual for nice men, it provides helpful hints on how to seduce a lady. The female reader is promised a sensuous secret *akin* to having an actual affair. Kensington is a never-never land of gourmet breakfasts for two; considerate, devoted husbands who have never cheated, not once, and equally faithful wives, who have only imagined extramarital affairs; financially solvent couples who have loved one another "passionately" for forty years and still screw three times a week; grandchildren who tumble into the house for a babysit just as Grandma has finished her smutty, clitoris-eating adventure with, of all people, a very stunned Henry Miller, who gets his comeuppance by being sent away before his sexual favors are reciprocated.

No doubt the real Henry Miller would have survived this rejection. In fact, he might have turned his temporary sexual adversity to advantage by encouraging the Kensington grandmother's efforts to create erotic literature. Had he met her earlier, he might have introduced her to his lover's patron, the Collector. However, the Kensington ladies who thought they could create democratic sexual turn-ons that had no victims, no oppressors, no injustice, and no violence ended up with a pallid good-girl feminine erotica that is hardly any turn-on at all. The Collector would not have paid them one penny for their efforts.

The Marquis de Sade would have liked nothing better than to pretend to believe in the Kensington utopia, with "the vain fancies that inhabited it: innocence, kindness, devotion, generosity, and chastity," and then to proceed to exhaust the anatomical possibilities of each of the Kensington Ladies, one by one, part by part, until the lucid minds that inhabited their bodies dissolved in abject voluptuousness and the flesh that covered their souls was degraded into the undifferentiated physical matter in which it originated. "Of what use is vice," he would ask, "if there were no virtue to harass?"

In defending his aesthetics, Sade wrote: "Who can flatter himself that he has put virtue in a favorable light if the features of the vice surrounding it are not strongly emphasized?" "But," counters Simone de Beauvoir, "he meant the very opposite: how is vice to be made thrilling if the reader is not first taken in by the illusion of good?"

The greatest illusions of good in the land of Kensington are the virtues of the bountiful dinner table. The Ladies were on to something in their capricious mixings of recipes and varieties of sexual experience. But they were hampered by the benevolences of good wives and the generosities of good mothers, and so when it came to the question of how to transform the succulence of a roasted lamb and the sugary voluptuousness of a chocolate fondue into an erotic orgy, they were stumped. On the other hand, Sade, who had based his entire ethic on the general interchangeability of bodily orifices and the absolute equivalences between gastrointestinal and genital pleasures, had no trouble with the intimate bond between sexual orgies and eating orgies. "There is no passion more closely involved with lechery than drunkenness and gluttony." During the eleven years of his last imprisonment, Sade found compensation for his enforced sexual starvation by devouring at each meal as much as four men and fattening his body into a monstrous perversity of human flesh. There came a point when his immense obesity prevented him from standing up or moving about his cell and also prevented "the exercise of those remains of grace and elegance that still lingered in his general comportment." De Beauvoir grasped the implacability of Sade's destructive aggression. She, who knew that he would never confuse any body part with actual human flesh nor sentimentally mistake the human flesh as an object of enchantment, tells how the Sadean interchangeability of lusts climaxed in the penultimate Sadean anthropophagous fantasies:

> To drink blood, to swallow sperm and excrement, and to eat children mean appeasing desire through destruction of its object. Pleasure requires neither exchange, giving, reciprocity, nor gratuitous generosity. Its tyranny is that of avarice, which chooses to destroy what it cannot assimilate.

What Sade cannot assimilate and what he wishes to destroy is any knowledge of the differences between the sexes. By abolishing all distinctions between one body part and another, by substituting infantile eating lust for genital desire, by destroying the gender identity of the object of desire and reducing her to a zero of mutilated flesh, Sade attempts to triumph over the humiliations of the primal scene. But the ultimate crime he is striving for can never be consummated. Because the flesh resists this reduction of itself into nothingness, the ideal pornographic climax is forever unrealizable. The Sadean hero is always frustrated. Even *Snuff* is not enough. Even the most heinous crimes are never equal to the absolute destruction the Sadean hero desires. "Ah," wails one of Sade's spokesmen, Jerome, "how many times, by God, have I not longed to be able to assail the sun, snatch it out of the universe, make a general darkness, or use that star to burn the world! oh, that would be a crime."

Surely there are women who are similarly consumed by a Sadean hatred of the human flesh, who are also interested in dissolving all distinctions and differentiations between men and women, children and adults. Until now, the closest approximation to masculine pornography has come from a few women who have managed to caricature the ultimate sadism of male pornography. They have responded to male misogyny by writing about the mutilation and destruction of male bodies. This literature, which depends for its effects on the mutilation of someone in the top-active-dominant-masculine position, does not serve as an erotic turn-on for anyone, female or male. But it certainly does lay bare the essential deception of male pornography, that making hate with an artful disguise is really making love.

Valerie Solanas decided to fight back against penis power by snatching the sun from the sky and burning up the phallocentric universe. She brought forth *SCUM Manifesto,* the platform of her one-woman Society for Cutting Up Men. In June 1968, after Maurice Giradias, a male publisher, convinced the destitute Solanas to sell him the rights to all her novels, theater pieces, and *SCUM* for five hundred dollars,

Solanas felt she had been sold short and judged that it was only fair game to kill a man as revenge for this injustice. The victim she selected was an artist and film director, the Pygmalion who had once directed her in a film, Andy Warhol. Warhol, who barely survived the five bullets she fired into his body, exhibited more sympathy with Solanas's plight than with traditional justice and magnanimously refused to press charges. Solanas was given a short prison sentence. Giradias, some years later, published *SCUM*.

In her *SCUM Manifesto*, Solanas proposes that the male was a biological accident. The male Y gene is an incomplete female X gene: "The male is an incomplete female, a walking abortion." Maleness is an organic deficiency. The only honest males are transvestites and drag queens, for the central desire of every male is to grow into his true self by becoming a woman. A male's genetic destiny is confirmed in his early and complete erotic dependence on his mother. Nature and nurture conspire to tie a male to femaleness for life. As Solanas summarizes the plight of the male, she gives a personal twist to some contemporary ideas on the developmental dilemmas faced by most little boys: "Every boy wants to imitate his mother, be her, fuse with her." "It never becomes completely clear to the male that he is not part of his mother, that he is he and she is she." To exist as a person, the male throughout history has overcompensated for his shameful feminine strivings with his sexist patriarchal philosophy that eventuates in war, submission-domination politics, money, prostitution, mental illness, high art, and culture.

There are two kinds of women, the atrophied ones—the female pimps, the daddy's girls, the big mamas—and SCUM women, who will devote their lives to the destruction of the male sex and paternal power. As a temporary measure, women will use sperm from sperm banks to reproduce among themselves and produce only females. After a while, when old age and death have been conquered, there will be no need at all for reproduction. Soon every living being will be an XX and the human species will have fulfilled its true destiny. Some men, those who have been clever enough to survive, will come to their senses. They will want to become female. They will conduct biological research and then "by means of operations on the brain and nervous system," they will be "transformed in psyche, as well as body, into women." The few remaining men, those who are too stupid or frightened to acknowledge their desire to be female, will be allowed to go voluntarily to a suicide center, where they "will be quietly, quickly, and painlessly gassed to death."

SCUM is a parody of what feminine pornography might be if it modeled itself on masculine pornography. The male genitalia were to Solanas, as the female genitalia were to Weininger, "the chief difficulty in the way of regarding men as theoretically beautiful." By doing away with males and male genitals, Solanas arrived at the heart of the Sadean aesthetic, which was to abolish all signs of differences between the sexes. In his culminating orgy, Sade performed his fifteen operations on fifteen fifteen-year-old girls, operations that effectively obliterated genital difference. With her wanton pen as scalpel, Solanas enacted the role of emasculating surgeon with a feminine glee. Solanas also caught the fairy tale netherworld of the pornography enterprise.

In her pose as the wicked witch, the self-assigned marshall of the multitude of scattered covens, Solanas proudly displayed her defiant and rebellious masculinity. However, Solanas was a female still, and with all the desperation of her masculine protest she, like most women who make a show of masculine bravado, was craving the love of a mother. In her heart of hearts, unknown even to herself, Solanas was the cleverest of good fairy godmothers. SCUM is an elaboration of the basic text of a fixated infantile primal scene, where all children are restored to the primordial mother. By eliminating the male genital organs, Solanas granted the infantile wish to obliterate the distinctions between the sexes. By doing away with paternity, she assuaged the mortifications of the differences between the child and parent generations. She granted to every mortified boy and girl the wish to deny the father's role in the mother's life. SCUM females can fuck the mother better than any incomplete female-daddy burdened with the deficiencies of virility. Males can fuse with mother, be mother, assume the mother's role in intercourse, even acquire through surgery the nerves, muscles, and genital organs of females, and all with impunity and without shame. The transformed males can join the SCUM revolution, participate as equals in the remaking of the order of the world where eventually there will no longer be a need to cut up men since the Y sex, the incomplete females, the genetic mistakes, will no longer exist. And even to the recalcitrant ones, Solanas does not withhold her magical powers. To men who choose to remain deficient XYs, she grants the penultimate snuffing, the passive surrender they crave but fear—the voluptuous petit mort of the gas chamber.

Solanas intuited that the dismemberment that the male witnesses from the position of the violating voyeur might very well be the self-dismemberment he unconsciously desires and longs for. The purveyors of pornography are businessmen and -women who are proficient in the basics of their simple trade—lechery and innocence, domination and submission, mutilation and torment. However, their stereotyped texts have more symbolic resonance than they imagine.

In the end, Valerie Solanas, whom nearly everyone dismissed as a mad girl, gave the most sensitive *interprétation du texte*. She revealed to the world the nasty secrets that the generous Ladies of Kensington in their gender-orderly households could not dare to know or even allow themselves to imagine. Like de Beauvoir, who saw beneath Sade's mask of virility and exposed his mission to destroy the object of desire, to obtain pleasure through a tyranny of avarice, "which chooses to destroy what it cannot assimilate," Solanas was attuned to the secret desires of the Collector who financed Anaïs Nin's house of literary prostitution. "Stick to sex," he had blurted in his little-boy bravado of virility. When Nin wanted to adorn her tales with flavors, whims, personal ties, enveloping caresses, the sandlewood smells of living flesh, she missed the crucial point of the Collector's mission. For what the Collector really craved, in the darkness of his soul, was the voluptuousness of humiliation, mutilation, death. The erotic, the sex, was merely the screen, the artful disguise.

Some men are more desperate than Sade or the Collector. They skip over the formalities of the scripts that would give an erotic semblance to their secret mission to obliterate all fleshly reminders of distinctions between the sexes. They inscribe directly on their own bodies what the ordinary, rigidly stereotyped pornographic texts keep discreetly veiled. Impatient with slow-moving, studiously plotted texts, the male who mutilates his body is enacting with his amateurish surgical paraphernalia, his knives and shards of glass and hooks and needles, the roles of Sadean surgeon and trembling patient. He makes no pretense of being a dominant male who secretly identifies with the degraded, submissive, obliterated female. He is sufficient unto himself; in one body, both dominant male and submissive female, both potent parent and humiliated child, both castrating father and castrated mother. He enacts his narrowly fixated primal scene fantasy directly on his body, obliterating any distinctions between penis and vagina, perhaps symbolically by removing a finger or a toe or an eye, perhaps directly by removing his testicles and penis.

Self-mutilation is a form of perversion in which the terrors and shameful and forbidden wishes of childhood are right out in the open, but it is even harder to decipher than an ordinary perverse script because the customary landmarks of plot, character, and scene are expressed in gestures that defy interpretation. Self-mutilation is the pornography of the mute. As we will see in the next chapter, self-mutilators have the words—some will even carve them out across the surface of their bodies—but they have lost the language of desire.

Every "normal" woman makes some attempt to carve or shape her body into the object of desire that will turn men on. These acts of self-beautification are in the interests of enhancing feminine graces and charms. They prove to the world and to women themselves that they are truly womanly women. These little cosmetic surgeries of everyday life are as much an essential ingredient of a stereotypically normal femininity as genital performance is an essential component of stereo-typically normal masculinity. In themselves they are not perversions. But like the urgent obsession with virility in a male perversion, when such aesthetic surgeries are preoccupations and are employed as a solution to gender conflict and are devised to allay anxiety and humiliation and act as disguises for a fundamental fear and hatred of the human flesh, we have a perversion. In the female versions of self-mutilation, the parents and children, bridegrooms and brides of the infantile primal scene are disguised as razors and sliced human flesh, tweezers and plucked hair, surgeons' knives and carved-away cartilage. The despair of having to be only one sex, the terror of the finitude of living only one life, aging, and dying, the infantile anxieties of annihilation, abandonment, separation, and castration that are usually held in abeyance by a perverse enactment are defiantly exposed in the perversions of self-mutilation. With self-mutilation, the aesthetic of erotic desire that traditionally masks the mask of death is only faintly discernible.

11

Mutilations

From an intricate package, she carefully unwraps a razor
blade. She always takes it everywhere. The blade smiles like a
bridegroom at a bride. She gingerly tests the edge; it is razor
sharp. Then she presses the blade into the back of her hand
several times, but not so deep as to injure tendons. It doesn't
hurt at all. The metal slices her hand like butter. For an
instant, a slit gapes in the previously intact tissue; then the
arduously tamed blood rushes out from behind the barrier.

The Piano Teacher

Charles Bovary enters Emma Rouault's life as a
healer of wounds. She enters his as a bleeder. He has come through the
night, the fourteen miles from Tostes to Les Bertaux, to attend to her
father's fractured leg. She assists him by sewing pads for the splint. She
pricks her fingers. As she raises them to her lips to suck the blood, she
captures the attention of Bovary, who had barely noticed her until
then. True to his medical calling, he studies her fingers and is pleased
by the gleaming, finely tapered, clean, ivory whiteness of her nails but
then is vaguely dismayed by her hand, which is too long, brownish,
lacking in softness, and dry at the knuckles. Bovary's anatomization of
Rouault's daughter goes on to include her eyes, the full lips that she

has the habit of biting, the curve of her head, her temple, her black hair that is divided into two sections by a fine part running down the middle of her head and fastened at the back by a tight bun, the neck, the tip of her ear, the rosy cheeks, and finally "the tortoiseshell monocle which she wore like a man, tucked between two buttons of her blouse."

As with every one of her illusions, Emma's marriage to Charles would only confirm her sense of herself as a creature with lofty aspirations but no wings to soar. True to his penchant for subverting what he seems to be celebrating, Flaubert glorifies Emma's attempts to soar above the mediocrities that surround her and then, one by one, undermines each of her romantic illusions. Emma's illusions, which at first make her empty life endurable, turn out to be as much a reflection of the fetishistic values of her social order as are the conventions she wishes to escape.

In the scenarios of self-mutilation that I am about to discuss, the perverse strategy is enlisted as a way of forestalling the expectable but emotionally painful adolescent process of mourning the lost illusions of childhood. Adolescence represents an inner emotional upheaval, a struggle between the eternal human wish to cling to the infantile past and the equally powerful wish to cut away from the past and get on with the future. An adolescent is not able to establish sexual intimacy with persons of her own generation unless she is first able to give up, gradually and slowly, the infantile aspects of her attachments to her parents. The purpose of adolescence is to retain what was valuable from the parent-child relationships and to say farewell to the infantile idealizations and dreams of perfection that stand in the way of a full realization of adult sexual and moral potentials. In mourning the illusions of childhood, an adolescent is recognizing the parents more as they actually are, giving up her infantile idealizations of them, and thereby arriving at more humane and flexible versions of femininity and masculinity. Thus, in achieving this difficult emotional separation from the parents, a child gains access to the sexual and procreative capacities of an adult. It is no easy task, even for an average adolescent, to reconcile the enormous physical changes of adolescence that reawaken in both sexes forbidden and shameful cross-gender wishes, fears of uncontrollable sexual excitement, and castration anxiety.

For the self-mutilator, who has already suffered a childhood of loss and deprivation and trauma, to accept that the childhood past is over and that there is no way of redeeming the failed hopes of this past would mean an unleashing of a violent hatred toward the depriving ones, which dashes all hope of a forgiving reunion with them. For such an adolescent, therefore, the emotionally painful process of mourning, with all its undercurrents of abandonment, separation, and castration, is unendurable. Because the self-mutilator did not feel secure within her body in childhood, to her the expectable adolescent anxieties coalesce into an insupportable mutilation anxiety. Her active and defiant gestures of self-mutilation are most directly a means of avoiding a passively suffered mutilation but also a method of forestalling final gender identity and denying that the illusions and hopes and dreams that made life endurable are lost forever—in this life at least.

All along the way, from Emma's accidental and delicate pricking of her fingers to her intentional and savage self-annihilation, the gradual erosion of her childhood illusions and dreams is expressed, if not by an actual wounding of *her* body, then by her participation in cycles of castration and restitution, with their underlying currents of abandonment and reunion, death and resurrection.

One evening, as she huddles in the coach that will carry her from Léon in Rouen back to Charles in Yonville, a blind beggar suddenly appears out of the darkness. Emma notices first the gaping bloody orbits that substitute for eyelids, then his skin that was peeling away in raw, red strips, then the liquid matter that oozes from his sores, the hardened green scabs, the black nostrils. She listens to his song about a girl who is longing for an embrace of love.* "Emma, overcome with exhaustion, shivered under her clothes and felt herself growing colder and colder down to her feet, with death in her soul." Emma has begun to detect Léon's mediocrity and the dreary domesticity of their once passionate love affair. The peeling away of the blind man's face signals the erosion of Emma's illusions and her increasing awareness that soon there will be no hope at all, no dream to sustain her or make life endurable. And only a few months later his song will be the last sounds she hears. Her long black hair, which in her moments of passion she had always loosened from its neat little bun, will be all undone, lying disheveled about her shoulders as she takes her parting breaths of life and cries out, "The Blind One!"

Earlier, when she begins to detect the muddy bottom that was belied by Rodolphe's majestic phallus, Emma turns again to Charles for her salvation. Emma's ambition to be the wife of a famous doctor inspires a monstrous mutilation. What could be more fitting than to have bungling Charles Bovary perform the awful deed? As for the sacrificial lamb, there should be someone who is akin to Emma, a person already in the demeaned, feminine position, a lowly servant with a body deformity that needs fixing. Who could be better than Hippolyte, the stableboy with a clubfoot? In keeping with *his* role as a doctor who is determined to label, categorize, and constrain every manifestation of abnormality, Homais is the Muse of the straightening contraption that will imprison Hippolyte's affront to normality. In keeping with *his* role of a man whose every longing is destined to mock him, Charles's attempt to repair a bodily defect results in a ghastly mutilation.

It is said that Flaubert's father, Dr. Achille-Cléophas Flaubert, the idealistic student of Bichat, had once sought unsuccessfully to cure a

---

* Vargas Llosa remarks that "a scribbled notation in Flaubert's manuscripts of *Madame Bovary* preserved in the Municipal Library of Rouen [indicates that] the picaresque melody that the Blind Man sings was taken from a book by Restif de la Bretonne" (p. 28). Restif de la Bretonne wrote extensively about fetishism and was himself a famous foot fetishist.

little girl of clubfoot by encasing her deformity in a contraption of metal and wood. Later, when he was an established and famous doctor, the surgery that his elder son Achille would perform on his thigh resulted in a gangrene that killed him. Charles Bovary begins his miraculous cure of Hippolyte by cutting the Achilles tendon and the anterior tibial muscle. He then encases Hippolyte's foot in an eight-pound contraption of metal and heavy wood designed by his own hands. Before the results are certain, Homais cannot restrain himself from publicizing the miracle taking place in Yonville. He composes a letter for the Rouen daily newspaper that concludes, "Is this not an occasion for celebration, that the blind will see, the deaf hear, the crippled walk?"

When the cast is removed, "the shape of the foot had disappeared into a swelling so enormous that the skin seemed about to burst open." A few days more in the straightening apparatus and matters had worsened. "A livid tumescence had spread over the entire leg and here and there were blisters oozing an inky liquid." A week later, the gangrene is creeping upward toward the knee. Finally there is no choice but to amputate at the thigh the leg that had become infected all the way to the groin. The surgeon Canivet, who has been summoned from Neufchâtel to perform the amputation, berates Homais for interfering in medical matters and mocks Bovary for his surgical folly. "Straighten clubfeet! How could anyone in his right mind think it possible to straighten clubfeet? That is like thinking you can make a hunchback straight."

Bovary's folly was an attempt at reparation, a wish to improve the looks of things, to remove an affront, to imprison an errant physicality. It was a cosmetic or aesthetic surgery, the type of surgery that many women of all ages willingly submit to with the aim of transforming their bodies into youthful objects of desire.

Every day pubescent girls and adult women across this nation, rich and poor alike, are carving away at their bodies for the sake of beauty: tweezings, depilations, starvation diets, hair cuttings, hair permings, hair straightenings, facial scrubs and acid abrasions, nail whittlings and cuticle trimmings, liposuctions, excisions of bony tissue, breast jobs and hip jobs and nose jobs. Are these commonplace acts that are consciously designed to repair and beautify the body unconscious self-mutilations, the equivalents of a body mutilation, a perversion? Whenever living flesh, the living body, or part of a body is deadened into a fetishistic object, we must suspect the perverse strategy at work.

It is never the behavior itself that determines whether an act is a perversion but the mental strategy that empowers the act and the unconscious fantasies that accompany it. For example, as I stressed in Chapter 8, the distinction between a genuine womanliness and a masquerade is never entirely clear. We are justified only in suspecting that a behavior *might* be perverse if it is designed to assuage anxiety and shame. If the behavior is also an act of vengeance against the depriving almighty ones of childhood and if it lends expression to forbidden or shameful cross-gender strivings, the perverse nature of the activity becomes more than a theoretical possibility. The atmosphere of risk, secrecy, and wrongdoing surrounding the behavior is also a clue to the perverse nature of an activity. In considering the possibility that some ordinary, everyday behaviors *might* be an expression of the perverse strategy, the difficulty as usual is with the off-putting term *perversion,* with its connotations of sin and moral transgression. However, if we remember that every human being is susceptible to the longings, anxieties, and mortifications that motivate the perverse strategy, the possibility that our everyday submissions to tweezer, facial scrubs, and the like are normalized variants of a perversion should not offend us but alert us to something important about our shared human plight. Contrary to what many doctors would like to believe and have us believe, there is no firm dividing line between the healthy and the sick or between so-called normal and abnormal behavior. Furthermore, a perversion, when it is successful, also preserves the social order, its institutions, the structures of family life, the mind itself from despair and fragmentation. For as horrifying as self-mutilation might be, the perverse strategy that empowers the behavior is aiming to prevent worse mayhem—homicide, black depression, utter madness. And though the mask of Eros that usually masks the grinning mask of Death is *barely* discernible in the most extreme acts of self-mutilation, there is still an erotic element, still a longing to realize one's illusions of perfection, still a wish to be reunited with some almighty one who gave love and then took it away.

Some women consciously set out to wound their bodies. These exceptional cases of deliberate self-inflicted mutilation give us a clue to what *might* be going on beneath the surface of our everyday acts of beautification, *when* and *if* those behaviors are aspects of a perverse strategy designed to keep unconscious the anxieties of abandonment, separation, and castration that might otherwise become conscious and unbearable.

A rare disorder found almost exclusively among females—adolescent girls particularly but also women of all ages—has been given the innocent-sounding diagnostic label *delicate self-cutting.* And since every adolescent girl is struggling with the same emotional dilemmas as the delicate self-cutter, among them separation from her parents, particularly her mother, trying to come to terms with the uncontrollable physical changes of puberty that are changing her irrevocably into a adult woman with sexual and procreative capacities that frighten her for reasons that elude her, having to suffer the loss of her childhood illusions and with them her dreams of perfection and self-perfectibility, she may at times and for a while force these awesome anxieties and mortifications to the background of her mind by tearing at the skin of her cuticles, rubbing the skin off the bottoms of her feet, plucking her eyebrows, splicing the split ends of her hair, pulling out chunks of her hair, even occasionally pricking her skin till it bleeds or making a delicate cut into her wrist. Though these actions give her a twinge of feeling that she is doing something not quite right, even sinful, she is able to lose herself in these bodily preoccupations and forget about the worries that would otherwise beset her. The little mutilations take up her mind and enable her to temporarily escape the frightening implications of being transformed physically and emotionally into a woman with the sexual and moral responsibilities of adulthood. The difference between the delicate self-cutter and the average girl, who will recover from the emotional turmoil of adolescence and be able to give up the bodily preoccupations that express the underlying nature of her worries but also effectively take her mind off them, is that the delicate self-cutter has suffered a childhood where these ordinary troubles of adolescence are experienced as threats to her very existence. The mind of the delicate self-cutter is too preoccupied with reliving and mastering the traumas of childhood to suffer the sexual and moral implications of growing up into adulthood.

The adjective *delicate* is meant to distinguish a typically female disturbance from an analogous rite of self-mutilation in males, which is called *coarse self-cutting*. The male self-mutilator suffers more extensively from the mutilation anxiety and forbidden cross-gender wishes that afflict the female delicate cutter, and as a rule he inflicts his body with more devastating damage. With the corresponding male disorder, many an adolescent boy will engage in self-mutilating activities, such as tying strings around his fingers and toes until they turn blue and almost fall off, tearing away at his cuticles until they bleed, plucking at his acne pimples until he creates open wounds and sores, tatooing or otherwise scarifying his arms and legs. And these mind-absorbing body preoccupations, as much as they are visible expressions of the boy's fears of mutilation, are also a means of taking his mind off some of the other expectable adolescent anxieties such as mourning the loss of his childhood illusions, separating from his parents, expiating guilt, and becoming a man with adult sexual and procreative capacities.

Although the male coarse cutter, like the female delicate cutter, is looking for relief from mutilation anxiety and the sexual and gender dilemmas that haunt his life, the violence of his attacks on his body can, and frequently do, eventuate in the very castration he is warding off and sometimes in death. Coarse cutting, where a knife or other mutilating instrument is used to penetrate through the skin surface down to tendons, veins, arteries, and bones, sometimes advances to severings or amputations of body parts, in which cases the diagnostic label is adjusted to *self-amputation*.

Any body part may be chosen for amputation. The least anxious of the self-amputators will limit their mutilations to symbolic equivalents of the male genital: hands, fingers, and toes are favored sites. Some finger and toe severers make a hobby of their self-mutilating activities and eventually join secret societies devoted to the practices and ideals of amputation. Here, in the safety of these therapeutic communities, fellow "hobbyists" can trade memories of their first experiments with self-amputation or recall the childhood origins of their current fetishistic lust for female amputees. Here they can share their collections of photographs of amputees and mutilations. They are able to share without shame the imaginary amputations that figured in their adolescent masturbation rituals: the fake peg legs that enabled them to hobble toward orgasm, the masturbatory excitements of cutting off arms and legs from the photographs of women. They enjoy particularly reminiscing about the unwitting doctors who gave their young patients their first lessons in the techniques of proper surgery. How exciting it had been to observe as the doctor applied his scalpel to the botched "small" halfhearted, incomplete, experimental self-amputations and carried them through to the "ultimate" professional amputation.

In the letters columns of various girlie magazines, fellow hobbyists can solicit sexual partners, exchange ideas, and share special preferences with others who have a "monopede mania." *Amputee Love,* an erotic comic book with a limited circulation and a highly select readership, is devoted to love among self-severers and amputees.

One coarse cutter, a Monsieur M, hired other men to mutilate his body. They were not professional surgeons. They followed the patient's instructions and were able to give him exactly what he wished. When near the end of his life Monsieur M was seen for a medical consultation with a psychiatrist, his right breast was virtually nonexistent; it had been burned with a hot iron and torn away. Strips of skin had been cut into his back to hold the hooks that would suspend his body so that he might hang in midair while being penetrated by a man. Molten lead had transformed his navel into a crater. His rectum had been enlarged into the shape of a vagina. Gramophone needles had been inserted into his testicles. The tip of his penis had been cut open with a razor to create yet another mock vagina.

Monsieur M had also instructed his mutilators to tatoo the entire surface of his body except for his face and hands. Tatooed on his buttocks were the obscene phrases that revealed a few of the forbidden cross-gender fantasies and shameful feminine wishes that motivated his self-mutilations:

I'm a dirty whore, I am fucked, long live masochism, I am a living shit, I have people shit and piss in my mouth and I swallow it with pleasure. I adore to receive blows over every inch of my body; hit me hard. I am a whore, fuck me. I am a prostitute. Help yourself to me like a she-animal. You'll really enjoy it. I'm the king of arse holes. My mouth and my arse are open and waiting to receive magnificent pricks.

The perverse strategy was not working as it should for Monsieur M. The unconscious wishes and the madness that are usually disguised in a perverse scenario were right out in the open. The crude symbolic handiwork achieved by Monsieur M's self-mutilations, other more desperately anxious men cannot articulate at all. The mute self-mutilators are loners; they never join amputee clubs or hire professional mutilators. They keep to their private delusional world. They have no patience with aesthetic niceties that substitute fingers and toes and other remote parts of the body for the genitals they wish to amputate. A delusional coarse cutter might retain some semblance of symbolization and gouge out his eyes. Very often, however, the disordered mind cannot achieve any compromise at all. The man will cut off, tear off, slash off his testicles, perhaps removing his penis as well. One man managed to keep his genitalia intact by going directly to a hormonal source of his sexual tensions. He cut out his adrenal gland.

Some transsexuals, men who believe they are females trapped in the bodies of males, grow impatient for the licensed sex-reassignment surgeries that will remove their genitals, replace them with mock female genitals, and thereby liberate the female within. They castrate themselves. Three decades ago, when the term *transsexual* first became headline news and sex-reassignment surgery became a fad, very few of the doctors who specialized in these surgical procedures thought to question whether they might be collaborating in a patient's unconscious wish to be castrated. They did not realize that only a small percent of the patients who applied for sex reassignment were genuine transsexuals. The doctors and the patients were blissfully unaware that they were participating in a Sadean operation, a doctor-patient perverse scenario.

The man who shares his amputation fantasies with fellow hobbyists, the man who tattoos the surface of his body with obscene words and phrases or with the serpents and swords that merely suggest his castration wishes or the valentines and cupids that hint at his unresolved and subsequently twisted desires for Mother give us a pretty good idea of the gender conflicts and anxieties that prompt these acts of self-mutilation or self-amputation. However, more usually the fantasy life of a coarse cutter is never revealed at all. He moves so swiftly from anxiety to self-mutilation that he experiences only the impulse to cut. Female self-mutilators are also prone to act rather than reflect on their emotional plights.

While any act of self-mutilation must be considered coarse and lacking in refinement, the delicacy of delicate self-cutting refers to the shallowness of the incisions and the control exercised in the act of self-mutilation. Unlike the careless, hasty, violent, deep gougings and organ removals inflicted on his body by the typical coarse cutter, the deliberately conceived light-handed incisions made by a delicate cutter barely penetrate the top layers of skin. The usual site of the cutting is the ventral surface of the wrist, but sometimes the arms, legs, torso, or face will be chosen. The cuts are carefully wrought, sometimes simple parallel lines but also intricate patterns; rectangles, circles, initials, even flowerlike shapes. After a while, as some of the young women grow more desperate, they advance to coarser mutilations: burning the surface of the skin with cigarettes and hot irons, scraping off the surface of the face with fragments of glass, gouging out chunks of flesh with knives. The delicate self-cutter is not entirely mute, but she has lost the connection between her actions and the language of desire.

Typically, the symptom of delicate self-cutting first appears some months immediately following the first menstruation. Thereafter, the cuttings or burnings or scrapings are a method of relieving the complex assortment of anxieties and tensions aroused premenstrually or during menstruation. Until it is brought to their attention, delicate cutters are unaware of any connection between the mortifications they inflict on their bodies and the mortifications they experience in reaction to their menstrual cycles. Few of them can recollect a traumatic reaction to their first menstruations, but most recalled distinctly that they were unprepared and that neither their mother nor anyone else had given them any advice or explanation about what it meant for a girl to become a woman.

Although the emotional connection between their first menstruation and their first self-cutting has been lost to them, these troubled adolescent girls and adult women can remember that they initiated their "experimentations" somewhere between the ages of twelve and fourteen. As they are relating to their therapist the details of these early, still halfhearted experiments, some delicate cutters will suddenly recollect a frightening and painful accident, occurring at age twelve or so, that resulted in broken bones, torn ligaments, and profuse bleeding. Thus, they allow into consciousness a memory that reveals yet simultaneously screens out the shock of menstrual bleeding.

Even before they menstruated, the first sightings of elevated nipples, breast buds, and the downy, not yet curly and coarse pubic hairs will usually have set off the alarms a few years earlier. And it is then that girls who had in the past been compliant good girls begin to smoke cigarettes, hang out with the ruffians, stay out all night, take dope, and once in a while think about cutting themselves or committing suicide.

For, in addition to these first external signs of pubescence, unwelcome changes will have taken place inside the body. These invisible, more cryptic changes, because they are so mysterious and have such a powerful impact on the body, are even more frightening than the elevated nipples and downy pubic hair. These events going on inside the body exacerbate an emotional disorganization that up till then these girls have managed to control. The shock of the menstrual flow is merely the culminating indignity, the final insult to the container called the body.

The adrenal and ovarian estrogens that brought out the initial signs of puberty have been silently at work effecting changes over the entire outer surface and also the inner surfaces and organs of the body. In combination with the adrenal androgens, these female hormones encourage the growth spurt that will now reshape a girl's body into a woman's body. There will be a rapid fat accumulation on the hips and thighs, a dramatic increase in the size of the wrist, the pelvis, the heart, the abdominal viscera, the thyroid, the spleen, and especially the long bones of the legs, arms, and trunk. The expansiveness of the growth spurt is alarming to these girls, who are already afraid that they will be unable to contain excitement or relieve tension or find comfort.

Soon the vagina increases in breadth and length. Fatty tissue develops in the pudendum area, thickening the outer, larger lips of the labia and causing them to grow over the smaller, inner lips, which will begin to protrude slightly. The clitoris doubles in length and thickness and, like the nipples, acquires the capacity of erectility. A mucoid substance from Bartholin's glands now lubricates the pudenda during masturbation, petting, and coitus. The uterus, which is tucked into the pelvic cavity, grows almost threefold from its childhood size. Estrogen stimulation causes the pelvic cavity to tip forward and its neck to become relatively shorter. As the uterus accommodates to the changing shape of the pelvis, the contours of the uterus change from cylindrical to pear-shaped. The uterine tubes grow longer and more opened. The thickness of the endometrium, the lining of the uterus, increases greatly. As pubescence proceeds, the cells of the endometrium become more differentiated. The time of the first shedding of the endometrium, or menarche, occurs at around thirteen years in the average American.

For the average girl, menstruation acts as an organizing experience that will consolidate her changing psychological feminine identity in harmony with the gradual physical feminization of her body. Until menarche, the more focused excitability of the clitoris, urethra, labia, and introitus have favored the recognition of these bodily zones as sources of sexual excitation and discharge. As I discussed in Chapter 3, we have very good reason to believe that infant girls are intuitively aware of their inner genital world but for psychological reasons soon learn to suppress or deny this awareness in favor of the more controllable and visible genitals. Until she menstruates, it is extremely difficult, if not impossible, for a girl to incorporate the vagina, uterus, and other inner genital structures into the schema of her body—no matter how brightly she recites the litanies of sex ed. Menstruation, on the other hand, calls attention to the inner genitals and in ways that make it extremely difficult to ignore or deny them. Therefore, menstruation represents a disruption of the childhood state of genital organization. The initial effect is shock and mental and physical disorientation, even for the well-prepared, less anxious, and conflicted girl. But the average girl recovers.

In hunter-gatherer societies, where it is a matter of survival to remain in close touch with the mysterious and uncontrollable forces of nature, there is the pretense and illusion that social rituals can control an otherwise capricious nature. The growing up of a child into womanhood or manhood is not left to chance. The adolescent's body is treated like a piece of wood whose surfaces can be trimmed, broken through, and written on and whose irregular projections can be carved away into whatever the society designates as womanly or manly.

In some hunter-gatherer societies females do not have their own puberty rites. The girl makes the transition into womanhood by playing an important role in her brother's initiation into manhood. For example, the culminating initiation rite of the Dakota Indian male was the sun dance. Erik Erikson describes how "young men would engage in the highest form of self-torture by putting through the muscles of their chest and back skewers which were attached to the sun pole by long thongs. Gazing directly into the sun and slowly dancing backwards the men could tear themselves loose by ripping the flesh of their chests open." On the other hand, the Dakota girl has been educated since early childhood to serve the hunter and to become a mother whose breasts will be freely available to all the tiny potential hunters and warriors of her village, except when one might try to bite her breasts, in which case she must thump the little warrior soundly on his head and let him rage with frustration until his next feeding. While the boy will be learning to treat his mother and her milky breasts with the utmost respect and to direct his devouring rage against animals, enemies, and loose sexual women, the girl will be trained to sleep with her thighs tied together to prevent rape. And if at puberty she can verify her chastity, she will be allowed to participate in the triumph of her brother's masochistic surrender to the sun god by bathing his wounds.

In other societies, a girl is given other messages about what it will mean to be a woman. At menarche, nettles and grass may be inserted into the vagina to "cause" the bleeding. Or the girl might be instructed to enlarge her labia by pulling and stroking or placing vegetable irritants, herbs, or leaves into her vagina. The lips of her vulva may be enlarged by an older woman who stretches them and lightly punctures the vaginal tissue in several places.

Almost all ritual initiations into womanhood and manhood entail mutilations that signify simultaneously the differences between the sexes and the imminent separation from the world of childhood: pulling out a tooth, cutting off the little finger above the last joint, cutting off the earlobe or perforating the earlobe or nasal septum, scarifying the face, chest, back, legs, and arms, excising the clitoris, perforating the hymen, subincising the penis, cutting off the foreskin. Along with these more or less permanent mutilations are certain temporary body transformations that carry the same symbolic messages: painting the body with menstrual blood or semen, paring the nails, pulling out the scalp hair, or cutting off a few locks.

In modern societies, the few adolescent rituals that remain are showpieces of a conformity that neither the adolescent nor her parents take very seriously. We do not pretend that we can control the biological changes of adolescence. Instead, some of our elders maintain the equally unfortunate illusion that the process of menarche, which extends over several years, will somehow or other gradually mold the girl into womanhood, enable her to separate from her parents, bring her errant masculine strivings under control, ensure that she will eventually submit to some socially normalized version of femininity. However, menarche, much as it organizes a girl's body image and gender identity, also causes great emotional turmoil. A girl during this phase of her life needs all the help she can get, especially a girl who has not been able to make any sense at all of the excitements and tensions that emanate from inside her body. The puberty rites of hunter-gatherer societies, misguided, frightening, and painful as they may be, at least focus some attention on the girl and enable her to feel secure in being a valued member of a social order that will always protect and guide her. And as capricious as her natural world may sometimes be, the girl is confident that the tribal lore is an expression of a larger cosmic order that nurtures and holds.

"Holding" is everything that a nurturing environment gives to an infant that sustains her and produces a sense of body wholeness and integration. When the environment of the baby fits itself to the baby's inborn energies, gestures, and movements, the environment holds the baby. For a baby there is no environment without a mother who interprets it. In the first weeks of life a baby is fleetingly aware of eyes that gaze into hers, a nipple in the mouth, a caress on the surface of her body. Each of these mothering gestures holds the baby. The infant's searching mouth meets the giving nipple, her tiny body fits into the mother's, which smells and feels like her own body, the top of her head comes to rest against a boundary. A baby and a mother educate each other with mutual cuing. The baby has a repertoire of grunts, sighs, coos, finger grasps, head turnings, cries, and fretting sounds that give the mother some idea of how she should hold the baby. The mother has a psychological past that has readied her to understand what the baby is trying to tell her. She moves her body in a way that makes the baby feel understood. If she doesn't get it quite right, the baby will shift her posture until her mother gets the point. The baby begins to experience a sense of power over her little universe.

With each good-enough interpretation from the mother, the baby takes into her own self a caregiving presence of wholeness and completion. The baby begins to associate safety and wholeness with the presence of her environment mother, who gradually becomes an internal caregiving presence. By three months the infant who feels that she is being held is less caught up in cycles of inner tension and relief. Even when uncomfortable or too much excited by her appetites and desires, the baby is able to anticipate the mother's smell, her touch, her look, her comforting presence. Her body fills up with pleasurable anticipation. She can wait. She confidently expects that relief will come. The arousals and excitements that come from inside the body are no longer such frightening events. What was once diffuse and ambiguous is focused by an anticipation of relief.

A daughter who had a mother who responded in a coherent, empathic way when she was an infant suffering from frustration, feeling irritable from the bodily tensions of hunger or teething or intestinal distress, or feeling alone and helpless about the unpredictable comings and goings of her parents is more able to proceed through the disorganizing physical and emotional experiences of adolescence with a conviction that disorganization is a temporary business, that there are coherent, manageable ways of expressing emotions and reliable modes of discharging inner tensions. Despite her feelings of disorganization, she is protected by a sense that she will not fragment and fall to pieces. She feels held and held together. Someone will understand. Relief will come.

On the other hand, nearly every one of the young women who is hospitalized or enters therapy with a history of self-cutting has suffered a childhood characterized by glaring deficiencies in the experience of being mothered and cared for.* The typical mother of the typical self-cutter was distant, unresponsive, self-preoccupied, and, as a result of her own intensely conflicted feelings about being a female, much less a mother; she was unable to involve herself in an emotional give-and-take with an infant. The mother was singularly unempathic to the degree of actually distorting and disconfirming whatever her baby did try to communicate. This mismatching between infant communication and maternal gesture was often concretely demonstrated by the ways in which the mother actually held her infant daughter. The skin contact and other tactile-kinesthetic experiences that bring the inner and outer surfaces of a baby's body to life were either minimally life-sustaining or penetrating and overstimulating. How does a child learn that her skin is an alive part if no one ever caresses it or rubs it or kisses it into

---

* The reader should understand that I am speaking of *typical* cases of delicate self-cutting and the *typical* mother-infant interactions that preceded the symptom. Always in alluding to typical cases, a writer aims for clarity and thus unavoidably excludes the many exceptions to the rule. Later in this chapter when I talk about trichotillomania, another self-mutilating symptom, the same caution applies. For I have also seen and heard of cases of self-mutilation where the parents were immensely supportive of their daughters both during infancy and during adolescence. In these atypical cases of self-mutilation, the adolescent and adult disorder was preceded by a history of painful childhood illnesses or painful surgical interventions that were unavoidable. The girl still may interpret the pain she experienced in childhood as the mother's fault for not protecting her, but the mother herself and the father had done everything possible to protect and comfort their child. Also, in the present, these mothers and fathers were much better able to communicate with their daughters than the parents of the more typical cases of delicate self-cutting or trichotillomania.

aliveness? One mother bragged about how she was able to breast-feed her daughter without ever having to touch her. Another responded to her eight-month-old daughter's breath holding by weaning her to the cup and instituting a toilet training that was enforced by frequent enemas. A failure on the part of a mother to sense a baby's needs creates in the infant a need to react prematurely and inappropriately in a desperate effort to provide for herself the missing mothering presence. Such gross interferences with an infant's gradual integration of an internal mothering presence will transform an ordinary experience of hunger or stomach distress or teething or longing to be held into overwhelming bodily experiences of "going to pieces," "falling forever." The confident expectation of tension relief, which slowly and reliably develops in the average child, fails to develop. By the time she learns to use words to communicate, a child who has not developed a sense of confident expectation feels hopeless about communicating her emotional needs or desires. As her mother did not respond appropriately to her physical gestures in infancy, so her mother continues to disconfirm rather than confirm her attempts at verbal communication during childhood. This same basic reluctance and sense of helplessness about using verbal means to communicate distress or longing, sadness, excitement, or joy encourages a reliance on motor gestures and motor action rather than on thoughts, fantasies, or words to relieve and express tensions. Action brings comfort. Waiting long enough to think or speak brings only more tension and more disorganization.

When the little girl would turn to her father for what she did not get from the mother, his nonempathic responses would exacerbate an already nightmarish situation. Usually he was an absentee father, or a cold and distant father, or an ineffectual father, or a violent, uncontrolled father who brutalized, sometimes raped, both mother and daughter—in some cases, all of the above. Later, because the self-mutilating girl has defensively idealized the father and masculinity, the mother takes the blame for everything. In a child's mind, Mother is the rightful caregiver, the one who is supposed to provide safety and protection. Moreover, daughters, especially, tend to identify with a mother's attitudes about caregiving, even when a kindly nanny or governess was the actual caregiver and the mother never went near the nursery except from six to eight in the evenings and on Sunday afternoons. Having a good nanny might help a lot to modify the effects of a mother's uncaring attitudes, but a child who senses that her mother doesn't care will have a hard time being able to treat her body with any sense of self-protection. Since the typical self-cutting girl does not anticipate care or help from anyone, she does not seek therapy until either she or her parents have been made frantic by her escalating and increasingly coarse self-mutilating behavior. Her cry for help must become a shriek before anyone pays attention.

From the self-cutting girls who gradually learned to trust that they might safely communicate their feelings to their therapists, we learn something about why a self-mutilation has the power to provide relief from menstrual tensions and the inner genital arousals that accompany the changes of puberty: "I felt the badness in me go out" or "It's like vomiting—you feel sick and spit out the badness." For one girl, the trickling of the warm blood, the sight of it oozing through "the gap in the skin," was like a calming voice saying, "It's all over now, honey. Don't worry, dear, everything is going to be all right." Another girl likened the blood that oozed gently from the self-made zipper to a voluptuous bath, a sensation of delicious warmth, "which as it spread over the hills and valleys of my body, moulded its contour and sculpted its form."

The self-mutilator treats her skin with a conscious indifference, much as some surgeons have been trained to regard the human body— as though it were dead. However, unconsciously, she is recapturing and also remedying the unsatisfied longings of infancy. As a deadened piece of flesh is brought to life by the cutting edge of the razor and the sight of blood, the girl is also expressing the haunting complexity of her confused identifications with her mother. She is relieved when the "mother-blood" warmly flows over her. The deadened mother and deadened daughter are resurrected and reunited in the act of self-mutilation. As the bad, dirty blood flows out, the daughter rids herself of her internal "bad" mother. At the same time she becomes a bleeder in an identification with the denigrated, castrated, bleeding mother. Moreover, the anticipated passive castration of menstruation is transformed into a controlled active one.

The selection of the skin surface as the site of mutilation is partly a compensation for the deprivation of skin contact during infancy. But more than that, the delicate cutter thinks of her skin as a container for the dangerous body substances and organs and all the insupportable arousals emanating from inside her body. Whereas the orifices of the body—mouth, nose, eyes, ears, anus, vaginal hole—are vulnerable to attackers from inside and outside, the skin can hold in, leak out, or fend off the dreaded attacking arousals in a controlled and manageable way. In the place of a cannibalization of the entire inside and outside of the body, there is a localized, focused, *delicate* mutilation.

As they approach womanhood, these girls are unable to anticipate any relief from menstrual tensions or the sexual excitements induced by the bodily changes of puberty. During adolescence they are possessed by a desperate need to define and protect the boundaries of their bodies. The menstrual blood is experienced as an ugly, demonic substance that could leak out of the body to cover the world if it were not contained and controlled. Similarly, for the self-cutter, emotions like sadness, anger, joy, and love are thought of as demonic substances that are meant to be controlled and then expelled or expressed through the body as though they were tears, vomit, nasal mucus, urine, feces, or menstrual blood. "The whole problem was feeling empty and alone." "I felt mad and couldn't take it anymore." "I was frustrated—like when I couldn't do anything about anything." "Everything was getting all fucked up, people were really fucking me up." "I felt shitty." "I felt so tense, I had to do something." Without a sharpening of the boundaries of the body, everything might leak out—the tears, the feces, the menstrual blood, the rage. Because she did not learn how to express her emotions except in the infantile terms of a devouring mutilation or a leaking out of bodily substances, the delicate self-cutter continues to associate any kind of inner arousal with a devouring or leaking-out experience. Moreover, she confuses one kind of inner arousal with another and therefore confuses rage with sexual arousal and sexual arousal with rage.

The premenstrual edema, which is mildly discomforting and slightly disorienting to most adolescent girls, produces in the self-cutter overwhelming sensations of bursting and dizziness, an experience of the body being invaded by alien forces, attackers that must be locked up, a nagging insupportable erotic excitement. For all these reasons the delicate cutter is especially prone to thinking of her genitals as vulnerable to attack and mutilation. She also has a powerful fear of genital penetration, which to her is the equivalent of a total body annihilation. As an infant she did not feel held together and protected from the impingements of the outer world. Now as menstruation is forcing an awareness of her inner genital organs, she feels desperate, frantic that relief will never come, that her body will fragment into nothingness.

The delicate cutter is convinced that only she herself and the inanimate objects she invests with the power to bring comfort and relief can be trusted. Long after childhood, most of these young women continue to cling to stuffed animals and furry bathrobes, even pieces of velvet or satin. That they had preserved these items of comfort means that these girls were not totally neglected or deprived of care, security, and self-esteem. They were held, but only at times and usually at the wrong time and the wrong place and always with a love that was given and then taken away without sense or meaning. Therefore, comfort and hurting and the conviction that she is a bad, dirty child deserving of punishment are confused forever in the girl's mind. Along with their fuzzy animals they also have a fierce attachment to the slicing razors, scratching safety pins, pinching clothespins, abrading shards of glass— the tender-hurting caregivers that have the power to comfort, soothe, and bring relief of bodily tension.

A great many delicate cutters, who were already suffering from deprivations in mothering and fathering, had also experienced during early childhood a variety of physical illnesses and injuries. Doubtless, many of these bodily afflictions were the body's direct response to unempathic caregiving while others were accidents that were the indirect outcome of parental negligence. The physical disturbances ranged from severe colic, eczema and other dermatitis, high fevers, breath holding, motor seizures, wounds that required stitches, injuries that required casts, and surgical interventions. In one study, 60 percent of the cutters had had surgery, hospitalization for severe illness, or lacerations requiring sutures before the age of five. One adolescent self-cutter, at six weeks of age, fell out of her carriage and was run over by a car; she sustained multiple fractures and internal injuries. Another, who at the age of three had spiked braces placed on her teeth to deter her from her persistent and frenzied thumb sucking, would at the age of fourteen supplement her self-cutting by biting off pieces, sometimes chunks, of the flesh and skin of her fingers. Whether they were purely organic or due to accidents or injuries or careless caregiving or outright failures of the ordinary parenting that is every child's birthright, these passively suffered torments will convince a child that she must take over her own mothering and never again passively endure any invasion of her body. During adolescence, she is desperate to find some way to actively relieve menstrual tension, to bring some organization to the disorganizing experience of becoming a woman. Delicate self-cutting is the action that brings quick and certain relief.

The first "experimental" cuttings are sparse and barely noticeable. Before long the girls are cutting more and more frequently, boldly and dramatically. The resulting scars are badges of defiance that some delicate cutters will later exhibit with pride. Others simply leave the scars exposed for all to see. However, the mutilation itself is a guilty, secretive, and lonely performance. The enactment is often precipitated by an unanswered phone call, the departure of a friend or lover or therapist, a caring face that turned away. These separations arouse all manner of terrifying feelings and emotions, which are unconscious and unexpressible—except by way of enactment. The anxiety about being abandoned by the person the girl depends on for survival is augmented by the terrors of bodily fragmentation.

"For reasons not known to the patient she felt very tense," one analyst reports; "following a period of tenseness she decided to be by herself; while alone, the tension mounted; she discovered that she had already cut herself." The delicate self-cutter suspends conscious awareness of her self and the world around her. The part of her mind that reasons and feels is asleep, allowing her to act unencumbered by the restraints of being a thinking person with flesh-and-blood body: "Like this isn't me. I'm just watching. I feel it ain't me doing it." The girl's observing self is detached from her experiencing self. She is depersonalized. But the part of her mind that acts is alert and in control. As some unbearable but unlocatable tension begins to overwhelm her, she numbs out or fogs away into an altered state of consciousness. In this regressed, semidepersonalized state of awareness, she methodically carves onto the surface of her skin the delicate incisions that will give some external focus and meaning to the mysterious arousals that flood, flutter, and pound against the inner walls of her body. With the sight of the flowing blood, the cutter is immensely relieved. She is better able now to think and feel and she is calmer because once again she has succeeded in repressing the fantasies and thoughts and emotions that have set the stage for her act of self-mutilation.

As much as they are attempts to hold anxiety in abeyance, the fragmentations of self that precede the small delicate cuttings are attempts to divert aggression away from the betraying loved ones who disappeared, turned away, went on vacation, didn't remember, gave love and then took it away, left an infant longing for an embrace of love.

One of the reasons a delicate cutter is unable to communicate her anxiety and rage and longing in words is that she has learned never to bother her parents with unpleasant thoughts or feelings. Until the first signs of puberty invaded their bodies, some of these girls were obedient, straight A students, quiet as clams, never troubling their parents with their worries. But shortly after her first menstruation, one such girl used a knife to scratch the letters LOVE on her thigh. The cuttings were neat, precise, and shallow, but quite deep enough to allow the blood to color LOVE a violent red. She told her therapist that she had actually had the impulse to carve right down to the bone. As she dramatized the gestures that described her original impulse, her usually sweet, innocent face was clouded over by "an almost palpable hatred." She confessed that she had really wanted to carve HATE into the bone of her thigh. She had restrained herself because HATE was not a very nice thing to feel or think, much less to put into words.

This delicate cutter was one of the nice good girls, a caricature of femininity, a flower child. Her body was twiggy—slender, delicate, childlike. Her manner was ingenuous, bemused, passive, and appealingly gentle. She would skip about the grounds of the hospital barefoot, every once in a while standing on tiptoe to hug a tree or gracefully crouching in the grass to smell the flowers. This conventional facade of charming innocence could abruptly fade into a sad mournfulness that was just as much a simulation of feeling as the feminine euphoria. Both facades were masking the empty space of feeling, the deadness inside, the total bewilderment about what she was allowed to feel or could feel. A casual observer would think this sweet, loving girl incapable of an aggressive action or nasty thought. She, like many other self-cutters, was also an anorectic and an occasional bingeing-vomiting bulimic. Before she entered the hospital she was a well-known neighborhood pothead, a secret user of the mind-altering drugs that would conquer her feelings of inner deadness. And on many a bright Sunday morning, as she was recovering from a night of alcoholic rampage, the neighbors were given a front-row view of her disheveled body sprawled across the length of her mother's soft, sweet-smelling petunia bed.

Other self-cutters are not such nice girls. They devise more palpably hateful ways of settling the score with their parents. These are the "punks" decked out with a masculine facade, tomboys with a vengeance. They masquerade in ripped-up, filthy jeans and smelly sweatshirts and hang out with the guys and ride revved-up motorbikes and join the pack at the neighborhood bars. The moment they saw those breast buds and pubic hairs, these girls were determined to prove that they were as different as possible from their stupid, depressed mothers. They were more manly and tough than their brothers and could beat up the biggest of them if they chose. "I was always told that I was aggressive and that my brother was afraid of me." Some would boast of being the father's favorite, the child who was put in charge of caring for the pathetic mother and the unloved siblings while the master of the household was away on one of his frequent business trips. "I was more a father to my brother and a husband to my mother than that big old Dad could ever be."

The unconscious purpose of these caricatures of femininity and masculinity is to forestall the challenges of growing up into a woman with a female, and now at puberty a feminized, body. They are also a terrified girl's method of denying how much she is still feeling like a helpless infant longing for a maternal embrace. As we saw earlier, she cannot trust that calming and holding embrace except in the act of a bleeding reunion with her good mother. Nor can she reconcile to her identifications with her "bad" mother except as a denigrated bleeder.

Unlike the average girl who over the course of growing up into womanhood is increasingly able to integrate her individualized, complex, and varied feminine and masculine identifications with the feminine and masculine aspects of both mother and father, the delicate cutter is arrested at an infantile either-or version of femininity and masculinity. Most self-cutters openly and defiantly assert their identification with males in a defensive devaluation of their femininity, which they equate with a degrading neediness. A few hide their forbidden and frightening masculine identifications under the cover of a caricature of femininity.

During therapy the fragility and superficiality of both gender identifications become evident. In the course of one hour, a delicate cutter
will suddenly become a passive, dependent, teary-eyed, helpless version
of her hated, denigrated mother and only moments later assert her
violent, macho independence in a caricature of her hated but idealized
father. Just as she will experience rapid fluctuations of affects and
moods, moving within moments from laughter to tears, from an excited flooding of feeling to a protective state of emptiness and deadness, from a height of elation to an abyss of depression, so the delicate
cutter will fluctuate between masculine and feminine gender stereotypes with the same lability. It is always dramatically evident that,
whether she is impersonating an infantile feminine ideal or a masculine
one, each delicate cutter is terrified by and violently opposed to the
gradual and irrevocable feminization of her childlike, gender-ambiguous body.

On one level, the dramatis personae in delicate self-cutting are a
child and a mother, and the primal scene entails a rectification of a
disturbed mother-infant relationship. Here the razor is experienced as a
trusted caregiver, the skin is the child who is waiting to be cared for
and given relief. In the bleeding that follows, a child has been reunited
with a good mother. On another level, as in most perverse scripts,
there is an unconscious primal scene entailing a bride and a bridegroom. Unlike most girls, who by adolescence have acquired a more
loving and tender interpretation of sexual intercourse, the delicate cutter still imagines that "doing it" entails a cutting up and mutilation of
the bride's body. Her self-mutilations are a furtive and guilty participation in a primal scene of primitive violence. The excluded child is
anyone who has hurt or humiliated her, anyone who gave her love and
then took it away. Her mother, her father, her therapist, the ward
nurse, the friend who hung up the phone must now stand by helplessly
as a captive witness to the violent things she does to her body.

Unconsciously, the razor that is her tender caregiver is also her
smiling bridegroom. In the half-conscious preparations for the self-

mutilating enactment, in the unwrapping of the razor, in the quiet, breathless moment just before the cutting edge penetrates her skin, the girl arrives at a state of suspenseful excitement akin to erotic arousal. The suspenseful eroticized excitement disguises any anxiety she might otherwise experience. Oh how sweetly brutal the razor-bridegroom is and how passively the vulnerable skin-bride opens herself to his mutilations. Afterward, when the blood flows out of the cuts, the girl is conscious of an extraordinary relief. She reassures herself that she will not be the *passive* victim of a violent penetration of the insides of her body.

The delicate cutter is not without a real sexual life. However, the sexuality she does allow are also mutilations of a sort. When as a young child she discovered the anatomical differences between the sexes, the fact of having a hole where boys have something else was taken as another sign of her lack, her damage, her defectiveness—the reasons why nobody could love her or care for her. Now as she arrives at womanhood she regards her menstruation as the confirmation that her sexual and procreative organs are damaged and vulnerable to further mutilation. The penis, on the other hand, is an instrument of violence, intactness, power. Soon after these girls begin their mutilation experimentations, they begin to seek out a man who will focus their terrifyingly diffuse inner genital sensations by raping them or otherwise brutally introducing them to sexual intercourse. Some of these girls have learned this lesson from a father or brother who, when they were approached for comfort, offered genital petting or sexual intercourse instead. But most delicate cutters come to this idea of seeking relief through a violent defloration all on their own. The idea is to achieve actively and in a controlled way something that would be terrifying if it were to be suffered passively. The relief experienced from their early experimentations in self-mutilation inspire these girls to hitchhike along highways or lonely roads to pick up truck drivers who will rape them. Others wander into seedy bars in search of a tough guy, a violent, sadistic man who will use his penis like a slicing razor. Some self-cutters have been raped four or five times by different men. Though these girls rarely, if ever, can allow the passive yielding to orgastic pleasure, these enactments of submitting to a violent penetration of their vaginas bring the same relief, calm, and relaxation as the self-inflicted body mortifications.

In a confusion of fantasies about the penis, which she alternately views as a vaginal mutilator or a powerful vaginal fixer or a solid fixture that can hold together the body and plug up its leaking-out feelings, the delicate cutter actively invites the brutal penetrations of her vagina that she fears. Though she seems as passive and expectant as her waiting and vulnerable wrist, she is actively controlling the penis and its owner much as she controls the razor or shard of glass that is her sweet comforter, her friendliest bridegroom.

If delicate cutters did not suffer so frequently from bouts of prolonged and diffuse bleeding, amenorrhea and drug-related menstrual disorders, they might become pregnant more often than they do. As it is, many delicate cutters are made pregnant by the boys and men who accept her invitations to be a macho penetrator. When the girls find out they are pregnant, they are as ambivalent about the little bit of life implanted in them as they are about their mothers and fathers or the very fact of having the sexual and procreative organs of a woman. The painful and frightening abortions they undergo, however, bring the same calm and relief as the body mutilations they inflict on themselves. For a while the girls feel less need of the erotic adventures that bring them the comfort of an actively controlled, violent sexual penetration.

In looking over the medical histories of delicate cutters, we discover that long after infancy and early childhood they continued to suffer from illnesses or injuries that required painful medical interventions. Starting with adolescence, "things just seemed to happen to my body." Beyond the "attacks" of appendicitis and the severe constipation that led to unnecessary medical interventions, sometimes surgery, and the numerous tennis, skiing, windsurfing, and motorcycle mishaps that led to broken limbs, most of these "things" were directly associated with gynecological problems: ovarian cysts, vaginal infections, and menstrual irregularities—excessive duration or amount of menstruation (hypermenorrhea), too frequent menstruation (polymenorrhea), nonmenstrual or intermenstrual bleeding (metrorrhagia), shedding of endometrial tissue to abnormal locations of the body (endometriosis). In the past, gynecologists tended to respond to these not altogether uncommon adolescent complaints in their customary ways. Depending on the diagnosis of the underlying causes, the medical interventions would vary from a continuous administration of oral contraceptive pills, ovarian function suppressors, ovulation inductions with gonadotropins, endometrial implants, and surgical interventions from limited excisions of the offending gonadal tissues to hysterectomies.

In other words, the medical profession would, unwittingly, collaborate with the delicate cutter's wish for an active genital mutilation. Fortunately, these days gynecologists will do everything possible to avoid radical medical interventions on the sexual and procreative organs of young women. Whenever feasible, the treatment of adolescent menstrual irregularities is limited to drugs that temporarily suppress or encourage menstrual flow. But even these relatively "conservative" medical recommendations are a compliance with the delicate cutter's need to actively control menstruation and sexual excitement.

In thinking about the medical histories of delicate self-cutters and the ways in which they sometimes induce doctors to collaborate with their unconscious wishes, I was reminded of another doctor-patient scenario called the Münchhausen syndrome, named in 1951 for the famous eighteenth-century impostor and teller of tall tales, Baron Karl Friedrich von Münchhausen. Münchhausens of both sexes are medical impostors, as skillful in producing symptoms that will get doctors to operate as any swindler, charlatan, magician, or guru is in convincing any "victim" who wants, for his or her own motives, to believe that something that is untrue is true. When an unnecessary surgical procedure takes place, two persons have participated in the enactment—a patient and a surgeon. As long ago as 1934, Karl Menninger, the late director of the Menninger Clinic, called attention to the doctor's motives in collaborating with what he then referred to as "polysurgical addictions."

Naturally, unconscious motives determine the surgeon's behavior in operating no less than the patient's behavior in submitting to the operation. A consideration of the unconscious motives of surgeons in general would lead us too far astray, although in passing we may point out the obvious conclusion that surgery is a very immediate sublimation of sadistic impulses. . . . But if surgery is truly a sublimation and not merely a neurotic disguise, objective factors alone, i.e., the realities of infection, deformity, haemorrhage, etc. will determine the decision to operate, so far as the surgeon is concerned. Unfortunately, even the most superficial inspection of surgical practice must dissuade us from this optimistic view . . . we realize that much surgery betrays evidences of being undisguised sadism.

Luckily, in modern hospitals surgeons are trained to be on the alert for the Münchhausen patient, the so-called hospital hobo who wanders from one hospital to another in search of a willing and consenting surgeon. These days, sophisticated diagnostic techniques enable doctors to detect the Münchhausen before an unnecessary surgery takes place. Even so, some medical impostors still escape detection, and there are always some doctors who are unconsciously ready to grant the unconscious wishes of the Münchhausen patient.

To the average pain-avoiding person, it may seem unbelievable that any human being would voluntarily undergo needless surgery or, furthermore, that she could all unconsciously induce her body to produce physical symptoms so convincing that a doctor would consent to cut open her body to repair or remove the offending body parts. Though Menninger referred to the Münchhausen syndrome as a polysurgical *addiction*, the sadomasochistic nature of the syndrome alone would suggest the perverse strategy at work. Münchhausens are driven by the repetition compulsion that lies at the heart of all perversions. Each time they produce a symptom that can convince a surgeon to perform a surgical "mutilation," they are unconsciously enacting a cycle of abandonment and reunion, castration and restitution, death and resurrection. Is the consenting surgeon merely an unwilling partner, an innocent victim who has been hoodwinked into submitting to his patient's requests? Or is the surgeon a Sade whose preoccupation with the aesthetics of surgery drives him to perform the mutilations his patients are petitioning for?

The unconscious motives of the Münchhausen patient are clearer. On the most obvious level, she or he is seeking out a surgery to forestall a punishment that is feared more than the surgery. The surgery represents the kind of bribery of the conscience that finds expression in many conversion symptoms and psychosomatic illnesses. The afflicted person fantasizes that she has committed a crime or wished to commit a crime. If the body part that is imagined as responsible for the crime is immobilized by paralysis or sufficiently punished by excruciating pain, the sufferer will have sufficiently atoned for her crime. Illnesses requiring surgical intervention have certain special advantages over other psychosomatic illnesses, advantages that bring them into the realm of perversion. In every instance, an other party has been seduced into assuming the responsibility for the mutilation. In this respect the cooperating surgeons are like the strict governesses, high priestesses, or spike-heeled flagellators of the SM parlor who are hired to perform symbolic castrations on the sexual masochist, who willingly pays the price to be saved from a worse fate. He avoids responsibility for his desire to be humiliated and castrated and bribes his conscience by being passively humiliated and castrated—but only symbolically and by the other who is now responsible—and all in the name of love.

Another predominant motive of the Münchhausen is more directly linked to love. The incisiveness, power, and strength of the doctor invokes in the patient the dependency of a child. As Menninger stated:

To those who crave the love of a father and will submit even to surgery in order to obtain it, we must add those whose acceptance of love from the father is conditioned by masochism such that they can only accept love from a father which is conveyed in the form of pain.

Six decades ago when Menninger wrote those words, analysts were still talking only about the love of a father. Now most analysts would call attention to the craving for mother love that is gratified in an unnecessary surgery. Certainly this desperate longing for mothering is a powerful motive for the delicate self-cutter, who can accept a maternal embrace only in the form of a body mutilation.

For some adolescent girls and adult women the prospect of childbirth is viewed as a mutilation of the body, very much reminiscent of the childbirth fantasies of childhood. One adolescent girl, who suffered from severe and painful constipation, applied for surgery insisting that there was something moving about in her bowels that had to be removed. When an alert internist recommended that psychological therapy would be more appropriate for her condition than surgery, she soon revealed to her therapist that she was convinced there was a baby inside that could be released only through the rectum or through a cutting of her abdomen.

Menninger tells of a woman who devised a long-term strategy that enabled her to be operated on thirteen times in thirteen years. First she fulfilled her childhood wish of marrying a doctor who would make slits in her tummy and give her many babies. She unconsciously chose for this husband-doctor a surgical specialist with wavering ethics that corresponded to his wavering attitudes toward the female body. He was one of those men who became a surgeon as a way of making reparations for his unconscious sadism. It was fairly easy to convince him to perform operations on his loved one. Shortly after their engagement, he operated on her appendix and charged his customary fee. Some months later, after the marriage was consummated, he removed her tonsils. Then in rapid succession came surgeries for the first of two ectopic pregnancies, a perineorrhaphy to correct the minor perineal tears she sustained during childbirth, the cutting open of a breast abscess, the removal of an infected toenail, and another perineal repair. Then since her husband confessed his ignorance of dentistry, she had three slightly impacted wisdom teeth removed by a dentist. After the pain from the unnecessary dental surgery subsided, she returned as quickly as possible to her surgeon-husband for another removal of her apparently recalcitrant tonsils, another ectopic pregnancy, an abortion, a curettage, and finally a cutting away of the fatty tissue around her abdomen, which she felt was too protuberant.

Sometimes these actively sought mutilations achieve merely a symbolic castration. The surgeons remove only limbs, tonsils, appendixes, toenails, teeth. There are times, however, when patients are able to convince surgeons to remove their testicles or ovaries, even when diagnostic tests demonstrate that these tissues are healthy. One may wonder how a doctor could justify to himself or his colleagues that he consented to operate on a patient's testicles or ovaries when it should have been obvious that a severe anxiety rather than a genuine physical illness was motivating the request. A patient's petition for surgery, no matter how bizarre, is often granted under the aegis of acceptable medical practice. In the not too distant past, the medical profession was recommending testicle removals, hysterectomies, or partial ovarian removals as therapy for manic depression, schizophrenia, neurotic anxiety, masturbation, exhibitionism, pedophilia, rape, homosexuality, transsexualism, and tuberculosis.

Cosmetic surgeries might seem to be another matter. After all, the petitioner for cosmetic surgery, 80 percent of the time a female, is seeking only an improvement in her appearance. This wholesome desire could hardly be considered in the category of an actively sought mutilation. Quite the contrary, her shortened nose, smaller breasts, larger breasts, high cheekbones, enlarged or shortened chin, liposuctioned thighs and abdomen will enhance her chances of attracting a suitor, getting married, and having babies. Most of the time, so far as we know, cosmetic surgery is undertaken by a woman or a man with the altogether understandable and reasonable motive of enhancing physical appearance. It is puritanical to ordain that any human being must endure the bodily imperfections that nature has given her. There is nothing holy or noble about having a de Bergerac nose or a hunchback or a clubfoot or heavy thighs or crooked teeth or crossed eyes. Some of these injuries to a person's self-esteem and sense of well-being cannot be altered by any amount of surgery. However, a great many can. And to insist fanatically on some moralistic submission to nature's laws could also represent a seduction and propitiation of the gods, just the sort of fantasy that is an aspect of the perverse strategy.

It is true, nevertheless, that cosmetic surgery is the method *some* women (and men) choose as a way of obtaining relief from mutilation anxiety. The surgery gives a focus to their diffuse fears of bodily damage and in the bargain repairs or removes the bodily imperfection that the woman unconsciously regards as the visible, outward sign of her defective and damaged genital organs. This unconscious anxiety about her sexual and procreative organs becomes particularly apparent when an adolescent girl or a woman with large breasts gets a doctor to cut them down to "normal" Twiggy size, for this aesthetic surgery also diminishes considerably the erotic sensitivity of the breast and the erectile capacities of the nipples, sometimes even removing the glands responsible for lactation.

In 1986, the American Society of Plastic and Reconstructive Surgeons reported that its members alone had performed nearly 600,000 aesthetic surgeries, about 150,000 more than in 1984. We will never know, of course, how many of these surgeries are unconsciously interpreted as mutilations. While women and men of all ages are volunteering in increasing numbers for cosmetic surgery, the most frequent applicants are adolescent girls and pre- and postmenopausal women. In both slices of generational time, the female body is undergoing hormonal upheavals and enormous metabolic changes that directly influence the growth of the sexual and procreative organs. Like the delicate self-cutter, many other young women interpret menstruation as a proof that their sexual and procreative organs are damaged. The premenstrual tensions and the flow of menstrual blood are signals of the feared mutilations still to come—genital penetration and childbirth. Menopause, on the other hand, is an announcement of the termination of the procreative life, the slow degeneration of the inner organs of the body, and eventual death. For some women, these finite inevitabilities, which all of us regard with trepidation, are interpreted as the ultimate mutilations and omens of the impending, absolute abandonment by the gods. In a propitiation to the gods, they submit to the surgeries that will temporarily conquer their fears of bodily degeneration and atrophy.

Trichotillomania, a mania for hair plucking, is another self-mutilating disorder that brings adolescent girls and women of all ages to the attention of the medical profession. Estimates of the number of Americans with trichotillomania range from two to eight million. Virtually all the patients are females. Until someone recognizes that they are afflicted with a psychological disturbance, these girls and women are treated for baldness with ultraviolet irradiation, vitamin injections, thyroid hormones, and topical and parenteral steroids. And even when doctors are willing to recognize the psychological nature of this disorder, they arrest any further inquiry into its psychological meaning by immediately categorizing it and labeling it as a "compulsive behavior," which simply tells us what the patient knows only too well—that when she has the urge to pluck out or tear out her hair, she cannot stop herself. This neat categorization of trichotillomania is like calling a perversion a paraphilia, which tells us only that the man is attracted to a deviant sexuality and cannot stop himself when the urge comes over him. (Of course, as we know, the attraction in a male perversion is not an attraction but a commission of a vaguely shameful, risky, and "sinful" activity to avoid anxiety and mortification.)

Though trichotillomania is less dramatic and horrifying than a delicate cutting into the skin, in its own way hair plucking can be equally mutilating of a body part. The typical site of attack is the scalp hair, but the mutilations may involve the eyebrows, eyelashes, facial hair, limb, breast, and abdominal hair or pubic hair. One reason why we are, at first, less horrified by these acts of body mutilation is that we think of hair as a body part that does not experience pain, forgetting that the skin surfaces from which the hairs are plucked are pain-sensitive. Moreover, in its psychological essence, hair plucking is as violent as skin mutilation and often succeeds in leaving temporary or permanent scars.

The young woman afflicted with trichotillomania does not tear out or rub away clumps of her hair in a frenzy. Her methods are inventive, one could say delicate. She is meticulous. Characteristically, individual hairs or small strands of hair will be pulled out one by one. While some young women are preoccupied with plucking out "superfluous" body hairs on the limbs, mustache, abdomen, and breast, most trichotillomaniacs select the scalp and eyebrow hair for their aesthetic surgeries. Individual hairs may be broken off at various lengths from the scalp, a disorder called trichokryptomania. The scalp may be rubbed until small strands of hair fall out. Strands of hair are tangled into a brush or comb and pulled out at the roots (epilated). A few of the girls who were especially involved in self-epilation reported how much pleasure they got from hearing the popping sound that indicated that the root sheath had come out. Some girls will suck or chew on the hairs that they pull out, pluck out, or rub out (trichophagy). Split ends are split up the length of a single hair as far as possible, and then another and another until every identifiable split end has been transformed into two hair strands. The time from the initial impulse to pluck, pull, split, or epilate to the termination of the enactment may be several minutes, an hour, or several hours. Once the plucking begins it is hard for the girl to stop. It is not unusual for a hair plucker, delicate and careful as she may intend to be, to end up with enormous patches of scalp baldness, requiring that she wear a wig.

Some hair pluckers recall with fury that their long hair was cut off by their mother or fashionably bobbed at a beauty parlor, despite tearful protests and at a time when having long flowing tresses or a bounteous ponytail had helped them to feel secure, intact, perfect, beautiful, and lovable. Almost all these young women are as obsessed with being overweight and losing weight as they are with plucking out their hair. They go on starvation diets, suffer from drastic fluctuations in weight, and some are bingeing-vomiting bulimics. Consciously the aim of all these various acts of body mutilation is to be a beautiful, desirable woman. Unconsciously, these young women are protesting the invasion of their bodies by the signs of approaching womanhood. Their heads are filled with frightening infantile fantasies about the mutilations that are entailed in sexual intercourse and childbirth. The prospect of separating emotionally or physically from their parents—especially the mother—would produce an overwhelming anxiety if a symptom could not take the place of the anxiety. What is needed is a symptom that gives expression to the unconscious fantasies that are producing the anxiety. Hair plucking takes the place of this terrible anxiety, for while she is plucking or tearing her hair the young woman is oblivious to all else. Furthermore, hair plucking, as we will see, is also a symbolic expression of separation, castration, and mourning.

The family situation for the typical trichotillomaniac is different from that of the typical delicate cutter, and the difference may account for the difference in the site of the mutilation enactment. The girl who is obsessed with hair plucking has not been neglected by her mother. She has, however, formed an especially conflictual attachment to a dominating and possessive mother. The father of the trichotillomaniac may not have been available to help the girl separate from the mother. Typically, he is somewhat stern and distant but nevertheless a more gentle and caring man than the father of the delicate cutter. But he has not made his presence sufficiently felt in the family structure. When he did try to be close to his daughter, the mother could not allow the girl and the father to express affection for each other. The father may be a successful or famous man. However, the mother, in a not-too-subtle competition with him, constantly denigrates his powers. The girl gets the impression from her mother that the father's powers are something to be envied and appropriated even though he is never allowed to employ them in the queen's domain.

It is clear that the mother cannot relinquish her emotional hold on this daughter and that she wishes her to be her personal possession forever. She infantilizes her and thwarts her moves toward autonomy. At the same time, she has given her daughter the unconscious message that she is to march forth into the world as the emissary of the mother's ambitions and desires. The girl is supposed to become a free and liberated woman so that she can express the mother's thwarted "masculine" ambitions and strivings. She is supposed to parent her mother by satisfying her unmet dependency needs and yet she is expected to remain attached to her mother in a childlike, subservient way. It is not too hard to appreciate how the tensions created by these maddening and irreconcilable demands would be quite enough to make anyone want to tear her hair out. Hair pulling becomes an ideal strategy for enacting these conflicts and yet keeping them concealed. As the entire family, but especially the frantic mother, become focused on the daughter's trichotillomania, they manage to disguise the unconscious content of the underlying scenario.

As the symptom progressed, mother became endlessly preoccupied with the ins and outs of the daughter's difficulty; she often behaved as if the hair-pulling was meant to shock and provoke her. Sometimes, the daughter's acting out indicated that such was the case. The pair indulged in incessant squabbling and power struggles over the ramifications of the symptom: whether the wig should be worn in the house, what to tell others about the hair loss, and the like. . . . . Father's role was similar to the part he took in other family affairs: he stood by helplessly while the women of the house battled it out.

To appreciate why I am considering trichotillomania a perversion equivalent in psychological meaning to the self-mutilations of delicate self-cutting, we would have to go beneath the surface of this manifest content, which could be interpreted as simply a dramatic and violent version of a typical adolescent struggle for individuation. While the separation conflicts are relatively close to the surface, the sexual and gender conflicts in trichotillomania are not as apparent.

Studies of the rituals associated with the cutting of hair confirm that hair has symbolic connotations of separation. In some hunter-gatherer societies, for example, it was customary to arrange a feast when the first-born son was weaned from the breast. At this celebratory weaning around the age of two, the boy's hair was given its first cutting and he was given his own name, events that were meant to signify his separate identity and his separation from the body of his mother. Later, as puberty approached, a lock of the boy's hair would be cut. When it grew back long enough to be braided, the boy was considered a man ready to assume his manly duties.

Throughout the ages, hair has been regarded as a symbol of strength, manhood, power, energy—virility. Alongside those associations to hair there is also the long-standing tradition of regarding hair as synonymous with the feminine virtues—docility, innocence, beauty. Hair, because it is closest to the soul or head, is regarded as the symbol of all that is noble, sacred, and clean. At the same time, because the pubic hairs are so close to the anus, hair is sometimes associated with all that is soiled, defiled, and dirty. In these various associations to hair there is in common a certain degree of ambivalence about whether hair represents human qualities that are admired or qualities that are denigrated.

Since both sexes have hair, including pubic hair, hair is an ideal body part onto which a person might displace conflicts about gender.

In the name of cleanliness but also in the belief that hair constitutes the source of a woman's sexual powers and her attractiveness to men, Orthodox Jewish women before they marry must clip the hair off their heads, and afterward and forevermore wear a wig. No doubt, the cutting of the Jewish bride's hair is also meant to subdue her independence and assertiveness—her masculine tendencies. The ceremonial clipping of a nun's hair is meant to ensure her spiritual marriage to God the Father and her obedience and submission to the rules of the church. That a woman's hair signified her potentially dangerous sexuality is clear enough in the image of Medusa, who is always represented in statuary and paintings with long, flowing serpents for hair. Since it was believed that witches owed their malevolent powers to their long strands of hair, their scalps were shaved before they were handed over to the torturers who were assigned to extract their confessions.

For our immediate purposes of appreciating the sexual and gender conflicts that are expressed in the perverse strategy of trichotillomania, we have only to recall that fur pieces and hair itself are among the favored fetishes of male perverts. The *coupeur des nattes,* for example, inflicts a symbolic castration on a woman, with the comforting idea that hair, unlike genitals, can be cut off but then grow back. By mutilating the part of her body that symbolizes her sexuality, the *coupeur de nattes* expresses his envy of the female. Then, in fear of her retaliation, he is eternally obliged to make reparations by fixing damaged women, either directly with his penis or by fashioning and cutting their hair, performing cosmetic surgeries.

Mr. R, the triumphant hair cutter we encountered in Chapter 5, could have a satisfactory orgasm only when he cut off or shaved off locks of his wife's hair. When his wife finally refused to submit to any further cutting of her hair, Mr. R shaved off all his own body hair. Until his hair grew in, he had difficulty attaining an ejaculation and was occasionally completely impotent. At that time he jokingly referred to himself as a Samson who was devoid of power without his hair. His analysis revealed his envy of the childbearing capacities of women and led him to the unsettling conclusion that his perversion represented his bisexual conflicts, his wishes to be both a castrated woman, a woman without hair, and a phallic male, a Samson with hair —a fusion within himself of female and male.

In trichotillomania the unconscious script that is expressed in acts of hair plucking also grants a wish to be both sexes. Analytic explorations of hair plucking reveal an uneasy compromise between the young woman's feminine and masculine wishes, strivings that are colored by a persistence into adolescence and adulthood of the infantile equations of castrated-female and phallic-male. In the role of the defiant, active hair plucker who captures all of her mother's interest and attention, the girl demonstrates that she is a powerful phallic male. By giving in passively to her compulsive urge and undergoing her aesthetic mutilation, she wards off any retaliatory maternal vengeance by demonstrating that she is really a powerless, castrated female who will never actually compete with her mother in the sexual and procreative arenas.

What we sometimes forget is that a girl's wishes to be defiant, strong, and dominating are in the service of winning her mother's love. Every once in a while, every little girl entertains the fantasy that if she were a powerful phallic being like her father she could satisfy her mother desires and be her lover forever. For a girl who cannot during adolescence give up her infantile attachment to her mother, that infantile fantasy retains an extraordinary power. The trichotillomaniac wants desperately to free herself from her bondage to her mother and yet is still wishing that somehow she can be powerful enough to fulfill and gratify her mother's longings and desires. Moreover, the girl equates her adolescent strivings for individuation with a ruthless destruction of the mother. In these circumstances it would be dangerous for both parties if the girl expressed her aggression directly. What better way, then, for a daughter to express her unconscious hostile aggression toward her possessive and dominating mother than to ruin her beauty by plucking out the part of the body that her mother seems to regard as the outward sign of a good, obedient daughter, a truly womanly woman. Since hair can serve as both a symbol of attachment to the mother and a detachment from her, hair plucking is an ideal symptom for expressing the individuation conflict of adolescence. As is the case in any perversion, the daughter's (or son's) conflicts over individuation from the mother are intimately bound up with her (or his) gender conflicts.

Each perversion highlights one or another facet of the perverse strategy. But as different as they are manifestly, there is latent in each perversion every facet of the perverse strategy, if only as whispered hints or background tonalities. In delicate self-cutting, some polysurgical addictions, and trichotillomania, the emotional dilemmas associated with the physical maturation of the sexual and procreative organs are particularly at issue. We can observe how these actively controlled mutilations hold at bay the anxieties and conflicts aroused by the psychological process of growing up out of childhood into adulthood.

A perversion is not a perversion until puberty, when the incest taboo demands a modification of the still tentative gender ideals and feminine and masculine identifications that were arrived at in childhood. During adolescence, the feminization and masculinization of the body in connection with genital maturity usually bring into question the simpler, more dichotomous gender ideals of childhood. However, in a perversion these challenges to infantile gender ideals are forestalled. As the passions of family life are transposed into larger cultural structures, an average adolescent gradually learns to establish sexual intimacy with partners who are exempt from the incest taboo. In every perversion, however, there is an unconscious primal scene enactment entailing an incestuous relationship with a parent of the same sex. By continuing to render issues of adult sexuality and gender in terms of infantile issues such as passive-active, clean-dirty, castrated-phallic, the perversions succeed in sidestepping the incest taboo. What we have is an adult who has achieved physical sexual maturity while retaining psychologically the dichotomous and caricatured gender ideals of childhood.

Thus the perverse strategy accentuates infantile gender ideals over the more advanced and less stereotyped, more mutable, and less rigidly fixed gender identifications embodied in more successful resolutions of adolescent process.

Nor should we forget that in the more expectable and ordinary modifications of the dichotomous gender ideals of childhood, the adolescent is also saying farewell to childhood and undergoing an unconscious mourning of her childhood illusions and her infantile idealizations of her parents. When during a person's childhood or adolescence a parent is neglectful, careless, and unpredictably available or does not allow any individuation from her, the process of adolescent mourning must be postponed, sometimes indefinitely. If a parent actually dies or otherwise disappears by virtue of a severe depression or divorce or abandonment, there is also likely to be a short-circuiting of the usual process of adolescent mourning. Unless a sensitive adult helps an "abandoned" child to understand the meaning of loss, it often happens that the child will never learn how to mourn, even when she becomes an adult. Instead of a gradual giving up of her childhood attachments and the illusions and hopes of perfection that are aspects of these attachments, she carries the dead or abandoning or depressed mother (or father) with her, always losing her again and then refinding her as she seeks a mothering embrace from an idealized, omnipotent mother in all her subsequent attachments.

In the New and Old Testaments there are frequent references to tearing the hair or letting it grow disheveled as a sign of grief. In ancient times, it was often not enough that the bereaved should weep copiously. The mourners would cut their faces and arms, rip their beards from their chins, and tear out their long tresses. To demonstrate the extent of their grief, some mourners would throw the bleeding locks they had ripped from their scalps onto the body of the corpse. In later, more civilized versions of these ancient memorial practices, the living ones would show their love for the dead by making keepsakes out of pieces of the departed one's hair.

Emma Rouault is sent to the convent at the age of thirteen. It is there that she learns of her mother's death. Hoping to comfort herself for this loss, Emma writes to her father requesting a memorial picture trimmed with locks of her mother's hair. After receiving her memorial picture, Emma writes to her father, this time asking that when she dies she be buried in her mother's tomb. With this hope of being one day reunited with her mother, Emma soon stops crying and is able to forget her sadness by immersing herself in adorations of the sweet Virgin. But she has not altogether forgotten her mother. Some weeks after Charles's first wife dies, Emma woos him by making a show of her continuing devotion to her dead mother. She takes him to the garden where on the first Friday of every month she picks flowers to put on her mother's grave. After she falls in love with Rodolphe, Emma thinks of her mother again. She insists that she and Rodolphe exchange locks of hair as a token of their eternal love. She tells him stories about her mother and asks questions about his, who had died twenty years before. Imitating a tender mother, Emma consoles Rodolphe for his loss as though he were a bereaved child. She gazes up at the moon and says, "I am sure our mothers are up there, together, shining down on our love."

When two years later, Rodolphe refuses to lend her the money that would save her from the clutches of L'heureux, Emma rushes from his château in a rage. Standing in the woods, she contemplates the cold, unresponsive château. Her rage gives way to stupor. Beneath her feet, the earth turns to water and its furrows envelop her like enormous black waves. She is now beset by a panic that obliterates every trace of Rodolphe's meanness of spirit and restores her idealization and all the hopeful illusions Rodolphe embodied. For to acknowledge the moral emptiness and fallibility of the person she has endowed with perfection would signify an end to the possibility of a reunion with a loving and forgiving fate. So even now as the truth is transparent to the naked eye, Emma is blind. Worse, she loses sight of her actual plight—a matter of money—and imagines that she suffers from want of Rodolphe's love. Emma feels as though her soul is draining out of her "like the mortally wounded, who in the agonies of death can feel life ebbing away through the bleeding wound." Unable to suffer the finality of the loss of her childhood illusions and dreams, Emma swallows arsenic and suffers instead an agonizing cannibalization of the insides of her body.

After Emma's death the mutilations of her body continue. At Charles's request Emma is to be buried in her wedding dress and veil and satin slippers. As Félicité lifts her head to place the wreath, Emma's head falls to the side and a stream of inky liquid oozes out of her mouth to stain her dress. The next day Charles makes another request. He asks for a lock of Emma's hair. Homais, ever ready to display his courage, volunteers to do the deed. He trembles so violently at the sight of the dead body that he knicks the scalp in several places and makes panicky wide cuts here and there, leaving white patches of scalp showing through the black hair. When Charles dies, little Berthe finds him leaning against the garden wall, his hands clutching a long lock of her mother's hair.

12

The Child as Salvation

When piety and maternal sentiment are wanting, and in their place are strong passions and intensely erotic tendencies, much muscular strength and a superior intelligence for the conception and execution of evil, it is clear that the innocuous semi-criminal present in the normal woman must be transformed into a born criminal more terrible than any man.

—*Lombroso and Ferrero,* The Female Offender

However much they might disagree about their prescriptions for a normal femininity, the experts on female desire have agreed that the perverse side of the female would show itself most clearly in the most intimate of all human destinies—motherhood. Merely by being born female, a woman is destined for some perversity or other—if she chooses motherhood and if she does not, if she rocks and hugs and kisses her child and if she does not. At the end of the nineteenth century, we were told that when a woman enjoys sex but declines motherhood, she is worse than a beast. We were warned of the terrible evils that might emerge from the Pandora's box if women did not contain their sexual fires and murderous potentials in the tender eroticisms of motherhood.

August Forel, the fin de siècle expert on the proper relations between men and women, saw the erotic tendencies of modern women as an omen of the regressive pull of the natural order:

> The modern tendency of women to become pleasure-seekers, and to take a dislike to maternity, leads to degeneration of society. This is a grave social evil, which rapidly changes the qualities and power of expansion of a race, and which must be cured in time or the race affected by it will be supplanted by others.

Now at the end of the twentieth century, word is out that even a mother is supposed to have an active and flourishing sexual life. Her "complete feminine development" now includes another duty: she must communicate to her child that her desire is not limited to responding with a sweet "Yes" to his longings or a frustrating "No" to his naughtinesses. From the beginning even as she nurses her baby and cleans his little bottom and tells him where and when he may eat or do his duty, she must indicate her desire for the phallus. It is the father's job to make his phallic function apparent to the child and the mother. He is not supposed to be merely another tender breast, for that sentimental version of the father effectively castrates him. Nor is the father merely the giver of babies. He is the giver of sexual pleasure. As a female British analyst recently proclaimed, "What is the function of the father? But, of course, to fuck the mother." In short, the latest prescription for preventing maternal depravity is that "a 'fucked woman' has a phallus and would not need to keep her child as one." When a father does not properly fuck the mother, she will turn to her children for the gratification of her erotic life. By making her child and his infantile desires the center of her own life, the mother will arrest the child's sexual and moral development. Moreover, if she focuses her erotic desires on her child, one day or another the mother will take vengeance for her crippled life by tormenting her child. Lest there be any remaining doubts about the relationship between a wife's sexual frustrations and her maternal perversities, contemporary French analysts have dispensed a chilling admonition:

> If the picture is at all aggravated by a woman's inability to satisfy the need dictated by sexuality, or if the object of satisfaction is not given her, then her child will fill in part the function of the love object. It is onto that real object that the impulse will be directed, in this case a perverse impulse on an oral or anal pattern, whose sadistic nuances will not be negligible, even though they do not irrupt publically [sic] in the stories that regularly appear in the back pages of the newspapers.

All of this emphasis on the phallic function of the father, though it is consciously intended to be a recognition of the active sexual life of the mother, does unconsciously manage to retain the old tyrannies in a new guise. Obviously, "the object of satisfaction" to be given to the mother is the penis. So the latest prescription for a normal femininity keeps the female in her place as the receiver of the phallic goods and strategically omits mention of her ambitions and strivings outside the network of family life. It is true that unless a child is given the sense of a difference between adult desire and infantile desire and a clear message from both parents that she or he is not the center of the mother's universe, the child will be deprived of any opportunity to resolve the feelings of envy, mortification, jealousy, and rage that are awakened by a recognition of the differences between the generations. She or he will be arrested at an infantile version of the primal scene with all its familiar infantile gender dichotomies—active-passive, clean-dirty, submissive-dominant, phallic-castrated. And it is also true that when a mother invests all her hopes and ambitions in her child she will cripple that child's sexual and moral life.

However, it does not follow that the solution to maternal perversity is that a wife accept the law of the phallus. In fact, there is nothing much new here. The structure of family life as we know it is based on the premise of the wife's duty to confirm her husband's virility and to communicate to her children the phallic function of the father. However, a mother does not abuse her children for want of a phallus, but out of a conviction that she is nothing at all without a powerful phallic-being in her life and out of the rage engendered by this idealization. When the conditions of family life are such that a woman has no other choice but to achieve her own personal salvation through her children or through her husband or her lover, that's when the violence begins. "I am nothing without you" is an echo from the infantile past, a perverse refrain that merely repeats and recycles the abuses and soul murders of childhood.

The close-knit family unit of mother, father, and children evolved in tandem with the discovery or, as some have preferred to call it, the invention of childhood. Childhood was invented in the eighteenth century in response to the dehumanizing trends of the industrial revolution. By the nineteenth century, when artists began to see themselves as alienated beings trapped in a dehumanizing social world, the child became the savior of mankind, the symbol of free imagination and natural goodness. Blake and Wordsworth and soon afterward Dickens and Twain became preoccupied with themes of childhood innocence. The image of the child was set in opposition to the prison house of civilization. By peering into the soul of the child, the artist hoped to refind some divine state of selfhood, that original True Self that had been smothered when man became a social being. Whatever was noble and pure and good about the human being could be found in the child.

In the decades when this idealized version of childhood was at its height, parents began to reason as artists. Parents were God's sculptors, the Pygmalions of the child's soul. They were supposed to prove their worth and perfection by molding a worthy and perfect child. The theory was that the parent's lost goodness could be refound in the goodness of the child. In her straightforward way of construing these mighty philosophical matters, whenever Emma Bovary despairs of finding her self in the arms of a man she has invested with magical phallic powers, she seeks her salvation through Berthe.

Little Berthe is a shadow-child. Before her mother dies, Berthe exists only on those rare occasions when Emma impulsively decides to breathe a bit of life into her. A month or two here, a few moments there, whenever Emma needs a refuge from her disappointing and frustrating life, she rouses her maternal instincts. Berthe will be her salvation.

The more she is tormented by her voluptuous meditations on Léon, the more vigorously Emma immerses herself in domesticity. She takes her household in hand. She goes to church. She supervises the maid, pointing out the girl's mistakes and patiently demonstrating the efficient, thrifty, and refined methods of homemaking. Now when Charles finishes work his slippers are warming near the fire; his nightcaps are folded and arranged in neat little piles; his shirts have all their buttons sewn on properly.

Emma makes sure to give to her baby some special motherly attentions at least once or twice each day. Her arms envelop Berthe in tenderness. She caresses her tiny body with admiring eyes. When company arrives, she has Berthe brought down from the nursery to be exhibited. She undresses her and shows off her dainty legs to the neighbors. The household rings with Emma's lyrical pronouncements on the joys of motherhood. Oh, how much Emma adores children! Berthe is "her consolation, her joy, her madness."

Every mother looks into her child's eyes for an image of her own goodness. But when she is expecting that her very soul will be saved by her child, we can be sure that violence is in the offing. The ambivalence of Emma's maternal zeal is soon made apparent:

Within she was full of envy, rage, and hatred. That dress with the proper pleats concealed a heart in mutiny . . . the fleshly appetites, the envy of wealth, the melancholy of yearning desire, coalesced into one suffering. Instead of turning her thoughts to other matters, she dwelled on her disadvantages and sought out occasions to keep her suffering alive. She was irritated by a badly served dish or a door left ajar, complained bitterly about the velvet she did not have, the happiness that had betrayed her, the illusions that had eluded her, her shabby, narrow house.

The contrast between Emma's inner turmoil and the calm fixity of the solid provincial furniture that surrounds her is unbearable. The chairs, the tables, the windows are the ugly sticks of wood that make up the bars of her prison. She would like to unsettle them, create chaos, destroy, murder. Her vengeful fury is unleashed.

Berthe is the target. When Berthe, who had been content with exploring the fringes of the window curtains, spies her mother huddled in her favorite armchair, she is suddenly possessed by a longing for her mother's touch, her look of love. She toddles over to her. She tugs at the edges of her apron. The distraught Emma, who wants only to be left undisturbed to luxuriate in her miseries, her erotic sufferings and frustrated sexual yearnings, shoves Berthe away, "Leave me alone!"

Berthe wants to obey. However, now that her infant heart has been awakened to the love of her sweet-faced mother, she cannot resist her urge to be close to the object of her desires. She leans her arms on her mother's lap, looking up into her face and wooing her with adoring looks. A bit of saliva drips out of Berthe's mouth onto the silk of Emma's apron.

Emma's fury intensifies. The expression of rage on her face is terrifying. Berthe bursts into tears. Her outpourings of love and anguish drive Emma wild. She screams out that Berthe must go away, leave her in peace. Berthe is frozen with fear. Emma pushes her aside with her elbow, accidentally throwing Berthe against a washstand. A brass hook cuts Berthe's cheek. The sight of her child's blood panics Emma. She is filled with anxiety and remorse about her wicked act.

That night when she sees Berthe sleeping peacefully, Emma realizes that once again she has wasted her virtue. She contemplates Berthe's face: "Two large tears had congealed at the corner of half-closed lids that exposed between the lashes two pale sunken pupils. The bandage had pulled the cheek to one side. 'Odd,' Emma thought, 'how ugly this child is.' "

Across the ocean, Bronson Alcott, the father of Louisa May and her elder sister, Anna, was looking to his children for his salvation. Alcott's experiments in childrearing were an exotic ambivalence of a liberalized Calvinist perfectionism and a visionary transcendental permissiveness. Holding little Anna's fingers over the flames to teach caution and encouraging her to run about stark-naked were both compatible with his evangelistic approach to raising children. Sometimes Alcott admitted to his confusion about the messages he was sending to his daughters. He was, however, completely confident about the goodness that entered his soul through his devotions to childhood innocence:

> Verily, had I not been called to associate with children . . . I should never have found the tranquil repose, the steady faith, the vivid hope, that now shed a glory and a dignity around the humble path of my life. Childhood hath *Saved* me. Once did I wander a little way from the Kingdom of Heaven, but childhood's sweet and holy voice hath recalled me, and now I am one with them in this same Kingdom, a child redeemed.

Around the time that Bronson Alcott in America was refinding his lost childhood innocence by becoming an educational reformer and Emma Bovary in France was purging her soul of adulterous passion through her devotions to motherhood, a Dr. Daniel Gottlob Moritz Schreber in Germany was writing a series of books on the healthy upbringing of children. His 1853 *The Harmful Body Positions and Habits*

of Children Including a Statement of Counteracting Measures was amplified five years later by *Education Towards Beauty by Natural and Bal-
anced Elevation of Normal Body Formation, of Life-Supporting Health, and
of Mental Ennoblement,* a volume containing diagrams of exercises and
corrective devices guaranteed to deter children from unnatural body
postures. He concluded his life's work with *The Family Friend as Educator and Conductor to Domestic Happiness, to Popular Health and to the
Refinement of Man, for the Fathers and Mothers of the German People.*

In the sense that all three hoped to find personal salvation through
parenthood, Emma Bovary, Bronson Alcott, and Daniel Schreber were
no different from countless other mothers and fathers. The strange
thing is that traditionally the mother-child relationship has been portrayed as a hotbed of potential perversity, whereas until very recently
the father-child relationship was seldom brought under such scrutiny.
For centuries, it had been tacitly allowed that a father might vent his
frustrations on his wife and children, beat and molest, even murder
them if they did not mirror his own lawfulness and power. Conceding
for a moment that the duties and little sensual exchanges of ordinary
mothering provide women with opportunity and excuse enough for
expressing their perverse inclinations, we would still have to question
the patriarchal values that have defined the shape of motherhood.
Though some would like to think otherwise, mothering is not an
instinctual, natural process. Mothering is learned and, unfortunately
more often than not, the lessons are conveyed in the spirit of some
primitive social gender stereotype of femininity, particularly that most
prevalent and abiding one—that a normal woman will find her true
self, her personal salvation, in motherhood.

The nineteenth-century bourgeois morality held that a good mother
should behave like Homais's wife. It fell to Madame Homais to make
sure that the Homais children mirrored to her husband the orderliness
of his own soul. The eldest, Napoléon, assists Homais in the laboratory,
Athalie embroiders caps for him, Irma cuts out neat paper circles for
covering jam pots, and little Franklin recites the multiplication table in

one breath. With the rare exception of artists like Flaubert, who depicted *la famille Homais* as the symbol of the decadence and fetishistic values of the modern world, no one would have considered the gender stereotypes that Madame Homais inflicted on her children as omens of perversity. Without hesitation most people then, and probably now as well, would have identified the adulterous Emma Bovary as the transgressor of family values and betrayer of her motherly duties—a pervert.

Emma's occasional impulsive and disastrous flings with salvation through motherhood were confined to Berthe. Though Emma dared to challenge the conventions of femininity that bound her, in the end she was trapped by them and had no power to control her own life, much less the world. The Alcott and Schreber nurseries, on the other hand, were experimental stations where childrearing methods could be tested out on the family children before they were applied to the children of the world. Those nurseries *were* hotbeds of perversion. Fortunately for the Alcott daughters, they had a mother who humored her husband in his peculiar notions of childhood but went about her daily mothering activities as she saw fit, with great inconsistency and, as her husband would complain, "the fondness and timidity of her heart." This was not true of the Schreber nursery, where the devoted mother of five children accepted the patriarchal rule of her godlike husband and lived to witness the soul murders of her two sons.

Alcott's fundamental philosophy was to respect the infant's whole nature and cooperate with it, "in due accordance and harmony with the laws of its constitution." Schreber's childrearing methods were based on the premise that the child's crude nature must be tamed, crushed if necessary. The parent must become the master of the child from the moment of birth and bring this otherwise wild and rebellious creature to a state of submissiveness before he reaches the fifth or sixth year of life. Manifestly, Bronson Alcott and Daniel Schreber were fathers of an entirely different breed. But they both had in mind nothing less than a design for perfecting mankind, and each saw himself as an apostle, if not a messiah, in the flesh.

Alcott proclaimed that "the parent, like the Divinity, should exert a special oversight over all the relations of the sphere in which he moves." A wise divinity, one who wished to bring out the natural goodness of the child, would spare the child's bottom. However, even as he sought to liberate children from the physical torments that the conscientious Calvinists of his day were addicted to, Alcott was imposing moral burdens on his daughters that, were it not for his wife's careless application of his principles of childrearing, might have proved more crushing to their spirits than an occasional spanking. Alcott's methods were designed specifically to give the parent a forceful and enduring access to a young child's soul. Alcott expected nothing less from his little girls than a moral perfection based on self-renunciation: "by and by you will love me well enough to give up your wants always."

One afternoon he extended this sermon on the relationship between love of others and renunciation by convincing the three-year-old Anna to surrender her personal rocking chair to her eighteen-month-old sister, Louisa. "Very good little girls give up their own wants to the wants of their little sisters whom they love."

The Alcott trademark was that his methods required no specialized equipment. He simply used the small events of domestic life as they came up or devised some manipulation of an everyday situation to bring home a spiritual lesson. Alcott was always vigilant, on the alert for a moral crisis to occur naturally. When the day went by without a natural crisis, his mind was ready with an invented one. Around the same time as the affair of the rocking chair, Alcott devised the trial of the apple.

One evening, Alcott placed an apple on the nursery table in full view of Anna and Louisa and then proceeded to engage them in a Socratic dialogue on the moral responsibilities of little girls. "Would you take an apple that belongs to someone else without asking?" he asked. Anna responded with a dutiful "No," and Louisa echoed her sister with a boisterous and enthusiastic "No."

However, Alcott was a patient father who appreciated the capricious nature of a child's conscience, and therefore the trial worked out much as he expected. He left the girls alone with the apple while he went to eat his dinner. When he returned, all that was left of the apple was its core. The moment her father approached the table, Anna recognized that she had been caught, but before she could admit her own naughtiness she eased her confession by describing in some detail Louisa's role as coconspirator. Her father did not grant his forgiveness all at once but first extracted from Anna the further confession that, in fact, she had not listened to her conscience, that she had acted while knowing that she was not doing the right thing. With a little more coaching from her father, Anna finally promised that next time she would mind her conscience, and Louisa promised the same.

Anna, who by then had gained considerable experience with her father's moral trials, was immediately cured of apple stealing. But Louisa could not resist. The next day another of her father's apples appeared. While her mother was in the room she said, "Me not take Father's apple. Naughty! Naughty!" When her mother left the room for a few minutes, Louisa devoured the entire apple, explaining later, "Me could not help it. Me must have it."

As transcendentalist divinity, Alcott preached that children's souls should be left open and susceptible to the physical and sensual wonders that surrounded them. His puritanical streak, with its emphasis on self-renunciation, was more in harmony with the marketplace mentality and workaday materialism that would soon be required to support the American economy and way of life. There would be less and less time for children to be little children as it became necessary for them to become little women and little men of the marketplace.

For all his desire to protect children from physical brutality and mental torment Alcott, with his own children, was a grand inquisitor, an ever-present vigilance and inescapable presence, "a wraparound father" who kept the inmates of his house of moral justice under constant surveillance. Fortunately for the children of the world, Alcott's child-observational diaries were sometimes far too abstract or on other days too lush with the minutiae of Anna's obediences and Louisa's little naughtinesses to be of interest or practical help to other parents.

Unfortunately, Dr. Schreber's books on childrearing achieved, if not a wide popularity, at least a general acceptance among German mothers and fathers. His instructions were practical, full of how-to hints and, because they were strict, rigidly organized, precisely scheduled, and left no room for deviation, imagination, or whimsy, parents could entrust themselves entirely to the methods he recommended. It was Schreber's absolute conviction that much moral and physical remediation could be accomplished in the course of an ordinary day. All that was required was that a parent be persistent and vigilant in following out Schreber's regimens and rules. Crying, whimpering, moodiness, and stubbornness could be eliminated once and for all during the first year of life. On the whole, everything a child did could be regulated and controlled. Schreber was not averse to manipulating daily events to enforce his moral philosophy. There was, for example, his trial of the pear.

The trial of the pear was meant to illustrate the art of renouncing, one of those numerous facets of child mental hygiene that is best accomplished during the first year of life. Dr. Schreber's training for renunciation was simple, straightforward, and effective. The nurse or nanny should hold the infant on her lap. She should be permitted—in fact encouraged—to eat whenever she was hungry—in full view of the child. But the child's hunger must never be gratified between his regular meals no matter how hard he might cry or plead for a bit of food or drink. Of course, Schreber did not understand that it is just this sort of teasing of a child that provokes sadistic and masochistic responses in the child. His theory was that submission to the parents' authority would be strengthened if the child became practiced in renunciation. Schreber was saying that *if there were no awakened desire there could be no experience of renunciation.* The exquisite morality underlying Schreber's little trial of the pear was twisted and misguided, but many of the parents who read his books were reassured by his high moral tone.

Imagine Schreber's dismay upon discovering that one of the nurses from his own household was unable to resist the pleas of a Schreber infant. When the child begged for a piece of pear that the nurse was eating, that kindly but weak-minded young lady broke off a tiny bit and gave it to him. This otherwise excellent nurse was fired immediately for her moral ineptitude. News of the pear incident spread to all the other nurses in Leipzig and Dr. Schreber had "no further trouble with any other such erring maids or nurses."

Dr. Schreber recognized that some parents might become over-enthusiastic in applying child disciplines. And although he was an antimasturbation zealot, he would have disapproved of mothers or fathers who physically *abused* a child, even if that child was sexually corrupt. But physical punishment, he insisted, was never unwarranted. It was an essential ingredient in the upbringing of a child no matter how obedient and submissive that child might be. Submission and renunciation must be fortified by guilt. The aim of punishment was not simply to stop bad behavior. It must be used in such a way as to bring about an acknowledgment of guilt. After he has been punished the child must ask for forgiveness. And only the punisher has the power to forgive a punished child. The child must shake the hand that has whipped him and ask for forgiveness.

Dr. Schreber started out his career as a medical Pygmalion who wanted to repair the bodies of crippled children. He devoted himself to designing devices that would strengthen and straighten their muscles and bones. But he soon realized that his mechanical devices might benefit the average child, who through habits of sloth and lackadaisical posture might inadvertently damage their bodies. Crucial to Dr. Schreber's theories of normal body formation was his doctrine that the bodies of children of all ages must be kept straight at all times—when they stood, sat, walked, played, lay down, or slept.

To ensure proper growth of the jaw and teeth, for example, Dr. Schreber devised a leather chin band that was held on to the head by a helmet of crisscrossing leather straps. The chin band kept the jaw and head straight. Another Schreber invention, one of his simplest but most effective, was the *Kopfhalter,* or head holder, which prevented the child's head from falling forward or sideways. The *Kopfhalter* consisted of a sturdy suspenderlike leather strip that could be buttoned onto the child's underwear at one end while a metal fixture at the other end was clamped onto the child's hair. If the child did not hold his head straight, he would be reminded by a sharp tug on his hair. The *Geradehalter,* a portable T-shaped metal contraption that could be screwed onto any desk at school or at home, was for preventing slumping while doing schoolwork. The horizontal bar pressed against the child's collarbone and the front of his shoulders to prevent forward movement or crooked posture. The long vertical bar that supported the horizontal bar and held it to the desk screw had an unforeseen side benefit. By pressing hard against the child's crotch, the vertical bar discouraged leg crossing and thigh pressing and other acts of moral degeneracy.

Dr. Schreber assured the public that he had always first tested his devices on his own children. As far as we know, Schreber's three daughters weathered their father's hygienic devotions. However, the two sons of the illustrious doctor, who envisioned himself as Gardener of the German spirit, were afflicted eventually with excruciating mental torments. At the age of thirty-eight, several weeks after being named a Gerichstrat (senior judge), the eldest, Gustav, took his life with a gun. The other, Daniel Paul Schreber, was in and out of mental asylums during the last twenty-seven years of his life.

Even before his children were born, Dr. Schreber had chosen as the epigraph to *The Book of Health,* "Bear in mind that a god resides in your body and that the temple at all times must be spared desecration."

Daniel Paul Schreber's detailed recollections of the tormenting and humiliating bodily sufferings performed on him by "God's penetrating Rays" were recorded in his *Memoirs of My Nervous Illness,* which he published at age sixty-one. The connection between Daniel Paul's mental torments and his father's straightening devices is painfully and tragically apparent. One of the most "horrifying" devices Daniel Paul described was the compression-of-the-chest miracle that would smash ribs and cause a lack of breath that would be transmitted throughout the boy's body. Then there was the "abominable" head-compressing machine, with which God's little devils (who resided within Daniel Paul's skull) would saw his skull to pieces, pull it apart, thin it, perforate it, and occasionally squeeze it into an elongated pear shape causing excruciating head pains. Even as Schreber was ready to leave the asylum, he continued to suffer from uninterrupted headaches, "hardly at all compared to the ordinary kind." Another of God's specialties was the coccyx miracle:

> This was an extremely painful caries-like state of the lowest vertebrae. Its purpose was to make sitting and even lying down impossible. Altogether I was not allowed to remain for long in one and the same position or at the same occupation; when I was walking one attempted to force me to lie down, and when I was lying down one wanted to chase me off my bed. Rays did not seem to appreciate at all that a human being who actually exists must be somewhere.

Several times in the course of his *Memoirs,* Schreber expressed his ambivalence toward this mysterious God, who with the ostensible motive of benefiting Schreber with his miracles, never seemed to grasp that he was performing his compressions, straightenings, and other miracles on a human being with a body and a soul capable of suffering. In this connection Schreber speculated on the tyrannical egoism of the being who directs the order of the world. "These egoistic actions have been practised against me for years with the utmost cruelty and disregard as only a beast deals with its prey." Apparently, his father, Dr. Schreber, had not grasped that his straightening miracles were being performed on a little child with human feelings.

Dr. Schreber was not alone in his missionary devotions to childhood. When it came to designing devices that would ensure the moral and physical "straightness" of the child, even the most prosaic parents could rise to imaginative heights. Masturbation was a never-ending source of inspiration. At night the child was chained or strapped or handcuffed to his or her bed so that all body movement was rendered impossible. During the day the lower part of the child's body could be locked into metal contraptions that served as underwear. Wealthy parents instructed the governesses and tutors to whom they entrusted their children that they should take any measure necessary to ensure sexual straightness. It was not uncommon for children to be sexually stimulated by their governesses and then bound up in leather straps or chains to ensure that they would not masturbate. Like a true saint, the child was tempted into desire and then humiliated into tormenting renunciation.

Masturbation anxiety had been a spritely specter in the minds of adults ever since the discovery of the child's "true nature." For at least two centuries previously, physicians had been acquainted with the various conditions that could be caused by onanism—hysteria, asthma, epilepsy, paralysis, melancholia, insanity. During the latter half of the nineteenth century and extending into the early part of the twentieth century, physicians turned their attention from mild cures to methods of total suppression. Restraining devices, severe punishments, and surgery were among the reputable medical cures.

Doctors wrote prescriptions for ergots, Sexine tablets, Paris Vital Sparks, and they recommended blistering, removal of nerves, and circumcision. For winding around the unruly penis were all manner of mechanical devices of rubber, wire, and springs. Catheters and tubes could be inserted within the penis. Companies made fortunes on the sale of electric belts and suspension apparatuses, many of which awakened even more exotic erotic fantasies than the child or adolescent could have conjured on his own and thereby stimulated more elaborate methods of onanism.

Moreover, since many middle-class parents were beginning to place themselves in a position of direct responsibility for the daily upbringing of their children, it was nearly impossible for them to continue to deny that girls might also be afflicted with the "solitary sin." When a girl sinned, she would not end up in the asylum or the grave. For her, the brothel beckoned. Far worse than madness or death were nymphomania, prostitution, barrenness, and bearing defective children. Clitoridectomy, a cure that removed the offending organ, was, mercifully, a brief fad. Nevertheless, blistering the thighs and genitals, "burial" of the clitoris beneath the labia, cauterization, and infilibration of the labia majora were frequently recommended.

In 1848, a Scottish physician who had familiarized himself with the immoralities of girls' boarding schools and convents devised a panty girdle with back laces and a front grillwork that could be sewn across the bottom. The girdle was fastened by belts to a pair of drawers and then secured by a padlock.

The sentimental falsification of the child's true nature, with which the discovery of childhood began, led to a fanatic savagery whereby child abuse could be politely disguised as socialization and mental hygiene. To ensure that children did not stray from their natural piety, they would have to be purged of those insidious unnatural passions that could so easily claim a child's soul. A parent had the absolute right to punish, even to occasionally whip a child for laziness, disobedience, rudeness, stealing, alcoholism, and masturbation. These punishments would have to result in death before anyone would intervene on the child's behalf.

In November 1899, *The Neue Freie Presse* of Vienna published "A Slowly Murdered Child." The article catalogued the abrasions, contusions, wounds and lacerations, and broken bones of five-year-old Anna

Hummel, a child physically brutalized by her mother, with her father's approval and encouragement, until "death had taken pity upon her." The parents were brought to trial, where it came out that they had also collaborated in devising other torments for Anna. They tied her to a chair and placed her day's food in full view where she could not reach it; they made her stand barefoot in icy water on freezing winter days; they forced her to eat her own excrement.

At first some of the good citizens of Vienna found a way to alleviate their horrified reactions. The Hummels were ignorant, lower-class parents, and as everyone knew the children of lower-class families were always the victims of their parents' moral corruption and disorderly, drunken lives. However, this comforting rationalization did not work for long, especially after people read about the starving, the icy water, the excrement. Surely, the passionate zeal with which Anna's mother and father had slowly and deliberately led her to her death seemed to betray some new kind of human depravity.

At the end of every century, people begin to speculate about the moral prospects of the century to come. So in 1899, the Viennese middle class began to worry about the larger import of little Anna's murder. Was this perverse parental scenario an omen of the apocalyptic sadisms that awaited humanity in the twentieth century? How could a mother and a father have calculated such unheard of sufferings for their child, invented "tortures which remind one at times of Dante's Hell"? In his summation to the jury, the prosecutor found just the right words to express the essential horror that was on everyone's mind:

In our times, eaten away by doubt and the mania for mockery, if there is still something of value, then it is faith in the mother. Everything gives way before the power of maternal love. It is the purest sentiment, but it is also stronger than anything else; it overpowers everything. This mother also had a child and she murdered it, no, not murdered, but butchered it with horrible tortures. Her deed makes a mockery of everything that is holy to human beings; one could almost doubt the omnipotence of mother love.

Two weeks later, the same prosecutor brought to justice the murderer of another little Anna. This Anna, the eleven-year-old daughter of a proper middle-class postal official, Rudolf Kutschera, had been tortured and abused to death by her stepmother, Maria Kutschera. After a brief but at times morally confusing trial in which the stepmother brazenly justified her brutal methods of childrearing as instructions in moral obedience, she was sentenced to hanging. Her husband, the widowed father of Anna who had colluded, approved, and never intervened on his daughter's behalf, got off with a mild sentence.

Maria Kutschera had physically abused all seven of her stepchildren. But the other Kutschera children had managed to survive. Evidently Anna had been the most trying child for Maria Kutschera, who when asked if she had loved her stepchildren replied, "Yes, and especially Annerl, she was my darling."

She accused Anna, the child who had died from her disciplines, of disobedience, dishonesty, alcoholism, theft, and sexual depravity. Of course, Anna had to be regularly beaten on her fingers. Those very fingers were always stealing the schnapps. The prosecutor described to the court the Kutschera family whip, used at one time or another on all the children, a Russian instrument with studded leather straps attached to a short leather handle. However, Kutschera insisted to the end, "I beat the children, but I didn't abuse them, only disciplined them."

By the end of the nineteenth century, the uncertain borders between discipline and abuse had become a convenient loophole for all sorts of parental perversities. From the beginning of human time, children had been subjected to infanticide, abandonment, Spartan strengthenings, cripplings, and sexual abuse by the adults entrusted with their upbringing. However, now that childhood and motherhood had become the icons of man's noblest aspirations, the abuse of children was justified in the name of advancing the march of human progress.

By claiming to act in the name of the child's salvation, any parent could justify even the most brutal acts of physical and mental punishment. The truth is that whenever a parent employs physical or mental torment to correct a child's behavior, we can be sure that the parent is actually seeking his or her own salvation.

Along the way, the twentieth century acquired the appellation Century of the Child. In 1959, a "Declaration of the Rights of the Child" was composed and circulated among the experts entrusted with the preservation of children's rights—judges, lawyers, policemen, day-care workers, teachers, social workers, psychologists, politicians. Twenty years later the trustees of children's rights celebrated the International Year of the Child. By that year the experts had been awakened to the realities of the "battered child syndrome" and were becoming acquainted with the psychology of the mothers and fathers who physically abuse their children.

Typically, both parents of an abused child have similar personal histories. Many of them are abused children grown to adulthood physically, but still children psychologically, still longing that maybe someday, someone will love them, still silently raging for the physical pain they had to endure in silence. Even those who had not been subjected to consistent physical torment grew up in households where they were continuously criticized, where their desires and feelings were always belittled or disregarded.

Statistics on *known* cases of child abuse reflect the role structures of the modern family. Mothers, the primary caregivers, are the primary abusers of infants and toddlers. Later, when the babies become children between the ages of five and twelve, they must leave the protecting warmth of the nursery and learn the ways of the world. It is then that fathers, the lawgivers, take over and become the chief abusers of their children.

From the point of view of a child who has been abused, the brutality of his mother is experienced as more devastating than the father's brutality. And even when the father is the one who does the whipping or punching, the child feels betrayed by the mother's failure to protect him against the father's attack. No matter what the Bronson Alcotts or the Daniel Schrebers might do or how far their messianic arms might reach, it is the Emma Bovarys who are likely to be accused of bestiality. Father is the lawgiver, the one who defines crimes and punishes transgressions. It is almost as though we expect that fathers, in their role of enforcing the laws of society, have every right to be as forceful as necessary, even brutal, if the child is recalcitrant to socialization. However, Mother is the universal symbol of caregiving, protection, nurturing, comfort, and mercy.

The three- or six-month-old baby who has had his clavicle fractured for crying too loud has not yet been indoctrinated into this cultural stereotype. His mind isn't yet making distinctions about the respective responsibilities of mothers and fathers. By the time a battered child is two or three and old enough to have fantasies about the abuse that has been inflicted on his body by mother *or* father, he will reckon that the-mother-of-the-good-nursery-breast should have protected him. However, a battered child mostly reckons that he must be the guilty one, for only a very wicked child is deserving of such terrible punishment. And so, until the day the abused child dies, he or she will yearn for a mother with caring arms, loving looks, smiles of admiration and approval, tenderness and mercy, a mother whose loving eyes will confirm that he is worthy of being loved. It is in this unquenchable thirst to be recognized as a worthwhile person that the recycling of child abuse from one generation to the next begins. The mother who was abused in childhood will be looking in the eyes of her baby for proof of her own worthiness. Later, when the once abused father takes over the socialization of his child, he will expect that child to prove that he is an important, respected, and manly man by obeying his every commandment and law, to the letter, on the double, with no back talk.

In any society where motherhood is considered a sacred duty, it is understandable that a mother might look to her child for a reflection of her own goodness. A battering mother, a woman who is still yearning for the mothering and nurturance she never had, is even more strongly inclined than an average mother toward estimating her own value by her capacity to satisfy the needs of her child. She feels mothered and nurtured when her child says "Yes" to her milk, her embraces, her soothing gestures, her commands for obedience, her restrictions. When the child says "No" or is naughty or doesn't look cheerful, the mother is reminded of the unhappy, unloved child she had been. The unspoken assumption is that the child has been put there to take care of the parent. "All my life nobody ever loved me. When my baby was born I thought he would. When he cried it meant he didn't love me. So I hit him."

One battering mother found a windup walking, talking doll that she recommended as the perfect child. This miraculous doll knew only a few words but they were just right: "Hello, I love you. Hello, I love you. Hello, I love you." Another perfect child was the two-and-a-half-year-old Timmy, who always washed the dishes, vacuumed the living room, and could even bake cakes for his mother when he had the proper mix. Timmy never made any trouble. He took care of himself. He could tie his own shoelaces and put on and button his own coat. Timmy did not entirely escape his mother's threats, slaps, punches, and angry glares, but he fared much better than his one-year-old brother, who had his arms broken and his ear nearly torn off for crying too much and having accidents in his pants.

Five-month-old Harry provoked his mother's attacks by always trying to get hold of the spoon while she was feeding him. He liked to mess around with the food before he put it in his mouth. His mother reported proudly how she had kept slapping his fingers until he learned not to poke them into his food. By the time he was eight months old,

Harry would sit in his high chair with his arms held high in the air, scanning his mother's face anxiously and rapidly gulping down every morsel of food she offered him.

Abused children learn fast. Sixteen-month-old Annie knew that when her unemployed father, the official caregiver of her home, said "Come here," she had better come right away. "If she doesn't come the minute I call her, I just give her a little tug on the ear to remind her." When Annie was hospitalized with multiple contusions and bruises on her face and head, her ear was lacerated and nearly torn away from her head. Her little brother Donald, aged three months, was hospitalized at the same time with fractures of the clavicle and femur and bilateral subdural hematomas.

Some abused children never get hit quite hard enough to require hospitalization. They are merely tormented daily by criticisms, belittlings, slaps, whacks, pokes, pinches. Occasionally they are burned with cigarettes or injured with various household appliances. Their bodies show bruises, burns, and minor lacerations but never fractures. Other infants are subjected to periodic attacks of yanking and hitting and punching of an intensity that results in bone fractures, massive bruising, major lacerations, and life-threatening internal injuries. Their bodies are often covered with welts from belts and electric cords and burns from hot appliances. Between attacks these children are often relatively well cared for.

While they are incapable of empathy, abusing mothers can be uncannily sympathetic to the sufferings of the child they are abusing. An abusing mother regards the child as a part of her own self and therefore experiences directly what the child is experiencing. She sees in her own hurting child the hurt child she once was. And while she didn't dare cry then for fear of more punishment, now she allows the tears to flow. "After I hit Johnny, I sat down by the crib and cried and cried. I felt as if I had hit myself."

As she gathers up her thoughts of childhood, every mother will call up two sets of memories, one set consisting of how it felt to be a child and the other of how she was cared for by her parents. Whether a mother realizes it or not, these parallel memories are informing the way she behaves with her own child. The average mother can conjure up an assortment of childhood recollections. They encompass a wide range of occasions from the marvelous times when she was an obedient, charmingly mischievous, beautiful, brilliant, lovable, and loved child to the disheartening and mortifying moments when she was hateful, smelly, messy, incompetent, and therefore dissatisfying, displeasing, and an affront to her parents' needs, desires, and values. However, the mother who batters her child has an exceptionally narrow view of her own childhood. She imagines that she always was a horrible creature who was rarely, if ever, able to please or satisfy her mother and father. She recalls her mother's voice as always demanding, criticizing, and punishing and her father as never protecting her from the abuses and torments of the mother. She recalls that when she got older her father took over the demanding, criticizing, and punishing and her mother never protected her from his brutality or helped her to understand that his rage wasn't her fault. Now as she approaches the job of caring for this tiny helpless baby of her own, she would insist that it is her imperative sacred duty to be a good mother, for if she can be a good mother, perhaps she will be absolved of her wickedness; perhaps now her mother will love her. Since her baby will be the means of proving her own value, her single-minded driven ambition to be proved worthy will take precedence over any realistic assessment of what a real baby can or cannot accomplish. She wants only to be a good mother and certainly does not want to hurt, injure, or murder her child. What then would provoke this excessively dutiful mother to repeatedly attack her child and each time come very close to murder?

The unconscious perverse scenario, the terrifying spectacle of an infant being beaten by his mother, begins with the baby's inability to comply with whatever it is the mother is trying so desperately to accomplish. It is not enough that he do what she wants, he also must not cry, he must not turn his head the other way, he must not say

"No," and, furthermore, he must attune his body to her gestures of mothering—all with a happy, contented face. When he does not, or cannot, she feels wounded and criticized. "When the baby keeps crying, it sounds just like my mother yelling at me and criticizing me." The infant is being seen by his mother not as a helpless child but as an unloving, critical parent. The crying baby, therefore, arouses in the mother the helpless fury she experienced when she was a baby who tried and tried to be the good "I love you" doll her mother so urgently needed. This rage, which she could never express or even allow herself to feel when she was an unworthy child, reduces the mother to feeling again that she is a bad, smelly, ugly, stupid child. The violence of the rage, the uncertainty of whose rage it is or where it is coming from, the sense that she is a wicked child about to be punished again in God knows what way overwhelms all reason and sanity. The mother's only safety now is to identify with her punishers, to live up to the expectations of the cruel and terrible *voice* that she carries in her head at all times. With all reason gone, now the *voice* gives permission to destroy the wicked and ugly child. In this terror and rage without boundaries or a restraining voice that forbids a mother to murder her child is a demonic force that explodes into drownings in hot water, burnings with cigarettes, punches in the face, whippings of the fingers or buttocks, yanks on the earlobes.

In this perverse scenario the spotlight is on the voice of conscience and the mother's sense of sin and worthlessness. Thus, as always in a perverse scenario, a conscious sense of wrongdoing is brought into the foreground to help the person assuage the insupportable anxieties and mortifications that would otherwise become conscious. The mutilation anxiety and the shame of being an unworthy, incompetent, impotent child who could never satisfy her mother's desires is held at bay by placating the voice of conscience with an actively controlled mutilation. The disobedient baby, after all, came from inside the mother and is still indistinguishable from her own self. If she mutilates him, she will be safe from the threatened mutilations of the voice. And since there are three generations united as one in this scenario—the disobedient baby now, the punishing mother of the past, and the unworthy, bad child of the past—the raging vengeance of the currently abusing mother is unconsciously directed against the almighty mother of the past but suffered by the helpless baby in the present. Another facet of the perverse strategy that comes vividly to life in this scenario is the desperate longing of the battering mother for a reunion with the good almighty one on whom her survival once depended and still does. For with all its demonic rage, the battering mother is still longing for approval, protection, and an embrace of love. Despite all she recalls about her mother's abuse and her father's collaboration, she must try to keep alive the image of a loving, protecting parent. And in every perverse scenario there is this longing to be reunited with the good parent.

In a Schreber-like scenario of guilt, the child who is tormented by a parent must call on that same parent for help and rescue. She must hold out her hands in forgiveness to the punishing parent. The child must break with what she has actually experienced and out of the desperation of being only a helpless, dependent child represent the abusing parent as good. For only the mental image of a good parent can help the child deal with the intensity of fear and rage that are the immediate aftermaths of these tormenting experiences. To survive the enormity of her own terror and rage, the child must treasure in some compartment of her mind the delusion of a godlike parent and some illusion and hope that one day all the terror and pain and hate will be transformed into love. But the voice of the punishing parent will make sure that every time the child reaches out to be loved, the child will experience a making of hate in the name of love.

The yearning for attachment is fundamental to human existence. A child will become emotionally attached to the person who cares for her, no matter how the caregiver does it. And, for better or worse, a child also becomes emotionally attached to the kind of care she receives. When the abused child grows up and looks about to make a new life for herself with new possibilities, she can't shake loose from the past. Unconsciously, she is convinced that the only way she will ever feel safe and worthwhile is in a relationship with an abusing parent.

The person she chooses as lover or husband does not look cruel or tyrannical. What she is consciously drawn to is his tender concern for her welfare. Isn't he always saying that all he wants to do is take care of her? However, what she is picking up unconsciously about this man is that he needs to see reflected in her eyes that he is adored and worshiped—at all times, under all circumstances, on the double, with no back talk, and especially when he is feeling that he is not worth much at all. The grand idea that she and she alone has the power to make her husband or lover happy seems so familiar, like an echo from the past. And each time she is able to make him happy she feels safe and loved, almost the way it was during those rare and beautiful moments when she succeeded in being the best little "I love you" doll for her mother. When the honeymoon is over and she knows with absolute certainty that she will be beaten if he's been out drinking with his pals or if the boss insulted him or if his co-workers made a joke at his expense or if he lost a bet at the racetrack, she will still keep trying, against all odds, to make this man happy in the hopes that he will take care of her and keep her safe. As one battered child, battered wife put it, "Feeling bad is something I know, it's safe, it's the smell of home."

The Century of the Child is drawing to its conclusion on an ominous note. No sooner had child development experts become aware of the physical abuse that some parents inflict on their children than another perversion of parenting, another violation of the differences between the child and adult generations, became too evident to be ignored.

What with all the other fascinating news in the 1948 Kinsey report on the sexual life of females, not too much was made of the incidental finding that nearly 20 percent of the women interviewed reported having had or having been invited to have sexual relations with adult men when they were little girls. However, by the late 1970s there was a professional periodical, *International Journal of Child Abuse and Neglect,* which each year would publish several articles on the sexual abuse of children. Each year the public got more and more used to hearing about the sexual abuse of children—by experienced pedophiles, child kidnappers, day care workers, and family members. When on August 25, 1985, the *Los Angeles Sunday Times* stated that at least 22 percent of the nation's adults had been victims of child sexual abuse, readers were shocked but not entirely unprepared for the news.

The statistics were the outcome of a nationwide survey conducted by I. A. Lewis, a reporter who was also highly experienced in poll-taking techniques. Of the 2,627 persons interviewed by Lewis's staff, 27 percent of the women and 16 percent of the men reported having been sexually abused in childhood. Fifty-five percent of the victims reported having sexual intercourse with an adult while they were children and 18 percent of those said that physical force or threats had been used to induce their cooperation. The other half of the victims were subjected to what is known as less serious sexual abuse—fondling, being confronted by exhibitionists, posing in the nude for photographs. The most vulnerable age for the victims was ten, and the typical abuser was about twenty years older than the victim.

Although there is no hard-and-fast rule about these matters, typically a four-or five-year-old who is sexually abused by an adult will be more seriously traumatized and permanently damaged emotionally than a teenage girl or boy who is similarly abused. Most states do distinguish between the statutory rape of older children—the age of consent varying from thirteen to eighteen—and the more serious crime of child molestation of prepubescent children. It *is* important to make these distinctions. But however old or young the child is and in whatever way he or she has been sexually abused, some adult has used and abused the body of a child for his own emotional needs, without any regard for the feelings or sensibilities of the child. To him, the child was a fetish, much like a lock of hair, a velvet bathrobe, a horse, a corpse. The adult did not seem to appreciate at all that a living, breathing child existed somewhere in the body he was molesting or raping.

It is clear that any adult who sexually abuses a child is involved in trying to disavow the differences between the child and adult generations. He is engaged in a perversion. The effects of his perversion on the child he has abused can vary. The sexual abuse of a child can be a one-time occurrence or can go on for years. Even a one-time occurrence, an almost accidental sexual encounter between, for example, a child camper and an older camp counselor, might, depending on the state of mind of the camper and the attitude and approach of the counselor, leave an indelible trauma. Sexual abuse can be inflicted on the victim in an atmosphere of violence or an atmosphere of "tenderness." A girl who had to endure repeated exposures to exhibitionists in playgrounds and on subway platforms will not suffer in the same way as a girl who is repeatedly forced to have intercourse with a child molester or a girl who is periodically seduced by a father whom she loves and adores. When the abusers are parents or other family members, the crime is incestuous sexual abuse. And with incest the psychological impact on the child victim varies considerably depending on whether the sexual abuser is a father or mother, an aunt or uncle or grandfather, or a same-generation sister, brother, or cousin. Once again, what seems to make an incestuous relationship traumatic is the state of mind that the sexually abused child brings to the situation and the attitude toward the child of the incestuous adult.

While current research reveals that some mothers, aunts, female neighbors, and female adolescent babysitters sexually abuse younger males, the vast majority of child sexual abusers are males and most of the abused are females. Nevertheless, many of these grown-up men, particularly the pedophiles, are especially fond of young boys. When the abuser is a stranger to the child, chances are he is a pedophile, a male who elevates his perversion to a virtue by proclaiming to the world that he is treating his child victim to an education in love and sex.

The pedophile is a "fixated" child molester, meaning that he is compulsively drawn to children and has no other options for his sexual life and that he has been predisposed to child molesting from childhood. Many pedophiles were sexually molested as children, and the others were subjected to various other physical and mental abuses by their parents. While it is customary to speak of the pedophile's attraction *toward* children, the fact is that he, like all male perverts, is drawn *away* from the adult female body and doesn't like to be reminded of the differences between the sexes. A child's body, particularly a boy child's body, keeps that unwelcome news hidden. And, more obviously than other perverts, pedophiles are preoccupied with obliterating all distinctions between the child and adult generations.

A pedophile's life is consumed by an unconscious fury toward the sacred morals of his society and a conscious contempt for any social distinctions that remind him of his banishment from the Garden of Eden. When he is not actually sexually molesting prepubescent children, he is photographing them in the nude and collecting and trading photographs of naked and seminaked children and pornographic tales of child lust with other pedophiles. Some of the molested and raped children grow attached to their adult molesters and will never betray them. Others are afraid to tell, and when they do tell chances are they will not be believed. To be convicted, a pedophile usually has to be caught "in the act."

In cases of incest, roughly ninety-eight times out of a hundred, a father is the offender and a daughter is his victim. Unlike pedophiles, who regard themselves as members of a sexual elite, fathers who sexually abuse their daughters are not proud of what they do and will make every effort to keep their activities secret. If his daughter finally gets up the courage to report his sexual seductions to her mother, the father will accuse the girl of lying; chances are the mother will believe him.

Like the Viennese citizens of 1899 who distanced themselves from the horrors of Anna Hummel's death by attributing her fate to her lower-class origins, most good Americans in 1990 would prefer to believe that incest occurs only in lower-class families from urban slums and ghettos and the backwoods of Appalachia. However, a great many incest families are middle class and look hypernormal. The neighbors are shocked when they learn that a jolly, hard-working family man with three children, two cars, a dog, and a well-trimmed lawn, faithfully married to his submissive, devoted, pie-baking, PTA wife has been sexually molesting his two daughters since they were toddlers. The striking thing about upper- and middle-class incest homes is that they are emulations of the gender caricatures that are celebrated on "Ozzie and Harriet," "The Cosby Show," "The Wonder Years," "Major Dad," and "Roseanne."* In these stereotypical Norman Rockwell TV households—overlaid with every cultural diversity that is currently popular—the mothers and the girls act just like *girls,* the fathers and the boys act just like *boys,* and everyone is laughing and crying and looking worried or startled at precisely the right moment, but emotionally nothing is going on. Nobody empathizes with the feelings or thoughts of anybody else and, like the dog and the barbecue, the children are used as props for the picture-perfect view of American family life. The robins and bluebirds are singing in the trees and under the neatly mowed lawn a hot jungle of perversity is flourishing.

The wives of incestuous fathers would much sooner punish their daughter for lying than take steps to protect the girl from the father's abuse. The wife is more interested in keeping up appearances of an ideal family and protecting her relationship with her husband than in

---

* Each TV season brings some new family sit-coms and cancels a few others. However, for all their surface differences, one TV family behaves just like every other TV family. Even the Newcomers to our planet, the Franciscos of "Alien Nation," succumb to the formulas. The program, designed as an allegory against bigotry, started off the fall 1989 season with a sense of social purpose—for example, Buck, the prototypical rebellious teenager, was reading *Madame Bovary* in the original French—but as the Franciscos and their Newcomer friends were gradually integrated into American society they, like every minority group represented on the TV sit-coms, became indistinguishable from their neighbors. TV critic Marvin Kitman, who championed the Francisco family and the socially responsible morality of the Newcomers, nevertheless lamented that "Alien Nation" sometimes might as well have been called "Ozzie and Harriet Go Bald." ("The Marvin Kitman Show," *Newsday,* May 7, 1990, p. 9.)

having the lord of the manor and breadwinner carted off to jail. In many small, close-knit communities where there are known instances of incest, families and neighbors would much rather handle the situation quietly without legal intervention. There are many more cases of incest in lower-class, middle-class, and upper-class American families than are reported.

Typically, fathers who sexually abuse their daughters are starved for loving affirmation and when the dependent, narcissistically wounded women they married begin to show even a spark of independence, these husbands turn in panic to their impressionable daughters. Psychological studies of the incest family frequently reveal that both father and daughter felt neglected by the mother, that both were hungry for affection. It is not unusual for the daughter to collaborate with her father in a version of the incest scenario that puts the blame on the mother. The mother is accused by the father for her aloofness and emotional unavailability, and the daughter will say that she too suffered from deprivation of motherly love. The daughter will say that the only time she felt worthwhile and safe was in the arms of her father. This version of things is a partial truth. The wife of an incest father plays the *role* of devoted mother but is more involved in salvaging her self-esteem by maintaining her husband's grandiose narcissism than in ensuring the welfare of her children. She is emotionally oblivious to her children's needs but highly attuned to her husband's emotional requirements. When she turns her admiring eyes away from him and stops baking pies, he regresses to incest.

In contrast to the fixated pedophile, the incestuous father is considered a "regressed" child molester, a "normal" man who has been reduced by situations of stress to a state of emotional neediness that provokes him to make his initial sexual advances toward his child. Almost always the father who sexually abuses his children has been insanely dependent on his pathetically dependent wife from the day they met. What he needed from her was her assurance that she regarded him as a mighty lord, the most important thing in her life, and that she derived all her emotional satisfactions through her relationship with him. She has to convey to him that she is nothing without him. As long as the couple maintains this rigid role division and balance of power, the father may never approach his children for sex. Typically what triggers an incest father's regression to incest is an alteration in the structure of his relationship to his wife. The wife's prolonged illness, her death, their separation or divorce, her showing some sparks of independence—losing weight, changing her hair style or mode of dressing, going back to school, spending long hours at a paid job or volunteer work instead of doing the laundry and dusting the furniture. Another precipitating factor is merely the stress of losing a job or professional prestige, especially when this degrading event necessitates the wife's going out to work and the husband's taking over the household duties. It is not unusual in such situations that this previously hypernormal husband and father, with however hidden a core of frantic need and terrible anxiety, will start to consume vast amounts of alcohol or become addicted to drugs. If he had been trying to inhibit any impulse toward having sexual relations with his children, the alcohol and drugs that at first satisfy his needs and calm his anxiety will eventually serve as disinhibitors. Sometimes, the first sexual approach toward one of his daughters occurs almost accidentally while the man is drunk and the child asleep. However, this first experience, which is immensely erotic and narcissistically gratifying, guilt-provoking and tormenting, as well as an outlet for the suppressed rage of childhood, contains all the emotional ingredients necessary to produce a perversion. All perversions are preoccupations that have an addictive, compulsive quality, and with incest the drug is always available because only a rare child will refuse her father's sexual advances.

In recent years a new breed of child molester has been identified—the *crossover* pedophile-incest father. Such a pedophile seeks out divorced or widowed women with children or marry women they identify as prospective mothers of their prospective child-lovers. They establish legitimate households with these women and thereby cross over from pedophilia to incest. The hero of *Lolita,* Nabokov's 1955 novel, now a bible for pedophiles, would be considered a crossover child molester. Humbert Humbert married Mrs. Haze, whose brazenly coquettish ways and willingness to adore him in favor of her child—"Just slap her if she interferes with your scholarly meditations"—signaled her readiness to become an incest mother. Humbert found Mrs. Haze's womanliness offensive to his elegant tastes, but he married her anyway to gain sexual access to her daughter, his nymphet dream girl. Humbert miscalculated about Dolores Haze's readiness to hand over Lolita, however. Lolita's mother had to die before Humbert could gain his prize. Humbert lamented the discovery of "normal" childhood and the injustice of laws against pedophilia and incest:

> We are not surrounded in our enlightened era by little slave flowers that can be casually plucked between business and bath as they used to be in the days of the Romans; and we do not, as dignified Orientals did in still more luxurious times, use tiny entertainers fore and aft between the mutton and the rose sherbet. The whole point is that the old link between the adult world and the child world has been completely severed nowadays by new customs and new laws.

An incest mother is a woman who is attracted to men who are hungry for adoration, men who they imagine are far above them intellectually and socially. The women who marry crossover pedophiles or those hearty heterosexuals who will one day regress to incest are referred to as incest mothers because they have an uncanny knack for choosing men who are potential incest fathers. As I have said, these men do not look like fiends or demons. They look more normal and refined than the average man. The image they project is of the ideal father, the head of the ideal household—a caricature of fatherhood. Law enforcement agents and mental health workers have considerable difficulty determining which of the men accused of child molesting might be actual abusers and which are being falsely accused. The incest mother, however, who knows unconsciously the type of man she needs for her own salvation, has emotional antennae that lead her directly to her man. More than one therapist specializing in cases of child sexual abuse has remarked on the diagnostic acumen of the incest mother: "It's like the man has the words 'child molester' painted on his forehead, but the letters are invisible to everyone else but the incest mother." Most likely the words the incest mother sees are "Love me, adore me, worship me."

A man who marries with the conscious or unconscious intention of begetting the offspring who will fulfill his grandiose fantasies starts training the selected child from her birth. He is the kind of father every little girl dreams of having. He bathes and diapers her with every tenderness, he buys her pretty clothes and dresses her every morning, he massages her body and brushes her hair and takes her to grown-up parties and encourages her to feel that her mother is a nobody, a woman he regards as a household slave and nothing more. A child will become attached to anyone who arouses strong and passionate emotions. What could be more exciting to a child than to be chosen by her daddy or granddaddy or stepfather, a man she regards as something of a god anyway, to be his favorite, his special little wifey? Moreover, when that god also knows just how to rub your little breasts and fondle your genitals and teaches you how to make head for him, the already passionate attachment that a child feels for her father is magnified by the charged eroticism of doing something behind her mother's back. It isn't until she becomes a teenager and realizes that all her friends have boyfriends their own age that the girl consciously recognizes anything peculiar about her dad or her relationship with him. Of course, she has been suffering from unconscious guilt all along, knowing that she has usurped her mother's place, knowing that the special love she feels for her daddy is their little secret, which she must never reveal to anyone.

When she becomes a woman she will be strongly identified with the mother who achieved her own existence and sense of value through a relationship with a godlike man. She grows up with a profound unconscious hatred of men but is nevertheless convinced that a certain kind of man, the man who survives on some woman's slavish devotion to him, is the only kind of man that can turn her on sexually. That certain kind of man is just the kind of man that might sexually abuse her children. She needs only to decipher the message inscribed on his godlike face: "Worship me, adore me, love me." And so begins a marriage between an emotionally needy child-wife and an emotionally needy child-husband, a family structure in which neither parent is capable of empathizing with what it means to be a needy, dependent child.

A child who has spent a lifetime being subjected to systematic, conscientious inflictions of sexual abuse, torment, neglect, and deprivation is overwhelmed by these traumas. Her mind is flooded with feelings and sensations that cannot be mastered in any ordinary human way. The average child who suffers only from the ordinary, expectable traumas of childhood will enlist her fantasy life as a way of working over these traumas and repairing them. However, the child who suffers from severe and repetitive traumas requires massive and mind-distorting defenses that impoverish her fantasy life. These mind-distorting defenses are the source of certain irreversible deformities of human thinking and feeling. When the torments of infancy and childhood require such massive defenses for a child to survive psychologically, the child's mind is crippled not only from the physical and mental torments she has suffered but from the survival mechanisms she had to enlist to continue to think and feel. The child goes on living, but her soul has been murdered.

The expression "soul murder" was first used in 1832 in a book that described the torments of Kaspar Hauser, a foundling brought up in total darkness and deprived of almost all human contact for nearly seventeen years. The author, Anselm von Feuerbach, a well-known German judge, accused the two foster parents of soul murder and said:

> It is the iniquity perpetrated against his spiritual nature which presents the most revolting aspect of the crime committed against him. His being excluded from all intercourse with rational beings. To withdraw from him all the nourishment afforded by what makes the human mind grow and flourish is a criminal invasion of man's most sacred and most peculiar property—the freedom and destiny of his soul.

Since Hauser's life was taken from him before his soul could be completely destroyed, he was said to be the subject of a partial soul murder, which according to von Feuerbach was any deliberate or careless destruction of one person's identity by another.

Most women and men who have been subjected to an unconsciously calculated soul murder or conscientious systematic physical and sexual abuse in childhood do not withdraw from the world or become psychotic, except as a last resort. When a child is overwhelmed by feeling or sensation, a typical defensive reaction is to shut off all emotional response until the situation that is giving rise to these unmasterable sensations is over. It is almost as though the child is thinking, "What is happening to me is so terrible that it must not be felt and I must not let it register on my mind." Of course the child is not thinking and cannot think when these traumatic situations occur. All he or she can do is react by shutting off the lights on reality. When these crises of being overwhelmed are recurrent or chronic, then the blanking-out or numbing-out defenses also will become chronic and irreversible. If she or he wants to survive at all, the child who is being abused or misused has little choice but to become a mechanical and obedient automaton. The less thinking or feeling the better.

An essential ingredient in this scenario is the tormented's relationship with the tormentor. Pedophiles, sexually abusing fathers, or battering mothers will complain that they were later agonized by remorse for the brutal and inhuman acts they perpetrated against an innocent and helpless child. They turn the soul murder into a soul saving. They insist that it was not sadism, but that their remorse compelled them to "save the child's soul." After all, little Annerl was Maria Kutschera's darling. What better way to save a child's soul than to make the child confess to her own guilt, to force the child to hold out her hand in forgiveness to her tormentor, to hack the sinning little body into pieces and bury it or burn it and scatter the ashes to the winds? What these maniacal soul savers recite about the sorry state of their own souls in the local newspapers and tabloids still shocks us. But now that *we* have faced the facts and turned the lights on to reality and recognized that physical and sexual abuse of children is not merely an ubiquitous childhood fantasy but events that could happen to any child, we are no longer so completely surprised.

Still, the fantasies of childhood do play a part. The child who suffers a soul murder has shut off her mind but retains nevertheless a shred of fantasy life, just enough to transform herself into the culpable one. Why does the child, if she or he survives the body torment and soul murder and soul saving, so willingly participate in the tormentor's scenario? The child, who is already ashamed of the wicked sexual feelings she is experiencing and the awful rage she has conjured but cannot express, has no way of grasping who the guilty party is. The powerful adult must be the good one and the child then must be the bad, dirty, sinful one. What results is an abiding confusion between victim and perpetrator, between good and bad, between innocence and culpability, between sexuality and sinfulness. After a while the borders between being a perpetrator and being a victim all but vanish.

As adults these tormented children find themselves bound by a compulsion to repeat the cycle of abuse with other tormentors. Each time there is the expectation "Maybe this time I will be loved and cared for." Very often, there is a reversal of roles, and the one who was previously tormented or sexually molested becomes the tormentor, the molester. "Now I will be the parent and I will do it better." As we have seen, sometimes the recycling of torment and soul murder occurs in the setting where it originally started—at home in the nursery. Some women who have been sexually and physically abused as children want only to refind their lost goodness by proving that they are good mothers. Others seem to unconsciously comprehend the extent of their murderous rage and protect their unborn children by never having them. When they have miscarriages and abortions they experience a strange sense of relief. At least they will not have to be the tormentor of a helpless child.

Little girls like Olympia (in Chapter 8) grew up to become *Raunch* centerfolds, porno stars, Hollywood starlets, go-go dancers, pinup girls, fashion model Elizas, call girls, prostitutes. Now multitudes of men (and women) will always adore and cherish their bodies. Some women who were abused as children seem to have an "instinctive" talent for realizing the perfect disciplinary gestures for a man who needs to be humiliated and abused in order to perform sexually. By being a dominating top in sadomasochistic scenarios with men who depend on her disciplinary ministrations to produce and maintain their erections, the woman is at once an abusing parent and a good parent who is able at last to please and satisfy her helpless child—and she will never actually murder that man who, after all, is only posing as a helpless child.

Protected by the rigid organization and precise rules that govern a reliable SM specialty house, one has endless opportunities for refinding the lost goodness of one's childhood—for realizing one's destiny as an abusing-good parent, an abused-good child. All the experiences of a tortured and tormented childhood can be reenacted in safety, with a sense of control, in settings and with paraphernalia for any socially acceptable disguise of the child-parent roles. There are operating tables set up in operating amphitheaters, doctor's offices with examination tables, schoolrooms, courtrooms, altars and other religious settings, harems, prisons, medieval torture chambers, even nurseries with cribs and playpens. One can choose from an assortment of special equipment: paddles, long and short whips that are braided, knotted, and studded, canes, chains, nails and needles, spears and arrows, knives, razors, surgical instruments, chains and wires and ropes for hanging or suspending the body, racks for stretching the body, dildos and adhesive tape for stuffing in the mouth, garments and materials for wrapping the body, bandages, leather coats, raincoats, hot irons, and hot wax for branding and burning. One can indulge in any infantilism and be whipped or paddled or wrapped in bandages or suffocated, or powdered or cuddled or fed with a milk bottle or nursed. In these settings using these props to perform one's personally conceived perverse scenario, any trauma of childhood can be transformed into a triumph of adulthood.

Once she has become proficient in her role as a stern governess, strict mother, whipping rider, injecting doctor, the same woman might dare the adventure of being a slave or a student or a helpless baby. Having realized that pain can be safely administered within the boundaries of a rigid scenario, she might entrust her body to the disciplinary ministrations of a "teacher," the operating techniques of a "doctor." Thus a woman who never trusted herself to any loving relationship will finally refind the painful relationship to her mother, but this time the pain and the punishment will bring love and forgiveness. She will allow her labia and nipples to be pierced by an experienced top who knows just how to administer pleasure, just how to discipline a woman's body in just the right way. In such a way the two beings are united, the two souls become one. The child is reunited with her good and loving mother. "Now I was the child again, and my mother did it right."

In every one of these perverse scenarios, whether the participants are disguised as doctor and patient, judge and prisoner, there is a parent and a child and a symbolic repetition of an act of perverse parenting.

Unlike the primal scene fantasies and playful enactments that could be aspects of any run-of-the-mill sexual relationship, these enactments are rigid and compulsive. They are preoccupations that govern the lives of the participants. The soul murders that these adult men and adult women suffered in childhood represented a violation of the generational differences. Some were raped and sexually molested, others were invited to the father's bed while the mother was excluded; still others knew from the time they were babies that they were expected to parent the parent and could never count on who was child and who was parent. So whether the participant assumes the bottom role of helpless child or the top role of parent-caregiver-lawgiver, he or she is identifying with both roles and hoping each time to rectify the traumas that were suffered passively as a child at the hands of a father and mother whose own lives were dominated by a perversion of their parenting roles. "Maybe this time it will come out right."

Not every sadomasochistic scenario involves sexual intercourse. Not every sadomasochistic scenario involves physical pain. Practitioners of S and M make a distinction between SM and BD, bondage-discipline. BD, they insist, is the *true essence* of sadomasochism. The giving and receiving of pain is merely a special subheading of the larger drama of dominance and submission:

> "Bondage" means that one person is "submissive" to another who is "dominant," or in more extreme cases he is a "slave" to a "master," or in the most extreme form he is in actual physical bondage: bound, tied up by the other. "Discipline" implies A) that commands are being given by the dominant person to the submissive one who is supposed to obey them, and B) that if he does not obey, or not sufficiently to the master's liking, he will be punished in some way, which fact can be used either as a threat to increase the obedience, or else for the sake of increasing the guilt and punishment itself.

The resemblances between parental discipline of a child and the bondage-discipline scenario are atrociously apparent. The SM parlor, with all its paraphernalia of torture and torment and bondage, is a routinized, stereotyped nursery. In a certain sense, the SM parlor provides a safer and more socialized nursery than the domestic nurseries where real fathers and mothers abuse real children.

When a father or mother is drawn toward a transgression of his or her parenting role, this perversion of parenting tends to take the form of a travesty, a desecration of every fundamental social value. It is an act of violence aimed at the basic structures of the social order. The physical or sexual abuse of a child by a parent is far less about a transfer of erotic desire, an attraction toward a deviant sexuality, than it is an expression of a unconscious, demonic fury aimed at the central structures of the social order. For if in childhood the mother did not protect the child from the father, or the father did not protect the child from the mother, later when the child becomes an adult, it will be society itself that she or he wishes to mutilate and demolish for not having protected her or him from the parent.

The way of life of every human society depends on the responsibility of an adult generation toward a child generation. Humbert Humbert was right that in certain aristocratic societies of "the Ancient World, B.C." these borders between child and adult generations were often violated. In most human societies, though, the father is assigned the role of upholding the moral order and representing in his person this order of the world. The mother is assigned the role of conveying an experience of moral order to her children with a tenderness, mercy, and compassion that will enable the children to leave their Garden of Eden and accept the law of the land, whatever that may be. When a father physically or sexually abuses his children, the lawgiving father is violating the very role assigned to him by his society and he will be regarded and treated as a criminal. When the caregiving and protecting mother abuses her children or looks the other way when the lawgiver abuses her children, she is violating her mothering role and will be regarded and treated as a virago who has violated her sacred duty.

Until recently there was a rule of thumb about fathers' rights. They were allowed to beat their children and wives as long as the instrument of abuse and murder was no thicker than their thumb. While we no longer accept this yardstick of justice and these days are always shocked and horrified when we hear that a father has abused or murdered his child or wife, there is still a lingering prejudice that brutality and sadism are consonant with maleness. We are shocked, yes, but not entirely shaken in our most sacred beliefs. But when a mother abuses or murders her child we are shaken to the roots of our being. We respond to this bestiality the way an abused child responds: "Mother should have protected me." On the surface, our modern societies have allowed a shift in these traditional roles of mother as caregiver and father as lawgiver. But unconsciously, we have not come very far from the view expressed by the prosecutor assigned to the case of the Hummels, the mother and father who in 1899 physically abused and murdered their little Anna. Yes, the prosecutor agreed, by committing so brutal a murder the father had transgressed the laws of his society. But it was the mother's violation of her sacred duty that was the ultimate horror: "Her deed makes a mockery of everything that is holy to human beings; one could almost doubt the omnipotence of mother love."

There is an omnipotence of sorts in the mother-infant relationship. But it is not at all what the Hummels' prosecutor had in mind. The yearning for attachment is the most powerful human force, so powerful that hardly any abuse inflicted on an infant or child can destroy that attachment once it has formed. Once the sparks of love are ignited they are hard to extinguish. When a mother rocks her child, kisses and strokes her, feeds her, bathes her, dresses and undresses her, through the thousand sensuous exchanges of everyday life a child is seduced into living in the world and accepting its laws and values. In a few years, the fantasies that the child begins to invest in those sensuous exchanges will charge them with erotic meaning and excitement. The father's presence in the mother's life will signify to the child that there is a lawfulness mightier than the tender laws of the nursery. As this unwelcome news of a higher moral order, with its insistence on the differences between the sexes and the generations, is gradually assimilated by the reluctant child, the sexual and procreative roles that the child is learning in the family will become central aspects of the way she interprets the social roles of her society. The child, as we know, is only too ready to interpret these adult social roles in an infantile way as clean-dirty, submissive-dominating, castrated-phallic, pure-virile. And if our social order perpetuates these infantile dichotomies, the perversions of parenting in our modern societies will take the form that they customarily do and always have.

When the child is sexually abused by the person she regards as lawgiver, she will defend this representative of the higher moral order with every means her childlike mind can muster. Since she still needs him to protect her, she will be the bad one, the sinner. She will be the transgressor, the one who is guilty of a crime. When boys and girls are physically abused by caregivers, they will defend those icons of mercy and compassion and prefer to think of themselves as the ugly, stupid child who was not worthy of care or tenderness or mercy. Abused children are always looking for someone to absolve them of crime, someone who will make them feel worthy and valuable. When they become parents, they will look to their own children for salvation. If they do not become parents, they will look to their husbands and lovers or their dominating tops in an SM parlor.

There is another force nearly equal to (some would say greater than) the omnipotence of mother-infant love. That force is the omnipotence of rage, of hostile, destructive aggression. Abused children are also always looking for a place to put the rage and fury they suppressed in order to preserve the godlike images of the caregivers and lawgivers on whom their very survival depended. What better way to express this suppressed and therefore volcanic hatred than to disguise it as an act of love! What better way to vent this helpless fury than to make a travesty of virility and purity! The crimes they commit and the perversions they enact as adults will be caricatures of the masculine or feminine virtues or, as in the perversions of parenting, reversals of these prototypes of the good parent—fatherly virility and motherly purity turned into vices. The lawgiving father tramples on the law and desecrates it. The caregiving mother shows no compassion or mercy, defiling everything that is most sacred in her society.

13
Little Soul Murders: Pure Girls and Virile Boys

Upon hearing a tale of soul murder, we react with horror. However, around the globe untold numbers of little soul murders are occurring each minute, not in SM parlors or mental asylums or concentration camps or prisons or the homes of parents who abuse and sexually molest their children, but in conventional and seemingly normal nurseries where all that parents consciously want are properly feminine little girls and properly masculine little boys.

Because children are helpless and utterly dependent on those who care for them, they feel safe, loved, and worthwhile when they are able to conform to the subtle and not so subtle indoctrinations into the gender role stereotypes that their well-meaning parents assume will produce well-adjusted, normal children. With these little touches of soul murder, a child is cut off from some part of his or her personal identity that might have flourished or an emotional response that might have blossomed into joy, nostalgia, concern, gratitude, mercy, compassion, erotic pleasure, passivity, mastery, voluptuousness, sadness, or a capacity to empathize with a person of the opposite sex.

In acquiring her feminine identity, every little girl will be giving up a small or large touch of the qualities, virtues, and talents that are defined in her society as masculine. We can never know what sort of woman she might have become had she been raised in a different social order and a different family structure with different parents. While most of these touches of soul murder are inevitable even in an ideal socialization and will produce some degree of gender conflict within the child, serious and devastating conflicts arise when parents are preoccupied with gender conformity in their children out of a terror of their own cross-gender strivings. What such mothers and fathers produce in their daughters or sons are caricatures of feminine purity and of masculine virility. However, these little soul murders of gender stereotyping are never completely successful, for those aspects of the child that have been repressed and cut off from any expression will continue to seek expression until one day, in adolescence perhaps or in middle age, the smoldering desires will perhaps erupt in a perversion or worse, in madness.

A baby is so ready to be what her mother wants her to be. A mother's trilling voice and glowing eyes tell her baby: "Oh what a beautiful baby you are. You are the best baby. See how my eyes light up when I hold you in my arms." The baby looks deep into the mother's eyes, coos and gurgles in harmony with her voice and sees herself mirrored as all the spectacular and powerful things that a best baby is. From then on, for the sake of sharing in the glory and power of a mirroring other, a baby will surrender something of her self: perhaps merely a touch or just some or a considerable portion of the power of gesture and action with which she was born. From then on, the anxiety of being separated from the mirroring other holds the baby's omnipotence in check, prevents her from running away with herself. Whenever she feels vulnerable, less than she would wish to be, reassurance is at hand. If she is a best baby and doesn't reach out to grab the spoon and mess around with the mushy stuff, if she just opens her mouth and receives the spoon and swallows and coos, the mirroring yes will light up: "What a wonderful baby you are. You are the best baby, the perfect little girl."

Anorexia is the outcome of one of those little soul murders of childhood in which, to survive, a child gives up aspects of the self she might have become and instead becomes a mirroring extension of the all-powerful other on whom her life depended. By the middle of the nineteenth century doctors were beginning to notice that many of the young women brought to their consultation rooms were starving to death. They had been the best babies, the perfect little girls, but now at puberty they were driving their mothers and fathers crazy and making them suffer the anguish of watching helplessly as their precious child wasted away. Most of these young women were the daughters of solid, prosperous upper-middle-class parents and came from homes where there was no shortage of food or love or attention. Yet the girls seemed to have no appetite and were dying of malnutrition. None of the boys in these families were similarly afflicted, and the other daughters were chubby, rosy, and contented with life.

The disorder was first given its label, *anorexia,* loss of appetite, by Ernest Laseque in France in 1873 and by Sir William Gull in England in 1874. Gull stressed the nervous anxiety that accompanied the loss of appetite—hence *anorexia nervosa.* Laseque thought of the disorder as a variety of hysteria, another typically female disorder, and called the disorder *anorexie hystérique.* Some years later, another French physician, Henri Huchard, discounted the hysterical origins and recommended the more inclusive label *anorexie mentale,* the term by which the disorder has been known ever since in Italy and France. In Germany the disorder is referred to as *Pubertatsmagersucht*—compulsive pubertal emaciation. The Germans have the right idea. Anorexia implies a failure of appetite, but the disorder actually has to do with compulsive self-starvation. The girls and women who are afflicted are preoccupied with eating, recipes, and food preparation and are hungry all the time.

Prior to the mid-nineteenth century there were only sporadic, isolated descriptions of illnesses resembling anorexia—a thirteenth-century monk, a sixteenth-century princess. In the twentieth century, as more and more cases came to their attention, physicians and psychologists were frustrated by their inability to solve the enigmas of this bizarre disorder. Because the doctors were focusing their attention on the most obvious and dramatic feature of the anorexia syndrome— eating or not eating—their theories concentrated on the "oral" components of the disorder. It took several decades for doctors to get to the deceptions that were hidden beneath the surface of the anorexia strategy, which, as we will see, uses the cover story of a conscious preoccupation with eating and appetite, *Fresslust,* as a disguise for unconscious genital lusts. And then, only in the 1980s did a few doctors begin to suspect that this typically female disorder might be a perversion.

While the doctors were figuring out how to classify and label this disorder, it got around that some 15 percent of anorectics died of starvation, and this fact, because it increased the anxieties of anorectics' families and their doctors, contributed to the blurring of everyone's vision about the underlying meaning of the refusal to eat and compulsive emaciation. When someone you love or care for is dying right before your eyes, you don't bother to worry about underlying meanings. When that someone is starving to death, you force-feed her by mouth or nasogastric tubes; you give her insulin therapy designed to bring on sweating, dizziness, anxiety, and eventually hunger; you coax her to swallow chlorpromazine to reduce her fear of eating; you anesthetize her so you can perform neurosurgery on her brain, the leucotomy that gets her to eat but turns her into a bulimic, a secret binger–vomiter. Through all this the anorectic is unconsciously victorious, for to her these mortifications of her flesh are a collaboration with her unconscious perverse scenario.

As psychologists became familiar with the details of the separation-individuation process, the mother-infant relationship began to be thought of as the key that would unlock the secrets of anorexia. Some were claiming that the anorectic is a girl who was unable during infancy to separate successfully from her mother. Now, at pubescence or puberty, when faced with the necessity to detach from her mother, she cannot imagine any existence away from the mother's mirroring eyes. This longing for oneness with the mother makes it impossible for the girl to engage the conflicts of adolescence. Other psychologists focused on the love-hate struggle between the anorectic and her family, especially the mutual ambivalence between daughter and mother. They said that the girl has regressed to the rapprochement subphase of separation; she clings to the mother and yet struggles to be free of her, much like a toddler in the throes of rapprochement.

Certainly there is some merit to these interpretations of the infantile etiology and ongoing dynamics of the anorexia syndrome. However, these well-meaning interpretations can and frequently do obscure the essential fact that anorexia is a solution to the dilemmas associated with becoming a woman. The anorectic is not an infant struggling with issues of separation-individuation but an adolescent or adult woman struggling to come to terms with genitality and female gender identity. The deception that she is only an innocent child struggling with infantile conflicts, a saint lacking in all sexual desires or shameful lusts of the body, is central to the anorectic's perverse strategy. The anorectic presents herself to the world as a sexless child in a caricature of saintlike femininity. Behind her caricature of an obedient, virtuous, clean, submissive, good little girl is a most defiant, ambitious, driven, dominating, controlling, virile caricature of masculinity. Although her mother consciously wanted a perfect good little girl, in her very determination to stamp out rebellion and active sexual striving, she was also communicating to her daughter her own repressed intellectual and sexual strivings, which throughout her own childhood and adolescence and adulthood she had been regarding as forbidden masculine wishes.

And it is these unconscious wishes of her mother that the anorectic is now symbolically enacting and granting to her, with a vengeance.

From a retrospective point of view, that is, from the patient's remembrances, her parents' reports, and the fantasies that come up during therapy, the picture of childhood that consistently emerges is that of the intelligent, compliant baby girl who all too easily and willingly surrendered her omnipotence, aggression, autonomy, independence, and rebelliousness for the safety and self-esteem of becoming a narcissistic extension of Mother. Yet from a prospective view, looking ahead from infancy to adolescence, no sensible clinical observer would predict from observations of a girl's relationship to her mother during infancy and childhood an anorectic solution to the dilemmas of adolescence.

As with any perversion or any other mental strategy, the origin or primary etiology of anorexia can explain very little except to say, that's probably how it all began. In biological organisms, no matter how lowly, where or how that organism begins its existence does not determine absolutely what that organism will be at maturity. The higher a plant or animal is on the *scala natura* and the longer its maturing process, the more opportunity the environment has to alter the initial or early shape of that organism. The human child is always growing and developing in new and often surprising ways, and her environment is always changing and eliciting new responses from her. That is why we are always surprised that some children from the worst imaginable childhood homes manage to overcome their traumas and lead relatively free and independent adult lives, whereas children whose infancy and early childhood were "idyllic" may succumb to severe mental disorders in adolescence and adulthood.

The typical anorectic *probably* was one of those perfect good little girls. Still, not every perfect good little girl who is subjected to the little soul murder of having to be a mirroring extension of the mother becomes an anorectic. In the intervening years, changes in the family's emotional constellation—the birth of another child, the father becoming a more active participant in the household, the mother's melancholic reaction to the death of her own mother, a move to a new neighborhood, the father's loss of professional prestige—and, most important, the flourishing during latency and early pubescence of temperamental, artistic, and intellectual qualities dormant during the infantile period can have the effect of alleviating, modifying, potentiating, or exacerbating the pathogenic possibilities set in motion by the little soul murders of infancy.

To return once again to my crochet needle analogy of human development, we know that adolescence is one of those crucial junctures of a life history that impel a reaching back to the infantile past. During the adolescent years when the body is changing rapidly and dramatically, a once sexually immature girl is noticing each day new signs that she is about to become a woman—just like her mother. Very soon she will no longer be a child who is excluded from the secrets and mysteries of genitality. She will be a member of an adult generation with the sexual and moral responsibilities of an adult. In her efforts to come to terms with her own sexuality, every young woman is reevaluating and taking stock of her parents' sexual life. It is in this adolescent striving to reevaluate and revise the past that the pathology of the anorectic's infantile relationships with her parents becomes apparent. A little girl who gathers all her self-esteem from believing that she is a mirroring extension of her mother will find it particularly difficult to tolerate the idea that her mother is a sexual being who experiences desire for the father. Until she is forced to notice the physical changes taking place in and on the surface of her own body, she has been able to disavow that males have the genital parts that excite desire in females, that females have the genital parts that excite desire in males. With her sexless, gender-ambiguous body and with her ghastly, off-putting emaciation, the anorectic mocks the power of adult sexuality.

As the conjugator of childhood and adulthood, adolescence is always a battleground on which the past and future contend for the soul of the individual. With the anorectic, the necessity to integrate genital functioning into one's gender identity induces a profound regression that arrests the individual in the past, blocking any potential movements into adulthood. If the biological changes of pubescence had not taken place, the dormant illness of infancy might not have revealed itself. If it were not for the psychological trials of adolescence, we might never have known that this best of all little girls, provided with every advantage by her consciously well intentioned family, had been subjected to a little soul murder and had been deprived of the authenticity of her being.

Until her changing body forced her to negotiate the dilemmas entailed in growing up from childhood to adulthood, the pathology in the anorectic's infantile history barely showed. In fact, as her parents were proud of announcing to everyone, she was good, clean, neat, polite, well behaved, delicate, cheerful and charming, smart in a dutiful, obedient way, but never challenging or controversial—the perfect feminine type.

Onset of anorexia in females is virtually nonexistent before the age of eleven. And although older women may become anorectic when their babies go to school or their husbands leave them or their mothers die, initial onset of anorexia is infrequent in women over twenty-five. Since babyhood the girl predisposed to anorexia has been relatively precocious in her physical and intellectual development. Pubescence and menarche are likely to commence about one or two years earlier than the average. Whether her pubescence begins early at age ten or late at age fourteen, the potential anorectic is not an anorectic until she tries to cope with the dilemmas of becoming a sexually active woman.

One of the first things that happens by the time the anorectic has lost 30 percent of her normal body weight is that her menstrual cycles either never begin or stop altogether. Then, after almost all the fat around her hips, thighs, and abdomen has vanished, the bones of her pubic region will protrude prominently. Then, because of the hormonal imbalances set in motion by starvation, her arms and legs and face and chest will be covered with downy hair. The hirsute, masculine, phallic look is not distressing to the anorectic, who now secretly cultivates in herself all the rebelliously active, phallic, masculine characteristics she had lost in herself on her way to becoming the perfect, virtuous, best little girl in the world.

One woman who eventually recovered recalled the very moment she had arrived at perfection. The force feedings and the chlorpromazine had failed to cure her and even encouraged her rebellion and heightened her erotic longings. She was on the brink of death. She didn't care anymore what her parents or her doctors thought about the state of her mind or the appearance of her body. She needed only her own mirror to reflect back the perfection she had been striving for and had finally achieved. "I got my wish to be a third sex, both girl and boy. Standing in front of the mirror, I saw a lovely attractive woman. My other self, the body outside the mirror, was a lusting young man preparing to seduce the girl in the mirror. I was having a love affair with myself."

It used to be completely acceptable for females to remain in a state of childlike dependency for their entire lives. Proper girls were not expected to know too much about the differences between the sexes. Only males and fallen women were supposed to be interested in sexual pleasure. The term *youth* was reserved for males, and only males were burdened with the dilemmas of growing up into adulthood. If she could have remained in the never-never land of childhood, this dutiful girl might have turned out to be a child-bride who satisfied her ambitions by acting the role of the efficient but scatterbrained female her husband required as wife so that he could be the strong, independent, smart, heroic male. She could have grown charmingly chubby from the joys of preparing dinners and having babies. Or she could have become a model citizen of a utopian society—a nunnery, a commune, a collective farm. There she would have enthusiastically accepted the drab uniform and number assigned to her. She would have flourished on the regimentation. Her excessive ambition to be a perfect good little girl could have been satisfied by obeying the rules better than anyone else. Her bodily mortifications, saintly asceticism, or puritanical self-sacrifice would have been a perfect disguise for her forbidden sexual lusts.

Like most upper- and middle-class adolescent girls growing up into womanhood in a Western society during the last half of the twentieth century, the potential anorectic has been granted permission to use her talents, to advance her intellectual ambitions, to do everything that a human being is meant to do in the course of a lifetime. She has been given license to pursue her sexual desires in any way she sees fit with any person she deems desirable. For most girls and boys, this sudden newfound freedom is frightening, a little too much to manage, a little too soon to assimilate without considerable conflict. But erotic and moral freedom is terrifying for a best little girl whose morality before adolescence was based on absolute obedience and submissions to exacting rules and regulations.

The onset of pubescence drove the girl out of her well-run, orderly, harmonious, smothering domestic cocoon. Once outside the cocoon, on a bicycle trip through Europe, during her first months in a new high school, on her way to college, the terror set in. She was going to have to separate from her parents and in the process become an independent, sexually functioning adult. All this was going to mean giving up her cherished unconscious fantasy that there were no real differences between the sexes or the child and parent generations. Now that the unwelcome news was forcing itself on her and she could no longer hide from the challenges of becoming an adult woman, what could she do? How could she suddenly acknowledge that sex counted for something, when all along she had been repeating to herself and to everyone else that she had abolished desire and longing.

The way that the parents of the anorectic behave toward one another help to perpetuate the infantile fantasy that there is no difference between the sexes. The father of the anorectic seems to care a great deal more about his job and position in the world than about sex. The mother seems to care only about her household and darling children.

The fathers of anorectic girls are usually fiercely ambitious in their professional roles and astonishingly passive and emotionally unavailable at home: "Oh, you better ask my wife about that. She takes care of feelings." These fathers expect polished performances from their children and wives but are content to let their wives rule the roost and dominate the trivialities of emotions and to mop up the untidinesses of the nursery. There is no sign anywhere of a desire between the parents.

A further confusion comes from the failure of the parents to make clear the differences between the child and adult generations. In fact, they have done their best to obscure those differences, if not with all their children, then certainly with the girl who becomes anorectic. In the family system that produces anorexia, the parents have enlisted this child as the third party in *their* marital life. It is she that stands between them. Because of their terror of their forbidden and shameful cross-gender strivings, mother and father have been unable to enjoy any sexual life together or to resolve the sexual tensions between them. When this perfect little girl comes along, she is a solution to their sexual dilemmas. First, as a little girl she is encouraged to believe that she is her mother's "everything" and that all her father cares about is maintaining order and getting ahead in business. Now as she arrives at adolescence and her body is changing into a functioning sexual body, the sight, merely the thought, of her budding breasts and her menstruation rekindles in her parents their erotic fantasies. That is, these fantasies would be stirred up if there was not something very dramatic going on in the family to distract them. The whole family therefore colludes in the fiction that the girl's problem is hunger, *Fresslust*, or the absence of it. She comes to the rescue of her parents now by focusing her parents' attention on her eating problems. Now nobody in the family has to acknowledge her sexuality or theirs.

Both parents are terrified, in their own ways, of unruly sexual and aggressive desires. Like Flaubert's Monsieur and Madame Homais, the anorectic's father and mother wish only "to eradicate, to forcibly conventionalize or to imprison whatever presumes to exist outside those categories and norms." The anorectic's brother might recite the multi-plication table backward and forward, and her sister might make pretty designs for her father to hang on the wall of his office. But both parents, more than either of them consciously realizes, have chosen this child as the one who must achieve perfection in all things—multiplica-tion and artistic designs and everything else. For her father she must be the A or A+ student who follows all the rules and memorizes all the dates and equations. For her mother she is to mirror the perfect little girl who obeys and never does anything wrong. For both parents, then, this chosen girl gets the rewards of love and admiration from her ability to follow rules and control her desires. What is such a girl to do when she arrives at puberty and every sight, sound, and movement reminds of her of sexual desire?

The *bête noire* of the anorectic is her awakening erotic longing. If her desires were to surface, the entire family would be destroyed. There is a solution. Perhaps if there were *no* desire in the self . . . ? Perhaps the physical body with its cravings so constantly excited by the phenomenal world could be mortified or obliterated? With her all-consuming interest in eating and not-eating, the anorectic is pretending that the last things on her mind are sex and genitals. This holier than thou, self-abnegating child is far too virtuous to entertain erotic thoughts or feelings. Since her parents denied their desire and strenu-ously hid any clue as to what those adult genitals were all about, as a child she was always wondering what went on between her parents. She knew that for all her perfection, her body was small and insignifi-cant compared to their bodies and she was as mortified as any child by these inescapable indications of her ineffectuality. She knew that her genital immaturity was excluding her from something. But in the absence of all signs of desire, what could that be? She participated in this mysterious primal scene by peeking at, staring at, scrutinizing her parents' bodies and wondering what the mighty giants did or did not do with those bodies.

Now as an adolescent, she reverses the direction of the arrow of desire. Now that she is starving, every day, everyone is peeking at, staring at, scrutinizing her body and and wondering whether or not she will or will not succumb to desire. Though her parents deny any interest in bodies, they are always looking at her body. The army of medical specialists summoned to cure her are always undressing her and examining her every body part. Everyone is preoccupied with how thin or fat her body looks and whether or not she has eaten. Even her therapist, who knows the vital importance of scrutinizing the fantasy life that motivates the girl's self-starvation, is seduced into caring more about whether she eats or doesn't eat and is always scrutinizing her emaciated body. The anorectic no longer envies the parents for their power over her. She no longer envies her therapist for having the power to cure. It is not she who desires and envies them. It is they who desire her. It is they who envy her for her power to humiliate and defeat them. Yes, she has reduced even her therapist to envy. The anorectic knows it and her therapist, if she is honest with herself, will acknowledge that she too is capable of infantile reactions. That way the therapist gets to know personally the bitter envy that motivates her patient's self-starvation. In everyday life the anorectic is experiencing herself as ineffectual and unable to live up to the expectations of her parents, her teachers, her friends, her therapist. But through her performance as a hunger artist the anorectic achieves immense power.

Anorexia is the best little girl's Academy Award performance. The audience is horrified yet spellbound, which in turn produces in the hunger artist a delusion of omnipotence. From the girl's point of view she is the consummate artist. The longer the illness lasts, the more self-absorbed the girl becomes. She is on the alert, on the go, sleeping only one or two hours a night. She is dizzy, faint with elation, exalted with the sense of her absolute attunement to the world around her. In her mystical unity with her physical surroundings the girl needs no others. She has reached a transcendental peak. The high that she now gets from her near-starvation and ceaseless physical movement is like a jolt of morphine. "You feel outside your body. You are truly beside yourself

—and then you are in a different state of consciousness and you can undergo pain without reacting. That's what I did with hunger."

Theologians are familiar with the moral excesses of physical ecstasies based on pain. They know of the spiritual delusions of the starving state and its sexual undertones. "The awareness of spiritual power is increased and with it the danger of losing sight of what is assigned to each one of us, the limits of our finite existence, of our dignity and our abilities. Hence the dangers of pride, magic, and spiritual intoxication." One of the trials of sainthood is to learn to distinguish between a true spiritual ecstasy and an earthly intoxication. And it is easy to confuse these states of mind, for in a spiritual ecstasy the saintly one believes that she or he is achieving a union with an almighty one who is referred as Beloved, Bride, Bridegroom, the Heavenly Breast. Even a casual reading of the lives of saints will reveal that the ecstasies of self-mortification can be employed as an avenue of expression for a forbidden sexual life.

Teresa of Avila struggled her entire life to distinguish between a genuine saintly rapture and what she deemed a "spiritual gluttony." As a novice she was compelled to extravagant self-mortification and as a nun took her inspiration from *The Song of Songs* and wrote of the nun's bridelike passion for the heavenly Bridegroom as a sort of divine intoxication, "a heavenly inebriation by which she is delighted and terrified at the same time. . . . Oh, thy breasts are better than wine." When she became Mother Teresa, she warned the sisters about the difference between *arrobamiento,* ecstasy, and *abobamiento,* a silly stupor, an exhibitionistic imposture that simply ruins the health and makes a mockery of the serious work of God. One of Teresa's prioresses observed to a lay sister who was constantly advertising her ecstasies, "We don't need you here for your raptures, but for washing the dishes."

The high of the anorectic's fasting state is an imposturous ecstasy, and her emaciation is not a victory over the passions of the body but an exhibitionistic display of these passions. The anorectic's self-mortification is her pride, her dubious triumph over the almighty ones who would have squelched in her every trace of mastery and rebellion. In her defiant self-starvation she is at last true to herself, to her inner voices, to the powers she surrendered in order to be a best little girl.

However, when the anorectic finally arrives at the altered state of consciousness brought on by the high of constant movement and starvation, she is once again the perfect little baby reunited with her almighty mother, her heavenly breast. "What a beautiful baby you are. See how my eyes light up when I hold you in my arms." But now, of course, she is not a baby anymore. All through childhood she went along with the family fiction that there is no desire, and now at adolescence her hirsute, fleshless, gender-ambiguous body is supposed to be a proof of this absence of earthly passions. But with all this fiction of no desire, the anorectic is plainly an adolescent with the awakening erotic desires of an adolescent, which always include an unconscious erotic longing for the parent of the same sex. So for all its saintliness, this baby-mother reunion is a disguised erotic union—of sorts. In the defiance of her hunger artistry, which has seduced the entire world to stare at her body with envy, the anorectic has granted the concealed masculine desires of the omnipotent one upon whom her survival depended and thereby seduced her conscience into granting an incestuous wish—and all under the cover of a saintly, good little girl, feminine perfection. Having always been the third party that stood between her parents and their desire, she had understood that the way to glory and perfection was through the fiction of being her mother's "everything." And by hook or crook, by death itself if necessary, she will render unto her mother the perfection she has been longing for and in that way be allowed to remain tied to her mother's apron strings forever.

In these confusing matters of God's ways, His mysterious order of the world, which we in our modern enlightenment call conscience, Daniel Paul Schreber, the head judge of the highest court of Dresden, is a guide worthy of every intricacy of the perverse strategy. Adolescence is *one* phase of life that inevitably impels a reaching back to revise the past. Marriage, parenthood, the death of a parent, middle age, the arrival at the time of life when procreation becomes an impossibility are other critical junctures in a life history that brings the past into the present, sometimes bringing with it new opportunities, fresh possibilities, a sudden burst of vigor, different and better interpretations of one's life history. However, sometimes at these critical junctures, the infantile traumas and little soul murders of childhood, which up till then had not prevented the living out of a fairly peaceful, even productive, successful way of life, press forward to claim the soul that had been so cleverly eluding the forces of justice. At these crucial moments in the life cycle, some parts of the self that had been suppressed in the interests of mental harmony and social adjustment begin to rebel and to stir up a cataclysmic disruption of the person's sense of identity and selfhood. One of the facets of the self that is challenged and brought up for revision during these moments of life crisis are the feminine and masculine gender identifications that were arrived at, without any seemingly exceptional conflict, during childhood and adolescence.

Daniel Paul Schreber, the younger son of Dr. Schreber, became a mental patient at Sonnenstein Asylum who was behaving like a howling infant one day and a mute fetus the next. Schreber, now a respected and eminent judge, invented for himself mental torments that only an immensely brilliant, law-abiding adult intimate with the fine points of corruption and justice could have invented. Nevertheless, he was still less than a child in some respects. In three different years, Judge Schreber was admitted to a mental hospital in November, very close to the exact date of his father's death. There is no question that the events that precipitated his first mental illness, a severe hypochondriasis, and the subsequent two attacks of a paranoid psychosis were connected directly to his ambivalent relationship to his father. The form of his bodily illnesses and the content of his hallucinations and delusions reflected the treatment he had received from that godlike father.

The first illness, hypochondriasis and an intractable insomnia, was precipitated by losing an election to public office and then being further humiliated by the press reports of his defeat: "Who has heard of Schreber?" Schreber recovered from that illness relatively quickly, within a year, and afterward lived in peace and contentment with his wife for eight more years. He described those happy years as rich in worldly honors "and marred only, from time to time by the repeated disappointment of our hope of being blessed with children." Though he and his beautiful wife had sexual intercourse, she had several miscarriages and Schreber was unable to become a father. The second illness, the one described in Schreber's *Memoirs,* began in late 1893 and was still in progress nine years later. During his last year of confinement, 1902, Judge Schreber had recovered enough of his sanity to enable him to compose a plea that he be released from the asylum. He was able to convince the court that he was competent to manage his own affairs. No doubt the writing of his *Memoirs,* which he began in 1900, helped considerably toward the restoration of Schreber's capacity to participate in life outside the asylum.

This second, and most devastating, illness *seemed* to begin on October 1, 1893, when Schreber had reached the age of fifty-one and was nearing the anniversary of his father's death at the age of fifty-three in November 1861. He had just assumed his position as Senatspräsident of the court of appeals in Dresden. The burden of this very impressive professional responsibility was made all the heavier and "demanded all the more tact in my personal dealings with the members of the panel of five Judges over which I had to preside as almost all of them were much senior to me (up to twenty years)." Schreber was given this awesome assignment of being in charge of these father figures just as he was trying to reconcile to the fact that he was incapable of fatherhood. The combination of circumstances aroused all the demons of his past and plunged Schreber into a profound psychosis. For the first few years in the asylum, the eminent Judge Schreber was so antisocial, violent, and destructive that he had to be confined to a padded cell at night and accompanied by three attendants during his afternoon walks through the asylum gardens, and he had to be forcibly fed. He was mute and immobile for long periods, repeatedly attempted suicide, suffered from unbearable insomnia, and was massively hallucinated and deluded about his body and his surroundings. This delusional state lasted for five years, until at last Schreber began to grasp the higher purpose of his mental torments.

Schreber resumed contact with the outer world in the guise of a transvestite. His recovery began when he began to think of himself as a voluptuous woman who was destined to be impregnated by God. Finally, the delusions and hallucinations of paranoia that had acted as a screen for the unconscious feminine wishes were replaced by a delusional transvestism. Fantasies that had been less acceptable and less available to Judge Daniel Paul Schreber's consciousness were freed— among them the wish to be a voluptuous woman with a womb ready to be impregnated by the Father.

A psychosis is often a screen for forbidden cross-gender wishes. On the other hand, a perversion, which always gives some expression to these forbidden wishes, is often the safety valve that prevents or at least minimizes the torment of outright madness. Moreover, how much more pleasurable it is to yield to perversion than to sink forever into the depths of madness. Schreber's recovery from utter madness could begin only when he found his safety valve, which was to allow his long-repressed, shameful feminine sexual wishes into consciousness. If the transvestite solution did not altogether heal Schreber's crippled soul or cure his psychosis, at least it brought to an end the worst of Schreber's torments. And this Schreber understood very well. As he put it, he was "faced with the choice of either becoming a demented human being in male habitus or a woman of spirit." Schreber decided on the latter and argued that it would be hard to imagine a reasonable man deciding otherwise. Once reconciled to the advantages of his exceptional femininity, Schreber improved and left the hospital protected by his unshakable conviction that his personal "unmanning" could now serve the higher purpose of the preservation of the species.

Out of the "absurd relations" between himself and God, Schreber had, at last, found a middle course.

Until the perverse strategy came to his rescue, Schreber endured seven years of mental torment in the mental asylum, trying to remain the manly, upright citizen his father had trained him to be. But right from the beginning of his stay at Sonnenstein, God's rays had mocked him by addressing him as "Miss Schreber." As those words were spoken in the demeaned "feminine" language of English, and in German had the connotation of "misshapen," Schreber's humiliation was devastating. During the first five years Schreber experienced only the ignominy of his threatened and imminent unmanning. Unmanning meant that his body might be sexually abused. Initially he had the conscious fantasy that his body was to be transformed into a female body and then left lying around for sexual misuse by his doctors and God's rays and afterward simply forsaken, left to rot. The Doctor Flechsig who was in charge of his treatment had become his new father-god. Schreber thought he was being tied to his bed with his clothes removed to make him more susceptible to the voluptuous sensations of womanhood. These sensations would be stimulated in him by the female nerves, which he imagined had already started to enter his body. He resisted the nerves of voluptuousness that were penetrating his body in great masses. He barked and bellowed and tried other devices to suppress the feminine impulses that these nerves were arousing in him. He enlisted every sense of manly honor. However, try as he might, the "soul voluptuousness" would get its way—especially when Schreber was lying in bed.

After a while the process of Schreber's fantasized unmanning was no longer merely imminent. It proceeded methodically and seemed to operate independently of the other tormenting miracles that were inflicted on his body. Schreber could feel his male organs retracting and softening. At times the softening approached a complete dissolution. Every day, somehow, a few more hairs from his beard and mustache would disappear. Owing to a contracting of the vertebrae and thigh bone, Schreber's entire stature was shrinking to female size. Despite his resistance, the soul voluptuousness was becoming so strong that he received the impression of a female body on his legs, bosom, and other parts. His internal sexual organs were being transformed into female sexual organs.

After a week or so of these imagined bodily changes Schreber's understanding of what his unmanning meant in the order of the world altered. "It was *common sense* that nothing was left but to reconcile myself to the thought of being transformed into a woman." What else could be envisaged as a further consequence of his unmanning? Nothing more nor less than fertilization by divine rays for the purpose of creating new human beings. The rays' contemptuous remarks no longer bothered him. "Fancy a person who as Senatspräsident allows himself to be f——d."

Now that he no longer felt compelled to deny his feminine strivings, Schreber proclaimed that he "wholeheartedly inscribed the cultivation of femininity on my banner." As he was preparing his release from Sonnenstein, Schreber carried his banner high and was arrogant about asserting his femininity before his fellow lawmakers. He insisted that he be allowed to exhibit his body for medical examination to prove his new feminine status. Schreber seemed to know just where a woman experienced her voluptuousness. He joyously asserted that his whole body was at last filled entirely with nerves of voluptuousness, "from the top of my head to the soles of my feet as is the case only in the adult female body, whereas in the case of a man, as far as I know, nerves of voluptuousness are only found in and immediately around the sexual organs."

As Schreber perceived it, the top half of his body, when it was naked, gave the decided impression of a female trunk, especially when he heightened the illusion by wearing feminine adornments. He could feel certain string of cordlike structures under his chest "where the woman's bosom is." These cords ended in nodular tissues, which were the nerves with which God's rays had filled him, the erotic female nerves in which lay the essence of divine creation.

Having accepted his perverse solution, Schreber loved to prance about his room half-naked. He stood in front of the mirror in a very low-cut vest decorated with gaily colored ribbons, gazing at his female bosom. He enjoyed himself by looking at pictures of naked women. He drew pictures of female nudes. He shaved off his mustache. He used every opportunity to cultivate his femininity. He bought sewing material and female toilet articles and took great pleasure in feminine occupations such as sewing, dusting, making beds, scrubbing his chamber, cleansing his body. His feminine longings increased. "If only I could always be playing the woman's part in sexual embrace with myself, always rest my gaze on female beings, always look at pictures of females." By the time Schreber began to write his *Memoirs,* his wishes for impregnation by God were coming true. The soul voluptuousness that had infiltrated his entire body had given him a readiness to conceive and be pregnant. The new life to come would grant to Schreber a state of *Kinderseligkeit,* Schreber's neologism for child-blessedness. He was almost certain that twice he had had a female genital organ, "although a poorly developed one" and on two occasions he was able to feel the quickening, the first signs of life of a human embryo. "By divine miracles, God's nerves, corresponding to male seed, had been thrown into my body." Fertilization had occurred. It was only a matter of time before Schreber would bless the world with God's child.

Schreber, no doubt, was familiar with the *fin de siècle* morality. It was unacceptable to the Senatspräsident that he would be unmanned, turned into a woman, merely to enjoy sexual intercourse. If not accompanied by fertilization, the unmanning would have meant that he had been given a female body for sexual purposes and sexual abuse only. Moreover, it was God who demanded *"constant enjoyment."* Schreber saw it as his duty "to provide Him with it in the form of highly developed soul-voluptuousness. . . . If I can get a little sensuous pleasure in this process, I feel I am entitled to it as a small compensation for the excess of suffering that has been mine for many years past."

> I must point out that when I speak of my duty to cultivate voluptuousness I never mean any sexual desires towards other human beings (females) least of all sexual intercourse, but that I have to imagine myself as a man and woman in one person having intercourse with myself or somehow to achieve with myself a certain sexual excitement which perhaps under other circumstances may be considered immoral but which has nothing whatever to do with any idea of masturbation or anything like it.

This cultivation of his femininity was Daniel Paul's triumph over the soul murders of his childhood and a fitting memorial to his father. Only now, as his sanity was partially restored, did Schreber remember how it had all begun. He recollected that it was not just the fact of being incapable of fatherhood or being elected to a high office with awesome responsibilities that had driven him mad. More frightening than these facts were the awful fantasies and shameful longings that these midlife crises had awakened in him. It was the return of the feminine longings he had managed to repress since childhood that had plunged Daniel Paul Schreber into his terrifying psychosis.

He recalled that one morning, soon after he was appointed to the highest office that a lawmaker might aspire to, while still in bed, half-asleep, half-awake, a peculiar sensation came over him. The sensation was accompanied by the thought "It really must be so lovely to be a woman succumbing to intercourse." The delusional world that Schreber erected to protect himself from this horrifying thought represented his frantic quest for a virility that would be spotless, untouched by feminine desire. "This idea was so foreign to my whole nature that I may say I would have rejected it with indignation if fully awake." How could such an idea have come to a Senatspräsident, a man who was happily married to a lovely woman, an upright man whose life was rich in worldly honors?

If we put together what we know about the common fantasies of childhood with Schreber's later delusions, we might reconstruct a general picture of the childhood fantasies that laid the groundwork for his adult mental torments. Not unlike most men, when he was a little boy Daniel Paul must have every once in a while wished to be in the position of his mother and have the father do to him whatever it was he was doing to his mother. Moreover, it was far too humiliating to think that his adorable mother, Paulina, might experience sexual desire for the grand Dr. Schreber, that she might desire the god of the nursery more than she desired her dear little Daniel Paul. Much more satisfying to conjure away the thought of his parents' mutual sexual excitement. Much better to imagine a passive mother submitting to a violent, aggressive father who demanded constant enjoyment. This is a common enough strategy for salvaging the self-esteem of a humiliated little boy who has been excluded from the parental bedroom. But in Daniel Paul's case, the behaviors of his actual mother and father and the prevailing gender mythologies in mid-nineteenth-century Germany exacerbated and perpetuated this common childhood fantasy of the succumbing mother and dominating father.

Throughout Daniel Paul's childhood, his father demanded absolute erectness, bodily firmness, and sexual cleanliness. Schreber's absolute surrender to his almighty father and Paulina's inability to protect her boy from the godlike physician, orthopedist, educator she worshiped made it impossible for the boy to bring his feminine strivings into harmony with a masculine identity. There was no place in his father's cult of virility for anything weak, childish, or feminine. And though she was a devoted mother, there was no place either in Paulina's concept of good mothering for disobedience to the rule of the father. The only solution for little Daniel Paul Schreber was to submit to his soul murder and try very hard to erase all traces of soul voluptuousness.

In his fifty-first year, with the psychotic regression that followed on the heels of the thought "It would be so lovely to be a woman succumbing," every thought and feeling that had been so ruthlessly stamped out by his father returned with a fury. Like all his bodily weaknesses and childish inclinations, Daniel Paul's femininity had remained as a pocket of rankling desire, a pollution on his soul, smoldering until at last it flared up to haunt him, forcing its voluptuousness into his body, as if from the outside world, through the medium of God's rays. Perhaps these forbidden feminine longings could have remained relatively silent, insinuating their presence in other, less threatening ways—disguised in certain weakenings of the body—like the insomnia and imaginary illnesses Schreber suffered during his first nervous breakdown or like the tension headaches, ulcers, and back troubles that afflict all those men (and women) who hold back tenderness, tears, and softness. Perhaps the unconscious wish to be fucked like a woman was already being expressed in Schreber's suspiciousness toward his rivals, in those fleeting notions that there were plots against him, in his tendency to doubt and a certain paralysis of the will. However, with Schreber, the crises of middle age had incited his imprisoned feminine longings to a state of murderous rebellion. Anything might happen if his fellow judges discovered his weaknesses. What might these father figures do to him when they discovered his impotence, the proof of his lack of virility? Poor Schreber would require more devious strategies than imaginary illnesses or headaches. Schreber reentered the asylum where he had gone for the first cure of his hypochondriasis. He resumed his treatments with Dr. Flechsig, who responded immediately with a sleep cure that only increased Schreber's suspicions that Flechsig was plotting against him, trying to lower his resistance in order to sexually abuse his body.

Three months later, after having successfully resisted Flechsig's plot to put him to sleep and penetrate his body, an event occurred that would precipitate Schreber's final descent into hell. "Decisive for my mental collapse was one particular night; during that night I had a quite unusual number of pollutions (perhaps half a dozen)." What was the masturbating judge to do? Was he not a traitor to his father's tireless campaign to eradicate masturbation? Had not his father declared that only "incessant vigilance" on the part of parents and teachers could stamp out "this insidious plague of youth . . . which makes the unfortunate stupid and dumb, fed up with life, overly disposed to sickness, vulnerable to countless diseases of the lower abdomen and to diseases of the nervous system, and very soon makes them impotent as well as sterile?" For his seditious pollutions, Schreber would surely be punished in the worst possible way. Surely castration was the only just punishment for such heinous crimes. And perhaps God might abandon him forever. After the night of Schreber's several pollutions, the visitations and communications with the tormenting supernatural powers began and never let up. And as his father had predicted, the pollutions initiated the first phase of Schreber's unmanning, his miraculous transformation into a woman.

Eventually, Schreber found the perfect way to bring his lowly and despicable feminine strivings into harmony with the higher commands of God. Now God would never leave him. God's rays would continue to torment him by dissolving his inner organs, forcing him to eat his own gizzard, preventing him from relieving himself, compressing his chest, squashing his vertebrae and skull, always with the implied threat of turning him over to the sexual abuses of Dr. Flechsig. But on that misty November morning when the pollutions gave Schreber his first inklings of the true purpose of his unmanning, these slight "inconveniences" no longer worried him. It was God's will. Still later he realized that God *demanded* of him that he must strive to give the "impression of a woman in the height of sexual delight." God *demanded* his right to "constant enjoyment," and it was Schreber's duty to provide Him with the most highly developed form of soul voluptuousness. Now that Schreber had realized the higher purpose of his voluptuousness, he could grant himself at night after the main meal and in the early morning upon awakening a full experience of sensuous well-being, erotic pleasure, onanistic release. Since Schreber's voluptuous-

ness now served the blessedness of motherhood, a twice-daily masturbation was not disgraceful. Armed with his holy mission, Schreber
would stand proudly before his fellow lawmakers and the medical
authorities to announce his transformation into a woman. The grandeur of being God's woman put on earth to perpetuate the species was
more than ample compensation for the shame of being transformed
into a voluptuous, sexually excited woman. At last, after a lifetime of
suppression, the errant and mischievous thought "How lovely to be a
woman succumbing to intercourse" found its proper place in the order
of the world.

Daniel Paul, called Paul during his childhood, was christened before
God with the destiny of becoming a mixture of his father, Daniel, and
his mother, Paulina. The naming in itself would not have created any
confusion if a mother had stood out in the little boy's mind as an
entity clearly separate from a father. But with her sons, Paulina always
acted as an agent of Dr. Schreber. She took in her husband's recommendations for childrearing and never questioned them. She believed
that no wife with common sense and good will wants to oppose the
decisive voice of a husband who declares himself with such certainty.
Schreber expected that Paulina would be as strict as he was with their
sons. And apparently she welcomed his masculine usurpation of her
maternal role. Why not? His rules seemed quite appropriate to the
upbringing of boys. And after all, was not her husband an authority on
childrearing? Even on those occasions when she might have been
tempted to hold her little Paul on her lap for a bit of cuddling or a
morsel of pear between meals, she would have felt it her duty to
subject him to a health-promoting trial of renunciation.

Anna Schreber, one of the three Schreber daughters, saw her mother's enthrallment with her father in a congenial light: "Father discussed
with our mother everything and anything; she took part in all his
ideas, plans and projects; she read the galley proofs of his writings with
him, and was his faithful, close companion in everything." As Paulina
was given more discretionary authority over the upbringing of her

three daughters, life did not turn out too badly for them. Besides, even the most manly and autocratic father does not find it an affront to his virility if his daughters are weak and *feminine*. While it was imperative that his sons should develop into strong, morally sound, healthy men free of weak, childish, or effeminate traits, Dr. Schreber was tolerant of and probably even subtly advocated physical delicacy, childishness, and feminine mannerisms in his daughters. It was quite enough for Schreber that his daughters walk and sit upright, that they fall asleep in a straight posture, that they pass his trials of renunciation, that they *not* masturbate, that above all they *not* grow up into one of those nasty, emancipated, masculine women. He approved that they adorn themselves with trinkets and frilly hats, that they emulate their mother's good housekeeping talents and her casual interests in music and art.

Anna, Sidonie, and Klara Schreber escaped the fates that eventually overtook their brothers. The decisive factor was that they were able, in fact, encouraged, to identify with Paulina, who was, in addition to being a highly respected woman in her community, an exemplary German wife. It was expected that her husband's honor and welfare should take precedence over the needs and well-being of her children. Paulina was not an emancipated, masculine woman. However, she idealized and venerated the power of men. She was born into a prestigious family of illustrious men, among them her grandfather, a legal scholar, and her father, a professor of medicine. She herself received an education suitable for a princess. Neither she nor her sisters attended the local schools, as it was considered more elegant to have a private tutor at home. Though Paulina never was much of a scholar, she was proud of her intellectual heritage and made no secret of her reverence for important and intellectually talented men. As a young woman growing up in Leipzig she was well aware that her parents entertained some of the most important doctors and lawyers of Germany. Till the day she died, at the age of ninety-three, she boasted about her personal association with Felix Mendelssohn and Franz Schubert. After his nine years at Sonnenstein, Daniel Paul retired to his mother's household, entrusting himself to her care while his wife patiently awaited the day when God might see fit to restore her husband's manhood. In the meantime she adopted a daughter.

Dr. Schreber thought he was stamping out his son's feminine weaknesses, but he was actually provoking their wishes to remain attached to their mother in an infantile way and their tendencies to identify with her femininity. Thus, the uncompromising male gender stereotypes that held sway in the Schreber nursery had exactly the opposite effect on his sons. Under Dr. Schreber's unrelenting tutelage and domination of his male children, an average and altogether commonplace boyhood fantasy of "submitting to the father as a mother would" became a powerful and eventually irrepressible erotic craving. The Schreber boys were not eased away from the kind nursery breast and gradually introduced to the meaning of boyhood and manhood. Instead little Gustav and Paul were wrenched away, abruptly and decisively, in order that they might be efficiently indoctrinated into their father's cult of virility. Daniel Paul's body submitted to the manhood his father inflicted on him, but his soul, which underwent only a partial murder, was left with an everlasting longing to be indistinguishable from a caregiving breast, a wish that he at last fulfilled at Sonnenstein. And so, like many sons and grandsons of that Ultimate Fatherland, where Schreberian-like doctrines of bodily and mental straightness were enlisted to preserve the order of the world, Schreber's own sons were never securely anchored in their masculine identity. At any moment they could be penetrated by the rays of God. So the sons of the fatherland were consumed by a need to repudiate, at all costs, even suicide and psychoses, even mutilation and mass murder, every shred of female voluptuousness.

Judge Schreber's fantasies of bodily dismemberment were harbingers of Auschwitz and Buchenwald. The cult of virility that inspired Dr. Schreber's soul murders of his own sons were part and parcel of an ethos that was dominant in Leipzig and throughout the German Empire. It was that same ethos that allowed Hitler's utopian visions of

Fatherland to enthrall and captivate so many German youths, boys and girls alike, during the 1930s. The emancipated German woman who in the 1920s had gained access to professions previously allowed only to men and was marching through the streets pestering with her feminist causes and worrying the men with her masculine tendencies was ordered back to the home. If the rule of the father were to prevail, the woman's proper interests were to be *Kinder, Küche und Kirche.*

The themes of body mutilation and moral torment that Schreber, the eminent judge, was able to express consciously in his *Memoirs* are usually unconscious in those who adopt a perverse solution to their mental sufferings. Perverts are aware that the perversion brings relief from some obscure anxiety or dread. They are aware that the perversion somehow replaces the dread with an exalted experience of being more valuable and more powerful than any ordinary mortal. After an enactment, they might feel ashamed for having yielded to temptation or sense a vague apprehension of doom, but they do not understand the reasons for these painful affects. They are unaware of the unholy bargain they have struck with the almighty tormentors who have traumatized them, deprived them, abandoned them, humiliated them, subjected them to the big and little soul murders of childhood.

With all the vengeful rage, all the making of hatred in the guise of love, there must also be room in a perversion for a seduction that will transform the tormenting aggressor into a beloved one. The unconscious dilemma would be "What forbidden act *may* I perform? What is it that will please my tormentor?" A perversion is a strategy for placating God, lawgiving father, protecting mother, or conscience, that inner voice of authority that represents the power of the gods.

It is fairly easy to understand that a perversion provides a way to express all variety of forbidden and shameful desires and that it should have the power to bring relief to a tormented soul. What is much harder to appreciate is that a perversion, an act that seems so directly to violate the laws of conscience, could also serve the function of appeasing, even pleasing, one's conscience. But if one thinks about these Faustian bargains from the point of view of a child who endures soul murder or an adult who still suffers the effects of these childhood traumas, such corrupt deals with conscience are plausible, in fact ineluctable. That our conscience should love us for doing something forbidden is no less plausible than anything else about perversion.

Since every part of the human mind participates in the construction of a perversion, conscience must also be enticed to give its permission. For how else could a perversion bring relief from suffering and yet still torment us sufficiently for our wickedness? In returning to the perverse strategy through the role of conscience, I return to the beginning.

Quite remarkably, it turns out that a perversion *is* a quest for ecstasy. But it is a caricature of spiritual ecstasy designed to seduce the love of some moral authority that is revered and idealized. Whether it is our conscience that we seduce into providing that ecstasy or some other godlike authority, the method and outcome are the same. The perverse strategy gives permission to an aspect of desire that expresses a godly ideal—for example, virility or submissiveness—while it keeps buried and hidden from consciousness those gender rebellions and frailties that might cause the authorities to punish and humiliate us. Moreover, in making these unconscious bargains that permit and condone the expression of a forbidden and shameful ecstasy, the pervert is seducing the almighty into a veiled, incestuous gratification. How does a transvestite, a man who in everyday life behaves in hypermasculine ways, get permission from his conscience to dress in the clothes of a woman? How did Judge Schreber, whose father's ideals of virility ruled his family, get permission from his conscience to be a woman succumbing?

To gain permission to substitute a perversion for the torments of psychosis, Schreber had first to convince his conscience, the almighty god-father inside him, the very father that he had both hated and loved as a little child, that he was living up to his responsibilities and duties.

Judge Schreber figured out that his most sacred duty was to satisfy God's need for constant sexual enjoyment. If he could satisfy God in this way, he could rest assured that God would never abandon him or mutilate his body. Even as a child, Daniel Paul Schreber had intuited, in the very vehemence with which his father tried to stamp out femininity, that almighty god's unconscious feminine strivings. Now as a transvestite, Judge Schreber was submitting to the almighty one just as a woman would and thereby giving to his father the virility *he* had so desperately needed. When he arrived at a state of feminine voluptuousness, Schreber could give to God every proof of *His* virility. He would give to *Him* not only in the pleasure of sexual intercourse with a woman of spirited voluptuousness but in the satisfaction of child-blessedness, by producing a child. By promising God this fulfillment of His virility, Schreber seduced Him into granting an incestuous wish. Judge Schreber did love his father and he knew all too well what *he* secretly desired.

With madness, the almighty is inflicting on one's body and soul the full extent of his wrath. And the soul is constantly tormented with not being able to figure out what He wants. With perversion the person has found the ecstasy He desires.

The fourteenth-century German mystic the Blessed Henry Suso (Heinrich Seuse) had almost gone mad from trying to figure out what the Lord desired of him.

> I used to be called his dear bride. Now, alas, I am not worthy to be called his poor washerwoman. In my deep shame I no longer even dare to raise up my eyes. . . . Who shall give me the expanse of heaven for my parchment and the depths of the sea for my ink, leaf and grass for my pen, that I might describe to the full the suffering of my heart and the irreparable desolation that this bitter separation from my Beloved has caused me? O, that I was ever born! What is left for me to do but cast myself into the abyss of bitter despair?

Suso had tried wearing a hair shirt and an iron chain. But he had bled like a fountain and had to give them up. He had tried an undergarment made of thongs into which a hundred and fifty pointed nails were attached and then rubbed his wounds with the oils that would attract stinging insects and vermin. But when he fell asleep his hands would push away the garment and scratch his itching skin. Then, at last, he found the way:

> He had someone make him two leather gloves and had a tinsmith fasten pointed brass tacks all over them. These he would put on at night. He did this so that, if in his sleep he tried to take off his undergarment or get some relief from the biting vermin, the tacks would prick him. And so it came to pass.

Dr. Daniel Gottlob Moritz Schreber, who as a youth was teased for his short, frail-looking, and sickly body, devoted his adult life and work to proving his virile masculinity. He cured crippled children of their deformities. He was the master of his children, but especially of his sons, whom he cured of their feminine and infantile weaknesses. Perhaps one day he would be remembered as the master of all the children of the German Empire. How could Dr. Schreber have understood that in his absolute repudiation of his weaknesses and femininity he would end up by externalizing onto his sons what he deemed as the lowly, crude, weak, and sweetly voluptuous parts of his own self? But his son Daniel Paul left to the world an appreciation of the twisted experience of a child who is chosen to be the victim of these fatherly projections. "God Himself was on my side in His fight against me."

14
Feminine, Masculine: The Codes of Perversion

I believe that ideas about separating, purifying, demarcating and punishing transgressions have as their main function to impose system on an inherently untidy experience. It is only by exaggerating the difference between within and without, above and below, males and female, with and against, that a semblance of order is created.

Mary Douglas, Purity and Danger

With the starry heavens God created a masterpiece. But with conscience God did an uneven piece of work. For no matter how advanced our moral life, conscience is never free of the earliest images of the parents from the infantile period of life. These idealized godlike parents embodied in conscience are never entirely humanized. They resist every attempt to replace them with more humane principles of protection and justice. Alongside our most advanced moral attainments, the early gods hold forth with their threatening surveillance and standards of impossible perfection. Though we are never sure what these prohibiting voices and scrutinizing eyes and pointing fingers want of us, we do our best to please and placate.

All children figure out that one sure way to win the protection and admiration of the almighty beloved ones is to live up to their ideals of gender. As adults they may wish to threaten and overthrow these implacable gods, but the frightened child within is cautious. If men continue to masquerade in their infantile caricatures of manhood and women continue to masquerade in their infantile caricatures of womanhood, perhaps the gods won't care because in this there is only a pretense of assuming the reins of power. If they disguise themselves as powerless children who are interested only in infantile pleasure, *Fresslust,* or defecation and urination, or exhibitionism and voyeurism, or submission and domination, perhaps the gods will not suspect an insurrection.

There has never been a time when human beings did not have a conscience or have to reckon with moral anxiety and shame. But in the earliest days of human history, when nature seemed so uncaring and harsh, so awesomely wild and unruly, and the societies that humans established could do so little to protect them from the capricious famines and droughts and storms and earthquakes and volcanoes and bolts of lightning, the inner voices of authority and protection were also experienced as uncaring, too harsh and implacable to tolerate as an inner part of one's own self. Conscience was more manageable when the forces of punishment and love could be imagined as residing in an external power. The totem gods or heavenly gods or God or the feudal lord were amenable to manipulation. The vengeful wrath of these allmighty ones could be placated with fetishes, magical potions, human and animal sacrifices, self-flagellations, sinners burned at the stake, and holy inquisitions that could sort out the saints from the sinners. Love and protection could be seduced with corn festivals and rain and sun dances and expeditions for the holy grail.

Only when we began to feel in greater control of the forces of nature and to recognize that society was an edifice of our own making meant to serve and protect us, and not the other way around, was it possible to acknowledge that the gods who punish and protect are as much part of our own selves as the wild desires and unruly passions that we regard with terror and awe.

Some things change. For those of us who have suffered only our "fair" share of mild deprivation and ordinary trauma, the prohibiting voices are more lenient, the scrutinizing eyes are more approving. But other aspects of conscience, the ideals of perfection we strive for, especially those primitive ideals of gender, seem never to change. The fault lines shift, creating a minor disturbance for a while, but then, as though nothing had ever happened, the fissured earth closes over. And sometimes, usually just after some stronger than usual upheaval, the old familiar gender ideals return, this time with an aftershock and virulence that send us scurrying for shelter. The primitive ideals of gender have been with us for so long that we still think of them, even now, as human destiny, as god-given, as nature's way. Some of us are convinced that any challenge to these ideals will offend the gods, causing earthquakes and tidal waves that will shatter and overrun the planet, destroying every sacred boundary between above and below, good and evil, clean and dirty, male and female. In observing the workings of conscience in the modern world, we might wonder if this latest version of authority—this inner representation of lawfulness and protection— is any kinder or more just in its dealings with human souls than the thunder gods and feudal tyrants of earlier societies.

The social agencies responsible for the regulation of sexuality and gender conformity have changed. And certainly, the experience for an individual person is very different if the enforcement of a gender conformity is left up to the tribal elders or the church or the community or, as nowadays, to the individual, who must deal only with his or her conscience. Nevertheless, the ideals of gender acquired by the free men and free women of the modern industrial world are not remarkably different from the ideals of masculine virility and feminine purity that the tribal elders demanded of the Dakota Indian children and brought home to every adolescent boy and girl through the sun dance puberty ritual. It would be hard to find a time in human history when the ideal of male virility and the ideal of female purity did not prevail. However, when those gender ideals are inscribed on the body in the form of scarifications and mutilations designed by tribal elders, the experience of arriving at gender identity is more decisive and less subject to conflict for the individual. The scarifications and mutilations are regarded by the tribe as visible proofs of moral obedience and of a youth's beauty and nobility. The conflicts and dilemmas that might have troubled the youth are resolved in the formal qualities of the scarifications: line-circle, above-below, clean-dirty, male-female, ancestors-descendants, past-future.

When the church was responsible for the regulation of sexuality and gender, the obeisant-sinner could deviate according to gender and then atone through confession or be suitably humiliated and punished according to gender-prescribed torments. In some ages, for example, burning or drowning was for witches and other religious heretics, mostly females and a few suspiciously feminine males; hanging or decapitation or drawing and quartering was for political rebels, mostly males and a few rebellious masculine females. When the community, the serfdom, the village regulated sexuality and gender, a similar situation of crime and punishment prevailed in that the agency of gender enforcement was an external social institution with some clearly stated premises of justice and punishment for all. To be sure, not one of these external regulating agencies survived very long after its system of justice failed to support the central political-economic structures of the society.

The freewheeling economics of the eighteenth and nineteenth centuries required a different sort of regulating agency. What was needed was a more personal institution where the system of justice would be enforced through the emotional immediacies of maternal love and paternal-power. A family structure of some sort has always been responsible for communicating social gender ideals to the child. However, it was only recently, toward the end of the seventeenth century, and only in some parts of the Western world, that the family actually took over from church and community to assume the authority and power of regulating sexuality and gender. While the males of these modern societies were not going to be trained to be voracious hunters like the Dakota, it was imperative that their virility be set free to exploit nature without too much shame or moral anxiety and to proudly embrace the masculine virtues of avarice and acquisitiveness that might one day make them rulers of the marketplace.

The females, on the other hand, were to be the guardians of the hearth. It was the females, the wives and the mothers, who were expected to represent virtue and innocence while the males were turned out into the marketplace to make real gold out of their unconscious Faustian bargains. Girls and women would not have to tie their legs together at night to prevent rape as the Dakota females did, but they were tied down just as effectively by a rule of conscience and ideal of womanhood that insisted on purity. Females knew that they must uphold in themselves the standards of sexual purity that would ensure the stability of the family. In this system of justice, it was a convention that lower-class females were going to form the ranks of prostitutes and that female domestic servants of all ages would also make themselves available to service the sexual needs of middle- and upper-class husbands married to household nuns whose sexuality was in the service of reproduction.

Burnings and drownings were no longer necessary. The errant aspects of female sexuality could be held in check by the internal regulating agency of conscience. It was sufficient that the guardians of the hearth grow up with an internal experience of conflict between their active erotic yearnings and their reproductive and household duties. The work ethic of the eighteenth- and nineteenth-century industrial-commodity societies required that children renounce in themselves those desires and those aspects of their identity that might turn a boy into a sexually passive, submissive, tender-hearted caregiver or a girl into an sexually active, masterful, strong-hearted lawgiver. In exchange for these renunciations, these ordinary little soul murders of childhood, the modern bourgeois family promised its children a successful and productive life and a fair share of the commodities offered in the marketplace. For a time, there was at least an apparent equity between what was given up of one's self in childhood and the rewards that were offered in adulthood. Conscience seemed to be on the side of those who obeyed. Conscience seemed to be paying off.

However, something else was in the air that threatened to subvert the rigidly dichotomized gender ideals that were enlisted to support this work ethic, payoff system of conscience. The seemingly impervious, steel-forged link between female sexuality and female procreative functions, which everyone had assumed as a god-given, eternal biological essence, was eroding. The scientific progress that had made possible the technologies of the modern industrial economy had also improved the lot of women and children, physically at least. For one thing, better medical care was available to middle- and upper-class families. As the infant mortality rate declined, women did not have to devote so many years of their lives to childbearing, childrearing, and child burying. Instead of bearing twelve infants of whom three might survive, a woman might bear only six and produce three survivors. Improved medical care also protected women from crippling illnesses and deaths during pregnancy and childbirth. Women were becoming a bit more comfortable with the use of commercial contraceptives and other long-standing folk methods of birth control. In the journals and tabloids, abortion medicines and equipment were advertised as freely as prescriptions for preventing masturbation, and sometimes the former was deceitfully advertised as the latter. Along with this technological control over what happened or did not happen to their bodies came the possibility for women of a fuller erotic pleasure, a sexuality relatively uncontaminated by the fear of death, a sexuality freed of the burdens of reproduction. And it was not too long before this freedom of erotic response in the female was seen as a threat to the order of the world.

Middle- and upper-class women began to have leisure time away from their household chores. Girls were given educations that made them literate enough to read romance novels and Rousseau. Some were even beginning to think about female social conditions and to speak up about women's place in human history. There had always been moments of bold interruption in women's silence about their bodies, their intelligence, their destinies, their rights. There had always been a few brave and powerful women who defied the gender conventions. Not until the eighteenth century, and more particularly the nineteenth century, did this trend toward female self-expression become at all commonplace.

However, the very sound of women's voices shook men down to their boots. Even in earlier ages when women were relatively powerless over their lives, the females voice, the female body, and female sexuality had always evoked in males a dread of death and castration. As much as women's purity had been venerated, so their sexuality had been feared. Now that women were speaking up, there was justification for fearing their sexual powers. Or so the virile men and their virtuous household nuns imagined.

For the more women are freed from the rigidly dichotomized roles of whore and madonna, streetwalker and household nun, witch and angel, the kinder and less arbitrary conscience becomes for men and women alike. However, to this day the female voice is heard as the call of the Siren, and whenever women speak up, men find new ways to denigrate and frighten them, to send them scurrying back the the shelters of motherhood and sexual purity. Women, unaccustomed to commanding their own bodies and destinies, also tremble before the cryptic powers they discover within themselves. Even the women who dare to make themselves heard then draw back because they are frightened of expressing the full range of their abilities and desires. Sometimes the bravest among them will subvert the causes they seem to be celebrating.

• • •

In November 1817, some three decades before Monsieur Rouault entrusted his thirteen-year-old daughter, Emma, to the town convent school, Madame Dupin de Francueil, otherwise a confirmed religious agnostic, committed her rebellious, recalcitrant thirteen-year-old grandaughter, Aurore, to the instruction of the pious English nuns of the Couvent des Anglaises. Aurore's father, a career soldier, had died when she was four. Before his death he had been a shadowy figure in her life, a dramatic presence who came and went for reasons that were mysterious to little Aurore. Her mother, whom Aurore had adored as a little girl, had let herself be robbed of her maternal authority by the wealthy and domineering paternal grandmother. The grandmother had bartered power for love and convinced Aurore's lower-class upstart mother to hand over her daughter to be raised as a girl of class. But Aurore, who longed only to be returned to the arms of her beloved mother, to live in a garret and make pretty hats the way her mother did, fooled her grandmother. She believed in God in the simple working-class way of her milliner mother and she refused to become a first-class woman.

Like Emma Rouault, Aurore Dupin would spend three years of her adolescence in a convent. Aurore started out her convent career by joining forces with the *diables,* the girls who held clandestine picnics where they ate the forbidden fruits smuggled in by the porter, the mischief-makers who filled the pianos with chicken bones and threw jam pies onto the ceiling. She soon became the maddest of these rebellious madcaps and came to be known by the other *diables* as *calipan,* a knickname derived from her unique brand of deviltry, which consisted of composing elaborate letters and passing them around the classrooms and chapels to her coconspirators, who delighted in the gossipy secrets contained in their *calipan*'s surreptitious literature. What the other *diables* did in the traditional nunnery *diable*-style, Aurore performed with a tranquil assurance that the nuns found charming. But then in her fifteenth year, after she had graduated to the senior class and been assigned her own cell, Aurore tired of the obviously illicit and took up a more devious corruption, a more sensual mode of deceiving and seducing the gods. The more her sexuality was awakened, the more deeply she absorbed herself in the lives of the hermits and martyrs. She loved God and now in direct communication with his works she could fully embrace the ideals of justice, tenderness, and holiness that He represented. As she looked back on her last year at the convent, Aurore reported, "Now at last I felt this communication suddenly established, as though some invincible obstacle had been removed between the source of infinite ardor and the subdued fire in my soul." Her friends, former *diables* on their way to becoming proper young ladies, wondered what had become of *calipan*. They dubbed the new Aurore a saint and soon "Saint Aurore" became a Teresa of Avila. Absorbed as she was in her extreme holiness, she had to invent sins to confess. She scrubbed the chapel floors. She no longer slept. She walked about in a trance. She ate only the tiniest morsels of the most tasteless food. Her once rosy, robust body paled and shriveled. She mortified her flesh by wearing a filigree necklace with sharp edges. The abrasions gave her no pain and when the sores became deep enough to bleed she at last understood what it was that God required of her. "In a word, I was living in ecstasy, my body was unfeeling. I no longer existed." As an adult, Aurore looked back on her *maladie sacrée* and appreciated its intimate relationship to her awakening adolescent sexuality. She understood then that the love of God and Christ was only without danger at ages when the passions are mute. She could recognize that in adolescence, when the soul is so susceptible to the corruptions of the body, the love of holiness and holy ones can be enlisted in the service of a perverse strategy. However, as an adolescent, she had understood nothing about these corrupt bargains where a forbidden ecstasy is granted to a saint who figures out what God requires of her. She had recognized only her spiritual hunger and the malady of holiness that had temporarily overcome her.

By the time she returned from the convent, Aurore had been cured of her religious fervor. She scandalized her neighbors by studying geology, mineralogy, medicine, and osteology. A handsome young medical student loaned her arm bones and leg bones and skulls to copy from and took to spending long evenings in Aurore's bedroom helping her with her medical studies. The neighborhood doctor loaned her a human skeleton so that she could explore every detail of anatomy. She kept the skeleton draped across a chest of drawers. She quickly learned how to fire a pistol, to ride cross-saddle, to delight in wearing trousers, vests, and Spanish sombreros when dashing through the countryside on her stallion. True, these outfits were far more comfortable than the narrow-skirted sheaths and flowered bonnets that were the custom for young ladies. But there was more to Aurore's triumph than simple relief. She admitted, indeed boasted, that she felt noble and glorious as she sallied forth, seated on a man's saddle, disguised as a young man. Her mischievous glee could not be contained when one day she dismounted from her wild steed, set up her pad, sketched a Gothic castle, and caught the attention of several well-skirted women who came out of the castle to observe the artist at work. These graceful women were as much taken by the charming offbeat looks of the rakish young artist as they were by his remarkable drawing, which looked exactly like the castle in every detail. "Would Monsieur agree to sell the drawing when he is finished?"

Her grandmother died when Aurore was seventeen, freeing her to choose for a husband anyone she wanted. Casimir Dudevant, a semi-retired army officer of twenty-eight, was not exactly the romantic hero that Aurore had been dreaming of, and he had only a miserable dowry, but he could be tender and playful and his frank, easygoing manners reminded her of her half-brother Hippolyte, who also did not think too much about emotions or the meaning of existence. "I have here a companion I like a lot, with whom I jump and laugh as I do with you." When she married Casimir Dudevant, Aurore had every intention of being a dutiful wife and mother. She knew she had the soul of an artist but was content to paint miniature designs on snuffboxes and sell them to her neighbors. Casimir tried hard to be a devoted and caring husband. Knowing how much his bride loved music, he bought her a piano. However, he could not abide the uppity pieces she played and after a year or so of enduring her musical entertainments, Casimir would simply leave the room with a scowl the instant Aurore's fingers touched the keyboard. He attempted to read the books she recommended but after a few paragraphs would doze off in his armchair. As for the philosophy, poetry, ethics, and other intellectual enthusiasms that moved her so, he could not even make a credible try. The marriage eroded from its lack of shared passions and then deteriorated altogether when she could no longer bear his blunt attempts at lovemaking. He took solace in the arms of her maid. Aurore fell madly in love with a nineteen-year-old poet, Jules Sandeau, and was meeting with him in Paris and Bourdeaux whenever she could get away from her two children. Aurore tried not to yield completely to this new passion and to be a good mother, if not an entirely good wife. She finally made the break with Casimir, joined her lover in Paris, and promised to return to be with her children for six months of every year. She more or less fulfilled that promise, depending on the progress of her love affairs.

The pitiful 300-franc allowance that she agreed to could hardly support Aurore in the Paris of the 1830s. However, she had claimed her right to sexual passion and her freedom to find out who and what she was meant to be. Aurore Dupin Dudevant and Jules Sandeau collaborated on a novel about an actress and a nun, a literary work meant to express the sexual and virtuous sides of woman's nature. Their publisher recommended to Aurore and Jules the joint nom de plume J. Sand. The novel was adored by the public and mocked by the critics for its obvious symbolism and mawkish sentimentality. Aurore decided to take a chance on expressing her talents without the collaboration of Sandeau. She wrote her own novel. This novel, *Indiana,* was a hit with the public *and* the literary establishment. Aurore adopted for her personal nom de plume the initial G., which soon became Georges, for the greek *georgias,* meaning husbandman. When she was a confirmed best-selling author, Aurore dropped the *s* in deference to her English fans and became forevermore George Sand.

Though Sand is usually remembered as an outlandish woman with lesbian inclinations who wore trousers and pantaloons, smoked cigars, and rolled her own cigarettes, the lover of Alfred de Musset, Frédéric Chopin, and countless other victims of her sexual lust, "a voracious nymphomaniac moving insatiably from the exhausted body of one genius to the next in vain search of an inexhaustible virility," her literary contemporaries regarded her as the muse of the 1848 revolution, the queen of a new literary generation, the finest female genius of any country or age, a sky lark singing in the profuse strains of unpremeditated art, the Christian soul par excellence. Within forty years, she authored sixty novels, several dozen plays, twenty-five of which were produced, thirty to forty thousand letters, and nearly as many essays. Elizabeth Barrett Browning felt she had to justify to her husband her immense regard for the mannish woman Sand, "in her good and evil together, I regard [her] with infinitely more admiration than all other women of genius who are or have been." Not that George Sand did not have her critics. Baudelaire, whose own erotic tastes ran to giantesses, pygmies, negresses, and women's feet and who would some years later be the first to identify the streak of virility in Emma Bovary, immediately perceived the bourgeois *femme évaporée* beneath the trousers of the social rebel George Sand. "She has the famous flowing style dear to the bourgeois. She is stupid. She is ponderous, she is long-winded; she has in moral ideas the same depth of judgment and the same delicacy of feeling as concierges and kept women."

At the age of sixty-one, already three times a grandmother and still spinning out novels, essays, and letters with careless ease and envious speed, George Sand became a close friend of Gustave Flaubert, who was forty-three and just commencing his seven-year drudging labor at *L'Education Sentimentale*, where as he did in writing *Madame Bovary*, he would sweat over every word. In the decade of their relationship these two friendly antagonists visited one another occasionally, embraced warmly when they met, and proclaimed their mutual admiration in every exchange of letters. They loved at a distance, more from his choice than hers, but their extensive correspondence revealed a slowly deepening intimacy. He was estranged from the world, embittered, and in need of consolation. She was ready, as always, with her warm heart and spritely enthusiasm. He insisted on the natural depravity of humanity. She insisted on natural goodness. For her, art was a means of touching and transforming the world. For him, art was an avenue of escape from the chaos of existence. She was a Romantic through and through and he a professed Realist, who was always struggling with his subversive romantic tendencies. She preached to her readers about political and social progress and believed completely in the ideals of democracy, even in the hypocritical and imperfect Bonaparte democracy. He regarded with suspicion everything about the industrial revolution and could not abide sanctimonious preachers of progress or the Bonaparte banalities they preached. She was always trying to seduce him toward a more generous view of humanity. He wanted to coax her toward his way of viewing the world and advised her to renounce her illusions, her faith in goodness. "Ah, dear good master, if you could only hate! That is what you lack, hate. . . . In spite of your great Sphinx eyes you have seen the world through a golden colour. . . . Cry out! Thunder! . . . Bedew us with drops of the blood of wounded Themis." Sand was roused by her dear friend's summons to arms. She printed her reply in *Réponse à un ami*. "And what you want me to stop loving? You want me to say that I have been mistaken all my life, that humanity is contemptible, hateful, that it always has been so and will always be so? . . . Humanity is not a vain word. Our life is composed of love and not to love is to cease to live."

Critics were puzzled by the easy intercourse between these two natural antagonists. Surely, they said, if you wanted to know what happened to a woman who read George Sand's romantic novels, you had only to examine the fate of Emma Rouault Bovary. The adulterous and passionate heroines of Sand's novels—Valentine, Indiana, Lelia —were Emma's models. The mocker of the bourgeois, Flaubert, had written a book inspired by Sand, the muse of adultery, the spirit of the 1840 bourgeois.

There was between Sand and Flaubert an intimacy, an immense respect, an abiding love. When Sand died at the age of seventy-two, the tough-hearted Flaubert was at the graveside weeping: "I cried like a baby at her burial not once but twice; first, when I embraced her little granddaughter, Aurore (whose eyes that day so resembled hers, it was like a resurrection), and then again when the coffin was carried past me." Turgenev wrote a letter of condolence to Flaubert: "She loved us both but you above all, which was natural. What a heart of gold she had! What absence of every petty, mean, or false feeling. What a brave man she was, and what a good woman!" After he recovered from his loss, Flaubert summed up his feelings: "One had to know her as I knew her to realize how much of the feminine there was in this great man, the immensity of tenderness to be found in this genius."

Sand, the epitome of the free woman to her own and later generations, never did acknowledge how much of the feminine there was in her masquerades as a man. She always did think of herself as an exception, a woman yes, but a woman exempt from the burdens of womanhood. Throughout her life she was a feminist elitist who defended the gender conformities of her age. Despite her occasional hot flirtations with women of artistic genius, exceptions like herself, she preferred the company, conversation, and attentions of men. She had little sympathy for the less-than-great female artists. About the poet Louise Colet, who, after her affair with Flaubert, took up with Sand's abandoned *enfant terrible* Alfred de Musset, Sand had this to say: "There are some who seek to be talked about in a certain way, there are others who seek to be talked about no matter how. The first like celebrity, the second like noise. Louise Colet was of this second category."

When she was in her late thirties, Sand expressed her views on the "feminine question" in *Lettres à Marcie,* six letters addressed to a fictional unwed girl of twenty-five. Sand approved that women should not have to remain in marital bondage to men who did not respect them. That was about as radical as Sand got about the rights of women. She condemned the then fashionable philosophy of free love and sexual liberty as a perverse remedy for the afflictions of a corrupt society. She professed that females were innately more noble than males. Women should not imitate men or try to acquire their kinds of power. It was the duty of females to cultivate their femininity and to speak in feminine voices about feminine issues. To make society a better place for all human beings, women should preserve in themselves the feminine ideals that stamp them as creatures purer and morally superior to men. If they were to participate in society at all, women were meant to be poets, painters, actresses, and musicians, certainly not politicians. Nor should a woman consider household chores inherently degrading. "The wife has the fatigues of housekeeping, the husband those of the establishment—two diverse yet equally necessary and thus equally noble ways of working for the family." Sand, who may very well have been searching all her life for the embrace of a tender mother; who still longed for the spritely, amusing mother of her childhood; who never forgave her mother for not fighting back hard enough when the dominating and tyrannical grandmother stole her little girl away—Sand put her faith in the woman-mother who is "all calm, kindness and serenity." She spoke against the woman-lover, that passionate, unstable, flighty creature who disrupted the calm of family life. She spoke against the woman-lawgiver. She preached:

> The role of each sex is traced, its task is assigned, and Providence gives to each the instruments and resources which befit it. . . . Women complain of being brutally enslaved, of being badly educated, badly advised, badly directed, badly loved, badly defended. All this is unfortunately true. But what confidence would women inspire if they were to demand by way of compensation, not

household peace nor the freedom of maternal affections, but the right to parade in the forum with sword and helmet, the right to condemn people to death?

Aurore Dupin was an adolescent who concealed her erotic yearnings in a masquerade of saintliness. George Sand was a feminist who hid her feminine longings beneath a cloak of masculine bravado. Yet she was always looking to find her true self in the arms of a man she endowed with phallic perfection. And, insofar as she would cut off locks of her hair to prove her endless devotion to her lovers or would abase herself before them as she readied herself to leave them or they threatened to leave her, she behaved like a typical extremely submissive woman. Though she was a rebel who refused to accept the bondage of the good housewife and good mother, Sand accepted the sexual mythologies of her day and would worry that she was exhausting and depleting her lovers with her voracious sexual appetites. At the same time, she threw herself into the role of nurturing mother to these petulant, sickly, dependent, egotistical poets and musicians, a few of them men of genius, others of plainly mediocre talent. The more needy they were, the more she ignored their failings, the more she was determined to give to them the tender and powerful mother they were yearning for. For several months Sand resisted falling into the arms of the beautiful but thoroughly dissipated and unreliable twenty-three-year-old Musset. One day, he quite inadvertently found the key to her heart. He wrote a farewell letter: "You should love only those who know how to love. I know only how to suffer. . . . Good-bye, George, I love you like a child." The next night she became mistress, housekeeper, sick-nurse and mother to her new little boy. Gossip had it that Sand would show up to her initial assignations with a jeweled dagger hanging from her trouser belt. This ornament assured Prosper Mérimée's impotence. On Alfred de Musset it had quite the opposite effect.

And so it generally went for feminists and feminist causes during the nineteenth and early twentieth century. In feminist essays on the rights of women, one could usually detect the writers' unreconciled conflicts between their own feminine and masculine strivings. On one side or the other, in one way or another, their preachings and doctrines reflected the infantile dichotomies of gender that had once oppressed them. Some were revolutionaries who marched to the wars and the barricades with their radical-minded brothers, often leading the way as the men followed. The next day they would be recommending to their downtrodden sisters the virtues of motherliness. Women longing for mothering posed as Big Daddys and women who longed to dominate and conquer found themselves posing as all-suffering saints and Big Mommas. It was all very confusing, one could say perverse. And, to some extent, it still is.

By the 1920s, it had become standard for successful professional women to masquerade in a caricature of womanliness to disguise their forbidden masculine ambitions. Joan Rivière's patient (discussed in Chapter 8) did some unconscious bargaining with her conscience and figured out a way to seduce her fierce and unforgiving conscience to permit her to express the ambitions and intellectual aspirations that her social order labeled as masculine. Her unconscious plot was simple. First, she would show her "mother" that "father" was on her side and would protect her from the mother's wrath. She would get her senior male colleagues to say that she was deserving of tribute. Then she would masquerade before them as a self-sacrificing, self-denigrating, submissive woman so they wouldn't think of her as one of those terrible emancipated women and steal her intellect away from her. Furthermore, she found in her adult social order a correspondence between her infantile solutions to gender conflict and the gender compromises that had been instituted to protect the order of the world against the emancipated woman. Her conscience was sufficiently against her but still enough on her side to calm any anxiety that she might be abandoned or mutilated for exhibiting her stolen trophies.

Now, more than half a century later, with all that has seemed to change, with all the progress that women have made in shifting the gender structures of their societies, there are more women like the Janet I describe in Chapter 8 than there were in Rivière's day. Some things have not changed. The infantile fantasies of a Janet can still find a comfortable place in the grown-up world, where it is still more acceptable for a woman to masquerade as a perfectly womanly woman than to compete with men, fair and square, on her ground or theirs. They are seen every day in analytic practices: brilliant women, successful and respected in their callings and professions, virtuosos of the womanly arts, but all the while interpreting their talents and ambitions as stolen trophies. Janet's infantile strategy of hiding her talents in a masquerade of womanliness, a caricature of femininity, fits perfectly with the order of the world, and therefore her conscience, which is also part of this scheme of things, gives her very little trouble. With the world still going along with her masquerade, even supporting and condoning it, why should a Janet, or anyone else, for that matter, question the kind of woman she has become?

Fortunately, for all that some things never change, there is a counterforce that resists these reactionary and soul-crippling solutions. Something in the human spirit wants to keep on growing and changing. Some women are too frightened of the powers they are discovering in themselves and are retreating to the old familiar shelters of purity and nurturing motherliness. But others are rewriting and revising the old scripts and questioning these stereotypes of femininity, and when they see them operating in their own lives they no longer accept that there is nothing to be done about this sorry state of affairs.

The Janets of our modern world are much more fortunate than the Sallys, Lillians, and Olympias, all the women for whom transvestism, homeovestism, and female impersonation are the best possible alternatives to the madness of never knowing what is wanted of one. The little soul murders of a Janet's childhood are comparatively minor and ordinary, nothing of a magnitude that would require her to enlist the massive defenses of numbing out and blanking out. Neither does Janet's conscience require that she actually dress up as this or that kind of woman or decorate her body as if it were a container for forbidden desires or treat her body like a fetish object or starve herself to death as the only way of displaying her rebellious masculinity. A Janet's perverse solution, her corrupt bargain with her conscience, is played out in her character structure. It is a solution to a gender conflict that takes place within Janet, and no one is any the wiser about what is going on in her mind, including Janet herself. She develops this character perversion that allows her a worthwhile intellectual life and a sexual life with a proper modicum of erotic pleasure but at the price of fitting herself into a gender stereotype of femininity that manages to keep her conscience on her side—most of the time. She looks perfectly normal, to herself and to everyone else.

Until Janet began to wonder why she felt compelled to behave like a foolish girl each time she finished giving a brilliant, authoritative lecture, her conscience never gave her much trouble. Some excruciating backaches, some humiliating fits of rage, a sleepless night after every grand performance, and that was it. Indeed, to question and analyze all this was far more troubling and threatening to her self-esteem than any backache or anxiety. It was frightening to peel away her mask of womanliness, painful to recognize her infantile deceptions and all that they were hiding, especially those corrupt deals with her conscience. When she decided to explore the woman she had become, Big Daddy Janet had to suffer the humiliating discovery that she was *only* a woman, just like her mother and sisters and less fortunate female colleagues. For a while, to forestall all this mortifying knowledge, she became a kleptomaniac who felt compelled to steal important books from her university library. After this symptom gave way, there were some terrible months when Janet was cutting her long and beautiful hair in outrageously unbecoming styles, shorter and shorter. She was also considering an unnecessary operation for her back condition until finally she understood these self-mutilations and mutilation fantasies as an attempt to ward off retaliation for her "crimes." In short, as Janet questioned her character perversion it came apart into a number of typical female perversions.

Eventually, though, Janet's spritely intelligence, courage, determination, and persistence in facing up to the lies hidden by her masquerade allowed her to experience and enjoy a fuller range of her abilities and desires. She began to feel convinced that what she possessed belonged to her and to no one else. The fame she had achieved was hers and not a stolen trophy. As she became less desperate to prove herself in the bedchamber, she could allow the ambiguities and uncertainties of a feminine *jouissance* into her erotic script. She gave up having to pay for who she was by a masquerade of self-sacrificing masochism. She no longer felt the need to placate her conscience by acting like a denigrated woman. And to Janet's surprise, she discovered that conscience was on her side anyway—and not so much against her as it used to be.

There has never been and never will be a social order that does not demand of a female child some conformity to some gender ideal of femininity. The social institutions assigned to regulate gender conformity have always been changing and will continue to change as the socioeconomic structures of society change. As I said earlier, until very recently the family was not given full authority over the regulation of sexuality and gender conformity. Nevertheless, however much the family system has changed or how much or little power it has had over the destiny of the child, throughout the ages the family was the social institution that mediated between the crude, unformed nature of the child and the society.

We are born as biological males or females, and from that moment of birth and perhaps even while still in the womb, the social qualities of femininity or masculinity that are prevalent in our social order will be transmitted through the medium of the family. The family, however, is no mere servant of society. The family has emotional interests of its own that go deeper than the temporary, superficial, and practical interests of society. In its enduring role as intermediary between child and society, the family has always seen as *its* own best interests an enhancement of emotional intimacies among its members, a preservation of the individual against intrusions of the larger social order. That is why in utopian societies, from Plato's *Republic* to Zamiatian's *We,* from the medieval monastery to the Israeli kibbutz, the first and crucial order of the day was to remove the infant from the subversively personal influences of the family. On its side, society cares almost nothing at all for the emotional life of its citizens. If the emotions of family life threaten a disturbance in the order of the world, the social authorities will not support that family system in the expectation that it will wither away; or so they hope.

Societies are created by persons, but once established societies are impersonal and interested only in preserving and maintaining their own structures. One of the most effective and powerful instruments of socialization is gender conformity. The social order impresses its structures on its citizens through its ideals of femininity and masculinity. Fortunately, the family is not without its power to resist what seems inimical to its more personal interests. The family may enforce the prevalent social gender conventions or try to subvert them. However, even with this power, no mother or father can simply indoctrinate a child into some socially approved feminine or masculine gender identity, even if she or he should want to attempt that little soul murder. A child's gender identity is formed on a day-to-day basis within the many subtle interactions between child and mother, father, siblings, grandparents, aunts, uncles, and the child's identifications with all of these family members, but primarily through his or her identifications with the lawgiving and caregiving functions of his or her parents. Moreover, as we have seen in the case of Schreber, the cult of virility that Dr. Schreber consciously inflicted on his sons' bodies and souls was no match for the unconscious feminine strivings that he unconsciously communicated to them. The muscle man who is always bullying and teasing his son, throwing him into the pool "to make a real man of him" is as likely to produce a frightened momma's boy as another imitation real man. For any father who is so intent on proving his masculinity is surely more than a little frightened of his feminine longings and ambitions. The mother of the anorectic may be trying very hard to produce an obedient and virginal little girl, but the girl will sense her mother's forbidden intellectual and erotic strivings and give them expression in a defiant self-starvation that makes a mockery of feminine purity. Whatever parents might consciously try to impose on their children in the way of gender ideals can easily be subverted by the mother's or father's own unconscious suppressed gender strivings.

Furthermore, a person's gender identity is also much more than a matter of these conscious and unconscious identifications learned in the context of family life. Some psychologists would like to reduce the complexities of gender identity to interpersonal relationships and family identifications and thereby spare themselves the riddles posed by human sexuality and the role it plays in gender identity. However, one of the most powerful subversive forces within the child and within the family is sexuality.

Ours is a special kind of sexuality that exists nowhere else in the animal kingdom. Technically, because of the uniqueness of our sexuality, we do not have to be dominated either by society or nature. On the contrary, in a divided allegiance, we are spared the total ruthlessness of each. Society opposes the tyrannies of nature, while nature, particularly the inherent flexibility of our sexuality, protects us from social domination. Other mammals are biologically programmed with instincts that fit them into a social order that never changes, or changes only slightly, from one generation to the next. They are born with sexual instincts that ensure heterosexual matings that must take place only at a certain time and only in a certain place. And when these instincts cannot find a suitable accomodation to some alteration in the environment, the species dies out. We humans, on the other hand, are capable of instituting vast alterations of our social and natural environments. The same is true of our sexuality, which can take many forms.

Human sexuality is *polymorphous,* which means literally a quality of being able to assume different forms. This polymorphous quality of human sexuality, which is largely a result of our especially long period of infant dependency and partly a feature of our rich fantasy life, makes us an animal species with a potential for a variety of feminine and masculine forms relatively independent of biological sex—femaleness or maleness. Our sexuality arises from many different bodily sources; our sexuality can seek satisfaction in many different ways and through any organ of the body; our sexuality can be attached to any person or object that we invest with erotic desire. It is very hard indeed for human beings to bring together all these components of sexuality, all these possibilities for satisfaction, and arrive at the so-called normality of genital sex with a partner of the opposite sex. Moreover, though we prefer to think otherwise, especially when we are in love, sexual desire does not reside in the object of desire, the loved one. Only the loving or desiring one can invest someone or something with desire. The man with the golden hairs and rippling arm muscles, the nymphet, the skin surface of the body, the curving neck, the black garter belt are not intrinsically beautiful or exciting. These potential objects of desire are not sexually exciting until someone invests them with erotic value and with fantasies of desire. Because human sexuality is more a matter of imagination and fantasy than of biology, nothing pertaining to our sexuality is predetermined. For this reason alone, the sexual intimacies that are generated within the family during the child's long period of dependency are always potential underminers of the gender conventions that support the structures of human societies.

Societies function on the basis of a precise gender differentiation, but there is nothing natural or god-given about all this. Gender roles are learned and are an effort on the part of society to channel and regulate an otherwise errant sexuality. In humans, the fact of being born male or born female is no guarantee of a masculine or feminine gender identity or of a heterosexual mating. The love of a woman for a man is no more biologically natural or imperative than the love of a woman for another woman. It is no more human to experience erotic desire for a person than to invest a fetish object with erotic desire. All of these outcomes of the human sexual "instincts" are possible, and all of them represent the vast possibilities of erotic response available to human beings. The polymorphous sexuality of the human being creates plights and dilemmas for all human beings and uncomfortable relations with the societies into which they are born.

It is often said that persons who are unable to identify the genitals as the principal sexual organs and coitus as the principal goal of erotic excitement are polymorphous *perverse*. However, as we have seen in this study of perversion, men and women are able to utilize penises and vaginas and heterosexual behavior to gratify all sorts of longings and desires and to alleviate all varieties of anxiety and suffering. This polymorphous sexuality of ours, though it causes considerable mischief and conflict, is part of the human factor that protects individuals from complete domination by the social order.

Society is always suspicious of deviant sexual trends among its members, and rightly so from the point of view of its interests. From a social perspective, it is best that male children should grow up with the masculine ways that perpetuate society's structures and that female children should grow up with the feminine ways that perpetuate society's structures. Social gender conventions are designed to capture, contain, and regulate the errant and inherently mischievous forces of human sexuality. However, outright suppression and containment and cataloguing are not the only effective methods of gender indoctrination.

The polymorphous quality of human sexuality is, on the one hand, a protection against gender stereotyping. On the other hand, this very flexibility and potential variability of the human sexual response makes it feasible for sexuality to be harnessed to any and all *social* causes. Sexuality, and therefore gender, can be manipulated to support any and all political and economic structures. More insidious, because they are harder to identify or oppose, are those methods of gender indoctrination that extract conformity by pretending to favor diversity. For example, society can achieve its aims of keeping everyone in his or her place with a trivialization of sexuality by posing this trivialization as erotic freedom. Whenever there are challenges to the prevailing gender conformities, the social order has it in its power to license sexual orgies where everything goes, or holy days and Mardi Gras where men may dress as women and women may dress as men, where children may act like grown-ups and grown-ups may act like children. These days, the popularization and commercialization of deviant sexualities is achieving the purposes of gender conformity and sexual repression just as effectively as the more obvious and direct methods of suppression that prevailed at the beginning of this century. Consumer sex is simply another artifact of the law of consumerism, the commodity fetishism, the perverse strategy that informs the political and socioeconomic structures of the modern world.

In this study of female perversion, we have been examining the ways in which social gender ideals of femininity and masculinity in modern industrial-commodity societies have shaped the perverse scenarios of modern men and women. What has been different in the twentieth century is not that perversions exist or that the perverse scripts we are most familiar with have been designed by males in the interests of maintaining the cult of virility. What is different, or seems to be different, is the paradoxical way in which the polymorphous sexuality of the human being is now being enlisted to preserve the economic and political structures of our modern world. In the twentieth century, something that had been latent in other centuries simply became more apparent. The feminine and masculine roles that are enacted in a perversion, male or female, epitomize in dramatic form the very social gender stereotypes and social role conventions that a perversion pretends to be subverting and undermining. As we know, there are many deceptions embedded in a perverse scenario.

One deception is that perversions are forces of revolution, ways of exploding the social gender stereotypes and creating new possibilities for human sexuality. However, by appearing to destroy every sacred boundary, perversions actually preserve and memorialize whatever is most conservative and reactionary in the human spirit. The story of perversion in the twentieth century began with what looked like an attempt to repress all sexualities that did not fall into the gender conventions of modern Western societies. The twentieth century is ending with an ingenious way of containing and regulating the gender ambiguities that are the lot of human beings. The medical profession is still consumed with cataloguing and recataloguing sexual aberrations. Sexologists are still at work trying to help every impotent man to become potent and every frigid woman to have vaginal orgasms. Whereas sexuality has been enlisted in previous eras to enhance procreation, saintliness, tenderness, intimacy, and romance, it is now in the service of erotic pleasure and so-called erotic freedom. Among the explicit ideals of modern westernized societies, along with the rights to free speech and a free press, is the ideal that every citizen is entitled to not only the same material commodities, but also the same fulfilling experiences of life—dignity, equality, and the pursuit of happiness. A free and liberated erotic life has become an ideal of this democratization of experience, a rigid conformity to which paradoxically tyrannizes people to be free about sex. On the other hand there is a dread of a rampant sexuality that might undermine the social order. Obviously, there is some conflict about this whole business of erotic freedom.

Some things are changing, among them our capacity to observe our own consciousness, our increasingly humane conscience, our belief in the moral perfectibility of the human race—all those facets of human evolution that have enabled us to resist the tyrannies of the past. These days, most parents from every social and economic class are consciously trying to instill in their children a mutual respect for members of the other sex, a tenderness and caring love that they hope will modify the dehumanizing and sadistic aspects of aggression. These same well-protected and well-cared-for children every day come in contact with the children of poverty, children like themselves except that they are homeless and, like many better-off children, also drug- and alcohol-addicted and victims of the sexual and physical abuse of the adults who care for them. Among the protected children are those who are already addicted to a hard-rock sadism that demeans women, slasher movies that snuff out women and children, pornographic comic book versions of Wonder Woman and Batman, and sadistically tinged, video games that are programmed to instill the virtues of virility— domination, control, exploitation. All children in our society are sur- rounded by media messages that glorify sadomasochistic sexuality. Eros is harnessed to consumerism as erotic messages, liminal, sublimi- nal, and supraliminal, are designed to sell clothing, cosmetics, perfume, automobiles, food, detergents. Eroticism itself is marketed with the same fanatic devotion that used to be given entirely to the marketing of domestic goods. Now any enlightened adult citizen or child can turn on her or his TV set or dial a porn number and participate in any and every sexual aberration she or he desires, provided the messages look and sound merely indecent but not wholeheartedly obscene.

Sex has become a commodity, and like any commodity, eventually the most outrageous styles soon achieve a widespread popularity. The modern industrial economy that originally derived its greatest support from the gender conformities of the bourgeois family is now turning its energies to the mass marketing of sexual perversion. The twentieth century is ending in an ironic conformity of sexual deviation that trivializes the meaning of erotic freedom. The ideal of perversion is the interchangeability of one body part for another, one person for an- other, an object for a person. This, however, is not erotic freedom. Our polymorphous sexuality gives us a freedom of erotic response. In a perversion, however, there is no freedom, but only a driven compul- sion, a rigid conformity to a gender stereotype, a posing of hatred as an erotic ideal. Erotic freedom cannot exist or flourish in a social climate of rigid gender stereotyping that uses gender ideals of virility and sexual performance as the measure of erotic freedom. For centuries, by denying and disavowing the nature of female sexuality, we have understood less than half the truth about human sexuality. By focusing exclusively on the perversions that males perform and not questioning the relative rarity of those perversions in females, we have been taken in by the lies of the perverse strategy and have therefore misapprehended the meaning of erotic freedom.

The strongest appeal of perversion is its capacity to provide individuals relief from troubling affects and emotions. During the perverse enactment a person might suffer a twinge of apprehension and afterward shame for having once again yielded to this bewildering impulse, but these mildly painful effects are nothing compared to the unconscious mortification, terrible anxiety, and awesome guilt he or she would otherwise experience. Perversions also serve a useful social purpose by regulating violence and sadistic destructive aggression. But perversions also forestall any possibility of understanding more about the motives for anxiety and guilt or the sources of human violence and sadistic rage. With the advent of mass market sexual deviation, everyone is given the opportunity to numb out psychological distress by participating in performances in which they or someone else is enacting the roles of helpless, dependent, humiliated infants and passive, humiliated, denigrated women. With this permission of a group social conscience to subjugate and dominate, there is an illusion of erotic freedom. But actually conscience, like Schreber's God, is on our side in its fight against us, intimidating us into a mindless conformity. Any sentiment or troubling emotion that might encourage us to rebel against these conformities of submission and domination is assuaged by commodity sex.

No one any longer has to deal with the human plight. And perhaps it is no accident that now when our human plight includes the possibility of global environmental disasters more uncontrollable in their effects than the hurricanes and volcanic explosions and famines and droughts that have always been a source of terror and awe or as horrifying as the racial genocides and nuclear holocausts of the first half of our century, perversion should become an underground social ideal. Though much has changed in the outward manifestations of our political and socioeconomic structures, the link between gender structure and social structure is no different in modern postindustrial societies than in traditional hunter-gatherer societies. If we want to challenge in any significant way the gender stereotypes that imprison the souls of males and females, we are very much mistaken if we imagine we can accomplish that end without identifying the duplicities embedded in the economic and political structures of our modern postindustrial societies.

In most of the female perversions, we can readily identify a collaboration between a woman's personal solution to the traumas of childhood and a social gender stereotype of femininity. This collaboration, present in all perversions, is most evident in kleptomania, the perversion that many analysts have proposed as the prototype of the female perversions. Here material goods are used to compensate for all kinds of infantile deprivations. The impulsive theft of material goods is always symbolically linked to some personal experience of deprivation. The trophy that is stolen—the library book, the dress, the necklace, the steak, the chocolate cake, the fur jacket, the emerald, the automobile, the pen—can be unconsciously equated with a breast or a penis or a loving father or a protecting mother. The theft is also an expression of a vengeful hatred and envy toward the depriving environment symbolized by the library or department store. If it were not for woman's marginal status in the economic order and for her social gender role as a primary consumer in that order, kleptomania could not be a typically female triumph over the traumas of childhood. Kleptomania and its more socialized but equally perverse variant, compulsive shopping, have their personal roots in all variety of infantile humiliations and soul murders. But as in all perversions, these infantile traumas find a correspondence in the social order.

Kleptomania, compulsive shopping, and shoplifting are a woman's psychological response to her deprivation of economic power in a social order where those with penises control the source and flow of economic goods. What I am emphasizing now, and have been suggesting throughout this book, is that an indoctrination of females to their socially and economically necessary gender roles has lent support to the perverse strategy of kleptomania and to every other perverse strategy that is typical of females.

In its initial stages, the commodity fetishism of modern industrial societies thrived on the imprisoning domesticity of women, who were trained from childhood to find the satisfactions of all their desires in material goods. In their roles as proper wives and good mothers, women were assigned the power of managing the household. They were allowed to be in charge of purchasing food and clothing, planning and serving meals, and decorating the sitting rooms with sofas and armchairs, the windows with lace curtains, the mantelpieces with trinkets and objets d'art. They were expected to inscribe on their bodies the decorations and ornaments that appealed to the eyes of men. Men were the rulers of the marketplace and women were the major consumers of marketplace goods. If women were to keep to their assigned gender roles, it was best that they should not think too much or feel too deeply. Every troubling emotion or moral torment could be smoothed away by material objects. Every social ambition or sexual desire could be satisfied by material objects. Every sentiment that might have encouraged women to rebel against their domestic imprisonment could be assuaged by a commodity.

L'heureux, Flaubert's happiness peddler who comes out of nowhere to dispense the illusory happiness of Algerian scarves and embroidered collars to the sexually imprisoned Emma Bovary, knew instinctively what the real Mayor Laughinghouse and the happiness peddlers of the megamall are now realizing in a more conscious, calculating way. It is not that L'heureux was incapable of calculation. He was a master of figuring out just how far and how much he could transform Emma's sexual hunger into a hunger for material goods. He would not have grasped the general principle that the polymorphous possibilities of human sexuality can be transformed into a narrow and "specific greed for an infinity of unnecessary commodities," but he understood concretely that he could turn a healthy profit from the unsatisfied yearnings of Emma Bovary.

As an intermediate step between the hand-to-hand peddlings of L'heureux and the monolithic happiness megamalls of our own age came the department store with its array of similarly unnecessary commodities that could similarly compensate for unsatisfied erotic longings. The department store was the economic institution that most clearly represented this nineteenth-century mechanization of desire. Men had become commodity-producing machines and women the buying machines that kept the men busy producing. By the 1870s the rampant consumerism of the good housewife caught the attention of feminist writers.

> The majority of women seem to consider themselves as sent into
> the world for the sole purpose of displaying dry goods; and it is
> only when acting the part of an animated milliner's block that
> they feel they are performing their appointed mission.

Though many writers were able to perceive the hidden corruptions underlying this female gender conformity, as long as most women accepted their roles of proper housewife and good mother they were regarded as normal. In 1987, in *Idols of Perversity,* Bram Dijkstra pointed to the unconscious hostility toward men that was expressed through women's willing submissions to their gender-appropriate role as the trained seals of a consumer society. Having little else to do with their lives but decorate, "nineteenth century middle-class women had transformed the characteristic trappings of their own marginalization from the productive life of their time into the raw materials for a direct attack on the men who had placed them in the gilded cage of conspicuous consumption." The lawgivers and heads of households were enslaved by the conspicuous consumption of their wives and their daughters, who were in training to be shoppers from the day they were born. Nevertheless, everybody put up with this arrangement of mutual hostility in the friendly guise of gender normality until one day women began to want to compete with men in the marketplace. They began to want real gold and real power. They began even to think. They began to question their demeaned position in society. Then and only then were they regarded as perverse.

Just as women were waking up to lies of their demeaning marginalization, men were realizing that the economic power they thought they had achieved was also a lie. The renunciations of childhood were not paying off. The middle-class merchant, who had once thought of himself as a mover and shaker of society, had become a bit player, a pieceworker, a paid employee of the massive commercial conglomerates, trade monopolies, and trusts that had come to dominate the turn-of-the-century marketplace. Dijkstra says:

> Only those with a truly ruthless hunger for acquisition could play leading roles, sit at the head of the table during the great feast of imperialist acquisition which was taking place everywhere and from which, on the material level, both the aristocracy and the middle class and the aristocrat were certainly benefiting greatly.

With all the financial rewards that accrued from this economy of freewheeling avarice, men, especially those who had benefited greatly, were vaguely aware that they had been duped. To obtain positions of power, they had "willingly submitted" to a social marginalization that placed them instead in positions not unlike the demeaned positions of women, slaves, and the working-class blokes who worked their factories and department stores. When these wealthy and well-bred, or at least well-fed and well-housed, men looked around for someone to blame for their marginalized status, the most obvious enemy was the emancipated woman, the gold digger who was trying to emasculate males by appropriating their gold and their power. Dijkstra links this economic marginalization of the average middle-class male to the flourishing of his masochistic sexuality. If the robber baron was the sadistic executioner, the tyrannical mover and shaker who controlled and curtailed other men's economic movement, and the average middle-class entrepreneur and professional and aristocrat and artist were merely his demeaned assistants, the unconscious infantile fantasy of being a submissive woman fucked by the powerful dominating father was becoming an all too conscious adult reality. How could a self-respecting man reaffirm his virility and still uphold the economic power structures from which he benefited greatly?

By the turn of the century, then, it had become commonplace to insist that woman, in her hunger for gold, was responsible for the manner in which the economic environment seemed to be changing. She had come to be seen as the secret force which had taken the reins of economic selfhood out of the hands of many whose fathers had still appeared comfortably in control of their own financial futures. Suppositions of this sort made her into an ideal surrogate executioner to the many masochistic executioner's assistants among the men of the turn-of-the-century middle class. Woman had become the victimizer of choice of the period's self-pitying marginalized male. By identifying her as the culprit he could forgo the search for other causes and by using her as an executioner's surrogate, he could indulge his pleasure in manipulating the supposed manipulator.

In the light of Dijkstra's argument, the myth that penis envy is the essential psychological motive of kleptomania can be viewed as a response by upper- and middle-class doctors to their own economic and social marginalization. Rather than question or disturb the economic and social structures from which they continued to derive some status and financial ease, they could attribute their demeaned positions to the avarice of the "penis-envying" female. Moreover, what Dijkstra says about the strategies underlying the sexual masochism of males is true of all perversions, male and female. *Perversions are psychological strategies that enlist social gender stereotypes as a way of forgoing the search for the sources of our shared human miseries and plights.*

When these same gender stereotypes are rationalized as the biological qualities that distinguish males from females, we can observe *in statu nascendi* every social force that would make of men and women something less than they could be. Always the easiest, but surely never the wisest, solution to the dilemmas of gender is to enlist some variant of biological determinism, particularly the essentialist philosophy that males and females are in their very biological essence masculine or feminine. Certainly, I am aware that a good argument in favor of biological essentialism can be derived from the fact that preponderantly males are drawn to the deviant sexualities we have traditionally labeled as perversions. How well the statistics on perversion and even my descriptions of male perverse scenarios and male pornography support the mythology that men are born to be brutes, sexual weirdos, and mutilators of female bodies. Why should I bother to argue against these apparent "facts," when I could instead use them to support the mythology that females are innately more noble and pure than males?

In current debates about the legitimacy of male pornography, we can observe the ways in which the essentialist point of view subverts a better understanding of gender. We hear, for example, that the culprit that causes men to turn to sexual perversions and pornography is the urgent and demanding penis. Women, on the other hand, derive their moral superiority and sexual restraint from the receptive and less demanding vagina. Females are designated as victims of the social order while males, the brutes who victimize women, are said to be born that way. Anyone who claims that masochism is an expression of female nature is a woman-hater. As everyone knows, female masochism is the result of women's socialization in a patriarchal society. On the other hand, sadism and men's sadistic fantasies are said to be *natural* outcomes of the male's innate violence and sadism. Male sexuality is "the stuff of murder, not love." Female sexuality is a confection of concern and caring. Everything complicated and interesting and potentially revolutionary gets boiled down to androgen-testosterone power and the abysmal ways in which those with androgen-testosterone power bully and demean the ones with estrogen-progesterone delicacies.

Alice Echols, who in 1983 adopted the Redstocking term *cultural feminism* to refer to this counter-penis, watered-down version of radical feminism, cut beneath the surface of the essentialist philosophy to expose the reactionary gender stereotypes hidden there. Cultural feminists, Echols argued, "define male and female sexuality as though they were polar opposites. Male sexuality is driven, irresponsible, genitally oriented, and potentially lethal. Female sexuality is muted, diffuse, and interpersonally oriented. Men crave power and orgasm, while women seek reciprocity and intimacy." The female style emphasizes love, tenderness, commitment. Male sexuality is selfish and violent. Female sexuality is more spiritual than sexual. The sexuality of genital contact is not central to women's lives. Men need to put their penises into vaginas, but women can do very nicely without that sort of sex, or in fact any sex at all.

As Echols is careful to point out, "to maintain that there exists a theoretical coherence to cultural feminism is not to suggest that it is monolithic." There are shades and variations. I, like Echols, would stress the serious dangers to women, politically and emotionally, of adopting a cultural separatist, female counterculture as a response to male domination. Nevertheless, in exploring the female perversions, I have come to agree with aspects of the cultural feminist position. A woman's sexual energies are not expressed through or dominated by one sexual organ, and therefore her eroticism is not channeled through any single part of her body or necessarily through the body itself. One could even argue, with some justification, that the reason the female is so terrifying and so often portrayed as a threat to the order of the world is her generous capacity for an enigmatic, unfocused, and therefore mischievously polymorphous sexuality. There is some merit to the idea that a female sexuality, more fully explored might be a force that could undermine the social order. This must be so or we would not be so determined to deny, disavow, and repress it. Furthermore, I would agree that men whose lives are dominated by a compulsive sexuality, a perversion, are so because of their driven and defensive, if I may be forgiven a neologism, their *monomorphous* focus on the penis. For those males, the state of the penis, tumescent *or* detumescent, carries the implications of aliveness *or* deadness, wholeness *or* fragmentation, identity *or* nonidentity, phallic *or* castrated.

However, it does not follow, as the more extreme cultural feminists insist, that sexual intercourse itself is a male invention designed to keep women on the bottom. My objections arise when some cultural feminists equate socially created psychological differences between females and males with the anatomical differences between the sexes and then reduce social-psychological characteristics to biological imperatives; when they lose sight of the exploitative social uses made of these so-called natural differences; when they muster their arguments in support of cultural mythologies that can only increase the hostility and warfare between the sexes.

The essentialist perspective on gender is not restricted to females. Some years ago, Ellen Willis warned women about the good male cops who extol the virtues of femininity and proclaim that feminine eroticism is more a fire in the heart and the soul than in the perineum. Says Willis, "The good cops stand ready to assure us that we are indeed morally superior to men, that in our sweetness and nonviolence (read passivity and powerlessness) is our strength." The good cops contrast the urgency of men's stiff penises with women's greater capacity, even when excited, to wait, to forgo, or even when necessary or appropriate to refuse sexual intercourse altogether. It is true that most women are not nearly so desperate as men to confirm their sense of self and identity through genital potency. Nevertheless, any argument that exaggerates and polarizes the differences between female sexuality and male sexuality ultimately confirms the social gender stereotypes of feminine and masculine that are the greatest threat to erotic freedom, and ironically the bedrock and foundation of the perverse strategy. When a man dons the good cop uniform, he invariably confirms what many sexually repressed women want to hear. And what he says does sound no different from any other ploy designed to keep women in their place. The good cops are always telling us that female sexuality is far nobler and humane than male sexuality, which should please and flatter us. However, these good cop arguments smack of the biological essentialism that engenders hopeless animosity between men and women. By asserting that "truly feminine" women care more about relationships than sex, the good cops who pose as our friends are recommending that we accept the infantile gender stereotypes of feminine purity and innocence on which perversion and the pornography enterprise thrive.

What makes a perversion a perversion is not the "kinky" sexuality that every adult may enlist to enliven sexual performance. Perversions are those ironic psychological strategies that enlist gender ideals of virility or purity as a means of dissolving, destroying if necessary, all boundaries between one body part and another, one sex and another, one generation and another. That females tend to express these infantile versions of sexuality and procreation in the perversions of purity and males in the perversions of virility has much more to do with primitive social gender stereotypes than with any essential biological destiny of females and males.

It is true that most of the characteristics we think of as innately feminine or innately masculine are social gender conventions that have prevailed over long periods of human history, almost since the beginning of human time, with only a few sparks of light in the vast sea of darkness. We can make a host of conjectures about what females or males might have been like given more wholesome and humane social environments. But we won't know what that "might have been" means until we question the social structures that exist in the present. To insist that biological sex comes with its innate built-in qualities of femininity and masculinity is as absurd as to insist that females were destined to be gatherers and men were destined to be hunters and that everything that came afterward in human social evolution was a colossal perversion of human destiny. Sociobiologists argue that particular traits of masculinity and femininity have been *ingrained* in human beings as a result of thousands of generations of life in hunter-gatherer societies. Even if it were true, as some scientists claim, that the only males who survived these centuries of social evolution were those who were dominant, aggressive, and sadistic and that only those females who were submissive and passive could go on to have families and reproduce, this would still not account for the persistence of social gender stereotypes. We know, for example, that human beings are immensely responsive to any change, for better or worse, in social gender conventions and that they will hungrily, if not always wisely, adopt any possibility that offers a greater freedom of erotic response. We know also that a social group that has existed for centuries on the basis of certain rigid gender conformities can deteriorate in two or three generations into a primal horde that puts its infants out to be devoured by leopards and steals food from the mouths of the elderly and the sick. On the other side, in some traditional agricultural societies, the custom of wrapping newborns in serapes until the age of two or three produced generations of dull, unimaginative, vacant-eyed children with little inspiration to change or alter the face of their society. But in only one generation, when such infants were given greater stimulation, they became more alert and rebellious parents whose own infants in the second generation became avid readers, talented musicians, physicians, and political leaders.

Very little about the human being, except eye color and blood type, is unalterable. For if we human beings have so altered the shape of nature and of the planet we live in; if we have mustered even the technological capacity to rocket off to other planets; if we have destroyed the hunter-gatherer cultures and extinguished the great auk, the bison, the wild ass, the mammoth, the woolly rhinoceros, the Irish elk, we must wonder why we did not strive to alter in any significant way the gender role stereotypes that have remained almost as they were in the sun dance puberty rituals of the Dakota—whom we also destroyed.

I speak with some hesitation about this entirety of human history, which has come to me secondhand and thirdhand from historians and social anthropologists, who disagree among themselves about the evolution of the human being. I do, however, speak with confidence about perversion in the context of the limited moment of human history that I am most familiar with. I include in that moment modern history, the history of our Western European industrial-commodity societies. From different perspectives entirely, Flaubert and Marx, independently, would respond to the Bonaparte and industrial revolutions by identifying the psychological alienation engendered by the commodity fetishism of bourgeois societies. It is in this socioeconomic context of the industrial revolution and its aftermath that I have been exploring the social gender ideals that underlie the male and female perversions.

Perversions have always existed. I have been addressing the perverse scenarios, male and female, that I have observed in my clinical practice. When I came to the various masquerades of feminine gender identity —the rare transvestism, the more commonplace homeovestism, female impersonation, womanliness—I pointed to the collaboration of the fashion and cosmetic industries with the fetishization of the female body and the trivialization of the female mental and sexual life. In my search for an understanding of the female perversions, I have come to believe that every perverse scenario is intimately related to the social and economic structures of our westernized industrial societies. The social gender stereotypes that are expressed in the perversions I have been writing about are reflections of those structures.

• • •

Flaubert composed *Madame Bovary* in the four and a half years between the autumn of 1851 and the spring of 1856. The chronology of events leading up to Emma Bovary's suicide spans the decade from 1837 to 1847, stopping just short of the political upheaval (Flaubert would have said "catastrophe") that would usher in the age of Homais, the categorizer and labeler. For Flaubert, Louis Bonaparte's rise to power in 1848 signaled the end of hope, magic, faith, and the philosophical reckonings with life and death that characterized the medicine of Bichat, his father's mentor. At the age of nineteen Flaubert wrote, "The day may come when all of modern science may collapse and people will laugh at us, and I wish they would." In his thirties, Flaubert put into Homais's mouth the caricatures of his own father's devotion to science and the scientific method. He railed against the coming of the factories and the railroads and saw in these technologies the end of nature as he knew and loved it. Flaubert was suspicious of social progress, especially of the technologies and economic structures that were implicit in the word *Progress*. Early in Flaubert's century, Jean Baptiste Fourier speculated about the effects of fossil fuel combustion on the earth's atmosphere and used the metaphor of the "hothouse effect." At the beginning of the twentieth century, Svante Arrhenius converted Fourier's mathematical speculations into the hard mathematics of physical chemistry, predicting that if the stepped-up production of carbon dioxide were to double from the pre-industrial level, the average global temperature would rise 9 degrees, heat waves in the mid latitudes would run as high as 130 degrees, the seas would rise several meters, and crops would wither. Flaubert had a point about the mindless progress of the industrial revolution.

In Emma Rouault Bovary, whose romantic illusions led her not to erotic freedom or a greater vision of human possibility but each day chained her more certainly to her demeaning feminine condition,

Flaubert exposed the narrowness of the illusions underlying the Bona-parte revolution, which simply replaced the grandiose tyrannies of aristocracy with the more commonplace tyrannies of the bourgeoisie. The industrial revolution was to him the source of a new kind of misery for human beings, a misery that had yet to be fully elaborated or defined.

Flaubert was profoundly and personally involved with the social constraints that are placed on human desire. He was appalled at the prescriptive gender normalities that were beginning to infiltrate the modern world. He viewed Emma's plights and dilemmas as the same for every human being, male and female. Flaubert chose as his protag-onist a certain female type of his day because he believed that women were particularly burdened by the gender conventions that also bur-dened him. In Emma we observe a woman struggling against the conformity of the Mme. Bovary in which she has been imprisoned. She has not submitted to domesticity, but in her rebellion against that commonly prescribed gender normality she daydreams herself right into a number of other stereotypes of femininity—the dissatisfied wife, the mad housewife, the seduced housewife, the romantic adultress, the extremely submissive woman, the commodity-hungry kleptomaniac, the emasculating temptress, the witch-mother. Emma finds herself within these feminine stereotypes and all the while experiences herself as a detachable, replaceable object that circulates from one man to another.

In his 1950 Foreword to *Madame Bovary*, Jacques de Lacretelle in-formed his readers that Flaubert's heroine had already given her name to a psychological concept: "Bovaryism is the mental state of one who under the domination of imagination and daydreams, fancies himself [*sic*] other than he is and ends by banning reality from his life. It is a sort of concentrated repressed romanticism that has no wings to soar and ends up more often than not in utter nihilism."

Some moments before Léon steps back into her life through the curtains of her box at the Rouen Opera, Emma was reflecting on her sufferings, trying to make sense of her life, thinking back on the happiness she might have had, and wondering why she had missed it. She was reviewing her past and coming to appreciate something about the reasons for her misery. What she understood was only a partial truth. But it was a good beginning. She had the thought that happiness might be a blend of virtue, tenderness, sensuality, and duty; and then the next, even more complicated counterthought that "such happiness must be a lie invented to cause the despair of all desire." However, Emma is so accustomed to finding a diversion from any serious or complicated human dilemma—an Algerian shawl, a bejeweled prayer bench, a love affair—that she finds it hard to get beyond her customary thought "If only I weren't a woman." And so it takes no more to dim the light of reason than the brandishing gestures and captivating presence of Edgar Lagardy, a tenor renowned for seducing women who ruined themselves for one night of his love.

He played to the crowds and always made sure to slip into his publicity a poetic phrase about his fascinating personality and the sensitivity of his soul. With a fine voice, an unshakable aplomb, more temperament than intelligence, more bombast than lyricism —he managed to elevate himself to the level of a marvelous charlatan, in whom there was something of both a hairdresser and a toreador.

For a few moments, Emma is scornful of his overstated machismo. In his black cloak, Spanish hat, silver gilt spurs, soft boots, and lace ruffle, Lagardy is a sorry image of manhood. Before too long, however, Emma is swept away by the poetry of his words, the fire of his passionate gestures. Now here was a man with an inexhaustible supply of love! How she might have found meaning in her life if only she had met *him* and loved *him*. "With him, she would have traveled through all the kingdoms of Europe, from capital to capital, ready to share his hardships as well as his triumphs, picking up the bouquets thrown to him, embroidering his costumes with her own hands."

So carried away is Emma that for a mad moment she is sure that Lagardy is looking at her. "She wanted to run into his arms, to take refuge in his power as if that power were love incarnate and to cry out to him, 'Carry me away, take me with you, let us leave! I am yours, all my passion and all my dreams are yours, yours alone.' "

Emma is possessed by the idea that she can change the reality of who she is by finding a new self in the arms of a powerful man. Emma's illusion of being fixed and transformed by a magical phallus is, to my mind, the most common manifestation of perversion in women, and it gives reason to all the other perversions of female desire. That central illusion, that particular method of defying and short-circuiting reality, is a psychological equivalent of the fetishistic perversions of men.

A woman, dissatisfied and disillusioned with everything the real world has offered to her, is possessed by the idea that a certain kind of person does have the power to fix her—a father, a priest, a husband, a teacher, a lover, a hairdresser, a toreador, a dry goods merchant, a fashion designer, a movie star, a surgeon, an analyst, a son or a daughter or female lover whom she invests with phallic power—and to bring her illusions to life and satisfy all her frustrated desires. He or she will compensate for the humiliations of her childhood and rectify the mortifications of her feminine condition. When that certain kind of person—the ultimate phallic being—is found, that is, created and invented by the woman, the erotomanic pursuit of this fictive phallic power assumes a force and intensity that eventually subsume and consume all a woman's strivings and ambitions.

Yes, an erotomanic pursuit of phallic perfection does succeed in circumventing and undermining reality. However, inevitably the pursuit of illusory moral and physical perfection becomes just another way of acquiescing to the conditions of being and possessing, submitting and dominating. The perversions of sexuality and gender, which so often are glorified as a rebellion against convention, always end up as a doleful expression of the slave-master relationships that preserve the structures of the social order.

Whenever she is too frightened to reveal her treasures to the world or even admit to herself the extent of her powers to know and understand, the slave of love uses the social conventions of her day to curtain the bars of her prison windows. Emma Bovary is always looking around herself trying to locate the sources of her misery. She is not able to look for herself within herself and so has no options but to search for who and what she is in a stereotype of femininity.

There is, though, a potential within each individual woman to arrive at more tempered versions of womanhood, perhaps not so far from Emma's fleeting notion of happiness. What it takes is the not inconsiderable courage to question the various aspects of womanliness that we have come to take for granted as the person we are. In this painful examination of the corruptions of our spirit it is also necessary to scrutinize the Faustian bargains we have made with the social world in which we live.

Along the way toward growing into a normal and socially acceptable womanhood we leave many of our possible lives by the wayside. But they are still there, haunting the life we have chosen to lead. Sometimes, like Emma Bovary, we will imagine that our real life is the life we didn't lead. We sense nameless feelings coursing through our breast and wonder what they could be. We imagine that once we might have played so many parts in the human comedy, that once we were true to ourselves and to our powers. For a woman now, as in Emma's day, to explore and express the fullness of her sexuality, her ambitions, her emotional and intellectual capacities, her social duties, her tender virtues, would entail who knows what risks and who knows what truly revolutionary alteration of the social conditions that demean and constrain her. Or she may go on trying to fit herself into the order of the world and thereby consign herself forever to the bondage of some stereotype of normal femininity—a perversion, if you will.

Notes

The following writings, referred to throughout this book, significantly influenced my interpretations of the female and male perversions.

ABRAHAM, KARL. "Manifestations of the Female Castration Complex" (1920). In *Selected Papers on Psychoanalysis,* translated by Douglas Bryan and Alex Strachey. New York: Basic Books, 1927. Cited as Abraham (1920).

DIJKSTRA, BRAM. *Idols of Perversity.* New York: Oxford University Press, 1986.

FLAUBERT, GUSTAVE, *Madame Bovary: Moeurs de Province.* Paris: A. Quantin, Imprimeur-Éditeur, 1885. English translations are mine. Cited as *Bovary.*

———. *Correspondance.* 13 vols. Paris: Louis Conrad, 1926. English translations are mine except where indicated otherwise. Cited as *Correspondance.*

FREUD, SIGMUND. *The Complete Psychological Works of Sigmund Freud.* Edited and translated by James Strachey. London: Hogarth Press, 1955–1974. Freud's complete works are traditionally referred to as the *Standard Edition,* a practice I use in these Notes.

———. "Fetishism" (1927). In vol. 21 of *Standard Edition.* Cited as "Fetishism."

KESTENBERG, JUDITH. *Children and Parents.* New York: Aronson, 1975.

———. "Outside and Inside, Male and Female." *Journal of the American Psychoanalytic Association* 16: 457–519.

KOHON, GREGORIO, "Fetishism Revisited." *International Journal of Psychoanalysis* 68: 213–28 (1987).

STOLLER, ROBERT. *Observing the Erotic Imagination.* New Haven: Yale University Press, 1985.

TANNER, TONY. *Adultery in the Novel.* Baltimore: Johns Hopkins University Press, 1979.

VARGAS LLOSA, MARIO. *The Perpetual Orgy.* Translated by Helen Lane. 1975. New York: Farrar, Straus and Giroux, 1986.

PROLOGUE

The immediate inspiration for the four doctors was Tony Tanner's essays on *Madame Bovary* in *Adultery in the Novel.* Perhaps the most significant influence on my thinking about the fetishistic undercurrents in *Madame Bovary* has been Tanner. I thank Professor Barbara Williamson for calling his work to my attention.

2 "In opposition to his wife's maternal tendencies": *Bovary,* p. 6.

2 "like a mill horse": *Bovary,* p. 9.

3 "To eradicate, to forcibly conventionalize": Tanner, p. 283.

4 "to that generation": *Bovary,* p. 369.

4 "the sum of the functions that oppose death," physical properties held back by vital properties, "Time wears them away": cited by Tanner, p. 320n, from François Jacob, *The Logic of Life* (New York: Pantheon Books, 1973), *passim.*

5   "You will dissipate at once," "to yield up their meaning": from Bichat, cited by Tanner, p. 321n. Tanner's reference is Michel Foucault, *The Birth of the Clinic* (New York: Pantheon, 1973), p. 146. Foucault's reference is Bichat, *Anatomie Générale,* Avant-propos, p. xcix.

5   "as sharp as his lancet": *Bovary,* p. 369.

5   "In the latter day bourgeois society": Frankfurt Institute for Social Research, *Aspects of Sociology* (1956), translated by John Viertel, Preface by Max Horkheimer and Theodor W. Adorno (Boston: Beacon Press, 1972), p. 131. I thank my friend and colleague Professor Joel Whitebook for referring me to the writings of the Frankfurt Institute.

Chapter 1   WHAT IS A PERVERSION?

9–18   The perverse strategy: My interpretations of the perverse strategy were informed by the following works:

Hans Sachs, "On the Genesis of Perversion" (1923), translated by Ruth B. Goldberg, *Psychoanalytic Quarterly* 50 (1986). Sachs emphasizes that the element of infantile sexuality that attains awareness is a detail that keeps unconscious an entire history of infantile sexuality, especially the incestuous wishes of the Oedipus complex. William Gillespie, "A Contribution to the Study of Fetishism," *International Journal of Psychoanalysis,* 21 (1940), and "The General Theory of Sexual Perversion," *International Journal of Psychoanalysis* 37 (1956). Victor N. Smirnoff, "The Fetishistic Transaction," in *Psychoanalysis in France,* edited by Serge Lebovici and Daniel Widlocher (New York: International Universities Press, 1980). Jean LaPlanche and J. B. Pontalis, "Fantasy and the Origins of Sexuality," *International Journal of Psychoanalysis* 49 (1968).

18–33   The basic psychiatric reference for my discussion of the paraphilias in *DSM* III and *DSM* III-R was Ethel S. Person's well-documented chapter "Paraphilias and Gender Identity Disorders," in *The Personality Disorders and Neuroses,* vol. 1 of *Psychiatry,* edited by Robert Michels, M.D., and Jesse O. Cavenar, Jr., M.D. (Philadelphia: Lippincott, 1985). Person has managed, quite remarkably, to convey the centrality of the fantasy life in the structuring of a perversion even though she was limited to presenting the *DSM* behavioral viewpoint. I also wish to thank Dr. Person for her valuable comments throughout the years that I was working on this book.

For the psychoanalytic perspective on the categories of male perversions, my primary reference was Otto Fenichel, "Perversions and the Impulse Neuroses," in *Psychoanalytic Theory of Neuroses* (New York: Norton, 1945).

25   "Mrs. Von Donajew may not only chastise": Leopold von Sacher-Masoch, *Venus in Furs* (1870). The complete text appears in Gilles Deleuze, *Masochism: Coldness and Cruelty,* (New York: Braziller, 1971), p. 220.

27   Marquis de Sade (1785), *The 120 Days of Sodom and Other Writings,* compiled and translated by Austryn Wainhouse and Richard Seaver with introductions by Simone de Beauvoir and Pierre Klossowski (New York: Grove Press, 1966). The culminating orgy: pp. 665–69.

32   The pedophile's perceptions of the female body: Charles Socarides, *The Preoedipal Origin and Psychoanalytic Therapy of Sexual Perversions* (Madison, CT: International Universities Press, 1988), pp. 455, 464.

34   Fetishism as the prototype of perversion: I owe much of my thinking about fetishism and the perverse strategy to an interview with Dr. Allan Bass, June 27, 1987.

34   a woman's full sexual identity and responding body: Tanner, pp. 287–88.

36   The passage on the Portuguese word *feitiço* and the allusions to Marx and Freud: Allan Bass, "On the History of a Mistranslation and the Psychoanalytic Movement," unpublished paper presented at the New York Psychoanalytic Society, February 1984. Bass cited the following Freud references: Sigmund Freud, "Leonardo da Vinci and a Memory of His Childhood," *Standard Edition,* vol. 11; Bernard Marsh and Hilda C. Abraham, eds. and trans., *The Letters of Sigmund Freud and Karl Abraham* (New York: Basic Books, 1965); and William McGuire, *The Freud/Jung Letters* (Princeton: Princeton University Press, 1974).

36   "commodity fetishism": Karl Marx, "Commodity Fetishism" (1847), *The Marx-Engels Reader,* edited by Robert C. Tucker (New York: Norton, 1972), pp. 215–25.

36   "the word is said": Bass, p. 27.

36   the list of fetishes: Stoller, pp. 16–17. Stoller was the first American psychiatrist to consider seriously the problem of sexual perversions in females. Stoller's down-to-earth way of assessing the psychological meaning of perversion as it exists in the

"real" world, that is, outside the psychoanalytic clinical situation, has been invaluable to me. I refer to some of Stoller's case histories in Chapters 8 and 9. I thank Dr. Stoller for his intellectual generosity and willingness to share his ideas with me.

37–40   Descriptions of male adolescence: Louise J. Kaplan, *Adolescence: The Farewell to Childhood* (New York: Simon and Schuster, 1984; New York: Touchstone, 1985), and Kestenberg, *Children and Parents,* pp. 371–76.

41   pushing forward the frontiers of the possible: Janine Chassequet-Smirgel, *Creativity and Perversion* (New York: Norton, 1986), p. 6.

Chapter 2   "A MEMORIAL TO THE HORROR OF CASTRATION"

44   "The most beautiful woman," "a terrible shyness": Francis D. Baudry, "Adolescent Love and Self-Analysis as Contributors to Flaubert's Creativity," in *Psychoanalytic Study of the Child* (New Haven: Yale University Press, 1980), 35:380–81. Baudry's translation is from Flaubert, *Correspondance,* 1:25.

44–45   "Take care not to ruin": letter to Ernest Feydeau, undated (beginning of February 1859), *Correspondance,* 4:312.

45   "probably no male human being": "Fetishism," p. 154.

47   "homosexuals from the rest of mankind": Freud, *Three Essays on the Theory of Sexuality* (1905), *Standard Edition* 7:145, footnote (1915).

47   "all human beings": *Standard Edition,* 7:146, footnote (1915).

47   "The exclusive sexual interest": *Standard Edition,* 7:146, footnote (1915).

47   "The disposition to perversions": *Standard Edition,* 7:171.

49   "But . . . a particular": "Fetishism," p. 152.

53   Metaphor of the crochet needle: I thank a suggestion from my editor, Nan Talese, who already understood all of this when we worked together on *Oneness and Separateness: From Infant to Individual* (New York: Simon and Schuster, 1977; New York: Touchstone, 1978).

56   From a very early time: The ages I use in my discussions of children's develop-
      ment are only approximate. There is wide variation among children in the ages at
      which they reach developmental stages.

60   The primal scene: Joyce McDougall, "Scène Primitive et la Scénario Pervers," in
      la Sexualité Perverse (Paris: Payot, 1972). McDougall's paper also influenced my
      interpretations of the case studies in Chapter 5.

64   "The horror of castration": Freud, "Fetishism," p. 154.

65   Prostitute interviews: I thank Lois Gould for sharing with me her research on the
      "kinky" garments requested by male customers of prostitutes.

72–74 The security blanket: My primary references are from D. W. Winnicott's exten-
      sive writings on transitional objects, in particular "Transitional Objects and Tran-
      sitional Phenomena," in Through Paediatrics to Psychoanalysis (New York: Basic
      Books, 1975).

73–74 Distinctions between transitional objects and sexual fetishes; little explorer: Phyllis
      Greenacre, "Perversions: General Considerations Regarding Their Genetic and
      Dynamic Background" (1968), in Collected Papers, vol. 1 (New York: Interna-
      tional Universities Press, 1971); "The Fetish and the Transitional Object" (1969)
      and "Transitional Object and the Fetish: With Special Reference to the Role of
      Illusion" (1970), Collected Papers, vol. 1; M. Wulff, "Fetishism and Object Choice
      in Early Childhood," Psychoanalytic Quarterly, vol. 15 (1946).

Chapter 3   THE FEMALE CASTRATION COMPLEX

78   "Her fate is one": Luce Irigaray, "Ce sexe qui n'est pas un," translated by Claudia
      Reeder for New French Feminisms, edited by Elaine Marks and Isabelle de Cour-
      tivron (Amherst: University of Massachusetts Press, 1980), p. 99. There is another
      pun I do not mention in the text: Irigaray is also saying that woman's sexual
      organ is not one but multiple, plural.

80   The drama of the three cigars: Abraham (1920), pp. 341–42. I have taken some
      liberty with this story and the later fate of the little dramatist (p. 344) but my
      interpretive version is true to the spirit of Abraham's paper.

82   "I have recently wondered": Bernard Marsh and Hilda C. Abraham, eds. and
      trans., Letters of Sigmund Freud and Karl Abraham, 1907–1926 (New York: Basic
      Books, 1965), December 3, 1924, p. 375.

83–84   Inner-genital phase: Kestenberg, Chapter 12, "The Development of the Young Child from Birth through Latency as Seen Through Bodily Movement," chap. 12 in *Children and Parents*. The inner-genital phase is described on pp. 246–53.

84   "Inner-genital sensations": Kestenberg, *Children and Parents*, p. 320.

84   "everything that moves": Kestenberg, *Children and Parents*, p. 321.

85   Separation-individuation: Margaret S. Mahler's extensive research and theoretical writings were brought together in *The Psychological Birth of the Human Infant*, coauthored with Fred Pine and Anni Bergman (New York: Basic Books, 1975). Mahler's interpretations of the separation-individuation process have been criticized by Daniel Stern. But his research, in fact, turns out to be a validation of her observations. For philosophical reasons Stern prefers to think of the human infant moving from separation to greater and greater unity or attachment to the mother. However, as I explain in *Contemporary Psychoanalysis* 23: 27–44, Stern has misinterpreted the process described by Mahler, which consists of two interweaving strands of development—attachment and separation—from birth onward. My version of the separation-individuation process appears in *Oneness and Separateness: From Infant to Individual* (New York: Simon and Schuster, 1977; Touchstone, 1978), where I make use of some of Stern's earlier observational studies that were brought together in *The First Relationship* (Cambridge: Harvard University Press, 1977).

85   By the middle of the second year: As I explained in Chapter 2, the ages that I cite in my discussions of children's development are only approximate.

96–105   The sections on female genital awareness, the female castration complex and primal scene interpretations are derived from my observational studies of infants, toddlers, and their families, from Kestenberg's observations, from the follow-up studies conducted by Mahler on the families in her original study, from the follow-up studies of children in my research nurseries, and from my clinical practice with female children, adolescents, and adults. I also recommend Eleanor Galenson and Herman Roiphe, *Infantile Origins of Sexual Identity* (New York: International Universities Press, 1981). After describing, in some detail, a genital awareness in male and female toddlers, the authors state on pp. 251–53 that their observational research strongly suggests, but does not definitively confirm, that such awareness would include an inner genital awareness, particularly in female toddlers.

Many female psychoanalysts have challenged the traditional view of the female castration complex. I mention one paper because the author's observations correspond to my own research and clinical experience, yet her interpretations are very different from mine: Doris Bernstein, "Female Genital Anxieties, Conflicts, and Typical Mastery Modes," *International Journal of Psychoanalysis* 71: 151–65 (1990).

Bernstein contrasts the traditional interpretation of female castration anxiety—"the fears and fantasies about lost, damaged or missing parts of the body" (p. 153) —with a constellation of genital anxieties—access, penetration, diffusivity—that she prefers to think of as dangers to bodily integrity rather than as castration anxiety. These fears and fantasies relating to the female genitals are prominent in females and I have, in fact, described them in this chapter. However, I think they *are* aspects of the female castration complex and do not feel that anything is gained by calling them something else merely to distinguish them from the traditional penis envy interpretation. More seriously, I object to Bernstein's perspective because it is symptomatic of a biological essentialism that is surreptitiously misogynist. I was saddened to learn of Dr. Bernstein's death in January 1990, for I find her work interesting and would have welcomed the opportunity to discuss our differences.

Chapter 4   OTHER MEMORIALS

109   "It is remarkable": Freud, "Infantile Genital Organization of the Libido" (1923), *Standard Edition*, 19:142n.

109   Anita A. Bell, "Some Observations on the Role of the Scrotal Sac and Testicles," *Journal of the American Psychoanalytic Association* 9: 261–86 (1961).

109   "in the areas of pleasure-unpleasure": Bell, p. 262.

110   "It's as though the scrotum": Bell, p. 273.

110   "Look, I have a nut": Bell, p. 271.

110   "Oh good, then I can make babies too": Bell, p. 271.

110   "See, there are two": Bell, p. 271.

110   Creation legends and cultural associations to the testicles: Bell, 278–79. Legend of Cronos: W. H. Auden, ed., *The Portable Greek Reader* (New York: Viking Press, 1948), pp. 53–54; also Joseph Campbell, *The Masks of God: Occidental Mythology* (New York: Viking Press, 1964).

111   "when the Pope": Bell, p. 278.

114   "extreme denial of the 'inside' ": Kestenberg, "Outside and Inside," p. 463.

116–17 The athletic supporter: "Fetishism," pp. 156–57.

118   "In conclusion we may say": "Fetishism," p. 157.

120   "The patient oscillated": "Fetishism," p. 156.

120   "the most important event": Freud, Preface to *The Interpretation of Dreams,* 2nd ed. (1908), *Standard Edition,* 4:xxvi.

121   "altogether the most perfect": Freud, "Femininity" (1933), *Standard Edition,* 23:133.

Chapter 5   PERVERSE SCENARIOS

123   "Men sometimes feel": Gay Talese, *Thy Neighbor's Wife* (Garden City, NY: Doubleday, 1980), pp. 115–16.

129–66 Case studies: To focus on the childhood events that gained expression in the perverse scenarios of Mr. G, Mr. R, Mr. B, and Mr. K, I have omitted any discussion of other unconscious themes and a number of significant technical elaborations. For these details, which give a more rounded appreciation of the infinite complexities of a perverse scenario, I refer readers to the original case reports.

129–38 Case of Mr. G: James Glover, "On an Unusual Form of Perversion," *International Journal of Psychoanalysis* 8: 10–24 (1924).

131   "a slackness of the mouth," a "derangement of hair or dress": Glover, p. 10.

132   "of falling and collapsing": Glover, p. 10.

132   "while they were hot and smelling": Glover, p. 16.

132   "Now go to Hell! I've finished": Glover, p. 11.

132   "ringing down the curtain": Glover, p. 11.

133   the game of "fetching mother's slippers": Glover, p. 11.

135   "I have lost my womanhood": Glover, p. 13.

135   "Get it over!" "Get it finished!" "Put it down!": Glover, p. 15.

137   "There is a tendency": Glover, p. 23.

138   "for her hypocrisy": Glover, p. 18.

138–39   Cases of lust murder: Richard von Krafft-Ebing, *Psychopathia Sexualis,* translated from the 12th German edition by Franklin S. Klaf (New York: Bell, 1965).

138   "I may say": Krafft-Ebing, p. 58.

139   "I had an unspeakable delight": Krafft-Ebing, p. 65.

140–43   Case of Mr. N: S. Nacht, R. Diatkine and J. Favreau, "The Ego in Perverse Relationships," translated by Joyce McDougall, *International Journal of Psychoanalysis* 55: 404–13 (1956).

144–45   Case of Mr. O: Otto Kernberg, "Malignant Narcissism and Its Relation to Perversion," unpublished manuscript, presented at the 27th annual Sandor Rado Lecture of Columbia University Center for Psychoanalytic Training and Research, June 4, 1984, pp. 26–27.

145–54   Case of Mr. R: May E. Romm, "Some Dynamics in Fetishism," *Psychoanalytic Quarterly* 99: 137–53 (1947).

145   "it may also signify": Romm, p. 138.

151   "I will cut my wife's hair," "I will cut her hair": My rendition of Romm's theoretical formulations on the unconscious fantasies underlying her patient's hair cutting scenario. Romm, pp. 138–39.

153   "attempting to take his mother": Romm, p. 145.

154–60   Case of Mr. B: Robert Bak, "Fetishism," *Journal of the American Psychoanalytic Association* 1: 285–98 (1953).

158   "a worm among Giants": Bak, p. 295.

158–59   "Historically, the pregenital identification": Bak, p. 286.

159   "dancing naked": Bak, p. 294.

159   "truly epic proportions," "How much I envied": Bak, p. 296.

160–66   Case of Mr. K: Kohon.

164   "The voyeurism of the mother": Kohon, p. 220.

165   "a gift cut from": Kohon, p. 220.

166   "exercising his authority," "attached, engaged, anchored": Kohon, p. 225.

Chapter 6   FEMININE STEREOTYPES AND THE FEMALE PERVERSIONS

168   "Her castration complex will thus": Abraham (1920), p. 344.

169   The vengeful bride: Abraham (1920), pp. 345–46.

171   Masculine women, "Such women do not, however": Abraham (1920), p. 347.

172   "I am the fortunate possessor": paraphrase of Abraham (1920), p. 348; "I must and shall receive": paraphrase Abraham (1920), p. 350.

173   "Just as male exhibitionists seek": Abraham (1920), p. 352. About the difference between the neurotic and perverse strategies, Abraham is correct in one respect. The man who exhibits his penis feels sinful, that he is doing something wrong, whereas the female with a swollen nose or fixed stare or parasol may be feeling anxious, that she is doing something worthwhile and good. Since some female perversions are expressed in a feminine stereotype of virtue and purity, the female's experience of pride in living up to the stereotype is the same as the male's experience of pride in his virility.

174   Phobias related to unconscious mutilation wishes; lovers of crippled and amputated men: Abraham (1920), p. 356.

176   Frigidity: Abraham (1920), pp. 359–62; "Frigidity is practically": Abraham (1920), p. 359.

176   an earlier paper of his: Karl Abraham, "Ejaculatio Praecox" (1917), Selected Papers, pp. 280–98. Cited as Abraham (1917).

176   "ejaculation with regard to the substance": Abraham (1917), p. 281.

176   "to what is for them": Abraham (1917), p. 283.

177   "Quite a number of those who suffer": Abraham (1917), p. 295.

178   "Ejaculatio praecox and female frigidity": Abraham (1917), pp. 284–85.

179   "In cases of frigidity": Abraham (1920), p. 359.

179   "It is these contractions": Abraham (1920), p. 359.

181–82   "The girl has primarily no feeling of inferiority": Abraham (1920), pp. 339–40.

186   Karen Horney, "On the Genesis of the Castration Complex in Women" (1922), in *Feminine Psychology* (New York: Norton, 1967).

187   "wrapped in a little cotton-wool": Susan Quinn, *A Mind of Her Own* (New York: Summit, 1987), p. 201.

187   "The conclusion so far drawn": Horney, p. 38.

191   Myths of primary femininity, past and present: In Horney's day some of the more popular works on primary femininity were written by a favorite teacher of hers, the sociologist Georg Simmel: *Weibliche Kultur* (Female Culture) in 1911 and later writings such as *Die Koketterie* (Flirtation) and *Das Relativ und das Absolut im Geschlechterproblem* (The Relative and the Absolute in the Problem of the Sexes). These and other essays have been collected in Georg Simmel, *On Women, Sexuality, and Love* (New Haven: Yale University Press, 1984). In his turn Simmel, like many other turn-of-the-century sociologists, was influenced by Bachofen, *Das Mutterecht* (Mother Right; 1861), in *Selections, Myth, Religion, and Mother Right* (Princeton: Princeton University Press, 1967).

Current myths of primary femininity as well as protests against those myths appear in nearly every contemporary collection of feminist thought. I highly recommend the following: Toril Moi, *Sexual Textual Politics* (London: Methuen, 1984); Elaine Marks and Isabelle de Courtivron, eds., *New French Feminisms* (Amherst: University of Massachusetts Press, 1980); Toril Moi, ed., *French Feminist Thought* (Oxford: Basil Blackwell, 1987); Ann Snitow, Christine Stansell, and Sharon Thompson, eds., *Powers of Desire* (New York: Monthly Review Press, 1983); Carole S. Vance, ed., *Pleasure and Danger* (London: Routledge and Kegan Paul, 1984).

An excellent review contrasting traditional psychoanalytic perspectives on female development with Horney's is Zenia Odes Fliegel, "Feminine Psychosexual Development in Freudian Theory," *Psychoanalytic Quarterly* 42: 385–409 (1973).

192–93   "Woman's intellectuality is to a large extent": Helene Deutsch, *The Psychology of Women* (New York: Grune and Stratton, 1944–45), 1:290–91.

197   Theory of female perversions: Wladimir Granoff and François Perrier, "The Problem of Perversion in Women and Feminine Ideals," and Victor N. Smirnoff, "The Fetishistic Transaction," in *Psychoanalysis in France,* edited by Serge Lebovici and Daniel Widlocher (New York: International Universities Press, 1980). While I am not in agreement with Granoff and Perrier about female sexuality, I do find their way of reasoning about the general issue of female perversion congenial to my theoretical and clinical viewpoints.

Chapter 7   THE TEMPTATIONS OF EMMA BOVARY

201   "It is better not": *Bovary,* p. 325.

201   "I dissect ceaselessly": Flaubert, letter to Ernest, December 1838, in Francis D. Baudry, "Adolescent Love and Self-Analysis as Contributors to Flaubert's Creativity," *Psychoanalytic Study of the Child,* 35: 380–81 (1980). Baudry translation from *Correspondance,* 1:19.

201   "Beneath beautiful appearances": Flaubert to Louise Colet, September 5, 1856, *Correspondance,* 1:294.

202   "I am in an entirely different world now": Flaubert to Louise Colet, February 8, 1852, *Correspondance,* 2:365.

203   "Save your eternally erect penis": Flaubert to Ernst Feydeau, undated (beginning of 1859), *Correspondance,* 4:312.

203   "I no longer have a penis": Flaubert to Louise Colet, April 13, 1854, *Correspondance,* 4:56.

204   "I could give a course": Flaubert to Louise Colet, August 26, 1853, *Correspondance,* 2:319–27. I thank Francis D. Baudry for the translation.

205   "yearning to live in town": *Bovary,* p. 150.

206   "little by little,": *Bovary,* p. 221.

206   "the eternal monotony": *Bovary*, p. 221.

206   "I am your servant": *Bovary*, p. 220.

206   "overflow into the emptiest of metaphors": *Bovary*, p. 221.

207   "And I'm so afraid": Wharton to W. M. Fullerton, early March 1908, *The Letters of Edith Wharton*, edited by R. B. Lewis and Nancy Lewis (New York: Scribner's, 1988), p. 134. Cited as *Letters*.

207   "because all the words in me": Wharton to W. M. Fullerton, early March 1908, *Letters*, p. 135.

207   "the stalest of platitudes": Wharton to W. M. Fullerton, June 10, 1908, *Letters*, p. 152.

207   "Drawing rooms are always tidy": R. W. B. Lewis, *Edith Wharton: A Biography* (New York: Fromm, 1985), p. 30. Cited as Lewis.

207   "Every character is a failure": Lewis, p. 31.

208   "This pinch of ashes": Lewis, p. 218.

208   "that lyrical region of adulteresses": *Bovary*, p. 188.

209   "that fever of happiness," *Bovary*, p. 187.

209   "so ardent they drove her mad": *Bovary*, p. 197.

209   "And so their great love affair": *Bovary*, p. 197.

210   "the instinct of feminine servitude": Richard von Krafft-Ebing, *Psychopathia Sexualis*, translated from the 12th German edition by Franklin S. Klaf (New York: Bell, 1965), p. 130.

210   "In women voluntary subjection": Krafft-Ebing, p. 130.

211   "numerous as the examples of male *Horigkeit*": Krafft-Ebing, p. 135.

211   "sexual bondage is not a perversion": Krafft-Ebing, p. 136.

211   Cases of sexual bondage: Mr. N, Krafft-Ebing, Case 223, p. 361; Mrs. X, Krafft-Ebing, Case 224, pp. 262–63.

212   "She got deeper and deeper": Krafft-Ebing, p. 263.

212   Extreme submissiveness: Annie Reich, "A Contribution to the Psychoanalysis of Extreme Submissiveness in Women" (1940) and "Narcissistic Object Choice in Women" (1953), in *Psychoanalytic Contributions* (New York: International Universities Press, 1973).

213   "reconciled to her own sexual role": Abraham (1920), p. 344.

217   "With the narcissistic entitlement": *Bovary*, p. 221.

218   The gone-away/come-back game is adapted from the *fort-da* game described by Freud, *Beyond the Pleasure Principle, Standard Edition*, 24:14–17.

224   "love nothing and no one except Lyova": Sofia Andreyevna Bers Tolstoy, *The Diary of Tolstoy's Wife: 1860–1891*, translated by Alexander Werth (London: Victor Gollancz, 1928), Moscow, January 17, 1863, p. 98. Cited as *Diary*.

224   "I can't find any occupation for myself": *Diary*, November 13, 1862; p. 87; "I have given my life to him": *Diary*, January 17, 1863, p. 98; "What was reverie": *Diary*, April 1, 1863, p. 104.

226   Edith Jones's brother Harry calls her John: Lewis, p. 26.

226–27 "I have wondered what stifled cravings": Lewis, p. 24.

227   "My life was better before I knew you": Wharton to W. M. Fullerton, mid-April 1910, *Letters*, p. 208.

227   "adopt a franker idiom": Wharton to W. M. Fullerton, October 1912, *Letters*, p. 281.

227   "between the essential and the superfluous": Wharton to W. M. Fullerton, June 8, 1908, *Letters*, p. 151.

227–28 "with all the heavy tin draperies": Wharton to W. M. Fullerton, October 1912, *Letters*, p. 281.

228   "from a long lethargy": Wharton to W. M. Fullerton, August 26, 1908, *Letters*, p. 161.

228   Fullerton compares Wharton to George Sand: Lewis, p. 222.

228   "the only possible sexual excitement:" Otto Fenichel, *The Psychoanalytic Theory of Neurosis* (New York: Norton, 1945), p. 352. Fenichel refers to extreme sexual submissiveness as a perversion more typical of females than males. He says that it represents a transitional state between infatuation and masochism (p. 352). Like Krafft-Ebing and Reich, Fenichel is distinguishing extreme submissiveness from masochism but also recognizing that it bears certain features that are similar. The literature on masochism is formidable. I will cite only my five favorite writings on the subject because they clarify, explicitly or implicitly, this crucial distinction between extreme submissiveness and sexual masochism: William H. Grossman, "Notes on Masochism: A Discussion of the History and Development of a Psychoanalytic Concept," *Psychoanalytic Quarterly* 15 (1986).

Theodor Reik, *Masochism and Modern Man* (New York: Farrar and Rinehart, 1941).

Otto Kernberg, "Clinical Dimensions of Masochism," *Journal of the American Psychoanalytic Association* 36: 4 (1988).

Sigmund Freud, "The Economic Problem of Masochism," *Standard Edition*, vol. 19.

Victor N. Smirnoff, "The Masochistic Contract," *International Journal of Psychoanalysis* 50 (1969).

233   "He was becoming her mistress": *Bovary*, p. 321.

233   "At last I have a real mistress": *Bovary*, p. 306.

233   "above all Angels": *Bovary*, p. 306.

233   "He rebelled against Emma": *Bovary*, p. 326.

233   "incapable of heroism": *Bovary*, p. 325.

234   "Bovary's mother kept him": *Bovary*, p. 6.

234   "It was he who could have been taken": *Bovary*, p. 33.

234   "the universe did not extend": *Bovary*, p. 38.

234   "infused into the veins," "virile blood," Vargas Llosa, p. 147n. Vargas Llosa cites a review that appeared in the October 18, 1957, *L'Artiste* and later was reprinted in Baudelaire's *L'Art romantique*.

234   "Like Pallas": Vargas Llosa, p. 145n.

235   "Beneath the exquisite femininity": Vargas Llosa, p. 140.

235   "Her gaze became bolder": *Bovary*, pp. 221–22.

236   "A man, at least, is free": *Bovary*, p. 102.

Chapter 8   MASQUERADES

237   "More clumsy I couldn't be": Virginia Woolf, *Orlando* (1928; New York: Penguin, 1946), p. 202.

237   "the silent and rather scornful woman," "I never appreciated": Nigel Nicolson, *Portrait of a Marriage* (New York: Atheneum, 1973), p. 116.

238   Description of Knole and Vita's family background: Victoria Glendinning, *Vita* (New York: Knopf, 1983), *passim*.

238   "The upper half of your face": Nicolson, pp. 34–35.

239   "something reserved, muted," "a central transparency," "Damn the woman": Nicolson, p. 212.

239   "the longest and most charming love letter": Nicolson, p. 202.

239   "the strength of a man": *Orlando*, p. 86.

239   "which can be worn indifferently": *Orlando*, pp. 86–87.

239   the costumes of Orlando, "China robe of ambiguous gender": *Orlando*, p. 141.

240   "Virginia by her genius": Nicolson, p. 208.

240   "Mother used to hurt my feelings": Nicolson, p. 4.

240   "Although the most incomprehensible": Nicolson, p. 6.

240   "as like a boy,": Nicolson, p. 5.

240   "stuffing their nostrils": Nicolson, p. 5.

240   "My armour. My swords and guns": Nicolson, p. 6.

241   "a lifelong daydream": Stoller, p. 154.

244   Two women cross-dressers: Stephen Greenblatt, *Shakespearean Negotiations: The Circulation of Social Energy in Renaissance England* (Berkeley: University of California Press, 1988), p. 66.

244   "so they say": Greenblatt, p. 66.

244   "for using illicit devices": Greenblatt, p. 66.

245   "like a man's": Greenblatt, p. 74, referring to Jacques Duval, *Des Hermaphrodites* (Rouen, 1603), pp. 404–5.

245   "There are not two radically different structures": Greenblatt, p. 74, referring to Duval.

245   Cross-dressing by females during the seventeenth and eighteenth centuries: David Underdown, *The London Review of Books,* September 14, 1989, p. 12, review of Rudolf Dekker and Lotte van de Pol, *The Tradition of Female Transvestism in Early Modern Europe* (New York: Macmillan, 1988). The reviewer and authors use the term *transvestite* in its general meaning of cross-dressing. However, it is uncertain and unlikely that all the women they describe were, technically speaking, transvestites.

245   "Male fears of 'women on top' ": Underdown.

246   "if the proper boundaries": Underdown.

246   Sally: "Transvestism in Women," in Stoller, pp. 135–56; eating the cake but saving the frosting: Stoller, p. 146; "at that fabulous moment": Stoller, p. 147.

247   "The neat part": Stoller, p. 142.

247   "I wear boots almost exclusively": Stoller, p. 143.

247   "yet mothered a child": Stoller, p. 147.

247   "It gives me a feeling of power to own them": Stoller, p. 147.

248   "The high point of each day": Nicolson, p. 194.

248   "Mother didn't soften": Nicolson, p. 8.

248   "Virginia is very sweet": Nicolson, p. 207.

249   George Zavitzianos is to be commended not only for his later bold inquiries into the previously unexplored perversion of homeovestism but also for his earlier courageous psychoanalytic treatment of Lillian. Many analysts might have assumed that Lillian's delinquency and profound character pathology would have made her "unanalyzable." However, if Zavitzianos had not ventured to make available to Lillian the unique benefits of an analysis, there is every likelihood that she would have maintained the antisocial and perverse behaviors that kept her deeper sufferings unconscious, and Zavitzianos might not have discovered the perversion of homeovestism. I owe Zavitzianos a special debt for his insights into homeovestism, a perversion that I had been observing in my female and male patients, appreciating the perverse strategy at work but never, until reading Zavitzianos, finding the language that would give these appreciations their full psychological meaning. I thank my colleague and friend Dr. William Grossman for calling his work to my attention. And if in my efforts to present brief, "narrative" renditions of the cases of Larry and Lillian I sometimes introduce a touch of my own clinical understandings, I have remained faithful to the spirit of Zavitzianos's studies. It was impossible here to render the extent of Zavitzianos's originality and the versatility of his theoretical understandings and therapeutic skill. I therefore refer readers to those of his writings that most influenced me, all of which appeared in volumes of the *International Journal of Psychoanalysis* between 1967 and 1977: "Problems of Technique in the Analysis of a Juvenile Delinquent," 48: 439–47 (1967); "Fetishism and Exhibitionism in the Female and Their Relationship to Psychopathy and Kleptomania," 52: 297–305 (1971); "Homeovestism: Perverse Form of Behaviour Involving the Wearing of Clothes of the Same Sex," 53: 471–77 (1972); "The Object in Fetishism, Homeovestism, and Transvestism," 58: 487–95 (1977).

249   Larry's case: Zavitzianos, 53: 473–75, 58: 489–90.

250   The distinctions among fetishism, transvestism, and homeovestism: Zavitzianos claimed that previous reports of male fetishism and transvestism by Freud (1927), Bak (1953), Gillespie (1940), and many others were actually cases of homeovestism. To put Zavitzianos's technical diagnostic distinctions briefly: fetishism represents a denial or warding off of a primary identification with the castrated mother; transvestism represents a wish to strengthen the identification with the castrated mother and to simultaneously repudiate that wish; homeovestism represents an identification with the idealized phallic parent of the same sex to overcome an unconscious identification with the castrated mother. Zavitzianos, 58: 492–93. I would describe homeovestism as an impersonation of the idealized phallic parent of the same sex to overcome shameful and frightening cross-gender identifications.

251   Lillian's case: Zavitzianos, 53: 472–73, 58: 491, 493.

251   "and anything that," "Lillian had a tendency": Zavitzianos, 53: 472.

254   The two Lillians: Zavitzianos, 48: 440–41, 53: 473.

255   Lillian's sexuality: Zavitzianos, 48: 440, 52: 301; "absorbed the boy's experience," "his power and his feelings": 48: 440.

256   "While performing the role": *Bovary,* pp. 216–17.

258   Olympia, "masochisma matches machismo," "the dumb blonde": "Centerfold," in Stoller, p. 87.

259   "I always thought I had the grace": Stoller, p. 81.

259   "Without the container": Stoller, p. 84.

259   Olympia's recollections of childhood, "favorite forms of entertainment," "I had quite a bit of difficulty": Stoller, pp. 74–75.

260   "Wouldn't it be interesting": Stoller, p. 78.

261   "So they are vulnerable": Stoller, p. 84.

262   Modern-day Pygmalions: Elizabeth Waites, "Fixing Women: Devaluation, Idealization, and the Female Fetish," *Psychoanalytic Quarterly* 51: 435–59 (1982).

265   "Cut out your sex life": Stoller, p. 75.

265   "All I am": Stoller, p. 76.

265   Quotations from the fashion industry: Michael Gross, "Designers Reveal the Woman Behind the Fashions," *New York Times,* November 24, 1987, p. B8.

268   Joan Rivière, "Womanliness as a Masquerade," *International Journal of Psychoanalysis* 10: 303–13.

268   "Of all the women," Rivière, p. 303.

271   "much as a thief will turn out his pockets," Rivière, p. 305.

278   "was worked to death," Rivière, p. 311.

Chapter 9   STOLEN GOODS

284   "Money is the universal means": Karl Marx, "On the Power of Money in Bourgeois Society" (1844), in *The Early Texts,* in Karl Marx, *Selected Writings,* edited by David McLellan (Oxford: Oxford University Press, 1977), pp. 110–11.

284   The psychoanalytic mythology: Traditionally, in psychoanalytic discourse, kleptomania is referred to as a female disorder, where the theft is motivated by "penis envy." Gregorio Kohon, for example, refers implicitly to this tradition when he says: "We find two groups of specific perversions which are exclusive to one sex: kleptomania, a perversion almost entirely found in females, motivated by envy of the penis, the wish to exercise a right to possess something that is felt to be denied; and fetishism and exhibitionism, almost exclusively male perversions, emerging as a response to the threat of castration." "Fetishism Revisited," *International Journal of Psychoanalysis* 68: 219 (1987).

However, while there are case studies where the impulsive theft of material goods is part of a patient's symptomatology, I was surprised when a search of the literature revealed not *one* theoretical essay devoted to kleptomania per se. Karl Abraham, in "Manifestations of the Female Castration Complex," refers to kleptomania as a neurotic disorder of the revenge type. About the best single summary of the dynamics of kleptomania appears in Otto Fenichel's chapter "Perversions and Impulse Neuroses" in *The Psychoanalytic Theory of Neuroses* (New York: Norton, 1945), pp. 370–71. In his characteristic thoroughness, Fenichel cites eighteen references for his one-page entry on "cleptomania," which he categorizes as an impulse neurosis. However, his references are to case histories, most of them in French or German, and these articles tell us nothing more substantive than appears in Fenichel's one-page entry.

292   "At a certain indefinite point," "may take over increasingly large areas": Tanner, p. 288.

292   "In *Madame Bovary* we see the first signs": Vargas Llosa, pp. 140–41.

293   "As this perverting power": Marx, "On the Power of Money," p. 111.

298   "leads more easily": Caesar Lombroso and William Ferrero, *The Female Offender*, Introduction by W. Douglas Morrison (New York: Appleton, 1903), p. 111.

299   "a conservatism of which": Lombroso and Ferrero, p. 109.

299   Deceitfulness of females and second-rate theories: Anne Campbell, *Girl Delinquents* (New York: St. Martin's, 1981), pp. 36–64; Carol Smart, *Women, Crime, and Criminology: A Feminist Critique* (London: Routledge and Kegan Paul, 1976), pp. 27–53. Also, Otto Pollak, *The Criminality of Women* (Philadelphia: University of Pennsylvania Press, 1950; New York: Barnes, 1961).

300   Citing Margaret Sanger: Pollak, p. 9.

301   "Woman's body, however": Pollak, p. 10.

302   "technical necessity": Pollak, p. 10.

302   "fits of veracity": Pollak, p. 12.

302   "these cases of so-called veracity": Pollak, p. 12.

302   "new riddles for pestered detectives": Pollak, p. 139.

302   "How often the accusation": Pollak, p. 159.

303   Pollak contends that: Pollak, p. 75.

303   "One can but marvel": Pollak, p. 147.

304   "trying to transform the vagueness": Tanner, p. 297.

306   "to find herself tranquil": *Bovary*, p. 44.

306   "stood out for her like comets": *Bovary*, p. 58.

307   Emma's wedding cake: *Bovary*, pp. 32–33.

307   "Their indifferent gaze": *Bovary*, p. 58.

308   Into that captious sieve: The idea is from Tanner, p. 347. Tanner cites Shakespeare, "a captious and intentible sieve," from *All's Well That Ends Well*, 1.3.

308   "He was clever": *Bovary*, p. 118.

309   "How much are they?": *Bovary*, p. 119.

309   "Emma will soon be unable": Tanner, p. 297.

310   "No, you mustn't": *Bovary*, p. 219.

310   "She nearly swooned": *Bovary*, p. 247.

311   "the same delicious words": *Bovary*, p. 248.

311   "Then you and I could arrange": *Bovary*, p. 315.

311   "It pains me," "Her ears rang": *Bovary*, p. 315.

312   "What a scene there was": *Bovary*, p. 318.

313   "Not a day passed that Trina": Dijkstra, p. 368.

313   "virgin whores of babylon," Eve and Pandora: Dijkstra, p. 364.

314   Venus–Pandemos, "idealistic aspirations": Dijkstra, p. 358.

314   Lulu, "created for every abuse": Dijkstra, p. 358.

314   "a fountain of life from which flows": Dijkstra, p. 366.

314   The Danae and Zeus: Dijkstra, p. 369.

314   Judith as a head–huntress: Dijkstra, pp. 376–79.

314   "sword blades gaping," "savage Nidularium blossom": Dijkstra, p. 360.

315   "The masochism, then": Dijkstra, p. 374.

316   Zuni fetishes: Frank Hamilton Cushing, *Zuni Fetishes,* facsimile edition, edited by Tom Bahti (1880; Las Vegas: KC Publications, 1966).

317   "to assist man" and descriptions of fetishes: Cushing, p. 6.

318   The department store: John D'Emilio and Estelle B. Freedman, *Intimate Matters: A History of Sexuality in America* (New York: Harper and Row, 1988), pp. 188–89.

318   "All our inventions and progress": Karl Marx, "Speech at the Anniversary of the *People's Paper,*" in *Surveys from Exile,* edited by David Feinbach (New York: Vintage, 1974), p. 300.

318   The megamall: All quotations are from Isabel Wilkerson, "Megamall: A New Fix for Future Shopping Addicts," *New York Times,* June 9, 1989, p. A14.

320   "amulets, sacred fountains": Gustave Flaubert, cited by Jean Paul Sartre, "La Conscience de Classe Chez Flaubert," *Les Tempes Modernes* (June 1966).

Chapter 10   FOR FEMALE EYES ONLY

321   "Man in his lust": Cited by Laura Lederer, ed., *Take Back the Night* (New York: Morrow, 1980), p. 21.

321   "The genitalia are the chief difficulty": Otto Weininger, *Sex and Character* (c. 1906; New York: AMS Press, 1975), p. 241. Weininger, a Jew who thought of

his Jewishness as a feminine weakness, was only a "self-proclaimed" philosopher, but he was taken seriously by a number of early-twentieth-century intellectuals. He committed suicide, at the age of twenty-three, shortly after completing *Sex and Character*, which would soon become a bible of the Nazis.

322   Men averting their gaze, the "aesthetics" of male pornography: Stoller, pp. 36–37.

323   "Liberated women publicize": Stoller, p. 37.

323   "There *is* a pornography just for women!": Stoller, p. 37.

324   Harlequin statistics and data: *The Harlequin Story: Harlequin Fun Facts* (Ontario: Harlequin, 1988).

326   "to sweep the reader away": *Harlequin Story*, p. 10.

326   "the publishing industry's answer," "They are juicy, cheap, predictable": Stoller, p. 39, citing article by Grover in *Wall Street Journal* (1980).

326   "in a dizzying succession": Stoller, p. 40.

326   "move about so much": Stoller, p. 40.

327   "captive dove trying": *Bovary*, p. 172.

327   "on the slice of white stocking": *Bovary*, p. 184.

327   "In my soul you are like a madonna": *Bovary*, p. 185.

327   "I am mad to listen": *Bovary*, p. 186.

328   After much simpering protestation: *Bovary*, p. 282.

328   "Scraps of paper fluttered": *Bovary*, p. 284.

328   "the bouregois stared": *Bovary*, p. 283.

328   "It was not without considerable": *Saturday Review*, July 1, 1857, p. 40. I thank Peter Gay for calling my attention to this review.

329   "The Trial of *Madame Bovary*," translated by Evelyn Gendel, in *Madame Bovary* (New York: New American Library, 1964), pp. 325–403.

329   "two words too late": "Trial," p. 361.

329   "otherwise one could recount" "his instincts from below," "The light pages": "Trial," p. 345.

331   "There was always love": *Bovary*, p. 41.

331   "soiling her hands": *Bovary*, p. 41.

331   "plucking daisy petals," "sultans with long pipes": *Bovary*, p. 43.

332   "In a less sexist society": Ann Barr Snitow, "Mass Market Romance: Pornography for Women Is Different," in *Powers of Desire*, edited by Ann Barr Snitow, Christine Stansell, and Sharon Thompson (New York: Monthly Review Press, 1983), p. 256.

333   "Having me urinate on them": *United States Attorney General's Commission on Pornography*, U.S. Department of Justice final report, 2 vols. (Washington, D.C.: Government Printing Office, July 1986), 1:793.

334   Anaïs Nin, *The Diary of Anaïs Nin*, vol. 3 (New York: Harcourt Brace and World, 1969). Hereafter cited as *Diary*.

335   "Leave out the poetry": *Diary*, p. 58.

335   "So I began to write": *Diary*, p. 58.

335   "Less poetry": *Diary*, p. 60.

335   "snobbish literary house": Anaïs Nin, *Delta of Venus* (1969; New York: Bantam, 1978), p. xii.

335   "As we have to suppress poetry": *Diary*, p. 157.

335   "For centuries we had only one model": *Delta*, p. xiv.

336   "color, flavor, rhythms, intensities": *Diary*, p. 177.

336   Pauline Réage, *The Story of O*, translated by Sabine d'Estrée (New York: Ballantine, 1965).

337   "Women at least are fated": *Story of O*, p. xxxiv.

337   Standard pornography formulas: *Story of O*, p. xvii.

337   "the tragic flowering of a woman": *Story of O*, p. xvi.

340   "The pornography industry has grown": *Commission on Pornography*, 2:1353.

341   "perversion, abortion, drug addiction": cited in *Commission on Pornography*, 2:1362.

341   "The 1980's have seen": *Commission on Pornography*, 2:1366.

342   Ann Snitow argued, "too much of what is infantile in sex": Snitow, p. 256.

342   "all social constraints": Snitow, p. 256.

343   Ellen Willis, "Feminism, Moralism, and Pornography," in *Powers of Desire*, p. 464. (First published in the *Village Voice*, October and November 1979.)

345   Organized crime and pornography: *Commission on Pornography*, 2:1042–53; land-lords, realtors: *Commission on Pornography*, 2:1043.

345   even minor infractions: *Commission on Pornography*, 2:1057.

345   "with the front bumper": *Commission on Pornography*, 2:1057–58.

345   dial-a-porn operations: *Commission on Pornography*, 2:1431–36.

346   "In New York, one Dial-A-Porn": *Commission on Pornography*, 2:1433.

346   five "pleasures": *Commission on Pornography*, 2:1431.

347   paperbacks under *A: Commission on Pornography*, 2:1548; films under *A: Commission on Pornography*, 2:1573; magazines under *A: Commission on Pornography*, 2:1505.

348   "from as young as one week": *Commission on Pornography*, 1:405.

348   Child pornography as a cottage industry: *Commission on Pornography*, 1:406–10.

349   Description of child pornography industry: Florence Rush, "Child Pornography," in *Take Back the Night*, pp. 71–80.

350   "Afraid to deal with women": Dijkstra, p. 195.

351   The history of "clean porn": Gay Talese, *Thy Neighbor's Wife* (Garden City, NY: Doubleday, 1980), pp. 45–49, 68–69.

352   "The hating way in which women": Laura Lederer, "Then and Now: An Interview with a Former Pornography Model," in *Take Back the Night*, p. 69.

352   Description of the snuff genre: Beverly LaBelle, "Snuff: The Ultimate in Woman-Hating," in *Take Back the Night*, pp. 273–74.

352   The Kensington Ladies Erotica Society, *Ladies' Own Erotica* (New York: Pocket Books, 1984).

353   "Do we really know": *Ladies' Own Erotica*, p. 1.

354   Grandma and Henry Miller: Sabina Sedgewick, "Solo Virtuoso," pp. 234–39.

354   Marquis de Sade, *The 120 Days of Sodom and Other Writings* (New York: Grove, 1966). Simone de Beauvoir's Introduction, "Must We Burn Sade?," was first published in *Les Tempes Modernes*, December 1951 and January 1952.

354   "the vain fancies that inhabited it," "Of what use is vice," "Who can flatter himself": Sade, p. 35.

355   "But he meant the very opposite": Sade, p. 36.

355   "There is no passion": Sade, p. 26.

355   "the exercise of those remains": Sade, p. 26.

355   "To drink blood": Sade, p. 26.

356   "Ah, how many times": Sade, p. 32.

356   Valerie Solanas, *SCUM Manifesto*, Introduction by Vivian Gornick (London: Olympia Press, 1968). Maurice Giradias was the publisher of Olympia Press. The Warhol story is in his Preface, p. xi–xii.

357   "The male is an incomplete female": Solanas, p. 3.

357   "Every boy wants": Solanas, p. 12; "It never becomes completely clear": Solanas, p. 14.

358   "by means of operations": Solanas, p. 38; "will be quietly": Solanas, p. 51.

Chapter 11 MUTILATIONS

362   "From an intricate package": Elfriede Jelinek, *The Piano Teacher*, translated by Joachim Neugrosschel (New York: Weidenfeld and Nicolson, 1988), p. 44.

362   Charles enters Emma Rouault's life: *Bovary*, pp. 16–17.

363   the tortoiseshell monocle: *Bovary*, p. 17.

365   "Emma, overcome with exhaustion": *Bovary*, p. 309.

365   "The Blind One!": *Bovary*, p. 375.

365–66 Dr. Flaubert encases a child's clubfoot in an iron boot: Vargas Llosa, p. 108.

366   "Is this not an occasion": *Bovary*, p. 206.

366   "the shape of the foot," "a livid tumescence": *Bovary*, p. 207.

366   "Straighten clubfeet": *Bovary*, p. 210.

368   Delicate self-cutting: The first case was reported by L. E. Emerson, who called it a perversion: "The Case of Miss A: A Preliminary Report of a Psychoanalytic Study of Self-Mutilation," *Psychoanalytic Review* 1: 41–54 (1914).

    The label *delicate self-cutting* was given by Ping-Nie Pao, "The Syndrome of Delicate Self-Cutting," *British Journal of Medical Psychology* 42: 195–205 (1969). In that same issue of *British Journal:* John S. Kafka, "The Body as Transitional Object: A Psychoanalytic Study of a Self-Mutilating Patient," pp. 207–12, and Edward M. Podvoll, "Self-Mutilation Within a Hospital Setting: A Study of Identity and Social Compliance," pp. 213–21.

Other significant clinical papers are the following: Stuart Asch, "Wrist Scratching as a Symptom of Anhedonia: A Pre-Depressive State," *Psychoanalytic Quarterly* 40: 603–17 (1971); L. Crabtree, "A Psychotherapeutic Encounter with a Self-Mutilating Patient," *Psychiatry* 30: 91–100 (1967). Shelley Doctors researched in depth the adolescent developmental issues associated with delicate self-cutting: Shelley Doctors, *The Symptom of Delicate Self-Cutting in Adolescent Females: A Developmental View,* doctoral dissertation, Ferkauf Graduate School, Yeshiva University, 1979. An abbreviated version of Doctors's thesis appeared in *Adolescent Psychiatry* 9: 443–60 (1981).

Since it is virtually impossible, outside a hospital setting, for any one psychoanalyst to treat a sufficiently large enough number of delicate self-cutters to arrive at generalizable conclusions, the clinician turns to colleagues to share experiences and insights. Therefore, I thank Drs. Pheema Englestein, Susan Scheftel, Shelley Doctors, and Howard Shevrin for sharing with me their theoretical and clinical insights.

370   Self-mutilation hobbyists: P. Wakefield, A. Frank, and R. Meyers, "The Hobbyist: A Euphemism for Self-Mutilation and Fetishism," *Bulletin of the Menninger Clinic,* 41: 539–52 (1977).

370   "the ultimate" professional amputation: "The Hobbyist," p. 541.

370   Magazine letters, *Amputee Love:* "The Hobbyist," pp. 547–48.

370   Description of Monsieur M's body mutilations: Michel de M'uzan, "Un Cas de Masochisme Pervers," *la Sexualité Pervers* (Paris: Payot, 1972), pp. 16–18; "I'm a dirty whore": M'uzan, p. 18. English translations are mine.

371   Self-castration: Karl Menninger, "A Psychoanalytic Study of the Significance of Self-Mutilations," *Psychoanalytic Quarterly* 4: 408–66 (1935); genital and adrenal self-castrations: Menninger (1935), pp. 445–52. List of references to self-castration: Menninger (1935), p. 459.

372   Sex-reassignment surgery: The most impressive and convincing critique of the controversy over sex-reassignment surgery is Jon K. Meyer, "The Theory of Gender Identity Disorders," *Journal of the American Psychoanalytic Association* 3 (1982).

372   Descriptions of delicate cuttings: Pao, Kafka, Podvoll, Asch, Doctors. In addition, H. Grunebaum and G. Klerman, "Wrist-Slashing," *American Journal of Psychiatry* 124: 527–34 (1967). Grunebaum and Klerman were still calling the symptom wrist slashing, but the patients they were describing were the delicate cutters discussed by Pao.

373   Methods and instruments: Grunebaum and Klerman, pp. 528–29. See also R.

Rosenthal, C. Rinzler, R. Wallsh, and E. Klausner, "Wrist-Cutting Syndrome: The Meaning of a Gesture," *American Journal of Psychiatry* 128: 1363–68 (1972).

373   Delicate self-cutting and menstruation: Doctors (1979), pp. 45–47, 240–50.

373   puberty changes: Louise J. Kaplan, *Adolescence: The Farewell to Childhood* (New York: Simon and Schuster, 1984; New York: Touchstone, 1985). Cited as Kaplan (1984).

375   Psychological and cognitive accompaniments to pubescence: Kestenberg, *Children and Parents;* Kestenberg, "Nagging, Spreading Excitment, Arguing," *International Journal of Psychiatry and Psychotherapy* 2: 265–97 (1973). Emotional reactions to menarche: Kestenberg, *Children and Parents,* pp. 290–99, 364–65.

375–76   Hunter-gatherer scarifications and mutilations: Kaplan (1984), pp. 28–31. 28–31.

376   Sun dance of the Dakotas: Erik Erikson, *Childhood and Society* (New York: Norton, 1950), pp. 130–32.

376   "young men would engage": Erikson, p. 130.

376   Girl sharing her brother's ritual: Erikson, p. 130.

376   Significance of ritual initiations: Kaplan (1984), pp. 28–31.

377–78   Holding: Louise J. Kaplan, *Oneness and Separateness* (New York: Simon and Schuster, 1977; New York: Touchstone, 1978), pp. 89–99 *passim,* as inspired by the writings of D. W. Winnicott. Cited as Kaplan (1977).

379–82   Mothers and fathers of delicate self-cutters: Asch, Crabtree, Doctors (1979; 1981), Kafka, Grunebaum and Klerman, Pao, Rosenthal et al.

380   mother who breast-fed without holding her baby: Pao, p. 197.

381   "I felt the badness": Grunebaum and Klerman, p. 529; "It's like vomiting": my clinical research; "the gap in the skin": Rosenthal et al., p. 1367; calming voice: my clinical experience.

381   self-made zipper: Kafka, p. 210. "which as it spread over the hills": Kafka, p. 209.

381   Identification with mother: Asch, pp. 614–17.

382   Leaking out of substances and feelings: Quotations from my clinical experiences and paraphrases from Doctors, Kafka. "I felt mad," "I was frustrated," "Everything was getting all fucked up": Doctors (1979), p. 184; "I felt shitty": Doctors (1979), p. 185; "I felt so tense": Peter Novotny, "Self-Cutting," *Bulletin of the Menninger Clinic* 36: 505–14 (1972), p. 505.

383   clinging to stuffed animals, fierce attachment to slicing razors: Doctors (1981), p. 221.

384   physical illnesses and surgeries in childhood: Rosenthal et al., p. 1363.

384   run over by a car: Rosenthal et al., p. 1363.

384   spiked braces: Kafka, p. 209.

385   "For reasons not known to the patient": Pao, p. 197; Semidepersonalized altered state of consciousness: Asch, pp. 608–9; "Like this isn't me": Doctors (1979), p. 190.

386   Girl who scratched LOVE on her thigh: Asch, p. 613; "an almost palpable hatred": Asch, p. 613.

386   Flower child: Asch, p. 605. Good girls who never bothered their parents: Interviews with Doctors, Englestein, and Shevrin confirmed my impression that there are two types of self-cutters, the so-called good girls and bad girls. Asch's patients seemed to be mostly of the good girl stereotype. Euphoric type: Asch, p. 605.

386   And on many a bright Sunday morning: my interpretation.

387   "I was always told": Pao, p. 197; "I was more a father": my clinical research.

389–90   Discovery of the anatomical differences: Doctors (1981), p. 451, Doctors (1979), pp. 196–200; attraction to violent and sadistic men: Asch, p. 604; deflorations and repeated rape: Doctors (1981), p. 450.

390   Frequent menstrual disorders: Rosenthal et al., p. 1364.

391   Typical menstrual disorders and remedies: The Merck Manual, 15th edition (Rahway, N.J.: Merck Sharp and Dohme, 1987), pp. 1687, 1698, 1700, 1701, 1723.

391   Münchhausen syndrome: The term was coined by R. Asher, "Münchhausen's Syndrome, Special Articles," Lancet 1: 927–33 (1957). Also B. Bursten, "On Münchhausen's Syndrome," Archives of General Psychiatry 13: 261–68 (1965); story of von Münchhausen: H. Spiro, "Chronic Factitious Illness," Archives of General Psychiatry 18: 569–80 (1968).

391–92   Karl Menninger, "Polysurgery and Polysurgical Addiction," Psychoanalytic Quarterly 3: 173–99 (1934). "Naturally, unconscious motives": Menninger (1934), p. 173. Another classical paper on the sadistic motives of doctors is Ernst Simmel, "The 'Doctor-Game': Illness and the Profession of Medicine," International Journal of Psychoanalysis 7:470–83 (1926).

392   Unconscious motives of polysurgical addicts: Menninger (1934), passim.

394   "to those who crave the love": Menninger (1934), p. 181.

394   Adolescent case: Menninger (1934), p. 182.

394   woman operated on thirteen times in thirteen years: Menninger (1934), pp. 182–83.

395   medical recommendations for castration: Menninger (1935), p. 451n.

397   Trichotillomania: John T. Monroe and D. Wilfred Abse, "The Psychopathology of Trichotillomania and Trichophagy," *Psychiatry* 26: 95–103 (1963); Harvey R. Greenberg and Charles A. Sarner, "Trichotillomania: Symptom and Syndrome," *Archives of General Psychiatry* 12: 482–89 (1965); Sadie H. Zaidens, "The Skin," *Journal of Nervous and Mental Disease* 113: 388–94 (1951a); Sadie H. Zaidens, Self-Inflicted Dermatoses and Their Psychodynamics, *Journal of Nervous and Mental Disease* 113: 395–404 (1951b). I did not discuss the infantile forms of trichotillomania because there is no convincing evidence of continuity between the infantile and adolescent forms of this disorder. However, see Edith Buxbaum, Hair Pulling and Fetishism, *Psychoanalytic Study of the Child*, 15: 243–60.

398   Methods of hair pulling: my observations and Greenberg and Sarner, p. 485.

399   Family background of trichotillomaniac: Greenberg and Sarner, pp. 485–86; Monroe and Abse, pp. 101–2; Zaidens (1951b), *passim*.

400   "As the symptom progressed": Greenberg and Sarner, p. 486.

401   The symbolic meaning of hair: Hyman S. Barahal, "Psychopathology of Hair-Plucking (Trichotillomania)," *Psychoanalytic Review* 27: 291–310 (1940); Charles Berg, "Unconscious Significance of Hair," *International Journal of Psychoanalysis* 17: 73–78; James G. Frazer, *The Golden Bough* (New York: Macmillan, 1923); Menninger (1934; 1935).

402   Orthodox Jewish women, nuns: Barahal, p. 301; Medusas: my interpretation; witches: Frazer, p. 680.

405–6   Emma and memorial picture: *Bovary*, p. 43.

406   "I am sure our mothers": *Bovary*, p. 196.

406–7   "like the mortally wounded": *Bovary*, p. 361.

Chapter 12   THE CHILD AS SALVATION

408   "When piety and maternal sentiment": Caesar Lombroso and William Ferrero, *The Female Offender* (New York: Appleton, 1899), p. 151.

409   "The modern tendency of women": August Forel, *The Sexual Question,* translated by C. F. Marshall (1906; New York: Physicians and Surgeons Book Co., 1925), p. 137.

409   The father's phallic function: Gregorio Kohon, "Fetishism Revisited," *International Journal of Psychoanalysis* 68: 225 (1987).

409   "What is the function of the father?," "a 'fucked woman' ": Kohon, p. 225.

410   "If the picture is at all aggravated": Wladimir Granoff and François Perrier, "The Problem of Perversion in Women and Feminine Ideals," in *Psychoanalysis in France,* edited by Serge Lebovici and Daniel Widlocher (New York: International Universities Press, 1980), pp. 259–60.

411   Discovery of childhood: Patricia Coveney, "The Image of the Child in English Literature," in *Rethinking Childhood,* edited by A. Skolnick (Boston: Little, Brown, 1976); Louise J. Kaplan, "Parenting: Alternatives and Continuities," in *Patterns of Supplementary Parenting,* vol. 2 of *Child Nurturance,* edited by Marjorie J. Kostelnik, Albert I. Rabin, Lillian A. Phenice, and Anne K. Soderman (New York: Plenum Press, 1982).

412   She takes her household in hand: *Bovary,* p. 122.

412   "her consolation": *Bovary,* p. 122.

412   "within she was full of envy": *Bovary,* p. 124.

414   "two large tears,": *Bovary,* p. 132.

414–15   Bronson Alcott: Charles Strickland, "A Transcendentalist Father: The Child-Rearing Practices of Bronson Alcott," *History of Childhood Quarterly* 1: 4–51 (1973). There were three Alcott children. Anna was born March 1831, Louisa eighteen months later in October 1832, and Elizabeth nearly five years later in 1835.

414   "Verily, had I not been called": *The Journals of Bronson Alcott,* selected and edited by Odell Shepard (Boston: Little, Brown, 1938), January 21, 1835, p. 55. Cited as Alcott.

414   The writings of Daniel Gottlob Moritz Schreber: From a bibliography of Schreber's writings (1839–1862) in Hans Israels, "The New Schreber Texts," in *Psychosis and Sexual Identity: Toward a Post-Analytic View of the Schreber Case,* edited by David B. Allison, Prado de Oliveira, Mark S. Roberts, and Allen S. Weiss (Albany: State University of New York Press, 1988), pp. 328–30. Cited as "Schreber Texts."

415   The Homais children: *Bovary,* p. 399.

416   "the fondness and timidity": Alcott, October 16, 1834, p. 47.

416   "in due accordance and harmony": Strickland, p. 5.

417   "the parent, like the Divinity": Henry Ebel, "Commentary" on Strickland's view of Alcott, *History of Childhood Quarterly* 1:55 (1973).

417   "by and by you will love me": Strickland, p. 40, from Bronson Alcott, *Alcott Family Manuscripts,* transcribed by Eyoke M. Strickland (Cambridge: Harvard University's Houghton Library), p. 276.

417   "Very good little girls give up": Strickland, p. 37, from *Alcott Family Manuscripts,* p. 200.

417–18   Trial of the apple: This is my narrative version of the trial as described by Strickland, pp. 41–42, from *Alcott Family Manuscripts,* pp. 156–59.

418–19   Grand inquisitor, "a wraparound father": Ebel, p. 54.

419   Dr. Schreber: William G. Niederland, *The Schreber Case* (New York: Quadrangle/New York Times Book Co., 1974), especially Chap. 7, "Schreber: Father and Son," Chap. 8, "Schreber's Father," Chap. 9, "The 'Miracled-Up' World of Schreber's Childhood."

419   Schreber's recommendations to parents: Niederland, pp. 56, 71.

419–20   Trial of the pear: As described by Dr. Daniel Schreber in *Das Buch der Gesundheit*

(The Book of Health) (Leipzig: Friedrich Volckmar, 1839), p. 64, cited in Niederland, p. 71.

420   "no further trouble": Niederland, p. 71.

420   the child must shake the hand: Dr. Daniel Schreber, *Kallipadie, oder Erziehung zur Schönheit* (Education Toward Beauty), p. 142, cited in Niederland, p. 56.

421   Dr. Schreber's equipment: Niederland, pp. 52–55 (with diagrams).

421   Gustav's suicide: Niederland, pp. 66–67; Daniel Paul Schreber's life: "Schreber Texts," pp. 209–10.

421   *Memoirs:* Daniel Paul Schreber, *Memoirs of My Nervous Illness* (1902), translated and edited by Ida Macalpine and Richard A. Hunter (1955), with a new introduction by Samuel M. Weber (1973) (Cambridge: Harvard University Press, 1988). Cited as *Memoirs.*

422   *compression-of-the-chest miracle: Memoirs,* p. 133.

422   *head-compressing machine: Memoirs,* p. 138.

422   *the coccyx miracle,* "this was an extremely painful": *Memoirs,* p. 139.

422   "these egoistic actions": *Memoirs,* p. 252.

423   Masturbation cures: G. Stanley Hall, *Adolescence* (New York: Appleton, 1904) 1: 453–63; Louise J. Kaplan, *Adolescence: The Farewell to Childhood* (New York: Simon and Schuster, 1984; Touchstone, 1985), pp. 198–200; Mary S. Hartman, "Child Abuse and Self-Abuse: Two Victorian Cases," *History of Childhood Quarterly* 1: 221–48 (1974); Stephen Kern, "Psychodynamics of the Victorian Family," *History of Childhood Quarterly* 1: 437–62 (1974).

424   "A Slowly Murdered Child": Larry Wolff, *Postcards from the End of the World* (New York: Atheneum, 1988), p. 50; "death had taken pity on her": Wolff, p. 47.

425   "tortures which remind one": Wolff, p. 51, citing *Neue Freie Press,* November 15, 1899.

425   "In our times, eaten away": the prosecutor of the Hummel case, Dr. R. von Kleeburn: Wolff, p. 67, citing *Arbeiter-Zeitung,* November 15, 1899.

426   The Kutschera case: Anna Kutschera's injuries: Wolff, pp. 115–16. "Yes, and especially Annerl": Wolff, p. 124, citing *Neue Freie Press,* November 29, 1899.

426   The Russian whip: Wolff, p. 122. "I beat the children, but I didn't abuse them": Wolff, p. 115.

427–33   "battered child syndrome": My primary reference for this section is Brandt F. Steele's classic paper "Parental Abuse of Infants and Small Children," in *Parenthood: Its Psychology and Psychopathology,* edited by E. James Anthony and Therese Benedek (Boston: Little, Brown, 1970). The vignettes of child abuse are my narrative versions of Steele's cases. The names given to the children are mine and the words of the parents are paraphrases of Steele. Cited as Steele.

     My other general references are Brandt F. Steele, "A Psychiatric Study of Parents Who Abuse Infants and Small Children," in *The Battered Child,* edited by Ray E. Helfer and C. Henry Kempe (Chicago: University of Chicago Press, 1968). Since the time that Steele wrote these essays, there have been countless books and reviews on the physical and sexual abuse of children. Among the most recent are *The Battered Child,* 4th ed., edited by Ray E. Helfer and Ruth S. Kempe (Chicago: University of Chicago Press, 1987). This edition contains an updated version of Steele's papers entitled "Psychodynamic Factors in Child Abuse." It also includes papers on the sexual abuse of children. I also recommend *Child Maltreatment,* edited by Dante Cicchetti and Vicki Carlson (Cambridge: Cambridge University Press, 1989), a complete technical report of recent research on child abuse and child sexual abuse.

429   "All my life nobody ever loved me": paraphrase of Steele, p. 455.

429   "Hello, I love you": doll attributed to battering mother: From Eda Le Shan, "The 'Perfect' Child," *New York Times Magazine,* August 27, 1967, cited by Steele, p. 451.

429   Timmy: Steele, p. 466.

429   Harry: Steele, p. 463.

430   Annie and Donald: "If she doesn't come the minute I call her": paraphrase of Steele, p. 472.

430   "After I hit Johnny": paraphrase of Steele, p. 472.

431   Emotional scenario leading up to the attack: Steele, pp. 470–71.

432   "When the baby keeps crying": paraphrase of Steele, p. 471.

435   Lois Timnick, "22% in Survey Were Child Abuse Victims," *Los Angeles Times*,
       August 25, 1986, pp. 8, 32. Nowadays, the sexual abuse of children is no longer
       confined to the back pages of magazines, newspapers, and tabloids, and there are
       numerous books on the subject. A recent publication that corresponds closely to
       my clinical understandings is an excellent nontechnical but psychologically so-
       phisticated summary of recent research on child sexual abuse, the psychology of
       the victims, and the victimizers, legal dilemmas, and treatment possibilities: John
       Crewsdon, *By Silence Betrayed* (Boston: Little, Brown, 1988; New York: Harper
       and Row, 1989). I highly recommend this volume, in which the distinctions
       between fixated, regressed, and crossover pedophiles and the psychology of the
       typical incest family and the incest mother are reported in greater detail.
           I also recommend Ramon C. Ganzarain and Bonnie J. Buchele, *Fugitives of
       Incest* (Madison, CT: International Universities Press, 1988), for its depiction of a
       psychoanalytically oriented group therapy process that brings out the issues I have
       discussed in this chapter.

441   Vladimir Nabokov, *Lolita* (1955), in *The Annotated Lolita*, edited by Alfred Appel,
       Jr. (New York: McGraw-Hill, 1970).

441   "Just slap her": Nabokov, p. 57.

441   "We are not surrounded": Nabokov, p. 126.

443   Soul murder: My references are to a classic paper on soul murder: Leonard L.
       Shengold, "Child Abuse and Deprivation: Soul Murder," *Journal of the American
       Psychoanalytic Association* 27: 533–60 (1979).

444   "It is the iniquity": Shengold, p. 535.

444   Systematic soul murder: Shengold, pp. 537–42. Mind-distorting defenses:
       Shengold, pp. 538–42.

444   blanking-out defenses: Shengold, p. 538.

445   "maybe this time I will be loved": paraphrase of Shengold, p. 542.

446–47   Descriptions of the settings and apparatuses were inspired by unpublished papers presented at psychoanalytic meetings by Robert J. Stoller.

448   " 'Bondage' means that one person is 'submissive' ": "Larry S." pseud., "S and M and the Revolution," *Come Out*, 1987.

450   "Her deed makes a mockery": Wolff, p. 67, citing *Arbeiter-Zeitung*, November 15, 1899.

Chapter 13   LITTLE SOUL MURDERS: PURE GIRLS AND VIRILE BOYS

455–56   Anorexia nervosa, historical accounts: John Sours, *Starving to Death in a Sea of Objects* (New York: Jason Aronson, 1980), pp. 207–17; Hilde Bruche, *Eating Disorders: Obesity, Anorexia Nervosa, and the Person Within* (New York: Basic Books, 1973), pp. 211–15; Jack L. Ross, "Anorexia Nervosa: An Overview," *Bulletin of the Menninger Clinic* 41 (5): 418–36 (1977); Mara Selvini Palazzoli, *Self-Starvation: From Individual to Family Therapy in the Treatment of Anorexia Nervosa* (New York: Jason Aronson, 1980), p. 5.

456   Hospital treatments: Sours, pp. 360–77; Hilde Bruch, *The Golden Cage: The Enigma of Anorexia Nervosa* (Cambridge: Harvard University Press, 1978), pp. 91–105.

457   Symbiotic and separation-individuation interpretations: Ross and Charles Chediak, "The So-called Anorexia Nervosa," *Bulletin of the Menninger Clinic* 41 (5): 453–74 (1977).

460   Age of onset: Center for the Study of Anorexia and Bulimia, *The Eating Disorder Bulimia* and *Anorexia Nervosa* (New York: Institute for Contemporary Psychotherapy, 1982); Sours, pp. 336–38; Bruch (1973), pp. 155–251.

461   "I got my wish": Bruch (1973), p. 98.

462   Precipitating events: Bruch (1978), pp. 57–71, and (1973), pp. 255–61.

463–64   "to eradicate, to forcibly conventionalize": Tanner, p. 283.

464–65   The perverse scenario: Derived from my clinical experience, consultations with colleagues, and especially Harold N. Boris, "On the Treatment of Anorexia Nervosa," *International Journal of Psychoanalysis* 65: 435–43 (1984), and "On the Problem of Anorexia Nervosa" *International Journal of Psychoanalysis* 65: 303–11

(1984). Boris does not explicitly state that anorexia is a perversion, but he is explicit about how a preoccupation with the obsessions and rituals associated with food and eating hold in abeyance the anxiety and shame the anorectic would suffer if she were to become aware of "longing, libido, and loneliness."

465   "You feel outside your body": Bruch (1978), p. 18.

466   "The awareness of spiritual power": Palazzoli, p. 75.

466   Teresa of Avila: Marcelle Auclair, *Saint Teresa of Avila,* Preface by André Maurois (1950; Petersham, Mass.: St. Bede's Publications, 1988). (Original English language translation by Kathleen Pond New York: Pantheon, 1953.)

466   "spiritual gluttony," distinction between *arrobamiento* and *abobamiento,* "We don't need you for your raptures": Stephen Clissold, *St. Teresa of Avila* (London: Sheldon Press, 1979), p. 115.

466   "a heavenly inebriation": From *Conceptions of the Love of God* (c. 1570) by Teresa of Avila, cited by Auclair, p. 241.

468–70   The case of Schreber: Daniel Paul Schreber, *Memoirs of My Nervous Illness* (1902), translated and edited by Ida Macalpine and Richard A Hunter (1955), with a new introduction by Samuel M. Weber (1973) (Cambri¹ɔe: Harvard University Press, 1988). Cited as *Memoirs.* All during his years of confinement, Daniel Paul Schreber took notes and wrote memos, which he would later use as verifications for his memoirs. But not until 1900 did he recover enough of his sanity to compose a consistent record of his mental torments. The memoirs were written from February to September 1900. The first postscript was written between October 1900 and June 1901, and the second postscript at the end of 1902, as he was writing his plea to be released.   Also, Zvi Lothane "Vindicating Schreber's Father: Neither Sadist nor Child Abuser," *Journal of Psychohistory* 16: 263–88 (1989). Lothane is critical of previous translations of Dr. Schreber's writings, which tend to exaggerate his cruelty. He portrays Dr. Schreber as a conscientious and caring doctor and one of the kinder fathers of his day—which may, unfortunately for the children of that day, be true.

469   "and marred only," "demanded all the more tact": *Memoirs,* p. 63.

470   "faced with the choice": *Memoirs,* p. 149.

471   Rays address him as "Miss Schreber": *Memoirs,* p. 119; transformation into a feminine body: *Memoirs,* pp. 147–49. Schreber entered the hospital at fifty-one; he

first became aware of the transformation of his body when he was fifty-three in November 1895, the thirty-fourth anniversary of his father's death.

472   "It was *common sense*": *Memoirs*, p. 148.

472   "Fancy a person": *Memoirs*, p. 148. Schreber considered words like *fucking* or *shitting* vulgar and insisted that he was only quoting the voices of the rays (*Memoirs*, p. 156).

472   "wholeheartedly inscribed": *Memoirs*, p. 149.

472   "from the top of my head": *Memoirs*, p. 204.

472   "where the woman's bosom is," sewing, dusting: *Memoirs*, p. 202.

473   "If only I could always": *Memoirs*, p. 210.

473   *Kinderseligkeit*, child-blessedness: *Memoirs*, p. 111. "By divine miracles": *Memoirs*, p. 43.

473   "*constant enjoyment*," "to provide Him with it": *Memoirs*, p. 209.

474   "I must point out": *Memoirs*, p. 208.

474   "It really must be so lovely": *Memoirs*, p. 63. Translation mine.

474   "This idea was so foreign": *Memoirs*, p. 63; Father's demand for absolute erectness: Niederland, pp. 63–67, 76–79, 82.

476   "Decisive for my mental collapse": *Memoirs*, p. 68.

477   "incessant vigilance," "this insidious plague of youth": Niederland, p. 73.

477   "impression of a woman": *Memoirs*, p. 208.

478–80 Paulina: Hans Israels, "The New Schreber Texts," in *Psychosis and Sexual Identity: Toward a Post-Analytic View of the Schreber Case*, edited by David B. Allison, Prado de Oliveira, Mark S. Roberts, and Allen S. Weiss (Albany: State University of New York Press, 1988), pp. 207–10. Cited as "Schreber Texts." Israels translates a poem written by Judge Schreber in honor of his mother's ninetieth birthday in 1905 (pp. 232–66). The poem celebrates Paulina (Louise Paulina Haase Schreber) and details the significant events of her life. Also, Robert B. White, "The Mother-Conflict in Schreber's Psychosis," in Neiderland, pp. 151–54.

478   "Father discussed with our mother": Niederland, "Further Data on the 'Historical Truth' in Schreber's Delusions," p. 96. The fates of Anna, Sidonie, and Klara Schreber: "Schreber's Texts," pp. 204–14.

483   Heinrich Seuse (1295–1366): Frank Tobin, ed. and trans., *Henry Suso: The Exemplar, with Two German Sermons,* with an Introduction by Frank Tobin (Mahwah, N.Y.: Paulist Press, 1989).

483   "I used to be called": Tobin p. 220, quoting Seuse from "Little Book of Eternal Wisdom."

484   "He had someone make him": Tobin, p. 88, quoting Seuse from "The Life of the Servant." ("And so it came to pass," my translation.)

484   Dr. Schreber's boyhood and manhood: Niederland, pp. 63–67.

484   "God Himself was on my side": *Memoirs,* p. 79n.

Chapter 14   FEMININE, MASCULINE: THE CODES OF PERVERSION

485   "I believe that ideas": Mary Douglas, *Purity and Danger: An Analysis of Concepts of Pollution and Taboo* (London: Ark Paperbacks, 1984), p. 4.

485   The contrast between the magnificence of the starry heavens and the uneven work of conscience: Freud, *New Introductory Lectures on Psychoanalysis, Standard Edition,* 22:61.

487–88   The social agencies responsible for gender conformity: John D'Emilio and Estelle B. Freedman, *Intimate Matters,* (New York: Harper and Row, 1988), pp. 15–52.

487   The sun dance ritual: See Chap. 11 in this book.

490   Improved medical care and contraception: D'Emilio and Freedman, pp. 59–61.

492–   Aurore: Curtis Cate, *George Sand* (Boston: Houghton Mifflin, 1975).
500

493 "Now at last I felt": Cate, p. 65.

493 "In a word": Cate, p. 66.

494 "I have here": Cate, p. 90.

496 "a voracious nymphomaniac": Cate, p. xxvii, describing gossip.

496 "in her good and evil together": Cate, p. ix.

496 "She has the famous": quoted in Cate, p. xv.

497 "Ah dear good master": *The George Sand–Gustave Flaubert Letters*, translated by Aimee L. McKenzie (New York: Boni and Liveright, 1921), pp. xxxv and 210. Cited as *Letters*.

497 "And what you want": *Letters*, pp. xxxvi and 212.

498 "I cried like a baby": *Correspondance*, 7: 311.

498 "She loved us both": Cate, p. 731.

498 "One had to know her": Cate, pp. xxv and 732.

498 "There are some who seek": Cate, p. 651.

499 *Lettres à Marcie*, "the wife has the fatigues": Cate, p. 419.

499– "The role of each sex": Cate, p. 419.
500

500 "You should love only those": André Maurois, *Lélia*, translated by Gerard Hopkins (New York: Harper and Brothers, 1953), p. 20.

515 "specific greed": Tanner, p. 288.

515 "The majority of women": Dijkstra p. 355, citing Abba Goold Woolson, *Women in American Society* (Boston, 1873), p. 103.

515 "Nineteenth century middle-class women": Dijkstra, p. 355.

516   "Only those with a truly ruthless hunger": Dijkstra, p. 354.

517   "By the turn of the century": Dijkstra, p. 371.

519–20   Alice Echols, "The New Feminism of Yin and Yang," in *Powers of Desire,* edited by Ann Snitow, Christine Stansell, and Sharon Thompson (New York: Monthly Review Press, 1983); "define male and female sexuality": Echols, p. 449. The term *cultural feminist* originated in the 1975 publication of the reconstituted Redstockings *Feminist Revolution* (reissued; New York: Random House, 1978).

519   "to maintain that there exists": Echols, p. 441.

520   "The good cops stand ready": Ellen Willis, "Feminism, Moralism, and Pornography," in *Powers of Desire,* p. 465.

524   "The day may come": Gustave Flaubert in *Souvenirs,* cited by Jean Paul Sartre in "La Conscience de Classe Chez Flaubert," *Les Tempes Modernes* (June 1966).

524   Fourier and Svante: William McKibben, *The End of Nature* (New York: Random House, 1989), pp. 8–9, 19.

525   I thank my colleague Dr. Sonia Riha for calling Lacretelle's Foreword to my attention. Jacques Lacretelle, new Foreword to 1857/1873 edition, *Madame Bovary* (Norwalk, CT: Easton Press, 1950), p. viii.

526   "such happiness must be a lie": *Bovary,* p. 260.

526   "He played to the crowds": *Bovary,* p. 258.

526–27   "With him, she would have traveled": *Bovary,* p. 261.

527   "She wanted to run": *Bovary,* p. 261.

Index

(f) indicates fictional characters

READ MORE IN PENGUIN

In every corner of the world, on every subject under the sun, Penguin represents quality and variety – the very best in publishing today.

For complete information about books available from Penguin – including Puffins, Penguin Classics and Arkana – and how to order them, write to us at the appropriate address below. Please note that for copyright reasons the selection of books varies from country to country.

In the United Kingdom: Please write to *Dept. JC, Penguin Books Ltd, FREEPOST, West Drayton, Middlesex UB7 0BR*

If you have any difficulty in obtaining a title, please send your order with the correct money, plus ten per cent for postage and packaging, to *PO Box No. 11, West Drayton, Middlesex UB7 0BR*

In the United States: Please write to *Penguin USA Inc., 375 Hudson Street, New York, NY 10014*

In Canada: Please write to *Penguin Books Canada Ltd, 10 Alcorn Avenue, Suite 300, Toronto, Ontario M4V 3B2*

In Australia: Please write to *Penguin Books Australia Ltd, 487 Maroondah Highway, Ringwood, Victoria 3134*

In New Zealand: Please write to *Penguin Books (NZ) Ltd, 182–190 Wairau Road, Private Bag, Takapuna, Auckland 9*

In India: Please write to *Penguin Books India Pvt Ltd, 706 Eros Apartments, 56 Nehru Place, New Delhi 110 019*

In the Netherlands: Please write to *Penguin Books Netherlands B.V., Keizersgracht 231 NL–1016 DV Amsterdam*

In Germany: Please write to *Penguin Books Deutschland GmbH, Friedrichstrasse 10–12, W–6000 Frankfurt/Main 1*

In Spain: Please write to *Penguin Books S. A., C. San Bernardo 117–6° E–28015 Madrid*

In Italy: Please write to *Penguin Italia s.r.l., Via Felice Casati 20, I–20124 Milano*

In France: Please write to *Penguin France S. A., 17 rue Lejeune, F–31000 Toulouse*

In Japan: Please write to *Penguin Books Japan, Ishikiribashi Building, 2–5–4, Suido, Tokyo 112*

In Greece: Please write to *Penguin Hellas Ltd, Dimocritou 3, GR–106 71 Athens*

In South Africa: Please write to *Longman Penguin Southern Africa (Pty) Ltd, Private Bag X08, Bertsham 2013*

READ MORE IN PENGUIN

WOMEN'S INTEREST

When a Woman's Body Says No to Sex   Linda Valins

Vaginismus – an involuntary spasm of the vaginal muscles that prevents penetration – has been discussed so little that many women who suffer from it don't recognize their condition by its name. Linda Valins's practical and compassionate guide will liberate these women from their fears and sense of isolation and help them find the right form of therapy.

Against Our Will   Susan Brownmiller
Men, Women and Rape

Against Our Will sheds a new and blinding light on the tensions that exist between men and women. It was written to give rape its history. Now, as Susan Brownmiller concludes, 'we must deny it a future'. 'Thoughtful, informative and well researched' – *New Statesman*

The Feminine Mystique   Betty Friedan

First published in the sixties, *The Feminine Mystique* was a major inspiration for the Women's Movement and continues to be a powerful and illuminating analysis of the position of women in Western society.

Understanding Women   Luise Eichenbaum and Susie Orbach

Understanding Women, an expanded version of *Outside In ... Inside Out*, is a radical appraisal of women's psychological development based on clinical evidence. 'An exciting and thought-provoking book' – *British Journal of Psychiatry*

Psychoanalysis and Feminism   Juliet Mitchell

The author of the widely acclaimed *Woman's Estate* here reassesses Freudian psychoanalysis in an attempt to develop an understanding of the psychology of femininity and the ideological oppression of women.